Blackstone's Guide to the

TRADE MARKS ACT 1994

Blackstone's Guide to the
TRADE MARKS ACT 1994

Ruth E. Annand, B.A. (Dunelm), Solicitor

Professor of Law, University of Bristol,
Associate with Humphreys & Co, Bristol

and

Helen E. Norman, LL.M. (Birmingham), Barrister, Gray's Inn

Lecturer in Law, University of Bristol
Consultant in European Law to the Solicitors' Information Group

BLACKSTONE
PRESS LIMITED

First published in Great Britain 1994 by Blackstone Press Limited,
Aldine Place, London W12 8AA. Telephone 0181-740 2277

ISBN: 1 85431 384 3

Reprinted 1998

British Library Cataloguing in Publication Data
A CIP catalogue record for this book is available from the British Library

Typeset by Style Photosetting Ltd, Mayfield, East Sussex
Printed by Livesey Ltd, Shrewsbury, Shropshire

Contents

14 The Community trade mark 235

Introduction: the need for a Community trade mark — The Community Trade Mark Office — Definition of a Community trade mark — Applying for a Community trade mark: registration procedure — Miscellaneous matters relating to registration — Maintenance of Community trade marks — Exploitation of Community trade marks — Rights conferred by a Community trade mark — Enforcing the Community trade mark right — Conclusion

15 International registration of trade marks 260

Introduction — The Madrid Agreement — The Madrid Protocol — Implementation of the Madrid Protocol in United Kingdom domestic law — Comparison between the Madrid system and the Community trade mark

Preface

The Trade Marks Act 1994 was described by Lord Strathclyde, speaking on behalf of the Government in the House of Lords, as:

> . . . both technical and complex, [but] of considerable importance to industry and commerce which wish to register and protect their trade marks.

The 1994 Act implements Directive 89/104/EEC of 21 December 1988 to approximate the laws of Member States relating to trade marks. In so doing, it lowers the threshold for the registrability of trade marks, thereby enabling the shapes of goods and of their packaging, sounds, smells and other sensory marks to be registered. It also broadens the scope of the infringement action to cover use of a registered trade mark on similar goods, and introduces the doctrine of dilution into United Kingdom trade marks law. Assignment and licensing of registered trade marks are deregulated.

On the international front, the Act will be of particular interest to multinational companies, in that it will enable the United Kingdom to ratify the Madrid Protocol. British firms will, for the first time, be able to obtain international registrations for their trade marks. The Act also provides better civil remedies for trade mark infringement and enhanced criminal penalties for counterfeiting, within the spirit of the recent agreement on the Trade-Related Aspects of Intellectual Property concluded as part of the Uruguay round.

Finally, the Act contains provisions linking the United Kingdom Trade Marks Registry into the Community trade mark system, expected to be fully operational in 1996.

The Act will be brought into force in stages. The new domestic trade marks law is scheduled to come into effect on 31 October 1994; the provisions dealing with the Madrid Protocol on 1 April 1995; and those relating to the Community trade mark early in 1996.

Countries which formerly based their trade marks laws on the United Kingdom model (for example, Hong Kong and India) are in the process of legislating in much the same terms as the 1994 Act.

The authors would like to express their thanks to Pat Jones and Marie Davies for their help in researching this book and to their husbands, Jonathan and Richard, for all their love and support.

Ruth Annand
Helen Norman
August 1994

CHAPTER ONE
Introduction to the Trade Marks Act 1994

Preliminary

By way of introduction to the Trade Marks Act 1994, this chapter will give a brief account of the historical background to United Kingdom trade marks law and will then set out those international conventions having an effect on the content of domestic trade marks law. It will go on to explain the various pressures for reform which led to the passing of the 1994 Act and will examine the nature and function of the trade mark in a consumer society. The chapter will conclude by discussing, in the context of a system which protects both registered and unregistered marks, the question 'Why register'?

Historical Background

Before 1875
The use of trade marks developed long before their legal protection. Marks were used either to show ownership of goods (witness the branding of cattle, from which the term 'brand name' comes) or commercial origin. Archaeological evidence has revealed the use of trade marks in ancient China and throughout the Roman Empire. During the Middle Ages, trade marks were widely used throughout Western Europe, either as a means of proving ownership of goods lost in transit or compulsorily, under the control of the craft guilds, as a means of preventing shoddy workmanship.

In the United Kingdom, the judicial protection of trade marks did not develop until the early nineteenth century, no doubt prompted by the effects of the Industrial Revolution. This brought about the separation of the producer from the consumer, with the consequent need to identify the source from which satisfactory goods had emanated.

As might be expected, the common law courts and the Court of Chancery each developed their own thinking on trade marks.

At common law, an action for damages for the wrongful use by the defendant of the plaintiff's trade mark was an extension of the tort of deceit. The rule was that although the defendant's goods need not be inferior to those of the plaintiff and although there need not be evidence of actual confusion on the part of the public, the issue of whether the marks were confusingly similar was a question of fact to be left to the jury. The key issue was whether the defendant *intended* to supplant the plaintiff by representing his goods to be those of the rightful owner of the mark (*Crawshay* v *Thompson* (1842) 4 Man & G 358).

In equity, the court was initially reluctant to award an injunction to restrain trade mark infringement, on the ground that to do so would create an unfair monopoly. However, by the time of *Knott* v *Morgan* (1836) 2 Keen 213, an injunction would be granted where the defendant fraudulently adopted the plaintiff's trade mark. An important change in thinking occurred in *Millington* v *Fox* (1838) 3 My & Cr 338, where the Lord Chancellor stated that the basis of equity's intervention was not fraud, but the property right in the mark.

Subsequent Chancery cases fell into two groups: those which treated trade mark infringement as a form of tortious liability, based on misrepresentation, whether fraudulent or innocent (*Burgess* v *Burgess* (1853) 3 De G M & G 896); and those which treated trade mark infringement as interference with a property right (*Leather Cloth Co. Ltd* v *American Leather Cloth Co. Ltd* (1863) 4 De G J & S 137).

Lest it be thought that such historical background is of no consequence today, nineteenth-century trade mark cases are still relevant, in that they form the basis of the tort of passing off. This is the common law means of protecting unregistered trade marks, and as a judge-made system is still developing. For example, in *Gillette UK Ltd* v *Edenwest Ltd* [1994] RPC 279, it was necessary for Blackburne J to refer to old cases in order to determine whether the defendant's innocence was a bar to the award of damages or an account of profits for trade mark infringement and passing off.

After 1875

Two major changes occurred in 1875. First, there was the enactment of the first Trade Marks Registration Act. This laid down a system of registration which has co-existed ever since with the common law means of protecting unregistered trade marks. The Act of 1875 and its successors treated the registered trade mark as a form of property to be protected by the action for infringement, whilst preserving the action of passing off in relation to unregistered marks.

Secondly, the Judicature Acts of 1873–5 fused the administration of common law and equity. This resulted in the equitable view of the protection of unregistered trade marks prevailing, but, as indicated above, there was some divergence in that view. Ultimately, cases decided after 1875 reverted to the notion that the protection of unregistered trade marks depended on the making of a misrepresentation, rather than interference with a property right. Both *Reddaway* v *Banham* [1896] AC 199 and *A. G. Spalding & Bros* v *A. W. Gamage Ltd* (1915) 32 RPC 273 state that there can be no property right in an unregistered name. Rather, what is protected is the goodwill of the business in which that name has been used.

The International Context of Trade Marks

The need for separate national registrations

Intellectual property rights are territorial in nature, that is, they result from rights granted under national legislation. Their effect is therefore limited to the territory of the State granting the right. In the case of intellectual property rights acquired by registration, that is, patents, trade marks and registered designs, it is necessary to seek registration in every country where protection is desired (the rule is different for copyright and unregistered designs).

Several international conventions exist which assist the applicant who wishes to register a trade mark in more than one country. These will be explained in turn.

The Convention of 14 July 1967 establishing the World Intellectual Property Organisation
The World Intellectual Property Organisation (WIPO) is an agency of the United Nations, based in Geneva. Its role is to promote intellectual property throughout the world, by educating and encouraging developing countries to adopt their own intellectual property laws and by putting forward proposals for the worldwide harmonisation of national intellectual property legislation.

WIPO is responsible for administering most (but not all) of the international conventions relating to intellectual property. In relation to trade marks, it administers the Madrid Agreement for the International Registration of Marks 1891 and the Madrid Protocol of 1989 which amends it. The latter will be incorporated into United Kingdom trade marks law by virtue of sections 53 and 54 of the Trade Marks Act 1994 and is explained in general terms below.

The Paris Convention for the Protection of Industrial Property 1883
This is the 'parent' intellectual property convention (and indeed the oldest). It has been revised several times, the current version being the Stockholm Revision of 1967. It covers all forms of intellectual property rights obtainable by registration, namely, patents, registered designs and trade marks (copyright and unregistered designs are covered by the Berne Copyright Convention of 1886).

Being a party to the Convention obliges a country to establish a national patent office and to publish information about its decisions. Hence in the United Kingdom separate weekly journals are published by the Patent Office on the subject of patents, registered designs and trade marks.

In relation to trade marks, the Convention obliges its signatories (known as 'Convention countries'):

(a) to protect well-known marks belonging to nationals of Convention countries (Article 6*bis*);

(b) to prevent the use and registration of 'armorial bearings, flags and emblems' of Convention countries (Article 6*ter*);

(c) to provide effective protection against unfair competition (Article 10*bis*); and

(d) to accept for registration any trade mark which has been duly registered in its country of origin (Article 6*quinquies* – the so-called '*telle-quelle*' obligation).

The wording of the Convention is quite broad, leaving a considerable discretion to its signatories. Consequently, the United Kingdom has never implemented the Convention as fully as it might. The 1994 Act will improve matters by expressly protecting for the first time well-known marks, and by transferring the prohibition on the registration of armorial bearings and flags from the Trade Marks Rules to the statute itself. However, there is still no express provision implementing the *'telle-quelle'* obligation, nor will the United Kingdom have a law of unfair competition, a matter of concern to those trade mark owners anxious to prevent the growing practice of supermarkets producing own-brand look-alikes.

The Paris Convention contains two provisions important in practice. These are the principle of national treatment (Article 2) and the system of claiming convention priority (Article 4).

National treatment National treatment means that each Convention country undertakes to give the same treatment to nationals (whether companies or individuals) of other Convention countries as it gives its own nationals. Thus a trade mark applicant from the United States of America or Hungary is guaranteed the same treatment by the United Kingdom Trade Marks Registry as is a British citizen. Conversely, a British citizen applying for a trade mark in Germany is given the same treatment by the German Patent Office as a German national.

Convention priority The system of Convention priority (of more significance in the patent system) means that where an application for a trade mark has been filed in one Convention country then any application made in another Convention country within the following six months can claim priority from date of the first application. Consequently, the validity of the second application is not affected by any third-party rights which arise in the meantime. The requirements for claiming Convention priority are explained in more detail in chapter 3.

The effect of the Paris Convention in national law Under United Kingdom law, an international convention binds the Crown only and its rules do not have the force of law unless and until they have been implemented by legislation. Parties before a court or before the Patent Office cannot rely directly on the Paris Convention (*CANADEL Trade Mark* [1980] RPC 535).

The Arrangement of Nice for the International Classification of Goods and Services 1957
Trade marks have to be registered for specific goods and/or services. The list of items for which a mark is registered is known as the 'specification'. To assist with the registration of and searching for trade marks, the Nice Arrangement divides goods into 34 classes and services into eight classes. It is left to countries which have adopted the Arrangement to decide whether they wish to permit applicants to file multiple class applications (as, for example, the Benelux Registry does) or to require applicants to file one application for each class of goods or services for which protection is sought (as used to be the position in the United Kingdom under the Trade Marks Act 1938, as amended).

The Nice classification can be found in appendix 4.

The Madrid Agreement for the International Registration of Marks 1891
The current version of the Madrid Agreement (the Stockholm revision of 1967) enables an individual or company established in one of the contracting States, once a 'home' registration has been obtained, to apply to the International Bureau at WIPO for an international registration. The Bureau will pass on the application to

the national trade mark offices of all contracting countries of the Madrid Agreement in which the applicant has requested protection. The Madrid system therefore provides a procedural short-cut for filing a batch of national applications by means of a single transaction.

Because the United Kingdom was not a signatory to the original Madrid Agreement, British firms have not been able to take advantage of this system of making a batch of trade mark applications. However, the United Kingdom has signed the Protocol which revises the Madrid Arrangement, so that once the United Kingdom's accession to the Protocol is ratified by the Trade Marks Act 1994, and once enough other countries have done likewise, this system will be available to British applicants. The latest information is that the Protocol is expected to be operative on 1 April 1995.

The workings of the Madrid system for the international registration of trade marks are explained more fully in chapter 15.

The Treaty of Rome 1957

The United Kingdom became a Member State of the European Communities on 1 January 1973 by acceding to the Treaty of Rome. Concerned as it is with the creation of, first, a common market, then, by virtue of the Single European Act 1986, a single market, and now, as a result of the Maastricht Treaty, a European Union, it might be thought that the EC would have little effect on domestic trade-marks law. In fact the opposite is the case.

Community law has had the following effects:

(a) The Court of Justice of the European Communities (which is charged with ensuring the enforcement of Community law and the correct interpretation of the Treaty and any secondary legislation made under it) has had to reconcile the territorial nature of intellectual property rights with the principle of the free movement of goods established by Article 30 of the EC Treaty. The resulting case law is explained in chapter 10.

(b) The Treaty prohibits conduct by commercial undertakings which infringes EC competition policy. Article 85 of the Treaty prohibits restrictive agreements and Article 86 prohibits the abuse of a dominant position. The way in which intellectual property rights are assigned, licensed or otherwise exploited may fall foul of these two provisions, which are discussed in chapter 11.

(c) As part of the task of achieving a single market (where internal national boundaries are ignored) the Council of the European Communities has adopted the First Trade Marks Directive of 21 December 1988 (Directive 89/104/EEC, OJ [1989] L40/1) on the approximation of national trade marks laws; and Council Regulation (EC) 40/94 of 20 December 1993, OJ [1994] L 11/1, on the Community trade mark.

References in this book to 'the Directive' and to 'the Regulation' are to these two items of Community secondary legislation.

The importance of the Directive   The Directive is intended to bring into line the national laws of the Member States by prescribing what can and cannot be a registered trade mark, the scope of the trade mark right, the obligation to use a trade mark, the grounds for revocation, and how a trade mark can be licensed. It leaves entirely to Member States the procedural details of applying for or revoking a trade mark or bringing infringement proceedings.

The Directive has had a major influence on the content of the Trade Marks Act 1994. In comparison with the previous United Kingdom legislation (the Trade Marks Act 1938, as amended) and as a consequence of the Directive, the new Act lowers the test for registrability of marks and broadens the scope of the infringement action. At the same time it makes it easier for third parties to challenge the validity of registered marks.

The Directive is drafted in language which may appear unfamiliar to a British lawyer. In keeping with the civil law tradition, it is written in terms of broad principle rather than specific detail.

Although most of the provisions of the Directive are mandatory, some are optional. This work will indicate where the United Kingdom has elected to implement an optional provision.

The role of the Court of Justice   Case law of the Court of Justice of the European Community concerning the implementation of EC Directives into national law has stressed that:

(a)   Directives *must* be used as an aid to the interpretation of any national legislation covering the same area, whether such legislation came before or after the Directive was passed.

(b)   Any national court which is unsure of the interpretation of national law based on a Directive has a discretion to refer the case to the Court of Justice for a preliminary ruling under Article 177 of the EC Treaty; a court of last resort must refer such a matter.

When asked to interpret a Directive, the Court of Justice, in keeping with the civil law tradition, will adopt the teleological style of interpretation, that is, it will consider the legislation in the light of its objectives, making use of working papers and discussions which preceded its enactment. Accordingly, much emphasis will be placed on the Commission's Explanatory Memorandum accompanying the first (1980) draft of the Directive. It is also likely that reference will be made to the minutes of the meeting of the Council of Ministers which adopted the Community Trade Mark Regulation. Both of these *travaux préparatoires* will be referred to throughout this book.

British lawyers and their clients will therefore have to accept that the meaning of the key provisions in the 1994 Act can no longer be conclusively determined by the Chancery Division, the Court of Appeal or the House of Lords. The only judicial body which has the authority to give a definitive interpretation of the Directive and any national legislation based on it will be the Court of Justice in Luxembourg. It is this body also which alone can decide, in any action brought by the EC Commission under Article 169 of the EC Treaty, whether the Trade Marks Act 1994 *correctly* implements the Directive.

National courts have a responsibility to ensure that Community law is enforced in Member States. Where a national court is satisfied that national legislation, whether primary or secondary, or a rule of common law, conflicts with the clear meaning of the Treaty of Rome or any legislation made pursuant to it, the court must 'disapply' (to use the language of the Court of Justice) the offending national law. As the House of Lords has made clear in *R* v *Secretary of State for Employment ex parte Equal Opportunities Commission* [1994] 2 WLR 409, the Divisional Court has jurisdiction to declare *any* rule of national law, whether derived from the common law, statute or delegated legislation, incompatible with Community law.

For the above reasons, the European dimension to the Trade Marks Act 1994 must be kept constantly in mind.

The Community Trade Mark Regulation This Regulation will lead to the establishment of an office which, in the Regulation is called 'the Office for Harmonisation in the Internal Market (Trade Marks and Designs)' but which will be referred to in this book as the 'Community Trade Mark Office'. It will be located in Alicante and, when operative, will allow applications to be made for a single trade mark effective throughout the whole of the EC. Such Community marks will, however, exist in parallel to national registrations. The Regulation is examined in detail in chapter 14.

The Pressures for Reform: the Background to the 1994 Act

The Trade Marks Act 1938 was the 10th such Act to be passed since the first legislation providing for the registration of trade marks in 1875.

The reform of the Act had been considered in detail by the Mathys Committee in 1974 (*British Trade Mark Law and Practice*, Cmnd 5601), but the only change recommended by that Committee which was implemented was the introduction of the registration of service marks in 1986. Even this was made unduly complicated. Registration of service marks was provided for in the Trade Marks (Amendment) Act 1984, but this in turn was amended and then implemented (along with other changes) by the Patents, Designs and Marks Act 1986. The result of the amendments was that there existed two parallel (but not identical) versions of the 1938 Act, one version dealing with marks for goods and the other dealing with marks for services. This dual legislation was both inconvenient and contradictory, and contained inconsistencies of wording (see *Re Dee Corporation plc* [1990] RPC 159).

The Government published a White Paper, *Reform of Trade Marks Law* (Cm 1203), in September 1990 (throughout this work, 'the White Paper'). This identified the following reasons why United Kingdom trade marks law was in need of a major overhaul:

(a) The 1938 Act was over 50 years old and unable to cope with changes in trading practices. The structure of the legislation following the amendments of 1984 and 1986 was unwieldy. The fact that the 1938 Act was stated to be a consolidating measure meant frequent recourse to earlier legislation or even pre-1875 case law.

(b) The need to ratify the 1989 Protocol to the Madrid Agreement of 1891.

(c) The advent of the Community Trade Mark Regulation, which obliges the United Kingdom Trade Marks Registry to cooperate with the Community Trade Mark Office in Alicante.

(d)   The obligation to legislate to bring United Kingdom domestic law into line with the Directive.

(e)   The need to incorporate the latest version of the Paris Convention into domestic law.

The Nature of the Trade Mark Right

Trade marks compared with other forms of intellectual property
Trade marks are included in the intellectual property triumvirate alongside patents and copyright. Most lay people (and some lawyers) frequently confuse the three concepts, yet despite their similarities there are significant differences between them.

The common denominator is that although each has its common law origins, all three are now regulated by statute whereby the 'right' is 'granted' to the 'owner' for the territory of the United Kingdom. The content of the statutory regime is often dictated by obligations which the United Kingdom has incurred by virtue of being a signatory to international conventions.

Intellectual property rights result from State grant   In the case of trade marks and patents (and also registered designs), Patent Office procedure results in a formal grant of protection after examination.

In the case of copyright, the system is somewhat different. The 'grant' is implicit and informal, arising automatically whenever a 'work' falling within the categories listed in section 1(1) of the Copyright, Designs and Patents Act 1988 (CDPA 1988) is created, provided:

(a)   it meets the criterion of being in permanent form (CDPA 1988 section 178); and

(b)   its author satisfies one of the criteria for being a 'qualifying person' (CDPA 1988, sections 153 to 159).

The same (copyright) principles apply to unregistered designs.

The nature of the patent right   The grant of a patent confers on the patentee for a maximum period of 20 years a monopoly to exploit a new and inventive product or process, and the right to stop others from making, disposing, using or importing a product, whether it is the subject of the patent itself or derived from a patented process, or from using the patented process itself.

The public interest in ensuring the patent system is not abused is achieved in various ways. Patents cannot be used to protect abstract ideas, only applied technology. While the guarantee of the fixed 20-year monopoly is said to reward ingenuity and provide an incentive to innovate, the price the patentee pays for this is being made to teach the invention, through sufficient disclosure in the patent specification, to the rest of the world. On expiry, anyone can use the information contained in the specification. Failure to exploit the patent will render the patentee open to compulsory licensing.

The nature of copyright   The copyright owner has the exclusive right, for the lifetime of the author plus 50, years to do or to license the 'restricted acts' listed in section 16 of the CDPA 1988 in respect of various categories of 'work' (such as books, plays, music, artistic works, films, sound recordings and broadcasts).

The copyright 'monopoly' is more limited than in the case of patents because of the need to prove copying on the part of the defendant. Consequently, where it can be proved that the work was created independently, the defendant will not be liable.

Liability for copyright infringement is imposed for both direct and indirect copying, for domestic as well as commercial activities, for authorising others to commit infringement, and for various forms of secondary infringement amounting to commercial dealings in infringing copies, provided in the last-mentioned case that knowledge is proved.

The public interest in the copyright system is based on the assumption that a person is entitled to claim ownership in the product of the intellect. In turn, this rewards creativity and, in the case of the 'entrepreneurial' copyright works, such as films and sound recordings, investment.

The underlying value judgment, therefore, for both patents and copyright is that a person's creativity and inventiveness improves the quality of life of his or her fellow human beings.

The nature of the trade mark right   At first glance, it is obvious that the trade mark right, unlike patents and copyright, is not theoretically limited in time. Provided the mark was properly obtained, renewal fees are paid, the mark remains in use and the owner does nothing which would invite another to commence proceedings for revocation of the mark, the right will last indefinitely.

Like the other two forms of intellectual property, trade mark registration confers 'exclusive rights', this time to the use of the mark *as a trade mark* to differentiate a product. But a trade mark owner who has adopted a non-invented word does not have the right to prevent the use of that word in all circumstances. The word is not taken out of the language. The only right is to prevent the use, in trade, of an identical or similar sign as a trade mark. As explained below, even the owner of an invented-word trade mark does not have unqualified exclusive rights in respect of it.

Because of the nature of the trade mark right, the arguments which may justify patents and copyright are of little relevance. The rationale of trade mark law lies in the economics of the consumer society. Judicial failure to perceive the difference between trade marks and other forms of intellectual property has led to a lack of understanding of trade marks.

The overlap with copyright   One of the major effects of the Trade Marks Act 1994 is that the definition of 'trade mark' in section 1 now expressly refers to 'designs' and 'the shape of goods or of their packaging'. This means that there may be dual protection for a design or shape, both under the law of trade marks and under the law of copyright and designs.

It is, however, accepted law that there can be no copyright in a single word or even a slogan, such 'work' being too minimal to cross the threshold for copyright protection. A trade mark which consists of an invented word does not attract copyright protection, even though it may, disjunctively speaking, satisfy the criteria found in section 3 of the CDPA 1988, of being 'original', 'literary' and 'work' (see

Exxon Corporation v *Exxon Insurance Consultants International Ltd* [1982] Ch 119).

The nature of the trade mark as a form of property

As explained above, one of the effects of the Trade Marks Registration Act 1875 was that a registered trade mark was treated as intangible personalty, protected by the action for infringement (see per Lord Diplock in *GE Trade Mark* [1973] RPC 297 at pp. 325–6). This approach is continued by sections 2 and 22 of the Trade Marks Act 1994, with the further extension of property rights to pending applications by section 27 (see chapter 11). However, this property right should be examined in more detail.

The commercial value of trade marks   The modern trade mark is endowed with many of the attributes of property. It confers the right to exclude others, and is capable of being licensed and transferred, whether by way of sale, charge or on succession.

Another attribute of an item of property is that it can be allocated a monetary value. The valuation of brands as part of a company's balance sheet is becoming common, sometimes as a means of fending off an unwelcome takeover bid.

Recent examples of brand valuation include Rank Hovis McDougall plc, which in 1991 calculated its brand names to be worth £583.5 million. The American business magazine *Financial World* concluded in its 1993 survey of brand names that MARLBORO was worth $39.5 billion, COCA-COLA worth $33.4 billion and INTEL worth $17.8 billion. The top 'British' brand was placed 22nd on the list: it was GUINNESS, allegedly worth $2.74 billion. The only non-American brands in the top 10 were NESCAFÉ and BACARDI.

Such property rights are not permanent   However, the property right in a trade mark is not necessarily permanent. In line with other registrable intellectual property rights, a trade mark can be declared invalid (and thus be deemed never to have existed) because of failure to meet the substantive requirements of registrability (see section 47 of the 1994 Act, and chapter 8).

Further, a trade mark, unlike other forms of intellectual property, is open to destruction by mismanagement. Failure by the owner to exercise proper control over the mark may expose it to revocation for non-use, generic use or misleading use (see section 46, explained in chapter 8). By contrast, failure to exploit a patent may result in compulsory licensing but not its destruction; failure to exploit a copyright will not affect the validity of the right, unless it is one of those limited categories of copyright work exposed to compulsory licensing.

Yet another point operates to differentiate the trade mark from other types of intellectual property. Whilst patents, designs and copyright can be owned by anyone, a trade mark serves to identify the goods or services of a particular commercial concern. The common law rule was that there was an indissoluble link between the mark and the goodwill of the business in which it had been used. This principle was eroded by the Trade Marks Act 1938, as amended, and the 1994 Act continues the process of dissolution even further. Nevertheless, it must be recognised that, because of the function of a trade mark (explained below) and its vulnerability to revocation (outlined above), the trade mark has to relate in some way to the business activity of its owner. For that reason it should not be regarded as capable of independent existence in the same manner as patents, designs and copyright.

The property right in unregistered marks   The common law view of the trade mark was that it was part of its owner's goodwill. If the trade mark were severed from the business, it could no longer exist. There is judicial authority (see *Reddaway* v *Banham* [1896] AC 199 and *A. G. Spalding & Bros* v *A. W. Gamage Ltd* (1915) 32 RPC 273) that there can be no property right in an unregistered mark, only in the goodwill of the business in which it has been used.

This suggests a contrast between registered and unregistered marks. Indications are, however, that this contrast may not continue to exist. Unregistered marks may, in due course and subject to judicial reconsideration, attract property rights, for the following reasons:

(a)   The 1994 Act, in section 56, by implementing the obligation in the Paris Convention to protect well-known marks, provides that the owner of such a mark can obtain injunctive relief 'whether or not that person carries on business, or has any goodwill, in the United Kingdom'. The provision protecting well-known marks therefore treats them as being independent of the goodwill of the business.

(b)   The Court of Appeal, in *Taittinger* v *Allbev Ltd* [1993] 2 CMLR 741, anticipating section 10(3) of the 1994 Act, has recently extended passing off to cover the dilution of an unregistered mark. Dilution is the gradual erosion of the mark's selling power. The action for dilution is based on the assumption that the trade mark is a valuable item of property in its own right and that it is a means for creating goodwill, rather than being part of goodwill.

The nature of the trade mark in creating a monopoly
British judges have expressed the opinion on several occasions that trade marks give rise to unfair monopolies (see, for example, *COCA-COLA Trade Marks* [1986] RPC 421 and *YORK Trade Mark* [1984] RPC 231). Such reaction appears to be a 'knee-jerk' response, as there is little accompanying analysis to substantiate this assertion.

It has often been pointed out that neither a registered nor common law trade mark creates a monopoly over language or product. The nature of the trade mark right is only to exclude others from using the same or similar name *as a trade mark*. Thus the word CAMEL, whilst registered as a trade mark for cigarettes, is free for use in ordinary language. Its registration or use does not stop other companies from manufacturing cigarettes. Equally, the adoption of a plastic lemon-shaped container for lemon juice does not pre-empt the creation of other plastic fruit-shaped containers for different products, let alone plastic containers generally, nor does it prevent the sale of lemon juice by another concern. In neither of the two examples does the adoption of the trade mark force the public to obtain the product in question from a single source of supply.

This presents an immediate contrast with patents, where the monopoly over product or process is absolute, and with copyright, where the qualified monopoly to reproduce the work in any material form is limited only by the need to prove derivation. A trade mark is a monopoly neither of a natural product nor of an invention nor of a work. Rather, it is a means of identification, established effectively by the use of advertising.

An economic analysis of trade marks   In the United Kingdom, there has been little academic and no judicial discussion of the relationship between trade marks and economic theory. In the United States of America, the extensive literature which exists on the subject has divided itself broadly into two camps:

(a)   Those who argue that by successfully differentiating a standardised product (even to the slightest degree) and achieving consumer brand loyalty through advertising, trade marks insulate a producer from price competition. This means that consumers will pay more for branded than for unbranded goods or services, and makes it harder for new manufacturers to enter the market.

(b)   Those who argue that the benefit of trade marks lies in providing information to consumers. Rather than investigating the attributes of all available goods or services to determine which one is best, the consumer relies on a brand name as an indication of consistent quality. The requirement for the producer to maintain such quality means that trade marks are self-enforcing. Inconsistency means that consumers will go elsewhere, unwilling to pay more for the branded than the unbranded product; consistency will lead to brand loyalty. All this presupposes the legal protection of trade marks. Confusion in the market-place will make it more difficult for consumers to purchase the product they desire; and free riding will eventually destroy the information capital embodied in the trade mark.

Which one of these two theories is correct? It may be that both are correct, so that there is a love–hate relationship between trade marks and competition. Generally speaking, however, the benefits to the consumer society of having brand names are perceived as outweighing the disadvantages of their anti-competitive effects.

Competition law considerations   In the light of the above economic analysis, it may be asked whether there are any competition law decisions concerning the monopolistic effects of trade marks. Such decisions as exist in EC competition law (there are none, so far as the authors know, in United Kingdom competition law) suggest that everything depends on the analysis of a company's market power, because it is this rather than the trade mark *per se* which may have an anti-competitive effect. Thus:

(a)   Where there is a highly competitive market with many brands, a relatively unknown trade mark for a product new to a particular geographical market (such as Canadian lager in the United Kingdom) will not pose a barrier to entry (*Re the Agreement between Moosehead Breweries Ltd and Whitbread & Co. plc* [1991] 4 CMLR 391).

(b)   Where the market consists of only a few producers and there is evidence of strong brand awareness in consumers, then trade marks may well create a barrier to entry. Examples of this were given in the House of Commons second reading debate on the Trade Marks Bill. Thus, in the detergents market, two companies, Procter & Gamble and Unilever, control 87 per cent of the market, the remainder being divided between 'own branders'; in the cornflake market, Kellogg's have a 57 per cent share; Nestlé has more than half the market share in instant coffee; and Pedigree has built up a 60 per cent share of the dog-food sector (*Hansard* (HC), 18 April 1994, cols 664–5).

Competition decisions have decided that such barriers to entry arise for several reasons. Consumers may be reluctant to try new brands; or new entrants may face the prohibitive capital costs of advertising their brands to build up a level of goodwill commensurate with that enjoyed by the supplier of the major brand (see *United Brands Co.* v *Commission* (Case 27/76), [1978] ECR 207; *Re the Concentration between Nestlé SA and Source Perrier SA* [1993] 4 CMLR M17).

(c) Where a company already occupies a dominant position in respect of its product, the ability (through corporate acquisitions) to control how a competitor uses its trade mark will amount to an abuse of that position (see *Warner Lambert & BIC SA* v *Gillette & Eemland* [1993] 5 CMLR 559). Again, it is the market power exercised by the dominant owner, rather than the strength of the brand name which is conclusive.

The Functions of Trade Marks

Changes in commercial practices
During the last 40 years or so there have been enormous changes in business practices in Western Europe:

(a) There has been a dramatic increase in advertising, on television and commercial radio, in newspapers and magazines, and on hoardings.
(b) The rise of the self-service shop has changed methods of selling and purchasing many products, particularly foodstuffs.
(c) Manufacturing and distribution methods have changed, the former becoming more centralised, the latter becoming more diverse.
(d) The volume of purchases made by individual consumers has increased. Instead of growing or making most of their needs, the average family today buys a vast range of goods, most of which would have seemed luxuries 50 years ago.

All this has led to the 'consumer society' in which the trade mark has played an ever-increasing role. A further, less obvious, factor is the ability of manufacturers to present the consumer with a bewildering variety of choice. Modern technology has led to diversification, because the cost of introducing short runs of goods has declined. Companies have discovered that different groups of consumers have different needs, desires and aspirations and are able to target their advertising at these specific groups, whether defined by socio-economic class or age. Pre-teens, teenagers, young professionals, 'baby-boomers', early-retired and so on have all become target groups for specialist products.

Schechter's theory
Frank Schechter, in his seminal work on trade marks, 'The Rational Basis of Trade Mark Protection' (1927) 40 Harv LR 813, took as his starting-point the orthodox definition that 'the primary and proper function of a trade mark' was 'to identify the origin or ownership of goods to which it is affixed'. He deduced that although

such definition may have been accurate historically, it was no longer so. Rather, he argued, the trade mark's prime function was not to designate source but to create and retain custom. Quoting from H.G. Wells about how the mark reached over the shoulder of the retailer and across the counter straight to the customer, he argued that 'the mark sells the goods'. From that he concluded that what matters is the selling power of the mark. The orthodox infringement action was insufficient. What was required was a form of action to prevent the destruction of the value of the mark by its use on non-competing goods.

The possible functions of a trade mark
As a result of Schechter's analysis, it came to be accepted that a trade mark may fulfil one or more of four functions:

(a)   to signify that all goods or services bearing the trade mark come from a single source (the indication of origin function);
(b)   to identify one seller's goods or services and distinguish them from goods or services sold by others (the product differentiation function);
(c)   to signify that all goods or services bearing the trade mark are of an equal level of quality, thus guaranteeing consumer satisfaction with the product (the guarantee function);
(d)   to promote the goods or services (the advertising function).

To what extent has legislation and case law recognised these functions?

The origin function   The common law view was that the *only* function of a trade mark was to indicate the source from which the goods or services emanated. The inconvenience of the origin function is that:

(a)   The average consumer neither knows nor cares about the precise identity of the originator of the product.
(b)   The trade mark cannot truly be treated as an item of property in its own right, and so cannot be licensed or assigned.

The first point received judicial recognition in cases such as *Powell v Birmingham Vinegar Brewery Co. Ltd* (1896) 13 RPC 235 at p. 250 and *Re McDowell's Application* (1926) 43 RPC 313 at p. 337: the source of goods, it was said, could be anonymous as long as the consistency of the supply was recognised. The second point has not really been dealt with until the Trade Marks Act 1994, which seeks to deregulate assignment and licensing.

Statutory recognition of the origin function can be found in section 68(1) of the Trade Marks Act 1938, which defined as trade mark as being:

a mark used or proposed to be used in relation to goods for the purpose of indicating . . . *a connection in the course of trade* between the goods and some person having the right . . . to use the mark, *whether with or without any indication of the identity of that person.* (Emphasis added.)

Over a period of time, this definition came to permeate every aspect of the 1938 Act, and consequently had a restrictive effect. Various provisions of the old Act received a narrow interpretation, including section 4 (the scope of the infringement action — see *Mars GB Ltd* v *Cadbury Ltd* [1987] RPC 387); section 26 (cancellation for non-use — see *KODIAK Trade Mark* [1990] FSR 49); and section 28 (licensing — see *Re American Greetings Corporation's Application* [1984] RPC 329).

The product differentiation function The definition of 'trade mark' found in Article 2 of the Directive and section 1(1) of the 1994 Act reflects the idea of the trade mark as differentiating one brand of goods or services from another. It suggests a move away from the indication of origin function, and in particular the inconveniences which that created in relation to assignment and licensing. It has not as yet received judicial recognition in the United Kingdom.

The guarantee function The existence of the guarantee function is alluded to by the 10th recital in the Preamble to the Directive. This in turn is derived from the ruling of the Court of Justice of the European Communities in *Hoffmann-La Roche & Co. AG* v *Centrafarm Vertriebsgesellschaft Pharmazeutischer Erzeugnisse mbH* (Case 102/77) [1978] ECR 1139 as to the 'essential function of a trade mark'. The guarantee function is not expressly mentioned in the 1994 Act.

United Kingdom case law has accorded only limited recognition to the guarantee function. In *A. G. Spalding & Bros* v *A. W. Gamage Ltd* (1915) 32 RPC 273, passing off was held to be available to prevent a retailer from describing goods as being of a better quality than was actually the case; consumer dissatisfaction would result in loss of business to the plaintiff.

The Court of Justice has alluded to the function of a trade mark in guaranteeing consumer satisfaction in *SA CNL-Sucal NV* v *Hag GF AG* (Case C-10/89) [1990] ECR I-3711, stating that a trade mark's essential function would be compromised if its owner could not prevent the circulation of goods bearing a confusingly similar name:

> . . . in this situation consumers would no longer be able to identify with certainty the origin of the marked product and the bad quality of a product for which he is in no way responsible could be attributed to the owner of the right.

There is a further allusion to the guarantee function of the trade mark in the most recent decision of the Court of Justice, *IHT Internationale Heiztechnik GmbH* v *Ideal-Standard GmbH* (Case C-9/93) *Financial Times*, 28 June 1994.

The advertising function The advertising function of a trade mark has never been referred to either in United Kingdom or Community case law. However, the advertising function of a trade mark is now protected by the right to bring an action for dilution, that is, to stop the gradual erosion of the selling power of a trade mark by its use on dissimilar goods. The dilution action is recognised by Articles 4(3), 4(4)(a) and 5(2) of the Directive, and is incorporated for the first time into United Kingdom trade marks law by sections 5(3) and 10(3) of the Trade Marks Act 1994.

Why Register?

As already indicated, United Kingdom trade marks law provides a dual system of protecting trade marks. The owner of a mark can choose either to register it, or to leave it unregistered and rely on the law of passing off to stop anyone who uses the same or similar mark in the course of trade.

The registration of trade marks is not, and never has been, compulsory. This begs the question, why register?

Reasons for registration
Registration of a trade mark is perceived to provide the following benefits:

(a)   Registration acts as prima facie proof of the plaintiff's entitlement to the mark.

(b)   Registration can be obtained before a mark is used, provided there is a bona fide intention to use.

(c)   Registration enables an action for infringement to be brought without proof of actual damage.

(d)   Registration enables an intending trade mark owner to ascertain what other marks have been adopted by competitors.

Disadvantages of not registering
By contrast, reliance on passing off to protect unregistered marks is perceived to have the following drawbacks:

(a)   The plaintiff has to prove entitlement to the mark, reputation in the mark and goodwill.

(b)   Passing off is not available for unused marks.

(c)   Passing off will only succeed upon proof of actual or likely damage to the goodwill of the business.

(d)   The evidential burden outlined above has to be satisfied each time an action is brought.

The drawbacks of registering
Registration is not totally advantageous. The applicant will have to satisfy the Registrar that the proposed trade mark is qualified for registration. This means that the proposed mark must satisfy the requirements of the 1994 Act, even though these are considerably less stringent than those found in the 1938 Act, as amended, and even though the registration procedure under the 1994 Act will be quicker and simpler than under its predecessor.

The basic requirements of the 1994 Act are that the proposed mark must be capable of graphic representation and must function as a trade mark (section 1(1); and see chapters 4 and 5). Further, the mark must overcome the absolute and relative grounds of refusal found in section 3 and section 5 (see respectively chapters 6 and 7).

All of this presumes, therefore, that the symbol for which the applicant is seeking protection has satisfied the minimal requirements for registration. Not everything which is placed upon goods or services in the course of trade reaches this threshold. During the passage of the Trade Marks Bill through Parliament, much time was spent debating the legal position of own-brand look-alikes. As will be explained in chapter 4, the various features which go, in combination, to make up the physical appearance of a successful product may not of themselves amount to a 'trade mark', either because they are not distinctive or they are generic to that type of product or because they are too imprecise. These objections mean that such features may not be capable of protection under passing off either; even if they are, the unpredictable nature of the action means that success cannot be guaranteed.

The influence of passing off on the law of registered trade marks
It should not be assumed that the dividing line between the protection of trade marks by registration and their protection by passing off is totally clear-cut. The Trade Marks Act 1994 will have an effect on both methods of protection. It will introduce passing-off notions into the law of registered trade marks; and it will effect changes to the tort of passing off itself. For these reasons, the protection of unregistered trade marks through the action for passing off will be examined first.

CHAPTER TWO
Unregistered and Well-known Marks

Introduction

In the United Kingdom, there is no obligation to register a trade mark. Protection has always been available at common law for marks *in use* through the action for passing off.

The Directive permits Member States to continue to protect used marks irrespective of registration by means of laws like passing off (see recital 4 in the Preamble to the Directive). The United Kingdom has accordingly taken the opportunity to include the optional provisions found in Articles 4(4)(b) and 6(2) of the Directive in the 1994 Act. These provisions enable, respectively, a used but unregistered mark to be treated as an earlier right for the purposes of the relative grounds of refusal (section 5(4)); and the owner of an earlier used but unregistered mark to plead the defence of earlier right to an infringement action (section 11(3)). Section 2 further provides that nothing in the Act affects the law of passing off.

Nevertheless, the 1994 Act will have important repercussions for the law of passing off, as follows.

Passing-off concepts are introduced into the law of registered trade marks
The 1994 Act requires, in various provisions, both the Trade Marks Registry and the courts to have regard to concepts developed by the case law relating to passing off. Passing-off concepts will be relevant in relation to:

(a) *The registration of trade marks.* When considering whether an earlier mark is to be treated under section 5(2) as a relative ground for refusing registration, the criterion is whether there exists a likelihood of confusion on the part of the public, which includes the likelihood of association with the earlier mark. Equally, in deciding under section 5(3) whether an earlier mark should count as a relative ground for refusal, even though it is registered for dissimilar goods, the issues to be considered include the reputation of the earlier mark. Under section 5(4), an earlier used but unregistered mark will be treated as a relative ground of refusal, but only where it would be protected by virtue of the law of passing off.

(b) *Trade mark infringement.* One of the key features of the 1994 Act is the way in which it expands the scope of the infringement action. Where the infringement action involves the use of the identical mark for identical goods or services, then liability is strict. In all other instances of infringement covered by section 10(2), the criterion is that there exists a likelihood of confusion on the part of the public, which includes the likelihood of association with the trade mark. Where the claim is for the infringement of a registered trade mark by dilution under section 10(3), then the reputation of the plaintiff's mark is the critical issue. As a result of this expansion of the infringement action, the practice of pleading passing off in the alternative will decline.

(c)   *Defences to infringement.* The defence to infringement found in section 11(3) (savings for prior rights) requires that the earlier used but unregistered mark must be capable of protection under the law of passing off.

(d)   *Invalidity.* Where a trade mark has been registered in breach of one of the relative grounds for refusal, it can be declared invalid under section 47(2), *inter alia*, because the conditions set out in section 5(2), (3) and (4) obtain. As already noted, these provisions incorporate passing-off notions.

Likely decline in importance of passing off
Despite its extensive utilisation in the 1994 Act, passing off as a separate cause of action is likely to decline in importance because of:

(a)   the registrability as trade marks under the 1994 Act of shapes, packaging, sounds, smells and other sensory marks;

(b)   the relaxed test for registrability which contemplates the acceptance of geographical names, descriptive words, laudatory epithets and generic marks, provided they are all distinctive in fact of the proprietor's goods or services;

(c)   the broadening in scope of the infringement action to cover the unauthorised use of the plaintiff's mark on goods or services outside the specification for which the mark is registered.

How passing off has already changed
Passing off has proved to be a flexible cause of action, ready in most instances to adapt to changing trading conditions. As a recent example, the decision of *Taittinger* v *Allbev Ltd* [1993] 2 CMLR 741 anticipated the provisions of the 1994 Act by recognising that an unregistered trade mark can be protected by the action for dilution, that is, the gradual erosion of the selling power of the mark by its use on dissimilar goods.

How passing off will have to change
Section 56 of the 1994 Act introduces for the first time into United Kingdom trade marks law express protection for well-known trade marks. The owner of such a mark is entitled to injunctive relief to stop the use of the same or a similar mark for the same or similar goods or services, even though the owner does not carry on business or have any goodwill in the United Kingdom. Although it is hard to predict at this stage, section 56 may in due course require the courts to reconsider the essential elements of passing off. This is explored more fully at the end of this chapter.

Role of passing off in the future
As far as trade mark owners are concerned, passing off as a cause of action will continue to have a role to play, although such role is likely to be confined to

matters outside the scope of the 1994 Act. Thus it can be expected to continue to protect the names of unique products such as 'Champagne' or 'Sherry', the themes inherent in advertising campaigns and (possibly) those aspects of the physical appearance of goods which do not qualify for registration as trade marks under section 1(1) of the 1994 Act.

However, if the Government does bow to the pressure brought to bear during the passage of the Trade Marks Bill and introduces in due course a law of unfair competition, then passing off will ultimately be absorbed into this wider form of protection.

The objective of this chapter is to give a succinct account of the law of passing off as it stands at the time of writing and to indicate how it might develop in the future under the influence of changes introduced by the 1994 Act.

Basic Elements of Passing Off

Today, the generally recognised starting-point for any discussion of passing off is the speech of Lord Diplock in *Erven Warnink BV* v *J. Townend & Sons (Hull) Ltd* [1979] AC 731 (*'ADVOCAAT'*). Lord Diplock identified five elements of the tort, as follows:

(a)   a misrepresentation;
(b)   made by a trader in the course of trade;
(c)   to prospective customers or ultimate consumers of the defendant's goods or services;
(d)   which is calculated to injure the business or goodwill of another;
(e)   which causes actual damage to a business or goodwill of the plaintiff or is likely to do so.

Lord Diplock added that the phrase 'calculated to deceive' does not imply that any intention on the part of the defendant is necessary, but rather that injury to goodwill must be a reasonably foreseeable consequence of the defendant's conduct.

Further, he pointed out the dangers of 'the undistributed middle': it does not follow that because all passing-off actions can be shown to possess these characteristics, all factual situations having these characteristics give rise to a cause of action for passing off.

Other judges (for example, Lord Oliver of Aylmerton in *Reckitt & Colman Products Ltd* v *Borden Inc.* [1990] 1 WLR 491, (*'JIF LEMON'*)) have preferred to analyse passing off in terms of the following:

(a)   the need for the plaintiff to establish reputation or goodwill;
(b)   a misrepresentation by the defendant, which need not be intentional;
(c)   resultant damage or likelihood of damage to the plaintiff's goodwill or reputation.

These basic elements of passing off will be analysed in turn.

Reputation
The existence of reputation is essentially a question of fact in each case, depending, *inter alia*, on the nature of the business, the area covered by it, the sort of customer and the type of goods or services provided.

The onus is on the plaintiff to satisfy the court that the mark has achieved public recognition, that is, it has acquired a secondary meaning.

At one time, passing off was the only method of protecting descriptive names. Thus in *Reddaway* v *Banham* [1896] AC 199, the House of Lords accepted evidence that the phrase 'Camel Hair Belting' had acquired a secondary meaning and was factually distinctive of the plaintiffs' goods, even though the phrase was incapable of registration as a trade mark. On the other hand, in *Burberrys* v *J. C. Cording & Co. Ltd* (1909) 26 RPC 693 the name 'Slip On' for raincoats had been used by others besides the plaintiffs; moreover, it became apparent that the plaintiffs had been using the phrase to describe a particular model of their garments, rather than to distinguish their goods from those of other traders and so relief was refused.

Now that the 1994 Act permits the registration of descriptive names, passing off is likely to be less important in this type of case.

Besides the volume of sales and the amount of advertising, the length of time and geographical area within which the mark has been used need to be considered. Again, this is a question of fact and it is not possible to predict in advance the extent of use required. In *Stannard* v *Reay* [1967] RPC 589, three weeks' use of the name 'Mr Chippy' on a mobile fish-and-chip van on the Isle of Wight was sufficient to sustain a passing-off action. There was clear evidence of a substantial drop in takings when the defendant commenced trading, prior to which the plaintiff had been the only such trader in what was a clearly defined, small locality (contrast *McCain International Ltd* v *Country Fair Foods Ltd* [1981] RPC 69).

Once acquired, such reputation may survive for some time after a business has moved or even closed down. There will come a point in time when it will be clear that the plaintiff has abandoned the reputation, in which case the defendant is free to adopt the plaintiff's mark (*Star Industrial Co. Ltd* v *Yap Kwee Kor* [1976] FSR 256). A descriptive name will require more effort to preserve after the business has closed (*Norman Kark Publications Ltd* v *Odhams Press Ltd* [1962] RPC 163).

Shared reputation   Normally, reputation must be exclusive to the plaintiff. However, there are instances where passing off has been allowed in cases of shared reputation.

In *J. Bollinger* v *Costa Brava Wine Co. Ltd* [1961] RPC 116, Danckwerts J decided that passing off was available to enable one of the 150 or so Champagne houses to stop the sale of Spanish sparkling wine under the name 'Spanish Champagne' because:

(a)   the name 'Champagne' denoted wine emanating only from a particular district of France made by a particular method and using grapes grown in that district; and

(b)   the name had acquired an extensive reputation and only wine producers from the Champagne district were entitled to use it (see also *H. P. Bulmer Ltd* v *J. Bollinger SA* [1978] RPC 79).

The same principle was used in *Vine Products Ltd* v *MacKenzie & Co. Ltd* [1969] RPC 1 to decide that because 'Sherry' meant a particular type of fortified wine produced at Jerez in Spain, there was no such thing as 'British Sherry' (although in this case the plaintiffs' delay in bringing the action disentitled them to injunctive relief). The unique qualities of Scotch whisky were recognised in *John Walker & Sons Ltd* v *Henry Ost & Co. Ltd* [1970] RPC 489.

The principle was confirmed in the *ADVOCAAT* case by the House of Lords, who added that it was not confined to drinks emanating from a particular locality, but applied equally where a product had a particular characteristic which had acquired public recognition. In the instant case it was agreed that the Dutch drink ADVOCAAT had a unique recipe, consisting of eggs and spirit, which was not the same as an egg-flip which utilised eggs and wine. Producers of the latter were restrained from calling their drink by the name ADVOCAAT (see also *Consorzio del Prosciutto di Parma* v *Marks & Spencer plc* [1991] RPC 351 in relation to PARMA HAM).

Shared reputation should be contrasted with the situation where a business has been split. Although neither of the two successors can sue each other for passing off (*Habib Bank Ltd* v *Habib Bank AG Zurich* [1982] RPC 1) each can sue a third party without joining the other as co-plaintiff (*Southorn* v *Reynolds* (1865) 12 LT 75; *Dent* v *Turpin* (1861) 2 J & H 139).

It must be questioned whether the passing-off cases on shared reputation will remain so significant given the ability under the 1994 Act to register collective marks (see chapter 13).

Misrepresentation

Lord Parker in *A. G. Spalding & Bros* v *A. W. Gamage Ltd* (1915) 32 RPC 273 at p. 284 explained the requirement of misrepresentation as follows:

> My Lords, the basis of a passing-off action being a false representation by the defendant, it must be proved in each case as a fact that the false representation was made. It may, of course, have been made in express words, but cases of express misrepresentation of this sort are rare. The more common case is where the representation is implied in the use or imitation of a mark, trade name, or get-up with which the goods of another are associated in the minds of the public, or of a particular class of the public. In such cases the point to be decided is whether, having regard to all the circumstances of the case, the use by the defendant in connection with the goods of the mark, name, or get-up in question impliedly represents such goods to be the goods of the plaintiff, or the goods of the plaintiff of a particular class or quality, or, as it is sometimes put, whether the defendant's use of such mark, name, or get-up is calculated to deceive. It would, however, be impossible to enumerate or classify all the possible ways in which a man may make the false representation relied on.

Misrepresentation was clarified in *H. P. Bulmer Ltd* v *J. Bollinger SA* [1978] RPC 79 where the Court of Appeal stated:

(a)   The misrepresentation need not be fraudulent or even intentional: an innocent misrepresentation will suffice.

(b)   The effect of the misrepresentation must be to make the public think that the defendant's goods or business are connected with the plaintiff. It must 'produce an association in the minds of the public' or make the public think that this is something 'for which the plaintiffs were responsible'.

A recent example of a misrepresentation which 'produced an association' in the minds of the public is *Associated Newspapers plc* v *Insert Media Ltd* [1991] 1 WLR 571, where the unauthorised insertion of advertising material into a newspaper was held to amount to passing off. Damage lay in the depreciation of the plaintiff's own advertising business.

Calculated to deceive It is not necessary to prove that the defendant intended to mislead the public, although evidence of fraudulent intent (which must be specifically pleaded) will go a long way to help the plaintiff.

It is for the court alone to decide whether the misrepresentation is likely to cause confusion amongst a substantial number of the public. The willingness of the courts to accept survey or opinion evidence is unpredictable. In *Taittinger* v *Allbev Ltd* [1993] 2 CMLR 741, Peter Gibson LJ approved as 'good sense' the idea that trade witnesses can give as admissible evidence their opinions on the likely reactions of others to the defendant's misleading use of the plaintiff's name (contrast the approach of the Court of Appeal in *H. P. Bulmer Ltd* v *J. Bollinger SA*).

This raises the question of the level of intelligence to be attributed to the 'consumer on the Clapham omnibus'. One judge has suggested that the criterion should be that of 'the moron in a hurry' (*Morning Star Co-operative Society Ltd* v *Express Newspapers Ltd* [1979] FSR 113). This was criticised in *Taittinger* v *Allbev Ltd*, although Peter Gibson LJ did concede that it was right to take into account the ignorant and the unwary. It is no defence to say that the intelligent or well-educated person would not be misled in those circumstances if there is clear evidence that those who are uninformed will be (per Danckwerts J in *J. Bollinger* v *Costa Brava Wine Co. Ltd*).

Damage to goodwill
The injury caused by passing off is normally diversion of custom (as in *Stannard* v *Reay*) and/or injury to business reputation because of the inferior quality of the defendant's goods (as in *A. G. Spalding & Bros* v *A. W. Gamage Ltd*). Damage must be more than minimal (see comments by Lord Fraser in the *ADVOCAAT* case and Slade LJ in *Stringfellow* v *McCain Foods (GB) Ltd* [1984] RPC 501). The plaintiff does not have to prove that damage has actually been suffered: a probability of loss suffices (see *H. P. Bulmer Ltd* v *J. Bollinger SA*). However, if the defendant's use of the deceptive material has gone on for many years and there is no evidence of any drop in the plaintiff's sales nor in any of the plaintiff's customers being misled, the court may decide that no passing off has occurred (*H. P. Bulmer Ltd* v *J. Bollinger SA*).

One case which may be viewed as something of an oddity is *Rolls-Royce Motors* v *Dodd* [1981] FSR 517. Here the defendant had built a car on which he placed a statuette similar to the 'Spirit of Ecstasy', with the famous 'R-R' logo also appearing on the brake pedal and gear lever; the car, however, was powered by a 27 litre Rolls-Royce Merlin aero engine. Whitford J granted an interlocutory injunction to restrain passing off, even though the defendant pointed out that he had not used the plaintiff's trade marks in the course of trade as he had not sold cars. Although the second of Lord Diplock's five elements was missing from the case, the damage to the plaintiff lay not in the diversion of custom, but in the tarnishing of their image by having their marks affixed to a home-made car.

On the orthodox analysis of tort law, if passing off is actionable without proof of damage, it must involve interference with a right of property. As was pointed out in chapter 1, this right of property has been repeatedly stated to lie, not in the name or trade mark in which the plaintiff has built up a reputation, but in the goodwill of the plaintiff's business (see Lord Herschell in *Reddaway* v *Banham* and Lord Parker in *A. G. Spalding & Bros* v *A. W. Gamage Ltd*). This view of passing off therefore reflects the indication of origin function of trade marks.

A recent decision of the Court of Appeal may make it necessary to reconsider:

(a)   the requirement of damage;
(b)   the function of the trade mark as an advertising tool rather than an indication of origin.

In *Taittinger* v *Allbev Ltd*, the defendants produced and sold a carbonated non-alcoholic fruit drink under the name 'Elderflower Champagne'. The Court of Appeal adopted the concept of dilution and decided that, despite minimal confusion, the use of the word 'Champagne' to describe the fizzy drink would debase the distinctive name 'Champagne', producing incremental damage to goodwill. The judgments all state that the loss was within the orthodox formula for passing off, but the recognition of dilution may signify the start of a move towards treating the common law trade mark as an item of property. The case anticipates section 10(3) of the 1994 Act in recognising dilution as a form of damage to the mark's advertising potential.

Another type of damage which might be recoverable is the loss of opportunity to license or franchise others. In *Lego System A/S* v *Lego M Lemelstrich Ltd* [1983] FSR 155, Falconer J accepted expert evidence to the effect that because of the strength of the reputation in the LEGO mark, the plaintiffs could well have wanted to franchise others to make plastic irrigation equipment even though at the time of the case the plaintiffs' only business concern was the manufacture of plastic toys.

The courts have been slow to recognise this loss of opportunity as a form of damage in cases of character or personality marketing (see *Stringfellow* v *McCain Foods (GB) Ltd* and *Lyngstad* v *Anabas Products Ltd* [1977] FSR 62). The problems caused by failure to recognise this as a head of damage are discussed in chapter 12. However, with full acceptance of trade mark licensing in the 1994 Act, the *LEGO* approach will be significant in assessing damages both for passing off and infringement of a registered trade mark.

The defence of 'no common field of activity'
As indicated above, standard descriptions of passing off utilise either Lord Diplock's five elements, or the threefold test of reputation, misrepresentation and damage. Nevertheless, certain cases have suggested that there is an additional element to be considered, namely, whether the plaintiff and defendant are in a 'common field of activity'.

The requirement of a common field of activity is taken to mean that plaintiff and defendant, broadly speaking, must be competing in the same line of business.

Reference to Lord Diplock's speech in the *ADVOCAAT* case shows no indication that a common field of activity is a requirement of passing off. Equally, Falconer J in *LEGO* expressly denied that this was so.

However, cases concerned with character and personality merchandising have in the past insisted that the absence of a common field of activity between plaintiff and defendant is fatal to the plaintiff's action. As explained in chapter 12, the assumption has been (probably incorrectly) that where, for example, the plaintiff makes a television series and the defendant sells goods bearing the name of one of the characters from that series, the public will *not* make the inference that the defendant has been licensed by the plaintiff.

A partial justification for this blinkered approach can be found in *Annabel's (Berkeley Square) Ltd* v *Schock* [1972] RPC 838. Russell LJ pointed out that it is a question of fact in each case whether there is likely to be confusion, and that this is far easier to establish in cases where there is some association between the plaintiff's and defendant's respective business activities.

As explained in chapter 12, the requirement of a common field of activity may well disappear as a result of the judicial recognition in *Mirage Studios* v *Counter-Feat Clothing Co.* [1991] FSR 145 that the public are well aware of the practice of character, personality and image merchandising. Indeed, Browne-Wilkinson V-C expressly stated that those decisions which had favoured the requirement would need to be reconsidered.

Extent of Protection for Unregistered Marks

Passing off has been developed by the courts to cover a wide variety of circumstances. In the words of Lord Parker in *A. G. Spalding & Bros* v *A. W. Gamage Ltd*, it is impossible to classify all the possible ways in which a false representation can be made. The following is a merely a convenient way of grouping the cases together to illustrate the multiplicity of ways in which passing off can be committed.

Use of plaintiff's personal or company name
The defendant's misrepresentation may consist of use of the plaintiff's name (or one similar to it) whether this is a personal name, a nickname (see *Biba Group Ltd* v *Biba Boutique* [1980] RPC 413) or a company name (see *Harrods Ltd* v *R. Harrod Ltd* (1924) 41 RPC 74).

But what of using one's own name? Although a person's own name may be used in connection with that person's own business, if a person with the same name has already established it sufficiently well in trade for it to have acquired a secondary meaning, any subsequent trader having the same name who starts up a new business using that name must make it perfectly clear to the public that the new business is not connected with that of the original trader. Further, it is not enough to take reasonable steps to differentiate the new business: those steps must be successful (see *Burgess* v *Burgess* (1853) 3 De G M & G 896, confirmed in *Boswell-Wilkie Circus* v *Brian Boswell Circus* [1986] FSR 479).

The apparent registrability of personal names in the 1994 Act means that this variety of passing off is likely to be less significant in the future.

Use of plaintiff's trading name
Passing off covers a misrepresentation made by using the plaintiff's trading name. Thus in *Brestian* v *Try* [1958] RPC 161, the defendant was enjoined from running a hairdressing salon under the name 'Charles of London' which was similar to the

trading name used by the plaintiff. Similarly, in *Clock Ltd* v *Clock House Hotel* (1936) 53 RPC 269, the plaintiff's road-house became known as 'The Clock' because of the building's main architectural feature, so that the defendants were enjoined from opening a new hotel five miles down the road under the name 'The Clock House Hotel'.

However, if the plaintiff has adopted a descriptive trading name which has yet to acquire a secondary, distinctive meaning, the slightest differentiation by the defendant when adopting a similar name will protect against a claim of passing off (*Office Cleaning Services Ltd* v *Westminster Window & General Cleaners Ltd* (1946) 63 RPC 39).

Again, with the relaxed standard of registrability (including the acceptability of names which are factually distinctive), this category of passing off is likely to diminish in importance.

Use of the plaintiff's trade mark

Until the introduction of the 1994 Act, this was the most fertile area of passing off, for a variety of reasons:

(a)   the inability under the 1938 Act, as amended, to register descriptive names or geographical names;
(b)   the inability (until 1986) to register marks for services;
(c)   the fact that under the 1938 Act, as amended, the trade mark infringement action was limited to the goods or services for which the mark was registered. Consequently, a registered trade mark could not be relied on where the defendant used it on similar but not identical goods or services, or where the defendant used it on dissimilar goods or services.

An example of the use of passing off to protect a descriptive name is *Reddaway* v *Banham*, already noted; an example of the protection of a geographical name is *Powell* v *Birmingham Vinegar Brewery Co. Ltd* [1897] AC 710 ('Yorkshire Relish'). In each case the issue was merely whether the unregistrable trade mark had acquired a secondary meaning.

Cases which illustrate the ability of passing off to protect the use of the plaintiff's mark on unrelated goods are the *LEGO* case (toys versus plastic irrigation equipment) and *Eastman Photographic Materials Co.* v *John Griffiths Cycle Corp* (1898) 15 RPC 105 (cameras versus bicycles). The reasoning in both these decisions was that because the trade marks had become household names, the public would assume, on seeing the marks on different goods, that the plaintiffs had expanded their businesses into new markets. As a result, the public would have bought the defendant's goods on the strength of that reputation.

Because the 1994 Act permits the registration of geographical and descriptive names and extends the infringement action to cover use both on similar and dissimilar goods or services (see sections 10(2) and (3) respectively), this variety of passing off will be virtually extinct unless the plaintiff chooses deliberately not to register the mark.

Nevertheless, cases formerly decided in this area will still have to be taken into account because the 1994 Act imports passing-off considerations into the law of registered trade marks. Those areas of registered trade marks law where passing off will need to be considered were listed at the start of this chapter.

Use of plaintiff's get-up
The prima facie registrability under section 1(1) of the 1994 Act of colours and of the shapes of goods and their packaging would seem to suggest that this is another area where passing off will decline. However, section 1(1) is likely to be limited to those aspects of the physical appearance of goods which are factually distinctive of the plaintiff and which are decorative not functional (see chapter 4).

Much of the debate on the new Act centred on the extent to which registration and/or passing off will be available to prevent supermarkets supplying their own-brand look-alikes in direct competition with branded goods. The issues surrounding the registrability of the 'look and feel' of branded goods is discussed in chapter 4.

During Parliamentary debates, two opposing views were put forward. Those in favour of price competition engendered by own-brand look-alikes argued that if a retailer copied the key features of a product, passing off would be available to protect the brand owner. By contrast, the British Producers and Brand Owners' Group argued that the onerous nature of the passing-off action and its unpredictability gave insufficient protection (for an example of a look-alike passing-off case where the plaintiff failed see *Cadbury Ltd* v *Ulmer GmbH* [1988] FSR 385). Attempts to introduce a provision into the Bill dealing with unfair competition were strenuously resisted by the Government.

It could be argued that the law of passing off would not prevent own-brand look-alikes because their commercial success depends on taking a *combination* of features, many of which are generic (for example, red lids for jars of decaffeinated coffee; or bright blue labels or bottles for bleach).

Under passing off, the issue is whether the get-up of the goods has become distinctive of the plaintiff (this will be the main issue under section 1(1) also). Contrast *F. Hoffmann-La Roche & Co. AG* v *DDSA Pharmaceuticals Ltd* [1972] RPC 1, where the green and black colour scheme of tranquilliser capsules was protected, with *Roche Products Ltd* v *Berk Pharmaceuticals Ltd* [1973] RPC 473, where the 'very ordinary appearance' of plain yellow, plain blue or plain white tablets was not. Even if the colour scheme adopted by the plaintiff has acquired a secondary meaning, for passing off to succeed the colour scheme must be visible at the point of sale (*Bostik Ltd* v *Sellotape GB Ltd*, *The Times*, 11 January 1994).

Examples of get-up formerly protected in passing off which would appear to be prima facie registrable include:

(a) the packaging of goods (see *William Edge & Sons Ltd* v *William Niccolls & Sons Ltd* [1911] AC 693 – washing blue sold in a little bag with a protruding stick, called 'dolly blue' by customers; and see also *Combe International* v *Scholl (UK) Ltd* [1980] RPC 1);
(b) the shape of a bottle (see *John Haig & Co.* v *Forth Blending Co.* (1953) 70 RPC 259 – the 'dimple' whisky bottle);
(c) the shape of a plastic container (see *JIF LEMON*).

False suggestion of superior quality
A. G. Spalding & Bros v *A. W. Gamage Ltd* provides yet another refinement of passing off. The defendants sold footballs which were correctly described as having been made by the plaintiffs, but sold them as a new and improved model when in

fact they were of unsatisfactory quality and had been disposed of by the plaintiffs as scrap. The defendants argued that passing off had not been committed as what had been supplied were goods originating from the plaintiffs and these had not been tampered with in any way. Nevertheless, the House of Lords had no doubt that the defendants' misrepresentation amounted to passing off, principally because of the elements of deception and damage to goodwill (see also *Wilts United Dairies Ltd* v *Thomas Robinson Sons & Co. Ltd* [1958] RPC 94 – the sale of out-of-date condensed milk; and *Sodastream Ltd* v *Thorne Cascade Ltd* [1982] RPC 459 – refilling gas cylinders for use in fizzy drinks machines).

This variety of passing off reflects the guarantee function of the trade mark and should be compared with decisions of the Court of Justice of the European Communities concerning the repackaging of goods by a parallel importer (see section 12(2) of the 1994 Act and chapter 10).

Geographical origin or composition of goods

As discussed under the heading 'Shared reputation', there is now a distinct group of cases where passing off is available to protect the name of a product which comes from a specific geographical location or which is made to a specific recipe, the location or the recipe imparting unique qualities to the goods.

These passing-off cases should be compared with the ability to register certification marks under section 50 of the 1994 Act (formerly section 37 of the 1938 Act, as interpreted by the decision in *STILTON Trade Mark* [1967] RPC 173) and collective marks under section 49 of the 1994 Act. Certification and collective marks are discussed in chapter 13.

Mention must also be made of EC Regulation 2081/92 (OJ [1992] L208/1) on the protection of geographical indications and designations of origin for agricultural products and foodstuffs. This enables Community-wide protection to be obtained by registration with the EC Commission of the names of regions, specific places, or, exceptionally, countries, which are used to describe an agricultural product or foodstuff, although wines and spirits are excluded, being covered by other EC Regulations. The product or foodstuff must originate in that region or place and must possess characteristics which are either exclusively due to the geographical environment (for designations of origin) or attributable to its geographical origin and/or the way in which the item is processed or prepared (for geographical indications).

Only groups of producers can make an application for registration, which must be accompanied by a detailed specification; opposition can be brought only by Member States (who must, however, consult with anyone having a legitimate economic interest); generic names are excluded from registration.

Registered names are to be protected against direct or indirect use or imitation or any other practice liable to mislead the public about the true origin of the product. Such registered names will also be a bar to the subsequent registration of a similar trade mark for the same type of product, although previous trade mark registrations obtained in good faith can continue to be used. Conversely, a designation of origin or geographical indication cannot be registered where, in the light of a prior trade mark's reputation or renown, registration is liable to mislead the consumer as to the true identity of the product.

Character merchandising
Because of the commercial importance of character merchandising and the separate treatment it received in the White Paper, it is dealt with separately in chapter 12 below.

False suggestion of professional endorsement
A passing-off action may lie where the defendant uses the name of the plaintiff, who is either a person or an organisation of some professional standing, in such a way as to suggest that the plaintiff has personally endorsed or sponsored the product. The cases seem to suggest that the court will fairly readily find that passing off has occurred where the plaintiff is a professional body or commercial enterprise. Thus in *British Medical Association Ltd* v *Marsh* (1931) 48 RPC 565 the defendant ran his chemist's shop with the letters 'BMA' over the door, thereby implying that his proprietary medicines were approved by the BMA, which professional body was granted an injunction to restrain the defendant's conduct. Another case is *Walter* v *Ashton* [1902] 2 Ch 282 where a cycle shop advertised its business in such a way as to suggest that it was in partnership with *The Times* newspaper.

However, where the plaintiff is an individual trying to protect his or her personality from being exploited without authorisation, passing off has been less successful (see *McCulloch* v *Lewis A. May (Produce Distributors) Ltd* (1947) RPC 58 and *Stringfellow* v *McCain Foods (GB) Ltd* [1984] RPC 501). Personality merchandising is discussed in chapter 12.

Advertising campaigns
In relation to the use of passing off to protect advertising campaigns, what is at stake is not the taking of copyright material (such as the script or music or costumes or sets), but the taking of the underlying theme or idea which cannot be protected under copyright law.

It was at one time thought that passing off could not be used to protect the theme of adverts. There is now, however, some slight authority that given the right set of facts, passing off might be available.

. In *Cadbury-Schweppes Pty Ltd* v *Pub Squash Co. Pty Ltd* [1981] RPC 429, the claim for passing off failed because the plaintiffs' campaign, using images of sportsmanship and nostalgia to promote 'old-fashioned lemonade', had not yet acquired sufficient distinctiveness; in any case the defendants had done enough to differentiate their product from that of the plaintiffs. In *RHM Foods Ltd* v *Bovril Ltd* [1983] RPC 275, the action was dismissed for procedural reasons although the court was satisfied as to the lack of probity on the defendants' part in seeking to copy features of the plaintiffs' BISTO advertising campaign. Lastly, in *Elida Gibbs Ltd* v *Colgate-Palmolive Ltd* [1983] FSR 95, Goulding J was prepared to grant an injunction on clear evidence that the defendants had deliberately set out to pre-empt the plaintiffs' new campaign which used a 'tree theme' to sell toothpaste.

It goes without saying that a trade mark used in an advertising campaign can be protected by registration, as can a slogan (see chapter 4). But the 'look and feel' of a campaign will not be within the scope of section 1(1) of the 1994 Act, nor is it within the scope of copyright protection. This therefore is an area of passing off likely to be of importance in the future.

'Reverse' passing off
As its name suggests, this version of the tort involves the converse of the normal set of facts. Instead of the defendant marketing goods or services as if they were those of the plaintiff, the defendant offers the plaintiff's catalogue as an example of its own products with a view to encouraging orders.

A recent example is *Bristol Conservatories Ltd* v *Conservatories Custom Built Ltd* [1989] RPC 455, where the court was satisfied that by showing prospective customers photographs of the plaintiffs' conservatories, the defendants were misappropriating the plaintiffs' goodwill. The case is a good example of the flexibility of the action for passing off in responding to different forms of commercial wrongdoing.

Again, this form of passing off is outside the scope of registered trade mark or copyright protection and hence is an area where passing off will continue to be useful.

Protection of Well-Known Marks

Although difficult to predict, one of the major effects on passing off of the 1994 Act will be the introduction of protection for well-known marks.

The obligation to protect well-known marks comes from Article 6*bis* of the Paris Convention. Prior to the 1994 Act, this had not been incorporated into United Kingdom trade marks law. However, it was often argued that:

(a)   the ability to register defensive marks under section 27 of the 1938 Act;

(b)   the fact that the owner of a used but unregistered mark could bring opposition proceedings under section 11 of the 1938 Act, as amended; and

(c)   the fact that the owner of a used but unregistered mark could sue for passing off;

went some way to meeting the United Kingdom's obligations in this regard. Nevertheless, restrictions (imposed as a result of case law) on the right of a foreign plaintiff to bring a passing-off action meant that this partial implementation of Article 6*bis* fell far short of what was required. The foreign plaintiff rule in passing off will be explained below.

Section 56 of the 1994 Act
Section 56 enables the owner of a well-known mark to do two things:

(a)   to restrain by injunction the *use* in the United Kingdom of a trade mark which is identical or similar to the well-known mark in relation to identical or similar goods or services (section 56(2)); and

(b)   (by combining section 56 with section 5 of the 1994 Act) to oppose an *application to register* a mark which is identical or similar to the well-known mark, and which is to be for identical, similar or dissimilar goods or services (see further chapter 7).

In each case, it is irrelevant whether or not the owner of the well-known mark carries on business or has any goodwill in the United Kingdom (section 56(1)). However, to get the benefit of section 56, the owner of the well-known mark must be entitled to the benefit of the Paris Convention, that is, the owner must be a national of or domiciled in or have a real and effective commercial establishment in a Convention country.

The ability to obtain an injunction under section 56(2) is subject only to a plea of acquiescence under section 48 of the 1994 Act. There is a saving in section 56(3) for the continuation of any bona fide use of a trade mark begun before the commencement date.

Section 56 therefore contemplates a mark which has been registered and/or used in another country, and where the reputation of that mark has spread to the United Kingdom as a result of advertisements in journals and newspapers or satellite television, or as a result of references to the mark in films or television programmes. There is no need for the mark to have been used in the United Kingdom. In the case of an application for injunctive relief under section 56(2), it will be for the court to determine whether the mark is 'well-known'. Survey evidence, however unacceptable it may formerly have been in passing-off cases, will be vital to establish that the public are aware of the mark.

The former 'foreign plaintiff' rule in passing off
The advent of section 56 will entail the complete revision of one aspect of passing off, namely, the ability of a foreign plaintiff to protect an unregistered mark in the United Kingdom.

The issue which previously the courts had to determine was whether a foreign plaintiff had to have:

(a)   an establishment in the United Kingdom; or
(b)   customers in this country who could be mislead by the defendant's misrepresentation; or
(c)   a reputation in the United Kingdom as a result of 'spill over' advertising.

United Kingdom cases eventually decided that reputation alone was not enough (*Alain Bernadin et Cie* v *Pavilion Properties Ltd* [1967] RPC 581). Although the foreign plaintiff need not have an establishment in the United Kingdom, there had to be some sort of business activity, whether this was the personal importation of goods by customers travelling abroad (*Panhard et Levassor* v *Panhard-Levassor Motor Co.* (1901) 18 RPC 405; *C & A Modes* v *C & A (Waterford) Ltd* [1978] FSR 126) or the ability of customers to effect hotel reservations in the United Kingdom for an overseas chain of hotels (*Sheraton Corporation of America* v *Sheraton Motels Ltd* [1964] RPC 202).

A further requirement emerged from the case of *Anheuser-Busch Inc.* v *Budejovicky Budvar NP* [1984] FSR 397. In relation to a passing-off action brought by the American producer of BUDWEISER beer against the Czechoslovakian producer of an identically named but slightly different product, the Court of Appeal held that the customers which the foreign plaintiff has in the United Kingdom must be part of the general public and not a separate and special category. Hence, the fact that the plaintiffs' product had been available only to American forces personnel and embassy staff meant that they were unable to sue for passing off.

The requirement that there had to be customers of the foreign plaintiff in the United Kingdom meant in effect that there had to be goodwill. Goodwill had traditionally been viewed by the courts as localised and confined to the territory of a particular country (see *Star Industrial Co. Ltd* v *Yap Kwee Kor* [1976] FSR 256), a rather anachronistic attitude in an era of international trade.

A more relaxed approach to the standing of the foreign plaintiff can be perceived in Australian cases. In *Conagra Inc.* v *McCain Foods (Aust) Pty Ltd* (1992) 106 ALR 465, the Federal Court decided that it was not necessary for a plaintiff to have a business presence within the jurisdiction. It sufficed that the plaintiff had a reputation, provided that there was likelihood of damage to that reputation as a result of the defendant's conduct.

Effect of section 56 on passing off

The immediate effect of section 56 is that it will no longer be necessary for a foreign plaintiff to establish that there is goodwill in the United Kingdom: reputation of the mark alone will suffice to obtain relief under the section.

However, on a wider front, it must be questioned whether section 56 will result eventually in a complete reformulation of passing off. It was explained earlier that whether regard is had to Lord Diplock's five essential elements, or the threefold test of reputation, misrepresentation and damage, goodwill traditionally has been an essential ingredient of passing off. Goodwill is relevant as regards the effect of the misrepresentation (there must be customers to be misled), as regards damage (loss of sales or tarnishing of image), and as regards the property right infringed by the defendant (passing off protects the property right in goodwill, not the mark).

If the presence of goodwill is not required for liability under section 56, but instead merely reputation, why should goodwill continue to be relevant for passing off generally? And if reputation alone suffices, does this not mean that the property right which is being infringed resides in the mark itself? Although this last point may seem heretical, it can be argued that it is entirely in accord with the recognition of the dilution of an unregistered trade mark in *Taittinger* v *Allbev Ltd* [1993] 2 CMLR 741. Dilution, as has been noted, exists not to prevent customer confusion, but to stop the erosion of the advertising power of the trade mark. The logical conclusion of dilution is that there is property in an unregistered mark.

CHAPTER THREE
Procedure for Obtaining Registration

Introduction

This chapter will give a brief overview of the procedure to be followed in obtaining registration of a United Kingdom trade mark under the 1994 Act and will highlight the main changes effected by the Act. This procedure should be distinguished from that applicable to the registration of Community trade marks (chapter 14) and international trade marks (chapter 15).

The Government's business compliance cost assessment in the Trade Marks Bill claimed that the simplification of national procedure at the United Kingdom Trade Marks Registry will save businesses £55 million in the first year of the Act, and £30 million a year thereafter. Reductions in staff at the Patent Office as a result of this simplification will, however, be offset by the need for more staff to be employed to deal with applications under the Madrid Protocol and the Community Trade Mark.

As recital 5 of the Preamble to the Directive makes clear, procedural matters pertaining to registration are left entirely to Member States. In some instances, however, changes to substantive law will, of necessity, have an impact on procedure. With a few exceptions, therefore, the changes to trade mark registration procedure are the result of government consultation with interested parties. These changes have, nevertheless, been largely influenced by the current policy of deregulation.

The Trade Marks Registry

The Register of Trade Marks
The Registrar (or, to give the full title, as section 62 does, the Comptroller-General of Patents, Designs and Trade Marks) is required by section 63 of the 1994 Act to maintain the Register of Trade Marks, on which are to be entered details of all registered marks and registrable transactions affecting them. The Register, which is computerised, is a public document open to inspection. The Registrar is empowered to supply certified or uncertified copies of entries on the Register.

Whereas under the 1938 Act, as amended, the Register was divided into Parts A and B (reflecting the two-tier level of protection under that Act), one of the significant features of the new Act is the creation of a single Register. The effect of this change to existing registrations is explained under the heading 'Transitional provisions' below.

Forms

As part of the supervision of the Register, the Registrar is empowered by the Act to determine which forms are to be used for registration and other proceedings (section 66) and the Registry's hours of business (section 80), although procedural rules for the conduct of Registry business and the fees to be charged are to be determined by the Secretary of State (sections 78 to 79). New Trade Marks Rules implementing the 1994 Act in practice can be expected in the autumn of 1994, prior to the anticipated implementation date of 31 October 1994.

Access to files

A new provision in the 1994 Act, section 67, empowers the Registrar, on request, to provide any person with information and documents relating to a trade mark application once the application has been advertised. This is similar to the practice in patent law and will be of assistance to those who wish to oppose the application or challenge the resulting registration later on. The other side of the coin is that arguments submitted by an applicant to the Registrar to deal with objections could well be used by a third party in subsequent proceedings for infringement, revocation or invalidity. Firms filing evidence of use of trade marks in support of an application (e.g., volume of sales, advertising expenditure) will need to consider whether any of the information supplied to the Registrar is to be treated as confidential.

Proceedings before the Registrar

Although hearings before the Registrar are relatively informal compared with court proceedings, section 68 provides that rules may be made empowering the Registrar to award costs in any proceedings before him. Under section 69, it is provided that rules may be made to determine the mode of giving evidence to the Registrar, either by affidavit or statutory declaration. Further, the Registrar is to be given the powers of an official referee of the Supreme Court as regards the examination of witnesses on oath, the discovery and production of documents and the attendance of witnesses.

All decisions of the Registrar are advertised in the weekly *Trade Marks Journal* published by the Registry (section 81). The Registrar is also required to produce an annual report (section 71).

Appeals

Under section 70, the Registrar is not taken to warrant the validity of any trade mark and is not subject to any other form of liability for the conduct of the Registry. However, under section 76, any *decision* of the Registrar (including any act in exercise of a discretion) can be appealed against either to an appointed person or to the court.

Appointed persons are to be those chosen by the Lord Chancellor under the terms of section 77. 'The court' means the High Court in England and Wales, the

High Court in Northern Ireland, and the Court of Session in Scotland (section 75). Unlike patents, there is (for the present) to be no specialist trade marks county court.

Where the appeal is to an appointed person, it can be referred by that person to the court in the circumstances referred to in section 76(2). Further appeal from either the appointed person or the court is possible (with leave) to the Court of Appeal, and thence (again with leave) to the House of Lords.

Under the 1938 Act, as amended, appeals were to a person appointed by the Secretary of State, or to the court. The 'person appointed' under the 1938 Act made a recommendation to the Secretary of State, who then made the decision, whereas under the 1994 Act, the decision will be made by the appointed person (see *Hansard* (HC/SCB), 17 May 1994, cols 13–14).

Preliminary Searches

Before filing a trade mark application, an applicant should ensure as far as possible that the mark is registrable, both in law and in fact. The legal requirements for registrability are discussed in chapters 4, 5 and 6 below. The applicant should also check that there are no prior rights which would prevent the registration of the mark, as these will amount to relative grounds for the refusal of the application under section 5 (discussed in detail in chapter 7).

Meaning of 'prior rights'
For the purposes of section 5, the phrase 'prior rights' means the following:

(a)   United Kingdom registered trade marks;
(b)   those international trade marks registered under the Madrid Agreement, protection for which extends to the United Kingdom;
(c)   Community trade marks;
(d)   pending applications for any of the foregoing;
(e)   later Community marks which derive priority from earlier national or international registrations;
(f)   registrations in any of the above categories which have lapsed during the preceding year;
(g)   marks entitled to protection under the Paris Convention as 'well-known trade marks';
(h)   unregistered but used United Kingdom marks, provided they are entitled to protection under the law of passing off; and
(i)   (of particular relevance to the applicant whose mark comprises pictorial elements or the shape of a product or of its packaging) any right existing under the law of copyright or designs, whether the latter are registered or unregistered (for an example under the 1938 Act of where the existence of a prior copyright prevented the registration of a trade mark see *OSCAR Trade Mark* [1980] FSR 429).

Therefore, although not mandatory, it is advisable to commence registration by making a preliminary search of the United Kingdom Trade Marks Register, which is open to the public. The search should reveal if there are any prior United Kingdom national trade marks and, in due course, if there are any international trade marks protection for which extends to the United Kingdom. The Register records both registrations and pending applications.

The search should be in respect of the goods and/or services for which the intending mark is proposed to be registered, and for any other similar goods and/or services (the test for what are viewed as similar goods or services is explained in chapter 7 below).

Once the Community Trade Mark Office is operational (which is expected to be in 1996), it will be necessary to conduct trade mark searches there as well, because a Community trade mark registration will be effective for all Member States, thus blocking any later national registration of a similar mark.

Further, once the United Kingdom has implemented the Madrid Protocol (which is expected to be six months after the 1994 Act becomes operational as regards domestic law), a United Kingdom applicant wishing to obtain an international registration based on registration in the United Kingdom will have to search both the international register and the national registers of those countries belonging to the Madrid Union to which trade mark protection is to be extended.

In the light of the above list of prior rights, the applicant should also check trade directories and specialist journals to see if:

(a)   there are any unregistered marks in use by competitors in the United Kingdom;

(b)   there are any well-known marks in use abroad whose reputation has spread to the United Kingdom;

(c)   there are any competitors using copyright material or designs which are similar in appearance to the proposed mark, if it involves a two-dimensional design or three-dimensional shape.

There are firms who specialise in conducting trade mark searches, not just of the United Kingdom Register but at other national and international registries, and for used but unregistered marks. No doubt their services will be much in demand once all the changes in the 1994 Act have been implemented.

In passing, it may be noted that the 1938 Act, as amended, enabled an intending trade mark applicant to seek the Registrar's preliminary but non-binding advice about whether the mark was registrable before filing a trade mark application. The 1994 Act unfortunately removes this facility, although the Registry continues to offer general advice to the public about how to register a trade mark.

Having made a preliminary search, the steps involved in obtaining the registration of a United Kingdom trade mark are:

Step 1:   filing the application.
Step 2:   examination.
Step 3:   acceptance.
Step 4:   publication.
Step 5:   opposition.
Step 6:   registration.

Application Procedure

Step 1: filing the application

Minimum requirements Under section 32, an application to register a trade mark must contain the following items:

(a) a request for the registration of the mark;
(b) the name and address of the applicant;
(c) a statement of the goods or services for which the mark is to be registered;
(d) a representation of the mark, which under section 1 must be 'capable of being represented graphically' (as explained in chapter 4) – such representation will have to fit into the 8 cm by 8 cm box on the application form; and
(e) a statement that the trade mark is being used by the applicant or with the applicant's consent (such as by a licensee) in relation to the goods or services specified, or that the applicant has a bona fide intention that it should be so used.

In addition the applicant must pay the appropriate application fee, plus any additional class fees where the application relates to more than one class of goods and/or services. Under current procedure, the applicant pays a composite fee (application fee plus registration fee) but the wording of section 40(2) requiring the applicant to pay a separate registration fee suggests that current practice will change.

Items (a) to (d) above are stated by section 33(1) to be the absolute minimum. An application is treated as being filed only when all of this information is supplied, or if it is supplied on different days, on the day when the last item is furnished. Section 33(1) therefore contemplates that the statement as to the use of the mark can be supplied later without affecting the filing date.

The date of filing is important because if registration is granted, it is deemed to run from the date when the application was made (section 40(3)). This enables the proprietor, once registration has been granted but not before, to sue for acts of infringement committed between the date of filing and the date when registration is granted, although criminal liability for counterfeiting a registered mark cannot arise until the application has at least been published in the *Trade Marks Journal*.

The statement of goods or services Trade marks can be registered only in respect of particular goods or services. An applicant should therefore request protection for specific items, for example, 'waterproofing chemicals for leather or textiles' (class 1) or 'lubricants and additives for lubricants' (class 4).

The choice of goods or services to be protected (usually referred to as the 'specification', although the 1994 Act talks in section 32(1)(c) about the 'statement') presents the applicant with a dilemma.

Under the 1938 Act, as amended, the temptation was to go for as wide a specification of goods or services as possible, because under that Act the right to sue for infringement was limited to the goods or services for which the mark was actually registered. The danger was that if the mark was not used in respect of all the goods or services within such a widely drawn specification, there was the risk of proceedings under section 26 of that Act for non-use. If the claim of non-use was upheld, the specification could be cut down by the court, or the entire registration could be lost (see, as an example, *KODIAK Trade Mark* [1990] FSR 49).

Under the 1994 Act, the dilemma is eased because section 10 extends the scope of the infringement action to cover use of the same or a similar mark on similar goods or services.

Nevertheless, there is still a danger in choosing too wide a specification of goods or services, in that section 46 enables any person to seek the revocation of a registered trade mark for non-use. Such revocation may be total or partial.

The classification of goods and services   Section 34 provides for goods and services to 'be classified for the purposes of registration according to the prescribed system of classification'. This is an oblique reference to the Arrangement of Nice for the International Classification of Goods and Services 1957 (as amended from time to time) (see appendix 4) which lists 34 classes of goods and eight classes of services.

Under the 1938 Act, as amended, the Nice classification was incorporated into the Trade Marks Rules as schedule 4 and it can be expected that a similar arrangement will occur when new Trade Marks Rules are made under the 1994 Act.

The standardisation of the classification of goods and services facilitates both the advertising of pending trade mark applications (pending applications are shown in the *Trade Marks Journal* class by class) and searching for prior marks. It also assists United Kingdom applicants with claiming Convention priority abroad (as explained below).

Multiple-class applications   Under the 1938 Act, as amended, and the Trade Marks Rules 1986, it was provided that where a mark was applied for in several classes, there had to be a separate application for each class concerned (which resulted not only in the payment of more fees but in the proliferation of applications). The White Paper, para 4.06, proposed that multiple-class applications be permitted, and this is reflected in section 32(4) of the 1994 Act which refers to the payment of 'such class fees as may be appropriate'. The Patent Office, in its briefing seminar on the new legislation, has explained how multiple-class applications will be advertised in the *Trade Marks Journal* (an advertisement for the trade mark will appear in each class section in the *Journal*) and entered on the Register (a single computer entry will be shown, listing all the relevant classes).

Reclassification   Prior to the 1938 Act, there were 50 classes of goods, this classification being preserved by schedule 3 to the Trade Marks Rules made pursuant to the 1938 Act. Although a trade mark proprietor could voluntarily 'convert' any pre-1938 registration to the schedule 4 classification under section 36 of the 1938 Act and although many pre-1938 registrations have now lapsed, there was nothing in the old Act whereby the Registrar could force trade mark owners to bring their old classifications of goods up to date. The White Paper estimated that there were about 23,000 trade marks still classified under schedule 3. Section 65 of the 1994 Act therefore gives the Registrar the authority to make rules for completing the process of compulsorily converting all schedule 3 registrations to the schedule 4 classification of goods.

Statement of use   Section 32(3) of the 1994 Act requires the applicant to file a statement that the mark is either in use, or that there is a bona fide intention to use. Use may be by the applicant personally or by a licensee.

Section 32(3) should be understood as a procedural version of the substantive requirement in section 3(6) that a trade mark application should not be made in bad faith (see the White Paper, paragraph 4.27). 'Bad faith' should be understood as covering at least two separate but related issues:

(a)   filing an application in the knowledge that another is entitled to the mark (see *KARO STEP Trade Mark* [1977] RPC 59 and *Wham-O Manufacturing Co.* v *Lincoln Industries Ltd* [1985] RPC 127); and

(b)   filing an application with the objective of trying to stop a competitor using the same or similar mark (see *Imperial Group Ltd* v *Philip Morris & Co. Ltd* [1982] FSR 92).

Both of these aspects are discussed in more detail in chapter 6 in relation to the absolute grounds for the refusal of a registration.

Step 2: examination
Section 37 of the 1994 Act states that the Registrar shall examine an application to determine whether it meets the requirements of the Act and any rules made thereunder.

The Registrar must be satisfied that:

(a)   what is applied for is a 'mark' under section 1 of the 1994 Act;

(b)   it is 'capable of distinguishing the goods or services of one undertaking from those of other undertakings' under the same section;

(c)   the application does not fail under one of the absolute grounds of refusal found in section 3, which include the objections that the mark is descriptive, deceptive, or contrary to law or public policy;

(d)   the mark applied for does not conflict with a prior right under section 5, whether this is an earlier registration, a prior used but unregistered mark or a prior copyright or design.

In connection with this last point, a search of earlier marks will be made by the Registrar (section 37(2)).

Registry practice in the past has involved making use of a wide range of reference books to decide if the mark is valid. These books included the *Oxford English Dictionary* (so as to see whether the mark has a descriptive or deceptive meaning); *Webster's New Geographical Dictionary* (for place names) and the London telephone directory (to check the frequency of a surname). If the mark included a foreign name, the appropriate foreign telephone directory, such as the Paris directory for a French name, or the Bonn or Frankfurt directories for a German name, used to be checked for the frequency of the occurrence of this name. This latter practice is likely to be discontinued given that surnames are now probably prima facie registrable, rather than prima facie unregistrable, as they were under the 1938 Act, as amended.

The practice of the Registry in determining whether an application meets the more relaxed criteria of the new Act will obviously take some time to evolve. It can be expected that the Registry will err on the side of caution in deciding whether to accept or reject an application. It will be reluctant to grant marks which might later be struck down in revocation proceedings by the court, and will also have to try to develop its practice in line with other trade mark registries in the European Community, given that the provisions in the Act governing whether a mark is registrable derive from the Directive. If different national registries appear to be developing different standards, then ultimately it will be for the Court of Justice of the European Communities to determine the correct approach under the Directive. Also, as the provisions in the 1994 Act on relative grounds for refusal (that is, conflict with earlier marks) correspond with the provisions on infringement, the Registry will obviously pay close attention to the developing case law in the latter area.

The applicant must be informed of any objections so that representations may be made to the Registrar or the application amended so as to overcome the objections. Unlike section 43 of the 1938 Act, as amended, there is no express requirement that an applicant has to be afforded a hearing at the Registry before an adverse decision is made. Nevertheless, a right to a hearing can be inferred from various provisions in the 1994 Act, such as sections 37(3), 68 and 69. Failure to reply to the Registrar or to overcome the objections will result in the application being rejected.

Step 3: acceptance

If there are no objections, or they are overcome, the application will proceed to the next two stages, namely acceptance by the Registrar and then publication.

The wording of section 37(5) of the 1994 Act coupled with the wording of section 38(1) should be noted: '*If* it appears to the Registrar that the requirements for registration are met, he *shall* accept the application' (section 37(5)); '*When* an application for registration has been accepted, the Registrar *shall* cause the application to be published' (section 38(1)) (emphasis added). Such wording suggests two differences between the 1994 Act and its predecessor in relation to the acceptance of an application, as follows.

Can an application be published before acceptance?   The wording of the 1994 Act, quoted above, indicates that the sequence of procedural steps to be followed is rigid, namely examination, acceptance and publication *in that order*. This should be contrasted with the position under the 1938 Act, as amended. The proviso to section 18(1) thereof enabled the Registrar in exceptional circumstances to advertise an application *before* it had been accepted finally, and, if necessary, to advertise it *again* after acceptance. Such treatment was normally reserved for those marks falling within section 9(1)(e) of the 1938 Act, as amended (see chapter 5 for an explanation of this provision).

This alternative sequence of steps would seem to have been abolished by the 1994 Act. (Note in passing the change of terminology: the 1938 Act, as amended, spoke of an application being advertised; the 1994 Act speaks of it being published.)

Does the Registrar have an overriding discretion?   The 1938 Act, as amended, made clear that there was no duty placed on the Registrar to register a mark. Under section 17(2) there was a residual discretion to reject an application. Often section 11 (which prohibited the registration of anything which would be 'disentitled to protection in a court of justice') was combined with section 17(2) as the reason for rejecting an application. Thus, for example, there was a recognisable group of cases where the Registrar decided that although there was no real risk of customer confusion between the mark applied for and a mark already on the Register, in the light of a risk of serious injury should the marks ever be confused, the later mark would be rejected (see *MOTRICINE Trade Mark* (1905) 24 RPC 585 and *JARDEX Trade Mark* (1946) 63 RPC 19).

At first glance, the 1994 Act appears considerably to restrict this discretion. The grounds for rejecting an application, being based on the Directive, are set out much more narrowly; and sections 37, 38 and 40 are all worded in a mandatory style.

However, close inspection of section 37(5) reveals that 'the Registrar *shall* accept the application *if it appears to him* that the requirements of the Act are met' (emphasis added). It is therefore submitted that although not expressed, there is still no automatic entitlement to the registration of a trade mark.

The White Paper, in paragraphs 3.10 to 3.12 stated that although the exercise of the Registrar's *discretion* would be removed, he would still need to exercise *judgment*: this would seem to be a rather semantic point.

Step 4: publication

Under section 38, when an application has been accepted, it will be published in the *Trade Marks Journal*. If no further objection is raised, the mark will be registered.

Step 5: opposition

Under section 38(2), any person may file opposition proceedings within the prescribed period (it is not necessary to show *locus standi*).

Under the 1938 Act, as amended, the opposition period was one month from the date of advertisement, but this period was always extendible without restriction.

The White Paper proposed in paragraph 4.19 that the opposition period under the new Act should be three months without the possibility of extension, to align the United Kingdom system with that of the Community trade mark and to enable the United Kingdom to ratify the Madrid Protocol, which imposes strict time limits on contracting States to complete the application procedure for international registrations. No time limit is specified in the Act itself but it will be prescribed in the new Trade Marks Rules and there is every indication from Patent Office briefings that the proposal in the White Paper will be implemented.

Under section 38(2), any opposition must include a statement of the grounds of opposition. An opponent may well want to exercise the right found in section 67 to inspect the Registry file relating to the trade mark application, in the hope of finding information which can be included in the grounds of opposition.

The usual grounds of opposition cover the same points as are of concern to the Registrar, as listed above, although the principal ground is usually conflict with a prior right.

Making written observations Section 38(3) provides an alternative approach to a person who does not want to go to the trouble of filing an opposition. It provides:

Where an application has been published, any person may, at any time before the registration of the trade mark, make observations in writing to the registrar as to whether the trade mark should be registered; and the registrar shall inform the applicant of any such observations.

A person who makes observations does not thereby become a party to the proceedings on the application.

Although clearly modelled on Article 41 of the Regulation, this provision does not follow the Community trade mark system exactly and hence may cause some uncertainty in its application:

(a)   The time limit in section 38(3) is different from that specified for opposition proceedings under section 38(2), in that the observations merely have to be made 'before the registration of the trade mark' (though for practical purposes the third party ought to be guided by the three-month rule).

(b)   The making of such observations *may* lead to the reopening of the case although, as section 38(3) states, the third party will not be involved. This is because section 40(1) does enable the Registrar to retract the earlier acceptance of the mark where 'having regard to matters coming to his notice since he accepted the application [it appears] that it was accepted in error'.

(c)   Even if the matter is *not* reopened by the Registrar, the third-party observations will be added to the Registry file on the application. This means that even though the mark proceeds to registration, such observations, if correct, would be ammunition in any subsequent invalidity proceedings under section 47. Because under section 47 an invalidly registered mark is deemed never to have been registered, any attempt by its owner to enforce the mark in infringement proceedings carries the threat of instant destruction as a result of any counterclaim which relies on the third-party observations.

(d)   Section 38(3) differs from Article 41 of the Regulation in two important respects:

(i)   Article 41 is confined to the making of observations about the absolute grounds of refusal; section 38(3) is not so restricted

(ii)   Observations under Article 41 do not give the Community Trade Mark Office the chance to reopen the case. Instead, the observations simply become part of the Office file on the application.

Contemplated changes to United Kingdom procedure   United Kingdom law has never in the past restricted an opponent merely to defending its own interests: hence any objection to an application may be raised in opposition proceedings. However, under the Community trade mark system, the term 'opposition' is restricted to an objection on 'relative grounds' and only the owner of the earlier right may bring an opposition. Any other person who objects to the mark on one or more of the absolute grounds of refusal is limited to making written observations to the Community Trade Mark Office, under Article 41, explained above. A person who makes such observations is not a party to proceedings and hence is not entitled to a hearing.

Clearly influenced by the Community trade mark system, the 1994 Act anticipates a further change in United Kingdom practice, but only after a significant period of time. Section 8 empowers the Secretary of State to make an order by statutory instrument under which relative grounds of refusal are not to be raised by the Registrar (so that in the future a search of prior marks may not be carried out by the Registry). Instead, relative grounds are only to be raised in opposition proceedings by the owner of the earlier right. Such an order may not be made until the Community Trade Mark Office has been in operation at least 10 years (it is not expected to start operations until 1996).

Unfortunately, the 1994 Act does not precisely follow the Community system, in two respects:

(a)   The making of an order under section 8 will not change the effect of section 38(3) explained above.

(b)   Section 38(2) does not restrict an opponent to raising relative grounds alone (see the White Paper, paragraph 4.18) and even when section 8 is operative, there will be no amendment to this provision either.

Step 6: registration
According to section 40(1), if there is no opposition to the publication of the trade mark application or if any opposition is overcome, the mark will then be registered, upon payment of the prescribed fee. The period of registration is calculated from the filing date, and under section 42, will be for 10 years. Registrations can be renewed under section 43 indefinitely for further periods of 10 years. Further detail about the process of renewal can be found in chapter 8.

The effect of registration   In one sense, the effect of registration can be regarded as procedural, as it confers the right to bring an infringement action under section 10 rather than having to bring a common law action for passing off which is preserved by section 2 in respect of unregistered marks.

Traditionally, passing off has been regarded as a much more burdensome form of action than trade mark infringement, because of the need to prove the reputation of the mark. The more favourable nature of the trade mark infringement action is reflected in section 72, which declares that the registration of a person as the proprietor of a trade mark shall be prima facie evidence of the validity of the original registration. This means that in infringement, revocation or invalidity proceedings the burden of proof is placed on the infringer or applicant for revocation or invalidity to argue that the mark should not be on the Register.

Miscellaneous Matters

Claiming Convention priority
The Paris Convention for the Protection of Industrial Property 1883, as revised at Stockholm in 1967, creates a system whereby an applicant for a patent, registered design or trade mark can claim what is known as Convention priority. This system is incorporated into domestic United Kingdom trade mark law by sections 35 and 36 of the 1994 Act, in terms not dissimilar to those found in section 39A of the 1938 Act, as amended.

Article 4 of the Convention provides that any person who has duly filed an application for, *inter alia*, a trade mark in a Convention country is to enjoy for the purposes of filing in other Convention countries a right of priority during the period of six months from the date of original filing. The conditions for this right of priority to apply are:

(a)   The applicant must be a person entitled to claim the benefit of the Paris Convention, that is, the applicant must be a national of a Convention country (if an individual), be incorporated in a Convention country (if a company) or be domiciled or have an effective industrial establishment in a Convention country.

(b)   The first application for the trade mark must be a 'regular national filing' (to be determined by the relevant national law), by which is meant that it must be possible from the documents filed to determine the date of the filing. The eventual outcome of this first national filing is, however, irrelevant.

(c)   The application from which priority is claimed must be the first one in *any* Convention country for that trade mark (though there is the possibility, under the strict requirements found in Article 4, Section C4, for a subsequent application covering the same subject-matter in the same country to be treated as the first filing if the previous first filing had been withdrawn, abandoned or refused, had not been published and had not been used as a basis to claim convention priority elsewhere).

(d)   Both the country in which the first filing occurs and the country or countries in which the subsequent filings are made must be members of the Paris Convention.

(e)   Both the first and any subsequent filings must be in respect of the same mark for the same goods (note that the 1967 version of the Paris Convention does not accord the benefits of Convention priority to service marks, although most Convention countries, including the United Kingdom, in practice do so).

Article 4 of the Convention goes on to provide that where priority is claimed in the case of a trade mark, the use of the mark (obviously, by another undertaking) during the priority period cannot affect the validity of the subsequent application for which priority is claimed, neither can an application for that mark by a competitor. In other words, third-party rights cannot be acquired during the six months of the priority period (and so cannot count as 'earlier trade marks' for the purposes of section 5 of the 1994 Act) although rights acquired by third parties *before* the date of first filing are not affected.

The right to claim convention priority can be passed on to a successor in title.

Section 35 of the 1994 Act follows the wording of Article 4 of the Convention closely, although some of the procedural details found in the Article as to how priority is to be claimed will be left to the Trade Marks Rules. However, in one instance, the wording of section 35 raises questions both in relation to the Paris Convention itself and to changes found elsewhere in the Act.

Section 35(1) states that 'A person who has duly filed an application for protection of a trade mark in a Convention country . . . has a right to priority, for the purposes of registering the same trade mark under this Act *for some or all of the same goods or services*' (emphasis added).

The contrast with the Paris Convention is that the Convention requires the later application to be for the *same* subject-matter. The wording of section 35(1) obviously permits an overseas applicant to apply for a *narrower* specification of goods or services than is found in the first national filing. However, it is not clear whether the converse would apply, that is, whether an overseas applicant could claim partial priority where the United Kingdom specification of goods is *wider* than that found in the first national filing, so that priority would be available only for goods covered by the first filing. Apparently, other convention countries do permit partial priority.

The other problem raised by provisions elsewhere in the 1994 Act relate to multiple priorities. Whereas the United Kingdom has now changed to the system of multi-class applications, many countries of the Paris Convention still insist on single-class applications. The 1994 Act does not specifically provide for an applicant to claim multiple priorities based on several applications in another Convention country for the same trade mark.

Besides the system for claiming Convention priority based on first national filings in other Convention countries (because in United Kingdom law international agreements are not capable of creating rights in domestic law, such countries have to be designated by Order in Council) the United Kingdom is party to reciprocal arrangements with some non-Convention countries whereby a right of priority similar to Convention priority can be claimed. The power to make an Order in Council for such reciprocal arrangements, including provisions for those who have filed trade marks in the Channel Islands, is contained in section 36 of the Act.

Section 55 enables the Secretary of State to make amendments to the Act by statutory instrument where such changes are occasioned by revisions or amendments to the Paris Convention.

Merger and division
Section 41 of the Trade Marks Act 1994 introduces two new concepts to United Kingdom trade marks law, namely, the division of one application into several applications, and the merger of separate applications or registrations into one application or one registration. Further details will be supplied in the Trade Marks Rules. These concepts have been prompted partly by accession to the Madrid Protocol and partly by the change to multi-class applications.

It is anticipated that the rules will provide for an applicant to request division of an application on payment of the appropriate fee. There will be no limit to the number of times an application can be divided or subdivided, although of course if the divided applications mature into registrations, it will be necessary to pay separate registration and renewal fees in respect of each of them, unless the separate registrations are later merged.

The main benefit of division is to enable an applicant (particularly, but not exclusively, in the case of multi-class applications) to deal with objections by separating out that part of the application which is contested from that which is not. This will allow the unchallenged part of the application to proceed to registration, whilst giving the applicant time to overcome the objections to the remainder.

In the case of merger, it will be possible to merge one or more applications or one or more registrations, although it will not be possible to merge applications with registrations. It is expected that the rules to be made under section 41 will limit merger to cases where the marks are the same, have the same date and are in the same ownership.

Series of marks

Section 41 of the 1994 Act, provides that rules may be made to provide for the registration of a series of trade marks. 'Series of trade marks' is defined as 'a number of trade marks which resemble each other as to their material particulars and differ only as to matters of a non-distinctive character not substantially affecting the identity of the trade mark'.

It can be seen that the above definition contemplates the registration of a group or 'family' of marks containing only minor variants.

This should be contrasted with section 21 of the 1938 Act, as amended, which provided for the registration of a series of trade marks in two situations. One was where the mark in question was a composite mark, with the proprietor being entitled not just to the mark as a whole but to each separate part of it, provided each part was capable of existing as an independent trade mark. The other situation was where the proprietor claimed to own several trade marks in respect of the same or similar goods or services and where the marks, although closely resembling each other, only differed either as to their respective goods or services; or as to the price or quality of the same; or as to any other matter of a non-distinctive character which did not substantially affect the identity of the trade mark; or as to colour.

The 1938 Act, as amended, went on to provide that in either case, such a series of marks were to be treated as associated trade marks. The latter phrase meant, in practical terms, that the group of marks had to be treated as a single entity and could only be assigned together, although use of one was deemed to be use of them all. The concept of associated trade marks has been abolished by the 1994 Act.

The definition of 'series of marks' in section 41 of the 1994 Act does not include the notion of a composite mark, nor does it require that the marks be for similar goods or services. Whilst by virtue of the wording of section 46(2), use of one of the series of marks will protect the rest of the 'family' from revocation proceedings, there is no restriction on assignment of the series to different owners. Although this could lead to similar marks being owned by competing enterprises, and hence to public confusion, the White Paper assumed in paragraph 4.45 that commercial good sense would ensure that this did not happen in practice.

Disclaimers and limitations

Section 13(1) of the 1994 Act provides as follows:

> An applicant for registration of a trade mark, or the proprietor of a registered trade mark, may—
>
>   (a)   disclaim any right to the exclusive use of any specified element of the trade mark, or
>
>   (b)   agree that the rights conferred by the registration shall be subject to a specified territorial or other limitation;
>
> and where the registration of a trade mark is subject to a disclaimer or limitation, the rights conferred by section 9 (rights conferred by registered trade mark) are restricted accordingly.

Section 13(1) presents a marked contrast with the equivalent provisions in the 1938 Act, as amended. As a number of sections of the 1938 Act have to be considered, it will be convenient to deal with disclaimers and limitations separately.

Disclaimers Under section 14 of the 1938 Act, as amended, the Registrar could require an applicant to disclaim any matter which was non-distinctive or common to the trade. Disclaimers could also be imposed on appeal or as a result of an application to remove the mark from the Register under section 32 of the same Act. Section 34 of the old Act also allowed a trade mark owner voluntarily to enter a disclaimer on the Register.

The consequence of having to disclaim matter was that the trade mark owner could not rely on such material in infringement proceedings. An extreme example is *DIAMOND T Trade Mark* (1921) 38 RPC 373, a case involving a composite device mark. The proprietor was required to disclaim all the component parts of the device (the diamond shape, the letter 'T' etc.) which left only the composite mark to be relied on in infringement proceedings; in other words, only a total copy of the mark could be prohibited by its owner.

However, for the purposes of opposing later similar marks, disclaimed matter in the prior registration was ignored when comparing a later conflicting application: see *GRANADA Trade Mark* [1979] RPC 303 and *L'AMY Trade Mark* [1983] RPC 137.

On examination section 13 of the 1994 Act seems rather illogical. Whereas under the 1938 Act, as amended, a disclaimer could be *imposed* by the Registrar or the court, thus determining the scope of the trade mark right at the outset, under the new Act all disclaimers are to be *voluntary*. This immediately begs the question why any trade mark applicant would wish to disclaim matter contained in the mark, except (as used to happen under section 34 of the 1938 Act, as amended) to overcome a challenge raised by a third party.

The White Paper suggested in paragraph 4.16 that disclaimers were of little value because they merely reflected the circumstances prevailing at the time the disclaimer was made. However, to leave the question whether an element of a composite mark confers any rights to be determined by a court in subsequent infringement proceedings introduces uncertainty. The insistence on voluntary disclaimers is even more surprising when it is remembered that the Community Trade Mark Regulation provides, in Article 38(2), for the imposition of a disclaimer in respect of a Community trade mark application.

Under section 13 of the 1994 Act, the effect of disclaimed matter is the same as it was under the 1938 Act, as amended: it cannot be relied upon in infringement proceedings.

Limitations In the 1938 Act, as amended, sections 17 and 18 enabled the Registrar or, on appeal, the court, to impose limitations on an application, 'limitation' being defined by section 68 as including limitations as to mode of use or as to the geographical area of use. The difference between disclaimer and limitation, therefore, was that a disclaimer related to the composition of the mark itself, a limitation on how it was to be used.

Another, more specific, kind of limitation was found in section 16 of the 1938 Act, as amended, which provided that a mark could be limited to one or more particular colours, but if there was no such limitation, then it was deemed to be valid for all colours. The Registrar's practice of asking for a limitation as to colour would happen only where the mark was inherently weak or where registration was obtained only by virtue of proving extensive use. The effect of such a limitation was that the proprietor could sue for infringement only where the exact colour scheme of the trade mark was copied (see *Smith Kline and French Laboratories* v *Europharm* [1988] FSR 115). If there was no restriction as to colour, then the proprietor could sue for infringement no matter what colour scheme was used by the infringer.

Limitations could also be imposed by the Registrar, under sections 12 and 26 of the 1938 Act, as amended, on an earlier mark, in cases where the owner of a later mark could establish honest concurrent use. Such limitations would act as a means of delineating, either by the method of use or the area of use, the two registrations, which would thereafter have to coexist on the Register.

As with a disclaimer, the trade mark owner could request a limitation to be entered on the Register under section 34 of the 1938 Act, as amended, and a limitation would effectively restrict the scope of protection of the mark in infringement proceedings.

By contrast, section 13 of the 1994 Act again seems enigmatic, because it provides for an applicant to agree to a limitation, rather than enabling the Registrar to impose one. The section is silent about what happens if the applicant does not agree! As with the old law, a limitation cannot be relied on in infringement proceedings.

Amendment

One major difference between the 1938 Act and the 1994 Act is the ability to get the Register amended after a trade mark has been registered.

Although section 64 of the 1994 Act enables any person having a sufficient interest to apply for the rectification of an error or omission in the Register (the effect of rectification being, unless directed otherwise, that the error or omission is deemed never to have been made), rectification may not be made in respect of any matter affecting the validity of the registration. In other words, rectification cannot affect the mark itself.

This is reinforced by the provision found in section 39(2) which permits an *application* to be amended only by correcting the applicant's name or address, errors of wording or copying, or obvious mistakes, provided the correction does not substantially affect the identity of the mark or extend the goods or services covered by the application. Equally, section 44 prohibits the alteration of a *registered* mark, apart from the limited exception of where the mark contains the owner's name or address and the alteration is limited to changing these details: even then, this must not substantially affect the identity of the mark.

All three provisions therefore impose pressure on the trade mark applicant to ensure that the mark is, from the outset, in the form in which it is to be used. Inability to amend means that if the mark is incorrectly specified in the application then that application will have to be abandoned and a fresh one made, thereby losing priority.

This is in contrast to the 1938 Act, as amended, which in section 35 allowed the proprietor (with the leave of the Registrar) to apply to add to or alter a registered trade mark 'in any manner not substantially affecting the identity thereof'.

Trade mark agents

Section 82 of the Trade Marks Act 1994, echoing section 65 of the 1938 Act, as amended, provides, in effect, that anyone dealing with the Trade Marks Registry may do so either in person or through an agent authorised orally or in writing.

The 1994 Act then goes on to re-enact, with minor changes, provisions on trade mark agents which first appeared in the Copyright, Designs and Patents Act 1988 in sections 282 to 284. Prior to 1988, there was no restriction on who could act for another in trade mark matters.

The 1988 Act, which removed the patent agents' monopoly and controlled the use of the descriptions 'patent agent' and 'patent attorney', can hardly have been expected to confer a monopoly on trade mark agents. That Act provided the client with freedom of choice, so that in trade mark cases, just as in patent matters, there was no restriction on who could act as a representative. However, the 1988 Act sought to control the use of the name 'registered trade mark agent'. This policy is continued by the 1994 Act.

Section 83 of the 1994 Act gives rule-making powers to the Secretary of State concerning the maintenance of the register of trade mark agents and provides that the term 'registered trade mark agent' means a person whose name is entered on that register. The converse power is to be found in section 88, which provides for the Secretary of State, by rule, to authorise the Registrar to refuse to recognise an agent, whether an individual, a partnership or a company. Under section 84, a person who is not so registered cannot be described as a registered trade mark agent, nor can a partnership carry on a business under any name which suggests that it is a firm of registered trade mark agents unless all the partners are registered trade mark agents or the partnership satisfies the conditions prescribed by the Secretary of State under section 85 for firms where not all the partners are so registered. Similarly, a limited company cannot carry on business under the description of registered trade mark agent unless all its directors are registered under section 83 or it satisfies conditions to be imposed under section 85. Contravention of sections 84 and 85 is a criminal offence.

The Act only protects the term '*registered* trade mark agent'. It has been suggested that this means that there is nothing to stop an individual, partnership or company claiming to be 'a trade mark agent' from doing business as such. This is in contrast to the position under the Patents Act 1977 as amended by the CDPA 1988, where the protected terms are 'patent agent' and 'patent attorney' without the addition of the word 'registered'.

Despite this anomaly, there is one major significance in someone being a registered trade mark agent. Under section 87, any communications between a client and a trade mark agent relating to the protection of any design or trade mark or in connection with passing off is privileged from disclosure in legal proceedings in the same way as communications between solicitor and client, provided the agent, whether an individual, a partnership or a company, is registered.

This professional privilege does not extend in the case of trade mark agents to anything involving patents, copyright or trade secrets unless this is incidental to the items mentioned in section 87 (there might be concurrent copyright existing in a pictorial trade mark). Similarly, the professional privilege accorded to patent agents by section 280 of the CDPA 1988 is limited to inventions, designs, technical information, trade marks and passing off, thereby excluding copyright. The benefit of section 87 is not confined to communications about the client's own trade mark, as the section refers to *any* design or trade mark, or *any* matter involving passing off.

In addition to the provisions of the Act, it should be noted that the Institute of Trade Mark Agents is the long-standing professional body for trade mark agents, providing training and examinations for its members.

As the 1994 Act largely repeats the earlier provisions of the CDPA 1988, schedule 3 to the 1994 Act provides that any rules made under the 1988 Act which were in force at the commencement date are to remain in force.

Trade mark attorney

Section 86, added to the 1994 Act during the Committee Stage in the House of Commons, creates an exception to the offences found in section 21 of the Solicitors Act 1974 and related legislation. It provides that no offence is committed by using the term 'trade mark attorney' in reference to a person who is not qualified to act as a solicitor but is a registered trade mark agent.

The provision, supported by the Institute of Trade Mark Agents, but opposed by the Law Society, was perceived to be commercially desirable in view of the low esteem given to those called 'agent' in, for example, the United States of America. The term 'trade mark attorney' parallels the adoption of the term 'European patent attorney' for those entitled to represent clients before the European Patent Office and should assist United Kingdom trade mark agents to receive the necessary accreditation with the Community Trade Marks Office.

Offences

As might be expected, the sanctity of the Register is protected by the imposition of criminal liability in respect falsely making entries thereon. Two sections are relevant.

Section 94 (which had a counterpart in section 59 of the 1938 Act, as amended) makes it an offence to make or cause to be made a false entry on the Register, with the *mens rea* of knowing or having reason to believe that it is false. This latter phrase, by analogy with similar wording which appears in the CDPA 1988, means that the defendant's state of mind is to be assessed on an objective basis, by reference to the knowledge of others in that line of business (*LA Gear Inc.* v *Hi-Tech Sports plc* [1992] FSR 121). The section also imposes criminal liability for making or causing to be made false copies of entries on the Register or producing such matter in evidence.

Section 95 (which again had a more convoluted counterpart in section 60 of the 1938 Act, as amended) makes it a criminal offence falsely to represent a trade mark as registered or falsely to represent the goods or services for which it is registered, again with the *mens rea* of knowing or having reason to believe that the representation is false, unless it can be shown that the reference to registration is to registration elsewhere than in the United Kingdom and that the mark was in fact so registered.

One difference between section 95 and its predecessor is that the 1938 Act referred only to the misuse of 'registered' or any other *word*, whereas the 1994 Act prohibits the use of any word or *symbol* (such as ®) to denote that a mark is registered when it is not.

The saving in section 95 for where the mark is registered elsewhere accords with the decision of the Court of Justice of the European Communities in *Pall Corp.* v *P. J. Dahlhausen & Co.* (Case C-238/89) [1990] ECR I-4827. Under German law, use of the symbol ® was prohibited unless the trade mark was actually registered in Germany. The defendants imported filters from Italy, where the manufacturers had legitimately affixed the symbol to the goods, and found themselves sued by the plaintiffs for unfair trading. The Court of Justice held that German law, by not recognising that the ® symbol might have been lawfully affixed to the goods in another Member State of the EC, infringed Article 30 of the EC Treaty.

The symbol ® is derived from the United States of America's Lanham Act of 1946 but seems to have been adopted universally as a convenient way of showing that a mark is registered. The use of the symbol ™, on the other hand, is commonly used to show that although a name is not registered, its proprietor regards it as a common law trade mark.

Transitional Provisions (Schedule 3)

Basic rule
Whilst it may seem fairly obvious that marks which complete their registration process before the effective date of the new Act (expected to be 31 October 1994) will do so under the old law, and that applications filed after this date will be dealt with under the new law, the position of applications which are still pending at the commencement date is not so straightforward.

It is estimated that at the commencement date there will be some 60,000 to 70,000 pending applications.

Pending applications to be dealt with under the old law
Schedule 3 to the 1994 Act provides, in paragraph 2, that an application for a mark which has not been finally determined before commencement shall be treated as pending. Paragraph 10 goes on to say that such a pending application shall be dealt with under the old law, hence it will be dealt with under the provisions relating to Part A or Part B of the Register as normal under the 1938 Act. When registered, it will be treated as an existing registered mark and transferred to the new Register. 'Finally determined' presumably means that the mark has been accepted and advertised and that the opposition period has expired without any objection being raised.

Conversion of pending applications
Paragraph 11 of schedule 3, however, enables any pending application under the 1938 Act which has not been advertised before the commencement date to be converted, at the choice of the applicant and upon payment of a fee, to an application under the 1994 Act.

Such conversion is irrevocable and, if chosen, results in the application being given a new application date, namely the commencement date of the 1994 Act.

Whether or not to convert a pending application will depend very much on the facts of each case:

(a)   A pending application dealt with under the old Act will have to meet more rigorous registration requirements, may be subject to the imposition of limitations or disclaimers by the Registrar but can be more easily amended under the provisions of the 1938 Act.

(b)   A pending application dealt with under the new Act would have a lower threshold of registrability to cross, but because of its new, later filing date may be subject to relative grounds of refusal which could not be raised before. Although no longer subject to disclaimers, it would not be capable of amendment. A converted application would also be subjected to the effects of section 67, that is, the contents of the Registry file created after conversion would be made available to third parties. Most importantly, however, conversion would mean the allocation of a new filing date and hence *loss of priority*.

Other transitional provisions relating to registration procedure

Transfer of marks to the new register   Paragraph 2(1) of schedule 3 provides for existing registered marks, that is, marks registered prior to the commencement date of the 1994 Act whether in Part A or Part B of the old Register, to be transferred on commencement date to the new, single Register.

This will result (as explained in chapter 8) in the effective 'demotion' of old Part A marks owing to the removal of the protection afforded to them by section 13 of the 1938 Act, as amended.

Section 13 had meant in effect that once a Part A mark had been registered for seven years, it could be removed from the Register only on the grounds that registration had been obtained by fraud or offended section 11 of the 1938 Act, as amended. With the repeal of the 1938 Act, this shield has been removed, and a mark may now be challenged under sections 46 or 47 of the 1994 Act regardless of how long it has been registered.

Registration and renewal periods   Schedule 3, paragraph 15, provides that the initial registration period of 10 years is to apply only to marks registered under the 1994 Act. Pending applications which are treated as 1938 Act applications by virtue of paragraph 10 will be accorded the initial registration period of seven years imposed by the 1938 Act, as amended. Any renewal falling on or after the commencement date of the 1994 Act will get the benefit of the new 10-year renewal period. Marks renewed before that date will be subject to the 14-year renewal period under the 1938 Act, as amended.

Conditions, disclaimers and limitations   Under sections 17 and 18 of the 1938 Act, as amended, the Registry had power to impose a condition on a registration either when accepting an application or after rejecting an opposition. Equally, conditions could be imposed in any appeal from the Registrar's decision.

A condition imposed under the 1938 Act, as amended, usually related to the manner or place of use of the mark: a good example of a condition is the case of *TONINO Trade Mark* [1973] RPC 568 (the mark to be used only for wines of Italian origin, otherwise it might be deceptive).

The grant of registration subject to a condition, unlike registration subject to disclaimer, did not have the effect of curtailing the trade mark owner's rights in infringement proceedings.

If the owner breached any condition, section 33 of the 1938 Act, as amended, enabled any person aggrieved or the Registrar acting *ex officio* to seek the removal of the mark from the Register.

Schedule 3 to the 1994 Act provides in paragraph 3(1) that any condition entered on the Register in relation to an existing registered mark immediately before the commencement of the Act shall cease to have effect.

Schedule 3, paragraph 3(3), goes on to state that any disclaimer or limitation entered on the Register in relation to an existing registered trade mark immediately before commencement shall be transferred to the new Register and have effect as if entered pursuant to section 13 of the 1994 Act.

Associated trade marks   Under section 23 of the 1938 Act, as amended, where the proprietor of a trade mark applied to register identical or similar marks for similar goods or services, the Registrar could at any time require that the marks be treated as associated marks.

The principal consequence of this was that marks once associated could not be assigned separately (unless the Registrar agreed to dissolve the association) because of the risk to public confusion if they were used by different proprietors for similar goods. The one benefit of association was that under section 30 of the 1988 Act, as amended, use by the proprietor of any one of the associated marks could be treated as equivalent to use of any other, thus protecting against cancellation for non-use.

The White Paper in paragraphs 4.44 and 4.45 came to the conclusion that the process of associating or disassociating trade marks caused unnecessary work for both the Registry and trade mark owners which was disproportionate to the consumer protection benefit of ensuring that similar marks did not fall into the hands of different proprietors. True to current deregulatory philosophy, the White Paper took the view that it would be the competing trade mark owners who had the most to lose from any confusion.

In implementation of this, the 1994 Act provides in schedule 3, paragraph 2(3), that any association of trade marks shall cease to have effect on the day the new Act becomes effective.

Series of trade marks   Schedule 3 provides that where a series of marks had been registered under section 21(2) of the 1938 Act, as amended, the marks are to be similarly registered in the new Register. However, unlike the old Act, such a series of marks will no longer be treated as associated marks (see above).

Amendments   Where an application to amend a mark registered under the 1938 Act is pending on the commencement date of the 1994 Act, paragraph 16 of schedule 3 provides that it shall be dealt with under the old law.

Defensive registrations   Section 27 of the 1938 Act permitted the proprietor of an invented-word trade mark which had become well-known to extend the registration to goods for which the mark was not used by making the appropriate application. A requirement of the section was that the mark had become so well-known that use on other goods would be likely to cause confusion. There was no equivalent provision for service marks.

Though little utilised, the benefit of section 27 was that where a trade mark was defensively registered, it could not be removed from the Register on grounds of non-use under section 26 of the 1938 Act.

The enlarged scope of the infringement action under the 1994 Act, together with the Directive's mandatory requirement that all trade marks be put to genuine use, renders defensive registrations redundant.

Schedule 3, paragraph 17, of the 1994 Act in effect removes the inability to challenge a defensive registration for non-use, by providing that a challenge under section 46 can be made in relation to an existing registered trade mark at any time after the commencement date. However, in the case of defensive registrations, such actions cannot be brought until more than five years have elapsed after that date. This gives the owner of such registration the opportunity to extend commercial activities to those goods in respect of which the mark has previously been unused, if so desired.

CHAPTER FOUR
Registrability I:
What Can Be a Trade Mark?

Introduction

The first question to address in considering the registrability of trade marks under the new regime is: what is a trade mark for the purposes of the 1994 Act? Once it is established that what the applicant is seeking to register is a trade mark, then the Act presumes that the trade mark is registrable unless there exists one or more of the grounds for refusal of registration described in chapters 6 and 7.

Definition of a Trade Mark (Section 1)

Section 1(1) of the 1994 Act broadly defines 'trade mark' to mean:

> any sign capable of being represented graphically which is capable of distinguishing goods or services of one undertaking from those of other undertakings

and goes on to provide that:

> A trade mark may, in particular, consist of words (including personal names), designs, letters, numerals or the shape of goods or their packaging.

The definition includes collective and certification marks which are dealt with separately at chapter 13.

The definition in section 1(1) follows the wording (although not in construction) of Article 2 of the Directive with which it must comply. Earlier drafts of the Directive contained no such definition: a trade mark was whatever Member States said it was in their laws. The present Article 2 was incorporated into the final version of the Directive in 1987 and parallels Article 4 of the Community Trade Mark Regulation from which it was taken.

The following extract from the Commission's Explanatory Notes (see COM (80) 635 final of 19 November 1980, reprinted in *Bulletin of the European Communities*, Supplement 5/80) on the draft Regulation shows the intended flexibility of the new definition:

No type of sign is automatically excluded from registration as a Community trade-mark. Article [4] lists the types of signs used most frequently by undertakings to identify their goods or services, but it is not an exhaustive list. It is designed to simplify the adaptation of administrative practices and court judgments to business requirements and to encourage undertakings to apply for Community trade marks.

Depending on the circumstances, therefore, the Trade-marks Office, the national courts or, in the last resort, the Court of Justice will be responsible for determining whether, for example, solid colours or shades of colours, and signs denoting sound, smell or taste may constitute Community trade-marks.

The United Kingdom Government endorsed this approach both in the White Paper (paragraph 2.06) and in subsequent Parliamentary debates on the Trade Marks Bill.

With this flexibility in mind, each phrase of the definition in section 1(1) of the 1994 Act will be considered in turn.

'Any sign'

'Mark' was defined by section 68(1) of the 1938 Act as including:

a device, brand, heading, label, ticket, name, signature, word, letter, numeral or any combination thereof'.

The definition was not exclusive but gave examples of the forms which marks commonly took. However, the definition was construed by the courts *eiusdem generis* to require something that could be applied to or attached to goods:

A mark must be something distinct from the thing marked. A thing itself cannot be a mark of itself. (*Re James's Trade Mark* (1886) 33 Ch D 392, per Lindley LJ at p. 395.)

This caused erstwhile difficulty over the registrability of the colour or colours of a product and precluded the registration of containers and shapes.

Against this background of restrictive interpretation many would have preferred to see specific mention of the following signs in the definition of 'trade mark' in section 1(1) of the 1994 Act.

Colours   It was finally decided by the House of Lords in *Smith Kline and French Laboratories Ltd* v *Sterling-Winthrop Group Ltd* [1976] RPC 511 that the colour or colours of products were marks capable of registration as trade marks under the 1938 Act. This and subsequent 'colour' cases decided under the 1938 Act may be indicative of the acceptability of colour marks for registration under the new law.

The *SKF* case concerned 10 applications by SKF to register as trade marks colour combinations for sustained-release drugs sold in pellet form within capsules. The applications were opposed by Sterling-Winthrop on the basis that each represented an attempt by SKF to register the whole external appearance of the respective drug itself and so none was a 'mark' within the meaning of the 1938 Act.

Lord Diplock rejected this argument. After referring to the overwhelming evidence of factual distinctiveness of the colour combinations concerned and to the concession made by Sterling-Winthrop that their use could be prevented in passing off, Lord Diplock observed:

> The colour combinations have thus been shown to serve the business purpose of a trade mark. They do precisely what a trade mark is supposed to do: they indicate to potential buyers that the goods were made by SKF and not by any other manufacturer. To the ordinary business man it would, I think, appear a strange anomaly in the law of trade marks if these colour combinations for drug capsules and their pellets were disentitled to the protection conferred by registration.

Lord Diplock then turned to the 1938 Act and concluded that there was nothing in that statute which excluded the registration of a mark which covered the whole external appearance of the goods: any visual symbol was capable of being registered provided it functioned as a trade mark. (Lord Diplock's reference to a *visual* symbol was because the 1938 Act, as amended, required a mark to be capable of printed or visual representation (section 68(2)).) The SKF applications should be allowed.

This was sufficient to dispose of the appeal but Lord Diplock felt obliged to deal with the dictum of Lindley LJ in *Re James's Trade Mark* quoted above, since it had been relied upon by the High Court of Australia in dismissing SKF's parallel applications under the Australian Trade Marks Act (in terms close enough to the 1938 Act to be of persuasive authority; *Smith Kline and French Laboratories (Australia) Ltd* v *Registrar of Trade Marks* [1972] RPC 519). Lord Diplock said that he doubted the relevance of *James* to the present appeal. (*James* concerned the validity of the registration of a device mark in the shape of a dome for blacklead and Lindley LJ's dictum was uttered in the context of whether the registration could be used to prevent other manufacturers making dome-shaped lead.) But if Lindley LJ's 'apophthegm' was of general application:

> the 'thing marked' in the instant case is the pharmaceutical substance in pellet form within the capsules and the 'mark' is the colour applied to one half of the capsule and the various colours applied to the individual pellets within the capsule.

Thus, the rule to emerge from *SKF* was that colours were registrable as trade marks provided they functioned as such. The White Paper points to this rule's continued applicability under the new law but with the caveat that most (if not all) applications for colour registration will have to be accompanied by cogent evidence of secondary meaning (evidence that the colour or colours are perceived by the public as distinguishing the applicant's goods or services).

The rule in *SKF* resembles that applied in the United States of America under the Lanham Act 1946. The Lanham Act contains a broad definition of what qualifies as a trade mark: colours are neither expressly included nor excluded. But in the famous case of *Re Owens-Corning Fiberglass Corp.* (1985) 774 F2d 1116, 227 USPQ 417, the United States Court of Appeals for the Federal Circuit held that OCF were entitled to register as a trade mark the colour pink for fibrous glass insulation. The evidence showed expenditure in excess of $122,000 by OCF to advertise their insulation by reference to the colour pink. The court was satisfied that the colour pink performed a trade mark function and that it had acquired a secondary meaning for insulation manufactured by OCF.

Since the *Owens-Corning* decision it appears that three conditions must be satisfied before a colour can be registered as a trade mark under the Lanham Act:

(a)   there must be no competitive need to use the colour for the goods or services (the 'colour depletion theory');
(b)   the colour must not serve a utilitarian or functional purpose (the 'functionality doctrine'); and
(c)   the colour must have acquired secondary meaning and not be purely ornamental.

Traces of the American color depletion theory and functionality doctrine can be found in the English case law decided after *SKF* on the registrability of colour marks under the 1938 Act. These themes might be expected to become more prevalent if applications for colour marks increase under the 1994 Act.

In *Unilever plc's Trade Mark* [1984] RPC 155, one of a series of cases concerning applications by Unilever to register as a trade mark the longitudinal red stripes of their SIGNAL toothpaste, Falconer J held, *inter alia*, that the stripes were functional in that they carried the mouthwash in the product and that red was one of a limited number of colours available to toothpaste manufacturers to use for this purpose. Hoffmann J made similar observations in rejecting further Unilever 'red stripe' applications in *Unilever Ltd's (Striped Toothpaste No. 2) Trade Marks* [1987] RPC 13. He also made the point that where, as in the present case, an application was for a very simple feature, which (in contrast to the colour schemes in *SKF*) was chosen *not* as a badge of origin, then it would be difficult for the applicant to prove that it had acquired a secondary meaning and was distinctive.

In *John Wyeth & Bro. Ltd's Coloured Tablet Trade Mark* [1988] RPC 233, the applicants applied to register as trade marks the colours blue and yellow respectively applied to tranquilliser drugs in tablet form (the single colour was applied to the whole surface area of the tablet). The applicants admitted that whilst their patent was in force, they had used the colours to denote the strength of the tablets. The applications were opposed by a generic drug manufacturer who wished to use the same colours on its products to indicate dosage. The applicants offered to limit their specifications to the colours applied to tablets of a particular and supposedly distinctive shape.

The Registrar held that although a single colour could be used as a trade mark it had to be considered separately from any shape: here the colours were not used as trade marks but to signify dosage. In any event, the colours blue and yellow were common in the pharmaceutical industry and could not acquire secondary meaning for pharmaceutical products.

Similarly, in *Smith Kline and French Laboratories Ltd's CIMETIDINE Trade Mark* [1991] RPC 17, an application by SKF to register as a trade mark the pale green colour of its CIMETIDINE tablet was refused by Peter Gibson J. It was common practice for pharmaceutical tablets to be supplied in a single colour and the evidence showed a single colour did not suffice to identify a given drug, let alone its source.

Sounds and smells (auditory and olfactory marks)   Sounds and smells were *not* capable of registration as trade marks under the 1938 Act, as amended. Section 68(2) of that Act demanded that a mark be visual, not sensory. In 1974, the Mathys Committee considered broadening the definition of 'mark' to include sensory signs. However, the Committee dismissed the idea on grounds of lack of demand and impracticality (*British Trade Mark Law and Practice*, Cmnd 5601, paragraphs 62–4).

Sounds and smells are prima facie registrable as trade marks under the new law *provided* they are capable of graphic representation (see below). This is acknowledged by the Minutes attached to the Community Trade Mark Regulation, and by the White Paper (paragraphs 2.11–2.12) and the Minister, Lord Strathclyde, at the Report Stage of the Bill in the House of Lords (*Hansard* (HL), 24 February 1994, cols 739–40) as far as United Kingdom trade marks law is concerned. Examples of sound marks discussed by the Lords were musical jingles and MGM's LION'S ROAR for films (*Hansard* (HL/PBC), 18 January 1994, col. 33). In the United States of America, the first 'smell' registration in history was granted in respect of embroidery yarn for 'a high-impact, fresh floral fragrance reminiscent of plumeria blossoms' (*Re Clark* (1990) 17 USPQ 2d 1238). (An interesting discussion by Bettina Elias of the problems, theoretical and practical, involved in trade mark protection for fragrances appears at (1992) 82 TMR 474.)

Although the issue has not so far attracted attention, there seems no reason why a distinctive taste should not be registered as a trade mark (YORKSHIRE RELISH sauce?) subject to the overriding requirement that it be capable of graphic representation. The same is true of distinctive 'feels'.

As with colours, sensory signs must be shown to be performing a trade mark function.

Graphic representation is a formality of registration. Section 103(2) of the 1994 Act makes clear that non-graphic use of sensory marks (for example, the audible use of a sound mark) can satisfy the user requirements in section 46(1) of the Act (see chapter 8) and can, if unauthorised, constitute infringement under section 10.

Slogans   Slogans were registrable as trade marks under the 1938 Act, as amended, and continue to be so under the 1994 Act. Consisting of words, perhaps coupled with a device, they are clearly capable of graphic representation. If confirmation is needed, this can be found in *Hansard* (HL/PBC), 13 January 1994, col. 11.

Slogans will be registrable under the new law only if they perform a trade mark function. Two cases decided under the 1938 Act may provide guidance.

In *HAVE A BREAK Trade Mark* [1993] RPC 217, Whitford J refused to allow Rowntree's application to register HAVE A BREAK for chocolate biscuits: the words were being used to advertise the well-known KIT KAT mark (HAVE A BREAK HAVE A KIT KAT) and not to differentiate Rowntree's products.

By way of contrast, registration of I CAN'T BELIEVE IT'S YOGURT for frozen yogurt and yogurt products was allowed in *I CAN'T BELIEVE IT'S YOGURT Trade Mark* [1992] RPC 533. The slogan was to be used on its own on products (that is, without any other trade mark) and it was fairly clear that the public would recognise it as the brand name.

Slogans which combine the functions of exhortation to buy and branding are probably trade marks but applications for registration of such slogans may need to be accompanied by evidence of use showing the latter function (per Robin Jacob QC in *I CAN'T BELIEVE IT'S YOGURT* at p. 537).

Logos/designs   Again, logos were acceptable for registration under the prior law, but specific confirmation of their prima facie registrability under the 1994 Act was sought, and given by the Minister, during debates on the Bill in the House of Lords (*Hansard* (HL/PBC), 13 January 1994, col. 8). Section 1(1) of the 1994 Act specifically refers to 'letters' and 'designs'.

The reference to 'designs' in section 1(1) is to two-dimensional designs, for example, the AQUASCUTUM house check design. Three-dimensional designs would come within the meaning of 'shapes' in section 1(1).

'The shape of goods or their packaging'
It has already been noted that the 1938 Act did not give an exclusive definition of 'mark'. In the *SKF* colour-combination case, Lord Diplock also observed that:

(a)   design registration and trade mark registration were not mutually exclusive (this point was conceded by Sterling-Winthrop); and
(b)   three-dimensional marks were not excluded from registration (see also Hoffmann J in *Unilever Ltd's (Striped Toothpaste No. 2) Trade Marks* [1987] RPC 13).

Lord Diplock gave as an example of a three-dimensional trade mark: 'a raised moulded pattern round the neck of a bottle containing the manufacturer's product'.

One year earlier, the Mathys Committee had recommended that shapes and containers should be expressly excluded from the definition of a 'mark' in the 1938 Act on competition grounds by creating an unfair monopoly (paragraphs 49–64).

Armed with Lord Diplock's example and the general reasoning in *SKF*, the Coca-Cola Company applied in 1976 to register the three-dimensional shape of its famous bottle. Coca-Cola's application was refused by the Registrar of Trade Marks and the courts all the way up to and including the House of Lords (*COCA-COLA Trade Marks* [1986] RPC 421).

Lord Templeman (with whom the other Law Lords concurred) set the tone for the House's decision by summarising the appeal as follows:

This is another attempt to expand the boundaries of intellectual property and to convert a protective law into a source of monopoly.

The shape of the COCA-COLA bottle had been accepted as a registrable design under the Patents and Designs Act 1907, the predecessor of the Registered Designs Act 1949, as a result of which the Coca-Cola Company had controlled use of the design for the 15-year monopoly period.

In Lord Templeman's view, the possibility of being able to register as a trade mark a container or a product of distinctive shape raised:

the spectre of a total and perpetual monopoly in containers and articles achieved by means of the Act of 1938. . . . A rival manufacturer must be free to sell any container or article of similar shape provided the container or article is labelled or packaged in a manner which avoids confusion as to the origin of the goods in the container or the origin of the article.

Lord Templeman cited with approval Lindley LJ's remark in *James*, which had been distinguished by Lord Diplock in *SKF*, and held:

> . . . the word 'mark' both in its normal meaning and in its statutory definition is apt only to describe something which distinguishes goods rather than the goods themselves. A bottle is a container not a mark.

The *SKF* case was peremptorily dismissed by the Lords as relating to the colour of goods and not the goods themselves or a container for goods.

There existed, therefore, under the 1938 Act, as amended, a strange metaphysical distinction between colour applied to a product, which was registrable as a trade mark, and the configuration of a product itself, which was not. Since liquid necessarily takes on the shape of its container, containers also had to be excluded from registration under the 1938 Act.

This rule had to be contrasted with the position in passing off. In *Reckitt & Colman Products Ltd* v *Borden Inc.* [1990] 1 WLR 491, the House of Lords were prepared to recognise Reckitt's *de facto* monopoly in the shape of its plastic JIF lemon-juice container; no amount of labelling by Borden could avoid the finding of passing off.

The situation has now been regularised by section 1(1) of the 1994 Act which includes the words 'the shape of goods or their packaging' in the definition of a trade mark. The potential for registering three-dimensional marks represents one of the most significant changes in United Kingdom trade marks law.

For the purposes of registration, an application for a three-dimensional mark must be described or depicted in two-dimensional form (because of the requirement for graphic representation), but use of the three-dimensional version will protect the mark against attack on the grounds of non-use in section 46(1) of the 1994 Act. Similarly, use of the three-dimensional mark without consent will amount to infringement within the meaning of section 10. Both these latter points are covered by section 103(2) of the Act.

In order to be registrable, the shape of goods or their packaging *must function as a trade mark*, that is, serve to identify the goods of one trader from competing goods of another trader. The White Paper spoke of registration recognising *de facto* monopolies in three-dimensional marks, not conferring them, and indicated that an application for the registration of a three-dimensional mark would need to be supported by evidence of use, showing that the mark had acquired trade mark significance amongst members of the relevant public (paragraph 2.18). Thus, although registration might in future be secured for the shape of the COCA-COLA bottle (given as an example in the House of Lords, *Hansard* (HL/PBC), 13 January 1994, col. 7) and the shape of the JIF lemon container, other successful applications for registration of three-dimensional marks are expected to be few and far between (White Paper, paragraph 2.13).

Furthermore, *no* amount of evidence of factual distinctiveness or secondary meaning can overcome the absolute ground for refusal of registration contained in section 3(2) of the 1994 Act. Section 3(2) excludes from registration as trade marks product shapes which: (a) result from the nature of the goods themselves; (b) are necessary to obtain a technical result; or (c) give substantial value to the goods. These exclusions are discussed in chapter 6 which deals with all the absolute grounds for refusal of registration under the 1994 Act. Suffice it here to say that useful comparisons can be drawn with the American 'doctrine of functionality' as it has been developed by Federal and State courts and tribunals in relation to the protection of product shapes.

Get-up/own-brand look-alikes 'Get-up' is a phrase used to describe product packaging as whole.

The COCA-COLA bottle and JIF lemon container provide rare examples of get-up which is so simple that only one, or at most two aspects, are involved. Get-up of this nature clearly falls within the *ordinary* meaning of the word 'sign' in section 1(1) of the 1994 Act. The most apposite definition of 'sign' given by the *New Shorter Oxford English Dictionary* (1993) is: 'a mark, symbol or device used to represent something, or distinguish the object on which it is put'.

Normally, however, product get-ups comprise a complex combination of design features and, sometimes subliminal, consumer images. So, for example, the overall get-up of a leading brand of shampoo might comprise: the name, which conveys the advantage of the product or the problem sought to be overcome (WASH AND GO, HEAD AND SHOULDERS); the shape of the container; the colour of the container; the shape and/or the position of the label; the colour of the label; the typeface of the name and principal product information on the label; the colour of the shampoo itself; and, perhaps, the shampoo's smell.

Whilst in themselves some aspects of get-up are not distinctive (and, indeed, may be generic: coloured lids on instant coffee jars?), in combination they often are. But such a combination of features cannot reasonably be said to be a 'sign' and registrable as a trade mark under the 1994 Act. Nor is it practicable that they should be. Manufacturers would have to apply for separate registrations to cover small variations in get-up for each product in a range (possibly in addition to applying for registrations for different word/device marks for each product in the range). Take, for example, the NESCAFÉ instant coffee range, which comprises: decaffeinated, regular, premium GOLD BLEND, strong dark-roast BLEND 37, Latin American ALTA RICA, and Colombian CAP COLOMBIE. Again, how would the 'trade mark' be represented in the application for registration? And what would the test for infringement be — a 'substantial part'?

As seen in chapter 2, protection for overall get-up can be achieved through an action for passing off. However, the cost and unpredictability of that action, coupled with the ever-increasing number of supermarket 'own-brand look-alike' products (products which resemble brand leaders in overall appearance, for example, SAFEWAY FONDANT FANCIES and MR KIPLING FRENCH FANCIES), led a group of major consumer goods manufacturers, the British Producers and Brand Owners' Group, to lobby the Government to introduce into the new trade marks law a provision against unfair competition under Article 10*bis* of the Paris Convention. (Benelux, Germany and France were cited as examples of countries within the European Union affording protection to product get-up through unfair competition laws.)

The Government resisted such a provision for the Trade Marks Act 1994. But growing support for the cause of the brand leaders may be indicative of future development.

'Capable of being represented graphically'
In order to qualify as a trade mark under the 1994 Act, a sign must be capable of being represented graphically. The limitation is necessary because it is included in Article 2 of the Directive. It is also present in Article 4 of the Community Trade Mark Regulation.

The requirement of graphic representation is necessary in order to enable interested parties to ascertain the scope of existing trade mark rights, either by consulting the *Trade Marks Journal* or by conducting a search of the Register, possibly from a remote location. This means that for the purposes of registration, a trade mark must be represented in a form which can be recorded and published. The requirement also aids owners of existing marks to check trade mark journals for new, similar applications.

In the case of a word and/or device mark the limitation will be satisfied by a facsimile of the mark. Two-dimensional representations of protected three-dimensional objects have long been familiar in patent and design law and should present no problem. Similarly, sounds can be represented in conventional notation or be described in words. Olfactory marks, tastes and feels might present initial problems but the American experience suggests that these types of marks can be described adequately in words.

As yet, the Trade Marks Registry has given no guidance on the representation of marks beyond that the mark must fit into the box on the application form which is 8 cm by 8 cm!

Section 103(2) of the 1994 Act makes clear that the phrase 'capable of being represented graphically' is no more than a procedural requirement of registration:

> References in this Act to use (or any particular description of use) of a trade mark, or of a sign identical with, similar to, or likely to be mistaken for a trade mark, include use (or that description of use) otherwise than by means of a graphic representation.

As well as confirming (by the back door) that three-dimensional and sensory signs do fall within the definition of a trade mark in section 1(1) of the Act, section 103(2) is of vital importance to the subjects of maintenance and infringement of registered trade marks which are dealt with in chapters 8 and 9 respectively.

'Which is capable of distinguishing goods or services of one undertaking from those of other undertakings'
In order to constitute a 'trade mark' under the 1938 Act a mark had to be used to indicate a connection in the course of trade between the goods and a person entitled to use the mark (section 68(1)). This was interpreted in the light of previous legislation to mean that a trade mark must be used to denote the source or origin of the goods concerned (*Bismag Ltd* v *Amblins (Chemists) Ltd* (1940) 57 RPC 209). (Section 3 of the 1905 Act (which section 68(1) of the 1938 Act replaced) specified the necessary trade connection as one of manufacture, selection, certification, dealing with, or offering for sale.)

Subject to the above requirement, it had been long settled that the actual source of the goods did not have to be known: all that was important was that the consumer recognised that goods bearing the mark emanated from the same source

(*Powell* v *Birmingham Vinegar Brewery Co. Ltd* (1896) 13 RPC 235 and *McDowell's Application* (1926) 43 RPC 313).

The 1938 Act defined 'service mark' as a mark used to indicate that a particular person was connected in the course of business with the provision of the subject services (section 68(1), as amended by the Trade Marks (Amendment) Act 1984). Arguably the business connection required was less rigid.

Section 1(1) of the 1994 Act *omits* a reference to an indication of a connection in the course of trade. A trade mark may consist of any sign provided it is *'capable of distinguishing goods or services of one undertaking from those of other undertakings'*. Section 1(1) seems to be applicable to identical goods or services from different sources.

Thus, the emphasis has shifted from the function of indicating a connection in the course of trade between goods or services and the proprietor of a mark (an *origin* function) to that of distinguishing goods or services of one undertaking from those of other undertakings (a *distinguishing* function). The new definition in section 1(1) should result in recognition of, and protection for, all the modern functions of a trade mark discussed in chapter 1, including those of advertising and promoting goods or services.

This raises the interesting question: does the 1994 Act permit registration of a trade mark for goods where trade in those goods is merely for the purpose of advertising the principal business of the applicant? *KODIAK Trade Mark* [1990] FSR 49, concerned Kodak Ltd's registration under the 1938 Act of the mark KODAK for clothing. Kodak used the mark on T-shirts in order to advertise photographic products. An application to revoke the registration on grounds of non-use succeeded: the mark was not being used as a trade mark (that is, to indicate origin) for clothing.

A related issue is whether registration may be achieved under the 1994 Act, where use of a mark in relation to goods is ancillary to the provision of a service, or use of a mark in connection with the provision of a service is ancillary to trading in goods.

The White Paper had the following to say about the phrase 'capable of distinguishing goods or services of one undertaking from those of other undertakings':

> The goods 'of' an undertaking can in this context only sensibly mean the goods which the undertaking makes or sells – in short, goods which it deals with in the course of trade – and not for example goods which it merely repairs or delivers. Likewise the services 'of' an undertaking means those services (banking, repairing, cleaning etc.) which the undertaking is in the business of providing. (Paragraph 2.22.)

Thus, although the opportunity has been taken in the 1994 Act to legislate for both trade and service marks under the umbrella term 'trade mark', the above passage indicates that the former divide between marks for goods and marks for services is to be maintained. (The passage also suggests that the United Kingdom courts might cling to the origin function of trade marks; see *Hansard* (HL), 24 February 1994, col. 733.)

The distinction between marks for goods and marks for services was first enunciated by the House of Lords in *Aristoc Ltd* v *Rysta Ltd* (1945) 62 RPC 65.

An application to register the mark RYSTA for stockings was refused, *inter alia*, on the ground that the applicants were in the business of repairing stockings: they were not trading in stockings.

The rule in *Aristoc Ltd* v *Rysta Ltd* did not exclude registration under the 1938 Act, as amended, of a mark in respect of goods supplied in the course of providing a service. The test was one of genuine trading in the goods concerned, as opposed to mere ancillary supply. In *VISA Trade Mark* [1985] RPC 323, the applicant provider of financial services was held entitled to register the mark VISA in respect of travellers' cheques and printed bank cards which it sold to customer banks. By way of contrast, in *ADD-70 Trade Mark* [1986] RPC 89, the applicant was not permitted to register the mark ADD-70 for insurance policy documents which were ancillary to its business of providing insurance services. These cases are expected to continue to apply under the new law.

Exactly the same test applied to services provided in the course of trading in goods – with one added complication. The definition of 'service mark' inserted into section 68(1) of the 1938 Act by section 1(7) of the Trade Marks (Amendment) Act 1984, as amended, required the provision of services to be *for money or money's worth*. (The definition of 'trade mark' in section 68(1) of the 1938 Act contained no such requirement: *GOLDEN PAGES Trade Mark* [1985] FSR 27.) Thus, in *GIDEONS INTERNATIONAL Service Mark* [1991] RPC 141, spiritual reward could not secure a registration for Gideon International in respect of its provision of free bibles to hotel rooms. The need for services to be provided for money or money's worth has been dropped from the 1994 Act.

Retail services An issue that was debated both before and during the passage of the Trade Marks Bill through Parliament was whether special provision should be made in the 1994 Act for the registration of trade marks in respect of retail services. The effect would be to extend the protection of trade marks law to a business name associated with a particular style of trading (additional to any goods registrations a trader may have).

The Arrangement of Nice for the International Classification of Goods and Services (see appendix 4) does not mention retail services but they could be included in Class 42 ('other services'). Registration for retail services is permitted in some other countries, including the United States of America, Australia, Hong Kong and South Africa. Community trade marks will *not* be available for retail services (Minute 1 to the Community Trade Mark Regulation).

Registration of retail service marks was not possible under the 1938 Act, as amended. In *Re Dee Corporation plc* [1990] RPC 159, Boots, Sainsbury's Homebase and Gateway made 'test' applications to register their marks for retail services in Class 42. The services in question included the provision of advice to customers, a selection of goods, a congenial atmosphere in which to shop, car-parking and checkout and credit facilities. The services were not separately itemised on customers' bills.

The main ground on which the Court of Appeal rejected the applications was that none of the activities referred to were provided for money or money's worth.

More importantly for present purposes the Court of Appeal held that:

(a) the activities were merely *ancillary* to the business of trading in goods in the stores;

(b)   the expression 'retail services' contained an inherent contradiction and was really another way of saying trading in goods; and

(c)   the specification 'retail services' was too imprecise to support a registration. (See also *Tool Wholesale Holdings (Pty) Ltd* v *Action Bolt (Pty) Ltd* [1991] RPC 251.)

Despite intense lobbying by the retail industry, the Government maintained its objections to retail services. The law remains as stated in *Dee* though without, of course, the requirement for money or money's worth. However, it must be said that the particular fear of retailers which prompted the *Dee* applications has been met by section 10(4) of the 1994 Act, which for the first time makes clear that using someone else's trade mark as the name of a business dealing in goods similar (or dissimilar where the mark is 'of repute') to those for which the mark is registered is infringement (see chapter 9).

Dee does not mean that retailers cannot obtain trade mark registrations under the 1994 Act for services provided in the course of trading in goods. Registration can be achieved in respect of a *specific* service provided that service is not simply ancillary to the principal business of retailing. Examples might include the provision in a supermarket of crèche or hairdressing facilities.

Intent to use   The United Kingdom has long permitted the registration of future as well as existing trade marks (express provision was first made in the Trade Marks Act 1905). The qualification under the 1938 Act, as amended, was that the mark had to be 'used or proposed to be used' in relation to the specified goods or services (section 68(1)). This phrase was interpreted by the Court of Appeal in *Imperial Group Ltd* v *Philip Morris & Co. Ltd* [1982] FSR 72 to mean use or an intention to use the mark with a view to deriving trading profit and prevented, *inter alia*, the registration of 'ghost' marks, that is, marks applied for in order to protect an unregistrable mark, or to block a competitor's use of a similar mark (in *Imperial*, for example, NERIT to guard against use of MERIT).

The definition of 'trade mark' in section 1(1) of the 1994 Act contains no requirement for use or intention to use. However, section 32(3) of the Act states that an application for registration of a trade mark must be accompanied by a statement of use or bona fide intention to use the mark in relation to the goods or services the subject of the application.

In the White Paper, paragraph 4.27, the Government stated that a mark applied for without bona fide intention to use would be treated under the new law as a mark applied for in bad faith. The latter is an absolute ground for refusal of registration in section 3(6) of the 1994 Act (see chapter 6). Since the issue is most likely to arise in connection with invalidity proceedings, it is discussed in detail in chapter 8. The *Imperial* case is likely to continue to be relevant under the new law.

Use by whom?   Under the 1938 Act, as amended, the use or intended use of the mark in the United Kingdom had to be by the proprietor of the mark or by a registered user (section 68(1)). A proprietor which did not intend itself to use the mark in the United Kingdom, but which intended to license another to do so, could apply for registration of its mark under section 29(1)(b) of the 1938 Act, as amended, provided it accompanied its application with an acceptable application to register that other user. (Section 17(1) of the 1938 Act, as amended, only permitted applications by 'the proprietor of a trade [or service mark] used or proposed to be used by him'.)

Again the definition of 'trade mark' in section 1(1) of the 1994 Act is silent on this matter. There has been considerable deregulation of licensing under the 1994 Act (see chapter 11) and section 46(1) reflects Article 10(3) of the Directive in providing that *any* use with the consent of the proprietor will count as use by the proprietor (see chapter 8). The former section 29(1)(b) application is now a thing of the past. Under section 32 of the 1994 Act, an application for the registration of a trade mark is to be by the 'applicant' who must declare that the mark is being used by the applicant or with its consent, or that the applicant has bona fide intention that it should be so used.

However, there remain incentives under the 1994 Act to register licences, which are discussed at chapter 11.

Transitional Provisions (Schedule 3)

By virtue of paragraph 1(2)(a) of schedule 3 to the 1994 Act, an application for registration of a mark is treated as *pending* on commencement of the Act, if it was made but not finally determined before commencement. The date on which an application was made for this purpose is the date of filing under the 1938 Act, as amended (see Trade and Service Mark Rules 1986, as amended, rules 3(2), 22(3)).

A pending application for registration is to be dealt with under the old law and, if registered, is treated as an 'existing registered mark' for the purposes of the transitional provisions in the 1994 Act (paragraph 10(1), schedule 3).

Alternatively, in the case of a pending application which has not been advertised in the *Trade Marks Journal* under section 18 of the 1938 Act before commencement, the applicant may by giving notice in the prescribed form to the Registrar, *irrevocably* elect to have its application determined under the new law (paragraph 11(1), (2), (3), schedule 3 to the 1994 Act). The advantages of this course of action are the wider definition of 'trade mark' and the relaxed test of registrability (see chapter 5). The disadvantages are wider relative grounds for refusal of registration (see chapter 7) and loss of priority (see chapter 3).

A summary of the old law on the subject-matter of this chapter is as follows:

(a) An applicant for registration under the 1938 Act, as amended, had to establish that what it was seeking to register was:

(i) a 'mark'; and
(ii) a 'trade mark' or a 'service mark'.

(b) 'Mark' was defined by section 68(1) of the 1938 Act, as amended, as including:

a device, brand, heading, label, ticket, name, signature, word, letter, numeral or any combination thereof.

Section 68(2) stated:

references to the use of a mark shall be construed as references to the use of a printed or other visual representation of the mark.

Colours fell within the definition of 'mark' (*Smith Kline and French Laboratories Ltd* v *Sterling-Winthrop Group Ltd* [1976] RPC 511), but not shapes or containers (*COCA-COLA Trade Marks* [1986] RPC 421). Sensory signs were not registrable marks because of the requirement for visual or printed representation.

(c)   'Trade mark' was defined by section 68(1) of the 1938 Act as:

a mark *used or proposed to be used* in relation to goods for the purpose of *indicating, or so as to indicate, a connection in the course of trade* between the goods and some person having the right either as proprietor *or as registered user* to use the mark, whether with or without any indication of the identity of that person. (Emphasis added.)

The important points to note were:

(i)   the mark had to be used or proposed to be used (*Imperial Group Ltd* v *Philip Morris & Co. Ltd* [1982] FSR 72);
(ii)   in the course of trading in goods (*Aristoc Ltd* v *Rysta Ltd* (1945) 62 RPC 65);
(iii)   as an indicator of the origin of the goods (*Bismag Ltd* v *Amblins (Chemist) Ltd* (1940) 57 RPC 209, *KODIAK Trade Mark* [1990] FSR 49);
(iv)   by the proprietor of the mark or a registered user.

(d)   The differences in the definition of 'service mark' in section 68(1) of the 1938 Act, as amended, were:

(i)   the business connection required was probably not so rigid ('to indicate, that a particular person is connected, in the course of business, with the provision of those services'); and
(ii)   the services applied for had to be provided for money or money's worth (*GIDEONS INTERNATIONAL Service Mark* [1991] RPC 141).

Registration for retail services was impossible under the 1938 Act (*Re Dee Corporation plc* [1990] RPC 159).

CHAPTER FIVE
Registrability II:
Distinctiveness: Capacity to Distinguish

Introduction

In order to qualify as a trade mark under section 1(1) of the 1994 Act, a sign must be *capable of distinguishing* the goods or services of the applicant for registration from competing goods or services in the market-place. A sign can perform this identifying function only if it is *distinctive*. Distinctiveness may arise in two ways:

(a) The sign itself may possess an innate capacity to distinguish, or *inherent distinctiveness*. This will be the case where a sign conveys no meaning to the consumer except in the context of the applicant's goods or services, or where the ordinary meaning(s) of the sign bears no relationship to the applicant's goods or services. The best example of the former is an invented word, like KODAK. An example of the latter might be APPLE for computers.

(b) Because of the use made of the sign, the consumer has come (or has been educated) to recognise the sign as identifying the goods or services of the applicant. In other words, the ordinary meaning of the sign has been displaced by a secondary meaning, or *factual distinctiveness*, when the sign is used in conjunction with the applicant's goods or services. The JIF lemon is, perhaps, the most well-known recent example of a sign which is distinctive in fact, but not by nature.

The 1994 Act recognises both types of distinctiveness as entitling the applicant to register its sign as a trade mark, subject to the proviso that there must not exist any of the absolute or relative grounds for refusal of registration listed in sections 3 or 5 respectively. Even then, certain of the absolute grounds for refusal of registration can be overcome by proof of the factual distinctiveness of the trade mark in use (proviso to section 3(1)); the relative grounds, by obtaining the consent of the conflicting trade mark or right owner to registration of the applicant's mark (section 5(5)).

By way of contrast, under the 1938 Act, as amended, a trade or service mark's suitability for registration was judged against the mark's possession of certain 'essential particulars' (listed as alternatives in section 9(1) of the 1938 Act, as amended). The extent to which an applicant could show that its mark comprised one or more of these particulars determined whether the mark was 'adapted to distinguish' for the purposes of registration in Part A of the Register (section 9(2)), or was 'capable of distinguishing' for the purposes of registration in Part B of the Register (section 10(1)). In assessing whether a mark was adapted to or capable of distinguishing, the tribunal was directed to have regard to both the inherent distinctiveness of the mark and its distinctiveness in fact (sections 9(3) and 10(2)).

The unfortunate consequence of this direction (probably unintended by the 1938 Act, *Joseph Crosfield & Sons Ltd's Application* (1909) 26 RPC 837, *WATERFORD Trade Mark* [1984] FSR 390) was that certain marks, in particular the names of countries or substantial towns and laudatory epithets, because of their lack of inherent distinctiveness, were treated by the English courts as being incapable of distinguishing *in law*, notwithstanding 100 per cent distinctiveness in fact (*YORK Trade Mark* [1984] RPC 231). Such marks were never registrable, even in Part B of the Register.

In the White Paper, the Government likened the criterion 'capable of distinguishing' in section 1(1) of the 1994 Act to the test governing the registrability of marks in Part B of the Register under the 1938 Act, as amended (paragraph 3.08). However, as section 3(1) of the 1994 Act confirms, descriptive, laudatory and geographical signs will no longer be excluded from registration as trade marks if they are shown to be distinctive in fact.

It was noted above that distinctiveness for the purposes of the 1938 Act, as amended, was measured against positive requirements, or 'essential particulars'. The Government observed in the White Paper that the Directive presumes that a trade mark is registrable unless objection can be taken to it on one of the grounds for refusal of registration listed in Articles 3 or 4: 'The adoption of this approach in the new law should make it easier to register a trade mark' (paragraph 3.07).

However, the fact of the matter is that the Government chose not to implement the compulsory provisions of Articles 2, 3 and 4 of the Directive as they stood. Article 2 specifies the signs of which a trade mark *may consist*, leaving Articles 3 and 4 to specify what cannot be registered. Section 1(1) of the 1994 Act, on the other hand, *defines* 'trade mark' as a sign which is capable of distinguishing, thus imposing a positive obligation on the applicant to show that what it is seeking to register *is* a distinctive trade mark, before the grounds for refusal of registration listed in sections 3 and 5 can come into play. Apart from anything else this creates an inconsistency between section 1(1) and the absolute ground for refusal of registration contained in section 3(1)(b) (noted by the House of Lords, *Hansard* (HL), 6 December 1993, col. 756): according to section 1(1) distinctiveness is a prerequisite to the existence of a trade mark, but section 3(1)(b) states that a *trade mark* which is devoid of any distinctive character cannot be registered.

Game plan for the chapter

Be this as it may, registration in the new single Register will comprise, for the major part, marks formerly considered acceptable in Parts A and B. Although the essential particulars are no longer in force, much of the case law and Registry practice surrounding them will remain relevant under the new law, not only in assessing the distinctiveness of a sign, but also in applying the absolute grounds for refusal of registration which in some instances negatively mirror essential particulars.

The game plan for this chapter is, therefore:

(a)   to examine what light the previous case law on section 10 of the 1938 Act sheds on the meaning of the phrase 'capable of distinguishing' in section 1(1) of the 1994 Act; and

(b)   to discuss what type of signs will, or might be considered to be, distinctive for the purposes of the new law, using the former essential particulars as guidelines.

The process in paragraph (b) above will be continued, where appropriate, into the account of the absolute grounds for refusal of registration in chapter 6, the objective being to give as clear a picture as is possible of the type of trade marks which will be acceptable for registration under the 1994 Act.

Registry practice
The Trade Marks Registry is currently developing new administrative procedures for, *inter alia*, the examination of trade marks, which it intends to circulate to interested parties before the 1994 Act comes into force. Expected changes over past procedure will be highlighted wherever possible.

Capable of Distinguishing (Section 1)

History of the 'capable of distinguishing' criterion governing Part B marks
The concept of Part B registrations was first introduced into United Kingdom trade marks law by the Trade Marks Act 1919. The purpose was to get on to the Register marks which were functioning as trade marks in the market-place, that is, were distinctive in fact, but which were treated as unregistrable because they lacked inherent distinctiveness. (In fact, this might have been one of the purposes of the 1905 Act: see the judgment of Fletcher-Moulton LJ in *Joseph Crosfield & Sons Ltd's Application* (1909) 26 RPC 837.)

Section 2 of the 1919 Act stated that any person who had made bona fide use of a trade mark for a period of not less than two years could apply to the Registrar for registration of the mark in Part B of the Register. Registration could be refused if, *inter alia*, the Registrar was not satisfied as to the use of the applied-for mark, or its *capacity to distinguish*. Part B of the Register was, therefore, initially concerned only with marks in use.

This policy changed with the introduction of the 1938 Act. The two-year minimum use period was abolished and the sole criterion for registrability in Part B became the mark's capacity to distinguish (section 10(1) of the 1938 Act, as amended). As stated above, in assessing whether a mark was capable of distinguishing the goods of its proprietor, the tribunal had to have regard to the extent to which:

(a)   the mark was inherently capable of distinguishing; and

(b)   'by reason of the use of the trade mark or of any other circumstances', the mark was capable of distinguishing in fact (section 10(2) of the 1938 Act, as amended).

The obvious objective of this change in the 1938 Act was to extend Part B to unused, as well as used trade marks (see the majority judgment of the Irish Supreme Court on similar legislation in *WATERFORD Trade Mark* [1984] FSR 390). Hence the direction to tribunals to take into account a mark's inherent capability of distinguishing (a lesser test of distinctiveness than 'adapted to distinguish' for Part A), or any other circumstances.

The judge-made by-product of the change was, of course, the utter exclusion from the Register of some geographical names and laudatory epithets, however distinctive in the market-place (*YORK Trade Mark* [1984] RPC 231). The reasoning of the House of Lords in *YORK* was that other traders must be free without improper motive to use such terms, but this ignored:

(a) the saving from infringement in section 8 of the 1938 Act, as amended (retained by section 11(2) of the 1994 Act) for bona fide use of a trader's name or address, or of a mark to describe goods or services or their place of manufacture; and

(b) that if a trade mark is 100 per cent distinctive in fact, as was the case in *YORK*, no competitor can have a legitimate motive for using it.

It is not intended to dwell on *YORK* in this chapter. Its effect has been overturned by the proviso to section 3(1) of the 1994 Act and further discussion is more conveniently sited alongside the descriptions of the absolute grounds for refusal of registration contained in section 3(1). (The point to repeat here is that marks which could never be distinctive under the 1938 Act may be 'capable of distinguishing' within the meaning of section 1(1) of the 1994 Act, provided they are distinctive in fact.)

Instead, it is proposed to devote the next section of this chapter to looking at other judicial pronouncements on the meaning of the criterion 'capable of distinguishing' for Part B marks under the 1938 Act, as amended.

What does 'capable of distinguishing' mean?

In fact, there were very few judicial attempts to define the phrase 'capable of distinguishing' in section 10(1) of the 1938 Act, as amended, and, in particular, to differentiate its meaning from 'adapted to distinguish' in section 9(2) (Part A marks). However, four cases involving descriptive or quasi-descriptive marks were generally accepted as providing (somewhat inconsistent) guidance on registration in Part B: three of the cases concerned unused marks; the fourth, a mark which was 100 per cent distinctive in fact.

Unused marks   In *SMITSVONK Trade Mark* (1954) 72 RPC 117, the applicants applied to register SMITSVONK for electric spark apparatus. 'Smit' is a Dutch surname, which at the time of the examination of the application appeared several times in the London telephone directory; 'vonk' is Dutch for spark. Therefore, translated SMITSVONK meant 'Smith's spark'. No use had been made of the mark.

Lloyd-Jacob J upheld the Registrar's decision that the mark lacked sufficient inherent distinctiveness for Part A:

So far as concerns section 10, however, in my judgment the matter has to be considered somewhat differently, that is to say, *the Tribunal must have in mind the potentiality that to some section of the trading community the mark might be regarded in that descriptive sense* [the Part A test], *but it has to consider whether on balance that potentiality is such as to cause the mark to be incapable of distinguishing,* or rather the potentiality is such as to deny the applicant the conclusion that he has established a prima facie case of capacity to distinguish. (Emphasis added.)

The judge found *as an issue of fact* that it was highly unlikely that those coming into contact with goods bearing the mark would perform the mental processes necessary to arrive at the conclusion that SMITSVONK was descriptive of the goods rather than a particular brand of those goods. He was therefore prepared to hold that the mark was inherently capable of distinguishing and should go forward for registration in Part B.

By way of contrast, in *H. Quennel Ltd's Application* (1954) 72 RPC 36, Lloyd-Jacob J held that the mark PUSSIKIN was directly descriptive of, and inherently incapable of distinguishing, cat food. Since the mark was unused, the judge turned his attention to seeing whether there were 'other circumstances' (the latter part of the requirement in section 10(2)(b) of the 1938 Act; see above) that could be relied upon by the applicants in support of the application:

The question to be decided [is] whether or not the mark applied for [is] such a word as other traders [are] likely in the ordinary course of their business and without any improper motive to desire to use . . . *whether the mark [is] a word so apt for normal description of the article that a monopoly in the use of it should not be 'acquired'.* (Emphasis added.)

There was no evidence to suggest that PUSSIKIN was newly coined: the applicants had failed to establish that registration of the mark would not unduly fetter 'the freedom of action of other bona fide traders'.

The test for unused marks seems to have synthesised by *American Screw Co.'s Application* [1959] RPC 344, also a decision of Lloyd-Jacob J. The applicants sought to register the mark TORQ-SET for screws, bolts and rivets and were refused registration in Part A because the mark had a direct reference to the goods. ('Torque' and 'set' are terms of art in relation to the subject goods.)

Nevertheless, as the judge observed, the order of the words in the mark was the reverse of the correct description (setting against torque): the mark was not 'apt for normal description'. The judge went on:

Part B of the Register is intended to comprise marks which in use can be demonstrated as affording an indication of trade origin *without trespassing upon the legitimate freedom of other traders.* (Emphasis added.)

and held that TORQ-SET was inherently capable of distinguishing the goods.

Used marks In *WELDMESH Trade Mark* [1965] RPC 590, the applicants already had a registration for WELDMESH in respect of steel wire mesh in Part B, but were now applying for registration of the same mark in Part A. It was conceded by the Registrar that since the date of the registration in Part B, the mark had become 100 per cent distinctive in fact. The applicants argued that such distinctiveness in fact could only have resulted from some innate quality in the mark, which was therefore 'adapted to distinguish' for the purposes of Part A.

Lloyd-Jacob J rejected this argument and explained the difference between the criteria for Part A and Part B marks as follows:

> Section 10 and Part B of the Register are concerned with an alternative method of registration for marks which can be shown to be capable of distinguishing the goods of the proprietor, and this is secured by *proof of the development of a secondary meaning which outweighs the apparently non-distinctive character of the mark when viewed in isolation.* It is, therefore, not unreasonable to regard the two expressions 'adapted to distinguish' and 'capable of distinguishing' as being deliberately chosen so as to direct the enquiry aright, the former emphasising that it is because of the presence of a sufficient distinguishing characteristic in the mark itself that distinctiveness is to be expected to result whatever the type and scale of the user and thus secure an estimation of a positive quality in the mark; *and the second that, in spite of the absence of a sufficient distinguishing characteristic in the mark itself, distinctiveness can be acquired by appropriate user, thereby overcoming a negative quality in the mark.* (Emphasis added.)

WELDMESH was so directly descriptive of welded mesh goods that it could not be registered in Part A: nevertheless use had overcome this negative quality in the mark for the purposes of Part B.

Lloyd-Jacob J's decision was upheld on appeal ([1966] RPC 220) and the above passage was cited with approval. Willmer LJ illustrated the difference between Part A and Part B marks by reference to a rough piece of wood: undoubtedly *capable* of being moulded by a carpenter into an elegant piece of furniture but not *adapted* for this purpose. Harman LJ dealt with the issue thus:

> I agree with the Registrar that the mark is clearly and directly descriptive of welded mesh goods. When he goes on to hold that the word is in fact 'adapted to distinguish' [sic] (which means distinctive of the applicants' goods) I again agree. This has been brought about by use and wont so that the distinctiveness now in fact exists, but it was not an inherent quality, but a quality conferred from outside. This, I think, is made clear by section 10. *The goods were inherently 'capable' of distinctiveness. This has been proved by the event.* It has come about by the events which have happened, and these prove the inherent capability. *If that did not exist, nothing could bring it into existence.* (Emphasis added.)

Conclusions   The following conclusions can be drawn from the above four cases on the meaning of 'capable of distinguishing' in section 10(1) of the 1938 Act:

(a)   The phrase 'capable of distinguishing' pointed to distinctiveness that could be acquired through use and was not necessarily an innate characteristic of the mark (although Lloyd-Jacob J and Harman LJ seemed to differ on the latter point).

(b)   In the case of an unused mark, where distinctiveness was not presumed (as with, for example, an invented word), capability of distinguishing was tested against 'aptness for normal description', or the legitimate need for other traders to use the mark (see recently, *MAGIC SAFE Trade Mark* [1993] RPC 470).

(c)   A mark's inherent capability of distinguishing could be proved by its distinctiveness in fact (again, Lloyd-Jacob J and Harman LJ seemed to disagree on this point in the case of a directly descriptive mark).

How far are these conclusions transferable to the test of 'capable of distinguishing' under the new law?

Section 3(1)(c) of the 1994 Act excludes from registration:

trade marks which consist exclusively of signs or indications which may serve, *in trade*, to designate the kind, quality, quantity, intended purpose . . . of goods or of rendering of services. (Emphasis added.)

This lends support to the second proposition that capability of distinguishing is to be tested against the need of other traders to use the sign.

The proviso to section 3(1) makes clear that descriptive *trade marks* are not registrable *unless* they are shown to be distinctive in fact, which appears to support Lloyd-Jacob J's view that use can overcome the negative quality in a mark. However, as was noted earlier in this chapter, section 1(1) of the 1994 Act departs from Article 2 of the Directive by *defining* 'trade mark' as a sign which is capable of distinguishing. Read together, sections 1(1) and 3(1) of the 1994 Act lean towards the Harman LJ view, that a descriptive mark which has acquired distinctiveness through use must have been inherently capable of distinguishing in the first place. (The ordering of Articles 2 and 3 of the Directive confirms the Lloyd-Jacob view.)

This does not cause the same uncertainty which existed under the 1938 Act about when such a mark could be accepted for registration: the proviso to section 3(1) of the 1994 Act states that registration can only take place once factual distinctiveness has been acquired. But, the lack of clarity in the new provisions is irritating.

It is to be noted that the proviso to section 3(1) does not allow the applicant to pray in aid of its application for trade mark registration circumstances other than factual distinctiveness (contrast section 10(2)(b) of the 1938 Act, as amended, cf. *PUSSIKIN*).

Signs Which Are (or May Be) Capable of Distinguishing

Since the level of distinctiveness required by the 1994 Act is 'similar to' that required of Part B marks by the 1938 Act, as amended (White Paper, paragraph 2.22), it will encompass signs which would have been acceptable for registration in either Part of the former Register (subject to what is said above).

The essential particulars governing the registrability of marks under the 1938 Act, as amended, will, therefore, continue to provide useful guidance to those choosing and/or assessing the registrability of trade marks under the 1994 Act. Although the essential particulars were expressed to apply only to Part A marks (section 9(1) of the 1938 Act, as amended), it was generally assumed that they also applied to Part B marks. There follows a brief résumé of the particulars, relevant case law and Registry practice.

Reference should be made to *Kerly's Law of Trade Marks and Trade Names*, 12th edition, for fuller discussion.

The 'essential particulars'

In order to be registrable under the 1938 Act, as amended, a mark had to consist of at least one of five alternative essential particulars listed in section 9(1). A mark which consisted of one or more of the first four particulars was presumed to be inherently distinctive. A mark which consisted of the fifth particular, 'any other distinctive mark', usually had to be supported by evidence of use.

The particulars were:

(a)   *Names represented as logos* – 'the name of a company, individual or firm represented in a special or particular manner' (1938 Act, section 9(1)(a)).

Protection only extended to the name *as represented*, therefore, the normal practice of the Registry was to require a disclaimer of the name. Disclaimer under the 1994 Act is voluntary (section 13(1)). 'Special or particular manner' necessitated something unusual in the way the mark was presented (*ROBIN HOOD Trade Mark* (1952) 69 RPC 125); ordinary type with mere fancy embellishments was not enough (*FANFOLD Trade Mark* (1928) RPC 199 and 325).

(b)   *Signatures* – 'the signature of the applicant for registration or some predecessor in his business' (1938 Act, section 9(1)(b)).

It had to be a real signature; just writing in 'copperplate' would not do (*BARRY ARTIST Trade Mark* [1978] RPC 793).

A famous example of a registered signature mark is the signature of Arthur Guinness which appears on the labels of bottles of Guinness stout and on the outside of cans of Guinness stout.

(c)   *Invented words* – 'an invented word or invented words' (1938 Act, section 9(1)(c)).

To summarise the extensive body of case law on this particular:

From a *negative* point of view an invented word could not:

(i)   contain an obvious allusion to the character or quality of the goods (*ARSENOID Trade Mark* (1916) 33 RPC 285);

(ii)   be a misspelling of a known word (*ORLWOOLA Trade Mark* (1909) 26 RPC 683, 850 – 'all wool');

(iii)   consist of two ordinary words conjoined even in a novel manner (*WELDMESH Trade Mark* [1965] RPC 590, [1966] RPC 220);

(iv)   be equivalent to a known word (*UNEEDA Trade Mark* (1902) 19 RPC 281 – 'you need a'); or

(v)   be the foreign equivalent of a known word (*DIABOLO Trade Mark* (1908) 25 RPC 565).

The *positive* aspects were:

(i)   an invented word did not have to be totally meaningless, but could contain a 'skilful and covert allusion' to the nature of the goods or services (*SOLIO Trade Mark* (1898) 15 RPC 476);

(ii)　the quantum of inventiveness was immaterial (*SOLIO*);

(iii)　obviousness of derivation, as opposed to obviousness of meaning, was irrelevant (*SOLIO*);

(iv)　true 'portmanteau' words could qualify as invented words (*WHIS-QUEUR Trade Mark* (1948) 66 RPC 105); and

(v)　an invented word could comprise two foreign words conjoined, provided the languages in question were not commonly known (*PARLOGRAPH Trade Mark* [1914] 2 Ch 103).

Invented words have always made the best trade marks, for example, KODAK and BOVRIL.

(d)　*Words having no direct reference to the character or quality of the goods or services* – 'a word or words having no direct reference to the character or quality of the goods, and not being according to its ordinary signification a geographical name or surname' (1938 Act, section 9(1)(d)).

Most applications for word or word and device marks under the 1938 Act, as amended, fell to be considered under this head.

Known words were perfectly acceptable as trade marks as long as they did not directly describe the goods or services. The test laid down in *CHARM Trade Mark* (1928) 45 RPC 421 was to consider the mark in relation to the goods or services in question to see what information about the goods or services it would convey to the average purchaser. Rejected on this basis were, for example, PALMOLIVE for soaps (*PALMOLIVE Trade Mark* (1932) 49 RPC 269); MILD for cigarettes (*MILD Trade Mark* [1980] RPC 527); and MONEYSWORTH for magazines (*MONEYSWORTH Trade Mark* [1976] RPC 317). Descriptiveness could be overcome by evidence of use for registration in Part B (*WELDMESH*).

Laudatory words were unacceptable for registration in either Part of the Register regardless of use (*YORK Trade Mark* [1984] RPC 231).

The known word could not be a geographical name, in the sense of indicating that the goods or services derived from a particular locality.

The registration of major geographical place names was barred altogether for goods (*Liverpool Electric Cable Co. Ltd's Application* (1929) 46 RPC 99; *YORK Trade Mark* [1984] RPC 231), but Registry practice was to allow, with geographical limitations, the registration of building society names for services (for example, Halifax, Woolwich).

Evidence of use could overcome objection to geographical names of lesser significance, but relevant considerations were whether the particular locality had a reputation for producing the goods or offering the services in question, or whether the goods were likely to be produced or the services offered there in the future. Thus, in *LIVRON Trade Mark* (1937) 54 RPC 327, the mark LIVRON was registered for tonic medicines, but was taken off the Register on it being shown that Livron was the name of a French town which had a pharmaceutical industry.

A geographical name which was clearly fanciful in relation to the goods or services concerned was acceptable for registration in Part A, the classic example being NORTH POLE for bananas. In *TIJUANA SMALLS Trade Mark* [1973] FSR 235, the mark was allowed for cigars since there was no tobacco industry in that part of Mexico, but in Part B, because its use in relation to the goods was not so obviously fanciful.

The overriding consideration in the case of geographical names was whether registration would be likely to inconvenience other legitimate traders wishing to indicate the geographical origin of their goods.

A similar consideration lay behind the exception from prima facie registrability of surnames. However, the exception was subject to Registry *de minimis* practice rules, which permitted the registration of uncommon surnames and surnames with well-known other meanings. Whether registration in such cases was allowed in Part A or Part B, depended on how many times the surname appeared in the London and relevant foreign telephone directories, up to maximum limits. Objections to a mark consisting of a surname could be overcome by evidence of use, usually resulting in Part B registration, although SMITHS is registered in Part A for crisps.

Changes under the 1994 Act are:

(i)   Descriptive words, laudatory epithets, geographical names indicating origin and generic trade terms are prima facie not registrable as trade marks (section 3(1)(c)). However, objections on these grounds may be overcome by evidence of use which establishes the factual distinctiveness of the mark before the date of application for registration (proviso to section 3(1)).

(ii)   There is no specific exclusion for surnames. Generally speaking, surnames are considered to lack inherent distinctiveness, so section 3(1)(b), which provides that 'trade marks which are devoid of any distinctive character' shall not be registered, may apply as a ground for refusal of registration, probably subject to similar *de minimis* rules. Again, evidence of use before the date of application for registration can overcome objections (proviso to section 3(1)).

(e)   *Any other distinctive mark* – 'any other distinctive mark, but a name, signature, or word or words, other than such as fall within the descriptions in the foregoing paragraphs (a), (b), (c) and (d), shall not be registrable under the provisions of this paragraph except upon evidence of its distinctiveness' (1938 Act, section 9(1)(e)).

Evidence of use had to be filed in order to register names, signatures or words which had failed to qualify under the paragraphs (a) to (d). It has already been seen that evidence of use could not overcome the presumed non-distinctiveness of laudatory words and some geographical names.

Paragraph (e) also included device marks, letters, numerals, monograms, portraits and other pictures and colour combinations. Usually, applications for registration of such marks had to be supported by evidence of use. Registry practice rules on the acceptability of letter marks was complicated and strict. New practice rules are expected to be more relaxed.

Shapes and sensory signs are registrable as trade marks under the 1994 Act, provided that they are capable of graphic representation and are shown to be distinctive (see chapter 4).

Transitional Provisions (Schedule 3)

These are the same as described in chapter 4. Briefly, the proprietor of an application for registration made under the 1938 Act, but not advertised before commencement, can irrevocably elect to have its application decided under the new law (paragraph 11). Otherwise, applications pending at commencement are dealt with on the basis of the 1938 Act (paragraph 10).

CHAPTER SIX
Registrability III:
Absolute Grounds for Refusal of Registration

Introduction

The absolute grounds for refusal of registration of a trade mark are set out in section 3 of the 1994 Act. They are intended to reflect the compulsory and optional provisions of Article 3(1), (2) and (3) of the Directive. Even though a sign may be capable of functioning as a trade mark, there may be reasons of public policy why its registration should be refused.

Until the United Kingdom Trade Marks Registry establishes a practice on the examination of applications for registration under the 1994 Act, it is difficult to judge what the perceived relationship (if any) will be between the so-called test for registrability in section 1(1) – 'capable of distinguishing' – and the absolute grounds for refusal of registration in section 3.

The Directive does not require relativity. Article 2 specifies the signs of which a trade mark may consist: Article 3 lists what cannot be registered as a trade mark. 'Capability of distinguishing' and the absolute grounds for refusal are independent elements of validity.

Nevertheless, the arrangement in the 1994 Act of the *definition* of a trade mark ('any sign . . . which is capable of distinguishing'; section 1(1)) and the absolute grounds for refusal of registration (section 3) suggests that:

(a) the absolute grounds for refusal, in particular, section 3(1)(c) and (d), contain examples of marks which are deemed to be incapable of distinguishing for the purposes of section 1(1) (see *Hansard* (HL/PBC), 13 January 1994, cols 12–13, Lord Peston); and

(b) capability of distinguishing is the overriding requirement for registration of a mark under the 1994 Act.

If this is the result of the drafting techniques employed, then sections 1(1) and 3 of the 1994 Act fail to implement Articles 2 and 3 of the Directive correctly.

Absolute Grounds for Refusal of Registration (Section 3)

Where do the absolute grounds for refusal come from?
The list of absolute grounds for refusal of registration is based to a large extent on Article 6*quinquies* of the Paris Convention. The 'shape' exclusions derive from Benelux trade marks law.

This is the first time in United Kingdom trade marks law that the absolute grounds for refusal have been presented collectively. Under the old law, they (or their equivalent) resided in different sections of the 1938 Act, as amended, in the Trade Marks Rules, or not all, or were part of the Registrar's discretion. The latter (apparently) no longer exists under the 1994 Act: the absolute grounds for refusal are limitative (Preamble to the Directive, recital 7); there is no room for the Registrar's former discretion (see White Paper, paragraphs 3.10 to 3.12).

In the Directive, the absolute grounds are expressed as grounds for refusal of registration *and* grounds of invalidity. The United Kingdom chose not to follow this approach for its new trade marks law. The grounds for invalidity are provided for separately in section 47(1) of the 1994 Act, but in any event mirror by reference the absolute grounds for refusal in section 3. Invalidity of a registered trade mark is discussed in chapter 8.

What are the grounds for refusal of registration?
Section 3 of the Trade Marks Act 1994 sets out absolute grounds for refusal of registration.

The absolute grounds for refusal can loosely be grouped under four headings:

(a)   Signs which cannot constitute trade marks.
(b)   Trade marks objections to which can be overcome by proof of distinctiveness in fact.
(c)   Signs or trade marks which cannot be registered, however distinctive in fact.
(d)   Trade marks applied for in bad faith.

Each grouping will receive comment in turn. But by way of preliminary, it is important to emphasise that for all the absolute grounds for refusal, each mark must be considered on its *individual merits*. A mark cannot be objected to merely because, for example, it consists of a geographical name or a surname, as was the case under the 1938 Act, as amended. But it may still be found that such a mark, examined on its individual merits, does serve in trade to describe, for example, the geographical origin of the goods, or is a generic trade name.

There seems to be nothing in the 1994 Act (nor the Directive) to prevent objection being taken to a mark on more than one of the grounds listed in section 3 (subject to what is said below).

Signs which Cannot Constitute Trade Marks (Section 3(1)(a))

The exact wording of the ground in section 3(1)(a) is: 'signs which do not satisfy the requirements of section 1(1)'.

This ground will, therefore, provide a bar to registration for those signs which do not satisfy the definition of a trade mark in section 1(1), that is:

(a) signs which are not capable of being represented graphically; and/or

(b) signs which are not capable of functioning as trade marks, that is, of distinguishing the goods or services of one undertaking from those of other undertakings.

Both of these requirements are discussed in chapters 4 and 5.

The meaning of 'represented graphically' is not yet clear. The only guidance issued by the Trade Marks Registry to date is that the mark must fit into the box on the application form, which is 8 cm by 8 cm. Of the 'new' marks, that is, three-dimensional and sensory marks, only olfactory marks are thought to present a problem, but there seems to be no reason why such marks should not be described in words, following the American experience (*Re Clark* (1990) 17 USPQ 2d 1238 – 'a high-impact, fresh floral fragrance reminiscent of plumeria blossom'). Word and/or device marks will continue to be represented by facsimile copy as under the 1938 Act, as amended.

An applicant seeking to register as a trade mark, in particular, a single colour, a shape, the packaging of goods, a slogan, an audible or an olfactory mark will need to demonstrate that the sign is capable of performing the function of a trade mark, as discussed in chapter 4.

In *YORK Trade Mark* [1984] RPC 231, the House of Lords held that certain words, in particular, laudatory epithets and some geographical words, were incapable *in law* of distinguishing, because they must be left in the public domain for other traders to use. Such words could never be registered as trade marks under the 1938 Act, as amended, however distinctive in fact.

It is strongly suggested that this would *not* be a permissible way of interpreting the 'capable of distinguishing' requirement in section 1(1), thus providing through section 3(1)(a) a *YORK* ban on the registration of geographical names and laudatory epithets. The proviso to section 3(1)(c) makes clear that objections to the registration of such words as trade marks can be overcome by evidence of use (see below).

Similarly, registration of a distinctive bottle shape cannot be refused registration under section 3(1)(a) on the grounds that, since all containers must remain free for traders to use, it is incapable of functioning as a trade mark within the meaning of section 1(1) (*COCA-COLA Trade Marks* [1986] RPC 421). A distinctive shape is registrable as a trade mark unless it falls within one of the exclusions in section 3(2) discussed below.

Section 3(1)(a) had no equivalent in the 1938 Act, as amended, other than the converse of the definitions of 'mark', 'trade/service mark' and 'use of a trade/service mark' in section 68.

Trade Marks Objections to which Can Be Overcome by Proof of Distinctiveness in Fact (Section 3(1)(b), (c) and (d))

'. . . *trade marks which are devoid of any distinctive character*' (*section 3(1)(b)*)
Attention has already been drawn (chapters 4 and 5) to the apparent inconsistency between the wording of this ground for refusal and the definition of 'trade mark' in section 1(1): the definition assumes a distinctive sign, but the ground for refusal speaks of a *trade mark* which is devoid of distinctive character.

The kind of mark (when examined on its individual merits) likely to be objected to under this head is, for example: a single letter or numeral mark; a single colour mark (*Smith Kline and French Laboratories Ltd's CIMETIDINE Trade Mark* [1991] RPC 17); a slogan which merely consists of an exhortation to buy or to use (*HAVE A BREAK Trade Mark* [1993] RPC 217); a device which is considered too simple to be distinctive (for example, a single star; *Unilever Ltd's (Striped Toothpaste No. 2) Trade Marks* [1987] RPC 13, red stripe in toothpaste); and a mark which does not consist *exclusively* of a description, a generic sign or a shape, but even with the addition of other elements, is considered devoid of any distinctive character. It is thought that marks consisting of a common surname might also be objected to under section 3(1)(b).

Even though a mark might be considered prima facie lacking in any distinctive character, it may be registered if the applicant can prove that it was distinctive in fact *before* the date of the application for registration (proviso to section 3(1)).

An applicant may voluntarily disclaim non-distinctive elements of a mark in order to overcome objections (section 13(1)(a); and see chapter 3).

The nearest equivalent in general terms to section 3(1)(b) in the 1938 Act, as amended, was the essential particular in section 9(1)(e).

'. . . *trade marks which consist exclusively of signs or indications which may serve, in trade, to designate the kind, quality, quantity, intended purpose, value, geographical origin, the time of production of goods or of rendering of services, or other characteristics of goods or services' (section 3(1)(c))*
Registration must be refused under section 3(1)(c) if a trade mark is *purely descriptive*, that is, consists *exclusively* of signs or indications which may serve *in trade* to designate particulars of the goods or services concerned as indicated in the ground. Marks which consist of a description *and* other elements cannot be refused registration under this head, but may be refused registration under section 3(1)(b).

The public policy objective is that trade descriptions should remain in the public domain. Therefore, registration will be refused even where a description as such is not known to the general public and, insofar as they are concerned, is not devoid of distinctive character.

The United Kingdom Registrar and courts are familiar with the concept of testing the registrability of a descriptive mark by reference to what other traders might want to use. There are many examples in the case law. Two contrasting cases will suffice to illustrate the point here.

In *POUND PUPPIES Trade Mark* [1988] RPC 530, the applicants sought registration for the mark POUND PUPPIES in respect of stuffed toy animals. Aldous J held that the mark was registrable, because 'pound puppies' was not the natural way an honest trader would describe toy puppies costing one pound.

By way of contrast, in *SUPERWOUND Trade Mark* [1988] RPC 272, registration was not allowed for SUPERWOUND in respect of guitar strings. The mark comprised a laudatory epithet conjoined to a descriptive trade term: the evidence established that 'wound' was used by the trade to indicate a particular type of guitar string.

The grounds for refusal in section 3(1)(c) yield to proof of factual distinctiveness of the mark acquired *before* the date of the application for registration (proviso to section 3(1)). The important effect is to overturn the House of Lords decision in *YORK Trade Mark* [1984] RPC 231, where an application for the mark YORK in respect of freight trailers and containers was refused, notwithstanding acceptance by their Lordships of evidence of use, which established that the mark was 100 per cent distinctive in fact of the applicants' goods (similarly overturned is the Court of Appeal decision in *Liverpool Electric Cable Co.'s Application* (1929) 46 RPC 99).

The decision in *YORK* also applied to bar laudatory epithets and initials from registration as trade marks under the 1938 Act, as amended (Lord Wilberforce's judgment in *YORK* was based, *inter alia*, on the decisions in *Joseph Crosfield & Sons Ltd's Application* (1909) 26 RPC 837 and *Registrar of Trade Marks* v *W. & G. Du Cros Ltd* [1913] AC 624, even though these cases were decided before Part B of the Register was created; see chapter 5). Again, objections to such marks under section 3(1)(c) of the 1994 Act can be overcome by evidence of use showing distinctiveness in fact.

As the Government acknowledged in the White Paper (paragraph 2.10), the proviso to section 3(1) is doing no more than recognising *de facto* monopolies. A descriptive mark which is 100 per cent distinctive in the market-place can (and could) be defended in passing off and cannot be used by other traders as a trade mark without improper motive. Section 11(2) of the 1994 Act makes clear that a trader does not infringe a registered trade mark by use of its own name or address, or an honest description of the nature or origin of its goods or services.

The proviso to section 3(1) will not greatly alter the more lenient approach which was adopted by the Registrar and the courts under the 1938 Act, as amended, towards marks consisting of descriptions other than as to origin or quality. Objections to such marks could be overcome by evidence of use (*Davis* v *Sussex Rubber Co. Ltd* (1927) 44 RPC 412; *WELDMESH Trade Mark* [1966] RPC 220).

Marks consisting of surnames constituted a specific exception to prima facie registrability under the 1938 Act, as amended (but objections could be overcome by evidence of use). There is no mention of surnames in section 3(1)(c), although they might fall within the phrase 'other characteristics of goods or services', or be considered devoid of any distinctive character for the purposes of section 3(1)(b) above.

It should be noted that 'signs or indications' under section 3(1)(c) includes not only written descriptions, but also descriptions in the form of pictures. In *Unilever plc's Trade Mark* [1984] RPC 155, the applicants sought to register as a device mark, a picture of a slug of toothpaste on a toothbrush. The application was refused as being a mere description of the goods.

There seems no reason in principle why section 3(1)(c) should not operate to exclude from registration descriptive colours, shapes, packaging and sensory signs.

Presumably, section 3(1)(c) applies to phonetic equivalents of descriptions (*Electrix Ltd's Application* [1959] RPC 283).

The grounds set out in section 3(1)(c) were formerly approximated by section 9(1)(d) and (e) and the converse of section 68 of the 1938 Act, as amended.

. . . *'trade marks which consist exclusively of signs or indications which have become customary in the current language or in the bona fide and established practices of the trade' (section 3(1)(d))*
Section 3(1)(d) provides an absolute ground for refusal of marks which the trade uses generically, that is, as the name of, or signification for the goods or services

concerned, for example, 'gramophone' (*Gramophone Co.'s Application* [1910] 2 Ch 423), 'shredded wheat' (*Shredded Wheat Co. Ltd* v *Kellogg Co. of Great Britain Ltd* (1940) 57 RPC 137) and 'linoleum' (*Linoleum Manufacturing Co.* v *Nairn* (1878) 7 ChD 834).

The ground applies only where the mark consists *exclusively* of a generic trade sign or indication (combination marks might be excluded under 3(1)(b)). The mark is tested against the current language and bona fide and established practices of the trade.

Again the mark need not be a generic name. Section 3(1)(d) applies to generic trade colours (*John Wyeth & Bro. Ltd's Coloured Tablet Trade Mark* [1988] RPC 233; *Smith Kline and French Laboratories Ltd's CIMETIDINE Trade Mark* [1991] RPC 17), generic shapes and packaging (coloured lids on instant coffee, plastic containers for washing-up liquid, milk cartons), generic picture or portrait marks (*Liebig's Extract of Meat Co. Ltd* v *Hanbury* (1867) 17 LT 298), generic devices and, if there are such things, generic sounds, smells, tastes and feels.

Even though a mark is prima facie excluded from registration by section 3(1)(d), it may be registered if it is shown to have in fact acquired distinctive character through use *before* the date of the application for registration (proviso to section 3(1)).

Section 3(1)(d) was approximated under the prior law by section 9(1)(d) and (e) of the 1938 Act, as amended.

Signs or Trade Marks which Cannot Be Registered however Distinctive in Fact (Section 3(2), (3), (4) and (5))

. . . *'A sign [which] consists exclusively of— (a) the shape which results from the nature of the goods themselves, (b) the shape of goods which is necessary to obtain a technical result, or (c) the shape which gives substantial value to the goods' (section 3(2))*

Copyright, patents, registered designs and design right are true monopoly rights, in the sense that material is removed from the public domain. They are exceptions to rules of free competition justified by the public good and are granted for finite terms. Trade marks are not true monopoly rights. They do not prevent *ordinary* use of material within the public domain and other traders are free to offer competing goods and services provided they do so under different marks. Trade marks are exceptions to rules of free competition justified by the concept of fair competition and are granted for indefinite terms.

However, when trade mark protection is extended to three-dimensional product shapes, as it has been by section 1(1) of the 1994 Act, the line between free and fair competition becomes less easy to define. Trade mark registration for a product shape can mean withdrawal of the product from the public domain. The absolute grounds for refusal in section 3(2) of the 1994 Act represent an attempt to reconcile the different objectives of free and fair competition with regard to the registration as trade marks of product shapes, and to ensure that the monopoly conferred by a copyright, patent or design is not abused by indefinite extension (White Paper, paragraph 2.20).

Section 3(2) reflects the compulsory provisions of Article 3(1)(e) of the Directive. The Benelux trade marks law was very influential in the drafting of the

Directive and the grounds for refusal in section 3(2) of the 1994 Act are, therefore, similar to those contained in Article 1(2) of the Uniform Benelux Trademarks Law 1971. They direct enquiry to whether the goods perform a function by virtue of their shape.

The grounds for refusal in section 3(2) also resemble the three limbs of the judge-made doctrine of 'functionality' as it applies to the protection of product shapes under American trade marks law (although it must be said that the doctrine is subject to different interpretations and applications by the different appeal and circuit courts).

Registration of product shapes as trade marks under the Lanham Act 1946 has been permitted since 1964 (*Re Minnesota Mining & Manufacturing Co.* (1964) 335 F2d 836), but is restricted to product shapes which do not fulfil an efficiency, utility or aesthetic function. But, in determining whether a product shape is functional, at least in the two former senses, the key element is whether other traders need to copy the shape in order to compete effectively.

Despite the differences in approach (which in any event usually coincide in result), it may be that the United Kingdom tribunals will look to decisions of the American courts, in addition to those of the Benelux courts, in order to assist them in the interpretation and application of section 3(2) of the 1994 Act.

Section 3(2) is expressed to apply to signs which consist *exclusively* of *shapes* falling within paragraphs (a), (b) or (c). If a mark comprises additional matter, it may still be refused registration under section 3(1)(b) if, taken as a whole, it is considered to be devoid of any distinctive character.

Section 1(1) of the 1994 Act includes the shape of goods *or their packaging* within the definition of 'trade mark'. The minutes attached to the Community Trade Mark Regulation contain the following statement on Article 7(1)(e), which is in identical terms to section 3(2):

The Council and the Commission consider that where goods are packaged, the expression 'shape of the goods' includes the shape of the packaging.

The statement indicates that section 3(2) of the 1994 Act must be read as applying also to signs which consist exclusively of the packaging of goods.

Section 3(2) appears not to affect the registrability as trade marks of purely two-dimensional designs. The point arose for consideration by the Benelux Court of Justice in *Burberrys* v *Bossi* (*BURBERRYS II*) [1992] NJ 596, which concerned the validity of the Burberrys 'tartan patterns' marks. The Court held that Article 1(2) of the Uniform Benelux Trademarks Law 1971 applied only to three-dimensional product designs.

The fact that a product shape or its packaging is protectable or has been protected by another intellectual property right does not mean that it is automatically excluded from registration as a trade mark by section 3(2). In the Benelux, this was confirmed by the Court of Justice in *Superconfex* v *Burberrys* (*BURBERRYS I*) (1991) 22 IIC 567; in America, by the Court of Customs and Patent Appeals in *Re Mogen David Wine Corp.* (*Mogen David II*) (1967) 372 F2d 15. The point was also stated by the Government in the White Paper (paragraph 2.20) and is in sharp contrast to the opening lines of Lord Templeman's judgment in *COCA-COLA Trade Marks* [1986] RPC 421 (see chapter 4).

Turning now to the specific exclusions in section 3(2): paragraph (a) – 'the shape which results from the nature of the goods themselves' – appears to be aimed at excluding from registration as a trade mark a shape which makes a product superior in performance. Examples might include the shape of a stapler, the shape of a paper-clip, the shape of a football, the face plate of a three-headed electric razor (*Re North American Phillips Corp.* (1983) 217 USPQ 926), the shape of a 'dunking' biscuit, the pillow shape of shredded wheat cereal (*Kellogg Co.* v *National Biscuit Co.* (1938) 305 US 111 — unfair competition), the rhomboidal shape of a coal cleaning table (*Re Deister Concentrator Co.* (1961) 289 F2d 496), the shape of a knife handle, or the shape of a tampon.

Paragraph (b) of section 3(2) – 'the shape of goods which is necessary to obtain a technical result' – will exclude from registration as a trade mark a shape which facilitates the manufacture or use of goods, their storage or distribution. Examples here might include the shape of a handled container for heavy liquids, the shape of a milk carton, the shape of a pump-action toothpaste tube, the shape of stacking flowerpots, the shape of a rim on the underside of china to protect against breakage and to aid gripping (*Re Shenango Ceramics Inc.* (1962) 362 F2d 287), the shape of the rim at the bottom of a plastic water bottle to aid stability, the shape of a see-through window on packaging and the shape of any product which needs to 'connect', for example, the face plate of an electric plug.

All the above examples assume that the shape of goods or their packaging serves a purely utilitarian purpose. If the shape is arbitrary or 'non-functional' (it may well also serve a utilitarian purpose) then it is not excluded from registration, for example, the DIMPLE BOTTLE for Scotch whisky (*Ex parte Haig & Haig Ltd* (1958) 118 USPQ 229; see also *Mogen David II*) or, indeed, the COCA-COLA bottle.

Section 3(2)(c) – 'the shape which gives substantial value to the goods' – is likely to prove the most controversial and troublesome exclusion to apply in practice. Potentially affected are the shape of jewellery, fashion garments, porcelain, china, ornaments, toys, shoes, luggage, handbags; in fact, the shape of any product where aesthetic considerations are likely to influence consumer demand.

The exclusion seems to involve an investigation of the motive of the consumer in buying the goods; whether the purchase of the goods is substantially due to their aesthetic appeal, for it is only then that freedom of competition is hindered (*BURBERRYS I*).

The difficulty comes with a product shape which is both aesthetically pleasing and functions as a trade mark, and lies in knowing whether and how to separate out the *values* attributable to the two. This is a different question than asking whether the product shape has acquired a secondary meaning. It is clear from the wording and organisation of section 3(2) that if a product shape gives substantial value to the goods (or, indeed falls within the other exclusions in section 3(2)) then distinctiveness in fact cannot lead to its registrability as a trade mark (on the similar exclusion in Article 1(2) of the Uniform Benelux Trademarks Law see *Adidas* [1986] BIE 208).

The difficulty in assessing 'substantial value' when an attractive product shape has *de facto* trade mark significance is illustrated by two Benelux cases involving cracker shapes. In *Wokkels* [1985] BIE 23, the Dutch Supreme Court acknowledged that the well-known spiral shape of a salty cracker increased its market value, but held that this did not affect the intrinsic value of the cracker itself. On the other hand in *Bacony* [1989] NJ 835 the same court held that differences in taste between competing crackers were so insubstantial that the shape of the cracker concerned was the only factor which determined its market value; the shape was, therefore, unregistrable. (The *Wokkels* approach was confirmed by the Benelux Court of Justice in *BURBERRYS II*; following the latter decision, *Bacony* was referred to the Benelux Court of Justice, but as far as the authors are aware no decision has been published.)

In America, aesthetic functionality has been discredited as a test for registrability of product shapes (*Re Mogen David Wine Corp. (Mogen David I)* (1964) 328 F2d 925; *Re DC Comics Inc* (1982) 689 F2d 1042), on grounds that effective competition is not hindered by precluding competitors from copying aesthetic product shapes. But aesthetic functionality remains as a defence to infringement and unfair competition.

In these areas the test (a restricted form of aesthetic functionality) appeared to be quite straightforward: if the consumer bought the goods because of the attractive shape, there was no protection; if, on the other hand, the consumer selected the goods for source-related reasons (that is, because of the trade mark significance) protection was available (*Vuitton et Fils SA* v *J. Young Enterprises Inc.* (1980) 644 F2d 769).

However, more recent decisions of the American courts indicate a return to foreclosure of competition as the basis for a finding of aesthetic functionality and denial of trade mark protection. Opinion seems to differ over whether foreclosure of competition should be judged according to the shape's contribution to the commercial success of the product (cf *Pagliero* v *Wallace China Co.* (1952) 198 F2d 339, applied in, for example, *Plasticor Molded Products Inc.* v *Ford Motor Co.* (1989) 713 F Supp 1329, 11 USPQ 2d 1023), or the availability of other product designs on the market (see, for example, *LA Gear Inc.* v *Thom McAn Shoe Co.* (1993) 988 F2d 1117, 25 USPQ 2d 1913).

Until there are decided cases on section 3(2)(c) of the 1994 Act (and in the absence of definitive ruling by the Court of Justice of the European Communities) it is difficult to predict the approach that will be adopted by the United Kingdom tribunals in interpreting the 'substantial value' shape exclusion.

However, it must be stressed in relation to all three paragraphs of section 3(2) that, if an exclusion applies, registrability is denied, however distinctive the sign in fact.

Section 3(2) had no equivalent under the 1938 Act, as amended: three-dimensional signs were held to be excluded by the definition of 'mark' in section 68(1) (*COCA-COLA Trade Marks* [1986] RPC 421).

'A trade mark [which] is— (a) contrary to public policy or to accepted principles of morality, or (b) of such a nature as to deceive the public (for instance as to the nature, quality or geographical origin of the goods or service' (section 3(3))
The possibilities in section 3(3) of the 1994 Act were formerly dealt with under section 11 of the 1938 Act, as amended, and/or under the Registrar's discretion.

Section 3(3)(a) excludes from registration a mark, which when considered on its individual merits, is contrary to public policy or morality. Examples of marks contrary to public policy might include: a mark containing a religious symbol; a mark containing the name or representation of a person, where consent had not been obtained from that person, or that person's legal representative; the emblem of a public body, even if such emblem was not protected by section 4 of the Act (see below); a mark which constitutes a risk to public safety.

In *JARDEX Trade Mark* (1946) 63 RPC 19, the applicants were refused registration of JARDEX for disinfectant, because of the presence of JARDOX on the Register for meat extract. There was a danger that the products might be stored together in hospitals and other institutions to which they were supplied (see also *MOTRICINE Trade Mark* (1907) 24 RPC 585).

Morality is to be judged against current thinking and susceptibilities. In *HALLELUJAH Trade Mark* [1976] RPC 605, the applicants were refused registration of HALLELUJAH for women's clothing on the ground that it would offend generally accepted mores and was therefore contrary to morality. Until recently, Registry practice was to refuse registration of marks consisting of explicit drawings or photographs of full frontal nudes or offensive rear views of nudes. However, in *Masterman's Design* [1991] RPC 89, Aldous J permitted the registration of a design for a kilted doll with mimic male genitalia under sections 3(3) and 43(1) of the Registered Designs Act 1949, which are in similar terms to the provisions presently under consideration.

Registration must also be refused under section 3(3)(b) of the 1994 Act if a mark is deceptive in relation to the goods or services concerned. Three instances of deception are mentioned in paragraph (b); deception as to nature, quality or geographical origin.

It was quite common under the 1938 Act, as amended, for objections to be made to a mark on the grounds of descriptiveness *and* deceptiveness: the mark either described the goods or service directly, or it was deceptive, in that it suggested characteristics which the goods or service did not possess.

The point is neatly illustrated by *ORLWOOLA Trade Mark* (1909) 26 RPC 683. The mark ORLWOOLA was held to be totally unsuitable for registration in respect of textile goods being directly descriptive of goods that were 'all wool' and deceptively misdescriptive of goods, such as cotton goods, which were not. Restricting the specification to goods of 'all wool' would have merely reinforced the descriptive objections. The conundrum for trade mark owners of choosing a mark which is not, on the one hand a description (objectionable under section 3(1)(c)), or on the other hand, a deceptive misdescription (objectionable under section 3(3)(b)) remains under the new law.

Other examples of marks deceptive as to nature from the prior case law include: CHINA-THERM for thermally insulated plastic containers, cups and tumblers (*CHINA-THERM Trade Mark* [1980] FSR 21); and SOFLENS for contact lenses, if used for 'hard' contact lenses (*SOFLENS Trade Mark* [1976] RPC 694). An example of a mark deceptive as to quality was SAFEMIX for thermostatically controlled valves, implying that the valves were safe under all circumstances, which was not true (*SAFEMIX Trade Mark* [1978] RPC 397).

Section 3(3)(b) of the 1994 Act will also prevent the registration of marks which are deceptive as to geographical origin. In *ADVOKAAT Trade Mark* [1978] RPC 252, for example, an application for registration of ADVOKAAT in respect of an alcoholic beverage from Belgium was rejected because the mark suggested a drink from Holland.

Under the 1938 Act, as amended, an objection based on deceptiveness as to geographical origin could be overcome by the applicant agreeing to a condition to registration: 'It is a condition of registration that the mark shall be used only in relation to goods manufactured in . . .' (see, for example, *TONINO Trade Mark* [1973] RPC 568). A mark could be expunged from the Register for breach of condition under section 33 of the 1938 Act, as amended. Registration subject to condition is not a possibility under the new law and there is no equivalent to section 33 of the 1938 Act, as amended.

Apart from the specific instances of deceptiveness mentioned above, section 3(3)(b) will also prevent the registration of marks containing unjustified references to protection by a patent, or registered design.

Obviously, the absolute grounds for refusal in section 3(3) cannot be overcome by evidence of use.

'A trade mark . . . use [of which] is prohibited in the United Kingdom by any enactment or rule of law or by any provision of Community law' (section 3(4))
Section 3(4) reflects the optional provisions of Article 3(2)(a) of the Directive. The possibilities relating to the United Kingdom were formerly dealt with under section 11 of the 1938 Act, as amended, or under the Registrar's discretion.

Section 3(4) of the 1994 Act will continue to prevent the registration of marks which are, for example: unlawful under the Trade Descriptions Act 1968 or the Hallmarking Act 1973; contain the words RED CROSS or GENEVA CROSS or the devices of such crosses (section 6 of the Geneva Conventions Act 1957), or the word ANZAC ('Anzac' (Restriction on Trade Use of Word) Act 1916); or comprise the name of a plant variety registered under the Plant Varieties and Seeds Act 1964 (*Wheatcroft Bros Ltd's Trade Marks* (1954) 71 RPC 43).

The phrase 'any provision of Community law' in section 3(4) will, *inter alia*, provide an absolute ground for refusal where a proprietor attempts to register and use different trade marks for the same products in different Member States within the European Economic Area, without legitimate reason for doing so. Since this ground is more likely to arise in connection with invalidity proceedings it is discussed in more detail in chapter 8. It is noted that there is a proposal for a Community Regulation on Hallmarking.

It goes without saying that section 3(4), if applicable, will prevent registration of a trade mark, however distinctive in fact.

A trade mark which consists of or contains a specially protected emblem (section 3(5))
The specially protected emblems to which this absolute ground for refusal refers are described in sections 4, 57 and 58 of the 1994 Act. They were formerly dealt with under section 61 of the 1938 Act, as amended, and under the Registrar's discretion.

Section 4 prevents the registration of marks including the Royal arms; representing members of the Royal Family or various types of Royal emblem; or representing the Union Jack or national flags. Rules may prescribe that the registration of marks including arms conferred by Crown grant of arms be prohibited.

Absolute grounds for refusal of registration are also provided for marks which consist of flags or other State emblems, or an emblem or name of an intergovernmental organisation which is protected by Article 6*ter* of the Paris Convention (sections 4(3), 57 and 58).

Trade Marks Applied for in Bad Faith (Section 3(6))

It is thought that section 3(6) of the 1994 Act will provide a ground for refusal of registration in the following circumstances:

(a)   *A mark applied for without bona fide intention to use in relation to the goods or services.* Section 32(3) of the 1994 Act requires an application for registration of a trade mark to contain a statement that the mark is being used by the applicant, or with its consent, in relation to the goods or services, or that the applicant has bona fide intention that the mark should be so used. In the White Paper, the Government stated that a mark applied for without bona fide intention to use would be treated as a mark applied for in bad faith (paragraph 4.27).

The ground in section 3(6) will therefore, cover: applications for 'ghost' marks, that is, marks applied for in order to protect an unregistrable mark, or to block a competitor's use of a similar mark (*Imperial Group Ltd* v *Philip Morris & Co. Ltd* [1982] FSR 72); and marks applied for speculatively, for example, in the event of future merchandising activities (see chapter 12).

(b)   *A mark applied for in the knowledge that it is someone else's mark.* Section 17(1) of the 1938 Act, as amended, used to provide that:

Any person claiming to be the proprietor of a trade mark used or proposed to be used by him . . . must apply . . . to the Registrar . . . for registration either in Part A or in Part B of the Register.

In *Loudoun Manufacturing Co. Ltd* v *Courtaulds plc* (1994) *The Times*, 14 February 1994, Aldous J held that section 17(1) merely required on the part of an applicant, an honest belief that it had a good claim to be registered. The fact that a third party might be able to stop the applicant using the mark, for example, through copyright, was irrelevant to the section (*KARO STEP Trade Mark* [1977] RPC 255 dissented from on this point).

However, there could be no bona fide claim to be registered under section 17(1) if the applicant was aware that someone else had a better right to ownership (*Casson's Trade Mark* (1910) 27 RPC 65, *ZOPPAS Trade Mark* [1965] RPC 381 – employee registering employer's selected trade mark).

Furthermore, because there were no appropriate sanctions, the wording of section 17(1) (coupled with the Registrar's discretion) was strained to prevent, under certain circumstances, registration in bad faith of a foreign mark with reputation in the United Kingdom (*Gaines Animal Foods Ltd's Application* [1958] RPC 312) and registration by an agent of a foreign mark without consent (*K SABATIER Trade Mark* [1993] RPC 97).

In *RAWHIDE Trade Mark* [1962] RPC 133, the applicant attempted to register the mark of a popular American television series, not known at the time in the United Kingdom, in respect of toys and games. The applicant's motive was to avoid paying royalties for the use of the mark. The application was refused, but there was also some doubt as to the applicant's intention to use (*RAWHIDE* was approved by Aldous J in the *Loudoun* case above).

The 1994 Act moves the United Kingdom closer to being a 'first to file' jurisdiction, although the registration of marks can be opposed or declared invalid on the basis of defensible prior rights, *inter alia*, in copyright and passing off (sections 5 and 47(2)). Owners of foreign marks which are well-known in the United Kingdom are, for the first time, given statutory rights to bring opposition and invalidity proceedings and to seek injunctive relief against use of their marks in the United Kingdom (sections 5, 6(1)(c), 47 and 56). Section 60 of the 1994 Act gives the proprietor of an overseas mark the right to apply for a declaration of invalidity where its mark is registered in the United Kingdom by an agent or representative without authority.

As to the role of section 3(6) where an application is made after commencement without bona fide belief in entitlement:

(a) The *Loudoun* principle remains true; in such circumstances, the onus is on the owner of the prior right to oppose or apply for a declaration of invalidity.

(b) Section 3(6) will need to be relied upon in opposition proceedings:

    (i) where an unused mark is chosen by an employer for its goods or services, but registered without consent by an employee (*Casson*; *ZOPPAS*);

    (ii) in a *RAWHIDE* situation where a foreign mark is not yet well-known in the United Kingdom; or

    (iii) where an agent applies to register an overseas mark without authority.

(c) It may well be that the Registrar will use section 3(6) at application stage where he suspects that a well-known mark is being applied for without consent.

(d) Section 3(6) will provide the owner of an earlier right or well-known mark with an additional ground in opposition or invalidity proceedings where an applicant knows that it lacks entitlement to registration because of that earlier right or well-known mark.

Section 3(6) is discussed in relation to invalidity in chapter 8.

The possibilities covered by section 3(6) were provided for by various sections in the 1938 Act, as amended: sections 11, 13, 17(1), 26(1)(a) and 68(1); and under the Registrar's discretion.

Transitional Provisions (Schedule 3)

These are the same as described in chapter 4. In short, the proprietor of an application for registration made under the 1938 Act, as amended, but not advertised before commencement, can irrevocably elect to have its application decided under the new law in which case the absolute grounds for refusal in section 3 of the 1994 Act will apply to the application (paragraph 11) (*note* the original application or priority date will be lost). Otherwise, applications pending at commencement are dealt with on the basis of the 1938 Act, as amended.

The corresponding old law has been indicated throughout this chapter. Section 9 of the 1938 Act, as amended, is also discussed in chapter 5.

CHAPTER SEVEN
Registrability IV:
Relative Grounds for Refusal of Registration

Introduction

In order to obtain registration under the Trade Marks Act 1994, the final hurdle to be overcome by the applicant is to convince the Registrar that no relative grounds for refusal exist. As the terminology suggests, such grounds do not relate to the intrinsic nature of the mark itself, but to whether its registration is prevented by the existence of another's prior rights – of which there may be none.

The relevant sections of the 1994 Act to be considered are: section 5, which contains the basic prohibition against registration where there exist relevant prior rights; section 6, which defines 'earlier trade mark'; section 7 (a belated addition to the Act), which provides a limited exception to the foregoing in cases of honest concurrent use; and section 8, which contemplates changes to the procedure whereby relative grounds of refusal may be raised, but only after a certain period of time.

Interpretation of the new provisions
Sections 5 and 6 are based on Article 4 of the Directive. It is unfortunate that the 1994 Act does not follow the construction of the Directive, but instead splits Article 4 between two sections. This makes the Act difficult to follow.

When interpreting sections 5 and 6, the Registrar and the courts will need to have regard to:

(a)   decisions on relative grounds for refusal under Article 8 of the Regulation by the Community Trade Mark Office;

(b)   decisions on relative grounds for refusal by other national registries and courts, especially in those Member States whose laws have clearly influenced the Directive, e.g., Benelux;

(c)   decisions of United Kingdom courts, and in due course, courts of other Member States, on questions of infringement – this is because, following the Directive, the relative grounds of refusal are a mirror image of the scope of the trade mark right (see chapter 9 for an explanation of the infringement provisions);

(d)   decisions on the invalidity of a registered mark made under section 47(2) of the 1994 Act.

Ultimately, the definitive interpretation of the Directive, and of any national law derived from it, can be given only by the Court of Justice of the European Communities, by means of a request for a preliminary ruling under Article 177 of the EC Treaty.

Although sections 5 and 6 bear some resemblance to provisions found in the 1938 Act, thereby inviting recourse to earlier case law, this should be done with caution, for the reasons stated above.

Procedure

Relative grounds for refusal of registration may be raised:

(a)   *ex officio* by the Registrar, as a result of the search of prior rights carried out under section 37(2);

(b)   by any person in opposition proceedings filed within three months of the advertisement of the trade mark application in the *Trade Marks Journal.*

This reflects United Kingdom procedure as it has been for the last century, with the Registry priding itself on the thoroughness with which it examines trade mark applications for conflict with prior rights. One of the benefits of this scrutiny is that, according to the White Paper, only 1–2 per cent of applications are opposed.

However, the 1994 Act contains the seeds of change. The system prevailing in some Member States of the EC (in particular, Germany) and adopted by the Community Trade Mark Regulation relies entirely on the filing of oppositions. So, whilst the Regulation provides for the Community Trade Mark Office to make a search of prior rights, and to notify both the applicant and the owners of these prior rights of the search results, the Office does not have the authority to reject an application on the ground that it conflicts with prior rights. Instead it is left to the owner of the prior right to institute opposition proceedings. The EC Commission has estimated that at least 80 per cent of applications will attract opposition, which is in stark contrast to the present position in the United Kingdom.

The White Paper discussed in some detail whether it would be appropriate for the United Kingdom to switch to an opposition-based system, but felt that it would impose too great a burden on small and medium-sized firms, and that the saving of costs to the Registry in not dealing with prior rights would be far outweighed by the extra costs in holding opposition hearings. Rather than close the door completely on the use of an opposition-based system, a compromise is offered by the 1994 Act. Under section 8, the Secretary of State is empowered to order that relative grounds for refusal cannot be raised by the Registry but only by the proprietor of the earlier right in opposition proceedings. Such an order can be made only after the Community Trade Mark Office has been open for business for a minimum of 10 years. As the Community system is not expected to be operative until 1996, it will be well into the next century before the United Kingdom considers abandoning its rigorous scrutiny of pending applications for conflict with prior rights.

Relative Grounds of Refusal: Sections 5 and 6

Introduction

Section 5 of the Trade Marks Act 1994 prohibits the registration of a trade mark in several distinct situations where prior rights exist. These prior rights comprise:

(a) earlier registered trade marks meeting the criteria set out in section 5(1) to (3);

(b) earlier used but unregistered trade marks meeting the criteria set out in section 5(4)(a);

(c) other earlier rights such as copyright or designs as provided for in section 5(4)(b). In the case of designs, these may either be registered under the Registered Designs Act 1949 (hereafter, RDA 1949) as amended by the Copyright, Designs and Patents Act 1988 (hereafter, CDPA 1988), or unregistered but protected under the provisions of Part III of the CDPA 1988.

Relative grounds for refusal: section 5(1) to (3)

The opening three subsections of section 5 provide as follows:

(1) A trade mark shall not be registered if it is identical with an earlier trade mark and the goods or services for which the trade mark is applied for are identical with the goods or services for which the earlier trade mark is protected.

(2) A trade mark shall not be registered if because—

(a) it is identical with an earlier trade mark and is to be registered for goods or services similar to those for which the earlier trade mark is protected, or

(b) it is similar to an earlier trade mark and is to be registered for goods or services identical with or similar to those for which the earlier trade mark is protected,

there exists a likelihood of confusion on the part of the public, which includes the likelihood of association with the earlier trade mark.

(3) A trade mark which—

(a) is identical with or similar to an earlier trade mark, and

(b) is to be registered for goods or services which are not similar to those for which the earlier trade mark is protected,

shall not be registered if, or to the extent that, the earlier trade mark has a reputation in the United Kingdom (or, in the case of a Community trade mark, in the European Community) and the use of the later mark without due cause would take advantage of, or be detrimental to, the distinctive character or the repute of the earlier trade mark.

Despite its complexity, it has to be said that the wording of section 5(2) is much clearer than when it first appeared in the draft Trade Marks Bill. The original version was based on the wording of Article 4(1)(b) of the Directive, which, because of the way in which it had been condensed during the process of revision, made little sense. Accordingly, section 5(2) has resorted to the wording employed in the first draft of the Directive.

Subsection (1) to (3) contain a number of permutations. For ease of explanation, the various possibilities are set out in tabular form below:

Table 7.1

Section	Mark	Goods or services	Additional requirement
5(1)	identical	identical	none
5(2)(a)	identical	similar	likelihood of confusion
5(2)(b)	similar	identical	likelihood of confusion
5(2)(b)	similar	similar	likelihood of confusion
5(3)	identical *or* similar	dissimilar	reputation *plus* detriment

The meaning of 'earlier trade mark'
The categories of earlier trade marks which may constitute relative grounds for refusal are as follows.

Earlier registrations   Section 6(1)(a) lists those earlier registrations which can bar a later application. They are:

(a)   *a registered trade mark:* by virtue of section 63(1) this means a mark entered on the United Kingdom national Register;

(b)   *an international trade mark (UK):* by virtue of section 53 this means a trade mark which has been registered with the International Bureau of WIPO under the Madrid Protocol, protection for which has been extended to the United Kingdom;

(c)   *a Community trade mark:* under section 51 together with Article 1 of the Community Trade Mark Regulation, this means a mark registered at the Community Trade Mark Office in Alicante, which mark is to have uniform effect throughout all Member States of the European Communities.

In contrast to the position under the 1938 Act, such earlier marks are no longer confined to domestic registrations.

Pending applications for national, international (UK) and Community trade marks   Section 6(2) provides that pending applications, provided they mature to registration, are to be treated as 'earlier trade marks'. In other words, the rule now is quite simple: the first to file prevails, as in the patent system.

Section 6(2) should be contrasted with the disorder inherent in section 12(3) of the 1938 Act, as amended. This provided that where separate applications were made by different persons for the same or confusingly similar marks for the same goods or goods of the same description or associated services (and vice versa for service mark applications), then the Registrar could refuse to register both applications unless their respective rights had been determined by the court or the parties had themselves managed to reach an amicable settlement. Further, in the absence of any agreement between the parties, the Registrar was not obliged to refer the matter to the court.

Section 12(3) was based on the unreal assumption that co-pending applications could *never* be separated. The fact of the matter was that the Registrar could usually find some means of determining the applications. Either there was a sufficient time gap between filing dates to enable the first application to be dealt with in the normal way; or the applications could be decided on the basis of who had first put the mark to genuine use (see *CARAVILLAS Trade Mark* [1981] RPC 381 for an illustration of both these points); or the two rival applications could be differentiated in some way, such as the fact that the goods were supplied to different sections of the public (see *BUD Trade Mark* [1988] RPC 535).

Section 6(2) of the 1994 Act therefore provides a total break with the past.

Lapsed national, international (UK) and Community marks   Section 6(3) provides that the term 'earlier trade mark' is to include lapsed marks. These are to continue to be taken into account for a period of one year after their expiry unless the Registrar is satisfied that there was no bona fide use of the earlier mark during the two years immediately before expiry. This represents no change to section 20(4) of the 1938 Act, as amended.

Later Community marks   Under section 6(1)(b), an application may be defeated by a (presumably) later Community trade mark based on an earlier national or international trade mark (UK) having an earlier priority date, the Community trade mark being effectively backdated (by virtue of Articles 34 or 35 of the Regulation) to the date of the earlier national or international registration.

'Well-known marks'   Close examination of section 5(1), (2) and (3) reveals these provisions consistently use the word 'protected' when speaking of 'earlier trade marks'. This raises the question whether the three subsections relate just to registered trade marks, or to unregistered marks as well. As was explained during the report stage of the Trade Marks Bill in the House of Lords, the word 'protected' was deliberately chosen for the sake of consistency with the Paris Convention (see *Hansard* (HL), 24 February 1994, col. 731). Further, if regard is had to the definition of 'earlier trade mark' in section 6, this makes clear that, with one exception, the earlier trade marks under the three subsections which operate to prevent a later application succeeding can only be marks which are entered (either as registrations, applications or lapsed registrations) on the relevant register, whether national, Community or international. The only category of unregistered mark which acts as a relative ground for refusal under section 5(1) to (3) is that of the 'well-known mark', as specified in section 6(1)(c).

The obligation to treat a 'well-known mark' as a relative ground for refusal stems from Article 6*bis* of the Paris Convention 1883, as amended, although the obligation has only been transposed fully into United Kingdom domestic law for the first time by virtue of the 1994 Act (the protection afforded under the 1938 Act to 'defensive registrations', which has now been abolished, can hardly be said to have met the United Kingdom's obligations under the Convention).

A 'well-known mark' is defined by section 56 as meaning one which is well-known in the United Kingdom and is owned by a person (whether an individual or a company) who is entitled to the benefit of the Paris Convention (this was explained in chapter 3 above) but who need not carry on business nor have any goodwill in the United Kingdom. Section 56 goes on to provide (as already discussed in chapter 2 above) that the owner of a well-known mark can obtain an injunction to restrain the *use* of an identical or similar mark for identical or similar goods or services where there is a likelihood of confusion with the 'well-known mark'. The corollary of this provision is section 6(1)(c) which entitles the owner to oppose an *application to register* a trade mark on the same basis.

The ability of the owner of a 'well-known mark' under section 6(1)(c) to oppose an application on the grounds listed in section 5(1) to (3) is therefore a new provision in United Kingdom law for which no guidance from earlier cases will be available. Even the case law relating to the foreign plaintiff in passing-off actions will be of no help, because that had insisted that the foreign plaintiff had to have customers in the United Kingdom, that is, the business had to have goodwill in this country, a requirement which is dispensed with by section 56. Reference to texts explaining the Paris Convention reveals that the 'well-known mark' does not have to be registered, as the basis of Article 6*bis* is the prevention of unfair competition and the promotion of consumer protection. Further, the 'well-known mark' does not have to have been used in the country where the owner seeks to oppose registration of a confusingly similar trade mark. It is sufficient if information which promotes the 'well-known mark' has caused it to acquire a reputation in commerce, even though the relevant product may not yet be available to members of the public.

According to the wording of Article 6*bis*, it will be for the United Kingdom authorities (in the case of section 6(1)(c), the Trade Marks Registry) to determine whether the mark is 'well-known'. At the time of writing, it is only possible to speculate about the evidential burden which the owner of the alleged 'well-known mark' will have to satisfy in order to mount a successful opposition under section 5.

However, as a 'well-known mark' need not have been used in the United Kingdom, but must merely have a reputation here, such evidence will have to relate to the publicity accorded to the trade mark (say) in journals, films and television programmes available in this country (the increasing use of satellite television will be relevant) and survey evidence of the degree of public recognition accorded to the 'well-known mark' (this is despite the general reluctance of both the Registry and the courts to accept survey evidence in trade mark cases). Presumably the extent of the use of the 'well-known mark' in another Convention country will be relevant.

Another question to be answered is what the relationship is between 'well-known marks', which are treated as 'earlier trade marks' by section 6(1)(c), and used but unregistered marks which are treated as a separate category of 'earlier right' under section 5(4)(a). As explained below, it is likely that because of the wording of section 5(4)(a) the owner of a used but unregistered mark which does not amount to a 'well-known mark' will have to put together sufficient evidence to indicate the probability of success in a passing-off action. By contrast, the owner of the 'well-known mark' would have to prove reputation and (if opposing under section 5(2)) likelihood of confusion, but not likelihood of damage to goodwill.

Further, because of the relationship between Article 2 and Article 6*bis* of the Paris Convention, as reflected in the wording of section 56 of the 1994 Act, there is possibly an element of reverse discrimination in the 1994 Act. From the wording of section 56, it is arguable that the obligation in Article 6*bis* of the Convention to protect 'well-known marks' only applies to nationals of *other* Convention countries. If this supposition is correct, the United Kingdom owner of an unregistered mark may be unable to rely on section 6(1)(c) and be forced to rely on section 5(4)(a), which imposes a higher evidential burden.

Be that as it may, it would be difficult to envisage a United Kingdom company which owned a mark which was well-known elsewhere but completely unprotected in the United Kingdom either by registration or use.

If the above supposition is wrong, the intending opponent seeking to rely on an unregistered mark as a relative ground of refusal will have to decide whether to claim that the mark is 'well-known' or to claim that use has been sufficient to support passing off. Either way, it will be necessary to wait for case law to clarify the difference between these two provisions.

The assessment of conflict with earlier trade marks: section 5(1)
Section 5(1) prohibits the registration of an identical mark for identical goods or services. Where there is this total overlap, there will be no need for the opponent to prove any likelihood of confusion. As long as the opponent's mark came first in time, there is an absolute right to stop a late-comer.

The assessment of conflict with earlier trade marks: section 5(2)
The situation under section 5(2) is not so clear-cut. As Table 7.1 above shows, the subsection covers the following eight permutations:

(a)   Where an earlier mark is protected in respect of goods, it will block a later application for:

    (i)   an identical mark for similar goods;
    (ii)   an identical mark for related services;
    (iii)   a similar mark for identical goods;
    (iv)   a similar mark for related services.

(b)   Where an earlier mark is protected in respect of services, it will block a later application for:

    (i)   an identical mark for similar services;
    (ii)   an identical mark for related goods;
    (iii)   a similar mark for identical services;
    (iv)   a similar mark for related goods.

In each case, however, there *must* exist a likelihood of confusion on the part of the public, which includes a likelihood of association.

The concept of similarity   The temptation for trade mark practitioners in the United Kingdom will be to assume that section 5(2) of the 1994 Act re-enacts section 12(1) of the 1938 Act, as amended. This had prohibited, in the case where a mark was registered for goods, the registration of the same or a confusingly similar mark for the same goods, for goods of the same description or for associated services. There was a similarly worded provision dealing with where the earlier mark was registered in respect of services.

However, it cannot be stressed too highly that section 5(2) of the 1994 Act is derived from the Directive, which in turn is based on Article 13A of the Uniform Benelux Trademarks Law of 1971 (see Minute 5 of the Minutes of the Council of

Ministers attached to the Community Trade Mark Regulation). Under Article 13A of the Benelux legislation, the concept of similarity is judged according to the likelihood of confusion or the likelihood of association in the minds of the public.

In assessing similarity, reference to the 10th recital to the Directive indicates that a broad test is to be applied, with the following matters, in particular, being relevant:

(a)   the recognition of the trade mark on the market;
(b)   the association which can be made with the used or registered sign;
(c)   the degree of similarity between the goods and services;
(d)   the degree of similarity between the trade mark and the sign.

Further, reference to decisions of the Benelux Court of Justice on the meaning of 'similarity' in Article 13A of the Uniform Benelux Trademarks Law of 1971 shows that the public, on seeing the later conflicting mark, do not need to be confused. What is required is that the public makes a mental link between the two marks, because the second mark conjures up some evocation of the first one (see the cases of *Union* v *Union Soleure*, Benelux Court of Justice, 20 May 1983 and *MONOPOLY* v *ANTI-MONOPOLY*, Dutch Supreme Court, 24 June 1977, discussed in chapter 9).

The impact of the Benelux approach to similarity has major implications for United Kingdom trade marks law:

(a)   By stressing the need to recognise the strength of the trade mark on the market and the mental images it produces, passing-off concepts will be imported into the law of registered trade marks. Even so, such passing-off notions will go beyond what has already been recognised by the judiciary, in that according to *H. P. Bulmer Ltd* v *J. Bollinger SA* [1978] RPC 79, 'producing an association' in the minds of the public meant making the public think that this was 'something for which the plaintiff was responsible', a reflection of the indication of origin function of trade marks. Benelux law has made it clear that the public are not concerned with the origin of the goods.

(b)   The assessment of similarity will differ from the test of 'confusing similarity' under section 12(1) of the 1938 Act, as amended. This was a somewhat sterile exercise in which only the notional, future use of both marks was considered (see Evershed J in *Smith, Hayden & Co. Ltd's Application* (1946) 63 RPC 63 at p. 71). The wording of the Directive, transposed into section 5(2), means that the extent of the previous use of the earlier mark will be relevant.

Similarity of goods and services   It will be remembered that one of the criteria for the application of section 5(2) of the 1994 Act listed in the 10th recital to the Directive, is the similarity of goods and services. The Registry are likely to continue to use the test laid down in *Jellinek's Application* (1946) 63 RPC 59 for comparing the similarity of goods, that is, to consider:

(a)   the nature and composition of the goods;
(b)   the respective uses to which they are put;
(c)   the trade channels through which they may be sold.

As the outcome of the *Jellinek* test was a question of fact in each case, it was not necessary for all three elements to be satisfied, although the nature of the goods tended to be the predominant requirement. Of the myriad cases decided under the old Act, two will suffice to illustrate the application of the *Jellinek* test. In *FLORADIX Trade Mark* [1974] RPC 583, an application for herbal elixirs was refused in the light of an earlier registration of FLURODIX in respect of dental preparations. Although the goods had different uses, their general nature was the same, in that both were put in the mouth. By contrast in *SEAHORSE Trade Mark* [1980] FSR 250, an application for the trade mark in respect of inboard marine engines exceeding 5,000 bhp was allowed despite the registration of the identical mark for outboard motors. The differences in the size and weight of the engines and the size of the craft in which they would be used (small boats versus ocean-going ships) meant they were not of the same description.

It must be stressed that the classification of goods laid down by the Arrangement of Nice 1957 and incorporated into the Trade Marks Rules was irrelevant under the *Jellinek* test. Goods in the same class may not be 'of the same description', whilst goods in apparently unrelated classes may well be so.

The *Jellinek* test was adopted by the Registry (though without judicial confirmation) to deal with the similarity of services, namely:

(a)   the nature of the services;
(b)   the respective services provided in respect of what, if any, articles;
(c)   the users of the services;
(d)   whether the two services could be provided in the course of normal business relations (for example, building society and estate agency services).

Basically, the test applied by the Registry under section 12(1), as amended, for assessing the similarity of associated goods and services was whether they could be provided by the same business (for example, stationery goods and photocopying services).

Similarity of marks   Again, the 10th recital directs the inquiry under section 5(2) of the 1994 Act to the similarity of marks. The tests used by the Registry under the 1938 Act, as amended, are likely to remain valid under the new Act. They are:

(a)   The idea of the mark is the prime consideration. This means that particular regard is to be had to the ideas and images conveyed by the mark. Thus in *Broadhead's Application* (1950) 67 RPC 209 the mark applied for, ALKA-VESCENT, was considered to convey the same information as ALKA-SELTZER (fizzy alkaline tablets).

(b)   Marks should be compared as a whole, disregarding matter common to the trade. There should not be a letter-by-letter comparison, rather the overall effect of the mark should be considered. Thus ERECTIKO was refused because it was too close to ERECTOR (*William Bailey (Birmingham) Ltd's Application* (1935) 52 RPC 136); by contrast *POL-RAMA* was allowed despite the presence of POLAR-OID on the Register (*POL-RAMA Trade Mark* [1977] RPC 581). Matter common to the trade is, in effect, substracted from both marks, so that PEPSI-COLA could be registered despite the presence of COCA-COLA; the suffix 'COLA' is common to many soft drinks and there is no similarity between PEPSI and COCA

(*Coca-Cola Co. of Canada Ltd* v *Pepsi-Cola Co. of Canada Ltd* (1942) 59 RPC 127).

(c)   The first syllable is the most important (although this test is subordinate to the requirement that marks be considered as a whole). Where the mark consists of one syllable, then the first letter is the most important. Hence *FIF Trade Mark* [1979] RPC 355 for non-alcoholic beverages was registrable in the face of JIF.

(d)   An aural as well as a visual comparison should be made of the marks and consideration should be given as to how the goods or services are to be ordered. Care needs to be taken with goods or services which might be ordered over the telephone, because of the risk of mispronunciation. There is less likelihood of confusion between marks where the goods or services are expensive and likely to be bought after negotiations between buyer and seller. Hence in *LANCER Trade Mark* [1987] RPC 303 it was held that there was no risk of confusion between LANCER and LANCIA for cars because of the way in which the goods were sold.

(e)   The court should always be guided by the 'doctrine of imperfect recollection'. The hypothetical customer will rarely be comparing the two marks side by side and probably remembers only one brand name and that imperfectly. Equally, allowance should be made for careless pronunciation by both customer and supplier.

(f)   The similarity of marks is essentially a 'jury' question. The Registry or court should therefore ignore its own specialist knowledge and approach the matter from the point of view of the potential customer. Instances of actual confusion may assist the court, although it is generally wary of survey evidence.

The above criteria are applicable not just to the relative grounds of refusal under section 5(2), (3) and (4)(a), but also to invalidity proceedings, infringement and passing off.

Assessment of conflict with earlier trade marks: section 5(3)
The wording of section 5(3) of the 1994 Act encompasses both the mandatory obligation of Article 4(3) of the Directive to prevent the dilution of Community trade marks and the option given to Member States by Article 4(4)(a) to prevent the dilution of national trade marks.

Section 5(3) appears, however, to extend dilution to two categories of earlier trade marks not covered by the Directive's dilution provisions, namely international marks (UK) and 'well-known' marks. Since the provisions of the Directive in relation to relative grounds are conclusive of the matter (see recital 10) the Act is in breach of Community law in this respect (though it may be queried whether the term 'national trade mark' under Article 4(4)(a) of the Directive includes international marks (UK)).

Section 5(3) is new to United Kingdom trade marks law and prohibits a later application if the following requirements are met:

(a)   the later mark is identical with or similar to an earlier mark;
(b)   the later mark is to be registered for goods or services which are not similar to those for which the earlier mark is protected;
(c)   the earlier mark has a reputation in the United Kingdom (if it is a national registration) or has a reputation in the European Community (if it is a Community trade mark);

(d)   the use of the later mark must be without due cause;

(e)   the use of the later mark must take unfair advantage of or be detrimental to, the distinctive character or the repute of the earlier trade mark.

It will be noted that unlike section 5(2), likelihood of confusion is *not* a requirement in section 5(3).

Section 5(3) should be compared with section 10(3) which provides for the right to stop dilution of a registered trade mark in the context of infringement proceedings. Both provisions owe their inspiration to the Uniform Benelux Trademarks Law of 1971, which in turn should be compared with legislation enacted in 22 States of the United States of America enabling the trade mark owner to prevent the dilution of a trade mark. This State legislation (there is no Federal anti-dilution statute in the United States of America) was inspired by the hypothesis of the late Frank Schechter, who argued ((1927) 40 Harv L Rev 813 at p. 825) that the only rational basis for trade mark protection lay in proscribing 'the gradual whittling away or the dispersion of the identity and hold upon the public mind of the mark or name by its use upon non-competing goods'. The action for dilution was the only way of preserving the mark's 'commercial magnetism', its unique quality and its effectiveness as an advertising tool.

Although in the United States of America, anti-dilution statutes have met with a considerable amount of judicial hostility and resistance, reference to case law there and in the Benelux shows that dilution can take two forms:

(a)   the blurring of the product identification of the mark by its use on dissimilar goods or services;

(b)   the tarnishing of the affirmative association which the mark has come to convey by its use on goods which might be regarded as unwholesome.

Schechter gave the following as an example of the 'blurring' effect of dilution: 'If you allow Rolls Royce restaurants, and Rolls Royce cafeterias, and Rolls Royce pants, and Rolls Royce candy, in 10 years you will not have the Rolls Royce mark any more' (this type of 'whittling away' of the trade mark should be contrasted with where the mark becomes generic for a particular product). An example of the 'tarnishing' effect of dilution, is the leading decision of the Benelux Court of Justice, *CLAERYN/KLAREIN* (1976) 7 IIC 420, where the owner of CLAERYN Dutch gin was able to restrain the use of KLAREIN for household cleanser.

Certain of the elements of dilution (namely 'reputation', 'due cause', 'unfair advantage' and 'detrimental to') require further elaboration. The element of reputation imports yet again passing-off concepts into the law of registered trade marks. Proof of sufficient reputation will impose a considerable evidential burden, covering, *inter alia*, the following matters:

(a)   the degree of inherent or acquired distinctiveness of the mark

(b)   the duration and extent of use of the mark in connection with the goods or services;

(c)   the geographical extent of the trading area in which the mark is used;

(d)   the channels of trade for the goods or services with which the mark is used;

(e)   the degree of recognition afforded to the mark;

(f)   the degree to which the same or a similar mark has been used by third parties.

Although the White Paper referred to marks of 'wide reputation', the 1994 Act simply refers to 'reputation'. It is therefore unclear what level of reputation will be required and whether dilution will protect only 'famous' marks. American courts have tended to favour only 'famous' marks, whereas Benelux courts have not been too concerned with the requirement of reputation. It remains to be seen which line of thinking the United Kingdom courts follow.

'Without due cause' has been narrowly interpreted by the Benelux Court of Justice in the *CLAERYN* case to mean 'necessity'. The phrases 'unfair advantage' and 'detrimental to' perhaps suggest a requirement of intention, but if a comparison with passing off is made, there is ample authority to the effect that intention to deceive the public is *not* an essential element of the tort. It will obviously take quite a few years until it becomes clear how the Registry and United Kingdom courts follow their European or American counterparts in adding detail to the bare bones of the dilution doctrine found in the 1994 Act.

Relative grounds for refusal: section 5(4)(a)
Given that United Kingdom domestic trade marks law has always conferred on the owner of a used mark the right to oppose a pending application, it is hardly surprising that the United Kingdom chose to adopt, in section 5(4)(a), the optional provision of Article 4(4)(b) of the Directive. Section 5(4)(a) provides that rights to a non-registered trade mark, provided they are acquired before the application or priority date of the later mark, and provided that the non-registered trade mark confers on its owner the right to prohibit the use of a subsequent trade mark, are to be treated as relative grounds of refusal.

The nearest equivalent to section 5(4)(a) in the 1938 Act, as amended, was section 11. This prohibited the registration of any mark which '. . . by reason of its being likely to deceive or cause confusion, [was] disentitled to protection in a court of justice'. Case law on section 11 could be useful in interpreting section 5(4)(a) of the 1994 Act, but differences (discussed below) between the old and new sections should be borne in mind.

The way in which section 11 of the 1938 Act was to be applied in the case of an opposition by the owner of a used mark was explained by Evershed J in *Smith, Hayden & Co. Ltd's Application* (1946) 63 RPC 71 at p. 101:

Having regard to the reputation acquired by the [earlier mark] is the court satisfied that the mark applied for, if used in a normal and fair manner in connection with any goods covered by the registration proposed, will not be reasonably likely to cause deception and confusion amongst a substantial number of persons.

The comparison under section 11, therefore, was between the *past* use of the opponent's mark and the *future* use of the mark applied for. Hence, the greater the use of the opponent's mark and the greater its reputation, the wider the area of protection which would be conferred on the mark. Decisions under section 11 therefore enabled the owner of the prior used mark to stop the registration of a mark for dissimilar goods, where the prior mark had acquired an extensive reputation. An example is *GOLDEN JET Trade Mark* [1979] RPC 19, where a three-pointed star trade mark was refused for clothing because of the use of such a device on Mercedes-Benz cars. It was also held that section 11 was wide enough to encompass not merely confusion between two marks, but confusion between a mark and a company name (*GE Trade Mark* [1973] RPC 297).

It could be argued that Evershed J's test was slightly modified by Lord Upjohn's judgment in *BALI Trade Mark* [1969] RPC 472. Lord Upjohn stated that the words 'having regard to the reputation . . .' should be replaced with the words 'having regard to the user of . . .', although the New Zealand case of *Pioneer Hi-Bred Corn Co.* v *Hy-Line Chicks (Pty) Ltd* [1979] RPC 410 suggested that reputation acquired solely by advertising but without actual trade was sufficient to found an objection under the section. This case also clarifies the meaning of the phrase 'substantial number of persons'. The requirement is to be sensibly applied, so that in a highly specialised industry, the actual number of persons misled need not be vast, as long as the number concerned is significant in that industry.

It seems reasonable to assume that section 5(4)(a) of the 1994 Act will be applied in similar fashion to section 11 of the 1938 Act and that like its predecessor it will protect a used mark against use on dissimilar goods where the strength of the reputation of the prior mark justifies this.

However, there are two differences between section 5(4)(a) and its predecessor, one obvious and one not so obvious:

(a)   The principal difference stems from the wording of the Directive. This requires that the owner of the earlier used mark must have 'the right to prohibit the use of the subsequent mark'. Section 5(4)(a) states that 'A trade mark shall not be registered if . . . its use in the United Kingdom is liable to be prevented by virtue of any rule of law (in particular, the law of passing off) protecting an unregistered trade mark'. The presence of this wording (whether or not it correctly reflects the Directive) has the effect of increasing the evidential burden imposed on an opponent seeking to rely on section 5(4)(a), in that an opponent must now show passing off. Under section 11 of the 1938 Act, as amended, it was not necessary for the opponent to show that a passing-off action would have been successful (see *BALI Trade Mark* and *GE Trade Mark*).

(b)   Section 5(4)(a) will be available only to the owner of an unregistered trade mark, whereas section 11 was available to the owner of a used mark, whether or not registered (see the facts of *Smith Hayden & Co. Ltd's Application*). This was vital to the owner of a trade mark registered under the 1938 Act in view of the fact that section 12(1) of that Act was limited to prohibiting a later registration for similar goods or services. The availability of dilution under section 5(3) of the 1994 Act means that the curtailment of the scope of protection for a used mark by section 5(4)(a) may be of little practical significance.

Relative grounds for refusal: section 5(4)(b)
Section 5(4)(b), in implementing the optional provision in Article 4(4)(c) of the Directive, puts into statutory form a ground for refusal which was formerly dealt with by the exercise of the Registrar's discretion under sections 11 and 17 of the 1938 Act, as amended.

The wording of the new provision prohibits the registration of a trade mark if its use would be prevented by virtue of an earlier right (other than those already mentioned in section 5) 'in particular by virtue of the law of copyright, design right or registered designs'.

It must be stressed that section 5(4)(b) is relevant only to marks which incorporate pictorial elements and three-dimensional shapes of goods or their packaging. This is because copyright, which exists to protect the categories of 'works' listed in section 1 of the CDPA 1988, cannot subsist in individual words, or short phrases or slogans, and because both design right (dealt with by Part III of the CDPA 1988) and registered designs (protected under the RDA 1949 as amended by Part IV of the CDPA 1988) are concerned to protect the shape of three-dimensional articles.

Specifically, artistic works, such as drawings, paintings and sculptures, protected by virtue of section 4 of the CDPA 1988, will be relevant to pictorial trade marks; and designs for the appearance of three-dimensional articles, whether having eye-appeal for the purposes of the RDA 1949, or whether relating to functional items by virtue of Part III of the CDPA 1988, will be relevant to trade marks consisting of three-dimensional shapes.

The effect of section 5(4)(b) is to enable the owner of a prior copyright or design to object to a later trade mark application where the trade mark reproduces the earlier work. The trade mark need not be an exact copy of the earlier work, provided that in the case of copyright and design right it reproduces a substantial part of the copyright or design. 'Substantial' here refers to the quality of what has been copied, rather than the quantity.

However, in the case of both copyright and design right, in order to succeed in an infringement action, the copyright owner has to prove that the infringer copied or had the opportunity to copy the work. It is not clear whether this requirement will be transported into section 5(4)(b) by virtue of the phrase 'its use is liable to be prevented', or whether the mere fact that someone else is entitled to the copyright or design right will suffice to defeat the trade mark application.

In the case of a registered design, section 7 of the RDA 1949, as amended, gives the registered proprietor the right to object to the application of the design or one 'not substantially different from it' to an article, but without the need to show copying, as the registration of a design confers an absolute monopoly right.

There are two cases decided under the 1938 Act which illustrate the way in which section 5(4)(b) might operate. In *KARO STEP Trade Mark* [1977] RPC 255, Whitford J upheld an application by the German copyright owner (who also owned the German collective mark registration) to revoke the registration of a composite trade mark, consisting of the words 'Karo Step' in a four-pointed star device. Holding that the device was an artistic work under the provisions of the Copyright Act 1956, he decided that section 11 of the 1938 Act enabled him to revoke the mark because had the registered proprietors continued to use it, their conduct would have amounted to copyright infringement and thus would have been 'contrary to law'.

In *OSCAR Trade Mark* [1979] RPC 173 the application to register the name OSCAR and a picture of the famous statuette was rejected on the grounds that the trade mark applicants did not own the copyright in the sculpture and their use of the trade mark would amount to infringement.

Both of these cases were based on the 'contrary to law' prohibition found in section 11 of the 1938 Act. Concern was expressed that the Trade Marks Registry was not the proper forum for determining whether use of the trade mark would amount to copyright infringement. It therefore remains to be seen whether such fears materialise under section 5(4)(b) of the 1994 Act.

Consent: section 5(5)
The owner of any of the earlier rights listed in section 5 can always give consent to the registration of the later trade mark. By providing this, section 5(5) implements the optional provision found in Article 4(5) of the Directive. In contrast to the 1938 Act, however, if such consent is given, it is no longer open to the Registrar to exercise overriding discretion and refuse the application. The consent of the owner of the prior right is therefore absolute.

Exception to Relative Grounds: Honest Concurrent Use

Temporary nature of the exception
Section 7 of the 1994 Act was added to the Trade Marks Bill by the Government during the Third Reading in the House of Lords, as a result of arguments raised during the Committee Stage. It creates an exception to section 5 by permitting a later mark to be registered where there has been honest concurrent use with an earlier trade mark or earlier right. This exception will, however, prove temporary, because section 7 will cease to have effect should an order be made under section 8. As explained at the beginning of this chapter under 'Procedure', such an order will introduce a switch to an opposition-only means of raising relative grounds for refusal but will happen at the earliest 10 years after the operational date of the Community trade mark.

Rationale behind section 7
Section 7 was felt by the Government to be necessary despite the existence of section 5(5) of the 1994 Act which enables the owner of an earlier trade mark or earlier right to consent to a later conflicting mark being registered. Section 7 will enable the Registrar to order registration of the second mark even where the owner of the prior right does *not* consent. Section 7 is confined to enabling the trade mark applicant (provided the requirements of the section are satisfied) to get round relative grounds for refusal. Section 7(4)(a) makes it clear that honest concurrent use cannot be a means of overcoming any of the absolute grounds found in section 3.

Mechanism for dealing with honest concurrent use
At first glance the wording of section 7(2) appears to be straightforward. It suggests that where relative grounds are raised by the Registrar, the applicant can refute them by pleading honest concurrent use. The Registrar is then obliged to accept and publish the application, leaving it to the owner of the prior right to bring opposition proceedings. The inference from the wording of section 7(2) is that such opposition would be determinative of the case, but that if no opposition is brought the owner of the prior right may still seek a declaration of invalidity under section 47(2).

However, examination of the explanation given by Lord Strathclyde for the insertion of the section into the 1994 Act reveals that section 7(2) does not give the complete picture. Claiming that the section provides a 'procedural mechanism' whereby the onus of raising relative grounds falls to the owner of the prior right rather than the Registrar, he stated:

> So far, that is the same as the position under the existing law. Under the new law, however, if there is opposition from the owner of the earlier mark, the Registrar will have to decide whether the grounds for refusal are made out. If they are based on subsection (1) of [section] 5 – that is, the marks are identical, and so are the goods or services concerned – then the application will have to be refused. The fact of honest concurrent use will not be sufficient to defeat the opposition. If, however, the opposition is based on subsection (2) of [section] 5, it is necessary to show a likelihood of confusion on the part of the public. In such a case the fact that the two marks have been concurrently used may well make it more difficult to establish that such a likelihood exists. Likewise, if the ground of opposition is that the later mark would take undue advantage of the earlier mark's reputation, the fact that the two have co-existed in the market-place may have a bearing on the outcome. (*Hansard* (HL), 14 March 1994, col. 71.)

This statement indicates that the filing of opposition proceedings by the owner of the prior right will *not* be conclusive. The Registrar will have to decide whether the two marks can coexist without any likelihood of confusion, at least where the opposition is based on section 5(2) or (3). The owner of the prior right may therefore find a later conflicting mark being admitted to the Register despite any arguments which have been made, although the right to seek a declaration of invalidity under section 47(2) is preserved.

Express reference to earlier law
Section 7 is unusual in making direct reference to its predecessor, section 12(2) of the 1938 Act, as amended. For once, recourse to earlier case law will be essential in interpreting the new provision. Section 12(2) of the 1938 Act, as amended, had stated that, in respect of trade marks, where there was honest concurrent use, or other special circumstances, making it proper for there to be conflicting marks on the Register, the Registrar could permit a later identical or similar mark for the same or similar goods and/or associated services. There was a parallel provision in respect of service marks.

Differences between the old and new Acts
Several differences can be perceived between section 7 of the 1994 Act and section 12(2) of the 1938 Act, as amended.

(a)   In enabling the Registrar to accept a later mark under section 12(2) where there had been honest concurrent use, the 1938 Act, as amended, conferred a discretion to impose any conditions or limitations. By contrast, the 1994 Act has done away with conditions, and limitations under section 13 can be imposed only with the agreement of the applicant, so the powers of the Registrar in attempting to differentiate the two marks are much reduced.

(b)   The wording of section 7 of the 1994 Act is narrower than that of section 12(2), in that it provides for honest concurrent use alone to be a derogation from section 5, rather than honest concurrent use 'or other special circumstances'.

(c)   Section 7 does clarify a point which had been in some doubt under section 12(2), despite a certain amount of relevant judicial authority. Under the 1938 Act, as amended, it was unclear whether section 12(2) was a derogation *only* from section 12(1) (which applied where the earlier mark was registered) or was a derogation *both* from section 12(1) *and* section 11 (which applied where the earlier mark had been used but not registered). Although the wording of the 1938 Act might have suggested that section 12(2) was a derogation only from section 12(1), with there being no exception to section 11 on the face of the Act, Megarry J *obiter* in *Berlei (UK) Ltd* v *Bali Brassiere Co. Inc.* [1970] RPC 469, relying on *Bass, Ratcliffe and Gretton Ltd* v *Nicholson & Sons Ltd* (1932) 49 RPC 88, held that section 12(2) overrode both section 12(1) and section 11. This was despite the earlier statement by Lord Wilberforce in *BALI Trade Mark* [1969] RPC 472 at p. 500 that if the later mark was deceptive under section 11 because of conflict with an earlier used mark, that was an absolute prohibition against registration of the later mark. Lord Wilberforce's comments were later doubted by Lord Diplock in *GE Trade Mark* [1973] RPC 297. Section 7(1) of the 1994 Act, by contrast, makes it clear that honest concurrent use can apply so as to allow registration of the later mark whether there is an earlier trade mark (as defined in section 6) or whether there is some other earlier right (as defined in section 5(4)). This means that both registered and unregistered but used prior rights are subjected to the exception.

Application of the old law: factors to be considered
The leading case on the application of section 12(2) is *Alexander Pirie & Sons Ltd's Application* (1933) 50 RPC 147, where Lord Tomlin listed the matters which should be taken into account by the Registrar in deciding whether to accept a claim for honest concurrent use. Under the new law, the Registrar will have to consider such matters only if the owner of the earlier mark brings opposition proceedings.
    The factors listed by Lord Tomlin were:

(a)   the extent of use in time and quantity and the area of the trade of the later mark;
(b)   the degree of confusion likely to ensue from the resemblance of the marks;
(c)   the honesty of the concurrent use;
(d)   whether any instances of confusion have actually been proved;
(e)   the relative inconvenience which would result if the second mark were to be registered.

No rule existed under the previous legislation as to the minimum period of time sufficient to establish honest concurrent use. In *Peddie's Application* (1944) 61 RPC 31, the Registrar stated that two years, three months' use was insufficient, but each case did depend on its own facts, and in *GRANADA Trade Mark* [1979] RPC 303, two years, 10 months' use on a very large scale was held to be sufficient.

Protection of the public interest
The overriding requirement under the 1938 Act, as amended, was the duty of the Registrar to protect the public interest. In the light of the Government's statement

that honest concurrent use will not overcome a section 5(1) objection, it must be assumed that the same will be true under the new Act. The key to a successful plea of honest concurrent use will therefore be whether the applicant can identify some factor which effectively differentiates the later mark from the earlier mark.

Examples of successful differentiation can be found in earlier case law. In *Bainbridge and Green's Application* (1940) 57 RPC 248, the parties traded in different geographical areas (a key issue in relation to conflicting marks for services, which tend by their very nature to be localised). In *Bass Ratcliffe & Gretton Ltd* v *John Davenport & Sons' Brewery* (1932) 49 RPC 88, the product, beer, was sold in different containers to different customers. In *BULER Trade Mark* [1975] RPC 275 the products, watches, could be separated by the price charged, the one being very expensive, the other very cheap. In each of the three cases, the products could be separated by reference to sales area, packaging or price.

Nevertheless, what mattered ultimately under section 12(2) was the protection of the public interest, and if the Registrar was not satisfied that this was being protected the later mark would be refused, as in *L'AMY Trade Mark* [1983] RPC 137.

Criticisms of section 7
The incorporation of section 7 into the 1994 Act can be criticised on grounds of internal and external inconsistency.

Internal inconsistency   The argument in favour of retaining an honest concurrent use provision in the new legislation was to the effect that such a provision had been part of United Kingdom trade marks law for over a century and ought to be preserved. Nevertheless, it is submitted that section 7 is illogical for a number of reasons:

(a)   Historically a provision on honest concurrent use may well have been justified when the system of registering trade marks was in its infancy, as it took businesses time to adjust to the concept of registering rights. The system of registration, when implemented in 1875, had to take into account the fact that whilst some businesses would register their marks fairly soon, others would continue to use their marks without registration and only consider the necessity for registration much later on. The forerunner of section 12(2) of the 1938 Act, as amended, was based on such an assumption, and also on the fact that trading conditions at the time were quite different from those of today. Businesses tended to be more localised and it was quite feasible for different proprietors in different parts of the United Kingdom to build up goodwill without cutting across each other's interests. This can hardly be true in the era of the Single Market and satellite television. Further, the commercial value of trade marks is generally appreciated today. Section 6(2) of the 1994 Act reflects the pressure on companies to get their product nationally recognised as quickly as possible. Can honest concurrent use fit in with a system which accords priority to the applicant who is first to file?

(b)   When section 7 is considered in the context of the 1994 Act as a whole, the ability to plead honest concurrent use in order to overcome relative grounds of refusal seems a hollow victory. As Lord Strathclyde pointed out in the Third

Reading Debate (see *Hansard* (HL), 14 March 1994, col. 71), the owner of the prior right will still be able to challenge the registration under section 47(2), subject to any plea of acquiescence under section 48. This begs the question: why should an applicant try to argue honest concurrent use under section 7 in the knowledge that the owner of the prior right can always challenge the registration later on? Surely this is a waste of time and money.

(c)   A further criticism of the Government's reasoning is this. The *old* law on honest concurrent use was concerned with whether there was any likelihood of confusion between the earlier mark and the mark applied for, such likelihood of confusion being appraised on the basis that the trade mark functioned as an indicator of origin. Section 5(2) of the 1994 Act, in transposing the Directive, contains the phrase 'likelihood of confusion on the part of the public, which *includes a likelihood of association*' (emphasis added). As already pointed out, the test for this, based on recital 10 of the Directive, will be considerably wider than under the old Act, a point overlooked by the Government when section 7 was introduced. To incorporate expressly a provision from the old Act when the new Act contains such a cultural revolution for trade marks seems short-sighted in the extreme.

External inconsistency: breach of European Community law   Despite statements to the contrary in the House of Lords' Third Reading Debate (see *Hansard* (HL), 14 March 1994, col. 71), by incorporating section 7 into the 1994 Act the Government is arguably in breach of various obligations imposed on the United Kingdom by virtue of European Community and international law:

(a)   Section 7 contradicts the mandatory wording of Article 4 of the Directive. Article 4 states explicitly that '*a trade mark shall not be registered*' (emphasis added) if it conflicts with an earlier trade mark or earlier right. Although Article 4(5) provides for the owner of the prior right to consent to the registration of the later conflicting mark, there is no other derogation in Article 4, other than in respect of the transitional arrangements which each Member State is allowed to make. Section 7 can hardly be regarded as being in this category. Given that the Directive imposes clear and unconditional obligations on Member States of the European Community with regard to their domestic trade mark laws, it is quite probable that it satisfies the criteria laid down by the Court of Justice of the European Communities for a Directive to have direct effect. If that is the case (indeed, the German Supreme Court has already decided that the Directive does have direct effect, although ultimately such a decision should be made by the CJEC), then the owner of a prior right who finds a later trade mark registered under section 7 should be able to rely on Article 4, either before the Registrar, on an appeal from the decision of the Registrar or in proceedings under section 47(2) for invalidity of the later mark. It is even possible to contemplate the owner of the prior right suing the owner of the later mark for infringement, and, when met by the defence of section 11(1) (which was introduced largely as a result of section 7 and which basically says that one registered proprietor cannot sue another registered proprietor), arguing that the later mark is invalid because it was registered in breach of the Directive. Alternatively, there is also the possibility of an action for judicial review, for, as has recently been confirmed in *R* v *Secretary of State for Employment ex parte Equal Opportunities Commission* [1994] 2 WLR 409, the Divisional Court has jurisdiction to declare both primary and secondary legislation to be incompatible with Community law, the only obstacle to such an action being the requirement under Order 53 of the Rules of the Supreme Court 1965 for *locus standi*.

(b)   It can be argued that section 7 is contrary to the Community Trade Mark Regulation. Article 1(2) of this establishes the unitary character of any Community mark, which is to have equal effect throughout the Community. If the United Kingdom Registry is to permit later national marks to come on to the Register (and it will be remembered that national trade marks, international trade marks (UK) and Community trade marks all count as 'earlier trade marks' for the purposes of section 5), then this must surely undermine any Community registration. As the Community trade mark is subject to national law only in the matter of infringement, the United Kingdom Registry would presumably be acting *ultra vires* in permitting a later national mark to be registered. The United Kingdom could well find itself taken before the Court of Justice by the Commission under Article 169 of the Treaty of Rome for breach of its obligations under the EC Treaty.

(c)   The same reasoning would apply to the situation where the owner of a prior international trade mark (UK) under the Madrid Protocol is forced to accept a later national United Kingdom domestic registration on the grounds of honest concurrent use. However, because of the status of the Madrid Protocol as an international convention, it will not have direct effect in United Kingdom law in the same way that the EC Treaty and EC secondary legislation do, so the ability of the owner of the earlier trade mark in such a case to argue that the second registration ought never to have been made is much weaker.

As indicated above, section 7 is not intended to be a permanent feature of United Kingdom trade marks law and should disappear if the United Kingdom abandons its rigorous scrutiny of earlier trade marks in favour of the opposition-based system found in Germany and elsewhere. Nevertheless, whilst it is on the statute book, for the reasons given above, there are cogent arguments for the proposition that it infringes, at the very least, both the Trade Marks Directive and the Community Trade Mark Regulation.

Transitional Provisions (Schedule 3)

Schedule 3, paragraph 10, provides, as already noted, that an application for registration made under the 1938 Act, as amended, which is pending on the commencement date of the 1994 Act is to be dealt with under the old law. This means that such an application will be subject to oppositions based on section 11 and section 12(1) of the 1938 Act, as amended.

An opposition based on section 11 would be to the effect that because of use which had been made of an earlier mark (whether registered or unregistered), the later application, if successful, would be likely to deceive or cause confusion and so be 'disentitled to protection in a court of justice'. In assessing the likelihood of confusion under section 11, the court would compare any past use of the opponent's mark with any notional, future use of the mark applied for (*Smith, Hayden & Co. Ltd's Application* (1946) 63 RPC 71).

An opposition based on section 12(1) would be to the effect that the existence of an earlier registered mark for goods prohibited the registration of a later application for the same or a confusingly similar mark in respect of the same goods, goods of the same description or associated services. There was a corresponding provision in respect of services. The likelihood of confusion under section 12(1) was assessed by considering the notional, future use of both marks (*Smith, Hayden & Co. Ltd's Application*).

An application which has not been advertised under the provisions of the 1938 Act, as amended, at the effective date of the 1994 Act may be converted into a 1994 Act application at the request of the applicant and upon payment of the appropriate fee (schedule 3, paragraph 11(1)). Conversion will mean loss of the original application or priority date (schedule 3, paragraph 11(3)).

In relation to the relative grounds for refusal, such conversion would be risky, for the following reasons:

(a)   Another competitor may well have filed a conflicting application in the meantime.

(b)   The categories of earlier rights in section 5 are considerably wider, though in practice marks registered under the Community and Madrid systems will not be operative until 1996 and 1995 respectively.

(c)   The assessment of similarity under the 1994 Act will be much wider than under the 1938 Act, with greater emphasis on the public perception of the two marks.

For these reasons, an applicant may well prefer to stay with the 1938 Act system of dealing with prior rights.

CHAPTER EIGHT
Maintenance and Loss of Registration

Introduction

Maintenance and loss of registration assume added importance under the new Act, not least because of the deregulation of assignment and licensing. The onus is placed firmly on the proprietor of a registered trade mark to observe basic rules of maintenance, if that registration is to remain in full force and effect. Essentially this means:

(a)   attending to renewal;
(b)   using the trade mark;
(c)   using the trade mark in accordance with the provisions of the 1994 Act.

Renewal (Sections 42 and 43)

The Directive contains no provisions of approximation concerning the renewal of a trade mark. Member States have a free hand to legislate in this area (Preamble, recital 7).

By virtue of section 42(1) of the 1994 Act, a United Kingdom trade mark registration lasts initially for a period of 10 years from the date of registration. The date of registration for this purpose is the date of filing of the application for registration (section 40(3)). The registration may be renewed at the end of the initial 10 year period and thereafter every 10 years (section 42(2)).

Under the Trade Marks Act 1938, as amended, the respective periods were seven and 14 years. The change brings the United Kingdom into line with the Community trade mark, most other national systems and the Protocol to the Madrid Agreement.

The mechanics of renewal are governed by section 43 of the 1994 Act. A renewal fee is payable (section 43(1)) and provision is to be made by rules for the Registrar to send a renewal notice to the proprietor before the expiry of the registration (section 43(2)).

If desired, renewal is effected by making a request for renewal and paying the renewal fee before the date on which the registration expires (section 43(3)). Provided these formalities are complied with, the right to renewal is absolute; it cannot be refused. The Government rejected in the White Paper the suggestion that a proprietor should be required to furnish proof of use in order to renew a registration (paragraph 4.31).

A grace period of not less than six months is allowed for late renewals, but only on payment of an additional fee (section 43(3)). This mirrors the system for renewal of patents under the Patents Act 1977, as amended (section 25(4); and see also Registered Designs Act 1949, as amended, section 8(4)).

Renewal takes effect from the expiry of the previous registration (section 43(4)) but if the request for renewal and appropriate fees are not received by the end of the grace period, the Registrar is under an obligation to remove the trade mark from the Register (section 43(5)). Under the Trade Marks Act 1938, as amended, the Registrar's power of removal for non-renewal in the prescribed manner was discretionary.

Section 6(3) of the 1994 Act provides that a trade mark whose registration expires shall continue to be taken into account for the purpose of determining the registrability of later marks during the 12 months following expiry, unless the Registrar is satisfied that there has been no bona fide use of the mark in the two years immediately preceding expiry. Section 6(3) will in the future cover not only expired national registrations but also expired international trade marks (UK) and Community trade marks. It is designed to protect the public against confusing or deceptive registrations and replaces section 20(4) of the Trade Marks Act 1938, as amended, which was, of course, limited to national registrations.

Restoration to the Register of a registration which has been removed for non-payment of renewal fees may be provided for by rules made under the 1994 Act, subject to such conditions (if any) as may be prescribed (section 43(5)). A restoration fee is likely to be charged in addition to the unpaid renewal fee.

The Trade Marks and Service Marks Rules 1986 stated that the Registrar had power to restore and renew a registration 'if satisfied that it [was] just to do so'. Lapsed patents are, on application by the proprietor, restored by order, provided the Comptroller is satisfied that the proprietor of the patent took reasonable care to ensure timely payment of any renewal and late payment fees (section 28(3)(a) Patents Act 1977, as amended; there is a similar restoration procedure for lapsed designs, see section 8A, Registered Designs Act 1949, as amended).

Whichever wording is chosen for the new Trade Marks Rules, it is thought that the case law on the restoration of lapsed patents will apply by analogy. Thus in *Ling's Patent* [1981] RPC 85, it was held that the proprietor of a patent is entitled to rely upon a renewal notice being sent to him by the Patent Office (section 25(5) Patents Act 1977). If it is not, and the patent expires, the failure to send the notice will be a ground for restoration of the patent. In *Textron Inc.'s Patent* [1989] RPC 441 a renewal notice was sent but ignored due to an oversight on the part of the proprietor's employee who had been given clear instructions on action to be taken over the overdue reminder; restoration was granted. (It should be noted that until section 28(3) Patents Act 1977 was amended by the Copyright, Designs and Patents Act 1988, a proprietor seeking restoration of a lapsed patent had also to show that non-payment of fees was due to 'circumstances beyond his control'.) Restoration was refused in the more recent case of *Electricité de France (EDF)'s Patents* [1992] RPC 205 where agents acting on behalf of the proprietor followed the incorrect procedure and consequently failed to file an application to restore within the prescribed period.

There was no time limit on the Registrar's power to restore a trade mark to the Register under the 1938 Act, as amended. Similarly there is no reference to a prescribed period in section 43(5) of the 1994 Act (contrast section 28 Patents Act 1977 and section 8A of the Registered Designs Act 1949, as amended), although one might be set by the rules.

Furthermore, the 1994 Act fails to deal with the *effect* of the restoration to the Register of a trade mark which has been removed for non-renewal; or, for that matter, the effect of renewal during the grace period of not less than six months (the 1938 Act, as amended, was also silent on these matters).

Section 9 of the 1994 Act confers exclusive rights on the proprietor of a *registered* trade mark. Therefore it is not safe to infringe a registration during the grace period (similarly, the anti-counterfeiting provisions of section 92 apparently continue to apply). This would accord with the position in relation to late renewal of patents and registered designs (but see section 62(2) Patents Act 1977). However, there is a saving in section 28A of the Patents Act 1977, as amended, for infringements begun after lapse and before restoration of a patent (see also section 8B of the Registered Designs Act 1949, as amended). Is the same true in the case of unauthorised use of a trade mark in the period between removal for non-renewal and restoration? A reading of section 9 and section 14 (action for infringement) of the 1994 Act suggests that the answer is in the affirmative. The authors know of no case on this point under previous Trade Marks Acts. Of course, failure to renew a trade mark registration is not as fatal as failure to renew a patent. The goodwill that has presumably been built up by the proprietor for its goods or services will protect the unregistered mark.

Renewals and restorations must be published in the manner prescribed by rules made under the 1994 Act (section 43(6)). Under the old regime, renewals and restorations were published in the *Trade Marks Journal* and this will continue to be the case for national registrations. Renewals and restorations of international registrations are published by WIPO in its bulletin, *Les Marques Internationales*. In the White Paper, the Government stated its intention to advertise international applications for registration (UK) in the *Trade Marks Journal* despite concurrent advertisement of such applications in *Les Marques Internationales* (paragraph 5.10). It is foreseeable that this practice will also be followed in the case of renewals and restorations. There is currently some controversy over whether WIPO should continue to publish a reproduction of the mark on renewal under the new regulations for the Madrid Agreement and the Madrid Protocol.

Transitional Provisions (Schedule 3)

The 10-year initial registration period laid down by section 42(1) of the 1994 Act applies only to trade marks which are registered pursuant to applications made after commencement (schedule 3, paragraph 15(1)). This includes trade marks which are registered pursuant to applications pending at commencement and converted into applications under the 1994 Act in accordance with paragraph 11 of schedule 3.

In any other case (including trade marks registered pursuant to applications pending at commencement but not converted as above) the old law applies, that is, the registration initially lasts for seven years from the date of the application to register (sections 20(1) and 19(1), Trade Marks Act 1938, as amended).

Where the renewal of *any* registration falls due on or after commencement sections 42(2) and 43 of the 1994 Act apply (schedule 3, paragraph 15(2)): the registration may be renewed for further periods of 10 years in accordance with the mechanisms set out in section 43 and detailed above.

In all other cases, that is, where renewal falls due before commencement, the old law applies (schedule 3, paragraph 15(2)). Renewal is governed by section 20 of the Trade Marks Act 1938, as amended, and rules 64 to 70 of the Trade Marks and Service Marks Rules 1986.

To summarise the position under the old law:

(a)   the Registrar is required to send notice of renewal to the proprietor between three months and one month before the renewal date (section 20(3); rule 64).

(b)   If renewal is required, the prescribed form must be completed by the proprietor and returned with the appropriate fee (rule 65).

(c)   Provided these formalities are complied with, the Registrar must renew the registration for a further period of 14 years from the expiration of the last registration (section 20(2)).

(d)   If no renewal fee is received, the trade mark is advertised as expired in the *Trade Marks Journal.* However, the registration can still be renewed within one-month of such advertisement on payment of an additional fee (rule 67).

(e)   If the renewal and late payment fees are not received by the end of this one-month period, the Registrar *may* remove the mark from the Register as of the expiration of the last registration (section 20(3); rule 68).

(f)   The Registrar has a discretionary power to restore to the Register a mark which has been removed for non-renewal. An application to restore is made on the prescribed form and must be accompanied by the renewal fee and a restoration fee (section 20(3); rule 68).

(g)   Renewals and restorations are advertised in the *Trade Marks Journal* (rule 70).

(h)   Section 20(4) provides that where a mark is removed from the Register for non-renewal, the mark shall be treated as a mark 'already on the Register' for the purpose of applications to register marks during the 12 months following removal.

The above transitional provisions apply regardless of when the fee is paid (schedule 3, paragraph 15(3)).

Loss of Registration (Sections 46, 47 and 60)

General
The continuance of trade marks on the Register has been a feature of United Kingdom trade marks law since the first Trade Marks Registration Act of 1875. Payment of a fee as the sole pre-requisite was first introduced by the Patents, Designs and Trade Marks Act 1883. Rights in a registered trade mark are, unlike other intellectual property rights, capable of indefinite duration. The classic example is Registered Trade Mark No. 1 (registered under the Trade Marks Registration Act 1875) which is still on the Register and was filed in the name of Bass & Co. for its red triangle label for beer.

The automatic right to renewal combines with several other factors to make the loss of registration sections of critical importance under the new law. These other factors include:

(a)   the likely increase in registrations having effect in the United Kingdom due to the relaxed test of registrability, ratification of the Madrid Protocol and the advent of Community trade marks;
(b)   the possible relinquishment of the substantive examination procedure;
(c)   the increased scope of the infringement action; and
(d)   the breadth of the anti-counterfeiting provisions.

The Preamble to the Directive states that one of the aims of the approximation exercise is to reduce the total number of trade marks registered and protected in the Community and, consequently, the number of conflicts which arise between them (recital 8). Lord Peston, during the second reading of the Bill in the House of Lords, pointed to the continued economic function of trade marks in the market-place and to the need to ensure in Committee Stage that the loss of registration provisions were tightly drawn.

The 1994 Act draws a distinction between grounds for revocation and grounds for invalidity of the registration of a trade mark, as required by the Directive. The grounds for revocation are set out in section 46 of the Act; the grounds for invalidity in section 47.

Who may apply?

Procedural rules for the bringing of revocation and/or invalidity proceedings are outside the scope of the Directive.

Section 47(4) of the 1994 Act provides that the Registrar may seek a declaration of invalidity in the case of bad faith in the registration of a trade mark. It is unclear whether this provision also covers bad faith in the registration of a registrable transaction, for example, an assignment or licence (see section 104 and section 63(1)). In all other cases an application for revocation or for a declaration of invalidity may be made by *any person* (section 46(4); section 47(3)).

This represents a substantial departure from the previous law. *Locus standi* for applications to rectify under the Trade Marks Act 1938, as amended, was afforded to the Registrar in the case of breach of condition of a registration (section 33), or fraud in the registration, assignment or transmission of a registered trade or service mark (section 32(3)); otherwise, the applicant had to be 'a person aggrieved' at the date of the application for rectification (*The Ritz Hotel Ltd* v *Charles of the Ritz Ltd* [1989] RPC 333).

Although the phrase 'person aggrieved' was widely interpreted by the courts to include any trade competitor whose business interests were adversely affected by the presence of a mark on the Register (*Powell's Trade Mark* (1894) 11 RPC 4), for example, a person charged with infringement or passing off, or a person whose application was opposed by the proprietor of the registration in suit, the abolition of the need to prove *locus standi* is welcomed by most interest groups. It cuts down on the issues capable of being pleaded and hence the cost of trade mark litigation. Fears have, however, been expressed over the increased scope for vexatious applications. The Act imposes no penalty on a person who attacks the registration of a trade mark without reasonable cause (although, of course, a costs liability might be incurred).

Rule 84(1) of the 1986 Rules provided that a person who was able to demonstrate an interest, for example, an equitable assignee, might be permitted to intervene in rectification proceedings. The new rules are expected to contain a similar intervener procedure.

Estoppel and acquiescence

In *JOB Trade Mark* [1993] FSR 118, a licensee was held to be estopped from applying for rectification under section 32 of the Trade Marks Act 1938, as amended, whilst at the same time claiming that its licence to use the challenged mark was extant. Presumably estoppel will continue to have this effect under the new law.

The effect of acquiescence has been statutorily prescribed by section 48 of the 1994 Act:

(1)   Where the proprietor of an earlier trade mark or other earlier right has acquiesced for a continuous period of five years in the use of a registered trade mark in the United Kingdom, being aware of that use, there shall cease to be any entitlement on the basis of that earlier trade mark or other right—
    (a)   to apply for a declaration that the registration of the later trade mark is invalid, or
    (b)   to oppose the use of the later trade mark in relation to the goods or services in relation to which it has been so used,
unless the registration of the later mark was applied for in bad faith.
(2)   Where subsection (1) applies, the proprietor of the later trade mark is not entitled to oppose the use of the earlier trade mark, or as the case may be, the exploitation of the earlier right notwithstanding that the earlier trade mark or right may no longer be invoked against his later trade mark.

Section 48 reflects the compulsory provisions of Article 9(1) and (3) of the Directive and the optional provision of Article 9(2) (by the inclusion of earlier rights). Article 9(1) actually speaks of 'a period of five successive years', but since this phrase has no meaning in the English language, nothing is thought to turn on the substitution of 'continuous' in section 48(1).

'Earlier trade mark' is defined in section 6 of the 1994 Act and means a prior registered trade mark, international trade mark (UK), Community trade mark (or prior application for any of these provided such application matures to registration), or a 'well-known' mark within the meaning of the Paris Convention; 'earlier right' is defined in section 5(4) and is a right protected by the law of passing off, copyright, design right or registered designs (section 104).

Four conditions must be satisfied before section 48(1) applies. There must be:

(a)   acquiescence on the part of the proprietor of the earlier trade mark or earlier right;
(b)   for a continuous period of five years;
(c)   in the use of a registered trade mark in the United Kingdom;
(d)   the proprietor being aware of that use.

The temptation of English lawyers will be to treat this as a combination of the equitable doctrines of acquiescence and laches, the latter being set at five years. Such a temptation should be resisted since the Preamble to the Directive makes clear that what is contemplated is *knowing toleration* of the use of a later mark for a substantial length of time (recital 11).

Contrast the modern approach to acquiescence at common law which was succinctly summarised by Oliver J in *Taylors Fashions Ltd* v *Liverpool Victoria Trustees Co. Ltd* [1982] QB 133 at pp. 151–2:

> Furthermore the more recent cases indicate, in my judgment, that the application of the *Ramsden* v *Dyson* (1866) LR 1 HL 129 principle – whether you call it proprietary estoppel, estoppel by acquiescence or estoppel by encouragement is really immaterial – requires a very much broader approach which is directed rather at ascertaining whether, in particular individual circumstances, it would be unconscionable for a party to be permitted to deny that which, knowingly, or unknowingly, he has allowed or encouraged another to assume to his detriment than to inquiring whether the circumstances can be fitted within the confines of some preconceived formula serving as a universal yardstick for every form of unconscionable behaviour.

A question arises as to where lies the onus of showing that the prior owner has been 'aware' of the use of the subsequent mark. Logic dictates that the onus is upon the person seeking to rely on knowing toleration (the owner of the later registered trade mark) to show that the prior owner was aware of the subsequent use for a continuous period of five years. This may be appropriate but it is an onus that the claimant may find hard to discharge.

Where section 48(1) applies, the prior owner is prevented from relying on its trade mark or other right in order:

(a)   seek a declaration of invalidity of the subsequent mark; or
(b)   bring an action for infringement and/or passing off against the subsequent owner or anyone using the later mark with consent (or in the case of a well-known mark, seek an injunction to restrain use of the later mark under section 56).

But the right to bring an application for revocation based on the earlier trade mark or right is not expressly excluded (this is also the case with Article 9 of the Directive).

The other side of the coin, prescribed by section 48(2), is that the subsequent owner cannot bring an action for infringement and/or passing off against the prior owner or anyone using the earlier mark with consent. But, again, section 48(2) does not exclude an application for revocation where the prior right is a registered mark.

The possibility of revocation in cases of 'acquiescence' will be explored below in connection with misleading use under section 46(1)(d).

Section 48(1) (and in consequence, section 48(2)) does not operate where the registration of the later trade mark was applied for in bad faith. The difficulty in interpreting the phrase 'bad faith', which knows no equivalent in English law, is explored below.

Choice of forum
Applications for revocation or for a declaration of invalidity by 'any person' can be made direct to the court or to the Registrar provided that no proceedings are pending in the court in respect of the registration (sections 46(4) and 47(3)). Where invalidity proceedings are initiated by the Registrar himself application must be made to the court (section 47(4)).

The Registrar has a discretion to refer an application for revocation or for a declaration of invalidity (that is, such an application which has been made to him) to the court at any time under sections 46(4)(b) and 47(3)(b) respectively.

'The court' is the High Court (England and Wales and Northern Ireland) or the Court of Session (Scotland) (section 75).

Appeals against Registry decisions
An appeal against the decision of the Registrar in revocation and invalidity proceedings, including as to the referral of an application to the court, lies to a person appointed by the Lord Chancellor to hear such appeals (section 77 of the 1994 Act; and see chapter 3) or, to the court (section 76).

Registrar's appearance in proceedings involving revocation and invalidity
Section 74 provides that the Registrar is entitled to appear and be heard in proceedings involving an application for revocation or a declaration of invalidity. The court may compel the Registrar's attendance. Unless otherwise directed by the court the Registrar may submit evidence, including as to Patent Office practice in like cases, by written statement. This section represents no material alteration to section 50 of the Trade Marks Act 1938, as amended.

Presumption of validity
Section 72 of the 1994 Act provides as follows:

> In all legal proceedings relating to a registered trade mark (including proceedings for rectification of the register) the registration of a person as proprietor of a trade mark shall be prima facie evidence of the validity of the original registration and of any subsequent assignment or other transmission of it.

This replaces section 46 of the Trade Marks Act 1938, as amended, and is in almost identical terms. The phrase 'including proceedings for rectification of the register' is thought to cover revocation and invalidity proceedings even though the term 'rectification' has a special meaning under the 1994 Act (see below).

Section 100 specifically puts the onus in non-use cases on the proprietor of the contested mark to show what use has been made of the mark. Otherwise the onus is on the applicant to establish a prima facie case for revocation or a declaration of invalidity.

Costs
The normal rule is that costs follow the event (that is, the successful party is entitled to an award of costs) whether the proceedings are before the court or the Registrar.

Provision is made in section 68(1) of the 1994 Act for rules allowing the Registrar to award costs to any party and fix an official scale of costs. In the past such costs have not been intended to compensate the parties for actual expense incurred and this practice is expected to continue. The rules may extend to orders for security for costs. Under the previous rules security for costs could only be ordered by the Registrar against foreign applicants.

Where a certificate of validity of contested registration is given by the court under section 73(1) of the 1994 Act costs can be recovered by the proprietor on an indemnity basis if the validity of the mark is unsuccessfully challenged in subsequent proceedings (section 73(2)). This does not extend to the costs of an appeal in the subsequent proceedings.

Extent and effect of revocation or invalidity

A registered trade mark may be revoked or declared invalid in whole or in part (sections 46(5) and 47(5)). This is in line with Article 13 of the Directive and represents no change over the previous law.

The effect of revocation is that the rights of the proprietor are deemed to have ceased to the extent of the revocation as from the date of the application for revocation, or if the Registrar or court is satisfied that the grounds for revocation existed at an earlier date, that earlier date (section 46(6)). It is not clear whether 'rights' includes rights at common law. The Trade Marks Act 1938, as amended, expressly provided that rights at common law were lost where a mark became generic within the meaning of section 15.

Where the registration of a mark is declared invalid, the registration is deemed never to have been made to the extent of the invalidity (section 47(6)). There is a saving for transactions past and closed.

The effects of revocation and invalidity are not the subject of a compulsory or optional provision in the Directive.

Procedure on applications to the Registrar

Application to the Registrar for revocation of a registered trade mark, or for a declaration of invalidity, or to intervene in such an application, should be made on the prescribed form.

Grounds for Revocation (Section 46)

Section 46(1) of the 1994 Act provides four grounds for the revocation of the registration of a trade mark:

(a)   that within the period of five years following the date of completion of the registration procedure it [presumably the trade mark, although the governing noun in section 46(1) is 'registration'] has not been put to genuine use in the United Kingdom, by the proprietor or with his consent, in relation to the goods or services for which it is registered, and there are no proper reasons for non-use;

(b)   that such use has been suspended for an uninterrupted period of five years, and there are no proper reasons for non-use;

(c)   that, in consequence of acts or inactivity of the proprietor, it has become the common name in the trade for a product or service for which it is registered;

(d)   that in consequence of the use made of it by the proprietor or with his consent in relation to the goods or services for which it is registered, it is liable to mislead the public, particularly as to the nature, quality or geographical origin of those goods or services.

Section 46(1) is intended to reflect the compulsory provisions of Articles 10(1), 10(3), 12(1) and 12(2) of the Directive. It is noted, however, that section 46(1) is couched in discretionary terms: 'The registration of a trade mark *may* be revoked' where, for example, grounds of non-use are made out, whereas Article 12 of the Directive is mandatory: 'A trade mark *shall* be liable to revocation if . . .' The court's or Registrar's powers of removal under the 1938 Act, as amended, were discretionary.

Non-use

Section 46(1) of the 1994 Act sets out two cases in which the registration of a trade mark may be revoked on the grounds of non-use:

(a)   where the mark has not been put to genuine use in relation to the registered goods or services within the five-year period following the date of actual registration (section 46(1)(a)); and
(b)   where, after the date of registration, genuine use of the mark in relation to the registered goods or services is suspended for an uninterrupted period of five years (section 46(1)(b)).

Those familiar with the prior law will immediately spot that there is no equivalent to section 26(1)(a) of the Trade Marks Act 1938, as amended. A younger than five-year-old registration cannot be attacked under section 46(1) of the 1994 Act on the ground that the applicant for registration never had bona fide intention to use the mark, and in fact did not so use it, in relation to the registered goods or services since the date of registration.

The White Paper stated that such a registration would be treated as one applied for in bad faith and hence liable to be declared invalid under Article 3(2)(d) of the Directive (the equivalent to section 47(1) of the 1994 Act) (paragraph 4.27). Nevertheless, it is difficult to see how the terms 'bad faith' and 'without bona fide intention to use' can be equated even in a case like *Imperial Group Ltd v Philip Morris & Co. Ltd* [1982] FSR 72 where the mark NERIT was registered solely to protect the unregistrable mark MERIT in case the proprietors wished in future to market a cigarette under the latter brand.

The key to the solution of the bad faith/no bona fide intention to use conundrum lies perhaps in the following sequence of events:

(a)   The original version of the Directive provided as an absolute ground for refusal/invalidity, disregard of national provisions concerning persons eligible to apply for/hold the registration of a trade mark.
(b)   There is no such absolute ground for refusal/invalidity in the compulsory provisions of Article 3(1) of the adopted Directive. However, the optional provisions of Article 3(2) permit Member States to legislate for the additional ground for refusal/invalidity that the registration of the trade mark is applied for in bad faith.
(c)   Such provision is included at sections 3(6) (refusal) and 47(1) (invalidity) of the 1994 Act. In addition, section 32(3) of the 1994 Act provides that an

application for registration of a trade mark must contain a statement of use or *bona fide intention to use* by the proprietor or with its consent in relation to the goods or services for which registration is sought.

(d)   It follows that applying for registration of a trade mark without bona fide intention to use in relation to the registered goods or services is tantamount to applying for registration of a trade mark in bad faith. This catches the proprietor in the *Imperial* case as well as the 'trafficker', that is, the opportunist who applies for registration of a trade mark with a view only to resale at a profit.

It was never an easy job in practice to remove a mark from the Register under section 26(1)(a) of the Trade Marks Act 1938, as amended. The onus of proof was on the applicant for removal and in *ROUND TABLE Trade Mark* (1990) SRIS 0/23/90, a mere assertion that the owner of the mark had bona fide intention to use was sufficient to defeat the application for revocation.

At least the position appears not to have been worsened by the 1994 Act. It can be extremely frustrating for an applicant for registration to find its way blocked by an existing unused registration which is not yet five years old. Indeed, the situation may have been improved if section 100 of the 1994 Act operates to reverse the burden of proof in such cases.

Section 100 is expressed to apply in proceedings involving a question of 'the use to which a registered trade mark has been put'. It remains to be seen whether section 100 will cover cases of no bona fide intention to use.

The five-year periods of non-use referred to in section 46(1) run from the date on which a mark is entered on the Register, not the earlier date of filing the application for registration. This represents no change over the previous law (see section 26(1)(b) of the Trade Marks Act 1938, as amended, as interpreted in *BON MATIN Trade Mark* [1989] RPC 537). The date of actual registration of a trade mark is stated on the certificate of registration.

Commencement or resumption of use after the expiry of the five-year period specified by section 46(1)(a) or (b) but within the three-month period immediately preceding the making of the application for revocation is disregarded unless preparations for the commencement or resumption began before the proprietor became aware that an application for rectification might be made (proviso to section 46(3)).

This three-month period of disregard is intended to facilitate negotiations between the parties by removing the risk that revocation proceedings will be frustrated by the proprietor immediately putting its mark to use. The period of disregard allowed under the 1938 Act, as amended, was one month.

The proprietor must show *genuine* use of the contested mark. Under section 26 of the 1938 Act, as amended, use had to be bona fide. 'Bona fide use' was interpreted by the courts to mean substantial and genuine use judged by ordinary commercial standards (*Imperial Group Ltd* v *Philip Morris & Co. Ltd* [1982] FSR 72; *CONCORD Trade Mark* [1987] FSR 209). Provided the use was of a genuine commercial nature, the user's motive was irrelevant (*Electrolux Ltd* v *Electrix Ltd* (1954) 71 RPC 23). The Government concluded in the White Paper that the change to the use of the word 'genuine' in the new law would be purely semantic (paragraph 4.29).

This may be a correct assumption. In *Levin* v *Staatssecretaris van Justitie* (Case 53/81) [1982] ECR 1035 the Court of Justice of the European Communities was asked to explain the notion of 'worker' in the context of Article 48 of the EC Treaty dealing with the freedom of movement of workers within the Community. The Court stated that the rules relating to the freedom of movement of workers covered 'only the pursuit of *effective and genuine* activities, *to the exclusion of activities on such a small scale as to be regarded as purely marginal and ancillary*' and 'guarantee only the free movement of persons who *pursue or are desirous of pursuing an economic activity*' (emphasis added).

Thus, a fake and relatively insubstantial launch of an existing product under the contested mark is unlikely to defeat an application for revocation for non-use (*Imperial*; *CONCORD* – cigarettes), whereas authentic commercial use for a new product or model will (*Electrolux* – cheaper model of vacuum cleaner), notwith-standing the fact that in both cases the reason for putting the mark into use was to prevent its use by a competitor.

'Use' for the purposes of section 26 of the 1938 Act, as amended, could be by advertisement (*REVUE Trade Mark* [1979] RPC 27) or by other real and determined preparations for placing goods or services on the market as in *HERMES Trade Mark* [1982] RPC 425, where the proprietor had placed orders with its component suppliers during the five-year period with a view to relaunch of the mark (for watches) which took place only afterwards. It is suggested that this will continue to be the case under the 1994 Act. The effectiveness of a single sale, however well evidenced (*NODOZ Trade Mark* [1962] RPC 1), is much more doubtful.

Section 103(2) of the 1994 Act defines 'use of a trade mark' to include 'use . . . otherwise than by means of a graphic representation' (section 1(1) requires a mark to be capable of graphic representation). Thus, playing a tune on a musical instrument would constitute use of a sound mark, assuming sounds are registrable as trade marks (see chapter 4). Verbal use of a word mark, for example, over the radio, would also count as use for the purposes of section 46(1)(a) and (b). Under section 26 of the 1938 Act, as amended, qualifying use had to be visual or printed because of the definition in section 68(2).

Section 46(2) of the 1994 Act follows Article 10(2) in providing that use for the purposes of section 46(1)(a) and (b) includes:

(a)   use in a form differing in elements which do not alter the distinctive character of the mark in the form in which it was registered; and

(b)   affixing the mark to goods or the packaging of goods in the United Kingdom solely for export purposes.

Section 30(1) of the 1938 Act, as amended, provided as a defence to an allegation of non-user, 'use . . . of the trade mark with additions or alterations not substantially affecting its identity'. In *HUGGARS Trade Mark* [1979] FSR 310 the Registrar refused to accept under section 30(1) the proprietor's extensive use of the unregistrable mark HUGGERS: HUGGARS was meaningless, whereas HUG-GERS was descriptive of the goods in question, namely clothing. By way of contrast, in *PELICAN Trade Mark* [1978] RPC 424, substitution of the letter 'K' for 'C' in the trade mark was held not to be an alteration affecting its identity. The case law on section 30(1) of the 1938 Act, as amended, may be indicative of the operation of section 46(2) of the 1994 Act despite the change in wording (and see also *Seaforth Maritime's Trade Mark* [1993] RPC 72 for permissible alterations to device marks under the 1938 Act, as amended).

The marking of goods in the United Kingdom for export purposes was formerly provided for in section 31 of the 1938 Act and was extended to service marks by the Trade Marks (Amendment) Act 1984: the use of a service mark as or as part of any statement about the availability or performance of services to be provided outside the United Kingdom constituted use. Section 46(2) of the 1994 Act does not mention use of a service mark for export trade (the same is true of Article 10(2)(b) of the Directive) and the conclusion must be that such use will not defeat an application for revocation under section 46(1)(a) or (b) of the 1994 Act.

The 1938 Act, as amended, also provided as defences to allegations of non-user: (a) use of an associated mark (section 30(1)); and (b) use of the mark on goods or services of the same description, or on related or associated services or goods, covered by some registration of the mark, except in cases of honest concurrent use (proviso to section 26(1)). Neither of these defences is available under the new law.

Non-user will, however, be excused under the 1994 Act if there are 'proper reasons for non-use' (section 46(1)(a) and (b)). No guidance is given in the Directive or in the 1994 Act as to what might constitute 'proper reasons' for non-use.

Section 26(3) of the 1938 Act, as amended, provided a defence where non-user was due to special circumstances in the trade. 'Special circumstances' had to affect the trade as a whole and not be particular to the business of the registered proprietor. Governmental import restrictions and the like provided the best example of qualifying reasons. Thus, in *Manus Akt.* v *R. J. Fullwood & Bland Ltd* (1948) 65 RPC 329, Swedish proprietors admitted five years' non-use of their British mark MANUS registered for milking machines but could point to a United Kingdom prohibition on imports, a Swedish prohibition on exports and a United Kingdom prohibition on the export of currency all of which were still in force at the time of the action.

During the Committee Stage of the Bill in the House of Lords an amendment was moved to include in the new legislation a definition of 'proper reasons for non-use' as: 'reasons determined by the Registrar or the court to be outside the reasonable control of the proprietor' (*Hansard* (HL/PBC), 19 January 1994, col. 84). The Government rejected the amendment on the grounds that:

(a)   the amendment appeared to extend the previously understood meaning of acceptable reasons for non-use of a trade mark, in that it could cover a proprietor's particular business difficulties; and

(b)   it was for the courts to interpret the expression 'proper reasons for non-use' in the Directive (*Hansard* (HL/PBC), 19 January 1994, col. 84).

This exchange of dialogue suggests that the 'proper reasons' defence to an allegation of non-user under the 1994 Act might be construed restrictively.

Under the 1938 Act a mark had to be used as a trade mark within the definition in section 68(1), that is, as an indication of origin of the subject goods. In *KODIAK Trade Mark* [1990] FSR 49, the applicants sought removal from the Register of the mark KODAK in relation to articles of clothing. Kodak Ltd relied on use of the mark on T-shirts supplied to retailers as part of a campaign to promote their photographic products. It was held that this was not use of the mark in a trade mark sense; the mark was used to advertise films and other photographic supplies and not to indicate the source of the T-shirts.

The 'KODIAK' problem was less likely to arise in connection with service marks because of the slightly different definition of 'service mark' in section 68(1) of the 1938 Act, as amended: the mark had to be used to indicate that a particular person was connected, in the course of business, with the provision of those services.

It is entirely unclear whether *KODIAK* will remain good law under the 1994 Act and depends on how far the courts are willing to recognise the wider functions of trade marks as being not only indications of source and quality but also means of promotion and advertising, 'carriers' of business goodwill.

The English courts have traditionally given precedence to the source theory of trade marks and might find comfort in the Preamble to the Directive which restates the main function of trade marks as guarantees of origin (recital 10). On the other hand the infringement criteria of the Directive (fully adopted by the United Kingdom) appear implicitly to accept that trade marks play a wider role in the modern market-place and that trade marks are worthy of protection in their own right (see chapter 9). Such implicit acceptance is also reflected in the definition of a trade mark: the trade mark serves to distinguish the product rather than distinguish the origin of the product (Article 2; and see section 1(1) of the Act) and is reinforced by the present Act which declares that a registered mark is a property right in personalty (sections 2(1) and 22) and can be dealt with in the same way as any other personal or movable property (section 24(1)).

The debate about the functions of trade marks is, of course, central to the application of the 1994 Act. It affects not only issues of maintenance and loss of registration, but also registrability, ownership, dealing and infringement.

The final version of the Directive was heavily influenced by the Benelux model which had long recognised the promotional and advertising value of trade marks. Other Member States, notably Germany, view the EC approximation exercise and the Community trade mark as heralding a new era of trade mark practice: an era in which the concept that the sole function of a trade mark is to identify the source of goods must be abandoned and the value of a trade mark as an independent industrial property right capable of being utilised in various ways recognised.

Only time will tell whether this will be the view of the United Kingdom courts and ultimately the Court of Justice of the European Communities. It may be indicative that during the passage of the Bill through Parliament, the Government steadfastly resisted attempts to introduce into the definition of a trade mark and the definition of infringement a requirement that a trade mark be used, or intended to be used, to indicate a connection in the course of trade.

One major change introduced by section 46(1)(a) and (b) of the 1994 Act (following Article 10(3) of the Directive) is that use of the trade mark with the proprietor's *consent* counts as use by the proprietor. Permitted use by a registered user was sufficient to defeat rectification proceedings under section 26 of the 1938 Act, as amended, provided such use was in accordance with the registered user agreement (section 28(2)). But the status of use by an unregistered licensee was less certain (*BOSTITCH Trade Mark* [1963] RPC 183). Controlled use of a 'house mark' by an associated company within a group of companies saved the mark in suit from expunction from the Register in *RADIATION Trade Mark* (1930) 47 RPC 37.

The points to note about consent for the purposes of section 46(1)(a) and (b) of the 1994 Act are:

(a) 'Consent' is not defined. Does consent have to be at the level of licence to use?

(b) The rights and remedies in relation to infringement set out in sections 30 and 31 of the 1994 Act are conferred only upon *licensees* who register their transactions (section 25(3)(b)).

(c) The 1994 Act (following the Directive) uses the word 'consent' (without definition) in several important sections including section 5(5) (relative grounds for refusal) and section 46(1)(d) (misleading use). The interrelation between these sections can be surmised but is not clearly spelt out. Query, for example, whether the type of use which may be the subject of consent under section 5(5) will also benefit the proprietor under section 46(1)(a) or (b).

(d) Notwithstanding the apparent lack of statutory regulation, proprietors are strongly advised to take adequate steps to ensure that use of their marks is controlled. Control should go both to the range *and* the quality of the 'licensed' goods or services *and* be effective rather than illusory. Uncontrolled user may not qualify as use with consent for the purposes of section 46(1)(a) and (b) (*JOB Trade Mark* [1993] FSR 118). In any event, the mark may be rendered generic or misleading and liable to revocation under section 46(1)(c) or (d).

Section 46(1)(a) and (b) refer to use 'by the proprietor or with his consent'. Section 25(1) requires, *inter alia*, assignments to be entered on the Register. Is the meaning of 'proprietor' in section 46(1)(a) and (b) restricted to the registered proprietor, or does it include an unregistered assignee? If not, what is the status of use by an unregistered assignee? Does it count as use with the 'proprietor's' consent?

A similar problem existed in connection with the prior law and it was confirmed in *TROOPER Trade Mark* [1994] RPC 26 that the Registrar or the court could take into account use by an unregistered assignee in determining rectification proceedings under section 26. The unregistered assignee should avail itself of the intervener procedure.

A problem can also be foreseen in connection with the provisions concerning co-ownership of a registered trade mark in section 23 of the 1994 Act, more fully discussed in chapter 11. 'Co-proprietors' are to hold as tenants in common in the absence of contrary agreement, which could theoretically lead to substantial fragmentation of ownership. Each co-proprietor is allowed to use the mark, either personally or through an agent, without seeking the consent of the other co-proprietor(s). It is nowhere stated in the 1994 Act whether use by one co-proprietor only will suffice to defeat an action for non-use.

The comment has been made that user inquiries necessitated by the 1994 Act reach unrealistic proportions because of the possibility of the requirement for 'genuine use' being fulfilled by a number of different unrecorded users. Such comment ignores the reversal of the burden of proof in non-user cases effected by section 100 of the 1994 Act:

> If in any civil proceedings under this Act a question arises as to the use to which a registered trade mark has been put, it is for the proprietor to show what use has been made of it.

Under the 1938 Act, as amended, it was for the applicant for revocation to show that a trade mark was not being used. As noted by the Government in the White

Paper, it is difficult and time-consuming to prove a negative, whereas if a trade mark is in fact being used it is relatively easy for the proprietor to demonstrate this (paragraph 4.30).

As was the case with section 26 of the 1938 Act, as amended, where there has been genuine use during the past five years for some only of the goods or services covered by a registration, application can be made under section 46 of the 1994 Act to limit the registration to exclude those goods or services on which the mark has not been used (for an example under section 26 of the 1938 Act see *Unilever plc* v *Johnson Wax Ltd* [1989] FSR 145). The applicant should specify the goods or services in respect of which non-user is alleged in order to enable the proprietor to adduce the appropriate evidence of use in support of its registration. If the application is put forward for the entire specification of goods or services but non-user is established only for some of the goods or services within that specification, the application for revocation may be prejudiced (*KODIAK Trade Mark* [1990] FSR 49).

Finally, it is noted that the 1994 Act contains no equivalent of Article 11 of the Directive prescribing sanctions for non-use of a trade mark in legal or administrative proceedings. In particular Article 11(1) (which appears to be compulsory) states that a trade mark cannot be declared invalid on the ground that there is an earlier conflicting mark if the latter does not fulfil the use requirements set out in Article 10. The problem is exacerbated by the fact that the United Kingdom chose not to enact Article 10 as a separate section but instead included its provisions in the grounds for revocation in section 46 (and in the case of Article 10(4), the transitional provisions in schedule 3). In other words the 1994 Act puts the onus on the subsequent mark owner to defend an application for a declaration of invalidity based on an earlier conflicting mark, by counterclaiming for revocation of the earlier mark on grounds of non-use. Arguably the 1994 Act fails to implement the provisions of the Directive in this respect.

Generic use
Section 46(1)(c) of the 1994 Act replaces section 15 of the 1938 Act, as amended, in dealing with the problem of a mark which, after registration, becomes the generic name of a product or service. In doing so it implements Article 12(2)(a) of the Directive.

In the United States of America rights in a mark can be lost through members of the public using the mark in a generic sense. This is not the case with section 46(1)(c) of the 1994 Act (nor was it the case with section 15 of the 1938 Act, as amended). A trade mark will only fall foul of section 46(1)(c) and be liable to revocation if it becomes the common name *in the trade* for a product or service in respect of which it is registered, as opposed to just a particular brand of that product or service. Famous marks lost in the United Kingdom through generic use by the trade include ASPIRIN and ESCALATOR.

Under section 46(1)(c) of the 1994 Act, generic use by the trade must be *in consequence of acts or inactivity* of the proprietor; section 15 of the 1938 Act, as amended, was not so limited. Furthermore, the 1994 Act increases the powers of a proprietor to prevent genericisation of its mark.

Genericisation can occur, *inter alia*, through unauthorised use of the same or a similar mark in relation to the same, similar or dissimilar goods or services. The old infringement action covered only use of the same or a similar mark in relation to the same goods or services (section 4, Trade Marks Act 1938, as amended); a proprietor had to pursue other miscreants, if possible, in passing off. The new infringement action is capable of embracing all the aforementioned activities (section 10, Trade Marks Act 1994). However, there is one anomaly: the protection conferred by section 10(3) of the 1994 Act upon marks of repute against use on dissimilar goods or services appears to be stronger than the protection conferred upon the same marks by section 10(2) of the 1994 Act against use on similar goods or services (because of the need to show confusion in 10(2) but not, it seems, in 10(3)). Yet the danger of genericisation resulting in either case is ambivalent.

This said, the position of proprietors of marks which tend to genericness is undoubtedly strengthened by the new provisions. Moreover, there existed under the prior law an added danger to proprietors of trade marks (as opposed to service marks). Generic use by the trade in relation to goods of the same description could lead to the mark's expunction from the Register under section 15(2) of the 1938 Act. The rule was particularly pernicious because, as mentioned above, it meant that a mark could be lost through use outside the registration and in ways which the proprietor, on the 1938 Act definition of infringement, could not stop. Thus, in *DAIQUIRI RUM Trade Mark* [1969] RPC 600, the mark DAIQUIRI RUM registered in respect of rum since 1922 was removed from the Register upon proof that 'Daiquiri' was used regularly by the trade to denote a particular type of rum cocktail. In relation to service marks the reference to 'same description' was omitted from section 15(2) thus eliminating for service marks the problem that arose in *DAIQUIRI RUM*. Such reference is also absent from section 46(1)(c) of the 1994 Act so that the 'Daiquiri rum' problem is no more.

The opening words of section 46(1)(c) of the 1994 Act: 'in consequence of acts or inactivity of the proprietor', serve as a useful reminder that genericisation usually occurs because the proprietor itself uses the mark as the ordinary name of the product or service, or permits widespread infringement. It can be avoided if the proprietor controls the ways in which its mark is used. Employees, licensees, franchisees and so on should be made to observe the following rules in all publicity material, other advertising literature, on labels, in business documents and correspondence – even in internal memoranda:

(a) A mark should be emphasised as compared with the surrounding text to show that it is a trade mark and not a descriptive term. Use capital letters for the mark or place inverted commas round it.

(b) A mark is a proper adjective; it should always be used together with the generic name of the product or service. It should never be used as a noun, nor as a verb. Furthermore, a mark should not be hyphenated, used in the possessive form or in the plural.

(c) A prominent indication, for example, by the use of an asterisk, should be given in each piece of printed material that the marks are the registered marks of X Company.

The symbol ® has no legal significance in the United Kingdom. However, use of the symbol does help to generate in the public mind an awareness that the mark is the subject of proprietary rights. The symbol should not be used unless the mark is registered in the United Kingdom or in the country of export (section 95; *Pall*

Corp v *P. J. Dahlhausen & Co* (Case C-238/89) [1990] ECR I-4827). The letters
TM are used to claim rights in an unregistered mark.

If use of the mark is licensed or otherwise authorised there should also be a
notice stating that the mark is used under licence from or with the authority of the
registered proprietor, X Company.

(d)   A company or trade name should be used to identify the overall business
of a company or person. A trade mark is associated with the products or services
of that company or person.

(e)   Any use by any other company or person of the same or a similar mark
and any other misuse of the mark (particularly in trade catalogues, directories,
dictionaries and so on) should be reported to the proprietor immediately and
actioned. It is unfortunate that the 1994 Act, unlike the Community Trade Mark
Regulation (Article 10), fails to give a specific right to control generic use in
dictionaries, encyclopaedias and the like.

Section 15(1)(b) of the 1938 Act, as amended, used to contain a narrowly
worded provision which dealt with the particular case of articles recently protected
by patents for which there was no other 'practicable' name. Such a provision was
inconsistent with Article 12 of the Directive and was not, therefore, carried forward
into the new law.

Where a mark is found to be generic within the meaning of section 46(1)(c) of
the 1994 Act the consequences are:

(a)   the registration of the mark may be revoked wholly or partially (it has
already been noted that Article 12(2)(a) is in mandatory terms); and

(b)   rights in the mark are lost to the extent of the revocation as from the date
of the application or, if the Registrar or court is satisfied that the grounds for
revocation existed at an earlier date, that date.

The consequences of genericisation under section 15 of the 1938 Act, as
amended, were comparable, except that section 15(2)(c)(i) specified that the
proprietor's rights in the mark were lost *both* under statute and common law.
Section 46(6) deals only with the cessation of a proprietor's rights under the 1994
Act. The current position of generic marks under the law of passing off can shortly
be stated thus: a defendant will not be restrained from using a generic (as opposed
to a descriptive) mark (for example, 'Native Guano' in *Native Guano Co.* v *Sewage
Manure Co.* (1891) 8 RPC 125) unless the defendant is using the mark as a false
trade description (*Erven Warnink BV* v *J. Townend & Sons (Hull) Ltd* [1979] AC
731) or the mark has attained a special geographic significance (*Taittinger* v *Allbev
Ltd* [1993] 2 CMLR 741). A detailed account of the law of passing off is outside
the scope of this book, although an outline appears at chapter 2. Reference should
be made to one of the major works in this area, for example, C. Wadlow, *The Law
of Passing-Off* (London: Sweet & Maxwell, 1990).

Misleading Use

Background   Apart from the specific powers of removal for non-use (section 26),
generic use (section 15) and breach of condition (section 33 – not carried forward

into the new law, see below), a general power to rectify entries in the Register was conferred on the court or the Registrar by section 32 of the Trade Marks Act 1938, as amended. A mark could be removed from the Register under section 32 where its registration was initially invalid or had subsequently become invalid. In either case, the registration had to be shown to be contrary to some other provision in the 1938 Act, as amended (*GE Trade Mark* [1973] RPC 297). The grounds most commonly relied upon were that the mark failed to comply with the requirements of sections 9 or 10 (distinctiveness), or that the mark offended sections 11 (deceptiveness) or 12 (conflicting prior registered mark), or that the applicant for registration was not entitled to apply under section 17.

In the case of a Part A mark, section 32 had to be read subject to section 13 of the 1938 Act, as amended, which stated that a Part A mark could not be challenged after it became seven years old except where the original registration was obtained by fraud or the mark offended section 11. This meant that a Part A mark with seven years' maturity could not be challenged, for example, on the ground that it was descriptive and should never have been registered (*Mars (GB) Ltd* v *Cadbury Ltd* [1987] RPC 387).

As for marks which offended section 11 of the 1938 Act, as amended, Lord Diplock explained in *GE Trade Mark* [1973] RPC 297 that two situations were envisaged:

(a)   where a mark was likely to deceive or cause confusion at the time when it was registered (for example, because of resemblance to another mark as in *BALI Trade Mark* [1969] RPC 472); and
(b)   where a mark had become likely to deceive or cause confusion since that date *by reason of some blameworthy act of the proprietor.*

In *GE* itself, two similar marks – GEC and GE – belonging to British and American companies respectively, were validly registered in respect of electrical goods. When imports of the American goods increased, the British company applied for rectification of the Register on the ground that the GE mark had become deceptive within the meaning of section 11 of the 1938 Act. The House of Lords refused to expunge the mark since such likelihood of confusion or deception as existed was through no fault on the part of the American proprietor.

Much of the territory formerly covered by section 32 of the 1938 Act, as amended, now falls within the grounds for invalidity set out in section 47 of the 1994 Act. In addition section 46(1)(d) provides for revocation of the registration of a trade mark where:

in consequence of the use made of it by the proprietor or with his consent in relation to the goods or services for which it is registered, it is liable to mislead the public, particularly as to the nature, quality or geographical origin of those goods or services.

This corresponds with the second situation identified by Lord Diplock in the *GE* case. Section 46(1)(d) contains identical wording to Article 12(2)(b) of the Directive.

Conduct justifying revocation under section 46(1)(d)   The first point to note about section 46(1)(d) is that there is no requirement for culpability. In *GE Trade Mark*, Lord Diplock explained that under the 1938 Act, as amended, expunction of a mark which had become deceptive since registration required blameworthy conduct because of the words: 'disentitled to protection in a court of justice' in section 11 of that Act. These words in turn resulted from the doctrine of honest concurrent use which had its roots in the 'common law' of trade marks, or more specifically in the rule that 'he who comes to equity, must come with clean hands'.

The doctrine of honest concurrent use is retained in section 7(1) of the 1994 Act *in name only* (see chapter 7). It no longer has anything to do with the equitable 'clean hands' doctrine and cannot be used to overcome objection to the registration of a later mark by a prior mark or right owner (this would be contrary to the Directive). Therefore, the *GE* case appears to have been overturned by section 46(1)(d) of the 1994 Act as to the need for blameworthy conduct on the part of the proprietor before a deceptive mark can be removed from the Register.

Secondly, the cancellation of a registered trade mark which has become misleading as to the nature or quality of the subject goods or services is well-embedded in United Kingdom trade marks law (although examples of the former were more frequently encountered at application/opposition stage, for example, *CHINA-THERM Trade Mark* [1980] FSR 21, misleading because it applied to thermally insulated *plastic* tumblers; *SAFEMIX Trade Mark* [1978] RPC 397, misleading because it implied a guarantee that the goods, thermostatically controlled valves, were safe in all circumstances).

In *Pimms' Trade Mark* (1909) 26 RPC 221, cited as an example by Lord Diplock in *GE*, the defendant restaurant proprietors dealt only in the plaintiff's 'Thorne Whisky'. They registered as a trade mark a label bearing the legend: 'Glen Thorne, Old Highland Whisky, Sole Proprietors, Pimms & Co.'. Later they stopped buying 'Thorne Whisky' but continued to supply their customers with other whisky under the 'Glen Thorne' label. The mark had been rendered deceptive by the defendants' own conduct and was ordered to be expunged.

Likewise rectification under the 1938 Act was ordered at the suit of French manufacturers in *K SABATIER Trade Mark* [1993] RPC 97. The manufacturers were the owners of the SABATIER registration in France but a former distributor had registered the mark in the United Kingdom without their knowledge. If the former distributor were to use the mark in connection with knives of another manufacturer this would lead to deception and confusion as to the nature and quality of the goods and such use would be 'disentitled to protection' within the meaning of section 11 of the 1938 Act. (Note that although it was held that SABATIER was the manufacturer's mark, challenge based on section 17 of the 1938 Act (applicant not the proprietor) was barred by section 13.)

In *SABATIER* use by the distributor on another manufacturer's knives would also have led to deception and confusion as to the trade origin of the knives. This sort of deception and confusion does not fall squarely within the remit of section 46(1)(d) of the 1994 Act and is discussed below.

Thirdly, the reference in section 46(1)(d) to use misleading as to geographical origin reflects increased European protection for geographical indications and designations of origin (see Regulation 2081/92 (EEC) on the Protection of Geographical Indications and Designations of Origin for Agricultural Products and Foodstuffs). Under the former Registry procedure, marks which were potentially deceptive as to geographical origin were often dealt with by condition at application stage: 'It is a condition of registration that the mark shall be used in relation only to goods manufactured in . . .' (see, for example, *TONINO Trade Mark* [1973] RPC 568). A mark could be expunged for breach of condition under section 33 of the 1938 Act, as amended. It is not possible to impose conditions under the 1994 Act and it follows that breach of condition is not a ground for revocation. Therefore a mark suggesting, say, casual clothing from America which is later applied to *haute couture* from France will have to be dealt with under section 46(1)(d) of the 1994 Act.

Fourthly, deception as to trade origin is not particularised as relevant public confusion in section 46(1)(d), leading once again to the conclusion that trade origin has been subsumed by the wider functions of trade marks in the 1994 Act.

Although case law on the subject was inconclusive, examples of deceptive use justifying expunction under section 32 of the 1938 Act, as amended, were thought to include licensing without effective quality controls (*BOSTITCH Trade Mark* [1963] RPC 183; *GE Trade Mark* [1970] RPC 339; *JOB Trade Mark* [1993] FSR 118) and 'trafficking', or dealing with a mark as a commodity in its own right (*Re American Greetings Corporation's Application* [1984] RPC 329; *Tradam Trading Company (Bahamas) Ltd's Trade Mark* [1990] FSR 200). These activities were considered to render a mark deceptive because of the resultant lack of connection in the course of trade between a particular origin and the goods or services in question. They might also lead to deception as to the nature or the quality of those goods or services but such deception was not expressed to be the determining factor.

The 1994 Act permits partial assignments of registered trade marks, both as to goods or services included in the registration, as to manner of use and as to locality. There are no statutory controls on the assignment of related marks, over licensing, or other use with consent, or over dealing with marks as security interests. The provisions on co-ownership were described as a 'minefield' by Lord Haskell in Committee Stage (*Hansard* (HL/PBC), 19 January 1994, col. 69). They appear to allow co-owners to use a mark separately without the agreement of the other co-owners. All contain the potential for public confusion, especially as to trade origin – if, a particular origin of goods or services is considered to be a relevant factor to today's purchasing public and one likely to lead to confusion if it is not consistent.

Certainly the White Paper concluded that certain assignments, licensing without quality controls and character merchandising could lead, 'in extreme cases', to revocation of a registered trade mark under section 46(1)(d) of the 1994 Act (paragraph 4.36). Arguably, that section does not purport to give an exhaustive definition of relevant public confusion and it will be interesting to see what importance (if any) the English courts attach to trade origin. Ultimately, of course, definitive interpretation must come from the Court of Justice of the European Communities.

In the meantime, it is clear that the 1994 Act puts the onus on the proprietor of a mark not to engage in dealings which endanger its registered trade mark. Indulging in unlimited, unrestricted and uncontrolled dealings will almost certainly have this effect, at least in terms of quality. The subject of assignment and licensing of marks is more thoroughly addressed in chapter 11.

Fifthly, the word 'public' in section 46(1)(d) is not defined in the 1994 Act. Assistance can perhaps be drawn from the New Zealand case of *Pioneer Hi-Bred Corn Co.* v *Hy-Line Chicks (Pty) Ltd* [1979] RPC 410. In that case, deception was said to result in a mark being 'disentitled to protection' within the meaning of the equivalent to section 11 of the 1938 Act, as amended, if a significant number of persons in the *relevant market* were deceived or confused.

Sixthly, the Australian case of *New South Wales Dairy Corporation* v *Murray Goulburn Co-operative Co.* [1991] RPC 144 provided a further persuasive example of blameworthy conduct which could lead to the expunction of a mark under section 32 of the 1938 Act, as amended: persistent failure to take action against infringers. This does not appear to be covered by section 46(1)(d) of the 1994 Act. Section 46(1)(d) speaks only of 'use' by the proprietor or with its consent rendering a mark misleading, not 'inactivity' by way of contrast with section 46(1)(c).

Seventhly, despite earlier authority for the proposition (*Woodward Ltd* v *Boulton Macro Ltd* (1915) RPC 32 173; *Pan Press Publications Ltd's Applications* (1948) 65 RPC 193), it was confirmed in *GE Trade Mark* [1973] RPC 297 that a mark could not be removed from the Register under section 32 of the 1938 Act, as amended, on the ground that it had ceased to be distinctive, unless it fell within the more limited provisions of section 15. This continues to be the case under section 46(1)(d) of the 1994 Act: a mark which has ceased to be distinctive can be revoked only if it has also become generic within the meaning of section 46(1)(c).

Earlier in this chapter, the question was raised whether an application for revocation could be grounded on an earlier trade mark or other right under the 1994 Act in cases of section 48 'acquiescence'. Were it not for the acquiescence, the normal course of action might be for the prior owner to apply for a declaration of invalidity of the later registered trade mark under section 47(2). The possibility of revocation is not, however, excluded by the wording of section 48. Assume facts similar to the *GE* case but after a period of five years' knowing tolerance on the part of the British proprietors (owners of the prior right) use by the American proprietors in the United Kingdom increases in volume and leads to the public being misled because the American mark is applied to electrical goods of cheaper quality. Confusion is as a result of 'use' by the American proprietor. There is no requirement for 'blameworthy conduct' in section 46(1)(d) (see above) and apparently no reason why a valid claim for revocation of the later mark cannot be made out.

It is thought, however, that the converse is not true: the American proprietor cannot apply for revocation of the earlier British mark (although this possibility is again not expressly excluded by section 48) because the confusion as to quality is not as a consequence of *use* by the British proprietor of its mark but as a consequence of its *inactivity* in failing to take action to prevent use of the later mark. This scenario does not appear to be within the ambit of section 46(1)(d).

Grounds for Invalidity (Sections 47 and 60)

Scheme
The Directive deals with grounds for invalidity alongside the absolute and relative grounds for refusal of registration of a trade mark in Articles 3 and 4. The 1994 Act prefers to handle the two separately (as does the Community Trade Mark

Regulation, Articles 51 and 52). The absolute grounds for refusal of registration are set out in section 3 of the 1994 Act (section 4 details the specially protected emblems referred to in section 3(5)); section 5, the relative grounds for refusal of registration (with 'earlier trade mark' being defined in section 6). Sub-sections (1) and (2) of section 47 then go on to specify the corresponding grounds for invalidity. Section 60 provides an additional ground for invalidity where an agent registers a mark without authority, thus reflecting Article 6*septies* of the Paris Convention.

Absolute grounds for invalidity
Section 47(1) of the 1994 Act provides that:

> The registration of a trade mark may be declared invalid on the ground that the trade mark *was* registered in breach of section 3 or any of the provisions referred to in that section. (Emphasis added.)

Therefore grounds for invalidity lie where a trade mark was registered in breach of any one or more of the absolute grounds for refusal of registration listed in section 3. The absolute grounds for refusal of registration are discussed in chapter 6.

The position under section 47(1) is comparable to the discretionary power of removal given to the Registrar and to the court under section 32 of the 1938 Act, as amended, where a mark was entered on the Register in breach of some other provision in that Act, for example, sections 9 or 10 which set out the distinctiveness requirements for Part A and Part B marks respectively, or section 11 which prohibited the registration of marks deceptive as to the character or geographical origin of the goods or services, contrary to law or morality, or a risk to public safety.

A mark which was registered under the 1938 Act, as amended, pursuant to an application made without bona fide intention to use in relation to the goods or services could be removed from the Register under section 32 because it failed to satisfy: (a) the definition of a trade mark in section 68(1); and/or (b) the application requirements of section 17(1). This was in addition to the specific power of removal contained in section 26(1)(a) of the 1938 Act, as amended (*Imperial Group Ltd* v *Philip Morris & Co. Ltd* [1982] FSR 72; *PALM Trade Mark* [1992] RPC 258).

The definition of a trade mark in section 1(1) of the 1994 Act no longer contains a requirement for use or proposed use but section 32(3) provides that an application for trade mark registration: 'shall state that the trade mark is being used, by the applicant or with his consent, in relation to those goods or services, or that he has a bona fide intention that it should be so used'. As explained earlier in connection with non-use, the Government has taken the view that a mark applied for without bona fide intention to use for the goods or services could be declared invalid under section 47(1) of the 1994 Act as being applied for in bad faith in breach of section 3(6).

Section 68(1) of the Trade Marks Act 1938, as amended, required a trade mark to be used or proposed to be used to *indicate a connection in the course of trade* between the goods and the proprietor (or permitted user). If an alleged trade mark was not intended to function as an indication of origin of the goods, it was not a trade mark for the purposes of the Act and could be expunged from the Register under section 32 (*Aristoc Ltd* v *Rysta Ltd* (1945) 62 RPC 65; *KODIAK Trade Mark* [1990] FSR 49).

The definition of a trade mark in section 1(1) of the 1994 Act does not appear to require a trade mark to be used as an indication of origin but, it is suggested, recognises the wider roles which trade marks may play in the market-place. If, however, such a requirement were to be imported by the courts into the new definition in section 1(1), a mark which did not, or was not intended to function as an indication of origin could be declared invalid as being registered in breach of section 3(1)(a) of the 1994 Act, which prohibits registration of 'signs which do not satisfy the requirements of section 1(1)'. It is respectfully submitted that this would be a retrogressive step. Moreover, the Government rejected at Committee Stage in the House of Lords, a proposed amendment to make clear in section 32(3) of the 1994 Act that use or intended use must be for the purpose of indicating a connection in the course of trade.

Arguably, a service mark has never had to function as an indication of origin. The definition in section 68(1) of the 1938 Act, amended by the Trade Marks (Amendment) Act 1984, required a service mark merely to indicate that: 'a particular person [was] connected, in the course of business, with the provision of those services'.

A further point that is worth express mention in connection with section 47(1) of the 1994 Act is that a ground for invalidity is provided where a proprietor is found to be in breach of Community law (section 3(4)) by registering and using different trade marks for the same products in different Member States of the EEA. The original version of the Directive contained a separate provision to this effect but it was deleted on the advice of the Economic and Social Committee and Parliament as needing no express enactment. The way that this would have been handled under the prior law (assuming appreciation of a Euro-defence) was that the defendant would not have been restrained from applying the United Kingdom mark to the parallel import from another Member State (*Centrafarm BV* v *American Home Products Corporation* (Case 3/78) [1978] ECR 1823).

One major difference between the old and the new law is that there is no provision in the 1994 Act for prescriptive validity (this would be contrary to the Directive). Section 13(1) of the Trade Marks Act 1938, as amended, stated:

> In all legal proceedings relating to a trade mark registered in Part A of the Register (including applications under section 32 of this Act) the original registration in Part A of the Register of the trade mark shall, after the expiration of seven years from the date of that registration, be taken to be valid in all respects, unless—
> (a)   that registration was obtained by fraud, or
> (b)   the trade mark offends against the provisions of section 11 of this Act.

Section 13(1) was stated not to apply where the original registration was obtained by fraud, where the mark offended section 11, or, by section 13(2), to Part B marks. It did not preclude rectification under section 26 (non-use) nor on the ground that the mark was not a trade mark within the meaning of section 68 (definition). But it did protect a Part A mark with seven years' maturity from attack on the ground that the mark should not have been registered because it was descriptive and non-distinctive for the goods or services within the specification (as in *Mars (GB) Ltd* v *Cadbury Ltd* [1987] RPC 387 – TREETS for confectionery).

The Register is, of course, no longer divided into two parts under the new law, but is a single Register with a lower test of registrability: the mark's capacity to distinguish. Nevertheless, the abolition of prescriptive validity is compensated for to a certain extent by section 47(1) of the 1994 Act (reflecting in part optional provision 3(3) of the Directive): evidence of use *after registration* can be taken into account where objection to a mark is taken under section 3(1)(b) – no inherent distinctiveness; section 3(1)(c) – descriptive signs, geographical names, laudatory epithets; or section 3(1)(d) – common trade terms.

The relevant time for determining validity *vis-à-vis* the absolute grounds for refusal of registration in the 1994 Act, is when the mark was 'registered'. Presumably this is the date of the filing of the application for registration (section 40(3)) as there is no reference in section 47(1) to the date of actual entry on to the Register (contrast section 46(1)(a)). This confirms that a mark which was distinctive at the date of registration cannot be declared invalid on the ground that it has subsequently ceased to be distinctive. Instead, an application for revocation must be made (if possible) on the more limited ground of genericisation provided by section 46(1)(c).

Relative grounds for invalidity
Section 47(2) of the 1994 Act states that a trade mark may be declared invalid on the ground:

    (a)   that there is an earlier trade mark in relation to which the conditions set out in section 5(1), (2) or (3) obtain, or
    (b)   that there is an earlier right in relation to which the condition set out in section 5(4) is satisfied,
unless the proprietor of that earlier trade mark or other earlier right has consented to the registration.

The use of the present tense in section 47(2) is problematical. It begs the question: when must the ground for invalidity be shown? At the date of registration of the later mark, or the date of application for a declaration for invalidity? Timing could be important to, *inter alia*, a finding of likelihood of confusion (5(2)), reputation in the United Kingdom (5(3)), or passing off (5(4)).

Section 47(2) speaks of certain scenarios set out in section 5 *obtaining or being satisfied*. Section 5 contains the relative grounds for refusal of registration and applies at the date of registration. The consequence of invalidity is that the registration is deemed never to have been made (section 47(6)). Article 4 of the Directive deals with grounds for refusal and invalidity together taken at the date of registration. Accordingly, the better view is that the relevant date for ascertaining relative validity under the 1994 Act is the date of registration and not the later date of application for a declaration of invalidity.

The relative grounds for refusal of registration under the 1994 Act are the subject of chapter 7. However, to aid better understanding of relative invalidity brief details of the circumstances in which registration of a later mark may be refused because of an earlier trade mark or other right are given in tables 8.1 and 8.2.

Table 8.1 Earlier trade mark (national registrations, international registrations (UK), Community trade marks, well-known marks

Section	Later mark	Goods/Services	Proof
5(1)	Identical	Identical	—
5(2)(a)	Identical	Similar	Likelihood of confusion/ association
5(2)(b)	Similar	Identical	Likelihood of confusion/ association
5(2)(b)	Similar	Similar	Likelihood of confusion/ association
5(3)	Identical	Dissimilar	Reputation + unfair advantage/dilution
5(3)	Similar	Dissimilar	Reputation + unfair advantage/dilution

Table 8.2 Earlier right (unregistered marks, copyright, design right, registered design)

Section	Later mark	Goods/Service	Proof
5(4)	—	—	Entitlement to restrain use by virtue of: passing off or copyright or design right or registered design

The relative grounds for invalidity under the 1994 Act are not available where the prior owner has consented to registration of the later trade mark (section 47(2)).

Furthermore, a prior owner loses the right to challenge the validity of a subsequent mark on the basis of its mark or other right after a period of five years' knowing acquiesence (section 48(1)).

It might be useful to compare the relative grounds for invalidity under the 1994 Act with the position under the prior law. Well known marks are considered separately.

(a) *New.* A mark is liable to be declared invalid if there is a prior registration (national, international (UK), Community trade mark) of an identical mark for identical goods or services (section 47(2)(a) of the 1994 Act). Honest concurrent use at the date of registration cannot provide a defence to invalidity proceedings (section 7(4)(b) of the 1994 Act).

Old. Under the 1938 Act, as amended, the later mark could be removed from the Register under section 32 as offending section 12(1). After seven years the original registration of a Part A mark could be attacked only under section 11 (section 13). A likelihood of confusion or deception would have had to be shown at the date of registration because of the *use* of the prior mark (*BALI Trade Mark*

[1969] RPC 472). Honest concurrent use at the date of registration might have provided a defence to invalidity (*GE Trade Mark* [1973] RPC 297). The earlier mark had to be a national registration and use for the purposes of section 11 had to be in the United Kingdom.

(b) *New*. A mark is liable to be declared invalid if there is a prior registration (national, international (UK), Community trade mark) of an identical mark for similar goods or services, a prior registration of a similar mark for identical goods or services, or a prior registration of a similar mark for similar goods or services. In each case a likelihood of confusion, which includes a likelihood of association, must be shown to have existed at the date of registration (section 47(2)(a) of the 1994 Act). There is no defence of honest concurrent use at the date of registration (section 7(4)(b) of the 1994 Act).

Old. Again, the later mark could be removed from the Register under section 32 of the 1938 Act, as amended, as offending sections 12(1) or 11, subject to section 13 and the defence of honest concurrent use. One further point of difference was that likelihood of confusion was presumed by section 12(1) in the case of an identical mark for goods or services of the same description.

(c) *New*. A mark is liable to be declared invalid if there is a prior registration (national, international (UK), Community trade mark) of an identical or similar mark for dissimilar goods or services, the prior mark has a reputation in the United Kingdom (or, in the case of a Community trade mark, in the Community), 'and the use of the later mark without due cause would take unfair advantage of, or be detrimental to, the distinctive character or the repute' of the prior mark (section 47(2)(a) of the 1994 Act). Again, honest concurrent use at the date of registration cannot provide a defence (section 7(4)(b) of the 1994 Act).

Old. There was no truly comparable ground for invalidity under the 1938 Act, as amended. Objection could be taken to a later mark under section 11 on the ground that it was likely to cause deception or confusion at the date of registration because of the past *use* of an earlier registered mark. There was no restriction under section 11 regarding goods or services but *likelihood of confusion* and *use*, as opposed to *reputation* of the prior mark in this country, were essential requirements (*BALI Trade Mark* [1969] RPC 472, Lord Upjohn correcting the terminology used by Evershed J in *Smith Hayden & Co. Ltd's Application* (1945) 63 RPC 97 when formulating the test under section 11). Honest concurrent use might have provided a defence to invalidity.

Invalidity of a later mark due to actual or potential dilution of an earlier mark is an entirely new concept to United Kingdom trade marks law.

(d) *New*. A registration may be declared invalid if, at the date of registration, a prior-right owner could have restrained use of the later mark in the United Kingdom, in particular, by virtue of the law of passing off, copyright, design right or registered design (section 47(2)(b) of the 1994 Act). Honest concurrent use at the date of registration cannot assist the proprietor of the later mark (section 7(4)(b) of the 1994 Act).

Old. The protection for unregistered marks is narrower than under the previous law. The owner of an unregistered mark could have taken objection to the validity of a later mark under section 11 of the 1938 Act, as amended, and needed only to show likelihood of confusion or deception at the date of registration, *not* fully fledged passing off (*Koyo Seiko Kabushki Kaisha's Application* [1958] RPC 112;

BALI Trade Mark [1969] RPC 472). But honest concurrent use at the date of registration might have provided a defence to invalidity.

Where copyright material formed the subject-matter of a trade mark registration, the mark could be expunged under section 32 of the 1938 Act, as amended, as being 'contrary to law' within the meaning of section 11, provided the copyright owner was entitled to United Kingdom copyright protection (*KARO STEP Trade Mark* [1977] RPC 255; *OSCAR Trade Mark* [1979] RPC 173). *Obiter dicta* of Whitford J in *KARO STEP* suggested that section 17(1) might have provided the copyright owner with a further ground for rectification. Section 17, which set out the procedure for registration of a trade mark, stated in subsection (1) that 'Any person claiming to be the proprietor of a trade mark . . . must apply in writing to the Registrar in the prescribed manner'. However, Whitford J's *obiter dicta* were dissented from by Aldous J in the most recent decision of *Loudoun Manufacturing Co. Ltd* v *Courtaulds plc* (1994) *The Times*, 14 February 1994: section 17 was not concerned with who was a mark's true proprietor; it only required the applicant to have a bona fide claim to be registered.

Now that shape registrations are a possibility, objections to validity based on design right or registered design are to be expected.

Conclusions
The main changes to the relative grounds for invalidity therefore comprise increased protection for national registrations, international registrations (UK) and Community trade marks 'of repute' and reduced protection for unregistered marks. In addition, honest concurrent use has no part to play in invalidity proceedings.

Well-known marks
Another major change is the introduction of protection for well-known marks within the meaning of Article 6*bis* of the Paris Convention. Irrespective of registration or use in the United Kingdom, the owners of such marks are entitled to object to the validity of a later registration which offends section 5(1), (2) or (3) of the 1994 Act.

Protection against registration of an identical or similar mark for dissimilar goods or services (section 5(3)) was extended to well-known marks as a result of a Government amendment to the Bill introduced at Report Stage in the House of Lords. Such protection is not allowed for in Article 4 of the Directive.

Marks registered by an agent or representative
Section 60 of the 1994 Act is a new provision which reflects Article 6*septies* of the Paris Convention. It enables the proprietor of an overseas mark to apply for a declaration of invalidity where its mark is registered in the United Kingdom by an agent or representative without authority. Alternatively the overseas owner can apply for rectification of the Register to substitute its name as the registered proprietor. Any such action must be taken within three years of the overseas owner becoming aware of the registration.

In fact, section 60 represents very little change over the prior law. The overseas owner could have applied under section 32 of the 1938 Act, as amended, to have the mark expunged or the Register rectified on the ground that the agent or representative was not the proprietor of the mark under section 17, or that the mark offended section 11 (*K SABATIER Trade Mark* [1993] RPC 97).

Discretion?

The Registrar or court had a discretion whether or not to order rectification under section 32 of the Trade Marks Act 1938, as amended. Section 47 of the 1994 Act similarly appears to confer discretionary power to declare a registered trade mark invalid. It is arguable that the Directive does not allow for such discretion.

Surrender (Section 45)

Section 45 of the 1994 Act provides that a registered trade mark may be surrendered by the proprietor in respect of some or all of the goods or services for which it is registered.

This takes the place of section 34(1)(c) and (d) of the Trade Marks Act 1938, as amended, which gave the Registrar power to cancel the entry of a trade mark on the Register or to limit the specification of goods or services at the request of the registered proprietor.

It can often be expedient for a proprietor to surrender or limit its registration especially when faced with the notion of revocation or invalidity proceedings.

A proprietor may also wish to surrender or relinquish a United Kingdom registration where it obtains an identical Community trade mark registration. The Community Trade Mark Regulation facilitates this by allowing the Community trade mark to claim 'seniority' from the earlier United Kingdom registration, so that the proprietor does not prejudice any of its rights (Articles 34 and 35). Seniority may, however, subsequently be lost if the surrendered or lapsed registration is declared invalid or revoked pursuant to the '*a posteriori*' procedure for attack set up by section 52(2)(b) of the 1994 Act.

Rectification or Correction of the Register (Section 64)

Section 64 of the 1994 Act provides (emphasis added):

(1) Any person having a sufficient interest may apply for the rectification of an error or omission in the register:

Provided that an application for rectification may not be made in respect of a matter *affecting the validity of the registration of a trade mark.*

(2) An application for rectification may be made either to the Registrar or to the court, except that—

(a) if proceedings concerning the trade mark in question are pending in the court, the application must be made to the court; and

(b) if in any other case the application is made to the registrar, he may at any stage of the proceedings refer the application to the court.

(3) Except where the registrar or the court directs otherwise, the effect of rectification of the register is that the error or omission in question shall be deemed never to have been made.

(4) The registrar may, on request made in the prescribed manner by the proprietor of a registered trade mark, or a licensee, enter any change in his name or address as recorded in the register.

(5) The registrar may remove from the register matter appearing to him to have ceased to have effect.

This section deals with alterations of entries in the Register. Section 44 of the 1994 Act deals with alterations to a registered trade mark itself.

Changes in proprietorship, the registration of licences and security interests, and amendment to, or removal of, registered particulars relating to a licence or security interest are covered by section 25 of the 1994 Act.

Correction of the Register was formerly provided for by section 34 of the 1938 Act, as amended.

Transitional Provisions (Schedule 3)

Applications pending on commencement (that is, made but not finally determined before commencement (schedule 3, paragraph 2(a)):

(a)   under section 33 of the 1938 Act, as amended, for expunction or variation of an existing registration for breach of condition (schedule 3, paragraph 3(1));

(b)   under section 26 of the 1938 Act, as amended, for revocation of an existing registration on grounds of non-use (schedule 3, paragraph 17(1)); or

(c)   under sections 32 or 34 of the 1938 Act, as amended, for rectification or correction of the Register (schedule 3, paragraph 18(1));

are to be dealt with under the old law and any necessary alterations made to the new Register.

In any other case:

(a)   By virtue of schedule 3, paragraph 2(1) to the 1994 Act existing registered marks are deemed, subject to the provisions of schedule 3, to have effect on commencement as if registered under the 1994 Act.

(b)   Schedule 3, paragraph 17(2), states that an application under section 46(1)(a) or (b) of the 1994 Act for revocation of an existing registered mark for non-use may be made at any time *after* commencement.

A specific exception is made in the case of old defensive registrations. No application to revoke a defensive registration for non-use may be made under section 46 until five years have elapsed from commencement. This is because there was no requirement of use or intent to use a defensive registration under the 1938 Act, as amended, and such a mark could not be challenged under section 26. Defensive registrations are not consistent with the Directive but the Government has taken advantage of Article 10(4)(b) of the Directive in order to phase them out over five years.

(c)   Since there is no contrary provision in schedule 3, the rest of section 46 of the 1994 Act, including sub-sections (c) and (d), applies to existing registered marks on commencement. An application for revocation of an existing registered mark on the grounds set out in either of those sub-sections may be made on, or at any time after commencement.

(d)   The new grounds for invalidity set out in section 47 of the 1994 Act apply to existing registered marks on commencement. Importantly, there is no saving for section 13 of the 1938 Act, as amended, in the case of existing marks that were registered in Part A of the Register. An application for a declaration of invalidity of an existing Registered mark under section 47 may be made on, or at any time after, commencement.

For the purposes of such invalidity proceedings, the provisions of the 1994 Act shall be deemed to have been in force at all material times (schedule 3, paragraph 18(2)).

However, no objection to the validity of an existing registered mark may be taken on the basis of section 5(3) (conflict with earlier trade mark registered for dissimilar goods or services) (schedule 3, paragraph 18(2), proviso).

(e)   An application for a declaration of invalidity or rectification of the Register under section 60 of the 1994 Act (mark registered by agent or representative) in relation to an existing registered mark may be made at any time on or after commencement, provided such application is not time-barred by that section.

(f)   The provisions of section 45 of the 1994 Act (surrender) apply to an existing registered mark on commencement.

(g)   An application for rectification or correction of the Register under section 64 of the 1994 Act in relation to an existing registered mark may be made at any time on, or after commencement.

Proceedings for revocation or rectification pending at commencement (to be determined under the old law)
A brief summary of the old law is as follows.

Non-use   Under section 26 of the 1938 Act, as amended, an application for revocation could be made to the court or to the Registrar by 'any person aggrieved', where:

(a)   the applicant for registration never had any bona fide intention to use the mark and did not in fact so use it, in relation to the goods or services, up to one month prior to the application to revoke (1938 Act, section 26(1)(a)); or

(b)   up to one month prior to the application to rectify there had been no bona fide use of the mark for a continuous period of five years in relation to the goods or services (section 26(1)(b)).

The period in section 26(1)(b) ran from the date the mark was actually entered on the Register. 'Use' for the purposes of section 26 had to be substantial and genuine use judged by commercial standards. Furthermore a mark had to be used as a 'trade mark' within the definition in section 68.

Defences to non-use included: use on goods or services of the same description covered by some registration of the mark (except in cases of honest concurrent use); use of an associated mark or a variation of the mark not substantially affecting its identity; and non-user due to 'special circumstances in the trade'. Use by a registered user counted as use by the proprietor (unless uncontrolled) (section 28(2)) but the position of use by an unregistered licensee was unclear.

Generic use   Any person aggrieved could apply to the court or to the Registrar under section 32 of the 1938 Act, as amended, for expunction of a mark which became generic within the meaning of section 15. This would happen where it became the well-known and established practice of the trade to use the mark as the ordinary name of the product or service in question. A trade mark (as opposed to a service mark) could be expunged if generic use by the trade was in relation to goods of the same description.

Deceptive use   A mark which became deceptive subsequent to the date of registration *because of the blameworthy conduct of the proprietor* could be removed from the Register under section 32 of the 1938 Act, as amended, upon application to the court or to the Registrar by any person aggrieved.

Breach of condition   Application could be made by any person aggrieved to the court or to the Registrar, or by the Registrar to the court, under section 33 of the 1938 Act, as amended, for removal or variation of the registration of a mark in cases of breach of condition. Conditions could be imposed under various sections of the 1938 Act, for example, section 17(2) (upon application) and section 28(5) (on registration of a permitted user).

Correction of the Register   A proprietor could apply to the Registrar under section 34 of the 1938 Act, as amended, to correct/cancel entries in the Register. A registered user could also require corrections.

Invalidity   Application could be made by any person aggrieved to the court or to the Registrar under section 32 of the 1938 Act, as amended, to expunge 'any entry made in the Register without sufficient cause'. This would cover a mark which was not a trade or service mark as defined by section 68; a mark which did not contain the essential particulars listed in section 9 or was not 'capable of distinguishing' within the meaning of section 10; a mark which was deceptive at the date of registration either on absolute grounds, for example, deception as to geographical origin, or on relative grounds (conflict with an earlier registered or unregistered mark) (section 11); a mark which conflicted with an existing registered mark under section 12(1); and disputed proprietorship (section 17(1)). Section 13 barred invalidity objections to a Part A mark with seven years' maturity except where (a) the registration was obtained by fraud, or (b) the registration offended section 11.

CHAPTER NINE
Infringement of Registered Trade Marks

Introduction

The statutory action for infringement of a registered trade mark traditionally provides the answer to the lay person's question: why register?

Until the 1994 Act, the advantages of the action for infringement of a registered trade mark over the action for passing off an unregistered mark would have been listed thus:

(a) capacity to protect an unused mark;
(b) avoidance of the need to prove reputation and goodwill in each action (including that the plaintiff is the proper owner of the mark); and
(c) avoidance of the need to show actual (or likely) damage to the plaintiff's business.

The disadvantage lay in the narrow scope of the infringement action.

Most of the advantages of the action for infringement are carried forward into the new law. However, with the broadening in scope of that action, notions of passing off are introduced. Practically this may have little effect, since infringement and passing off have long been pleaded together in trade mark 'infringement' cases. Nevertheless, the changes impact fundamentally on the nature of the infringement action and in turn have already influenced the future development of passing off. In *Taittinger* v *Allbev Ltd* [1993] 2 CMLR 741, the Court of Appeal was prepared to recognise as an actionable head of damage in passing off, actual or likely dilution of the name CHAMPAGNE and a shift in emphasis away from goodwill towards reputation in the United Kingdom is likewise expected (departing from the rule in *Anheuser-Busch Inc.* v *Budejovicky Budvar Narodni Podnik* [1984] FSR 413).

The statutory action for infringement is only available in respect of a registered trade mark. Common law rights to an unregistered mark in passing off are preserved (section 2 of the 1994 Act).

The Directive
It is important to stress that the Directive stakes out the minimum and maximum permissible boundaries of an infringement action, albeit by optional provisions in

the case of the latter. The EC Treaty objectives of free movement of goods and services are facilitated by ensuring that registered trade marks enjoy the same protection under the laws of all the Member States (Preamble, recital 9).

Matters of evidence and the onus of proof in infringement actions are left to national authorities to determine (Preamble, recital 10). In the United Kingdom, the onus is on the plaintiff to show that the defendant has infringed its mark.

Scheme of the infringement provisions in the 1994 Act
Infringement is dealt with by sections 9 to 13 of the 1994 Act. These sections define the nature of the monopoly rights conferred upon a proprietor by registration of a trade mark (section 9); what acts of invasion of those rights by unauthorised parties amount to the tort of infringement (section 10); what acts are saved from being infringements (sections 11 and 12); and the effect of registration of a trade mark subject to disclaimer or limitation (section 13).

This chapter describes the substantive law of infringement under the 1994 Act, that is, sections 9 and 10. Defences to infringement and remedies are discussed at chapter 10.

1994 Act and Directive compared
The Directive sets out the substantive law of infringement in a different way from the 1994 Act: the statement of rights conferred by a trade mark in Article 5 of the Directive *includes* entitlement to prevent specified infringing activities; as compared to the separate declaration of rights and definition of acts amounting to infringement in sections 9 and 10 respectively of the 1994 Act. Thus, Article 5(1) of the Directive begins by stating that:

The registered trade mark shall confer on the proprietor exclusive rights *therein*. The proprietor shall be entitled to prevent . . . . (Emphasis added.);

But section 9 of the 1994 Act says:

(1)   The proprietor of a registered trade mark has exclusive rights in the trade mark which are infringed *by use of the trade mark* in the United Kingdom without his consent.
The acts amounting to infringement, if done without the consent of the proprietor, are specified in section 10.
(2)   References in this Act to the infringement of a registered trade mark are to *any such infringement of the rights of the proprietor*. (Emphasis added.)

There are two possible explanations for the differences in approach:

(a)   Drafting technique. This is the view taken by the Government (*Hansard* (HL/PBC), 18 January 1994, col. 24).
(b)   The exclusive rights conferred by section 9(1) are narrower than those conferred by Article 5(1), in which case the Government has recreated the same problem that existed in connection with section 4(1) of the Trade Marks Act 1938, as amended. The general words of section 9(1) appear to be narrower than the acts of infringement specified in section 10.

Rights Conferred by Registered Trade Mark (Section 9)

Nature of the rights
Before 1938, successive Trade Marks Acts merely gave the proprietor of a mark the 'exclusive right' to use the mark, leaving the precise ambit of that right to be determined by the courts. In *Irving's Yeast-Vite Ltd* v *Horsenail* (1934) 51 RPC 110 the House of Lords held that the exclusive right conferred by section 39 of the 1905 Act had to be construed in the light of the definition of a trade mark contained in section 3 of that Act. Section 3 required a trade mark to be used by the proprietor to indicate a commercial connection with the goods, which led their Lordships to conclude that the infringement action covered only traditional acts of piracy, that is, where the defendant uses the plaintiff's mark to indicate a commercial connection between the defendant and the defendant's goods. The particular defendant in this case had engaged in a primitive form of comparative advertising which the plaintiff proprietors were powerless to prevent.

The Goschen Committee of 1934 (*Report of the Departmental Committee on the Law and Practice Relating to Trade Marks*, Cmd 4568) advocated a much broader definition of infringement which was not limited to protecting a trade mark's indication of origin function and recognised the harm that 'other uses' could do to the 'goodwill in' or 'reputation of' the mark.

However, when the recommendations of the Goschen Committee were transposed into law, the result was 'fuliginous obscurity' (Lord Mackinnon in *Bismag Ltd* v *Amblins (Chemists) Ltd* (1940) 57 RPC 209 at p. 237). Section 4(1) of the 1938 Act appeared to confer an exclusive right in substantially the same terms as its predecessor, section 39 of the 1905 Act, but also described, in paragraph 4(1)(b), infringing activities which were clearly not trade mark piracy. The scope of the former infringement action was thus rendered at best unclear (at worst, no further forward), although the better view was that section 4(1) provided for two types of infringement: (a) piracy (unauthorised use of the plaintiff's mark to indicate the trade origin of the defendant's product); and (b) comparative advertising (*Chanel Ltd* v *Triton Packaging Ltd* [1993] RPC 32).

The point of this brief historical foray is that although exclusive rights in a registered trade mark are now *declared* rather than conferred by section 9(1) of the 1994 Act, the language employed by that declaration is arguably no wider than the general wording of section 4(1) of the 1938 Act and, *ipso facto*, that section's predecessors. This is because of the reference in section 9(1) of the 1994 Act (absent from Article 5(1) of the Directive) to the exclusive rights in a mark being infringed 'by use of the *trade mark*' without the proprietor's consent.

Two separate but linked issues arise, which are fundamental to the scope of the new infringement action and will be discussed in the forthcoming sections:

(a) To what extent are the exclusive rights declared by section 9(1) restricted to protecting a trade mark's function as an indicator of origin?

(b) Can the proprietor of a registered trade mark control the use of non-trade mark matter?

During debates on the Bill in the House of Lords, Lord Peston twice moved an amendment to insert the following words at the end of the first sentence of section 9(1):

In particular, the proprietor has the exclusive right to use the mark on or in relation to the goods or services for which it is registered in the course of business so as to indicate a commercial connection with such goods or services.

The Minister's response on rejection of the amendment at the Report Stage in the House of Lords might be important for *Pepper* v *Hart* [1993] AC 593 purposes:

> As a matter of general trade mark law it is implicit that use of a registered trade mark must be *trade mark use* in order that the rights given by the Bill may be enforced. . . . Therefore, in our view the amendment is unnecessary. (Emphasis added.) (Lord Strathclyde, *Hansard* (HL) 24 February 1994, col. 733.)

At Lord Peston's request, the Minister also confirmed that what was said in the White Paper on this matter still represented the Government's view. The White Paper stated (at paragraph 3.26):

> A broad definition [of what uses of a conflicting mark should constitute infringement] is 'use of the mark, *in the course of trade, in relation to* the goods or services concerned'. (The words emphasised are found both in *Section 4 of the 1938 Act* and [sic] in Article 5 of the Directive.)

At the risk of being pedantic, none of this appears to make sense. If the exclusive rights in section 9(1) of the 1994 Act are to use a mark to indicate trade origin and 'infringement of a registered trade mark' means infringement of those exclusive rights (section 9(2)), there is a mismatch with section 10. Section 10 defines 'infringement of a registered trade mark' to include, as will be seen, unauthorised uses which are not 'trade mark use'. The inevitable conclusion is that Article 5(1) of the Directive has not been correctly implemented in this regard.

When may infringement proceedings be commenced?
Infringement proceedings cannot be commenced before the date on which the trade mark is actually entered on to the Register (section 9(3)(a)). This date appears on the front of the registration certificate.

However, damages for infringement can be recovered from the date of filing the application for registration (section 9(3)). In the case of a mark registered on an application claiming priority under the Paris Convention, the latter means the date on which the application for registration is filed in the United Kingdom.

Under the 1994 Act, jurisdiction to hear infringement proceedings is allocated to the High Court (England, Wales and Northern Ireland) and the Court of Session (Scotland) (section 75).

Territorial limitation
A proprietor can sue only in respect of infringements occurring within the United Kingdom including the Isle of Man (sections 9(1), 107 and 108). This may cause difficulties in connection with exports under section 10(4)(c). In *George Ballantine & Son Ltd* v *Ballantyne Stewart & Co. Ltd* [1959] RPC 273 it was held that although the infringing act must occur in the United Kingdom (in that case use of a label incorporating the plaintiffs' mark) likelihood of confusion (see below) is to

be considered in relation to the public in the country where the goods are to be sold.

Counterclaim for revocation or invalidity of registration

Under section 4 of the 1938 Act, as amended, the exclusive right arising from registration was subject to the limitation that the registration must be valid. No such limitation is contained in section 9(1) of the 1994 Act, although section 72 provides (in similar terms to section 46 of the 1938 Act, as amended) that in all legal proceedings relating to a registered trade mark, the registration of a person as proprietor of a mark shall be prima facie evidence of the validity of the registration.

The grounds for revocation or invalidity of a registered trade mark are set out in sections 46 and 47 of the 1994 Act respectively and are discussed in detail in chapter 8. Although nowhere stated in the 1994 Act, it must be implicit that these grounds can be pleaded by way of counterclaim to an action for infringement. The Community Trade Mark Regulation is more helpful in making this point clear (see Articles 50, 51 and 52, and Article 96).

Title to sue

Section 14(1) states that an infringement of a registered trade mark is actionable by the proprietor of the trade mark.

An exclusive licensee has the right to bring infringement proceedings in its own name, *but only* if, and to the extent that, it is given, by the terms of the licence, the rights and remedies of an assignee, and the licence so permits (section 31(1)). The proprietor must be made a party to the action (section 31(4)) and is subjected to no liability for costs if added as defendant (section 31(5)). The rule applies equally where a proprietor sues in relation to an infringement in respect of which its exclusive licensee has a concurrent right of action, but does not prevent the granting of interlocutory relief to either party alone (section 31(4) and (5)).

In any other case, a licensee (exclusive, with no right of action in relation to the particular infringement, or at all; sole; or non-exclusive) has the right (*subject to the terms of its licence, or the terms of a superior licence*) to call upon the proprietor to take infringement proceedings in respect of any matter which affects the licensee's interests. If the proprietor either (a) refuses to take action, or (b) fails to take action within two months, the licensee may bring the proceedings in its own name, provided the proprietor is joined as plaintiff or added as defendant (again the proprietor cannot be made liable for costs if added as defendant and, again, interlocutory relief may be granted on an application made by the licensee alone) (section 30(1) to (5)).

It is important to note that no licensee has any of the above rights unless an application to register its licence has been made in accordance with section 25 of the Act (section 25(3)(b)).

Acquiescence

By virtue of section 48(1) the proprietor (including a licensee with a right of action under sections 30 or 31 above) of a prior mark loses the right to sue for infringement where it knowingly tolerates the use of a later registered trade mark for a continuous period of five years, unless the later registration was applied for in bad faith.

Where section 48(1) applies the owner of the later mark cannot sue the prior owner for infringement of its later registered trade mark (section 48(2)). The subject of acquiescence is dealt with in chapter 8.

Infringement of Registered Trade Mark (Section 10)

The following table summarises the arrangement of infringement under the new law:

Table 9.1

	Same goods/ services	*Similar goods/ services*	*Dissimilar goods/ services*
Same mark	10(1)	10(2)(a)	10(3)
Similar mark	10(2)(b)	10(2)(b)	10(3)

In addition, contributory infringement of a registered trade mark is provided for in section 10(5) and certain forms of comparative advertising are deemed to be registered trade mark infringement by section 10(6).

Types of infringement
Section 10(1) and (2) of the 1994 Act reflect the compulsory provisions of Article 5(1) of the Directive and section 10(3) the optional provisions of Article 5(2), as follows:

(1)   A person infringes a registered trade mark if he uses in the course of trade a sign which is identical with the trade mark in relation to goods or services which are identical with those for which it is registered.
(2)   A person infringes a registered trade mark if he uses in the course of trade a sign where because—
(a)   the sign is identical with the trade mark and is used in relation to goods or services similar to those for which the trade mark is registered, or
(b)   the sign is similar to the trade mark and is used in relation to goods or services identical with or similar to those for which the trade mark is registered,
there exists a likelihood of confusion on the part of the public, which includes the likelihood of association with the trade mark.
(3)   A person infringes a registered trade mark if he uses in the course of trade a sign which—
(a)   is identical with or similar to the trade mark, and
(b)   is used in relation to goods or services which are not similar to those for which the trade mark is registered,
where the trade mark has a reputation in the United Kingdom and the use of the sign, being without due cause, takes unfair advantage of, or is detrimental to, the distinctive character or the repute of the trade mark.

There is some departure from the wording of the Directive in section 10(2) of the Act. The corresponding clause (9(2)) in the Bill as first published followed, almost to the letter, Article 5(1)(b) of the Directive, but was later amended by the Government in order to avoid use of the words 'identical' and 'identity'; 'similar' and 'similarity' within the same section. The amendment was thought necessary in view of the English style of interpreting legislation and seems to be of no consequence beyond clarification of the provisions.

Certain words and phrases in section 10(1), (2) and (3) call for common consideration before each of the sub-sections is discussed in turn.

'Sign' – trade mark use; use of non-trade mark matter
In order to constitute infringement under section 4 of the Trade Marks Act 1938, as amended, the defendant's use had to be as a trade mark or in a trade mark sense. Three cases decided under the old law illustrate this point.

In *Mars (GB) Ltd* v *Cadbury Ltd* [1987] RPC 387, the mark TREETS registered for confectionery was held not to be infringed by use of the words 'treat size' on packaging for Cadbury's miniature WISPA chocolate bars. The words were being used to describe the nature of the product and not as a trade mark.

Similarly, in *Mothercare (UK) Ltd* v *Penguin Books Ltd* [1988] RPC 113, use of 'Mother Care/Other Care' as the title of a book addressing the issue of working mothers was held not to infringe the registration of MOTHERCARE for books: the title was being used as a description for the contents of the book and not in a trade mark sense.

In *Unidoor Ltd* v *Marks and Spencer plc* [1988] RPC 275, application by Marks and Spencer of the slogan COAST TO COAST as decoration to T-shirts did not infringe the plaintiff's registration of COAST TO COAST in respect of articles of clothing.

The authors know of only one case decided under the prior law which suggested a different rule. In *News Group Newspapers Ltd* v *Rocket Record Co. Ltd* [1981] FSR 89, Slade J held that there was an arguable case that the defendants' song and record title, 'Page Three', infringed the News Group's registration of PAGE THREE for 'tapes and discs, all bearing audio and video recordings'.

There is a view that the word 'sign' in section 10(1), (2) and (3) (and Article 5(1) and (2) of the Directive) brings the use of non-trade mark matter within the new definitions of infringement. It is submitted that this is unlikely, because:

(a)   The definition of a trade mark in section 1 of the 1994 Act (Article 2 of the Directive) requires a sign to be capable of product differentiation.

(b)   The definition of 'sign' in the *New Shorter Oxford English Dictionary* (1993), is: 'a mark, symbol or device used to represent something, or distinguish the object on which it is put'.

(c)   If recourse is had to the Directive, the Preamble, recital 10 states that the rationale for infringement where there is use of an identical or similar sign for identical or similar goods or services is, in particular, to guarantee the trade mark as an indication of origin; and.

(d)   It is obviously the Government's view (see quote from *Hansard* above) that in order to infringe a mark, there must be trade mark use.

The dividing line between trade mark use and use of non-trade mark matter becomes more difficult to draw when one is considering the use of a 'famous' word or device mark as decoration on, say, articles of clothing. Under the old law, the case of *KODIAK Trade Mark* [1990] FSR 49, suggested that this was not trade mark use and, therefore, not infringement (see also *Unidoor Ltd* v *Marks and Spencer plc*). But the 1938 Act, as amended, only recognised the indication of origin function of a trade mark.

It is thought that such use of a 'famous' mark in relation to dissimilar goods or services, can now be restrained under section 10(3) of the 1994 Act, because that subsection recognises the advertising and promotional value of marks (see also paragraph 3.17 of the White Paper). The position in relation to identical or similar goods or services, where such use is not found to amount to trade mark use, is less clear.

Business names A loophole in the previous law was that there was no infringement where use was not of the proprietor's mark but of the proprietor's business name containing that mark (*Pompadour Laboratories Ltd* v *Frazer* [1966] RPC 7; *Duracell International Inc.* v *Ever Ready Ltd* [1989] FSR 71). This loophole appears not to have been plugged by the new provisions, unless a business name is considered to be a 'sign'.

'In the course of trade'
These words also appeared in sections 4 (infringement) and 68 (definition of a trade mark) of the 1938 Act, as amended. In *M. Ravok (Weatherwear) Ltd* v *National Trade Press Ltd* (1955) 72 RPC 110, the defendants incorrectly attributed ownership of the plaintiff's mark for the registered goods to a third party in their *Trade Marks Directory*. Lord Goddard held that this was not infringement under section 4 because the defendants had not used the mark in the course of trade *in the registered goods*. They had used the mark in the course of their *own* trade as publishers of a trade directory. Previously, in *Aristoc Ltd* v *Rysta Ltd* (1945) 62 RPC 65, the House of Lords had made the same point in another context (registrability of a mark for stocking repairs).

The ruling in *Ravok* was particularly irksome to proprietors trying to control misuse of their marks in newspaper editorials, trade magazine articles and the like in the fight against their marks becoming generic.

Section 10(1), (2) and (3) of the 1994 Act each contain the words 'in the course of trade' and 'in relation to' the goods or services concerned. It seems that the *Ravok* ruling, however inconvenient, may continue to be applicable under the new law.

The Community Trade Mark Regulation gives a proprietor the specific right to control generic use of a Community trade mark in dictionaries, encyclopaedias and reference works (Article 10). The first published draft of the Directive contained a similar right but this was dropped from the final Directive. Regrettably such a right is absent from the 1994 Act.

In *CHEETAH Trade Mark* [1993] FSR 263, the defendant tried to argue that use in invoices rendered subsequent to the sale of goods was not infringement under section 4 of the 1938 Act, as amended, because it was not use in the course of trade. The point was considered unarguable. Use of a registered trade mark on invoices, delivery notes and other business papers is specifically covered by section 10(4)(d) of the 1994 Act.

'*Use in relation to*'

In *AUTODROME Trade Mark* [1969] RPC 564, the plaintiffs had a registration for AUTODROME in respect of motor cars. The defendants named their car show-room 'Autodrome'. This was held not to be infringement under section 4 of the 1938 Act because it was not use in relation to the goods (see also *Harrods Ltd* v *Schwarz-Sackin & Co. Ltd* [1986] FSR 490).

Following *AUTODROME*, fears were expressed that a trader could adopt someone else's trade mark as the name of its shop selling goods for which the mark was registered and escape liability for infringement by refraining from using the mark on or near the goods. This led to an unsuccessful bid by several retailers to register their marks for 'retail services' (*Re Dee Corporation plc* [1990] RPC 159).

The situation is now covered by section 10(4)(b) of the 1994 Act which provides that: '. . . a person uses a sign if . . . he offers or exposes goods for sale, puts them on the market or stocks them for those purposes under the sign, or offers or supplies services under the sign'.

Under the 1938 Act, the words 'use in relation to' clearly included affixing the mark to goods or their packaging and use in advertising or other promotional material. Paragraphs (a) and (d) of section 10(4) of the 1994 Act confirm that this continues to be the case under the new law.

Section 10(4)(c) provides that use for the purposes of section 10 includes importing or exporting goods under the sign. Use of a mark in the United Kingdom for export trade in goods was formerly covered by section 31 of the Trade Marks Act 1938 and was extended to services by the Trade Marks (Amendment) Act 1984. Section 10(4)(c) does not cover use of a mark in the United Kingdom in respect of services to be provided abroad, but section 10(4) does not purport to be an exclusive definition of types of use.

Non-graphic use   Section 103(2) states that:

> References in this Act to use (or any particular description of use) of a trade mark, or of a sign identical with, similar to, or likely to be mistaken for a trade mark, include use (or that description of use) otherwise than by means of a graphic representation.

The definition means that a mark can be infringed by oral use (for example, over the radio) and deals with a particular problem identified during the Parliamentary debates on the Bill, that is, non-graphic use of a sound or smell mark. The example discussed by the House of Lords was the use of a sound mark by playing it on a musical instrument. (The definition in section 103(2) is thought to be necessary because section 1(1) requires a 'trade mark' to be capable of graphic representation.)

A mark could not be infringed by oral use under the 1938 Act, as amended, because section 68(2) defined 'use' of a mark as requiring 'printed or other visual representation'.

Identical sign for identical goods or services (section 10(1))

Liability is strict in the case of use of an identical sign for identical goods or services: there is no need for the plaintiff to show a likelihood of confusion.

The same was true of such infringement of a Part A mark under section 4 of the 1938 Act, as amended. However, section 5(2) of the 1938 Act, as amended, barred a plaintiff from obtaining relief for infringement of a Part B mark, if the defendant could show that the use complained of was likely neither to deceive nor to cause confusion; and the use complained of was not likely to be taken as indicating a connection in the course of trade. The former section 5(2) defence was rarely used to any effect (but see *Marc A. Hammond Pty Ltd v Papa Carmine Pty Ltd* [1978] RPC 697) except in comparative advertising cases (as to which, see below).

Identical sign for similar goods or services (section 10(2)(a)); similar sign for identical or similar goods or services (section 10(2)(b))

Infringement under section 4 of the 1938 Act, as amended, extended to use of a *nearly resembling* mark for goods or services within the registration (that is, identical goods or services). 'Nearly resembling' was defined by section 68(2) of that Act as 'a resemblance so near as to be likely to deceive or cause confusion'. Although the onus was on the plaintiff to prove near resemblance, the enquiry carried out by the court was rather artificial, the comparison being between the plaintiff's mark as registered and the defendant's mark as it appeared in actual use (for a recent example see, *Portakabin Ltd v Powerblast Ltd* [1990] RPC 471). Accordingly, considerations arising out of the way in which the plaintiff might have used its mark, for example, differences in get-up, though relevant to passing off, were not relevant to infringement, unless of a Part B mark to which a plea under section 5(2) of the 1938 Act, as amended, was raised.

One of the major changes introduced by the 1994 Act is the extension of infringement by section 10(2) to use in relation to similar goods and services. However, whether the use complained of is of an identical mark in relation to similar goods or services (section 10(2)(a)) (not covered under the previous law); of a similar mark in relation to identical goods or services (section 10(2)(b)) (covered by section 4 of the 1938 Act, as amended); or of a similar mark in relation to similar goods or services (section 10(2)(b)) (not covered under the previous law); the plaintiff must show that *there exists a likelihood of confusion on the part of the public, which includes the likelihood of association with the trade mark.*

These new criteria for infringement will undoubtedly introduce passing-off type considerations and evidence (including survey evidence) into the action for infringement of a registered trade mark. The 10th recital of the Preamble to the Directive sets out the particular factors (whilst acknowledging that there may be others) which tribunals in Member States should take into account when assessing likelihood of confusion, as follows:

(a)   'recognition of the trade mark on the market';
(b)   'the association which can be made with the used or registered sign';
(c)   'the degree of similarity between the trade mark and the sign'; and
(d)   '[the degree of similarity] between the goods or services identified'.

The broader than traditional approach taken by the Directive towards likelihood of confusion is based on the Benelux Court of Justice's interpretation of the concept of 'similarity' embodied in the infringement criteria of Article 13A of the Uniform Benelux Trademarks Law 1971. The Minutes of the Council Meeting at which the Community Trade Mark Regulation was adopted contain the following statement on Article 9(1)(b) of the Regulation, which is worded in exactly the same terms as Article 5(1)(b) of the Directive, in turn encapsulated in section 10(2) of the 1994 Act: 'The Council and the Commission note that ''likelihood of association'' is a concept which in particular has been developed by Benelux case-law'.

In the leading case of *Union* v *Union Soleure*, Decision of 20 May 1983, Case A 82/5, [1984] BIE 137, the Benelux Court decided that:

> . . . there is similarity between a trademark and a sign when, taking into account the particular circumstances of the case, such as the distinctive power of the trademark, the trademark and the sign, each looked at as a whole and in relation to one another, demonstrate such auditive, visual or conceptual resemblance, that associations between sign and trademark are evoked merely on the basis of this resemblance.

In other words, the public does not need to be *confused*. The mere fact that the public on perceiving the sign establishes a mental link ('association') between the sign and the trade mark is enough in order to reach a finding of similarity.

An example given by a Dutch commentator illustrates how the above rule might operate in practice (Harmeling, *Successful Strategies in Trademark Litigation*). Suppose OMO-HENKEL is registered for washing detergents and a competitor starts marketing its detergents using the sign OMO-UNILEVER. It is unlikely that the public will be confused as to the origin of the products, since the two companies, Henkel and Unilever, are well-known. There can be no doubt, however, that the public will form a mental link between OMO-HENKEL and OMO-UNILEVER because of the use of OMO in the trade mark and the sign. Under Benelux law the courts would accept that OMO-UNILEVER infringes OMO-HENKEL.

A truer-to-life example is provided by the case of *MONOPOLY* v *ANTI-MONOPOLY* [1978] BIE 39 and 43 (Dutch Supreme Court), where use for similar products was concerned (games). The second game was of a totally anti-capitalistic nature and it was highly improbable that any person would think that the two games originated from the same company. Nevertheless the court ruled that there was infringement: the public when seeing or hearing ANTI-MONOPOLY would think of MONOPOLY therefore the danger of association was made out.

Earlier in this chapter, the issue was raised of how far a proprietor's exclusive rights under the new law are limited by the origin function of a trade mark. Clearly, Article 5(1)(b) of the Directive, which section 10(2) of the 1994 Act seeks to implement, contemplates infringement occurring in circumstances not involving traditional source confusion. Therefore, it is reasonable to assume that the section 10(2) definitions of infringement are aimed at protecting the wider integrity of a trade mark.

The guidelines previously applied by the United Kingdom courts and the Registrar of Trade Marks in assessing similarity of goods or services, or related or associated services or goods (relative grounds for refusal of registration only) and in comparing marks (relative grounds for refusal of registration and infringement) have been described at chapter 7. It is a matter for speculation to what extent these former guidelines will be used by the courts in determining infringement under section 10(2) of the 1994 Act. However, it must be remembered that under section 10(2) the onus is on the plaintiff to show infringement of its registered trade mark; whereas in opposition proceedings under section 5(2) of the 1994 Act it is for the applicant for registration to show no likelihood of confusion (in the new wider sense).

Identical or similar sign for dissimilar goods or services (section 10(3))
Section 10(3) takes advantage of optional Article 5(2) of the Directive in extending infringement to use of an identical or similar sign in relation to *dissimilar* goods or services. The conditions for such protection are:

    (a)   the registered trade mark has a reputation in the United Kingdom;
    (b)   the use of the sign is without due cause; and
    (c)   the use of the sign takes unfair advantage of, or is detrimental to, the distinctive character or the repute of the registered trade mark.

Likelihood of confusion is *not* a condition for protection.

This recognises *dilution* of a trade mark and was included in the Directive at the instigation of the Benelux countries. There was no equivalent under the previous United Kingdom trade marks law. The Benelux case law on dilution under Article 13A(2) of the Uniform Benelux Trademarks Law 1971 is expected to be influential in interpreting section 10(3). The United Kingdom courts may also turn to decisions of the American courts under State dilution laws (as yet there is no Federal action for dilution of a trade mark).

What is meant by dilution in this context? In his seminal article, 'The Rational Basis of Trademark Protection' (1927) 40 Harv L Rev 813 at p. 825, Frank Schechter described dilution as: 'the gradual whittling away or dispersion of the identity and hold upon the public mind of the mark or name by its use upon non-competing goods'.

The harm addressed by section 10(3) is twofold:

    (a)   The 'blurring' of the distinctiveness of a mark into non-distinctiveness. BUICK aspirin, KODAK pianos and BULOVA gowns were given by the New York Legislature as examples of what might be called 'dilution by blurring'. The following were held to be infringement under Benelux dilution law: DUNHILL glasses, APPLE advertising services and MARLBORO cosmetics.

    (b)   The destruction of the positive associations a mark has come to convey to the public. The most blatant cases occur where a mark is associated with an unwholesome context. An example, again from New York State dilution law, is the defendant who sold a 'joke' fake AMERICAN EXPRESS card which contained a condom and the phrase NEVER LEAVE HOME WITHOUT IT. But this type of harm can result from use on seemingly innocuous products. Thus in the leading Benelux Court of Justice decision of *CLAERYN/KLAREIN* (1976) 7 IIC 420, the owner of CLAERYN Dutch gin was able to prevent Colgate using KLAREIN for liquid cleanser: both marks had an identical pronunciation in the Dutch language.

The doctrine of dilution comprises a third type of harm which is not covered by section 10(3) (or by Article 5(2) of the Directive). Use of an identical or similar sign for *competing* goods or services can lead to genericisation of a mark and its 'death' (see chapter 8). In cases involving similarity of marks and/or similarity of goods or services, the plaintiff must show *likelihood of confusion* in order to succeed in an infringement action under section 10(2). It is strange that protection against use on competing goods or services (section 10(2)) should be weaker than protection against use on non-competing goods or services (section 10(3)).

In order to succeed in an action for infringement under section 10(3), the plaintiff must prove that its mark has *reputation* in the United Kingdom. There is no requirement that the mark be *used* in the United Kingdom (although if the user requirements in section 46(1) are not met, the mark will be liable to revocation). This is to be contrasted with the present (but perhaps not future) 'foreign plaintiff rule' in passing off (*Anheuser-Busch Inc.* v *Budejovicky Budvar Narodni Podnik* [1984] FSR 413) and will be of obvious benefit to the owners of suitable marks abroad seeking to extend their businesses to the United Kingdom.

It is a matter for speculation what type of marks the United Kingdom courts will protect against dilution under section 10(3). The White Paper spoke of marks which have acquired a 'wide reputation' and referred to the practice of using 'familiar' marks to decorate T-shirts (paragraph 3.17). The trend under American State dilution laws is to protect only 'famous' marks, for example, MARLBORO, COCA-COLA, NESCAFÉ, BUICK, TIFFANY'S and PAMPERS; whereas reputation has not so far been treated as an important criterion under Benelux law.

The International Trademark Association (formerly the United States Trademark Association) has suggested to the United Kingdom Government (14 February 1994) the following practice guidelines for determining reputation for the purposes of section 10(3) (and section 5(3) – relative ground for refusal of registration):

(a)   the degree of inherent or acquired distinctiveness of the mark,
(b)   the duration and extent of use of the mark in connection with the goods or services,
(c)   the duration and extent of advertising and publicity of the mark,
(d)   the geographical extent of the trading area in which the mark is used,
(e)   the channels of trade for the goods or services with which the proprietor's mark is used,
(f)   the degree of recognition of the proprietor's mark in its and the defendant's trading areas and channels of trade,
(g)   the nature and extent of use of the same or similar sign by third parties.

These guidelines are, of course, very similar to the considerations taken into account by the United Kingdom courts in passing-off cases.

The defendant will not infringe under section 10(3) if its use is with 'due cause'. 'Due cause' is not defined by the Act and will need to be determined by the courts on a case-by-case basis. The words 'due cause' in Article 13A(2) of the Uniform Benelux Trademarks Law 1971 have been interpreted narrowly (*CLAERYN/ KLAREIN*): there must be 'necessity' for the defendant's use, for example, in connection with accessories or spare parts, or the defendant must have a prior right to use the sign. The problem is that such 'due causes' are listed as specific *defences* to infringement in section 11 of the 1994 Act (see chapter 10).

Finally, it was noted above that likelihood of confusion is *not* necessary to a finding of infringement under section 10(3). Section 10(3) clearly recognises a registered trade mark as industrial property worthy of protection in its own right (see also recital 9 of the Preamble to the Directive).

Contributory infringement (section 10(5))
By virtue of section 10(5):

> A person who applies a registered trade mark to material intended to be used for labelling or packaging goods, as a business paper, or for advertising goods or services, shall be treated as a party to any use of the material which infringes the registered trade mark if when he applied the mark he knew or had reason to believe that the application of the mark was not duly authorised by the proprietor or a licensee.

There was no such provision under the 1938 Act, as amended, but old case law suggested that printing or otherwise dealing in labels or packaging bearing a trade mark with the intention that they be used on non-genuine goods was itself infringement. Section 10(5) confirms that this is the case under the new law.

The test for liability is whether the third party 'knew or had reason to believe' that the application of the trade mark was unauthorised. This covers actual knowledge and, by analogy with the similar standard of knowledge required for secondary infringement of copyright under the Copyright, Designs and Patents Act 1988 (*LA Gear Inc.* v *Hi-Tech Sports plc* [1992] FSR 121), knowledge which the circumstances surrounding the application of the mark would suggest to a person of the defendant's calling.

Printers and designers should clearly get an indemnity and warranty from all who place orders for labels, packaging or promotional material in order to protect themselves from being caught by section 10(5).

Comparative advertising (section 10(6))
Section 10(6) deals with comparative advertising and proved to be one of the controversial provisions of the new law.

Comparative advertising means advertising which compares the merit of the product or service being advertised with that of a rival. Within the specific context of trade marks, the term is used to describe advertising made by trader A, in which trader A refers to the product or service of trader B by trader B's trade mark.

There are disparate views on the merits of comparative advertising both within the United Kingdom and the rest of Europe (see COM (91) 147 final). Trade mark owners would, of course, prefer to be able to restrain *any* unauthorised use of their marks in comparative advertising. The United Kingdom Government stated in the White Paper that in the interest of better consumer awareness it was committed to allowing comparative advertising, subject to the proviso that 'an advertiser should not be free to ride on the back of a competitor's trade mark' (paragraph 3.28).

In fact in the United Kingdom, legal control of the wider practice of comparative advertising is small. False or misleading statements may be actionable in trade libel (for a recent example see, *Compaq Computer Corporation* v *Dell Computer Corporation Ltd* [1992] FSR 93), and price comparisons and credit advertisements are controlled by the Consumer Protection Act 1987 and by the Consumer Credit (Advertisements) Regulations 1989 respectively. But, for the major part, comparative advertising is regulated by voluntary codes, the most important being the

British Code of Advertising Practice ('BCAP'), administered by the Advertising Standards Authority ('ASA').

By way of contrast, until the 1994 Act, use in comparative advertising, however truthful, of a trade mark registered in Part A of the Register was trade mark infringement under section 4(1)(b) of the 1938 Act, as amended (*Bismag Ltd* v *Amblins (Chemists) Ltd* (1940) 57 RPC 209; *Chanel Ltd* v *Triton Packaging Ltd* [1993] RPC 32).

The European Commission has published a Draft Directive on comparative advertising (OJ [1991] C 180/41). The subsequently amended proposal (see COM (94) 151 final of 21 April 1994) is to amend Directive 84/450/EEC on misleading advertising (implemented in the United Kingdom by the Control of Misleading Advertisements Regulations 1988) and permit comparative advertising subject to the limitations that the advertisements are not misleading, will not cause confusion between the goods or services of the advertiser and its competitor and do not 'discredit, denigrate or bring contempt on a competitor or his trade marks . . . or capitalise on the reputation of a trade mark . . . of a competitor'.

The proposal means little change in United Kingdom practice since these limitations are already present in the BCAP. However, section 4(1)(b) of the Trade Marks Act 1938, as amended, could no longer have remained law.

Comparative advertising is *not* trade mark infringement under either Article 5(1) or (2) of the Directive, or section 10(1), (2) or (3) of the 1994 Act. The Minutes attached to the Community Trade Mark Regulation make clear that 'use in advertising' in Article 9(2) of the Regulation (the equivalent to Article 5(3) of the Directive and section 10(4) of the 1994 Act) does not include use in comparative advertising.

Nevertheless, Article 5(5) of the Directive states that Article 5:

shall not affect provisions in any Member State relating to the protection against the use of a sign other than for the purposes of distinguishing goods or services, where use of that sign without due cause takes unfair advantage of, or is detrimental to, the distinctive character or the repute of the trade mark.

The Government has interpreted Article 5(5) as entitling the United Kingdom to legislate that comparative advertising may constitute trade mark infringement. Section 10(6) states:

Nothing in the preceding provisions of this section shall be construed as preventing the use of a registered trade mark by any person for the purpose of identifying goods or services as those of the proprietor or a licensee.

But any such use otherwise than in accordance with honest practices in industrial or commercial matters shall be treated as infringing the registered trade mark if the use without due cause takes unfair advantage of, or is detrimental to, the distinctive character or repute of the trade mark.

Since the Directive makes no mention of comparative advertising, doubts have been expressed about the justification for the inclusion of section 10(6) into the new law. Furthermore it is considered unwise to legislate on this topic in view of the imminent adoption of the Directive on comparative advertising.

As to justification, it seems that Article 5(5) was included in the Directive in order to preserve the infringement criterion in Article 13A(2) of the Uniform Benelux Trademarks Law 1971:

all *other use* of the mark or similar sign in the course of trade without due cause and under circumstances likely to cause prejudice to the trademark owner.

Article 13A(2) has been interpreted by the Benelux courts to cover use of a mark in comparative advertising.

Comparative advertising can constitute trade mark infringement under section 10(6) of the 1994 Act only if it: (a) is contrary to 'honest practices in industrial or commercial matters'; *and* (b) without due cause, takes unfair advantage of, or is detrimental to, the distinctive character or repute of the trade mark.

The first requirement has been criticised for being additional to the criterion in Article 5(5) of the Directive and difficult to predict in meaning. Does the phrase 'honest practices in industrial or commercial matters' refer to the standards applied by bodies like the ASA, or to practices pertaining in the particular industry concerned, for example, the motor trade which takes a fairly relaxed attitude towards comparative advertising subject to prior notification of the trade mark owner? Again, there are different forms of comparative advertising ranging from simple price tables, through to 'knocking copy', where one product is specifically denigrated (*News Group Newspapers Ltd* v *Mirror Group Newspapers (1986) Ltd* [1989] FSR 126), and 'smells, tastes or looks like . . .' advertising, where products are clearly distinguished but which trade mark owners would regard as tantamount to piracy (*Chanel Ltd* v *Triton Packaging Ltd* [1993] RPC 32).

Section 10(6) is probably aimed at the latter types of comparative advertising, but trade mark owners legitimately fear that the meaning of section 10(6) will only be determined at their expense, through costly litigation.

In the Government's defence, it may be that the 'honest practices' limitation in section 10(6) was unavoidable. If the words 'without due cause' in section 10(6) are interpreted by the courts, as indicated above, to apply only in cases of necessity or prior right then, in the absence of the limitation, comparative advertising by reference to a trade mark could never escape being infringement (as per the Benelux experience). This would have obviously frustrated the Government's intention as stated in the White Paper and, furthermore, would be contrary to the spirit of the forthcoming Directive on comparative advertising.

'Own-brand look-alikes'

During debates on the Trade Marks Bill a strong Parliamentary lobby was mounted in order to secure protection for brand leaders against 'own-brand look-alikes', that is, products carrying retailers' brands which resemble manufacturers' leading brands in overall appearance. An example given in the House of Lords was Procter & Gamble's HEAD AND SHOULDERS anti-dandruff shampoo and Sainsbury's HEADWAY anti-dandruff shampoo.

At first, protection was sought through an additional head of infringement. This was obviously contrary to the Directive since it amounted to extending infringement to cover unregistered get-up. Much more promising was an amendment to introduce an action for unfair competition based on Article 10*bis* of the Paris

Convention but this was strongly opposed by the Consumers' Association. The amendment was not accepted for inclusion in the 1994 Act. However, the support commanded by the proposed amendment, especially in the House of Lords, might be an indication of the shape of future legislation.

Transitional Provisions (Schedule 3)

Schedule 3, paragraph 4, provides a classic example of the pitfalls involved in the United Kingdom style of drafting legislation in order to implement a Directive. Paragraph 4(1) states that:

(a)   the new substantive law of infringement applies in relation to an existing registered mark (that is, a mark registered under the 1938 Act, as amended, immediately before commencement (paragraph 1(1)), or an application for registration which was accepted for registration on the basis of the old law (paragraph 10(1)) *as from commencement* of the 1994 Act;

(b)   *but*, the right of a proprietor to bring an action for infringement (section 14) applies in relation to infringement of an existing registered mark committed *after the commencement* of the 1994 Act;

(c)   *and* the old law continues to apply to infringements committed *before commencement.*

What of infringement of an existing registered mark committed *on the day of commencement*? Is that day a free for all?

This little peculiarity seems to have arisen from the difference in approach noted at the beginning of this chapter: that is, the Directive's statement of rights conferred by a trade mark includes the right to take action for infringement whereas the 1994 Act's declaration of exclusive rights does not.

Moving on from this point, paragraph 4(2) of schedule 3 provides (in accordance with compulsory Article 5(4) of the Directive) that:

It is not infringement of—
(a)   an existing registered mark, or
(b)   a registered trade mark of which the distinctive elements are the same or substantially the same as those of an existing registered mark and which is registered for the same goods or services,
to continue after commencement any use which did not amount to infringement of the existing registered mark under the old law.

Paragraph 4(2) preserves the much narrower scope of infringement under the old law in respect of 'existing uses' continued after commencement and also the savings and exceptions to infringement set out in sections 4(2), 4(3), 4(4), 7 and 8 of the 1938 Act, as amended (see chapter 10). It is not possible to avoid the saving by re-registering a trade mark under the new law. Note, however, that section 5(2) of the 1938 Act, as amended, did not provide a 'defence' to infringement of a Part B mark under the old law: it merely barred the proprietor's right to a remedy. Any such existing use cannot be continued under the transitional provisions of paragraph 4(2).

A brief summary of infringement of a trade mark under the old law is as follows:

(a)   A Part A mark was infringed if it was used in the course of trade *as a trade mark* (that is, to indicate the origin of the defendant's goods or services) in relation to goods or services *within* the registration (section 4(1)(a) of the 1938 Act, as amended).

(b)   A Part A mark was also infringed if it was used commercially for the same goods or services in comparative advertising (section 4(1)(b) of the 1938 Act, as amended). The scope of the phrase 'importing a reference' in section 4(1)(b) was otherwise unclear, although use which suggested that the proprietor was 'responsible' for the defendant's goods or services might have sufficed for infringement (*News Group Newspapers* v *Rocket Record Co. Ltd* [1981] FSR 89).

(c)   A Part B mark was infringed in exactly the same way (section 5(1) of the 1938 Act, as amended), but section 5(2) precluded a remedy for infringement if the defendant proved that its use involved no likelihood of confusion and no inference of trade connection with the proprietor or its goods or services. Section 5(2) meant that there was no point in suing in respect of use of a Part B mark in comparative advertising.

A summary of the savings and exceptions to infringement under the old law can be found in chapter 10.

Licensees
The right of a licensee under section 30 of the 1994 Act to call upon the proprietor to take action against infringers (and, in specified cases of default, to bring infringement proceedings in its own name) applies to licences granted before commencement, but only in respect of infringements occurring after commencement (schedule 3, paragraph 6(1)).

Well-Known Marks (Section 56)

By virtue of section 56(2), the proprietor of a trade mark which is entitled to protection under the Paris Convention as a well-known trade mark may restrain by injunction the use in the United Kingdom of a trade mark where:

(a)   the trade mark, or an essential part of the trade mark, is identical or similar to the well-known trade mark; and
(b)   the use complained of is in relation to similar goods or services; and
(c)   the use complained of is likely to cause confusion (query whether this is confusion in the wider sense, to include likelihood of association).

The right to an injunction is lost if the proprietor knowingly acquiesces in the use of the trade mark in the United Kingdom for a continuous period of five years (section 48; and see chapter 8). Furthermore, the right cannot be used to prevent any bona fide use of a trade mark begun before the commencement date of section 56.

Section 56(1) defines 'a trade mark which is entitled to protection under the Paris Convention as a well-known trade mark' as:

a mark which is well-known in the United Kingdom as being the mark of a person who—

(a)   is a national of a Convention country, or

(b)   is domiciled in, or has a real and effective industrial or commercial establishment in, a Convention country,

whether or not that person carries on business, or has any goodwill, in the United Kingdom. (Emphasis added.)

The protection of well-known marks is irrespective of registration *or* use in the United Kingdom.

Section 56 gives effect to the United Kingdom's obligation under Article 6*bis* of the Paris Convention. There was no equivalent provision under the old law.

CHAPTER TEN

Defences to and Remedies for Trade Mark Infringement, including Counterfeiting

Introduction

A defence to a claim of trade mark infringement has the effect of removing liability from the defendant and should be contrasted with a counterclaim, where the defendant seeks to question the validity of the plaintiff's trade mark under the provisions of sections 46 and 47 of the 1994 Act (explained in chapter 8). Defences to a claim of infringement should also be distinguished from arguments raised by a defendant as to why a particular discretionary remedy should not be granted for reasons of equity: these are discussed in this chapter.

The defences to infringement found in the 1994 Act all have their counterparts in earlier legislation and, with one exception, all reflect the provisions of the Directive. Because of the Directive, there are subtle differences in wording between the old and new Acts, so that care should be taken when using cases decided under the old law.

The various statutory defences will be examined in turn. However, because of the importance of the defence of exhaustion of rights in relation to the parallel importation of trade-marked products, this will receive a more detailed and separate treatment.

General Defences (Sections 11, 13 and 48)

Use of another registered mark (section 11(1))
Section 11(1) (which has no counterpart in the Directive) provides that a registered trade mark is not infringed by the use of another registered trade mark in relation to goods or services for which that other mark is registered. This provision, which was inserted during the Report Stage of the Bill in the House of Lords, was felt by the Government to be necessary to protect the owners of concurrent registrations which had been entered on the Register pursuant to the honest concurrent use provisions found in section 12(2) of the 1938 Act, as amended.

When the Government subsequently amended the Bill further by including, in section 7, a new (albeit temporary) provision on honest concurrent use, no reference was made to section 11(1). It must, however, be assumed that section 11(1) applies to registrations made pursuant to section 7 of the 1994 Act.

Section 11(1) must be read in the light of:

(a)   section 47(2), which provides for a mark to be declared invalid if it was registered in breach of an earlier right; and

(b)   section 47(6), which provides that if a mark is declared to be invalid, the registration is deemed never to have been made.

It may be noted that by virtue of schedule 3, paragraph 18(2), section 47 is to apply to existing registered marks as if it had 'been in force at all material times'. It therefore is irrelevant for the purposes of section 11(1) whether the registration by virtue of honest concurrent use was obtained under the 1938 Act, as amended, or under the 1994 Act.

The combined effect of section 11(1) and section 47(6) can be illustrated by the following example. Suppose two identical or similar marks, A and B, are on the Register in respect of similar goods, and that the owner of trade mark A sues the owner of trade mark B for infringement. The owner of trade mark B would raise the defence contained in section 11(1). The owner of trade mark A would then reply by seeking the cancellation of trade mark B, which, if successful, would mean that trade mark B has never existed. The defence in section 11(1) is therefore erased and the owner of trade mark B becomes liable for infringement.

The only caveat is that section 48 provides that five years' acquiescence in the use of a later registered trade mark by the owner of the earlier right debars the seeking of a declaration that the later mark is invalid (unless the later applicant acted in bad faith). The owner of the later mark in such a situation is conversely not allowed to challenge the earlier right.

Hence, in the example given, where the owner of trade mark A has known about the use of trade mark B and has done nothing to stop it for the requisite period of five years, the defence in section 11(1) becomes, in effect, absolute.

Section 11(1) had its counterpart in section 4(4) of the 1938 Act, as amended. Section 4(4) provided that use of one of two or more registered trade marks, being identical or confusingly similar, was deemed not to be infringement of the other or others. Like its successor, the defence was limited to where the second proprietor used the mark on the goods or services for which it was registered. Thus if the second proprietor started to use the mark on goods for which it was *not* registered, but for which the first proprietor's mark *was*, the defence would not be available (see *Gor-Ray Ltd* v *Gilray Skirts Ltd* (1952) 69 RPC 99).

As section 10 of the 1994 Act broadens the scope of the trade mark right to enable the proprietor to sue for infringement where the same or a similar mark is used on similar goods, rather than on the goods of the registration, it is likely that section 11(1) of the 1994 Act will be used more frequently than its predecessor, with a consequent increase in actions for invalidity under section 47(2).

Use of own name or address (section 11(2)(a))
Section 11(2)(a) provides that a registered trade mark is not infringed by 'the use by a person of his own name or address'. Although it might be thought that the mere use by a trader of his own name or address could not be 'trade mark use'

(whatever that may now mean), where such name or address is used in connection with the supply of goods and services it may amount to misrepresentation for the purposes of passing off, or to infringement of a registered mark. The defence is therefore based on public policy, but has to be understood in the light of the proviso which qualifies the whole of section 11(2), explained below.

Section 11(2)(a), although based on Article 6(1) of the Directive, looks not dissimilar to section 8(a) of the 1938 Act, as amended. This provided that no registration should interfere with:

> any bona fide use by a person of his own name or of the name of his place of business, or of the name, or of the name of the place of business, of any of his predecessors in business.

The new defence in section 11(2)(a) is therefore much narrower than under the previous law.

A similar provision is to be found in Article 12 of the Community Trade Mark Regulation. Minute 7 of the Minutes of the Council of Ministers attached to the Regulation states that the defence is available only to natural persons, not companies.

During the Committee Stage of the Bill in the House of Lords, the Government rejected attempts to have the requirement of good faith included in section 11(2)(a), as it was in its predecessor. The Government's view was that the wording of the proviso sufficed to import a requirement equivalent to good faith (*Hansard* (HL/PBC), 18 January 1994, cols 44–5).

Use to describe the goods or services (section 11(2)(b))
Section 11(2)(b), again based on Article 6(1) of the Directive, allows a trader to use another's registered trade mark to describe various attributes of a product, such as its quality, intended purpose or geographical origin. To give an example, the maker of fashion garments may wish to indicate that they consist of a particular fabric, the trade mark for which is owned by a textile manufacturer. The maker of a soft drink may wish to tell consumers that it contains a particular brand of artificial sweetener. Such use of another's trade mark is permissible, again as long as it complies with the proviso to section 11(2).

Section 11(2)(b) had a predecessor in section 8(b) of the 1938 Act, as amended, which stated that no trade mark registration should interfere with the use by any person of any bona fide description of the character or quality of the goods, provided that such description did not 'import a reference'. At first glance, therefore, section 8(b) appeared to create a circular argument, in that it stated that it would not amount to trade mark infringement to describe the quality of goods unless that description amounted to trade mark infringement. The key to understanding the section, however, was again the presence of the phrase bona fide. Case law explaining this is discussed in the context of the proviso to section 11(2) of the 1994 Act below.

Spare parts and components (section 11(2)(c))
Finally, section 11(2)(c), derived from Article 6(1) of the Directive, enables a third party to use another's trade mark where it is necessary to indicate the intended

purpose of a product or service, in particular, for accessories or spare parts. Such a defence is particularly important for those who manufacture replacement parts for consumer goods or cars. Again, the defence is subject to the proviso explained below.

The counterpart in the 1938 Act to section 11(2)(c) was section 4(3)(b). This provided that there was deemed not to be trade mark infringement where the registered trade mark was used in relation to goods adapted to form part of, or to be accessory to, other goods, provided such use was reasonably necessary and provided that neither the purpose nor the effect of the use of the mark was to indicate a trade connection with the third party. The objective of such qualifications appeared to be to stop a trader making unfair use of another's trade mark to sell a replacement product.

Proviso to section 11(2)

The three defences found in paragraphs (a), (b) and (c) of section 11(2) are all subject to the requirement that the use of the plaintiff's mark by the defendant is 'in accordance with honest practices in industrial or commercial matters'. This phrase is copied directly from Article 6(1) of the Directive and has no precise counterpart in earlier United Kingdom trade marks law, although similar qualifications were imposed, as explained above, on legitimate use of a registered trade mark under section 4(3)(b), section 8(a) and section 8(b) of the 1938 Act, as amended.

The problem with the proviso is the phrase 'honest practices', which is not defined anywhere in the 1994 Act. Concern was expressed during the Committee Stage of the Bill in the House of Lords that the phrase would be difficult to interpret. As Lord Oliver of Aylmerton pointed out, whilst it may be possible to establish *as a fact* what is an industrial or commercial practice, 'honesty' depends on the defendant's state of mind. By way of reply, the Government pointed out that the phrase has been part of the Paris Convention since 1910, where it is used in connection with the prohibition on unfair competition; the British judiciary should be able to allocate a meaning to it (*Hansard* (HL/PCB), 18 January 1994, col. 43). Ultimately, as it is a phrase derived from the Directive, United Kingdom courts will be able to seek the guidance of the Court of Justice of the European Communities in Luxembourg on the meaning of the phrase.

A further difficulty connected with the interpretation of the proviso is the extent to which earlier cases will be of help, as the equivalent sections in the 1938 Act each had somewhat different wording. Such authority as there is shows that there is a fine dividing line between making legitimate use of another's mark and free-riding on that other trader's goodwill.

With regard to the defence found in section 11(2)(a) (use of own name), such authority as existed on its equivalent in section 8(a) of the 1938 Act, as amended, focused on the meaning of bona fide. In *Baume & Co. Ltd v A. H. Moore Ltd* [1958] Ch 907, the defendants had sold watches marked with the phrase 'Baume & Mercier, Geneva' which indicated the Swiss manufacturers of the product. The plaintiffs sued for infringement of their trade mark BAUME. The Court of Appeal stated, *obiter*, that the defence in section 8(a) was a subjective one. A trader was either honest or dishonest and there was no such thing as constructive dishonesty; if therefore a trader honestly applied its own name to goods which had been made personally, then the plaintiff would not be able to sue for trade mark infringement, but only passing off.

An example of where the defendant had used the name dishonestly is *Teofani & Co. Ltd* v *Teofani* (1913) 30 RPC 446. The plaintiffs had over 20 years' use of their name for cigarettes (which they had eventually registered as a trade mark) and sought to stop the defendant from using the same name on a rival product. The court agreed with the plaintiffs that what the defendant had been trying to do was to cash in on an unusual surname which had achieved wide public recognition. The defendant's motives in using a personal surname in the circumstances were dishonest.

A more recent example of the old section 8(a) defence is *Provident Financial plc* v *Halifax Building Society* [1994] FSR 81. Comments by Aldous J in an interlocutory hearing again suggest a subjective approach to the issue of good faith.

In relation to the defence found in section 11(2)(b) of the 1994 Act (use to describe goods or services), cases decided under section 8(b) of the 1938 Act, as amended, stressed the need to inquire into the defendant's motives in using the plaintiff's trade mark, as well as the manner of use. In *IZAL Trade Mark* (1935) 52 RPC 399, the defendants sold toilet rolls in wrappers printed with the slogan 'medicated with IZAL' in prominent letters. When sued for infringement by the proprietors of IZAL (which was registered for disinfectants) the defendants pleaded the forerunner to section 8(b) as a defence, claiming that the slogan was a bona fide description of their goods. The court decided that because of the size of the lettering used by the defendants, the use of the plaintiffs' mark was not bona fide.

More recently, Megarry J in *British Northrop Ltd* v *Texteam Blackburn Ltd* [1974] RPC 57 decided that the wording of the defendant's list of spare parts for the plaintiff's looms did not get the benefit of section 8(b) of the 1938 Act, as amended. The phrase used by the defendant ('every part shall be inspected and approved by engineers with many years experience in the manufacture of NORTH-ROP parts'), even if bona fide, was an attempt to use the plaintiff's mark to obtain a benefit from the reputation enjoyed by the plaintiff's goods. The inference must be that the defendant was trying to 'free ride' on the plaintiff's goodwill. Megarry J suggested that the defendant should have worded its price list differently to get the benefit of section 8(b).

Both the *IZAL* and *NORTHROP* cases seemed to import a degree of objectivity into section 8(b) of the 1938 Act which is lacking from section 8(a) of the 1938 Act, as interpreted by the cases explained above. Even though the use of the plaintiff's mark may be an *honest* description of the defendant's product, the method of use raises question marks about the defendant's motives.

Although the defence in section 11(2)(c) of the 1994 Act (spare parts) had a counterpart in section 4(3)(b) of the 1938 Act, there was no authority on the meaning of the earlier provision. It could be argued, however, that section 4(3)(b) was analogous with section 8(b) of the 1938 Act, so that the *NORTHROP* case could be used for guidance.

Returning to the 1994 Act, the proviso to section 11(2) applies to all three defences, thus providing the uniformity missing from the 1938 Act. It remains to be seen whether the courts do have difficulty in interpreting 'honest practices in industrial or commercial matters' and whether they adopt a subjective test for the meaning of the phrase. Cases like *IZAL* and *NORTHROP* could be of assistance in suggesting a more objective appraisal of the defendant's conduct.

Prior rights (section 11(3))

Section 11(3), based on Article 6(2) of the Directive, provides that a registered trade mark shall not be infringed by the use in the course of trade in a particular locality of an earlier right which applies only in that locality. The wording of section 11(3) does not match the wording of the Directive exactly. Article 6(2) of the Directive provides that the trade mark shall not entitle the proprietor to prohibit a third party from using an earlier right. Whilst it may seem pedantic to argue that there is a difference between 'shall not be infringed' and 'shall not entitle the proprietor to prohibit', procedurally there is a difference between raising a defence to an infringement action (which is what section 11(3) implies) and claiming that the plaintiff has no cause of action because the trade mark right does not entitle the plaintiff to sue (which is what the Directive implies).

Section 11(3) then goes on to define 'earlier right' for the purposes of the section. This suggests that, contrary to section 104 (the list of defined expressions), 'earlier right' in section 11(3) does not have the same meaning as in section 5(4) of the 1994 Act, which deals with used but unregistered marks as earlier rights for the purposes of relative grounds of refusal.

For the purposes of section 11(3), an 'earlier right' means an unregistered trade mark or other sign which has been *continuously* used in relation to goods and services from a date prior to the use of the registered trade mark or its registration, whichever was earlier. Further, the earlier right is to be regarded as applying in a locality if its use there would be protected by the law of passing off.

This definition of 'earlier right' needs closer examination. The word 'locality' is not defined in the 1994 Act (possibly because it is derived from the Directive, so that any definition might be perceived as narrowing the effect of the Directive). It begs the question whether the whole of the United Kingdom could be a 'locality'. The Directive merely states that the right must exist within the limits of the territory in which the earlier right is recognised.

Equally, 'continuous' is not defined (this time it is a word which is *not* present in the Directive). It may be asked whether this means the same as the phrase 'uninterrupted use' which appears in the revocation provision, section 46. In any case, the requirement that the use be 'continuous' does not appear in section 5(4), dealing with an earlier right being a relative ground for refusal of registration.

Finally, it should be noted that the owner of the earlier right is required by section 11(3) to satisfy the court that the unregistered mark would be protected by the law of passing off, with the consequent evidential burden which this entails. This appears to reflect the requirement of the Directive that the earlier right must be 'recognised by the laws of the Member State in question'.

Section 11(3) had a counterpart in the 1938 Act, as amended, namely, section 7. At first glance, the latter provision (ironically) appears to accord better with the Directive than its successor, as its opening words were 'nothing . . . shall entitle the proprietor . . . to interfere with' the use of an earlier right. Section 7 of the 1938 Act did not confine itself to marks used only in a locality, nor did it require the owner of the earlier right to satisfy the court that passing off would be made out. It did, however, require that the use of the earlier mark be 'continuous'. This was interpreted to mean more than just occasional, though not necessarily 'every week or even every month' (*Smith, Bartlet & Co.* v *British Pure Oil Grease and Carbide Co.* (1934) 51 RPC 157 at p. 163). However, because section 11(3) of the

1994 Act requires that the owner of the prior right be in a position to bring a passing-off action, 'continuous' may now be a more stringent criterion.

Registration subject to disclaimer or limitation (section 13)
Section 13 of the 1994 Act provides that the rights of a trade mark owner conferred by section 9 are restricted by any disclaimer or limitation affecting the registration. Further, registrations effected under the law prior to the coming into force of the 1994 Act will have any disclaimers or limitations carried forward (schedule 3, paragraph 3(2)).

The principal difference between disclaimers and limitations imposed under the old law and those accepted under the new law is that under the 1938 Act, as amended (and earlier Acts), the Registrar could *impose* a limitation or disclaimer as a condition of granting registration, so that the trade mark owner had to accept such a restriction on his rights. Under section 13 of the 1994 Act, both are voluntary. A disclaimer may be offered by the proprietor, and any limitation can only be imposed by agreement. The significance of limitations and disclaimers (which were explained fully in chapter 3) is consequently much reduced.

The *effect* of section 13 should therefore be contrasted with the effect of its predecessor, section 4(2) of the 1938 Act.

Acquiescence (section 48)
Section 48 of the 1994 Act, based on Article 9 of the Directive, provides that after five years' continuous acquiescence in the use of a registered trade mark, the owner of an earlier trade mark or other earlier right, provided there was awareness of that use, ceases to be entitled to apply for a declaration that the registration of the later mark is invalid, or to stop its use, unless the owner of the later mark was acting in bad faith.

The section therefore contemplates that the later mark was allowed on to the Register in circumstances where:

(a)   the owner of the earlier right either did not oppose the later mark, or entered an unsuccessful opposition from which no appeal was made; and
(b)   that there has been five years' use of the later mark with the knowing toleration of the owner of the earlier right, without any attempt to get it cancelled or to sue for infringement.

The plea of acquiescence (see chapter 8) should be understood in the context of section 11(1) of the 1994 Act, explained above, and should be contrasted with the plea of delay when an interlocutory injunction is sought, explained below.

Parallel Imports of Trade-marked Products: the Defence of Exhaustion of Rights (Section 12)

The meaning of 'exhaustion of rights'
The defence of exhaustion (which applies to all types of intellectual property rights) states that once goods which are the subject-matter of a trade mark, patent or copyright have been placed in circulation, the intellectual property owner can no longer object to any subsequent dealings in those goods. The doctrine applies

not just where it is the intellectual property owner who has personally marketed the goods, but where a subsidiary company, licensee or some other person having consent has done so.

Thus, where legitimate goods have been supplied to a wholesaler, in the absence of any contractual provision, the trade mark owner cannot rely on the trade mark right to object to their resale to a particular retailer, or likewise stop the retailer from supplying them to the public in a particular way.

This principle is easy to comprehend if the facts are confined to a trade mark owner whose mark is registered in one country and who does business only in that country. Others can be stopped from copying the mark, but no objection can be raised to goods to which the mark has been affixed by the proprietor. However, if the trade mark owner is a multinational company doing business in many countries of the world and marketing local variations of its products under trade marks which are the subject of multiple national or international registrations, then the picture is more complex.

The meaning of parallel imports
The key to understanding the defence of exhaustion of rights in relation to international trade in goods depends on two related concepts, namely, the territorial nature of intellectual property rights and the difference between infringing imports and parallel imports.

Territorial nature   Intellectual property rights, whether patents, designs, copyright or trade marks, and whether based on legislation or case law, are territorial in nature, that is, they depend for their existence on the laws of a particular country. There are several consequences of this:

(a)   The rights of the intellectual property owner exist only in the territory of the country which 'grants' the right.

(b)   Consequently, an infringement action is only possible in respect of infringing conduct within that same territory. Thus, it is not possible to sue in English courts for the infringement in the United States of America of a copyright which is only recognised in that country (*Tyburn Productions Ltd* v *Conan Doyle* [1991] Ch 75). Equally, an action cannot be brought in Scottish courts for the infringement and passing off of a United Kingdom trade mark in Italy (*James Burrough Distillers plc* v *Speymalt Whisky Distributors Ltd* [1991] RPC 130).

(c)   Conversely, national law, because of its territorial nature, will entitle the intellectual property owner to use the right to keep out of the territory goods imported from another country.

Parallel imports   When goods are imported into the United Kingdom, it must be determined first whether they have originated from a third party who has no connection with the intellectual property owner and who consequently does not have the latter's consent to put the goods into circulation in the exporting country. If this is so, then they are regarded as infringing imports. Intellectual property rights can be utilised to stop their commercial distribution and, if they are counterfeit goods, the intellectual property owner (in the case of trade marks and copyright) can call on the assistance of HM Customs & Excise to prevent their importation (see below).

However, if the imports originated with the intellectual property owner (that is, they were marketed by the owner, or with consent, or by a related company or a licensee, in the exporting country) then they will be viewed as parallel imports. Whether a United Kingdom trade mark owner can use intellectual property law to prevent such parallel imports (the price of which frequently undercuts the price of the domestic product) depends on whether the goods are being imported from a country which is a member of the European Economic Area (the 12 EC Member States plus five of the EFTA countries, Austria, Finland, Iceland, Norway and Sweden) or not.

Parallel imports from within the European Economic Area (section 12)
Section 12(1) of the 1994 Act (copying, albeit not exactly, the wording of Article 7 of the Directive) provides:

A registered trade mark is not infringed by the use of the mark in relation to goods which have been put on the market in the European Economic Area under that trade mark by the proprietor or with his consent.

The difference in wording between the 1994 Act and the Directive is that the Act uses the phrase 'is not infringed' whereas the Directive states that 'the trade mark shall not entitle the proprietor to prohibit'. The same difficulty was encountered in relation to the defence in section 11(3), explained above.

Nevertheless, the simple provision in section 12(1) in effect means that a trade mark owner *cannot* use a United Kingdom registered trade mark to prevent parallel imports emanating from other countries in the EEA. It reflects three decades of case law in which the Court of Justice of the European Communities has sought to reconcile the objectives of the Community with the territorial nature of intellectual property rights. The court has achieved this reconciliation principally by its interpretation of two key Articles in the EC Treaty, namely Articles 30 and 36 (see appendix 5).

Objectives of the European Community   The Treaty of Rome 1957, as amended by the Single European Act 1986, sought to create a common market, the objective of which was to promote trade within a number of countries without the hindrance of barriers to trade. The opening Articles of the Treaty state that the Community shall have as its objectives, amongst others, the removal of restrictions on the import and export of goods, the establishment of a common customs tariff, the abolition of obstacles to freedom of movement for persons, services and capital and a system for ensuring that competition is not distorted.

Article 30   The Community's objective of removing restrictions on the import and export of goods is dealt with in more detail by Articles 30 to 36 of the Treaty. The most important of these is Article 30 (probably one of the most litigated Articles in the entire Treaty) which provides that:

Quantitative restrictions on imports and all measures having equivalent effect shall be prohibited between Member States.

This has been interpreted to mean that any trading rules enacted by Member States which are capable of hindering, whether directly or indirectly, whether actually or potentially, intra-Community trade, are prohibited. Over the years, a large body of case law has identified which national laws are contrary to Article 30. These range from provisions dealing with labelling and origin marking to price controls, banning the sale of goods unless they comply with certain local technical requirements and reserving names, symbols or shapes of containers for domestic products. The Court of Justice has made it clear that goods which are lawfully marketed in one Member State must be accepted in other Member States even if they do not meet local requirements. Free movement of goods can be stopped only on very narrow and specific grounds, found either in Article 36 of the Treaty or in the case law of the Court.

The exception found in Article 36   Article 36 provides for several exceptions to the principle of free movement of goods, including 'restrictions and prohibitions' which are for 'the protection of industrial and commercial property'. The phrase 'industrial and commercial property' can be equated to intellectual property.

It might be thought that this saving enables intellectual property rights to be used to prevent the free movement of goods in all cases, but the Court of Justice has made it clear that this saving must be read in the light of the second sentence of Article 36, namely, that such protection must not amount to a means of 'arbitrary discrimination or a disguised restriction on trade between Member States'.

To summarise the extensive case law, this means that, thanks to Article 36, the owner of an intellectual property right can rely on the protection given by national law to prevent infringing imports (as defined above), but because of the importance of Article 30, no objection can be made to the importation of goods put in circulation in another Member State. Any attempt by the owner of the right to stop such parallel imports will be a 'disguised restriction on trade' and contrary to the objectives of the single market.

This principle is, of course, the defence of exhaustion outlined above, but it is Community-wide exhaustion. The Court of Justice has justified the defence of exhaustion of rights by saying that the specific aim of intellectual property (whether patents, copyright or trade marks) is only to allow the owner to control the first marketing of the goods covered by that right. Once that first marketing has occurred, anywhere in the EEA, the proprietor of the right should not be able to object to subsequent dealings in the goods (including their movement across national boundaries) unless they are tampered with in some way.

Case law of the Court of Justice of the European Communities   The Court of Justice has considered the doctrine of exhaustion of rights in cases involving trade marks, patents, copyright and designs. The principles decided in the cases are of universal application, so that, for example, a rule laid down in a case involving patents is equally applicable to trade marks and vice versa. Copyright cases, however, should be treated with a degree of caution because of the nature of copyright as a bundle of rights rather than a single right.

The principal points emerging from the case law can be summarised thus:

(a)   Early cases were decided on the basis of competition laws because Article 30 had a lengthy transitional period. Hence, in *Établissements Consten SA* v

Commission (Cases 56 & 58/64) [1966] ECR 299 an agreement between the German manufacturer of consumer goods and its French distributor under which the latter was allowed to register Grundig's trade mark in its own name in France and then use the mark to keep out lower-priced imports from a German distributor was held to infringe Article 85. It amounted to a deliberate attempt to use trade mark rights to insulate national markets from price competition by parallel importers.

(b)   Once Article 30 was fully operational, the Court was quick to establish the principle of Community-wide exhaustion in *Deutsche Grammophon Gesellschaft mbH* v *Metro-SB-Grossmärkte GmbH & Co. KG* (Case 78/70) [1971] ECR 487. The Court held here that a German record company could not rely on copyright to stop a supermarket from selling sound recordings bought from the record company's French distributor, even though the price of such records undercut the price at which they were sold by the German distributor. The Court went on to state that there is a distinction between the existence and exercise of intellectual property rights. In the case of the former, the specific subject-matter of the intellectual property right gives the owner the right to put goods in circulation for the first time, and consequently, under Article 36, to take action against infringers. In the case of the latter, any attempt to exercise the intellectual property right to control subsequent dealings in legitimate goods will be contrary to Article 30 and not justified under Article 36.

(c)   The doctrine of exhaustion was taken further by *Centrafarm BV* v *Sterling Drug Inc.* (Case 15/74) [1974] ECR 1147) and *Centrafarm BV* v *Winthrop BV* (Case 16/74) [1974] ECR 1183), joined cases involving the attempt to stop the parallel importation of pharmaceuticals from the United Kingdom into Holland by relying on both trade marks and patents. The Court ruled that for the purposes of exhaustion, a corporate group should be taken to be a single entity. Thus it was irrelevant that the trade marks were owned in the United Kingdom by one subsidiary and in Holland by another. A trade mark owner in Member State A (Holland) cannot exercise rights conferred by national law in such a way as to prevent the importation of products bearing the same mark and lawfully marketed in Member State B (the United Kingdom) by the trade mark owner or with the consent of the trade mark owner. The indirect effect of the decision was to expose multinational companies to price competition, as in most cases the parallel importer was exploiting differential pricing created by the intellectual property owner.

(d)   The most criticised decision of the Court was, however, that in *Van Zuylen Frères* v *Hag AG* (Case 192/73) [1974] ECR 731 ('*Hag I*'). The case concerned the attempt by the owner of the CAFÉ HAG trade mark in Belgium to keep out imports originating from the German manufacturer of the same product. The Benelux registration had originally been in the name of the local subsidiary of the German company, but had been subjected to Government appropriation after the Second World War. The Court ruled that because the Benelux and German registrations had a common origin, the German HAG coffee must be treated as a parallel import. The fact that consumers might be misled was irrelevant.

When there is no exhaustion of rights   After the decisions in *Deutsche Grammophon*, *Centrafarm* v *Winthrop* and *Hag I*, the approach of the Court appeared to soften and a series of exceptions to the defence of exhaustion was developed, as follows:

(a) *Non-EEA goods*. In *EMI Records Ltd* v *CBS United Kingdom Ltd* (Case 51/75) [1976] ECR 811, the Court said that Article 30 did not apply to goods coming from outside the Community. Consequently, domestic trade mark law could be used to stop imports of records bearing the COLUMBIA trade mark from the USA. The decision appears to create a 'fortress Europe' situation, as exhaustion of rights will apply only to goods moving *between* Member States. The Court also stated that an agreement in 1918, dividing the trade mark between the two rival record manufacturers, whereby EMI got the mark in Europe, CBS elsewhere, was 'spent' for the purposes of Article 85.

(b) *Infringing imports*. Where the goods originate from an unconnected third party, who has no legal or economic links with the trade mark owner, then trade mark rights can always be used to keep out the third party's products (*Terrapin (Overseas) Ltd* v *Terranova Industrie C. A. Kapferer & Co.* (Case 119/75) [1976] ECR 1039), even if the trade mark in question has a descriptive element (*Deutsche Renault AG* v *Audi AG* (Case C-317/91) *Financial Times*, 7 December 1993).

(c) *No consent*. There is no consent to the marketing of the goods where they have been marketed by another under the terms of a compulsory patent licence (*Pharmon BV* v *Hoechst AG* (Case 19/84) [1985] ECR 2281); nor where the trade mark was appropriated and given to the third party without consent. This last point is the result of the decision in *Hag II* (*SA CNL-Sucal NV* v *Hag GF AG* (Case C-10/89) [1990] ECR I-3711), where the Court expressly departed from its previous ruling in *Hag I* in a case involving the reverse set of facts. Because the ownership of the mark had been involuntarily changed, there could be no consent on the part of the trade mark owner, so that the Benelux goods could therefore be stopped. *Hag II* has recently been extended by the Court to cover the situation where the trade mark owner voluntarily assigns the trade mark to another enterprise (*IHT Internationale Heiztechnik GmbH* v *Ideal-Standard GmbH* (Case C-9/93) *Financial Times*, 28 June 1994). The key issue in both *Hag II* and the *IHT* case was the risk of consumer confusion between two products emanating from different sources.

The importance of consent The Court in the cases of *Pharmon* v *Hoechst*, *Hag II* and *IHT* stressed the importance of determining whether the intellectual property owner *actually* consented to the marketing of the goods in the country of export. Consent is the key factor in the defence of exhaustion. Consequently, the following issues are of no concern in determining whether consent exists:

(a) *Whether national protection is available*. The intellectual property owner cannot argue that goods are infringing imports merely because they were marketed in a Member State where legal protection was not available. If the goods were put in circulation in that country by the owner, regardless of protection, then the owner must accept the consequences (*Merck & Co. Inc* v *Stephar BV* (Case 187/80) [1981] ECR 2063). The converse is also true: if the third party takes advantage of the lack of protection in the exporting Member State, any lack of consent by the intellectual property owner means that the goods will be infringing imports when they reach the importing Member State (*EMI Electrola GmbH* v *Patricia Im- und Export* (Case 341/87) [1989] ECR 79; *Warner Bros Inc.* v *Christiansen* (Case 158/86) [1988] ECR 2605).

(b) *Disparities of national law.* The court has equally been dismissive of the argument that differences between national laws of themselves raise an artificial barrier to trade which the trade mark owner is trying to exploit. Such differences must be tolerated until the Commission's harmonisation programme is completed (*Thetford Corp.* v *Fiamma SpA* (Case 35/87) [1988] ECR 3585; *Industrie Diensten Groep BV* v *Beele* (Case 6/81) [1982] ECR 707; *Keurkoop BV* v *Nancy Kean Gifts BV* (Case 144/81) [1982] ECR 2853). The only exception is where national law itself operates to discriminate between patent licensees on the basis of nationality (*Allen & Hanburys Ltd* v *Generics (UK) Ltd* (Case 434/85) [1988] ECR 1245).

Comparison with the 1938 Act   Section 12(1) of the 1994 Act should be contrasted with section 4(3)(a) of the 1938 Act, as amended. This was to the effect that the trade mark right was deemed not to be infringed where it was used in relation to goods if those goods had been marked by the proprietor or registered user, or if the proprietor had expressly or impliedly consented to the use of the mark.

Because of the definition of 'trade mark' in section 68(1) of the 1938 Act, the section 4(3)(a) defence of exhaustion of rights was confined to the use of United Kingdom registered marks. Thus, the section could not apply where goods marked in another country with a mark registered in *that* country were imported into the United Kingdom (*Castrol Ltd* v *Automotive Oil Supplies Ltd* [1983] RPC 315).

However, because of the supremacy of Community law, the cases outlined above meant that section 4(3)(a) had to be read in the light of Article 30 of the EC Treaty as regards imports coming from another Member State of the Community.

The exception to exhaustion (section 12(2))
Section 12(2) provides:

> Subsection (1) does not apply where there exist legitimate reasons for the proprietor to oppose further dealings in the goods (in particular, where the condition of the goods has been changed or impaired after they have been put on the market).

This reflects Article 7(2) of the Directive, which in turn is based on a specific group of cases decided by the Court of Justice dealing with the repackaging of pharmaceutical products.

In *Hoffmann-La Roche & Co. AG* v *Centrafarm Vertriebsgesellschaft Pharmazeutiscker Erzeugnisse mbH* (Case 102/77) [1978] ECR 1139 the importer took packets of the tranquilliser VALIUM as sold in the United Kingdom, repackaged the tablets so that they would be acceptable in Germany and added the trade mark together with its own name and address to the repackaged goods. The re-affixing of the trade mark was held by the Court of Justice to undermine the function of the trade mark in guaranteeing the quality of the goods, so that they became infringing imports. The Court went on, however, to provide guidelines for the parallel importer who wishes to repackage goods without incurring liability for trade mark infringement.

The importer in *Centrafarm BV* v *American Home Products Corporation* (Case 3/78) [1978] ECR 1823 overstepped the line even more. Not only were the goods repackaged, but the mark was changed from that registered by the trade mark owner in the country of export to that registered in the country of import. Again, the importer was held to infringe the latter registration. The Court accepted that the trade mark owner had good reason to have different marks in different Member States, but added the warning that if different marks were chosen simply to partition the single market, the parallel importer would be at liberty to change the marks without incurring liability.

In *Pfizer Inc.* v *Eurim-Pharm GmbH* (Case 1/81) [1981] ECR 2913 the parallel importer did follow the Court's earlier guidelines, with the result that it did not commit trade mark infringement.

Section 12(2) of the 1994 Act should be contrasted with section 6 of the 1938 Act, as amended. This provided that where a written contract imposed obligations as to how a trade mark was to be used in relation to goods, then breach of those obligations would be deemed to infringe the trade mark. The section specifically dealt with such conduct as altering the condition of the goods, altering the trade mark, applying another trade mark to the goods or the addition of other matter likely to injure the reputation of the trade mark. However, section 6 was confined to written contracts. Hence, when the goods came into the hands of a third party not having privity of contract with the trade mark owner or registered user, the section would not be available.

It can thus be seen that section 12(2) of the 1994 Act is considerably wider than its predecessor in enabling the trade mark owner to object to the conduct of third parties who in some way tamper with the goods or the trade mark.

Imports from outside the European Economic Area

How are parallel imports from outside the EEA dealt with under the 1994 Act? The answer has to be that there is no specific provision. Guidance, though, can be found in several places:

(a) Because of the wording of section 12(1) and the fact that it refers only to goods coming from the EEA, it can be inferred that the defence of exhaustion of rights does not apply to goods coming from any country other than a member of the EEA.

(b) Reference to the commentary on the 1984 draft of the Directive and Regulation (see COM (84) 470 final of 31 July 1984) reveals that the Commission decided against legislating for the international exhaustion of rights, and settled instead for Community-wide exhaustion. The Commission was no doubt influenced by the ruling in *EMI* v *CBS* that Article 30 had no application to non-EEA goods.

(c) Case law decided under section 4(3)(a) of the 1938 Act, as amended, had ultimately determined that there was no international exhaustion of rights. Such case law is outlined below.

For these reasons, therefore, parallel imports from a country other than a member of the EEA *can* be stopped by relying on a United Kingdom registered trade mark.

Cases decided under the 1938 Act   Cases in which it was necessary to apply section 4(3)(a) of the 1938 Act, as amended, focused on two issues: the exact scope of the section, and the issue of consent.

(a) *The scope of section 4(3)(a).* Because of its use of the phrase 'the right to the use of a trade mark given by registration as aforesaid' (referring back to the opening words of section 4(1)), section 4(3)(a) was interpreted as having territorial effect. It applied only to marks entered on the United Kingdom Register. Therefore, where goods which were imported from a non-EEA country bore a trade mark registered in that country, section 4(3)(a) could have no application, even though there might have been a parallel registration for the identical mark in the United Kingdom (*Castrol Ltd* v *Automotive Oil Supplies Ltd* [1983] RPC 315, *Colgate-Palmolive Ltd* v *Markwell Finance Ltd* [1989] RPC 497, and *Wellcome Foundation* v *Attorney-General for Hong Kong* [1992] EIPR D-263, the last-mentioned applying the same interpretation to marks entered on the Hong Kong Register).

(b) *The issue of consent.* The trade mark owner was free to stipulate, in the case of goods marketed elsewhere than the EEA, that such goods were intended for a particular market and were not to be exported therefrom. Such a contractual stipulation would negative any consent to the sale of the goods elsewhere. Where there were variants in the goods, whether due to climatic conditions or for some other reason, these variations pointed to there not being consent (*Castrol*; *Colgate*), although the absence of differences between the products was not fatal because of the territorial interpretation of section 4(3)(a) (*Wellcome*).

Unregistered marks   A trade mark owner may seek, in the alternative, to rely on passing off to prevent parallel imports. If there are differences between goods produced by the trade mark owner for the domestic market and the imported goods, such difference may well lead to consumer disappointment and confusion, with resultant damage to goodwill. Passing off will therefore be made out (*Colgate*).

The Revlon Case   The decision of the Court of Appeal in *Revlon Inc.* v *Cripps & Lee Ltd* [1980] FSR 87 stands out as not being in accord with the above cases. It propounded the notion of worldwide exhaustion of rights, an objective subsequently abandoned by the EC Commission when preparing the Directive and Regulation (see above). For this reason it should be treated as unsound.

Remedies for Trade Mark Infringement (Sections 14 to 21)

General remedies (section 14)
Unlike its predecessor, the Trade Marks Act 1994 in section 14 states what remedies are available for trade mark infringement. The section, however, does nothing more than restate the common law position. The remedies referred to by the section are as follows:

(a) *Damages.* As trade mark infringement is a form of statutory tort, the purpose of an award of damages is to restore the plaintiff financially to the position it would have been in had the wrong not been committed. Although in copyright and usually, but not always, in patents, the method of calculation is based on a reasonable licence fee, this is generally regarded as unsuitable for trade mark infringement. The starting-point is the lost sales revenue suffered by the plaintiff. With the deregulation of licensing, it remains to be seen whether loss of opportunity to license will become a recognised head of loss (see chapter 12). In contrast to the other two forms of intellectual property, the defendant's innocence is no bar to damages being awarded (*Gillette UK Ltd* v *Edenwest Ltd* [1994] RPC 279).

(b) *Account of profits.* Whilst damages are the common law method of providing compensation, an account of profits is an equitable remedy and hence is discretionary. A plaintiff cannot claim both forms of compensation and has to elect for one or the other. An account of profits has the disadvantage of being treated by the court as condoning all past acts of infringement. However, its method of calculation, although not straightforward, aims to make the defendant hand over all profits made from the acts of infringement. Depending on the defendant's volume of sales and the costs of setting up the enterprise, it could provide better compensation than damages. For an example of how the remedy works in the case of copyright infringement, see *Potton Ltd* v *Yorkclose Ltd* [1990] FSR 11. An account of profits will not be awarded in cases of innocent trade mark infringement (*Gillette UK Ltd* v *Edenwest Ltd*).

(c) *Injunctions.* A distinction must be drawn between an injunction granted by the court after trial of the action (a final injunction), which will be awarded only where there is clear evidence that the defendant will continue to infringe and where damages will not be adequate to compensate the plaintiff, and an interlocutory injunction. The latter, governed by the principles laid down in *American Cyanamid Co.* v *Ethicon Ltd* [1975] AC 396, is a court order granted between the issue of the writ and trial, intended to preserve the *status quo* until the trial of the action. In practice, the decision to award a plaintiff an interlocutory injunction is often accepted by the parties in intellectual property disputes as conclusive of the matter and the case is taken no further.

In *American Cyanamid Co.* v *Ethicon Ltd*, Lord Diplock said that an interlocutory injunction may be granted if:

(i)   the plaintiff establishes that there is an arguable case;

(ii)   the plaintiff cannot be compensated in damages at the trial if an injunction is not granted to stop the defendant's infringement;

(iii)   the defendant can be compensated in damages if the court ultimately finds against the plaintiff; and

(iv)   the balance of convenience favours the granting of the remedy.

Matters relevant in considering the last issue are: the relative size of the parties, their ability to pay damages, the level of investment undertaken by either party, and the risk to the defendant's employees if the product cannot be sold. If the plaintiff is successful in seeking an interlocutory injunction, a cross-undertaking in damages will be required, that is, a promise to compensate the defendant for lost business should the defendant ultimately be successful in the main trial.

Other interlocutory remedies available in intellectual property actions include *Anton Piller* orders (a court order instructing the defendant to admit the plaintiff's solicitor to premises which are under the defendant's control with a view to taking evidence of the infringement which might otherwise be destroyed) and *Mareva* orders (a court order freezing the defendant's assets to ensure that they are not dissipated in an attempt to frustrate the plaintiff's right to compensation).

All equitable remedies (account of profits, injunctions, *Anton Piller* orders and *Mareva* orders) are discretionary. The court will consider, amongst other factors, whether the plaintiff has acted promptly to protect its interests (delay will be fatal), whether the plaintiff's own conduct is faultless and whether the award of an equitable remedy would cause hardship to the defendant. An equitable remedy will not be granted if it cannot be supervised by the court. Damages, however, being a common law remedy, are not discretionary.

Erasure of offending sign (section 15)

Section 15 of the 1994 Act sets out in statutory form another remedy which was recognised as part of the court's inherent jurisdiction in trade mark infringement cases, namely, the power to award that the infringing sign be 'erased, removed or obliterated' from any infringing goods, materials or articles in the defendant's control.

Such an order can only be made once there is a finding that infringement has been committed, and the remedy is in the court's discretion. If the court believes that the order will not be complied with, it can instead order the goods to be delivered to another person for the purpose of removing the infringing sign.

Delivery up of infringing goods, materials and articles (section 16)

Section 16 of the 1994 Act puts into statutory form the court's power to order *a person* to deliver to the trade mark owner any infringing goods, materials or articles which are in that person's possession, custody or control *in the course of a business*. The request for delivery up of infringing copies must be made by the trade mark owner. The wording of section 16 is similar to that of section 99 of the CDPA 1988. This latter section has been interpreted to mean that an order for delivery up can be made against an innocent retailer which has infringing copies in its possession (*Lagenes Ltd v It's At (UK) Ltd* [1991] FSR 492).

A court order under section 16 must be made within six years of the application of the trade mark to the infringing goods or materials, or the manufacture of the infringing articles, unless the trade mark owner was prevented by fraud or concealment from discovering the infringement (section 18).

Destruction or forfeiture of infringing goods (section 19)

Once infringing goods, materials or articles have been delivered to the trade mark owner, then a further application may be made for their destruction or forfeiture under section 19. In deciding whether to make an order under section 19, the court must take into account other remedies which might be available to the trade mark owner and any licensee.

Anyone else who might have an interest in the goods is to be notified. Such a person might include a supplier of raw materials who has an interest in the goods by virtue of a retention of title clause; or, in the case of pirated copyright works to which a counterfeit trade mark has been affixed, the owner of the relevant copyright.

If an order is not made under section 19, the goods are to be returned to the person in whose control they were prior to the making of the order under section 18.

Meaning of 'infringing goods, materials or articles' (section 17)

Section 17, obviously inspired by section 27 of the CDPA 1988, provides definitions of 'infringing goods' (section 17(2) and (3)), 'infringing materials' (section 17(4)) and 'infringing articles' (section 17(5)). It should be read in conjunction with the remedies provided by sections 15 and 16, and with the acts of infringement stipulated by section 10, in particular the act of contributory infringement found in section 10(5).

The definitions of 'infringing materials' and 'infringing articles' (the former comprising labelling, packaging, business papers and advertising material, the latter comprising items such as printing blocks which enable a trade mark to be replicated) are straightforward and should be seen as a useful clarification of the remedies available to the trade mark owner.

The definition of 'infringing goods' is, however, problematical. This definition, as already indicated, is borrowed from section 27 of the CDPA 1988. There, the definition of 'infringing copy' appears in the context of provisions dealing with liability for the secondary infringement of copyright, such provisions prohibiting the sale, hire, distribution, possession in the course of trade, and importation of infringing copies of a copyright work.

The Trade Marks Act 1994 does not create any specific form of liability for secondary infringement, simply because the nature of the trade mark right (the right to stop the use of the same or similar sign in the course of trade) is quite different from the basic copyright right (the right to stop the work being copied). Subsections (2) and (3) of section 17 therefore sit awkwardly in the 1994 Act. In view of the nature of the trade mark right, was there really any need to define 'infringing goods'?

Further, the section refers in the definition of 'infringing goods' to 'goods [which] are proposed to be imported into the United Kingdom and the application of the sign in the United Kingdom to [which] . . . would be an infringement of the registered trade mark' (other than those governed by an enforceable Community right). This tortuous provision causes two difficulties.

First, by referring to imported goods other than those covered by Community law, it hints at the defence of exhaustion, which is surely unnecessary in view of the detailed case law subsisting behind section 12, explained above. Secondly, by using the phrase 'would be an infringement of the registered trade mark', it conjures up cases relating to parallel imports of copyright works (such as *CBS United Kingdom Ltd* v *Charmdale Records Distributors Ltd* [1981] Ch 91). In view of the differences noted above between the trade mark right and the right subsisting in copyright, such terminology appears inappropriate.

The position of the licensee (sections 30 and 31)

Section 31 of the 1994 Act provides that an exclusive licensee is to have the same rights and remedies and be subject to the same defences as the trade mark owner. Consequently, the licensee can bring infringement proceedings in its own name, subject only to the terms of the licence. The exclusive licensee's rights are to be concurrent with those of the trade mark owner, so that the court, when awarding damages, must take account of any other pecuniary remedy available to the other party. No account of profits can be directed if the other party has been awarded a pecuniary remedy; and any account of profits which is directed can be apportioned between trade mark owner and exclusive licensee.

In the case of a non-exclusive licensee, section 30 enables such a person to bring infringement proceedings in its own name where the trade mark owner has refused or failed to respond to a request to start such proceedings. Where the trade mark owner does bring the proceedings, any loss suffered by the licensee is to be taken into account by the court when calculating damages. The court can direct the proceeds of any pecuniary remedy to be held on behalf of the licensee.

Certificate of contested validity

Under section 73 of the 1994 Act, where a defendant has raised as a defence the issue of whether the trade mark is valid under section 47, but the court has rejected that claim, the trade mark owner can request the court to issue a certificate to the effect that the mark is valid. If the validity of the mark is questioned in later proceedings and the trade mark owner obtains final judgment, costs will be calculated on an indemnity basis (section 73 refers to costs being 'solicitor and client' costs, although the Rules of the Supreme Court indicate that the proper calculation would be on an indemnity basis). Section 73 repeats almost verbatim section 47 of the 1938 Act, as amended.

Threats

A new provision in the 1994 Act is section 21, which is based on the equivalent provision found in section 70 of the Patents Act 1977, as amended.

Section 21 provides that where a trade mark owner makes groundless threats of infringement proceedings, 'any person aggrieved' (that is, the person to whom the threats are made) can ask the court for relief under the section. The relief available to the victim of the threats is a declaration that the threats are unjustifiable, an injunction to restrain the continuance of the threats and damages in respect of any loss sustained by the threats.

The onus is placed on the trade mark owner (the defendant in the 'threats' action) to show that the conduct of the victim of the threats (the plaintiff) constituted infringement. Even then, the plaintiff in the 'threats' action may still succeed if the court is convinced that the trade mark is invalid or liable to be revoked.

A 'threats' action is not available to a person who is alleged to have applied the mark to goods or their packaging, or who has imported goods or who has supplied services. Section 21 therefore protects not the 'primary' infringer, but the category of persons who might be sued for infringement under section 10(4), such as wholesalers, retailers and distributors.

Section 21 primarily affects how correspondence prior to the commencement of infringement proceedings is worded. It specifically provides (in section 21(4)) that the mere notification that a mark is registered does not amount to a threat. Further, it does not apply to passing off, which is often pleaded in the alternative to trade mark infringement, nor does it apply to the threat of criminal proceedings for counterfeiting.

Notification to Customs and Excise
The worldwide trade in counterfeit goods (that is, imitation goods which bear a copy of a registered trade mark) has been estimated to be worth 5 per cent of the total of world trade, and developed countries have been trying for some time to persuade developing countries (where most counterfeiting is practised) to take steps to suppress the activity. Whilst agreement on anti-counterfeiting measures was reached in the Trade-Related Aspects of Intellectual Property Agreement (TRIPS) as part of the recently-concluded renegotiation of the General Agreement on Tariffs and Trade (GATT), United Kingdom and Community law have both for some time enabled a trade mark owner to stop the importation into the United Kingdom of counterfeit goods by asking HM Customs and Excise to help.

As regards goods coming into the United Kingdom from countries outside the European Economic Area, section 89 (largely repeating the provisions of section 64A of the 1938 Act, as amended) entitles the owner or licensee of a registered trade mark to give written notice to Customs and Excise that infringing goods, materials or articles are expected to arrive in the United Kingdom and requesting that they be treated as prohibited goods. Such goods cannot then be imported, otherwise than for private and domestic use, the penalty being forfeiture.

Section 90 gives Customs and Excise power to make the necessary regulations dealing with the type of evidence of counterfeiting which may be required, the payment of fees by the trade mark owner and the giving of security. Under section 91, information obtained by Customs and Excise may be passed on to local trading standards officials to enable them to bring a criminal prosecution under section 92 of the Act.

As regards counterfeit goods being imported into the United Kingdom from other countries of the EEA, EC Council Regulation 3842/86 (which is in the process of being revised, and which also covers pirated copyright goods such as videos and sound recordings) contains similar provisions, albeit in greater detail.

Criminal Liability: Counterfeiting (Sections 92, 93, 97 and 98)

Criminal liability for trade mark infringement
As part of the move to deal more effectively with counterfeit goods, section 92 of the 1994 Act provides for criminal liability in respect of trade mark infringement. Such liability is not entirely new, as section 300 of the CDPA 1988 inserted section 58A into the Trade Marks Act 1938, which contained a similar range of offences.

The new section is entitled 'unauthorised use of a trade mark', but is targeted at those who seek to make and sell counterfeit goods. Concern has been expressed, however, that its provisions may be drafted too widely, so that, for example, someone who buys fake LEVI'S jeans whilst on holiday abroad and then later, having tired of them, decides to sell them at a car boot sale, would commit an offence.

The scope of section 92
Section 92 provides that an offence is committed where, without the consent of the trade mark proprietor, a sign which is identical to or likely to be confused with a registered trade mark is applied to goods or their packaging, or where goods bearing such a sign are the subject of commercial dealings, or are in the possession

of the defendant. The defendant's conduct must be with a view to making a gain or with the intent of causing loss to another.

Similar offences are created for those who apply the mark to materials such as labels, business papers and advertisements and for those who make or possess articles (such as printing blocks) which enable copies of the trade mark to be made.

Criminal liability for counterfeiting is confined to where the infringing sign is used in respect of the goods for which the trade mark is registered or to where the trade mark has a reputation in the United Kingdom and the counterfeiting takes unfair advantage of such reputation. In other words, there is no liability for using the registered mark on related goods unless the mark has a reputation. The defendant can escape liability by satisfying the court of the existence of a belief on reasonable grounds that such use was not an infringement of the registered trade mark. The wording of the defence suggests an objective test.

The problem of 'brand copies'

Hopefully, the wording of the defence in section 92 will overcome the problem encountered by the Divisional Court in *Kent County Council* v *Price* [1993] 9 EIPR D-224. Price had been charged under the Trade Descriptions Act 1968 (but not under section 58A of the Trade Marks Act 1938) with applying a false trade description to goods, in that he had sold counterfeit T-shirts. A sign on his market stall stated that these were a 'brand copy'. The court held that his conviction had been rightly set aside by the Crown Court on the ground that the disclaimer negatived the false trade description. The phrase 'brand copy' (which admits trade mark counterfeiting) may well operate to impose liability under section 92.

Trial

The offence of counterfeiting can be tried either by a magistrates' court or the Crown Court. The latter can impose an unlimited fine and/or up to 10 years' imprisonment.

Enforcement of section 92

The enforcement of section 92 is given, by section 93, to trading standards officers employed by local authorities. Previously such enforcement was given to them by section 58D of the 1938 Act, as amended, so the new Act makes no change in practice. Recent press reports indicate that, at the moment, one of the main areas of activity for trading standards officers under the Trade Descriptions Act 1968 is seizing counterfeit trade-marked goods and pirated copyright goods at car boot sales.

By virtue of section 93, trading standards officers are authorised to use all the powers conferred on them under the Trade Descriptions Act 1968 (notably the power to make test purchases and the power to enter premises to inspect and seize goods) when enforcing section 92 of the Trade Marks Act 1994.

Forfeiture

Section 97 of the 1994 Act (which replaces the provisions of sections 58B and 58C of the 1938 Act) gives to those investigating and prosecuting trade mark counterfeiting the new power to apply to courts in England, Wales and Northern Ireland for an order of forfeiture in respect of any infringing goods, materials or articles which have come into their possession.

An application for forfeiture can be made either in the course of criminal proceedings for counterfeiting, or, if no such proceedings are brought, by way of complaint to a magistrates' court. Unlike the previous law, therefore, the ability to seek a forfeiture order does not depend on there being a successful conviction for counterfeiting, although under section 97(3) the court has to be satisfied that an offence has been committed, either under the 1994 Act, the Trade Descriptions Act 1968 or the Theft Act 1968.

If a successful application for forfeiture is made, the goods are to be destroyed in accordance with the court's directions, although, as an alternative, the court may release the goods to a specified person, on condition that the offending sign is removed. Presumably, such goods could then be released on to the market. Section 98 creates similar powers for Scottish courts.

Partners and company directors

Under section 101 of the 1994 Act, criminal proceedings for an offence alleged to have been committed by a partnership are to be brought against the partnership in the name of the firm. However, where a partnership is found guilty of an offence, every partner in the firm can also be prosecuted and punished unless they can prove that they were ignorant of or tried to prevent the offence being committed. Under the same section, where a company commits an offence under the Act, any director, manager, company secretary or similar officer who consented or connived at the offence is equally guilty of an offence.

Transitional Provisions (Schedule 3)

As explained in chapter 9, the transitional provisions relating to infringement and defences thereto are not straightforward.

The basic scheme is set out in paragraph 4(1) of schedule 3. This provides that the sections of the 1994 Act dealing with the effects of registration (that is, sections 9 to 12) apply to existing registrations 'as from the commencement of this Act'. Section 14 (the right to bring infringement proceedings, and the basic remedies available) applies in relation to the infringement of an existing registered mark committed *after* commencement. Does this mean that the commencement date does not count, thereby creating an amnesty for trade mark infringers? Otherwise, the old law continues to apply in relation to infringements committed *before* commencement.

Therefore, the basic rule is that it is the date of the commission of the infringing act which determines whether the old or new law applies.

With regard to defences to infringement, schedule 3 paragraph 4(2), provides that it is not an infringement of an existing registered mark to continue after commencement *any use* which did not amount to infringement of the existing registered mark under the old law. The saving cannot be circumvented by re-registering under the 1994 Act the same or substantially the same trade mark for the same goods or services. Basically, this means that the various defences found in the 1938 Act, as amended, are carried forward. By way of recapitulation, these defences were:

(a)   *Section 4(2).* This provided that a 1938 Act registration did not extend to matter which was the subject of a disclaimer or limitation. Such disclaimers and limitations are in any event carried forward to the new Register by virtue of paragraph 3(3) of schedule 3 to the 1994 Act.

(b)   *Section 4(3)(a).* This was the exhaustion of rights defence, now found in section 12 of the 1994 Act.

(c)   *Section 4(3)(b).* This was the 'spare parts' defence now found in section 11(2)(c) of the 1994 Act.

(d)   *Section 4(4).* This was the saving for concurrent registrations now found in section 11(1) of the 1994 Act.

(e)   *Section 7.* This was the savings for prior rights, now found in section 11(3) of the 1994 Act.

(f)   *Section 8(a).* This was the saving for the use by a trader of its own name or address, now found in section 11(2)(a) of the 1994 Act.

(g)   *Section 8(b).* This was the saving for using the trade mark to describe goods or services, now found in section 11(2)(b) of the 1994 Act.

Where any of these defences applied before commencement date, the *continued use* of the existing registered trade mark in such a manner will not amount to infringement. Such statutory defences will continue to be applied in accordance with the interpretation of the 1938 Act, as amended, and not in accordance with the wording of the 1994 Act.

One point which must be made about the application of paragraph 4(2) of the 1994 Act is this. It refers expressly to 'use which did not amount to infringement' under the old law. This should be distinguished from where use of a trade mark *was* infringement, but because of the wording of the 1938 Act, as amended, *no remedy was available* to the plaintiff. The one example of this which occurred in the 1938 Act was section 5(2). This provided that in the case of a mark entered on Part B of the Register, *'no injunction or other relief'* would be granted where the defendant could show that the use of the mark would not be likely to deceive or cause confusion or be taken as indicating a connection in the course of trade. It had been judicially confirmed that section 5(2) was not a defence, but 'went only as to relief' (per Whitford J in *Thermawear Ltd* v *Vedonis Ltd* [1982] RPC 44). Schedule 3 to the 1994 Act is silent as to the survival or otherwise of section 5(2) in relation to the continuation after commencement of the infringement of a Part B mark.

With regard to remedies for infringement, as indicated above, most of the remedies (including remedies against counterfeiting) referred to in the 1994 Act were in fact available under the 1938 Act, as amended. Paragraph 5 of schedule 3 states, however, that the remedy found in section 16 (an order for delivery up) is to be available whether the infringing goods, materials or articles were made before or after the commencement date. By implication, sections 18 and 19, which are dependent on section 16, must also be available.

CHAPTER ELEVEN
Assignment and Licensing of Trade Marks

Introduction

When first enacted, the Trade Marks Act 1938 was considered to be a radical provision in that, for the first time, it permitted:

(a) the owner of a registered trade mark to dispose of it independently of the goodwill of the business in which it had been used, subject to certain procedural requirements; and

(b) the owner of a registered trade mark to license another to use that mark, subject again to certain requirements, both procedural and substantive.

These changes had the potential to enable registered trade marks to evolve from functioning merely as indicators of origin to becoming the means of 'creating and retaining custom'. However, for a variety of reasons this evolution failed to happen, with the result that the law on the assignment and licensing of trade marks fell short of commercial reality.

The White Paper (in paragraphs 4.34 to 4.39) recognised that the public has grown accustomed to goods or services being supplied under licence from the trade mark owner through a variety of commercial arrangements, including franchise agreements. It also recognised that a registered trade mark is a valuable piece of property, the value of which depends on its reputation with the public. Whilst this value may be diminished through misleading or generic use (see chapter 8), the White Paper considered that it should be the responsibility of the owner rather than the Registrar to ensure it is not devalued. It is, said the White Paper, in the owner's best interests to ensure that the mark is fully yet properly exploited.

The White Paper accordingly proposed a further liberalisation of the law relating to the assignment and licensing of registered trade marks. With one exception (explained below), the Trade Marks Act 1994 fulfils the promises contained in the White Paper. However, it should not be assumed that there has been total deregulation of assignment and licensing. Certain procedural requirements must still be observed with regard to the recording of such transactions. Further, despite the reforms of assignment and licensing of registered trade marks contained in the 1994 Act, such transactions must be considered in the light of European Community law, in particular the rules on free movement of goods and on competition law.

This chapter will therefore consider: how the 1994 Act treats the registered trade mark as an item of personal property (sections 22, 23, 26 and 27); how registered trade marks are to be assigned (sections 24 and 25); how registered trade marks are to be licensed (sections 28 to 31 inclusive, plus section 25); and the impact of Community law on the foregoing.

Trade Marks as Personal Property (Sections 22, 23, 26 and 27)

The Directive
The Directive is silent on what property rights are to be ascribed to trade marks. This is hardly surprising in view of Article 222 of the EC Treaty, which declares that 'This Treaty shall in no way prejudice the rules in Member States governing the system of property ownership'. By implication, therefore, it is left to Member States to decide what property rights flow from trade marks.

A similar approach can be perceived in the Community Trade Mark Regulation, which provides for the law of the Member State where the Community trade mark owner is domiciled or established to determine the property rights in such a mark (Article 16 of the Regulation; and see chapter 14).

Registered trade marks as personal property
Section 22 of the 1994 Act simply declares that a registered trade mark is personal property (in Scotland, incorporeal movable property). Section 22 should be seen as amplifying the somewhat circular statement in section 2, which is to the effect that a registered trade mark is a property right obtained by registration under the 1994 Act.

By contrast, the 1938 Act, as amended, was silent as to the nature of the property right in a trade mark. Section 22 of the 1994 Act should not, however, be taken as introducing any change in the law: it merely confirms what had previously been understood, namely that trade marks are a form of intangible personalty.

Co-ownership
Section 23(1) provides that where a registered trade mark is granted to two or more persons jointly, each of them is entitled, subject to any agreement to the contrary, to an equal undivided share in the trade mark.

This provision, described during the House of Lords discussion of the Bill as a 'bit of a minefield' (*Hansard* (HL/PBC), 19 January 1994, col. 69) is modelled on section 36 of the Patents Act 1977, as amended. In effect, where two or more persons are entitled to a trade mark, the section creates a tenancy in common (despite the presence of the word 'jointly'). This means that each owner is deemed to have an identifiable share of the mark.

Section 23 goes on to explain some of the consequences of this co-ownership:

(a)   each co-owner is entitled, for its own benefit and without the consent of the other, to do any act which would amount to infringement of the registered trade mark (section 23(3)); but

(b)   one co-owner may not, without the consent of the other(s) license or assign the mark (section 23(4)); and

(c)   any co-owner can bring infringement proceedings, although the action may not continue unless the other co-owner is either joined as a plaintiff or added as a defendant. A co-owner who is added as a defendant does not incur any liability for costs. A single co-owner can always seek interlocutory relief (section 23(5)).

Section 23 is, however, silent on whether use by one co-owner accrues for the benefit of the other.

Section 23(6) provides that nothing in the section affects the mutual rights and obligations of trustees or personal representatives: such persons, of course, hold property as joint tenants.

Section 23 should be compared with section 63 of the 1938 Act, as amended. This had provided:

> Where the relations between two or more persons interested in a trade mark are such that no one of them is entitled as between himself and the other or others of them to use it except—
> (a)   on behalf of both or all of them, or
> (b)   in relation to an article with which both or all of them are connected in the course of trade,
> those persons may be registered as joint proprietors of the trade mark, and this Act shall have effect in relation to any rights to the use of the trade mark vested in those persons as if those rights had been vested in a single person.
>
> Subject as aforesaid, nothing in this Act shall authorise the registration of two or more persons who use a trade mark independently, or propose so to use it, as joint proprietors thereof.

Despite its obscure wording, section 63 of the 1938 Act, as amended, had the merit of creating a joint tenancy of a trade mark. Thus no single owner could point to a specific share of the mark, and if one died, ownership of the mark passed automatically to the survivor or survivors. Further, section 63 made it clear that use by one owner was deemed use by all.

Returning to section 23 of the 1994 Act, it creates a danger of fragmented ownership reminiscent of pre-1925 land law by imposing a tenancy in common where a trade mark is the subject of co-ownership. One example will suffice to illustrate the potential nightmare. Suppose that A and B are co-owners of a registered trade mark. A might hand over its share (with B's consent) to C and D. Later, B might hand over its share to E and F. The process might be repeated several times over. Section 23 contains no restriction on the number of times the co-ownership of a registered trade mark might be split.

Given that the trade mark is an important marketing tool it is difficult to envisage *why* any co-owner would agree to such fragmented ownership. This would surely devalue the trade mark, and might render it deceptive for revocation proceedings (although it is by no means clear whether section 46(1)(d) of the 1994 Act covers deception as to trade origin – see chapter 8). Further, the need to get the consent of all the co-owners to an assignment or licence would prove highly inconvenient, albeit necessary.

In response, it must be said that the philosophy of the White Paper, as explained above, is that it should be left to the trade mark owner to look after the value of the mark by not entering into transactions which render it deceptive.

It is possible, however, to envisage ownership becoming fragmented through the death of one or more of the co-owners, with the trade mark devolving to different people under the law of succession.

The conclusion to be drawn from section 23 is that a tenancy in common is a totally inappropriate form of co-ownership for a trade mark, and that it would have been better to continue the scheme of joint tenancy favoured by the 1938 Act. By copying a provision derived from patent law (where there is no technical objection to the tenancy in common of a patent, with each owner taking a quantified share of the benefit of the invention), the 1994 Act ignores the fact that a trade mark is conceptually quite different from a patent (see chapter 1).

It must be noted, though, that the effect of section 23 is stated to be 'subject to any agreement to the contrary'. Co-owners are therefore free to stipulate that their trade mark is subject to a joint tenancy.

Trusts and equities
Section 26 of the 1994 Act provides that no notice of any trust is to be entered on the Register, although any equitable interest existing in a trade mark can be enforced in like manner as in respect of any other personal property. Such provision is virtually identical to section 64 of the 1938 Act, as amended.

Property rights in trade mark applications
Section 27 of the 1994 Act provides that the provisions of sections 22 to 26 inclusive are to apply equally to applications for trade marks, with modifications where necessary. It may be queried whether this provision does not conflict with section 2 of the Act, which declares that a registered trade mark is a property right *'obtained by registration . . .* under this Act'. Nevertheless, as the White Paper pointed out (in paragraph 4.47), it was felt to be inconvenient that pending applications could not be assigned under the 1938 Act, as amended. The 1994 Act overcomes this inconvenience, but at the expense of logic.

Unregistered marks
The 1994 Act is silent (as was its predecessor) as to the nature of the property right in an unregistered trade mark. *Dicta* from passing-off cases such as *Reddaway* v *Banham* [1896] AC 199 and *A. G. Spalding & Bros* v *A. W. Gamage Ltd* (1915) 32 RPC 273 suggested that the property right in the case of an unregistered mark lay in the goodwill of the business in which the mark had been used, rather than in the mark itself. Given the likely impact of the 1994 Act on passing off (see chapter 2), this principle may require reconsideration by the courts.

Transitional Provisions (Schedule 3)

Schedule 3, paragraph 7, provides that section 23 of the 1994 Act is to apply to an existing registered mark which was previously the subject of joint ownership as from the commencement of this Act. However, as long as the relationship between the co-owners satisfies the description in section 63 of the 1938 Act, as amended, there is taken to be an agreement excluding the operation of section 23(1) and (3) of the 1994 Act.

Paragraph 7 appears to create a degree of uncertainty, because whether an existing registered mark is subject to a joint tenancy or tenancy in common will ultimately have to be decided by the court by reference to section 63 of the 1938 Act, as amended.

Assignment of Trade Marks (Sections 24 and 25)

The Directive
The Directive is silent on the ability to assign a registered trade mark, again in consequence of the effect of Article 222 of the EC Treaty (see above). The ability to assign a national trade mark is dependent on the domestic property law of each Member State.

The basic provision
The principal provision in the 1994 Act dealing with the assignment of registered trade marks is section 24. This declares in subsection (1) that a registered trade mark is transmissible by assignment, testamentary disposition or operation of law in the same way as other personal property. The subsection then adds that the mark can be transmitted in connection with the goodwill of a business or independently thereof.

Though using more modern wording, this provision differs little from that found in section 22(1) of the 1938 Act, as amended. This latter provision, considered to be revolutionary, had abrogated the common law rule that a trade mark could not be disposed of independently from the goodwill of the business in which it had been used. 'Goodwill' was usually taken to mean 'the attractive force which brings in custom' (*Commissioners of Inland Revenue* v *Muller & Co.'s Margarine Ltd* [1891] AC 217 at p. 222, per Lord Macnaghten).

The common law principle that a trade mark, whether registered or unregistered, could neither be assigned separately from its owner's business (nor indeed licensed) had been definitively established by the House of Lords in *Bowden Wire Co. Ltd* v *Bowden Brake Co. Ltd* (1914) 31 RPC 385. Such prohibition was based firmly on the origin function of a trade mark, so that if the link between the mark and the business were broken, the mark would become deceptive and hence 'disentitled to protection in a court of justice' (*Pinto* v *Badman* (1891) 8 RPC 181). Attempts to get round the common law rule by trying to segregate a portion of the goodwill and allocate it to a particular mark were firmly rejected (*Re Sinclair Ltd's Trade Mark* (1932) 49 RPC 123). However, there was nothing to stop a trade mark owner from dividing the business and assigning marks along with that part of the goodwill which had been divested, provided the business which was retained was in different goods (*Sunbeam Motor Car Co.'s Application* (1916) 33 RPC 389).

Partial assignment
Section 24(2) of the 1994 Act enables an assignment of a registered trade mark to be total or partial, partial assignments being stated to be:

(a)   those which relate to some but not all of the goods or services for which the mark is registered; or
(b)   those which relate to the use of the mark in a particular manner or particular locality.

The 1938 Act, as amended, had provided in section 22(2) for there to be an assignment for some of the goods or services for which the mark was registered, in line with the *Sunbeam* case noted above.

The 1994 Act, however, breaks new ground by enabling there to be a partial assignment as to locality or a partial assignment as to manner of use.

Having a partial assignment as to locality would not have been possible under the 1938 Act, as amended, except where the two proprietors had separate export markets (section 22(4) and (6)). It is a point on which, as indicated, the Directive is silent, but given that the Directive permits a trade mark to be *licensed* for part of a Member State (which is enacted in section 28 of the 1994 Act, explained below), then it seems logical for the 1994 Act to permit a partial *assignment* on the same basis. On the other hand, to fragment a trade mark between different owners for different parts of the United Kingdom would surely render the mark deceptive. Customers, after all, are highly mobile and are likely to assume that goods or services bought in one part of the country come from the same source as those bought in another part.

It is even more difficult to envisage a partial assignment as to the *manner of use*, as distinct from a partial assignment as to *some of the goods or services*. Whilst a licence as to manner of use might be appropriate for a patent, it goes against the fundamental nature of a trade mark. Such division of the mark would be likely to confuse consumers.

This raises two points of contrast between the 1994 Act and its predecessor:

(a) the 1938 Act, as amended, contained a public interest provision rendering *ineffective* any assignment which caused public deception or confusion (section 22(4) and (6)); and

(b) the 1938 Act also contained a mechanism whereby the parties to a proposed assignment could seek the Registrar's advice as to whether it might be against the public interest (section 22(5)).

It is interesting to note that the White Paper in paragraph 4.45 promised that any new legislation would retain:

(a) a provision making *void* any assignment which would be likely to deceive or cause confusion; and

(b) a provision enabling the parties to seek the Registrar's view on this question.

The 1994 Act does neither of these things.

Furthermore, as explained in chapter 8, it is unclear whether section 46(1)(d) is available to enable the revocation of a trade mark which has been the subject of a partial assignment resulting in deception to the public as to trade origin. If it is ultimately decided that the section is so available, then the effect of a deceptive assignment under the 1994 Act will be different from the effect of a deceptive assignment under the 1938 Act.

Under the 1994 Act, the partial yet deceptive assignment operates to transfer the mark to the new owner. There is the risk that it may be subject to a revocation action (admittedly involving the expense and uncertainty of litigation). Alternatively, customers may simply be deterred from a repeat purchase of the goods or services, with the risk of a resultant loss of business for the assignee (which would be in line with the deregulatory philosophy behind the 1994 Act). By contrast, under the 1938 Act, as amended, a deceptive assignment was stated to be ineffective (see above).

Examination of the Community Trade Mark Regulation reveals that although Article 17 permits the assignment of a Community trade mark with or without goodwill, and for all or some of the goods or services for which it is registered, such assignment has to be for the whole of the Community. No other form of partial assignment is permitted. Further, the Community Trade Mark Office has the power to refuse to register a partial assignment where it will mislead the public, unless the assignee agrees to limit the registration in some way (recital 10 of the Preamble to the Regulation, plus Article 17(4)).

Formalities
Section 24(3) of the 1994 Act requires the assignment of a registered trade mark to be in writing, signed by the assignor. This does not represent any change in the law as found in section 25(1) of the 1938 Act, as amended. Section 24(4) of the 1994 Act also enables a registered trade mark to be assigned by way of security.

The need for registration
In addition to the need for an assignment to be in writing, section 25(1) of the 1994 Act requires any 'registrable transaction' (that is, any assignment, licence, grant of security, assent or court order transferring a registered trade mark or any right in or under it) to be entered on the Register. The application is to be made by the person claiming to be entitled to the trade mark by virtue of a registrable transaction (for example, an assignee or chargee) or by any other person claiming to be affected by such a transaction.

Until recorded an assignment will be ineffective 'as against a person acquiring a conflicting interest in the registered trade mark in ignorance of it' (section 25(3)(a)). It is not clear from the wording to what extent this is a reflection of the bona fide purchaser rule found in the law of real property.

The 1938 Act, as amended, was silent as to the effect of an unrecorded assignment on a third party. Section 25(3) provided that an unrecorded assignment 'shall not be admitted in evidence in any court in proof of the title to a trade mark unless the court otherwise directs'. Section 25(3) therefore dealt with the position of the assignee who wished to bring infringement proceedings, but did not clearly spell out how priorities in a trade mark were to be determined.

Under the 1994 Act, an application to record *any* registrable transaction must be made within six months of the date of the transaction or as soon as practicable thereafter, otherwise the new owner or licensee cannot claim damages or an account of profits in respect of any infringement committed between the date of the transaction and the date of its registration (section 25(4)).

There is no longer any special procedure for the registration of assignments without goodwill. The 1938 Act, as amended, provided in section 22(7) that before an assignment without goodwill could be recorded, the assignee had to apply to the Registrar (within six months of the date of the assignment) for directions as to the advertisement of the assignment. Once the assignment had been so advertised in appropriate trade journals (for example, the assignment of a trade mark for a herbicide might well be directed to be advertised in *Farmer's Weekly*), then the assignment could be recorded. Failure to seek the Registrar's directions rendered the assignment ineffective. Assignments with goodwill were not subject to this procedure.

Unregistered marks

The 1994 Act declares in section 24(6) that 'Nothing in this Act shall be construed as affecting the assignment . . . of an unregistered trade mark as part of the goodwill of a business'.

At first glance, this would appear to restate the common law rule that unregistered marks are irrevocably linked with goodwill and cannot be assigned without it. Under section 22(3) of the 1938 Act, as amended, unregistered marks could be assigned without goodwill alongside registered marks, provided they were assigned at the same time, for the same goods and to the same person. This meant that a 'portfolio' of marks, some registered, some not, could be handled together and prevented the reduction in value of the registered marks had the unregistered marks been left with the original owner.

The 1994 Act contains *no* equivalent provision. Perhaps it was assumed that with the more liberal registration regime, there would be fewer unregistered marks. Nevertheless, it would seem that there is a gap in the new law.

Transitional Provisions (Schedule 3)

Schedule 3, paragraph 8(1), provides that assignments occurring after commencement are to be dealt with under section 24 of the 1994 Act. The old law continues to apply to transactions before the relevant date. The key date determining which law governs the *making* of an assignment is therefore the date of the transaction.

Existing entries made under section 25 of the 1938 Act, as amended, are to be transferred to the new Register (paragraph 8(2)).

Regarding the *registration* of those assignments already executed before commencement, three permutations are possible:

(a)   An application to record an assignment which is pending at the commencement date is to be treated as an application under section 25 of the 1994 Act (paragraph 8(3)).

(b)   An application to record an assignment under the 1938 Act which 'has been determined . . . but not finally determined' (this phrase presumably means 'not actually entered on the Register') is to be dealt with under the old law and then transferred to the new Register (paragraph 8(4)).

(c)   An assignment in respect of which no application to record has yet been made is to be dealt with under the new Act (paragraph 8(5)).

Such pre-commencement assignments are in most cases, therefore, dealt with under the 1994 Act. However, the effect of *failure* to register is dictated (illogically) by the old law. Paragraph 8(6) provides that the effect of the failure to register is that prescribed by section 25(3) of the 1938 Act, *not* section 25(3) and (4) of the 1994 Act. As already noted, section 25(3) merely provided that the unregistered assignment could not be used as proof of title in infringement proceedings and did not deal with any other effect on third parties for failure to register.

One further change which must be noted is that schedule 3, paragraph 2(3), abolishes the concept of associated marks (see chapter 3). In consequence, the obligation to assign associated marks as if they were a single entity has also disappeared. For an example of the old law restricting the assignment of associated marks, see *PHANTOM Trade Mark* [1978] RPC 64.

Licensing of Trade Marks (Sections 28 to 31 and 25)

The Directive
Article 8 of the Directive provides as follows:

1. A trade mark may be licensed for some or all of the goods or services for which it is registered and for the whole or part of the Member State concerned. A licence may be exclusive or non-exclusive.
2. The proprietor of a trade mark may invoke the rights conferred by that trade mark against a licensee who contravenes any provision in his licensing contract with regard to its duration, the form covered by the registration in which the trade mark may be used, the scope of the goods or services for which the licence is granted, the territory in which the trade mark may be affixed, or the quality of the goods manufactured or of the services provided by the licensee.

Article 8 therefore contains a clear statement of principle that a registered trade mark may be licensed, in whole or in part. It further clarifies that a licensee who breaches the terms of the licence is to be treated as an infringer of the trade mark. Article 8 should be read in conjunction with Article 10(3) of the Directive, which states that use of a trade mark with consent is deemed to constitute use by the proprietor.

By contrast, the 1994 Act contains no such statement of principle. Instead, rules equating to the provisions of Articles 8 and 10(3) have to be gleaned from sections dealing with revocation (section 46), the procedural rights of licensees (sections 30 and 31), the registration requirements (section 25) and the courts' powers to grant remedies for infringement. It is a matter of regret that there is no equivalent in the 1994 Act to Article 8(2).

The right to license a registered trade mark
Section 28(1) of the 1994 Act may be considered to be the nearest provision to Article 8 of the Directive. Rather than state that a trade mark can be licensed, it provides that a licence to use a registered trade mark may be general or limited (note the use of the word 'limited' rather than 'partial' which appears in Article 8).

Section 28(1) then goes on to explain that a limited licence may cover:

(a)   use in relation to some but not all of the goods or services for which the trade mark is registered; or
(b)   use of the trade mark in a particular manner or a particular locality.

The idea of a licence being limited to some of the goods or services for which the mark is registered, or limited to use in a particular locality is in accordance with the spirit of the Directive. A limitation as to manner of use is not in the Directive and arguably raises the same problems as an assignment which is so limited (see above).

Section 28(4) states that where the licence so provides, a sub-licence may be granted. Thus it is up to the proprietor to decide whether sub-licensing is permissible. A trade mark proprietor is entitled to stipulate that no sub-licences may be granted, or granted only with prior approval.

Section 28 of the 1994 Act should be contrasted with section 28 of the 1938 Act, as amended. This avoided the use of the word 'licence' and instead talked about 'registered users'. This was probably because prior to the 1938 Act, any licence would render a registered trade mark invalid (*Bowden Wire Co. Ltd* v *Bowden Brake Co. Ltd* (1914) 31 RPC 385) unless the arrangement could be regarded as the use of a trade mark, subject to quality control, as the house mark of a group of companies (*RADIATION Trade Mark* (1930) 47 RPC 37). Nevertheless, it was judicially recognised that section 28 of the 1938 Act, despite its terminology, did involve licences of trade marks (see *Re American Greetings Corporation's Application* [1984] RPC 329, per Lord Brightman).

The 1938 Act, as amended, provided in section 28(1) that any person other than the registered proprietor 'may be registered as registered user' of a trade mark and, in section 28(2), that such use ('permitted use') was deemed to be use by the proprietor. It may be noted in passing that section 28(2) of the 1938 Act ironically accords better with Article 10(3) of the Directive than does the 1994 Act.

Formalities
Section 28(2) of the 1994 Act states that a licence is not effective unless it is in writing, signed by or on behalf of the grantor. This is a matter left by the Directive to national law.

The 1938 Act, as amended, did not expressly state that a registered user agreement had to be in writing, but this could be inferred from the requirements of section 28 of that Act and from the Trade Marks Rules relating to the procedure for recording registered user agreements.

The need for registration
Section 25 of the 1994 Act, it will be remembered, requires all 'registrable transactions', including licences, to be registered. The application to register may be made either by the person claiming to be entitled to an interest in or under the registered trade mark by virtue of the transaction, or any other person claiming to be affected thereby. The wording of the provision is thus flexible enough to allow either the licensor or the licensee to apply to register the licence.

The importance from the point of view of the licensee of promptly registering a trade mark licence cannot be stressed too highly. The consequences of failing to record are spelled out in section 25(3) and (4). They are:

(a)   The transaction is 'ineffective as against a person acquiring a conflicting interest in or under the registered trade mark in ignorance of it' (section 25(3)(a)), the word 'it' presumably referring to 'transaction'.

(b)   A person claiming to be a licensee does not get the benefit of sections 30 and 31, which confer certain procedural advantages in relation to infringement (section 25(3)(b)).

(c)   Unless an application to register the licence is made within six months of the making of the transaction, or if the court is satisfied that it was not practicable so to do, as soon as practicable thereafter, then the licensee is not to be awarded any pecuniary remedy for acts of infringement committed between the date of the transaction and the date of registration (section 25(4)).

Registration under the 1938 Act   Section 25 of the 1994 Act should be contrasted with section 28 of the 1938 Act, as amended. Section 28(4) contained the procedure to be followed where it was desired to record someone as registered user of a trade mark. The key features were:

(a)   Both parties had to make *joint* application to the Registrar under the 1938 Act. Under the 1994 Act *either* party may apply.

(b)   The application under the 1938 Act *had* to show the degree of control to be exercised by the proprietor over the registered user. In practice, the Registrar accepted one of three things as evidence of control: either that the parties were in the relationship of parent and subsidiary; or that the mark was being licensed as part of a patent licence; or that there existed contractual provisions entitling the proprietor to exercise control over the quality of the goods or services.

As the Registrar examined the registered user agreement only once, when the application to record it was made, there was no means of ensuring that quality control was *in fact* exercised, whether initially or subsequently. For the purposes of section 28 of the 1938 Act, as amended, it sufficed that the *possibility* of control was present in the agreement.

The sort of contractual provision acceptable to the Registrar was one entitling the trade mark proprietor to enter the registered user's premises (at reasonable hours) to inspect the manufacture of goods or to take samples, or to inspect the quality of services provided.

Under the 1994 Act, there is no obligation to satisfy the Registry about quality control. It is left to the trade mark owner to ensure that the mark is applied to goods or services of the correct standard.

(c)   Even if the parties satisfied the requirements of section 28(4) of the 1938 Act, as amended, regarding quality control, the Registrar had a discretion to refuse to record the registered user agreement if it was contrary to the public interest. By contrast, the 1994 Act imposes a duty to record a licence, with no discretion conferred on the Registrar in this respect.

(d)   The exact scope of the 1938 Act, as amended, remained unclear for some time because it contained no statement of the *consequences* of failing to register a user agreement. However, in *BOSTITCH Trade Mark* [1963] RPC 183, Lloyd-Jacob J pointed out that the wording of section 28(1) was permissive, not mandatory. Therefore there was no obligation to register a user agreement, and failure to register could not affect the validity of the agreement.

The conclusion as to the interpretation of the 1938 Act reached in *BOSTITCH* should be contrasted with the wording of section 25 of the 1994 Act, which as noted above, clearly spells out the consequences of failing to register a trade mark licence.

Effect on third parties
In determining whether a trade mark licence binds third parties, two conflicting provisions of the 1994 Act need to be reconciled. First, section 28(3) provides that unless the licence states otherwise, 'it is binding on a successor in title to the grantor's interest'. Secondly, section 25(3) provides, as noted above, that until an application to register a licence has been made, the transaction 'is ineffective as against a person acquiring a conflicting interest in or under the registered trade mark in ignorance of it'.

In the absence of any definition in the 1994 Act of the phrase 'successor in title' in section 28(3) and of the phrase 'a person acquiring a conflicting interest' in section 25(3), it must be assumed that the effect of the licence on a third party varies, depending on whether the mark is subsequently acquired by succession or purchase. A person *inheriting* a trade mark will always be bound by a licence (subject to what the licence says). By contrast a *purchaser* will be bound only if the licence is recorded *or* there is notice, but will not be bound if there is failure to record *and* the purchaser is ignorant.

In practical terms, this means two things:

(a)   A licensee should *always* seek to register a trade mark licence immediately, so as to ensure its binding effect on any subsequent purchaser.

(b)   Any purchaser of a business which owns intellectual property rights should ensure that the contract of sale contains appropriate undertakings as to whether any licences have been granted. If the vendor warrants that no licences have been granted and some have, or the vendor discloses only some of the licences that have been granted, then at least the disappointed purchaser will have a claim for breach of contract.

By contrast to section 25(3) of the 1994 Act, the 1938 Act, as amended, was silent as to the effect of an unregistered licence on third parties.

The meaning of exclusive licence

Section 29 defines an exclusive licence as being one which excludes all other persons, *including the proprietor*, from using the mark. An exclusive licence must therefore be distinguished from a sole licence (where there will be no other licensees, but the licensor reserves the right to exploit the mark personally); and from a non-exclusive licence (where the licensor reserves the right both to grant further licences and exploit the mark personally).

There is no such thing as a 'sole and exclusive licence' (a phrase often inserted into commercial agreements), because it is a contradiction in terms.

Section 29 only defines exclusive licences, with non-exclusive licences being defined by implication. Sole licences are not defined at all.

Section 29(2) further provides that the exclusive licensee 'has the same rights against a successor in title who is bound by the licence as he has against the person granting the licence'. The words 'who is bound by the licence' must be taken to cross-refer to section 28(3) which provides for a licence to bind successors unless it provides otherwise. Therefore, where the licence is silent, the exclusive licensee will have the same rights against the successor as it had against the original trade mark owner.

However, if the 1994 Act is examined closely, it does not confer any 'right' on the exclusive licensee which can be exercised 'as against' the owner. Rather, the Act provides for the licensee to have *concurrent* rights, remedies and defences against third parties *with* the owner. The 'rights' referred to in section 29 must therefore be contractual rights, which the licensee has by virtue of section 28(3) anyway!

Rights of the exclusive licensee

Section 31 of the 1994 Act borrows largely from sections 101 and 102 of the Copyright, Designs and Patents Act 1988 by declaring that the exclusive licensee is to have the same rights and remedies as if the licence had been an assignment. Subject to any terms of the licence, such a licensee can bring infringement proceedings in its own name. However, the rights and remedies are to be *concurrent* with those of the proprietor (section 31(2)): in this respect, an exclusive licence is *not* the same as an assignment, because were the transaction an assignment, the assignor would cease to have any further rights in the mark.

Where the exclusive licensee does bring proceedings in its own name, the defendant can raise any defence which would have been available had the action been brought by the proprietor (section 31(3)). It is not clear from the wording of section 31(3) whether the defendant can also raise any counterclaim for revocation or invalidity, under sections 46 and 47 of the 1994 Act, against the exclusive licensee as could have been raised against the proprietor. Common sense must mean that this is so, otherwise the mandatory effect of the Directive in this regard is undermined.

Further, the right of the exclusive licensee to bring infringement proceedings is limited by the obligation, contained in section 31(4), to join as plaintiff or add as defendant to the infringement proceedings the proprietor of the trade mark. A correlative duty is imposed on the trade mark owner who commences infringement proceedings in respect of a trade mark which is the subject of an exclusive licence. Being added as a defendant will not make the owner or licensee, as the case may be, liable for costs (section 31(5)). Neither party, however, is prevented from seeking interlocutory relief on its own.

Where there are such concurrent rights, the court is directed by the terms of section 31(6) to take into account, in assessing damages, the terms of the licence and any pecuniary remedy available to either party in respect of the infringement. Further, the court has power to apportion an account of profits between the parties, or to direct that one party to the proceedings holds the proceeds of any pecuniary remedy on behalf of the other.

A trade mark owner seeking the remedy of delivery up under section 16 must notify any exclusive licensee before applying for a court order.

It must be stressed that the procedural benefits conferred by section 31 apply only where the licence has been registered in accordance with the terms of section 25 of the 1994 Act. Further, the whole of section 31, and in particular subsections (4) to (7), are subject to any contractual provisions to the contrary.

By contrast with sections 29 and 31 of the 1994 Act, section 28 of the 1938 Act, as amended, did not distinguish between the different types of licence and so did not accord any special treatment to exclusive licensees. Further, in section 28(12), the 1938 Act reflected orthodox property law theory concerning licences, by declaring that the registered user was not to acquire any property right to a trade mark. This should be contrasted with the fiction embodied in section 31(1) of the 1994 Act.

Rights of licensees other than exclusive licensees

If the terms of the licence do not entitle a licensee to bring infringement proceedings in its own name, then section 30(2) of the 1994 Act entitles the licensee to call on the proprietor to institute infringement proceedings. The same right is also to be available to a sub-licensee. Only if the proprietor refuses to institute infringement proceedings, or fails to do so within two months of the request, can the licensee institute proceedings 'in his own name as if he were the proprietor' (note the difference in wording between section 30(3) and section 31).

Although the licensee can seek interlocutory relief, the action may not otherwise continue unless the proprietor is either joined as plaintiff or added as defendant. Being added as defendant will not incur liability for costs (section 30(4) and (5)).

Again, as in section 31, the court is directed by section 30(6) to take into account any loss suffered by a licensee where the infringement proceedings are brought by the proprietor, and may give directions as to the extent to which any pecuniary remedy is to be held by the plaintiff on behalf of licensees.

Rather contradictorily, although the opening words of section 30 declare that the section is not to apply where the licensee can bring proceedings itself, the closing words of the section state that 'The provisions of this section apply in relation to an exclusive licensee . . . to the extent that he has, by virtue of section 31(1), the rights and remedies of an assignee as if he were the proprietor of the registered trade mark'. It is thus unclear whether sections 30 and 31 are mutually exclusive or complementary.

Again, it must be stressed that the procedural benefits conferred by section 30 only apply where the licence has been registered in accordance with the terms of section 25 of the 1994 Act. Likewise, the whole of section 30 is subject to any contractual provision to the contrary.

Under section 28(3) of the 1938 Act, as amended, a registered user could call upon the proprietor to take infringement proceedings. Only if the proprietor refused, or neglected to do so within two months of the request could the user bring infringement proceedings in its own name, adding the proprietor as defendant. Section 28(3) was otherwise silent as to the rights and remedies of, and defences against, the registered user who did bring such proceedings.

Need for control by the licensor
From the above discussion, it will have been noted that the 1994 Act contains no stipulations as to how a trade mark should be licensed. In particular, no mention is made in the Act about the issue of the control to be exercised by the trade mark proprietor over the licensee. The philosophy of the Act would seem to be that this is a matter for contractual arrangements between the parties, as determined by commercial requirements.

This is in marked contrast to the 1938 Act, as amended, which raised the issue of quality control in two instances, namely:

(a)   by requiring proof of the entitlement of the proprietor to exercise quality control over the user to be furnished when applying to register the user agreement (section 28(4)); and

(b)   by requiring the Registrar to refuse to register a user agreement if 'it appears to him that [it] would tend to facilitate trafficking in a trade mark' (section 28(6)).

This last-mentioned provision was interpreted to cover the extensive licensing of a trade mark, so that the mark became a commodity in its own right, despite the presence of contractual obligations to maintain quality control (*Re American Greetings Corporation's Application* [1984] RPC 329). 'Trafficking' was perceived to be contrary to the indication of origin function expressed in section 68(1) of the 1938 Act, because there would be no connection in the course of trade between the trade mark owner and the myriad goods made by the various licensees. The reputation in the mark would accrue not to the owner but to the licensees, thus rendering the mark deceptive under section 11 of the same Act.

Can it be assumed that because the 1994 Act makes no reference to quality control that the issue is no longer relevant to trade mark licences? It can be argued that the converse is in fact the case, for two reasons:

(a)   If a trade mark owner indulges in the uncontrolled licensing of a registered trade mark, so that licensees can apply the mark to goods of inferior quality, the registration is open to revocation proceedings under section 46(1)(d) on the grounds that the mark has become deceptive as to quality. A further argument might be (as was the case under the 1938 Act) that such uncontrolled licensing renders the mark deceptive as to trade origin, though it remains to be seen whether section 46(1)(d) applies to this (see chapter 8).

(b)   If a trade mark owner indulges in the uncontrolled licensing of a trade mark with no attempt to contact the licensee, such use may amount to a 'bare' licence. Under the 1938 Act, as amended, this was held to result in the use of the trade mark not accruing to the proprietor, even where the user agreement was registered, so that the mark was open to attack on the grounds of non-use (*JOB Trade Mark* [1993] FSR 118). It must remain a matter of speculation whether the same would be true under the 1994 Act. However, it could be argued that such uncontrolled use is not 'genuine' use for the purposes of section 46(1)(a), thus making the registration vulnerable to revocation proceedings for non-use (again, see chapter 8).

The conclusion must therefore be that a trade mark owner would be extremely unwise to permit the mark to be licensed without a suitable degree of quality control.

Licences of unregistered marks

By virtue of Article 1, the Directive is only concerned with the licensing of registered trade marks. Equally, the wording of sections 28 to 31 of the 1994 Act refers constantly to the licensing of a *registered* mark. The situation under the 1938 Act, as amended, was identical.

This raises the question whether statute has, by implication, changed the common law rule prohibiting the licensing of unregistered marks. Two possibilities present themselves. Either the common law rule still prevails, so that a licence renders the mark unenforceable, according to the principle of *Bowden Wire Co. Ltd* v *Bowden Brake Co. Ltd* (1914) 31 RPC 385; or a licence is now acceptable, provided there is sufficient quality control, in line with the decision in *RADIATION Trade Mark* (1930) 47 RPC 37.

There is little judicial authority on the point, other than *obiter dicta* at first instance and in the Court of Appeal in *GE Trade Mark* [1970] RPC 339, the matter not being considered in the subsequent appeal to the House of Lords. The consensus emerging from this case is that providing quality control is *in fact* exercised, a licence does not render an unregistered trade mark invalid.

Transitional Provisions (Schedule 3)

Schedule 3, paragraph 9(1), of the 1994 Act provides that sections 28 (licensing) and 29 (definition of exclusive licensee) are to apply only in relation to those licences *granted* after the commencement date. The old law is to continue to apply to licences granted before commencement. Any licence is therefore governed by the law in force when it was made. There must therefore be a strong temptation to renegotiate trade mark licences after commencement in order to get the benefit of the more liberal scheme of the 1994 Act.

As regards the registration of licences, paragraph 9(2) provides that existing entries for registered users are to be transferred to the new Register and treated as if made under section 25 of the new Act. Pending registered user applications are likewise to be treated as if made under section 25 of the 1994 Act (paragraph 9(3)).

Registered user applications which have been 'determined by the registrar but not finally determined' are to be dealt with under the old law (paragraph 9(4)).

European Community Law Considerations

Introduction
Chapter 10 has already explained how the objectives of a single market are diametrically opposed to the territorial nature of intellectual property rights, and how it has been necessary for the Court of Justice to reconcile Articles 30 and 36 of the EC Treaty (see Appendix 5) by developing the defence of exhaustion of rights.

The assignment and licensing of national trade mark registrations in different Member States need to be examined in the context of Article 30 and in the context of EC competition policy. Article 30 will be relevant where an assignee or licensee wishes to stop parallel imports of goods from another Member State. Competition policy will be relevant as regards the contents of agreements relating to trade marks (whether such agreements are licences or delimitation agreements) and as regards whether ownership of a trade mark is anti-competitive.

Free movement of goods
Article 30 of the EC Treaty establishes the principle of the free movement of goods. In the case of infringing imports, Article 30 gives way to Article 36, thereby enabling the trade mark owner to prevent the importation of a competitor's product (*Terrapin (Overseas) Ltd* v *Terranova Industrie C. A. Kapferer & Co.* (Case 119/75) [1976] ECR 1039, *Deutsche Renault AG* v *Audi AG* (Case C-317/91) *Financial Times*, 7 December 1993). In the case of parallel imports, whether Article 30 prevails over Article 36 now depends on whether the trade mark was the subject of a licence or an assignment.

Article 30 and trade mark licences   Where a trade mark is the subject of parallel national registrations in different Member States, each registration being licensed to a local subsidiary or distributor, Article 30 will apply so as to prevent the local trade mark owner and/or the licensee from relying on national law to restrict the importation of goods put on the market in another Member State with the consent of the trade mark owner (*Centrafarm BV* v *Winthrop BV* (Case 16/74) [1974] ECR

1183). The significance of the *Winthrop* case is the willingness of the Court of Justice to treat a corporate group as a single entity. Thus, the marketing of pharmaceutical products by one of the group in the United Kingdom was deemed to be with the consent of the whole group, and thereby exhausted the group's rights to object to any further dealings in the products anywhere in the European Community.

The outcome, however, would be the same whether the mark was registered by the parent company and licensed to local subsidiaries, or registered by the local subsidiaries in their own names, or registered by a manufacturer and licensed to local distributors. In any event, Article 30 prevents the use of trade mark rights to reinforce national boundaries so as to prevent parallel imports. A subsidiary or distributor cannot be shielded from the price competition which parallel imports bring.

The principle established in *Centrafarm BV v Winthrop BV* is reflected in Article 7 of the Directive and Article 13 of the Community Trade Mark Regulation.

Article 30 and trade mark assignments   The case law of the Court of Justice has recently gone through a significant change in regard to the relationship between trade mark assignments and the free movement of goods, *with the result that assignments are now to be treated differently from licences.* Because of the change in direction in the thinking of the Court of Justice, its four key decisions will be dealt with chronologically.

(a)   Initially, the Court had held in *Sirena Srl v Eda Srl* (Case 40/70) [1971] ECR 69 that where a trade mark had been assigned in one Member State, the assignee could not rely on the rights given by national law to keep out imports originating from the licensee in another Member State. The case was decided on the basis of Article 85 (at the time, Article 30 was not fully effective). The Court was criticised for ruling that a pre Second World War assignment of the trade mark had continuing effect.

(b)   The Court went one step further in *Van Zuylen Frères v Hag AG* (Case 192/73) [1974] ECR 731 ('*Hag I*'), where it ruled that the Government appropriation of the CAFÉ HAG trade mark in Belgium after the Second World War did not affect the operation of the defence of exhaustion of rights. Even though the original German owners of the Belgian trade mark did not consent to its seizure, the parallel registrations in Germany and the Benelux had a common origin. The subsequent owner of the Benelux registration could not rely on its trade mark rights to keep out German imports of the product. It mattered not that there might be customer confusion brought about by the differences in quality between the German and Benelux product.

(c)   *SA CNL-Sucal NV v Hag GF AG* (Case C-10/89) [1990] ECR I-3711 ('*Hag II*') involved the same set of facts but with the parties reversed, that is, the German trade mark owner sought to rely on its German trade mark rights to keep out imports of coffee from the Benelux. The Court expressly departed from its ruling in *Hag I*, preferring to stress the absence of consent to the Government appropriation of the mark and the risk of customer confusion by having two versions of the product in circulation in the Community. The common origin principle was discredited.

(d)   The unanswered question was whether the principle of *Hag II* extended to voluntary assignments of trade marks. The Court had already undermined the *Sirena* case by its decision in *EMI Records* v *CBS United Kingdom Ltd* (Case 51/75) [1976] ECR 811. This was to the effect that an agreement which subdivided trade mark rights, entered into before the operative date of the Treaty of Rome, would be caught by Article 85 only where there was clear evidence that the parties to that agreement continued to act in concert after the common market came into force. Such concerted practice would not be inferred merely from the exercise of trade mark rights.

The Court of Justice has now in effect overturned the *Sirena* decision, by extending the principle of *Hag II* to voluntary assignments. In *IHT Internationale Heiztechnik GmbH* v *Ideal-Standard GmbH* (Case C-9/93) *Financial Times*, 28 June 1994, the court ruled (contrary to the opinion of the Advocate-General) that the German subsidiary of the original trade mark owner could rely on national trade mark rights to keep out of its territory goods marketed by the successor in title to the assignee of the trade mark in France. The absence of consent by the German trade mark owner to the marketing of the goods in France and the risk of customer confusion were key issues for the Court.

The major impact of the *Ideal-Standard* decision will be to undermine still further the Community trade mark. By shielding a trade mark assignee from parallel imports, the decision enables companies to fragment the ownership of national rights within the Community. By contrast, a Community trade mark has a unitary character and can only be assigned for the whole of the EC (Article 1 of the Regulation). It must be stressed, however, that the assignment in *Ideal-Standard* was forced upon the trade mark owner by economic conditions. The case does *not* deal with the position where a trade mark owner deliberately assigns national rights with a view to partitioning national markets.

Competition law

The competition law provisions of the Treaty of Rome, namely, Articles 85 and 86 (see appendix 5), outlaw two forms of conduct which could distort competition within the single market, restrictive agreements and the abuse of a dominant position. These will be considered in turn as they apply to assignments and licences of trade marks.

Article 85   Article 85 renders void any agreement, decision or concerted practice between undertakings which may affect trade between Member States and which has the object or effect of preventing, restricting or distorting competition within the common market.

The Article also provides for the Commission to grant exemption to any agreement which satisfies the pro-competitive criteria in Article 85(3). Secondary legislation made under the Treaty confers powers on the Commission to investigate breaches of competition policy, to make formal decisions and to impose fines and other sanctions on those who breach Articles 85 and 86. Where parties to an agreement wish to have it declared compatible with competition policy (so-called negative clearance) or to have it exempted under Article 85(3) because it has pro-competitive benefits, they must notify the agreement to the Commission.

To ease the administrative burden of dealing with notifications, over the years the Commission has legislated (by virtue of powers conferred on it by the Council of Ministers under Article 87) to produce a series of Regulations containing block exemptions. These provide a series of 'templates' for common forms of agreement, such as exclusive distribution and exclusive purchasing agreements. Provided the parties draft their contracts to include the permitted clauses and to avoid the prohibited clauses found in these 'templates', then the agreements are exempted from the effects of Article 85. If, however, the contract cannot comply with the terms of a block exemption, it still has to be notified to the Commission.

It was originally assumed that Article 85 was targeted at horizontal agreements, that is, at cartels existing between independent undertakings occupying similar positions in the market, for example, price-fixing agreements between manufacturers, or market-sharing agreements between distributors. It was also assumed that vertical restraints such as agreements between a manufacturer and distributor were not inimical to the objective of free competition and so were outside the scope of Article 85.

Most forms of intellectual property licences are vertical restraints. It therefore came as a surprise when the Court of Justice of the European Communities ruled in 1966 that Article 85 did indeed apply to vertical restraints, the ruling occurring in the context of a trade mark agreement.

Since then, intellectual property agreements, particularly patent licences, have come under a great deal of scrutiny by the Commission and the Court, and are specifically the subject of block exemptions dealing with patent licences, know-how agreements and franchise agreements. Although the number of court and Commission decisions on trade mark agreements is relatively small when compared with those on patent licences, it is nevertheless necessary to consider such agreements in the context of both vertical and horizontal restraints on competition.

Vertical restraints   In *Établissements Consten SA* v *Commission* (Cases 56/64 and 58/64) [1966] ECR 299 the Court accepted the Commission's argument that a distribution agreement infringed Article 85 where it:

(a)   obliged the distributor to sell minimum quantities of the manufacturer's goods and to refrain from selling competing brands;

(b)   conferred territorial protection on the distributor; and

(c)   permitted the distributor to register the manufacturer's trade mark and use it to keep goods from other distributors out of its territory.

Trade mark rights were being used to obstruct parallel imports and the parties' conduct was an abuse of trade mark legislation.

Subsequently, the Commission has been prepared to accept that sometimes (depending on the nature of the product) it may be acceptable for a limited degree of territorial exclusivity to be conferred on a trade mark licensee, although absolute territorial protection can never be granted (*Re the Agreements of Davide Campari-Milano SpA* [1978] 2 CMLR 397).

Although the Commission and Court of Justice have often examined the contents of patent licences to see if individual clauses (other than territorial restrictions) are anti-competitive, this has rarely happened with trade mark licences, possibly because trade marks are not perceived by the Commission to be as monopolistic as patents.

One trade mark licence which was examined by the Commission was that in *Re the Agreement between Moosehead Breweries Ltd and Whitbread & Co. plc* [1991] 4 CMLR 391. The agreement contained a no-challenge clause in respect of the trade mark, meaning that the licensee could not question the validity of the trade mark without being in breach of contract. Although such clauses are generally prohibited in patent licences as being anti-competitive (because if the patent is invalid, then anyone can use the technology in it without paying royalties), the Commission decided in this case that the clause was outside the scope of Article 85. The trade mark was relatively new and unknown to the United Kingdom market (as was the product, Canadian lager) and hence was not a barrier to entry to other firms in what was a highly competitive market anyway.

Horizontal restraints   One type of horizontal agreement involving trade marks is what is known as a trade mark delimitation agreement. This will occur where two rival concerns each own the same or similar marks for the same or similar products but for different geographical areas within the EC. Rather than litigate to determine which undertaking has the better right, they agree to compromise the dispute by drawing up a contract laying out their respective trade mark rights. The EC Commission and the Court of Justice have had occasion to consider such agreements several times, so that their legal standing is fairly clear. The rules can be summarised thus:

(a)   Where the two companies are unconnected and where each has independently acquired trade mark rights, the marks being identical or similar and for competing goods, so that there is a genuine dispute, then the Commission may view such an agreement as outside the scope of Article 85 (*Re Penney's Trade Mark* [1978] 2 CMLR 100).

(b)   Where, however, the trade mark has a common origin and the two owners agree to divide trade mark ownership along national boundaries, then Article 85 will be infringed (*Re the PERSIL Trade Mark* [1978] 1 CMLR 395).

(c)   Even where the parties are unconnected, a trade mark delimitation agreement may still fall foul of Article 85 if it completely prevents the parties from marketing their goods in the other's territory (*Re the Agreement of Sirdar Ltd* [1975] 1 CMLR D93).

(d)   The trade mark rights relied on by the parties to the delimitation agreement must be valid, so that, for example, an agreement based on a dormant registration which is liable to revocation for non-use will infringe Article 85 (*BAT Cigaretten-Fabriken GmbH* v *Commission* (Case 35/83) [1985] 2 CMLR 470).

Care, therefore, needs to be taken when drafting trade mark delimitation agreements to ensure that the rights on which they are based are valid, that the no-challenge clauses are limited to five years (because of what is now Article 10 of the Directive) and that they are not in effect a market-sharing agreement in which national trade mark rights are used to partition the single market.

Franchise agreements   Franchising is a particular type of licence involving trade marks and other intellectual property rights, such as know-how and designs, which has developed considerably in recent years, to the extent that it is now the subject of a block exemption under Article 85, to be found in Commission Regulation 4087/88.

Franchising is a method of distributing goods or supplying services by a series of individual agreements governing a common business format. A product of standard appearance and which is easily identifiable is sold in uniform premises using the same business methods; or a service is provided relying on standardised procedures. These arrangements are encountered frequently, for example, in the hotel and catering industries, vehicle hire, hairdressing and photocopying.

The Court of Justice in *Pronuptia de Paris GmbH* v *Pronuptia de Paris Irmgard Schillgallis* (Case 161/84) [1986] ECR 353 identified the basis of the franchise system. It enables the franchisee to operate as an independent business while using the name and know-how of the franchisor. It can be distinguished from a distribution agreement because it involves the transfer of intellectual property rights, for which the franchisee pays. Therefore, in order for a franchise agreement to function properly, it is essential that the franchisor is able to lay down a common business format to which all franchisees should adhere, and that obligations relating to the integrity of the intellectual property rights should be imposed. As a result of this analysis, the EC Commission has basically adopted a benevolent attitude to this type of contract, because it is capable of stimulating economic activity. Franchising improves distribution without the need for major investment by the franchisor, and provides incentives for the franchisee because it enables ready entrance to the market under a name which has already achieved public recognition. This results in a benefit to consumers, again through improved distribution coupled with the existence of traders personally interested in the efficient operation of their business.

Regulation 4087/88 permits agreements which:

(a) exclude the franchisor from granting rights to third parties within the contract territory;

(b) oblige the franchisee to operate only from the licensed premises;

(c) prevent the franchisee from soliciting customers outside the contract territory (though 'passive' sales can be dealt with); and

(d) oblige the franchisee not to deal in competing goods and services.

Other restrictions may be permitted *insofar as they are necessary* to protect intellectual property rights or to maintain the reputation of the network. This category of clause includes an obligation not to engage in a similar competing business, to use best endeavours to sell the goods, to offer minimum ranges of the goods, to achieve minimum turnover, to meet objective quality control standards and to pay a fixed proportion of revenue towards advertising.

Banned clauses are those which:

(a) prevent the franchisee from using know-how after termination of the contract where such information has become generally known;

(b) allow the franchisor to determine selling prices (as opposed to recommending them);

(c) prevent the franchisee from challenging the validity of the intellectual property rights (though the franchisor can treat such conduct as a breach of contract);

(d)   stop the franchisee supplying goods to customers because of where they live.

The block exemption applies only to franchises for the distribution of goods or the supply of services (including master franchises), but does not apply to industrial franchises where the franchisee produces goods, nor to wholesale franchises.

Article 86   Article 86 prohibits any conduct which is an abuse of a dominant position within the common market or a substantial part of it, if that conduct affects trade between Member States.

The Article envisages an undertaking which has market power (that is, the ability to behave independently of its competitors, the size of market share not being conclusive) in the relevant product or service market. The finding of market power depends on a detailed economic analysis. An undertaking which finds itself in such a position has a special responsibility not to allow its conduct to impair genuine undistorted competition in the single market, and any failure to discharge this responsibility will amount to an abuse.

The Court of Justice has stated on several occasions that the mere ownership of intellectual property rights is not caught by Article 86 (*Parke Davis & Co.* v *Probel* (Case 24/67) [1968] ECR 55; *AB Volvo* v *Veng* (Case 238/87) [1988] ECR 6211). However, patents, copyright and trade marks may be combined with other factors leading to market power, in which case their exercise may amount to an abuse of a dominant position.

Most of the cases involving intellectual property rights and Article 86 have related to patents or copyright, but there are a few involving trade marks.

In *OSRAM/AIRAM* (reported only in the 11th Report on Competition Policy) the Commission hinted that it might be abusive for a firm in a dominant position to register a trade mark knowing that a competitor already uses that mark. In *Chiquita/Fyffes* (see Commission press release of 4 June 1992) the Commission took the view that an agreement between Fyffes and Chiquita that Fyffes would not use its trade mark on mainland Europe for 20 years infringed both Articles 85 and 86. The breach of Article 86 lay in the fact that its inability to use the mark would hinder Fyffes in its competition with Chiquita in the banana market.

Most recently, in *Warner Lambert & BIC SA* v *Gillette and Eemland* [1993] 5 CMLR 559, the Commission found that an agreement concerning the transfer and delimitation of trade mark rights infringed Article 86 and ordered divestiture of the mark.

In this case, the worldwide rights to the WILKINSON SWORD trade mark had been purchased in a management buy-out funded by Gillette, the manufacturer of the rival product. The purchaser and Gillette then divided the WILKINSON SWORD trade mark rights so that the mark was owned by the purchaser in the EC and the United States of America and by Gillette elsewhere.

The Commission's objection to the deal under Article 86 was based not on the strength of the WILKINSON SWORD trade mark but on the fact that it had been acquired by a company (Gillette) which controlled 70 per cent by volume of the market in wet-shaving products in the EC as a whole. The abuse of dominant position was because Gillette had acquired a substantial shareholding in its principal competitor; further, the terms of the funding agreement, enabled Gillette to restrict the purchaser's ability to use the trade mark to advertise its products outside America or the EC.

Gillette was ordered to sell its equity interest in the purchaser to an unconnected third party and to re-assign to the purchaser the trade mark rights for the rest of Europe outside the EC.

The implication of the WILKINSON SWORD case is that company acquisitions by firms dominating a particular product or service market which restrict the ability of competitors to use intellectual property rights will be scrutinised by the Commission under Article 86.

CHAPTER TWELVE
Character Merchandising

What is Character Merchandising?

. . . the use of characters, locations, names, titles and logos from television series, feature films or other entertainment programmes for promotions and the sales of products and services. It is alleged that modern buying habits are highly responsive to image-related advertising. If carefully chosen merchandise is marketed in overt association with a popular film, television series, celebrity, fictitious character or the like, that merchandise will enjoy a greater consumer demand than could have been expected for the unadorned product. (*Lorimar Productions Inc.* v *Sterling Clothing Manufacturers (Pty) Ltd* [1982] RPC 395 per Van Dijkhorst J at p. 398.)

Character merchandising is the name given to describe the business of applying an image of a character (name or likeness; real or fictitious) to a product or service. Character merchandising occupies a separate chapter of this book, not only because of its commercial importance, but also because it received special consideration by the Government in its review of United Kingdom trade marks law.

Cartoon characters provide the most obvious illustrations of merchandisable images. Some of the Walt Disney characters are enduring examples of such images and there are shops worldwide which sell exclusively Walt Disney related merchandise. But the popularity of other characters tends to be short-lived, which makes the industry both fast-moving and ever-changing. Electronic video images are the latest craze, with Sega's 'Sonic the Hedgehog' being described as 'the world's sexiest supermammal'; last summer JURASSIC PARK birthday cakes were all the rage.

Character merchandising is, however, not limited to fictitious characters. It extends to any personality or image that is capable of being transferred from its original medium and applied to a product or used in connection with a service, for example, Nancy Kerrigan ice-wear, or TAKE THAT T-shirts.

The objective of this image association is, of course, to make the product or service more marketable; to make the product or service more attractive to the consumer. It goes without saying that character merchandising is a multimillion-pound business and often results in greater profits to the image owner than its principal line of business, be that films, entertainment, sports or whatever. The Rolling Stones world tour is expected to net up to £40 million directly, with sales of souvenirs and memorabilia taking the profits to more than £300 million (*Sunday Times*, 10 April 1994).

Image owners do not normally manufacture or provide merchandised goods or services themselves. They license others to use their images in connection with those goods and services. Obviously, no manufacturer of goods or provider of services will enter into a licence agreement and pay royalties if it is free to use the image in any event. The viability of character merchandising, therefore, depends upon there being protectable rights in an image.

In the United Kingdom image owners have traditionally sought protection in three different areas of law:

(a) copyright;
(b) registered trade marks; and
(c) passing off.

This chapter seeks to give an up-to-date account of the various forms of protection available in character merchandising. In the past, protection has been patchy. An important consideration, therefore, is: what improvements may be expected to result directly or indirectly from the introduction of the Trade Marks Act 1994?

Copyright

Artistic works
Many cartoon characters start life in comic strips, the character having been developed from concept drawings. As long as the character is original, in the sense of not having been copied from another source, copyright may subsist in the drawing as an artistic work under the Copyright, Designs and Patents Act 1988, *irrespective of artistic merit* (sections 1(1)(a) and 4). The same is true where the original character takes the form of a puppet, toy or doll (a sculpture).

Initial ownership of copyright vests in the 'author' (the creator) subject to freedom of contract and subject to works made in the course of employment (sections 9 and 11 CDPA 1988).

Duration of copyright in artistic works is at present normally the author's life plus 50 years (section 12 CDPA 1988), but will be extended to the author's life plus 70 years when Council Directive 93/98/EC on the term of protection of copyright is implemented in the United Kingdom.

However, it is important to note that where an artistic work is exploited by making by an industrial process copies of the work and marketing such articles (as will often be the case where an image owner licenses the image for use on merchandised goods or services), the copyright period is reduced to 25 years from first marketing (section 52 CDPA 1988). Furthermore, in the unlikely event of a character drawing, puppet, toy or doll being treated as a design document or a model recording a design for anything other than an artistic work, copyright protection is removed in respect of articles made to that design (section 51 CDPA 1988; the point has not arisen for consideration).

Copyright in an artistic work will be infringed, *inter alia*, by copying the work or issuing copies of the work to the public without the copyright owner's permission (sections 17 and 18 CDPA 1988). Importing and otherwise dealing in infringing copies with knowledge amounts to secondary infringement of copyright (sections 22, 23 and 27 CDPA 1988).

Thus, applying an unauthorised copy of an original artistic work to, for example, a T-shirt would constitute infringement. The subsequent sale of such T-shirts to the public would amount to issuing copies to the public, which is also infringement.

The main advantage of copyright protection as far as character merchandising is concerned is that the definition of infringement covers reproduction of an original artistic work in any material form (section 17(2) CDPA 1988). In other words, a two-dimensional work can be infringed by a three-dimensional copy and vice versa. In *King Features Syndicate Inc.* v *O. and M. Kleeman Ltd* [1941] AC 417, POPEYE dolls and brooches were held to be infringing reproductions of the plaintiff's comic strips. Copying may be of the whole or a substantial part of an artistic work; direct or indirect (section 16(3) CDPA 1988).

The new self-help remedy in section 100 of the CDPA 1988 has proved a most effective way of seizing 'bootleg' souvenirs and memorabilia sold outside the venues of pop concerts.

An image owner may have difficulties in establishing copyright infringement where the defendant merely takes the idea of its character; generally speaking, copyright exists to protect the expression of ideas, not the ideas themselves. However, in *Mirage Studios* v *Counter-Feat Clothing Co. Ltd* [1991] FSR 145, the defendants took the concept of humanoid turtles and produced their own designs for aggressive sporting turtles. Browne-Wilkinson V-C nevertheless held that there was an arguable case of infringement of copyright in the plaintiffs' NINJA TURTLES drawings.

Literary works

Copyright subsists in original literary works (sections 1(1)(a) and 3 CDPA 1988), but there can be no copyright in a single word or name. In *Francis Day and Hunter Ltd* v *Twentieth Century Fox Corporation Ltd* [1940] AC 112, it was held that there was no copyright in the song title: 'The Man Who Broke The Bank At Monte Carlo'. Similarly, it was held in *Exxon Corporation* v *Exxon Insurance Consultants International Ltd* [1982] Ch 119, that there was no copyright in the word mark EXXON despite the vast amount of research and effort which went into its creation.

The lack of copyright in single words and names represents a serious gap in terms of character merchandising. It means that titles of television series (DAL-LAS, NEIGHBOURS), theatrical or musical productions (CATS, SUNSET BOUL-EVARD) and sporting events (WIMBLEDON) fall outside the protection of United Kingdom copyright law. The problem is particularly acute for real personalities who may wish to merchandise their names; in the United Kingdom, there is no right to personality as such.

Photographs

Real personalities may be able to get some mileage out of the copyright which subsists in original photographs as artistic works, provided the copyright in such photographs has been assigned to them (sections 1(1)(a), 4, 9 and 11 CDPA 1988).

Copyright protection will be available if the personality or his or her agent is the owner of the copyright in the photograph and that photograph is applied to a range of goods or services without consent. But this does not stop the unauthorised exploiter from taking an independent photograph of the personality and applying it to the goods or services concerned (see *Lyngstad* v *Anabas Products Ltd* ('ABBA') [1977] FSR 62). Furthermore, the copyright in photographs is very limited. In *Merchandising Corporation of America Inc.* v *Harpbond Ltd* [1983] FSR 32, a portrait of Adam Ant wearing his new 'Prince Charming' look was held not to be infringement of the copyright in the photograph on which it was based. Also, it was held in that case that there is no copyright in face make-up because it is too transitory in nature.

Films
Films are copyright works (section 1(1)(b) and 5 CDPA 1988). The first owner of copyright in a film is the person who undertakes the necessary arrangements for making the film, usually the producer (sections 9 and 11 CDPA 1988; but see Council Directive 92/100/EC on rental and lending rights, which considers the principal director to be the author of a film, although Member States can provide that others may be considered as co-authors). Taking a photograph from a film to be used, for example, to prepare a representation for transfer printing on T-shirts, will be infringement of copyright in the film (*Spelling-Goldberg Productions Inc.* v *BPC Publishing Ltd* [1981] RPC 283; section 17(4) CDPA 1988).

Moral rights
The possibility of relying upon the moral rights conferred by the CDPA 1988 on authors of artistic works and directors of films should not be overlooked by the image owner in the character merchandising equation, despite the limitations on and exceptions to these rights.

The rights are: the right to be identified as author or director (section 77); the right to object to derogatory treatment of work (section 80); the right to object to false attribution (section 84); and the right to privacy in commissioned photographs (section 85). Reference should be made to one of the specialist works on copyright, for example, *Copinger and Skone James on Copyright*.

Registered Trade Marks

Trade Marks Act 1938, as amended
The difficulties presented to character merchandising by the 1938 Act, as amended, were both practical and legal in nature:

(a) *The time taken to secure registration.* The popularity of images tends to be short-lived. Yet the average time span between application and registration of a mark was 18 months to two years, even where no opposition was involved. Oppositions could be drawn out interminably. Although it was possible to commence proceedings after registration for infringements occurring during the application period, a trade or service mark application could not be relied upon to obtain interlocutory relief.

(b) *Multi-class applications were impossible.* The rule was one registration per goods or services in a class (section 3). Therefore, several applications had to be made where the mark was to be merchandised for a variety of goods and/or services.

(c)   *The definition of 'mark' (section 68(1))*. Three-dimensional marks were not registrable under the 1938 Act, as amended (*COCA-COLA Trade Marks* [1986] RPC 421); nor were sensory marks, for example, musical jingles.

(d)   *Rectification for non-use*. Section 26 of the 1938 Act, as amended, provided for the expunction of a mark from the Register which was applied for without bona fide intention to use in relation to the goods or services, or which was not put to bona fide use in relation to the goods or services for a continuous period of five years. There were two particular problems here.

First, although use by a registered user accrued to the image owner proprietor (section 28(2)), the status of use by an unregistered licensee was unclear. Furthermore, the case of *JOB Trade Mark* [1993] FSR 118 suggested that uncontrolled use by a registered user might not be effective to fend off an attack on the grounds of non-use.

Second, there was the question of whether use of an image on merchandised goods or services amounted to trade or service mark use within the meaning of the 1938 Act, as amended, that is, use to indicate origin (section 68(1)). Application of a slogan as decoration to T-shirts was held not to amount to trade mark use in *Unidoor Ltd* v *Marks & Spencer plc* [1988] RPC 275. In *KODIAK Trade Mark* [1990] FSR 49, Kodak Ltd's use of KODAK on T-shirts to advertise its photographic products was ineffective to save its registration in respect of clothing from expunction for non-use.

(e)   *Rectification for deceptive use*. Licensing without effective quality control could lead to removal of a mark from the Register under section 32 of the 1938 Act, as amended (*GE Trade Mark* [1973] RPC 297). This could happen whether the licence was registered or unregistered, but at least in the case of the former, the Registrar had to be satisfied that mechanisms for quality control were in existence at the date of application for registration of the permitted user (section 28(4)).

(f)   *Trafficking*. In view of the registered user system, the obvious way to proceed under the 1938 Act, as amended, for an image owner wishing to merchandise its image, was to apply for trade or service mark registrations accompanied by appropriate applications to register permitted users. However, section 28(6) of the 1938 Act, as amended, instructed the Registrar to refuse an application for registration of a permitted user, if it appeared to him that the grant of registration would tend to facilitate trafficking in a mark.

In *Re American Greetings Corporation's Application* [1984] 1 WLR 189, applications to register the fictitious character 'Holly Hobbie' in respect of 12 classes of goods, each accompanied by a user agreement, were refused by the House of Lords under section 28(6). The quality control provisions in the user agreements were illusory given the size of the proposed merchandising activities. There would be no connection between the proprietor of the mark and the goods upon which the mark was to be used. Therefore, the grant of registration would facilitate trafficking.

Although the House of Lords' decision in *Holly Hobbie* came as rather a shock to trade mark practitioners, its lessons were soon learned. When setting up merchandising operations, registered user applications were not to be made all at one go and effective quality control provisions were the name of the game.

(g) *Narrow scope of infringement.* One of the biggest drawbacks of registered trade mark protection under the 1938 Act, as amended, was the narrow scope of the infringement action. Counterfeiters use popular images on all kinds of merchandise. Under the 1938 Act, as amended, infringement extended only to unauthorised use of a mark in relation to goods or services within the registration (section 4). Use had to be as a trade or service mark which raised the same issues as mentioned in paragraph (d) above.

Trade Marks Act 1994

Character merchandising should be greatly facilitated under the Trade Marks Act 1994 for the following reasons:

(a) *The time taken to secure registration.* The streamlining of administrative procedures within the Trade Marks Registry, coupled with the unification of the Register and the lowering of the threshold of distinctiveness required for registration of a trade mark, should result in an improvement in the time taken to secure registration.

The time limit within which oppositions may be brought will be prescribed by rules and is expected to be three months from the date of publication, with no provision for extension (section 38(2); White Paper, paragraph 4.19).

Relinquishment of the substantive examination procedure would, of course, represent a substantial saving in time. Section 8 of the 1994 Act gives the Secretary of State power to do this, but not until at least 10 years have elapsed from the date upon which Community trade marks may first be filed at the Community Trade Mark Office (section 8(5)).

(b) *Multi-class applications.* The rule of one application per class of goods or services has been abandoned. It is possible under the new law for an application for registration of a trade mark to be in respect of any number of classes (section 32 sets down what an application must contain, essentially the mark and a list of the goods and services for which protection is sought).

(c) *Definition of 'trade mark'.* The definition of 'trade mark' in section 1(1) of the 1994 Act is intended to be open-ended. The shape of goods and their packaging are specifically mentioned in the list of examples of signs of which a trade mark may consist. Both the Government and the Patent Office have confirmed that sensory signs, for example, auditory and olfactory signs, may be registrable as trade marks. The overriding requirement is that signs must be capable of graphic representation (see chapter 4).

The possibility of registering three-dimensional signs could be of great value to owners wishing to merchandise fictitious characters. However, the absolute ground for refusal of registration of shapes which give substantial value to the goods, might present a serious hurdle (section 3(2)(c)). It cannot be overcome by evidence of use. Are three-dimensional images of popular characters (JEMIMA PUDDLEDUCK or POOH BEAR) bought by members of the public solely because of their eye appeal, or because of their association with well-known and well-loved characters? (see further, chapter 6).

It might be significant that, in the White Paper, the Government pointed to a 'legitimate fear' that registration of trade marks: 'could be used to obtain a back door extension of the protection conferred under copyright law'. The Government concluded, however, that this was not sufficient reason for taking character merchandising out of the realm of registered trade marks and creating instead a *sui generis* character right (paragraph 4.43).

(d) *Satisfying the user requirements.* Section 46(1) of the 1994 Act provides that a trade mark can be revoked if it is not put to genuine use in the United Kingdom within a period of five years from the date on which it is registered, or if it is not put to genuine use for a continuous period of five years. These grounds for revocation are discussed in detail in chapter 8. Points to note in the present context are:

(i) *Any use with consent* will accrue to the proprietor of the mark, that is, use by an unregistered licensee will be effective to fend off an application for revocation of the mark on grounds of non-use (section 46(1)(a) and (b)).

(ii) The question of whether uncontrolled use will also have this effect is unclear. Image owners are advised to include effective quality control provisions in merchandising licences, not only to avert attack on grounds of non-use, but also to protect their marks from revocation on grounds of deceptive use (see below).

(iii) The continued applicability of cases like *KODIAK* under the new law is also unclear. Section 1(1) of the 1994 Act merely requires a trade mark to be capable of product differentiation. It does not require that a trade mark should necessarily perform the function of indicating the origin of goods or services, although in character merchandising it seems perfectly feasible to argue that the application of the image to the goods or services indicates to the consumer that the goods or services are manufactured or offered under licence from the image owner. In other words, the trade mark is guaranteeing to consumers that they are getting what they want: genuine image bearing products.

(iv) Merchandised goods or services should bear the legend: 'produced under licence from the trade mark owner X'.

(e) *Revocation for deceptive use.* The system of licensing under the 1994 Act has changed to one of self-regulation. The onus is placed on the proprietor of a mark to ensure that it does not render its mark deceptive through use. Deceptive marks may be revoked under section 46(1)(d) of the Act.

Character merchandising has been advanced by express recognition in the 1994 Act of a trade mark as an independent industrial property right (sections 2 and 22). It has also been acknowledged that character merchandising *per se* does not result in confusion as to trade origin, because the public are conversant with the idea of goods or services being produced or offered under licence (White Paper, paragraph 4.36).

Nevertheless, widespread and indiscriminate licensing of merchandising rights will almost certainly lead to deception as to the quality of goods or services produced or offered under the mark. The importance of choosing licensees with care, including quality control provisions in licence agreements and policing the quality of merchandised goods and services, cannot be overemphasised if the image owner is to maintain its registered trade mark.

(f) *Registration of licensees.* There are incentives under the 1994 Act to register merchandising licences.

Only a registered licensee has rights in relation to infringement (sections 30 and 31). An unregistered licence will not bind a subsequent purchaser without notice, and there is no entitlement to damages or an account of profits for infringements occurring after the date of the licence, unless the licence has been registered within six months of its creation (section 25(3) and (4)).

The registration of licences under the 1994 Act is a formal procedure and involves none of the detailed investigations by the Registrar which took place under the 1938 Act, as amended. Attending to the registration of merchandising licences is a step which should not be overlooked.

(g) *Trafficking*. Following on from paragraph (f) above, there is no equivalent to section 28(6) of the 1938 Act, as amended, in the new law. But the caveat is that purely speculative registrations of trade marks may be declared invalid as having been applied for in bad faith (section 47(1); White Paper, paragraph 4.41).

(h) *A wider definition of infringement*. The owner of an image which is registered as a trade mark will benefit greatly by the extended scope of the new infringement action (section 10 of the 1994 Act). Infringement is no longer limited to use of the same or a similar mark for the same goods or services, but covers use on similar goods or services where there is a likelihood of confusion and, in cases of marks of repute, use on dissimilar goods or services which, without due cause, takes unfair advantage of, or is detrimental to, the distinctive character or the repute of the trade mark (see chapter 9).

Furthermore, the protection conferred on well-known trade marks by section 56 of the 1994 Act will assist owners of foreign images whose reputations have travelled before them to set up merchandising activities in the United Kingdom.

The conclusion must be that the Government's review of character merchandising has led to a successful outcome.

Passing Off

In the past, image owners have frequently had to resort to the law of passing off in order to defend their characters or their personalities against unauthorised exploitation. In particular, copyright cannot be used to stop a defendant taking a name and, in the absence of registered trade mark protection (which in any event only covered use on the same goods or services under the 1938 Act, as amended), passing off offered the only hope of a remedy.

It is suggested that passing off will continue to play an important role in character merchandising despite the increased opportunities for registered trade mark protection offered by the 1994 Act. The popularity of images can be sudden and unexpected, and plans for merchandising activities involving the registration of trade marks may not have come to fruition, or may not be considered worthwhile.

This said, the United Kingdom courts have shown a marked reluctance to find for a plaintiff image owner in passing off. Traditionally, passing off exists to protect the goodwill in a business. The principal business of an image owner is entertainment, films, sports and so on. It usually has no direct involvement in the manufacture or provision of the goods or services which it merchandises. Therefore, the image owner has been unable to establish one or more of the following ingredients of passing off:

(a) a misrepresentation which is calculated to deceive;

(b)   that the consumer relied upon the misrepresentation in purchasing the defendant's goods or services (although this was not one of Lord Diplock's five requirements in *Erven Warnink BV* v *J. Townend & Sons (Hull) Ltd* [1979] AC 731); and

(c)   actual or likely damage to relevant business goodwill as a foreseeable consequence of the misrepresentation.

There is no *rule* that the plaintiff and the defendant must be trading in the same or related fields in order to succeed in passing off (*Lego Systems A/S* v *Lego M Lemelstrich Ltd* [1983] FSR 155). But, in character merchandising cases the lack of a common field of activity has proved a potent defence.

The United Kingdom courts have been slow to recognise that licensing, or the opportunity to license, can supply the vital link between the activities of the plaintiff image owner and the defendant (in the sense that the image owner can be regarded as just one step removed from the manufacturer or provider in the chain of getting goods or services on to the market) and that loss of royalties constitutes relevant damage.

In fact, the latter presents a 'Catch 22' situation for a plaintiff image owner where, as is usual, interlocutory relief is sought (*American Cyanamid Co.* v *Ethicon Ltd* [1975] AC 396); even if the plaintiff can show an arguable case of passing off, loss of royalties is quantifiable damage. This is one reason why image owners should always include quality control provisions in any licences which they grant. (Another is to foster a link between themselves and the merchandised products.)

The recent case of *Mirage Studios* v *Counter-Feat Clothing Co. Ltd* [1991] FSR 145 (*'NINJA TURTLES'*) is thought by many to have achieved a breakthrough in this area; some feel that the decision has created confusion. Passing off develops through the case law. In order to assess the present-day position of an image owner in passing off it is necessary to look briefly at:

(a)   the main character merchandising cases before *NINJA TURTLES*;

(b)   *NINJA TURTLES* itself;

(c)   subsequent developments, including the impact on passing off of the Trade Marks Act 1994.

Cases prior to NINJA TURTLES

Fictitious characters   The only case prior to *NINJA TURTLES* in which plaintiff image owners succeeded in passing off was *Shaw Brothers (Hong Kong) Ltd* v *Golden Harvest (HK) Ltd* [1972] RPC 559, which involved the film character, 'The One-Armed Swordsman'. The report of the case is unclear, but it seems that both the plaintiffs and the defendants were in the same line of business; they were both film producers.

However, in other cases in the 1970s, plaintiff image owners were spectacularly unsuccessful. In *Wombles Ltd* v *Wombles Skips Ltd* (*'WOMBLES'*) [1977] RPC 99, the plaintiffs were the assignees of the copyright in the book and drawings of the WOMBLES. The plaintiffs' main business consisted of granting licences (with quality control) to use the drawings on a variety of goods including waste-paper baskets. The WOMBLES were famous for keeping Wimbledon Common free of litter. Walton J refused to grant the plaintiffs an interlocutory injunction to stop the defendant using the word WOMBLES on its rubbish skips and as part of its trading name. There was no common field of activity; no one seeing a WOMBLES skip would think it had anything to do with the plaintiffs. If he was wrong in this, the plaintiffs existed only to exploit rights commercially and, if they won at trial, they could be adequately compensated by an award of damages.

The case of *Tavener Rutledge Ltd* v *Trexapalm Ltd* (*'KOJAK'*) [1977] RPC 275 illustrated the danger of an unauthorised user being first to acquire reputation in the United Kingdom. The plaintiff unlicensed user of the word KOJAKPOPS for lollipops was granted an injunction to restrain the licensees of Universal Studios (maker of the television series KOJAK featuring a New York detective who has a habit of sucking lollipops) from entering the market with a brand of lollipops called KOJAK LOLLIES. The licence from Universal afforded no defence; it was 'writ in water'. The defendant had failed to show that Universal could have sued the plaintiff for passing off, because of the lack of common field of activity.

Walton J held that in order to succeed in passing off in these circumstances, a plaintiff would have to show that public awareness of character merchandising was such:

(a)   that the public would, on seeing the character, immediately think that the defendant's product was licensed by the plaintiff;

(b)   that the public would know that licensors like the plaintiff exercised quality control over licensed products; and

(c)   that the public bought the product in reliance on this guarantee of quality.

This was a heavy burden of proof to discharge.

A glimmer of light began to penetrate the gloom in *IPC Magazines Ltd* v *Black and White Music Corp.* [1983] FSR 348. The plaintiff sought an interlocutory injunction to restrain the defendants from releasing a record named after, and containing a song about, the plaintiff's science fiction cartoon character JUDGE DREDD. JUDGE DREDD enjoyed a cult following and, by the time of the motion, both the drawings and the name had been the subject of a small number of merchandising agreements. The plaintiff argued damage under two headings:

(a)   to the reputation of its character; and

(b)   to its existing licensing operations, by encouraging others to use the character without seeking licences.

Goulding J was prepared to accept that members of the public might be confused into thinking that the record was authorised and approved by the plaintiff, that is, he was prepared to hold that there was an arguable case of misrepresentation. But the plaintiff had failed to show damage in respect to heading (a) – the record was 'no worse' than others in the charts; and, heading (b) was too far fetched. As regards the loss of opportunity to license the defendants' record, an award of damages representing lost royalties could be made if the plaintiff succeeded at trial.

Personalities   Real personalities appeared to fare no better in passing off.

In *McCulloch* v *Lewis A. May (Produce Distributors) Ltd* (1947) 65 RPC 58, a well-known entertainer who broadcast under the name UNCLE MAC failed to restrain the defendants from selling cereal under the name UNCLE MAC and by reference to the slogan: 'Uncle Mac loves children and children love Uncle Mac'. There could be no passing off in the absence of a common field of activity.

Similarly, in *Sim* v *H. J. Heinz Co Ltd* [1959] RPC 75, it was held not to be passing off to include the impersonated voice of Alastair Sim in television advertisements for HEINZ foods.

More recently, in *Lyngstad* v *Anabas Products Ltd ('ABBA')* [1977] FSR 62, the pop group ABBA failed to restrain the distribution and sale of T-shirts, key-rings, medallions and other memorabilia bearing the name and, sometimes, a photograph of the group. The group had not engaged in any significant merchandising activity. Oliver J held that there was no real possibility of confusion (because of the different fields of activity of the group and the defendants); no evidence to suggest that members of the public would think that the group exercised quality control over the products; and the loss of opportunity to license was 'hypothetical' and not relevant damage.

South Africa   The South African courts adopted a similar approach in passing off to character merchandising cases.

In *Lorimar Productions Inc.* v *Sterling Clothing Manufacturers (Pty) Ltd* [1982] RPC 395, the plaintiff producers of the television series DALLAS failed to prevent use of the title of the show and individual names of the characters on clothing and in respect of restaurant services, despite their having a huge merchandising business, *inter alia*, in respect of clothing and drinks.

Van Dijkhorst J held that the plaintiffs had no reputation in clothing and restaurants and therefore no relevant goodwill to protect. Furthermore, they had failed to show an actionable misrepresentation; there was no evidence upon which to base an assumption that the man in the street knew about character merchandising and no evidence of actual confusion. The latter findings were all the more questionable in view of the judge's definition of character merchandising which was cited at the beginning of this chapter.

Australia   The Australian courts have displayed a more lenient approach to the practice of character merchandising. To summarise the developments in their law of passing off:

(a)   In *Henderson* v *Radio Corporation Pty Ltd* [1969] RPC 218, it was accepted that a common field of activity is not an essential requirement for passing off. At common law passing off is established on proof of misrepresentation, that is, that 'A is falsely representing his goods as the goods of B, or his business to be the same or connected with the business of B'; it is not necessary to prove actual damage to invoke the assistance of equity and obtain an injunction; it is enough that the plaintiff has been deprived of his right to approve the product for a fee.

Thus, in *Henderson* itself, well-known professional ballroom dancers were held entitled to prevent the sale of a dance music record which carried a photograph on the sleeve of them dancing.

(b)   Objective misrepresentation was supplied in the case of *Children's Television Workshop Inc.* v *Woolworths (NSW) Ltd* [1981] RPC 187, in the sense that it was accepted that the public are familiar with the practice of character merchandising and will believe that an image-bearing product is produced under licence from or with the approval of the image owner.

(c)   In *Hogan* v *Koala Dundee Pty Ltd* (1988) 83 ALR 187 ('*CROCODILE DUNDEE I*'), Pincus J questioned the reality and the need for objective misrepresentation, that is, that the public believe that a merchandised product is licensed; he is said to have extended the tort of passing off to cover the intentional misappropriation of personality.

(d)   Finally, in *Pacific Dunlop Ltd* v *Hogan* (1989) 87 ALR 14 ('*CROCODILE DUNDEE II*'), it was recognised that the misrepresentation need not be direct; 'image filching' can constitute passing off. The defendant in this case used a 'spoof' of the 'knife scene' in the film CROCODILE DUNDEE to advertise his GROSBY LEATHERZ shoes on television.

At this juncture, a little more needs to be said of the case of *Children's Television Inc.* v *Woolworths (NSW) Ltd* [1981] RPC 187, because Browne-Wilkinson V-C used it to distinguish the English authorities in *NINJA TURTLES*.

The plaintiffs in *Children's Television Workshop* were the producers of the television series SESAME STREET and the creators of the MUPPETS. The MUPPET characters had been licensed in Australia for a wide variety of products including plush soft toys. All licensed products were manufactured under the plaintiffs' strict quality control. The defendants commissioned the making of cheap imitation MUPPET soft toys and sold them through their WOOLWORTHS stores. The plaintiffs sued the defendants for passing off. Copyright protection was *not* available because the design of the MUPPETS should have been registered under the Designs Act 1906 and Australian law did not, at the time, provide for concomitant copyright and design protection.

Helsham CJ granted the interlocutory relief sought. In effect, he treated the case as one of classic passing off. He held:

(a)   The plaintiffs had established a reputation in fact; the evidence showed that the public would recognise the toys as the MUPPET characters from SESAME STREET.

(b)   The plaintiffs had on the evidence established a reputation in law; the public were aware of the practice of character merchandising and would associate the toys with the plaintiffs: 'in the sense that it is its imprimatur, by licence, that permits the character merchandising or image related merchandising in dolls to take place'.

(c)   The parties were operating in a common field of activity; both were concerned with getting MUPPET toys on the market, albeit via a licensing agreement in the case of the plaintiffs.

(d)   The defendants were passing off their goods as those of the plaintiffs, or 'in more refined terms' as being made under licence from the plaintiffs.

(e)   The defendants' toys were 'lousy imitations' but in any event the plaintiffs' lost benefit of the defendants' royalties justified the grant of injunctive relief.

NINJA TURTLES

In *Mirage Studios* v *Counter-Feat Clothing Co. Ltd* [1991] FSR 145, the plaintiffs had conceived the characters TEENAGE MUTANT NINJA TURTLES and owned the copyright in the drawings. They did not manufacture or market goods themselves, being concerned mainly with the creation of cartoons, films and videos depicting the characters. However, a major part of the plaintiffs' revenue was derived from royalties received under various licensing agreements to those wishing to use the characters to sell goods (over 150 of such licences had been granted in the United Kingdom). Each licence contained quality control provisions. The plaintiffs' characters were a great commercial success.

Counter-Feat Clothing also made drawings of humanoid turtles (in sporting guise) relying on the concept rather than the plaintiffs' actual drawings. But they turned out to be similar in appearance to the plaintiffs' characters. The defendants licensed their drawings to certain clothing manufacturers for reproduction on casual wear.

The plaintiffs applied for interlocutory injunctions on the grounds of copyright infringement and passing off. Browne-Wilkinson V-C granted the relief sought:

(a)   It was appropriate to consider the strength of the plaintiffs' case because the balance of convenience was even and damages would not be an effective remedy for either party (*American Cyanamid Co.* v *Ethicon Ltd* [1975] AC 396).

(b)   There was an arguable case in copyright.

(c)   The five essential requirements propounded by Lord Diplock in *Erven Warnink BV* v *J. Townend & Sons (Hull) Ltd* [1979] AC 731 could be made out (as indicated below) and the plaintiffs *would succeed* at trial with their claim of passing off:

(i)   The defendants had misrepresented that goods bearing their TURTLES were produced under licence from the plaintiffs. This was because the public had mistaken the defendants' TURTLES for the plaintiffs' TURTLES and they: 'expect and know that where a famous cartoon or television character is reproduced on goods, that reproduction is the result of a licence granted by the owner of the copyright or owner of other rights in that character' (*a misrepresentation*).

(ii)   The defendants' misrepresentation was made in the course of their trade: 'since the representation of the defendants' TURTLES on goods licensed by them must be made by or with the authority of the defendants' (*made by a trader in the course of trade*).

(iii)   The defendants' misrepresentation was made to prospective customers of the defendants: 'because they [the goods] are being presented for sale to such customers' (*to prospective customers of it*).

(iv)   An important part of the plaintiffs' business consisted of licensing the copyright in their NINJA TURTLES drawings. The plaintiffs would obviously lose royalties if the unauthorised exploitation of the drawings was allowed (*calculated to injure the business of the plaintiff*).

(v)   More importantly, and because the public linked TURTLE goods with the plaintiffs, the value of the TURTLE image and therefore the licensing right would be significantly reduced by the affixing of the TURTLE picture to inferior goods and inferior materials. This damage was plainly foreseeable (*which causes actual damage*).

(vi)   Although the plaintiffs were not in the business of making or selling goods, the public connected TURTLES with them. There was sufficient link between the goods sold and the plaintiffs to support passing off (*even though Lord Diplock's five requirements are satisfied in any particular case, there is not necessarily passing off*).

(vii) There was no need to show that the public relied upon the misrepresentation that the defendants' TURTLE pictures were licensed by the plaintiffs in purchasing the goods.

Where to from NINJA TURTLES?

The points to note about Browne-Wilkinson V-C's decision in *NINJA TURTLES* are as follows:

(a) Objective misrepresentation was accepted – but the plaintiffs produced ample evidence of public awareness of character merchandising.

(b) The need for subjective misrepresentation, that is, that the public relied upon this misrepresentation in purchasing the goods, was denied.

(c) There *was* a common field of activity; both the plaintiffs and the defendants were in the business of licensing pictures of TURTLE characters. *Neither* was actually concerned in the manufacture or selling of the goods. Yet, in his judgment, Browne-Wilkinson V-C seemed to treat the defendants, but not the plaintiffs, as being involved in the selling of the goods.

(d) The plaintiffs were able to show merchandising activities on a vast scale based, *inter alia*, in the United Kingdom. Browne-Wilkinson V-C considered this evidence 'critical'.

(e) It was also vital to the outcome of the case that the plaintiffs were licensing copyright material, that is, existing property rights.

Since passing off exists to protect the *goodwill* in a business, it is difficult to see why the existence of copyright material was regarded as essential. But it seems to have enabled Browne-Wilkinson V-C to separate out the plaintiffs' business of merchandising from their business of making films and videos, for the purposes of assessing relevant damage.

(f) The existence of copyright material also enabled Browne-Wilkinson V-C to distinguish the English authorities (*WOMBLES*; *KOJAK* and *ABBA*) because these were concerned with the licensing of names (no copyright, therefore no separate business in licensing their use) and to express his preference for the Australian authorities, chiefly the *MUPPETS* case.

With respect, Browne-Wilkinson V-C's preference for the Australian cases may have been based on a false assumption; by licensing others to reproduce their characters on goods (and by failing to register a design), the plaintiffs in *MUPPETS* had deprived themselves of the right to rely upon copyright protection against those who did the same without consent (see also *Hutchence v South Seas Bubble Co. Pty Ltd* (1986) 64 ALR 330).

(g) The plaintiffs produced evidence of quality control provisions in their licensing agreements. This was important to the issue of forseeable and unquantifiable damage.

The *lessons* to be learned from *NINJA TURTLES* are that in order to succeed in passing off in character-merchandising cases:

(a)   A plaintiff must be able to produce evidence that the public are aware that goods or services bearing its image are produced under licence.

(b)   A plaintiff must be able to show merchandising activities on a large scale in the United Kingdom.

(c)   A plaintiff must be licensing copyright material.

(d)   The existence of quality control provisions in a plaintiff's merchandising agreements will be crucial to a finding of unquantifiable damage for the purposes of the grant of interlocutory relief.

Developments since NINJA TURTLES   In *NINJA TURTLES*, Browne-Wilkinson V-C said of the *ABBA* case, after dealing with *WOMBLES* and *KOJAK*:

> It may be that different factors apply in such a case, though those cases may, given the change in trading habits, require reconsideration on a future occasion if the evidence before the court is different.

Was he opening the way for protection in 'personality'-merchandising cases based on use of the name alone?

In *Kaye* v *Robertson* [1991] FSR 62, such a possibility was denied by the Court of Appeal to Gordon Kaye in respect of an article published in the *Sunday Sport* impliedly with his consent. Mr Kaye was 'not in the position of a trader in relation to his interest in his story'. The Court of Appeal's observations in *Kaye* v *Robertson* have, *inter alia*, prompted the calls for new laws on privacy.

In *Taittinger* v *Allbev Ltd* [1993] 2 CMLR 741 at 755, Peter Gibson LJ said:

> It seems to me no less obvious that erosion of the distinctiveness of the name champagne in this country is a form of damage to the goodwill of the business of the champagne houses.

This decision of the Court of Appeal appears to be a pre-emptive recognition at common law of the action for dilution of a registered trade mark by use on dissimilar goods or services, introduced by section 10(3) of the Trade Marks Act 1994, and, by implication, of a right of property in an unregistered mark.

If the form of property protected by the law of passing off is hereafter to be property in a mark, rather than in the goodwill of the business, perhaps the lessons which emerged from *NINJA TURTLES* identified above can be forgotten.

CHAPTER THIRTEEN
Certification and Collective Marks

Background

Under Article 7*bis* of the Paris Convention signatory States undertake 'to accept for filing and to protect collective marks belonging to associations the existence of which is not contrary to the law of the country of origin, even if such associations do not possess an industrial or commercial establishment'. The Article is unclear in several respects, not least as to the meaning of 'collective mark', and has been interpreted by national legislations in different ways.

Until the 1994 Act, the United Kingdom maintained that it fulfilled its obligations under Article 7*bis* of the Paris Convention by virtue of provisions in the 1938 Act, as amended:

(a)   permitting the registration of 'certification trade marks'; and

(b)   facilitating the licensing of trade and service marks through the registered user system.

By way of contrast, most continental European legal systems opted to recognise and make available registration for 'collective trade marks'. The United States of America chose to protect both certification and collective marks in the Lanham Act 1946.

As far as the United Kingdom is concerned, certification and collective marks have different objectives. The function of a certification mark is to indicate that goods or services comply with certain objective standards (concerning, for example, material, safety or quality); whereas the function of a collective mark is to indicate who is entitled to use the mark (for example, members of the association which owns the mark). Whilst a collective mark might also imply a guarantee of quality (assured by the rules governing membership of the proprietor association), it does not have to. A collective mark is, therefore, more akin to an ordinary trade mark.

The Community Trade Mark Regulation provides for the registration of a Community collective mark (but not a Community certification mark) which will have legal effect in the United Kingdom (Articles 1(2) and 64(1)). The Directive assumes that the trade mark laws of Member States may continue to authorise the registration of certification marks or collective marks, or both (Article 15).

In the White Paper, the Government announced its intention to provide for collective marks in the new United Kingdom trade marks law. However, certification marks would be retained alongside collective marks because of the different function they perform (paragraph 5.04).

The Government's intentions have been given effect in the 1994 Act by section 49 and schedule 1 for collective marks; and section 50 and schedule 2 for certification marks.

Certification marks have been a feature of United Kingdom trade marks law for many years. They were first introduced by the Trade Marks Act 1905 under the guise of 'standardisation trade marks' (section 62). Perhaps the best-known examples are the WOOLMARK of the International Wool Secretariat and the KITE mark of the British Standards Institute.

This chapter deals with certification marks first; collective marks second.

Certification Marks (Section 50 and Schedule 2)

Registrability
Section 50(1) of the 1994 Act defines a certification mark as follows:

> A certification mark is a mark indicating that the goods or services in connection with which it is used are certified by the proprietor of the mark in respect of origin, material, mode of manufacture of goods or performance of services, quality, accuracy or other characteristics.

The previous definition of 'certification trade mark' was contained in section 37 of the 1938 Act. Points of difference are:

(a)   A certification mark may for the first time be registered in respect of *services*. Section 37(1) of the 1938 Act was not extended to services by the Trade Marks (Amendment) Act 1984, nor by any subsequent amending legislation.

(b)   There is no requirement in section 50(1) of the 1994 Act that a certification mark be used 'in the course of trade'.

Section 50(2) of the 1994 Act goes on to state that:

> The provisions of this Act apply to certification marks subject to the provisions of schedule 2.

This has the rather peculiar effect of introducing a *further* definition of 'certification mark' into the new law. By virtue of schedule 2, paragraph 2, section 1(1) of the 1994 Act reads:

> In this Act a 'trade mark' means [in relation to a certification mark] any sign capable of being represented graphically which is capable of [distinguishing goods or services which are certified from those which are not].
>
> A trade mark may, in particular, consist of words (including personal names), designs, letters, numerals or the shape of goods or their packaging.

Section 1(1), as amended by schedule 2, therefore, adds the further requirements that a certification mark (as defined in section 50(1)) must be:

(a) capable of being represented graphically (as described in chapter 4); and
(b) capable of distinguishing in the specified manner (as discussed in chapter 5).

The effect is to extend the forms which a certification mark can take to include product shapes and packaging and sensory marks (previously excluded from registration by section 68 of the 1938 Act) and to lower the threshold of distinctiveness which a certification mark must possess in order to qualify for registration. Under the 1938 Act, a certification trade mark could only be registered in Part A of the Register and had to be shown to be 'adapted to distinguish' (that is, to be inherently distinctive), although there were older cases which suggested that the level of distinctiveness required of such a trade mark was somewhere in between Part A and Part B (*British Cycle and Motorcycle Manufacturers' and Traders' Union Ltd's Application* (1923) 40 RPC 226; cf. *Sunbeam Motor Car Co. Ltd's Application* (1916) 33 RPC 389 and *Bagots Hutton and Co. Ltd's Application* (1916) 33 RPC 357).

A certification mark is applied for in a similar manner to an ordinary trade mark *except* that:

(a) The applicant for certification must not itself carry on a business involving the supply of goods or services of the kind certified (schedule 2, paragraph 4; cf. proviso to section 37(1) of the 1938 Act).
(b) The applicant for certification must file with the *Registrar* regulations governing the use of the mark (schedule 2, paragraph 6(1); compare section 37(7) of the 1938 Act discussed below).

The certification mark itself is examined by the Registrar for registrability in the normal way. The absolute and relative grounds for refusal in sections 3 and 5 of the 1994 Act apply, subject to the following modifications:

(a) In accordance with Article 15(2) of the Directive, schedule 2, paragraph 3(1), permits the registration of geographical names as certification marks, notwithstanding the absolute ground for refusal in section 3(1)(c) (see chapter 6 and 'infringement' below).
(b) A certification mark must be refused registration if it is liable to mislead the public as to the character or significance of the mark, in particular, if the public are likely to take the mark as being something other than a certification mark (schedule 2, paragraph 5(1)). In order to overcome an objection made on this ground, the Registrar may require the mark to include an indication on its face that it is a certification mark (cf. schedule 1, paragraph 1(3) to the 1938 Act) and amendment of the mark is permitted for this purpose (schedule 2, paragraph 5(2); constituting a limited exception to section 39(2)).

The only reported case involving the registrability of certification trade marks under the 1938 Act was *STILTON Trade Mark* [1967] RPC 173. An association of cheese makers applied for the registration as a certification trade mark of STILTON in respect of a type of cheese made in and around the village of Melton Mowbray. The Registrar refused the application on the grounds that the association had failed to prove that only cheese made in the area was sold under the mark and that the mark could be deceptive if used by cheese makers within the area in relation to cheese other than 'Stilton'.

On appeal, Pennycuick J allowed the application. There was prima facie evidence that the mark had not been used on cheese coming from outside the Melton Mowbray area; and use could be confined to 'Stilton' cheese through certified users being bound by appropriate regulations of the association.

Some concern was expressed by the Earl of Harrowby during debates on the Bill in the House of Lords, that the absolute ground for refusal in section 3(1)(c) of the 1994 Act for marks describing the quality of goods or services could operate to render certification marks unregistrable. The Minister gave his assurance that this would not be the case (*Hansard* (HL), 24 February 1994, col. 729).

A major change in the procedure for registration of a certification mark is that the regulations governing use of the mark are to be filed with, examined and approved by, the Registrar (that is, a 'one-stop' procedure) (schedule 2, paragraph 8(1)). Under the 1938 Act, such regulations had to be referred by the Registrar to the Consumer Affairs Division of the Department of Trade and Industry, for examination as to whether they complied with prescribed requirements. The need for referral meant that applications for certification marks could take up to 10 years to process.

The Government's decision to entrust to the Registrar complete responsibility for certification marks was made during the passage of the Bill through Parliament and in the interests of streamlining the administrative procedures (the original version of the Bill empowered the Secretary of State to delegate the task of examining the regulations to an appropriate body; and see White Paper, paragraph 5.04). It is noted that both the Moloney Committee of 1962 (*Final Report of the Committee on Consumer Protection*, Cmnd 1781) and the Mathys Committee of 1974 (*British Trade Mark Law and Practice*, Cmnd 5601) recommended that the 1938 Act scheme for joint processing of applications for certification trade marks should be retained).

The regulations governing use of a certification mark must address the following issues (schedule 2, paragraph 6(2)):

(a)   who is authorised to use the mark;
(b)   the characteristics to be certified by the mark;
(c)   how the certifying body is to test those characteristics and to supervise the use of the mark;
(d)   the fees (if any) to be paid in connection with the operation of the mark; and
(e)   the procedures for resolving disputes.

Further requirements may be imposed by rules.

Although not incorporated in statute, former practice was to insist that a certification mark be open to all potential users provided they were prepared to meet the requisite standards and be subject to inspection. It is thought that this practice will be continued by the Registrar.

The competition aspects of arrangements regarding use of certification marks are discussed below.

A certification mark may proceed to registration only if the Registrar is satisfied:

(a)   that the regulations:

(i)   contain the prescribed particulars; and
(ii)   are not contrary to public policy or to accepted principles of morality;
and

(b)   that the applicant is competent to certify the goods or services concerned (schedule 2, paragraphs 7(1) and 8).

Under the 1938 Act, the Consumer Affairs Division had to be satisfied that the regulations were *to the public advantage.*

Condition (b) above was discussed by the Court of Appeal in connection with an application made under section 62 of the Trade Marks Act 1905 in *Union Nationale Inter-Syndicale des Marques Collectives' Application* (1922) 39 RPC 346. The application was for the certification marks UNIS and UNIS FRANCE to indicate goods made in France. The court held, *inter alia,* that competence to certify was established even though the proprietor itself did not affix the mark, nor make any investigation as to the origin of the goods. It was enough that the regulations of the association had to be complied with by any authorised person using the mark.

Once the application is accepted for registration it proceeds to publication in the normal way, except that the regulations are also published. An additional ground for opposition and/or observations is that the regulations do not comply with the conditions for registration set out above (schedule 2, paragraph 9).

The regulations governing use of a certification mark are open to inspection in the same way as the Register (schedule 2, paragraph 10).

Any subsequent amendments to the regulations governing the use of a certification mark need to be approved by the Registrar and published in the *Trade Marks Journal* (schedule 2, paragraph 11).

Normally, the applicant for a certification mark will be a trade association or semi-public body, but there appears to be nothing in the 1994 Act to prevent a sole trader from applying for a certification mark, provided an appropriate certification system can be established.

Assignment
The Registrar's consent must be obtained to any assignment or other transmission of a certification mark (schedule 2, paragraph 12).

Infringement
Section 37(3) of the 1938 Act sets out a separate regime for the infringement of a certification trade mark, but this merely mirrored infringement of an ordinary trade mark as stated in section 4 of the 1938 Act.

The provisions relating to infringement of a registered trade mark in the 1994 Act apply by reference to certification marks (sections 1(2), 50(2) and schedule 2, paragraph 1). However, paragraph 3(2) of schedule 2 states that the registration of a mark which serves in trade to designate the geographic origin of goods or services (see above) cannot be used to prevent use of the name 'in accordance with honest practices in industrial or commercial matters'.

The following sections of the 1994 Act apply in relation to an authorised user of a registered certification mark as in relation to a licensee of a trade mark (schedule 2, paragraph 13):

(a)   section 10(5) – contributory infringement by printers or designers who apply a certification mark to labels or other promotional material knowing that application of the mark was not authorised by the proprietor or an authorised user (see chapter 9);

(b)   section 19(2) – order as to disposal of infringing goods, material or articles; adequacy of other remedies (see chapter 10); and

(c)   section 89 – authorised user may request Customs and Excise to treat infringing goods, materials or articles as prohibited goods (see chapter 10).

Where infringement proceedings are brought by the proprietor of a certification mark, the court is directed to take into account any loss suffered or likely to be suffered by authorised users (schedule 2, paragraph 14). An authorised user of a certification mark has no right to bring infringement proceedings in its own name (compare collective marks, below).

Grounds for revocation
The grounds in section 46 of the 1994 Act apply to certification marks in the same way as to ordinary trade marks (see chapter 8). In addition, schedule 2, paragraph 15 provides a ground for revocation of a certification mark where:

(a)   the proprietor has commenced trading in the goods or services of the kind certified;

(b)   the mark has become liable to mislead the public as to its character and significance, in particular if it is likely to be taken as something other than a certification mark, because of the way in which it has been used by the proprietor;

(c)   the proprietor has failed to observe or secure observance of the regulations governing the use of the mark;

(d)   the regulations have been amended and no longer comply with paragraph 6(2) of schedule 2, detailing prescribed contents, or are contrary to public policy or accepted principles of morality; or

(e)   the proprietor is no longer competent to certify goods or services for which the mark is registered.

A rare reported case on the revocation of a certification trade mark under the 1938 Act is *SEA ISLAND COTTON Certification Trade Marks* [1989] RPC 87. The case turned on whether the proprietor of the mark, the West Indian Sea Island Cotton Association ('WISCA'), had ceased to be competent to certify the goods, in the sense that it had failed carry out sufficient checks when new certificates were issued to Japanese traders and when existing certificates were renewed to other traders. The learned deputy judge held in similar terms to the Court of Appeal in the *UNIS* case, namely, that there was no obligation on WISCA personally to inspect the goods to be certified when new certificates were issued. Furthermore, WISCA did not have to check whether the mark was being applied in accordance with the regulations each time a certificate was renewed. It was enough that authorised users were bound by regulations which enabled WISCA to investigate any breach. No instances of breaches had been put to the court: the application for revocation failed.

Grounds for invalidity
The normal grounds for invalidity in section 47 of the 1994 Act apply to certification marks. A certification mark may be declared invalid on the further ground (schedule 2, paragraph 15) that at the date of registration:

(a)   the proprietor was carrying on a business involving the supply of goods or services of the kind certified;
(b)   the mark was liable to mislead the public as to its character or significance, in particular, if it was likely to be taken as something other than a certification mark;
(c)   the regulations governing use failed to comply with schedule 2, paragraph 6(2), detailing prescribed contents, or were contrary to public policy or accepted principles of morality; or
(d)   the proprietor was not competent to certify the goods or services for which the mark is registered.

Collective Marks (Section 49 and Schedule 1)

The collective mark is an entirely new animal as far as the United Kingdom is concerned and its introduction in the 1994 Act is the direct result of the Community collective mark (see above). The scheme set up for the registration of collective marks under the 1994 Act is similar to the one for the registration of certification marks, but variations are necessitated by the different functions of the two types of mark.

Registrability
Section 49(1) defines a collective mark as:

a mark distinguishing the goods or services of members of the association which is the proprietor of the mark from those of other undertakings.

'Association' is not defined. Under Article 7*bis* of the Paris Convention, 'association' is generally understood to include traders' and manufacturers' associations, but not Government departments (compare Article 64 of the Community Trade Mark Regulation).

The 1994 Act applies to collective marks subject to schedule 1 (section 49(2)). By virtue of schedule 1, paragraph 2, section 1(1) of the 1994 Act requires a collective mark to be:

(a)   capable of being represented graphically; and

(b)   capable of distinguishing goods or services of members of the association which is the proprietor of the mark from those of other undertakings.

A collective mark may comprise a three-dimensional or sensory sign (as well as more traditional signs, for example, a word or words and/or a device) subject to the above requirements.

There is an exception to the absolute ground for refusal in section 3(1)(c) of the 1994 Act, in that a geographical name may be registered as a collective mark even though it serves in trade to denote the origin of the goods or services concerned. Such a registration cannot, however, prevent use by other traders 'in accordance with honest practices in industrial or commercial matters' (schedule 1, paragraph 3).

An additional absolute ground for refusal is provided by schedule 1, paragraph 4: a collective mark must not be registered if it is liable to mislead the public as to its character or significance, in particular if it is likely to be taken as something other than a collective mark. The Registrar may insist that the registration includes an indication that the mark is a collective mark (schedule 1, paragraph 4).

As for a certification mark, regulations must be filed with the Registrar pursuant to an application for registration of a collective mark (schedule 1, paragraph 5(1))). The regulations must specify:

(a)   the persons authorised to use the mark;
(b)   the conditions of membership of the association;
(c)   the conditions of use of the mark (if any), including any sanctions against misuse.

The competition aspects of collective marks are discussed below.

The examination of the regulations carried out by the Registrar is likely to be less lengthy than for certification marks. Collective marks may therefore prove to be more attractive to applicants. However, before registering a collective mark, the Registrar must be satisfied that the regulations:

(a)   contain the above prescribed particulars; and
(b)   are not contrary to public policy or accepted principles of morality in the United Kingdom (schedule 1, paragraphs 6 and 7).

Both the mark and regulations are published on acceptance in the *Trade Marks Journal*. The matters mentioned in the preceding paragraph may form the basis of opposition or observations (schedule 1, paragraph 8).

The regulations governing the use of a collective mark are open to public inspection (schedule 1, paragraph 9). No amendment to the regulations is effective unless and until the amended regulations are filed with, and approved by, the Registrar (schedule 1, paragraph 10).

There are no special restrictions on the assignment of a collective mark.

Infringement: rights of authorised users
Sections 10(5), 19(2) and 89 apply in relation to an authorised user of a collective mark as in relation to a licensee of a trade mark (see above, the similar provisions for certification marks).

In addition (schedule 1, paragraph 12), an authorised user of a collective mark has the right, subject to contract, to call upon the proprietor to take infringement proceedings in any matter where its interests are affected. If the proprietor:

(a)   refuses to take action; or
(b)   fails to take action within two months of being called upon to do so;

the authorised user may bring infringement proceedings in its own name as if it were the proprietor. In such a case, the actual proprietor must be joined as plaintiff or added as defendant, and generally incurs no liability for costs if added in the latter capacity. This does not prevent the granting of interlocutory relief to an authorised user alone.

Where a proprietor brings infringement proceedings, the court is directed to take into account any loss suffered or likely to be suffered by authorised users (schedule 1, paragraph 12(6)).

Grounds for revocation

Section 46 applies equally to collective marks. A collective mark may also be revoked on the ground that (schedule 1, paragraph 13):

(a)   the mark is liable to mislead the public as to its character or significance, in particular, if it is likely to be taken as something other than a collective mark, because of the way in which it has been used by the proprietor;

(b)   the proprietor has failed to observe or secure observance of the regulations governing the use of the mark; or

(c)   the regulations have been amended and no longer comply with schedule 1, paragraph 5(2), detailing prescribed contents, or are contrary to public policy or accepted principles of morality.

Grounds for invalidity

The grounds for invalidity in section 47 of the 1994 Act apply to collective marks. A collective mark may be declared invalid on the further ground (schedule 1, paragraph 14) that at the date of registration:

(a)   it was liable to mislead the public as to its character or significance, in particular, if it was likely to be taken as something other than a collective mark; or

(b)   the regulations governing use failed to comply with schedule 1, paragraph 5(2), detailing prescribed contents, or were contrary to public policy or accepted principles of morality.

Competition Law

Use of a certification or collective mark may have implications under both United Kingdom and EC competition law.

United Kingdom competition law

The Restrictive Trade Practices Act 1976, as amended, contained in schedule 3, paragraph 4(1), a limited exception from the Act for an agreement relating to the use of a certification trade mark. This exception was subject to the provisos that the regulations for the use of such a mark had been approved by the Secretary of State and that the agreement did not contain any of the restrictions forbidden by sections 6 and 7 of that Act.

The Trade Marks Act 1994, schedule 4, paragraph 7, substitutes a new paragraph 4 in schedule 3 to the Restrictive Trade Practices Act 1976. This has the effect of continuing the previous exemption, except that it now covers both collective and certification marks.

EC competition law

Section 5 of the Restrictive Trade Practices Act 1976 declares, in effect, that the Act is to apply to an agreement notwithstanding that the agreement may be valid or void under EC competition law. Thus, whilst an agreement relating to a collective or certification mark may be exempted from the effects of domestic competition law, its validity under EC competition law will be a separate issue.

Whilst there are several decisions by the EC Commission and Court of Justice relating to individual trade mark licences (see chapter 11), the authors know of no decision relating to collective or certification trade marks.

However, by analogy with those decisions which have examined the status of copyright collecting societies under EC competition law (see, for example, *Re GEMA* [1971] CMLR D35), individual provisions in agreements relating to collective or certification trade marks would have to be examined in the light of the following provisions in the EC Treaty: Article 7 (no discrimination on the grounds of nationality); Article 30 (no restrictions on the free movement of goods); Article 85 (no agreements which restrict competition within the common market); and Article 86 (no abuse of dominant position within the common market).

Further reference should be made to one of the specialist texts on competition law, for example, R. Whish *Competition Law*, 3rd edition (London: Butterworths, 1993).

CHAPTER FOURTEEN
The Community Trade Mark

Introduction: the Need for a Community Trade Mark

The conflict between the single market and national intellectual property rights
In trying to reconcile the objectives of a single market (in which internal national boundaries are disregarded) with the territorial nature of intellectual property rights, the EC Commission and Court of Justice have had to consider several factual situations where the ownership or exploitation of intellectual property has created a barrier to trade.

Where a single trade mark owner has parallel registrations in each Member State, the doctrine of exhaustion developed by the Court of Justice means that national rights cannot be relied on to prevent parallel imports bearing that trade mark, unless valid reasons exist for the importation to be opposed (such as repackaging which affects the condition of the goods: *Hoffmann-La Roche & Co. AG* v *Centrafarm Vertriebsgesellschaft Pharmazeutischer Erzeugnisse mbH* (Case 102/77 [1978] ECR 1139). The doctrine of exhaustion applies also where trade mark ownership is divided between different members of a corporate group, so that the group is treated as a single entity (*Centrafarm BV* v *Winthrop BV* (Case 16/74) [1974] ECR 1183). For a fuller discussion of exhaustion of rights, see chapter 10.

Other situations exist where the ownership of national trade mark rights may create a barrier to trade:

(a)   where contractual arrangements, such as distribution agreements or trade mark licences, have resulted in the trade mark right being used by a licensee to keep out parallel imports;

(b)   where the previous sale or appropriation of the trade mark has resulted in the same mark being owned in different countries by unconnected companies;

(c)   where a trade mark owner chooses different brand names for the same product in different countries;

(d)   where national laws have differing concepts of what is registrable, of the scope of the trade mark right and what amounts to a confusingly similar trade mark;

(e)   where, as a result of independent creation, conflicting trade marks exist in the hands of independent enterprises in different Member States.

The case law of the Court of Justice has solved some of these problems already.

(a)   Distribution agreements and licences of trade marks are subject to the controls of EC competition policy (*Établissements Consten SA* v *Commission* (Cases 56 & 58/64) [1966] ECR 299).

(b)   Where the ownership of trade marks is fragmented between unrelated enterprises, it is necessary to distinguish several possibilities:

(i)   Trade mark ownership worldwide is split so that the mark is owned inside the EEA by one corporate group, but outside the EEA by another. Here Community law can have no application (*EMI Records Ltd* v *CBS United Kingdom Ltd* (Case 51/75) [1976] ECR 811) because Article 30 of the EC Treaty is concerned only with trade *between* Member States.

(ii)   Trade mark ownership is split as a result of government appropriation. The doctrine of exhaustion has no application (*SA CNL-Sucal NV* v *Hag GF AG* (Case C-10/89) [1990] ECR I-3711) because neither party has consented to the use of the mark by the other.

(iii)   Ownership of the mark has been voluntarily fragmented among different enterprises within the EEA after the creation of the single market. The Court of Justice has recently ruled that because of the risk of public confusion, where goods bearing the same or similar mark emanate from different enterprises, the subsidiary of the assignor can prevent the successor to the assignee from importing goods into its territory, as long as the assignment was not created with the objective of fragmenting the single market (*IHT Internationale Heiztechnik GmbH* v *Ideal-Standard GmbH* (Case C-9/93) *Financial Times*, 28 June 1994).

The legislative solution
In relation to the other cases, listed above, where the territorial nature of trade mark rights conflicts with the philosophy of the single market, the EC has adopted a two fold strategy, namely the harmonisation of national law by means of a Directive and the creation of pan-European rights by means of a Regulation.

The problem of the diversity of national law has to a certain extent been solved by the Trade Marks Directive establishing the basic criteria for registrability, infringement, invalidity and revocation. However, although all Member States will eventually legislate to bring their national laws into line with the Directive, such legislation will operate in the context of varying legal systems and traditions. Furthermore, linguistic differences between Member States will result in a proposed trade mark receiving different treatment at the hands of different national registries.

The opinion of the Commission in proposing a Regulation for the creation of a single trade mark for the whole of the Community has been from the start that this is the only way to overcome the remaining problems of conflicting marks being owned in different Member States by unconnected enterprises (see *Terrapin (Overseas) Ltd* v *Terranova Industrie C. A. Kapferer & Co.* (Case 119/75) [1976] ECR 1039) and to stop a trade mark owner choosing a different mark for different countries (see *Centrafarm* v *American Home Products Corporation* (Case 3/78), [1978] ECR 1823). The concept of a unitary trade mark (which means that the mark will have the same effect throughout the whole of the EC) will also stop any voluntary assignment from fragmenting the trade mark right among different enterprises.

The objective of this chapter will be to explain in outline how the Community trade mark system will work (at the time of writing the implementing regulations are not available in final form) and to assess whether the assumptions underlying the Regulation are valid.

History of the Community Trade Mark Regulation

Discussions for the creation of a Community-wide trade mark can be traced back to 1964, when the Commission proposed a Convention for the Community Trade Mark, to run parallel to the Community Patent Convention (although the latter was not agreed until 1975 and has still not been implemented). Further proposals emerged in 1976 in a document entitled 'Memorandum on the Creation of a EEC Trade Mark' (see *Bulletin of the European Communities* Supplement 8/76). In the meantime, the Court of Justice had developed the doctrine of exhaustion to resolve some of the conflicts between the single market and trade mark rights. It was not until 1980 that the Commission adopted the twofold strategy of bringing national laws into line and creating a Community-wide right. The draft Directive and Regulation published in that year were subsequently amended in 1985 and 1984 respectively, with the final versions of each (both containing further substantial amendments) being agreed late in 1988 and late in 1993.

Legal basis of the Regulation

The Community Trade Mark Regulation has as its legal basis Article 235 of the EC Treaty, the implied powers provision. Any legislation based on this Article has to be agreed by unanimous vote in the Council of Ministers, which may explain why the Regulation took so long to emerge. The significance of the choice of a Regulation as the legislative vehicle for creating a Community-wide right is that under Article 189 of the EC Treaty such legislation is directly applicable in all Member States, that is, it has uniform effect throughout the EC and has automatic legal force without the need for intervening national legislation. Unless indicated otherwise, all references in this chapter to Articles are to those of the Regulation.

The Community Trade Mark Office

One of the main tasks of the Regulation is to provide for the creation of the Community Trade Mark Office (officially, the Office for Harmonisation in the Internal Market (Trade Marks and Designs)). It will be referred to throughout this chapter as 'the Office'.

Status of the Office

The Office (to be sited in Alicante, Spain) is to have legal personality (Article 111), so that it can acquire property and be a party to legal proceedings. It will enjoy the normal privileges and immunities accorded to other EC institutions (Article 113) and its staff will be subject to the EC Staff Regulations (Article 112). It is subject to the same contractual and non-contractual liability as other EC institutions (Article 114 together with Article 215 of the EC Treaty).

Organisation of the Office

The Office is to be overseen by a President, assisted by one or more Vice-Presidents (Article 119), who is answerable to the EC Commission for those aspects of the conduct of the Office not subject to judicial review by the EC Court of First Instance (Article 118). The management of the Office is entrusted to an Administrative Board, composed of a representative from each Member State plus one representative from the Commission (Articles 121 and 122). Financial control of the Office is delegated to the Budget Committee (Articles 133–139).

Under Article 125, the Office itself is to be subdivided into Examiners (see Article 126), an Opposition Division (see Article 127), a Cancellation Division (Article 129) and an Administration and Legal Division, the latter being responsible under Article 128 for decisions not falling within the competence of the other three, in particular the making of entries on the Register. Decisions of Examiners, the Opposition Division, the Cancellation Division and the Administration and Legal Division are all subject to an appeal to the Boards of Appeal (Article 130), the members of which must be independent (Article 131). No examiner, member of any of the Divisions or member of any of the Boards of Appeal can take part in a case if he or she has a personal interest therein or has previously been involved as a representative of one of the parties (Article 132).

Languages

Although the working languages of the Office are to be English, French, German, Italian and Spanish, an application for a Community trade mark can be filed in any of the official languages of the EC (currently nine, soon to be 12). All publications by the Office and all register entries are likewise to be in all EC official languages, for which the EC's official translation service is to be used (Articles 115, 116 and 117). However, an applicant, when filing an application, must indicate a second language which must be one of the languages of the Office. Oppositions and cancellation proceedings must be in one of the languages of the Office. Article 115 contains detailed rules for determining which is to be the language of the case where an opponent or applicant for cancellation chooses a language different from that of the first or second language of the applicant. The parties may agree, however, to use any official EC language as the language of the case.

Public inspection of the Register and files

Under Article 83, the Office is to keep a Register of Community trade marks which is open to public inspection. Files kept by the Office are not open to inspection prior to the publication of an application without the applicant's consent (Article 84). However, in the case of a third party who has been notified that once a Community trade mark application has been completed, infringement proceedings will be started against it, the files can be inspected without consent. Once an application has been published, files relating to the application can be inspected on request, subject to any restrictions which may be imposed by virtue of the implementing regulations, presumably on the basis of confidentiality.

Official publications

The Office is required to publish periodically a *Community Trade Marks Bulletin* (containing details of marks which have been registered as well as any other matter required to be published under the Regulation) and to publish an *Official Journal* containing notices and general information (Article 85). The Office is required to cooperate with the courts or authorities in the Member States (Article 86). In particular, national trade mark registries and the Office are to exchange official publications.

Legal representation

Legal representation
Although Article 88(1) states that it is not mandatory to be represented before the Office, it goes on in Article 88(2) to provide that businesses which are not domiciled or which do not have either their principal place of business or a real and effective industrial and commercial establishment in the Community must be represented before the Office, other than in filing an application. Firms which are domiciled or established in the Community, together with related enterprises, may be represented by an employee. Thus an American or Japanese company having a European subsidiary could be represented by an employee of that subsidiary (Article 88(3)).

Representation before the Office can be undertaken only by legal practitioners qualified in one of the Member States to act in trade mark matters, or professional representatives whose names appear on the list maintained by the office. To be entered on the list of professional representatives, a person must:

(a) be a national of one of the EC Member States;
(b) have a place of business or employment in the Community; and
(c) be entitled to act as an agent before the Trade Mark Registry of the Member State in which that business or employment is located.

Definition of a Community Trade Mark

The meaning of 'trade mark'
Article 4 of the Regulation is worded almost identically with Article 2 of the Directive:

> A Community trade mark may consist of any signs capable of being represented graphically, particularly words, including personal names, designs, letters, numerals, the shape of goods or of their packaging, provided that such signs are capable of distinguishing the goods or services of one undertaking from those of other undertakings.

Accordingly, it contains the same basic criteria of 'any sign', which is 'capable of graphic representation' and 'capable of distinguishing', explained in chapters 4 and 5 in relation to the implementation of the Directive into United Kingdom law.

Absolute grounds
Article 7(1) of the Regulation closely follows the wording of Article 3(1) of the Directive. Reference should be made to chapter 6 which explains the incorporation of this aspect of the Directive into United Kingdom law. The Community Trade Mark Regulation likewise prohibits the registration of the following:

(a)   signs which do not conform to the requirements of Article 4 of the Regulation (Article 7(1)(a)) (note the slightly different wording in Article 3(1)(a) of the Directive);

(b)   trade marks devoid of any distinctive character (Article 7(1)(b));

(c)   descriptive trade marks (Article 7(1)(c));

(d)   trade marks consisting of customary terms (Article 7(1)(d));

(e)   shapes resulting from the nature of the goods themselves, shapes necessary to achieve a technical result and shapes giving substantial value to the goods (Article 7(1)(e));

(f)   trade marks contrary to public policy or to accepted principles of morality (Article 7(1)(f));

(g)   trade marks which are deceptive (Article 7(1)(g));

(h)   trade marks which are to be refused under Article 6*ter* of the Paris Convention (State and intergovernmental organisation emblems) and similar badges, emblems or escutcheons of particular public interest (Article 7(1)(h) and (i)).

Like the Directive, the Regulation provides in Article 7(3) that paragraphs (b), (c) and (d) of Article 7(1) shall not apply where the trade mark has become distinctive in consequence of the use which has been made of it.

Article 7(2) states that the absolute grounds of refusal are to apply even though such grounds obtain in only part of the Community. For the Community trade mark applicant, the need to find a trade mark which is neither descriptive, deceptive nor contrary to public policy in all the official languages of the Community will pose a considerable hurdle, even more so when the Community is enlarged in 1995.

Unlike Article 3 of the Directive there is no reference in Article 7 of the Regulation to applications made in bad faith. It is, however, an express ground of invalidity under Article 51.

Article 11 entitles the proprietor of a trade mark which has been registered in the name of the proprietor's agent or representative to oppose the use of such mark if authorisation has not been given, unless the agent justifies such use. This provision implements in part Article 6*septies* of the Paris Convention, the rest of this Article being implemented in Article 8(3) of the Regulation.

Relative grounds
Article 8 has its counterpart in Article 4 of the Directive, which was explained in the context of United Kingdom law in chapter 7. The wording of the two provisions is not identical, but such differences as exist can be explained by the fact that the Directive is dealing with the problem of bringing national laws into line, whereas the Regulation is concerned with the creation of a pan-European right.

Article 8 treats as prior rights:

(a)   previously registered Community, national, Benelux or international trade marks (the last-mentioned need only be registered in one Member State to count as a prior right);

(b)   applications for any of the above;

(c)   trade marks which are 'well-known' marks within the meaning of Article 6*bis* of the Paris Convention, provided they are well-known in one Member State;

(d)   unregistered trade marks, provided that they are 'of more than mere local significance', provided the rights to such marks were acquired before the application or priority date of the Community application and provided the law of the relevant Member State would allow the proprietor of the earlier right to prohibit the use of the subsequent trade mark. In the context of United Kingdom law, this means that the owner of the earlier unregistered mark must be in a position to succeed in a passing-off action. Clarification will be needed from the Office and ultimately from the Court of Justice as to the meaning of the phrase 'of more than mere local significance'.

As with the Directive, Article 8 of the Regulation contains a number of permutations in relation to earlier marks which are either registered, pending applications or 'well-known'. As before, these permutations are set out for convenience in tabular form:

Table 14.1

Article	*Mark*	*Goods or services*	*Additional requirement*
8(1)(a)	identical	identical	none
8(1)(b)	identical	similar	likelihood of confusion
8(1)(b)	similar	identical	likelihood of confusion
8(1)(b)	similar	similar	likelihood of confusion
8(5)	identical *or* similar	dissimilar	reputation *plus* detriment

Although Article 8 of the Regulation, unlike its counterpart in the Directive, makes no reference to a prior copyright or design being treated as a relative ground for refusal, the existence of such a prior right is a ground of invalidity under Article 52.

A further ground of objection under Article 8(3) is where a trade mark is registered by an agent in the agent's name without the consent of the proprietor.

The opening words of Article 8(1) emphasise that the relative grounds for refusal can be raised only in opposition proceedings. This is in accordance with the style of procedure adopted by the Regulation (modelled on the German system) whereby the Office will carry out a search for prior rights, will notify the applicant of the outcome and will equally notify the owners of the prior rights of the publication of the later application, but will not reject an application on relative grounds. It is left to the owner of the prior right to bring either opposition proceedings under Article 42 of the Regulation, or (after registration) invalidity proceedings under Article 52. The owner of the prior right can, of course, consent to the registration of the later mark (Article 52(3)) and may also be prevented from seeking its cancellation for invalidity where there has been acquiescence for a period of five successive years in the use of the later Community trade mark (Article 53).

Applying for a Community Trade Mark: Registration Procedure

The final version of the detailed rules which will govern the procedures of the Office are not available at the time of writing. Article 140 of the Regulation provides for the making of implementing regulations which will deal, *inter alia*, with such matters as fees and late payment thereof, alteration of the register, registration of assignments and licences, the provision of certificates and certified copies of the register and inspection of files. Such implementing regulations are to be prepared by the EC Commission and agreed by a special committee, composed of representatives of the Member States (Article 141). If this committee cannot reach an opinion, the implementing regulations are to be decided by the EC Council of Ministers.

As in the case of a national application, it is advisable to ensure that a proposed Community trade mark is registrable in law (that is, it complies with Article 7, explained above) and is registrable in fact (that is, it does not conflict with any of the prior rights listed in Article 8). The intending applicant should therefore institute searches of such prior rights in the appropriate Community, national and international registers. Thereafter the steps to be taken in obtaining a Community trade mark are as follows:

Step 1: filing the application.
Step 2: examination.
Step 3: official search.
Step 4: acceptance and publication.
Step 5: opposition.
Step 6: registration.

Step 1: filing the application
A Community trade mark can be obtained only by registration (Article 6) and not by use. Accordingly, an application for a Community trade mark must be filed either at the Office or at a national trade mark registry (in the case of the Benelux countries, this will be the regional registry established under the Uniform Benelux Trademarks Law 1971) (Article 25(1)). If the application is filed at a national trade mark registry, it must be forwarded to the Office within two weeks (Article 25(2)).

The application has to contain, under Article 26, a formal request for registration, information identifying the applicant, the list of goods or services for which protection is requested and a representation of the trade mark. It must also comply with any requirements laid down in the implementing regulations. The list of goods and services must be classified in accordance with the Nice Agreement (Article 28).

Under Article 5, the applicant must be one of the following:

(a)   a national of one of the EC Member States;
(b)   a national of one of the other States belonging to the Paris Convention for the Protection of Intellectual Property;
(c)   a person domiciled in the EC or in one of the Paris Convention countries;
(d)   a national of a country which, although not a party to the Paris Convention, accords reciprocal protection to nationals of all EC Member States.

Failure to comply with Article 5 is an express ground of invalidity under Article 51.

The filing date of the Community trade mark application is the date on which all the documents required by Article 26 are filed, provided the application fee is paid within one month of this date (Article 27). Under Article 46, in the case of a successful application, the mark is registered for 10 years from the filing date.

As with national trade mark applications, a Community trade mark application can claim the benefit of Convention priority in accordance with Article 4 of the Paris Convention (claiming Convention priority in relation to a national trade mark application was explained in chapter 3). Accordingly, Article 29 of the Regulation reproduces the requirements of Article 4 of the Convention in relation to claiming Convention priority for a Community trade mark. Under Article 30, the applicant who wishes to claim Convention priority is required to complete the appropriate declaration. The effect of claiming Convention priority is explained by Article 31. The priority date is deemed to be the filing date as regards determining which prior rights take precedence, if any. Article 31 should, however, be read in the light of Articles 27 and 46 set out above. It is the filing date (and not the priority date) which becomes the eventual registration date.

The Community Trade Mark Regulation enables a trade mark applicant to claim Convention priority in the converse situation, that is, to claim priority from the date of filing a Community application when making a subsequent national filing (Article 32), although this benefit is limited to subsequent filings in the Member States only.

The Regulation also enables the applicant to claim six months' priority in the case of goods or services which have been displayed at an officially recognised international exhibition falling within the terms of the Convention on International Exhibitions 1928 (Article 33).

Finally, where the Community trade mark applicant is the proprietor of a national registration (including a Benelux registration), or an international registration effected in one of the Member States under the terms of the Madrid Agreement, for the identical mark in respect of the identical goods or services, seniority can be claimed from the earlier mark (Article 34). Seniority means that where the earlier mark is surrendered or allowed to lapse, then the owner of the Community mark is deemed to continue to have the same rights as it would have had if the national registration had not ceased to exist. Seniority cannot be claimed where the earlier national mark is revoked or declared invalid. Seniority can be claimed either at the time of the application for, or after registration of, the Community mark (Article 35). It can be expected that the first users of the Community system will be enterprises which already have parallel registrations in all the Member States. Such applicants are likely to want to claim seniority from their national rights.

Step 2: examination
An application for a Community trade mark is subjected under Article 36 to an examination to determine whether the formal requirements of the parent Regulation and the implementing regulations have been met, and to determine whether the appropriate fees have been paid. The applicant is to be given a period of time (to be prescribed in the implementing regulations) to remedy any deficiency, otherwise the application will be refused. The application may also be refused under Article 37 if the applicant is not a national of an EC Member State or of one of the Convention countries.

The application is next subjected to a substantive examination to ensure it complies with Article 7 (absolute grounds). In the case of non-distinctive matter which could give rise to doubts as to the scope of protection, the Office may, as a condition of registration, require the applicant to disclaim any exclusive right to the non-distinctive element (Article 38). An applicant is entitled under the same Article to withdraw or amend the application or to make observations before the application is refused.

Step 3: official search

Provided the application complies with the formal requirements of the Regulation and the applicant satisfies the criteria of Article 5, the Office will next make a search of prior Community marks to see if any relative grounds of refusal exist (Article 39). At the same time it will transmit a copy of the application to those national trade mark offices which have indicated that they wish to carry out a search of prior national marks. National offices who do carry out such a search must send their search results within three months. The Community and national search reports are then sent to the applicant. Once the application has been published, the owners of any prior Community registrations or applications will be notified of the application. No mechanism exists in the Regulation for notifying the owners of prior national rights, which will be disadvantageous to small and medium enterprises.

Step 4: acceptance and publication

Provided the application meets the formal and substantive requirements of the Regulation (including the status of the applicant) and provided one month has elapsed from the sending of the search reports to the applicant, the application will be published in the *Community Trade Marks Bulletin* (Article 40). Thereafter, under Article 41, third parties may submit written observations to the Office as to why the application should not be registered, in particular as to the grounds of absolute refusal found in Article 7. Such observations are passed on to the applicant. The making of written observations does not give the third party *locus standi* before the Office, so that there is no entitlement to a hearing.

Step 5: opposition

Any opposition to a Community trade mark application, which must be based solely on Article 8 (relative grounds), must be within three months of publication (Article 42). Those entitled to bring opposition proceedings are:

   (a)   the owner or licensee of an earlier Community, national, Benelux or international registration or application which meets the criteria of Article 8(1);
   (b)   the owner of a 'well-known' trade mark;
   (c)   the owner or licensee of the same or similar mark registered for dissimilar goods where the prior mark (whether Community or national) has a reputation (respectively, in the Community or Member State) and use of the mark applied for would be detrimental to the earlier mark;
   (d)   the proprietor of a trade mark which has been wrongfully registered by an agent in breach of Article 8(3);
   (e)   the owner of any unregistered trade mark which would amount to a prior right under Article 8(4).

Any opposition must be in writing which must specify the grounds of opposition: it may be supported by further evidence filed by the opponent. Where an opposition is filed, the parties are to submit written observations to the Office (Article 43). If challenged by the applicant, the owner of a prior Community or national mark which has been registered for at least five years and which is the basis of the opposition must furnish proof of genuine use of the mark. Article 43 empowers the Office to invite the parties to make a friendly settlement, but if it concludes that Article 8 does prevent the application from succeeding, whether in whole or in part, it will reject the application. Notice of such rejection is to be published in the *Community Trade Marks Bulletin*.

Any final decision by any department of the Office is subject to appeal (Article 57). Such appeal has suspensive effect and can be brought by any party to proceedings before the Office (Article 58). This will not include a third party who makes written observations under Article 41. Appeals must be brought within two months of the notification of the decision appealed against (Article 59), and the written grounds of appeal must be supplied within a further period of two months. In the case of an appeal which is not opposed by another party, the department of the Office whose decision is contested may rectify the decision of its own volition (Article 60).

Appeals are heard by the Board of Appeal, which can invite the parties to make observations (Article 61). The Board of Appeal can exercise the powers of the department responsible for the original decision, or can remit the case for further consideration (Article 62). Any decision of the Board of Appeal is subject to judicial review, to be brought within two months, under the provisions of Article 173 of the EC Treaty (Article 63 of the Regulation). The jurisdiction to review decisions of the Board of Appeal is conferred on the Court of First Instance of the European Communities (recital 13 of the Community Trade Mark Regulation together with Council Decisions 88/591/ECSC, EEC, EURATOM and 93/350/EURATOM, ECSC, EEC).

Article 44 provides that the applicant may withdraw the application at any time, or may restrict the list of goods or services. Otherwise, the application may only be amended by correcting errors of wording or copying or obvious mistakes, provided such an amendment does not substantially change the mark or add to the list of goods and services. This is in line with the limited power to amend a registration contained in Article 48.

Step 6: registration
Where a Community trade mark meets the requirements of the Regulation and the opposition (if any) is overcome, it will be registered for a period of 10 years (Article 45), such period being calculated from the filing date (Article 46).

Miscellaneous Matters Relating to Registration

Decisions of the Office
The Regulation provides in Article 77 that all decisions of the Office must be notified to those concerned. Further, under Article 73 any decision must contain a statement of reasons. In all its dealings the Office is to take into account the principles of procedural law generally recognised in the Member States (Article

79), so that the principles of natural justice must be observed. The Court of Justice has developed a considerable body of case law on this subject.

Hearings

Although the Office can examine facts of its own motion, in opposition proceedings it is limited to evidence and arguments raised by the parties, provided such evidence was submitted on time (Article 74). The Regulation provides, in Article 75, for the holding of oral hearings, either at the instance of the Office itself or at the request of the parties. Such hearings are to be private in cases relating to applications and oppositions, but public in the case of appeals from the foregoing decisions and in the case of cancellation proceedings.

Evidence

Article 76 empowers the Office to obtain relevant evidence by a variety of methods, including oral hearings, documents, expert opinion and sworn statements. The Office may commission one of its staff to obtain evidence or may issue a witness summons. Where a witness or an expert is to give evidence orally, the parties are entitled to attend and put questions to them.

Restoration of rights

Where the applicant for or owner of a Community trade mark, or any other party to proceedings before the Office, cannot meet any of the prescribed time limits in spite of the exercise of all due care, the right in question can be re-established by complying with the procedure laid down in Article 78. The restoration of rights following failure to meet a deadline is not available to an applicant who does not comply with Article 29 (Convention priority) or the owner of a prior right who does not meet the deadline in Article 42 for filing an opposition. The restoration of rights is not to prejudice any third party who in good faith has placed goods on the market or supplied services under a sign identical or similar to the Community mark in the period between the loss of rights and the publication of the restoration of those rights. Such a third party may oppose the restoration of rights.

Costs

Article 81 provides for the losing party in opposition proceedings to bear the costs thereof, although costs can be apportioned in cases where each party succeeds on some of the points raised. A party to opposition, revocation or invalidity proceedings, or to an appeal, who withdraws, or (where that party is the trade mark owner) fails to renew a Community mark, or surrenders the same, bear the other side's costs. Costs may be mutually agreed. On request, the Office shall fix the costs. Any decision by the Office as to costs is to be enforceable under national law (Article 82).

Community collective marks

Articles 64 to 72 of the Regulation provide for the registration of Community collective marks. No reference appears in the Regulation to certification trade marks. A Community collective mark is defined as:

> a Community trade mark which is described as such when the mark is applied for and is capable of distinguishing the goods or services of the members of the association which is the proprietor of the mark from those of other undertakings.

Collective marks can only be the subject of applications by associations of manufacturers, producers, suppliers of services or traders (provided that they have the legal capacity to undertake obligations) and any legal persons governed by public law (that is, State enterprises and the like). In other words, a collective mark cannot be owned by an individual.

Article 64(2), by way of derogation from Article 7(1)(c), permits collective marks to consist of signs indicating the geographical origin of goods, though the registration of such a name is not to entitle the owner to prevent a third party from using such a sign in the course of trade, provided such use is in accordance with honest practices in industrial or commercial matters.

An application for a collective mark must be accompanied by the submission of the regulations which will govern its use (Article 65). Such regulations are to be entered on the Community register and can subsequently be amended.

A Community collective mark can be refused on the same grounds as a Community trade mark, and on the additional grounds that:

(a)   the applicant does not satisfy the requirements of Article 64;

(b)   the collective mark's regulations are contrary to public policy;

(c)   the public are likely to be misled into thinking that it is something other than a collective mark (Article 66).

Other minor differences between a Community trade mark and a Community collective mark are:

(a)   Written observations under Article 41 objecting to the application for a collective mark can include comments on the additional grounds of refusal found in Article 66 (Article 67).

(b)   Use of the collective mark by any person having authority to use it will satisfy the use requirements of Article 15 (Article 68).

(c)   The rights of licensees conferred by Article 22 apply to every person who has authority to use the collective mark (Article 70).

(d)   Additional grounds of revocation are that the proprietor has not taken reasonable steps to prevent the collective mark being used contrary to its regulations, that its use has resulted in its becoming deceptive within the meaning of Article 66, or that its regulations have been recorded in the register when they do not comply with the requirements of Article 65 (Article 71).

(e)   An additional ground of invalidity is that the collective mark has been registered in breach of Article 66 (Article 72).

Conversion into national application

Articles 108 to 110 enable the proprietor of a Community application or registration to request its conversion into a national trade mark application, either where the application has been refused or withdrawn or where a registration has ceased to exist. Conversion is not available where:

(a)   the Community registration has been revoked for non-use, unless the mark has been used in the Member State for which conversion is requested;

(b)   grounds for the refusal, revocation or invalidity of that mark exist in the Member State for which conversion is requested.

Conversion will be appropriate in cases where a Community application or registration cannot live up to the requirement that it must have a unitary character, that is where it is valid only in some but not all Member States.

A converted application will enjoy the application or the priority date of the Community mark, and any right of seniority enjoyed by it in that Member State.

A request for conversion must be filed within three months of the notification of the decision of the Office refusing the application or cancelling the registration; or within three months of the withdrawal of the application or failure to renew by the proprietor; or within three months of the decision of a national court cancelling the registration.

The request is to be filed with the Office, specifying the Member States where protection is desired. If the conditions of the Regulation are fulfilled, the request is then passed on to the relevant national trade mark registries. Thereafter, it will be treated as a national application but cannot be subjected to formal requirements of national law which are additional to those required by the Regulation itself, other than the payment of necessary fees, the indication of an address for service and the provision of any necessary translation and representation of the mark.

Maintenance of Community Trade Marks

Many of the practical issues discussed in chapter 8 concerning the maintenance of a United Kingdom national registration apply equally to a Community trade mark registration. The provisions in the Regulation dealing specifically with the maintenance of a Community mark are as follows:

Renewal
Under Article 47, a Community trade mark is to be renewed for a further period of 10 years at the request of the proprietor upon payment of the prescribed fee. The Office will advise the proprietor in good time of the need to renew. Renewal must be within six months of the expiry date; failing this, renewal can be within the following six months provided an additional fee is paid. Renewal can be in respect of some only of the goods or services for which the mark is registered.

Alteration of a Community mark
Article 48 confers a limited power of alteration, worded in the same way as in the 1994 Act in respect of domestic registrations. Basically, a registered trade mark cannot be altered either during registration or on renewal, unless the mark includes the name and address of the proprietor and the change to that name or address does not substantially affect the identity of the mark. Such alteration is to be published. Article 48 therefore operates as a reminder that the mark should be carefully chosen at the outset, so that the registration matches the mark actually in use.

Requirement of use
Article 15, which is the equivalent of Article 10 of the Directive and which expands on recital 9 of the Regulation, requires that a Community trade mark be put to genuine use within the Community within the period of five years from registration, otherwise it may be revoked under Article 50. A Community trade mark is also liable to be revoked if it has not been put to genuine use for an

uninterrupted period of five years. In both instances the owner can argue that there were proper reasons for non-use.

It is not clear from the wording of Article 15 whether a Community mark has to be used in every single Member State, or a majority of Member States, or just one Member State, to maintain its validity. Guidance may be found from the ability to convert a Community trade mark into a national application under Article 108. The Article states that where the mark has been revoked for non-use in the Community, it can be converted if it has been put to genuine use in the Member State concerned. The inference would seem to be that to retain validity as a Community trade mark, use in more than one Member State is required. However, Minute 9 of the Minutes of the meeting of the Council of Ministers agreeing the Community Trade Mark Regulation states that genuine use in one Member State is to be treated as genuine use in the Community.

Article 15 states that use with the consent of the proprietor is deemed to be use by the proprietor, and also explains that 'use' for the purposes of the Regulation includes use of the mark in a different form, provided its distinctive character is not altered and use of the mark for export purposes. The need for the mark to be used in a form not substantially different from the form in which it was registered should be seen as a corollary to Article 48 prohibiting the alteration of a mark.

The positive obligation to use a Community mark found in Article 15 should be contrasted with the way in which the 1994 Act merely includes non-use as a ground of revocation.

Surrender

A Community trade mark can be surrendered in whole or in part in accordance with Article 49. The most likely instance of this happening is where the owner of a Community mark opposes a later application for a similar mark but when challenged cannot show genuine use of the mark for all the goods or services for which it is registered. Partial surrender would therefore enable the Community mark to survive in respect of goods or services for which it has been used. Surrender may have implications as regards the payment of costs under Article 81 in the context of opposition proceedings before the Office and so should be offered sooner rather than later.

Revocation

The grounds for revocation, contained in Article 50, are as follows:

(a) Failure to put the mark to genuine use in the Community for a continuous period of five years unless there are proper reasons for non-use. The mark will not be revoked if between the expiry of the five-year period and the filing of the application to revoke, genuine use has recommenced, unless this was within the three-month period prior to the application and the proprietor became aware that the application to revoke might be filed.

(b) Where, as a result of the acts or inactivity of the proprietor, the mark has become the generic name of the product or service for which it is registered.

(c) Where, as a result of the use of the mark by the proprietor or with his consent, the mark is liable to mislead the public.

(d) Where the proprietor no longer satisfies the requirements of Article 5 as to status.

Revocation of the mark may be total or partial, and may be sought by means of an application to the Office under Article 55 or by way of counterclaim to infringement proceedings before a national court under Article 92.

An application to the Office for revocation can be brought by any natural or legal person, including any group or body set up to represent the interests of manufacturers, producers, suppliers of services, traders or consumers (Article 55). It can thus be seen that a Community mark is open to revocation proceedings brought by someone other than another trade mark proprietor or applicant. An application to revoke will be inadmissible if the issue has already been adjudicated upon by a court in a Member State by way of final decision.

The application to the Office to revoke a Community mark must be supported by a written statement and the appropriate fee. The application will be examined by the Office, which must invite the parties to submit their observations. The Office may invite the parties to reach a friendly settlement, otherwise it will decide the revocation issue for itself. If the mark is revoked, in whole or in part, then the mark ceases to have effect from the date of the application to revoke unless an earlier date is fixed by the court or Office at the request of the parties (Article 54).

Where a national court hears a counterclaim for revocation under its jurisdiction granted by Article 92, such counterclaim can be based only on the grounds specified in the Regulation (Article 96). Such a counterclaim cannot be raised where the Office has already reached a final decision in the matter. The national court is obliged to notify the Office both of the filing of the counterclaim for revocation and of the outcome of the case. Alternatively, the national court may stay the infringement proceedings at the request of the trade mark owner and ask the defendant to submit an application for revocation to the Office; if this is not done within the prescribed time limit, the counterclaim is deemed to be withdrawn.

Invalidity

A Community mark can be declared invalid under either Article 51 or 52. As with revocation, invalidity can either be the subject of an application to the Office under Article 55 or the subject of a counterclaim to infringement proceedings heard by a national court pursuant to its jurisdiction under Article 92. The procedure in each case is identical to that for revocation explained in the previous section, with two exceptions:

(a)   Whilst an application for invalidity under Article 51 (which covers breach of Articles 5 and 7 and applications made in bad faith) can be brought by the same persons who can challenge for revocation, an application for invalidity under Article 52 can only be brought by the owners of earlier trade marks or other prior rights (Article 55(1)), in other words there is restricted *locus standi* under Article 52.

(b)   Where a Community trade mark is found invalid, it is deemed not to have had the effects conferred by the Regulation from the outset (Article 54(2)). By contrast, the revocation of a Community trade mark means that it is deemed not to have had the effects conferred on it by the Regulation from the date of the application to revoke. In other words, whilst revocation is prospective in its effect from the date of the application to revoke, invalidity is totally retrospective. Neither, however, can affect a final decision on infringement reached prior to the decision to revoke or invalidate the mark, or a contract which has been performed prior to that decision, subject to any national laws on unjust enrichment.

Further, where the application for a declaration of invalidity is brought by the owner of an earlier Community or national mark, the proprietor of the same can be required to furnish evidence of use of the mark: failure to do so will result in the invalidity proceedings being rejected (Article 56).

The grounds of invalidity in the Regulation are as follows:

(a)   that the mark was registered in breach of Article 5 (which concerns the status of the applicant (Article 51(1)(a));

(b)   that the mark was registered in breach of Article 7 (absolute grounds of refusal), except that where the mark should have been refused because it was non-distinctive, descriptive or customary, account may be taken of any intervening use which has rendered it distinctive in fact (Article 51(1)(a) and 51(2));

(c)   that the mark was applied for in bad faith (Article 51(1)(b));

(d)   that there existed an earlier Community, regional, national or international registration or application for the same, or a 'well-known' mark, amounting to a conflicting prior right under Article 8 (Article 52(1)(a));

(e)   that the trade mark had been the subject of an unauthorised application by the proprietor's agent contrary to Article 8(3) (Article 52(1)(b));

(f)   that there existed an unregistered but used earlier mark which satisfies the criteria of Article 8(4) (Article 52(1)(c));

(g)   that there existed some other prior right recognised by national law, that is, a right to a name, a right of personal portrayal, a copyright or some other industrial property right (Article 52(2)).

In respect of a claim for invalidity under Article 52 (prior rights), the owner of the prior right will be bound by any consent given to the registration of the later Community mark. The prior right owner will also be prevented from claiming invalidity where there has been five years' acquiescence to the later Community mark (Article 53, equivalent to Article 9 of the Directive) although the owner of the later Community mark is unable to challenge the prior right.

Exploitation of Community Trade Marks

The provisions of the Regulation dealing with the exploitation of Community trade marks should be contrasted with sections 22 to 31 inclusive of the 1994 Act, discussed in chapter 11.

Property rights

Because of the unitary effect of the Community trade mark declared by Article 1 of the Regulation, some mechanism is required for determining which system of property rights should govern such a mark. The EC Treaty itself does not deal with rules of ownership and indeed declares in Article 222 that the property laws of Member States are not to be prejudiced by the Treaty itself.

Article 16 of the Regulation provides this mechanism. It states that a Community trade mark is to be dealt with in its entirety and for the whole area of the

Community as if it were a national trade mark registered in the Member State where the proprietor has a seat or domicile or an establishment. Thus a Community mark owned by a German company will attract the German property rules applicable to German national registrations; a Community mark owned by an Irish enterprise will be treated as if it were an Irish national registration. Where the proprietor does not have a domicile or establishment within the Community, then a Community mark will be governed by Spanish law. Hence owners of Community trade marks who are not EC nationals or domiciles will be bound by the provisions of the Spanish trade mark legislation concerning property rights in trade marks.

Article 16 further provides that where two or more persons are entered on the Community Register as joint proprietors, then it is necessary to see whether the first one has a domicile or establishment in the Community, in which case the law of the Member State of the first-named applicant will apply; if not, then the status of the second-named applicant is examined to see if they get the benefit of the Article. Only if none of the joint proprietors is a Community-based enterprise will the mark be treated as a Spanish national mark.

It has been noted that section 23 of the 1994 Act creates a tenancy in common of a United Kingdom national mark which is the subject of co-ownership. By contrast, Article 16 of the Regulation refers expressly to 'joint proprietors'. This raises the possibility that a Community mark which attracts the operation of United Kingdom law by virtue of Article 16 would be subject to a joint tenancy, whilst a purely national United Kingdom mark would attract the opposite regime under section 23.

Article 24 states that the provisions of Article 16 and the other provisions in the Regulation dealing with property rights in Community marks are to apply also to pending applications for the same.

Assignment
Article 17 governs the transfer of ownership of a Community trade mark and should be contrasted with the provisions of the 1994 Act dealing with the same issue. The use of the word 'transfer' in Article 17 is intended to cover both voluntary assignments and transfers by operation of law.

The Article declares that a Community mark can be transferred separately from any transfer of the undertaking (that is, without goodwill), and can be transferred for some or all of the goods or services for which it is registered. The Article also deals with the converse situation: where an undertaking is transferred as a whole, this is deemed to include a transfer of the mark as well unless there is a clear express or implied agreement to the contrary.

A Community trade mark can only be voluntarily assigned in writing, signed by both parties, otherwise it will be void. Any transfer must be entered on the Community register and published. Until the assignment is recorded, the successor in title may not invoke the rights arising from the registration.

One particular point of contrast between the Regulation and the 1994 Act arises by virtue of Article 17(4), which reflects Recital 10 of the Regulation. This enables the Office to refuse to record a transfer of a Community mark where it is clear from the documentation submitted to it that the transfer is likely to mislead the public concerning the nature, quality or geographical origin of the goods or services in respect of which the mark is registered. The Office's objections can be overcome only by the successor agreeing to limit the registration to goods or services in respect of which it will not mislead. Although a similar power was conferred on the United Kingdom Trade Marks Registry by the 1938 Act, as amended, this was removed as part of the deregulation approach to trade marks found in the 1994 Act. The philosophy of the 1994 Act would appear to be that the parties themselves have a sufficient self-interest in ensuring that a trade mark assignment is not deceptive. The Community approach is clearly much more interventionist.

The assignment of a Community mark to its rightful owner can be demanded where it has been registered without authorisation by the agent of the proprietor (Article 18).

Other property dealings

A Community trade mark can be given as security, independently of the undertaking owning it, or be the subject of other rights *in rem* (Article 19). It can also be levied in execution (Article 20) and be the subject of bankruptcy proceedings in the Member State whose laws govern its property rights (Article 21). Any such proceedings affecting the ownership of the mark must be recorded in the Community Register.

Licensing

Article 22, in like manner to Article 8 of the Directive, provides that a Community mark can be licensed for some or all of the goods or services for which it is registered and for the whole or part of the Community. Such licence may be exclusive or non-exclusive. Unlike section 28 of the 1994 Act, the Regulation does not provide for there to be a partial licence as to 'use of the trade mark in a particular manner'.

Where the licensee breaches the terms of the licence as to duration, form of use, scope of goods or services, the territory of use or the quality of the goods or services, the proprietor can invoke the rights conferred by the registration (Article 22(2)).

The procedural status of the licensee of a Community mark is not as advantageous as that of a licensee of a United Kingdom national mark. The licensee of a Community mark can bring infringement proceedings in its own name only where the owner consents. However, an exclusive licensee can bring infringement proceedings where the owner, after a formal request, does not bring such proceedings within an appropriate period (Article 22(3)).

Where the proprietor of the Community mark brings infringement proceedings, the licensee is entitled to intervene in order to obtain compensation for any damage which it has suffered (Article 22(4)).

Article 22(3) and (4) should be contrasted with sections 30 and 31 of the 1994 Act.

Registration of transactions

Article 23 provides that transfers, mortgages and licences of Community marks will bind third parties in all Member States only once they have been recorded on the Community Register, unless the third party who acquired rights after the date of the transaction knew of the transaction at the time of acquisition. There is an exception for third parties who acquire a Community trade mark by way of transfer of the whole of the undertaking. The effect of any levy of execution on a Community mark or of any declaration of bankruptcy affecting the same is to be governed by the law of the relevant Member State.

Rights Conferred by a Community Trade Mark

The wording of the Regulation follows closely that of the Directive in spelling out the scope of the Community trade mark right. Reference should therefore be made to chapter 9 for a detailed discussion of the key words found in the Directive and incorporated into United Kingdom domestic law by sections 9 and 10 of the 1994 Act. Article 14 makes it clear that the effects of a Community trade mark shall be governed solely by the terms of the Regulation, although the procedural details of infringement are to be determined by national law, as explained below. This means that while the Regulation delegates the handling of infringement actions to the courts of Member States, when deciding whether a Community registration has been infringed they are to have regard only to the terms of the Regulation and avoid incorporating domestic notions of infringement. No doubt this will prove a fertile source of references to the Court of Justice of the European Communities for guidance as to the meaning of the Regulation.

Infringement of a Community mark
Article 9 of the Regulation, which is virtually identical to Article 5 of the Directive, declares that a Community mark shall confer on the proprietor exclusive rights therein, entitling him to prevent all third parties not having his consent from using in the course of trade any 'sign' which is identical or similar to the Community trade mark 'in relation to' the same, similar or dissimilar goods or services, subject to certain requirements. Like Article 5 of the Directive, the wording of Article 9(1) of the Regulation is not very clear, but a number of permutations can be identified, as follows:

Table 14.2

Article	Mark	Goods or services	Additional requirement
9(1)(a)	identical	identical	none
9(1)(b)	identical	similar	likelihood of confusion
9(1)(b)	similar	identical	likelihood of confusion
9(1)(b)	similar	similar	likelihood of confusion
9(1)(c)	identical *or* similar	dissimilar	reputation *plus* detriment

A number of questions can be raised concerning the interpretation of Article 9(1), as follows:

(a) The phrase 'in the course of trade' is not defined anywhere in the Regulation, but reference to recital 7 of the Regulation shows that the Commission regards the main function of the trade mark as an indicator of origin (which would suggest that 'in the course of trade' might be taken to mean 'trade mark use' in the sense formerly encountered in the United Kingdom in the context of the 1938 Act, as amended); by contrast, the definition of 'trade mark' in Article 4 of the Regulation points to the product differentiation function, whilst the recognition of the dilution action in Article 9(1)(c) points to a recognition of the advertising function. It will be for the Court of Justice to determine whether 'in the course of trade' is limited to 'trade mark use' or can include non-trade-mark matter.

(b)   Equally the phrase 'use in relation to' is not defined in the Regulation although some guidance can be found in Article 9(2) which declares that the following, *inter alia*, may be prohibited under Article 9(1), namely, affixing the sign to goods or packaging, offering the goods, putting them on the market or stocking them for such purposes or offering or supplying services thereunder, importing or exporting goods under that sign, or using the sign on business papers and in advertising. The latter variation again points to the recognition of the advertising value of trade marks, so that non-trade mark matter may be within the scope of Article 9. Further, Article 10 gives the proprietor of the Community mark the right to control the way in which the trade mark appears in dictionaries, encyclopaedias and other reference works so as to ensure that it does not become generic, though such right does not extend to periodical publications.

(c)   The concept of 'similar mark' will have to be developed in the context of a Community rather than national registration, although again recital 7 of the Regulation gives some indication of the matters to be considered. Ultimately, the Court of Justice will have to interpret the concept. It remains to be seen whether the court will follow British thinking on what is a 'similar mark' (as explained in chapter 7) or follow some of the more bizarre cases decided in Germany.

(d)   The concept of 'similar goods' will also require the development of Community case law, although again recital 7 contains some guidance.

(e)   It is relatively easy to predict that 'likelihood of confusion', which is to include a likelihood of association, will be interpreted in accordance with the jurisprudence of the Benelux Court of Justice, as explained in chapter 9.

(f)   It may also be predicted that in relation to the Community trade mark, there will be much reference to Benelux cases on dilution, given that Benelux trade marks law has provided much of the inspiration for the Directive and Regulation.

It should be noted that there is no saving in the Regulation concerning comparative advertising which uses a Community trade mark, nor is there any mention of the acts of contributory infringement proscribed by section 10(5) of the 1994 Act.

Defences
Defences to the infringement of a Community trade mark are set out in Articles 12 and 13. They can be summarised thus:

(a)   A third party is not to be prohibited from using its own name and address (Article 12 (a)).

(b)   A third party is not to be prohibited from using the Community mark to indicate the characteristics of the goods (Article 12(b)).

(c)   A third party is not to be prohibited from using the trade mark where this is necessary to indicate the intended purpose of a product or service, in particular accessories or spare parts (Article 12(c)).

Defences (a), (b) and (c) are subject to the proviso that such use is in accordance with honest practices in industrial and commercial matters.

(d)   A Community trade mark shall not entitle the proprietor to object to its use in relation to goods which have been put on the market in the Community by the proprietor or with its consent, unless there exist legitimate reasons to oppose the further commercialisation of the goods, especially where the condition of the goods is changed or impaired (Article 13).

These defences all have their counterparts in the Directive, and reference should be made to chapter 10 for an explanation of their equivalents under the 1994 Act.

Although there is no express saving (and hence no defence) for prior rights, Article 106 does permit the owners of earlier rights to sue under national law for infringement of their rights by a later Community mark, in addition to opposing the registration of such mark under Article 8 or seeking to have it cancelled for invalidity under Article 52. The same right is given by Article 107 to the owner of a used but unregistered and localised mark. In each case, however, the right to sue for infringement or passing off under national law is subject to any plea of acquiescence under Article 53.

Enforcing the Community Trade Mark Right

Enforcement is left to national law
Rather than create a special Community court to deal with litigation about a Community mark, the Regulation leaves the enforcement of the Community trade mark right to national law, and in so doing adopts the relevant provisions of the Brussels Convention on Jurisdiction and the Enforcement of Judgments in Civil and Commercial Matters 1968 (Article 90).

The designation of 'Community trade mark courts'
A preliminary requirement is that each Member State, under Article 91, must designate 'as limited a number as possible' of first and second-instance courts to deal with Community trade mark litigation, this to be communicated to the Commission within three years of the effective date of the Regulation. Such 'Community trade mark courts' (as they will be called) are required by Article 97 to apply the provisions of the Regulation to a trade mark case, and apply their own national law only to matters not covered by the Regulation. Matters which are not covered by the Regulation include rules of procedure (Article 97(3)), sanctions for trade mark infringement (Article 98), interim measures (Article 99) and appeals (Article 101). All of these issues are therefore left to national law to determine.

The jurisdiction of Community trade mark courts
The designated Community trade mark courts are given exclusive jurisdiction, by Article 92, to deal with infringement actions, threats of infringement (if recognised by national law), declarations of non-infringement (if recognised by national law), claims for damages and counterclaims for revocation or for a declaration of invalidity of a Community mark. Such courts are to treat the Community mark as valid unless validity is put in issue by the defendant (Article 95).

Determining the proper forum

Article 93 contains detailed rules for determining which of the Community trade mark courts should hear actions covered by Article 92. The primary forum is the court in the Member State where the defendant is domiciled or, failing that, in which the defendant has an establishment. Failing that, it is to be the court of the Member State where the plaintiff is domiciled or, failing that, where the plaintiff is established. If none of the foregoing criteria apply, Spanish Community trade mark courts will have jurisdiction. All of this is subject to any agreement between the parties that a different Community trade mark court will hear the dispute, or to the defendant entering an appearance before a different Community trade mark court. In all of these situations, the relevant court has jurisdiction to deal with acts of infringement committed anywhere in the Community (Article 94).

Cases may also be brought before the Community trade mark court of the Member State where the act of infringement was committed, but in this instance the court's jurisdiction relates only to acts of infringement committed within that Member State (Articles 93(5) and 94(2)).

Applications for interim relief can be sought in any of the courts in any of the Member States, even if the substantive issues can only be tried in one particular Community trade mark court (Article 99).

The detailed rules set out in Articles 93 and 94 will clearly involve a degree of 'forum shopping' by a potential plaintiff determined to get the best possible protection for a Community mark. The cost and simplicity of trade mark proceedings in each Member State will need to be considered.

Stay of proceedings

Article 100 contains detailed rules concerning the stay of proceedings where the issue of validity is before another Community trade mark court or the Office. Article 105 contains detailed rules for determining which Community trade mark court should decline to hear a case where two causes of action, involving the same parties, are brought in different Member States, one based on a Community mark and the other based on a national mark.

Referrals to the Court of Justice

The one unifying factor implicit in the Regulation is that any questions about its interpretation can be determined only by the Court of Justice of the European Communities by virtue of its jurisdiction under Article 177 of the EC Treaty. Designated Community trade mark courts and lawyers using them should be aware of the desirability of referring such questions to the Court of Justice, so that the Regulation can maintain its uniform effect throughout the Community.

Conclusion

The unitary character of the Community trade mark

Article 1 of the Regulation declares that the Community trade mark is to have unitary effect. This simple statement suggests a degree of uniformity which a Community trade mark does not in fact possess. It is possible to identify what are the consequences of this unitary nature, but equally the limitations created by the Regulation itself must be stressed.

Consequences of the unitary nature A Community mark is a single registration having effect in all the Member States. Only the Office is empowered to grant such a registration so that there should be a consistent standard when dealing with issues of registrability, including opposition proceedings brought by the owners of prior rights. By virtue of the Regulation, the rights conferred on the proprietor are to be the same throughout the EC, with standardised defences to an infringement action. The trade mark can be transferred only as a single entity.

The Regulation's limitations The initial choice of mark has to overcome the absolute and relative grounds of refusal not just at Community level but at national level as well, and therefore has to be a commercially viable choice in all the Member States. The mark is vulnerable to challenge on absolute or relative grounds by anyone anywhere in the EC, whether before or after registration. It must be put to genuine use 'in the Community' (whatever that may mean). The exact nature of the property right in the mark is to be determined by local not Community law. The enforcement of a Community mark is left to national courts who are to determine infringement actions and, where raised, counterclaims for revocation and invalidity. If the registration is successfully challenged, the mark is lost for the whole of the Community, unless the challenge relates only to the width of the statement of goods and services or unless it can be converted into a national application.

Parallel existence with national registration schemes
Recital 5 of the Regulation states that the Community trade mark system will not replace the trade marks laws in Member States. There will be no compulsion to register at Community level, indeed many undertakings will not want a Community registration. Small and medium enterprises often have very localised businesses, particularly in the service sector. National registration will therefore continue to be the best commercial option for them and the Regulation does not interfere with this freedom of choice.

Overlap with the Madrid Agreement for the International Registration of Marks
Once the Community trade mark system is operative, a trade mark applicant who wishes to obtain registration protection in more than one country will have a tactical choice to make. Apart from the consideration of cost and the intended geographical scope of the applicant's marketing operations, much will depend on whether the chosen trade mark is linguistically acceptable in all the Member States of the Community and whether there are any prior Community, regional, national or international registrations blocking the way. The applicant can:

(a) File separate national applications in those countries where it is intended to supply goods or services under the mark. This will entail translation costs and the appointment of local agents to effect the registrations, but has the advantage that each national application can be considered on its merits, and if the mark is not acceptable locally for linguistic reasons a different name can be chosen.
(b) File an application for a Community trade mark at the Office in Alicante. The application will have to be in one of the official Community languages, with one of the Office languages designated as the second language of the applicant.

The agent for the application can be an employee if the business is domiciled or established in the Community. One application will produce a single registration effective in all Member States. The drawback would be that the mark would have to be acceptable linguistically in all Member States (what is an invented word in one language could be descriptive, deceptive or contrary to public policy in another). Further, the Community application could be barred by a national registration existing in just one of the Member States, or by a used but unregistered mark in another. The Community registration will be vulnerable at any time to attack by way of a counterclaim brought in any of the Member States' national courts designated as trade mark courts: such attack, if successful, will destroy the whole registration.

(c)   Once an application has been filed in the applicant's home country, file an application under the Madrid Agreement (as amended) for an international registration, which is to extend to countries belonging to the Madrid system which are designated by the applicant. The procedural short-cut offered by the Madrid system enables a single application to result in a batch of national applications, each of which will be dealt with locally on its own merits. Even if the application is rejected in one country, it can still continue in all the others. A further advantage is that the amended Madrid system has only two languages (French and English) and does away with the need to appoint agents in each country where the mark is to be protected. The Madrid system is explained in further detail in chapter 15 which contains a more detailed analysis of why trade mark applicants may find it more attractive than the Community trade mark system.

Is there a need for a Community trade mark?

The Community trade mark system will be of interest to those undertakings which do business throughout the EC. The economies of scale in obtaining a single registration for all Member States will clearly be an attractive proposition, but the downside will be the need to find a mark acceptable throughout the Community. Initially, the system may be used by firms which already have parallel national registrations throughout the EC, but even then there will be problems where the proprietor has, for entirely legitimate reasons, chosen a different name for the same product in different Member States. Whilst the unitary character of the Community trade mark militates against such a practice, the ability to seek national registration instead leaves enterprises free to do so. Equally, the continued existence of national registrations will mean that it will still be possible for independent companies to register conflicting marks in their respective countries, so that such national rights will continue to be a barrier to trade. It therefore seems unlikely that the existence of the Community system will resolve the problems identified at the start of this chapter.

Consequently, it remains to be seen whether there will be much demand for the Community trade mark or whether businesses will continue to use national and/or international registrations to meet their commercial needs. Equally, time alone will tell whether the Commission's optimism about the value of a Community system of trade mark registration is justified.

CHAPTER FIFTEEN
International Registration of Trade Marks

Introduction

The need for an international system

As already explained in chapter 10, intellectual property rights have a territorial effect. This means that because they depend for their existence on statutory or judicial protection conferred by the law of a particular country, such protection is limited to the territory of that State. In an age when trade in goods is worldwide, this has one serious drawback for the intellectual property owner who wishes to sell products in more than one country. It will be necessary to obtain a separate registration for all the relevant patents, designs or trade marks to be applied to these products in each country where business is to be done. This obviously adds to the costs of doing business, as separate registration fees will have to be paid, applications will have to be made in the local language and professional advisers will have to be appointed in each country where protection is needed (some countries insist that transactions at their Patent Office can be effected only by local firms of lawyers).

A particular problem encountered in relation to obtaining trade mark protection in more than one country (and about 135 countries now have some sort of trade marks law) is that different countries have different approaches to the registration of trade marks. In many countries, there is no system of substantive examination and merely 'depositing' a trade mark application at the local trade marks registry suffices. The filing of an application therefore results in almost instantaneous registration. The validity of such a 'deposit' registration will be considered only in court proceedings, usually by way of a counterclaim to an infringement action.

An alternative system of registration is that found in Germany, and adopted by the Community Trade Mark Regulation. Here there is a formal examination of the trade mark application to see whether it complies with the definition of 'trade mark' and a substantive examination to see whether the mark is barred by any of the absolute grounds of refusal. However, although a search of prior rights is made, it is left to third parties to raise such relative grounds of refusal in opposition proceedings.

Finally, there is what might be termed the 'common law' system of trade mark registration, found in the United Kingdom, the United States of America and in many Commonwealth countries. Here the examination of a trade mark application is much more rigorous, as is the search for prior rights. As a consequence an application may be rejected by the Trade Marks Registry on both absolute and relative grounds of invalidity.

These different approaches to trade mark registration mean that the time taken to obtain registration varies enormously. A 'deposit' registration can often be obtained in a matter of days. On the other hand, an application which has been subjected to the common law system of rigorous scrutiny can take several months, if not years.

A further factor which businesses find puzzling is that even national systems which examine trade mark applications have different standards of what amounts to inherent deceptiveness or inherent descriptiveness, and of whether there is a likelihood of confusion with a prior mark. Thus a mark which has been success-fully registered in one country may be refused registration in another, even if both countries use the same language. It is of no concern to the registry of the latter country that the mark is acceptable elsewhere (*GLASSCAN Trade Mark* [1994] RPC 23).

Clearly, where the trade mark is to be registered in countries having different languages it should be remembered that a word which may be innocuous (or even meaningless) in English may have a derogatory meaning in French or Japanese or Arabic.

All of this begs the question why it has not been feasible to come up with a standardised trade mark procedure, with agreed definitions of what is deceptive or confusingly similar, and with some sort of procedure which would enable the intending trade mark applicant to obtain registration in a number of different countries simultaneously.

In response to these questions it must be pointed out that both the Paris Convention for the Protection of Industrial Property 1883 and the Trade-Related Aspects of Intellectual Property Agreement signed in March 1994 as part of the GATT negotiations contain statements as to what amounts to a trade mark. Both oblige signatory States to give protection to signs which satisfy these criteria. The choice of national procedure has, however, always been regarded as an issue of national sovereignty (and hence very sensitive). For this reason, national registries are keen to preserve their own standards of examination and adjudication and no attempt has ever been made (nor is likely to be made) to dictate how trade mark applications should be handled.

Further, it is easy to overlook the fact that trade marks, being a means of communication, have to function as part of the language and culture of the country where the goods or services are supplied. The intending trade mark applicant must therefore consider the impact of the mark not just in its country of origin but as it will appear to customers on the other side of the world.

Regional systems
As regards any attempt to provide for the international registration of trade marks, there are three 'regional' systems which enable one trade mark application to result in a single registration effective in more than one country. They are: the Uniform Benelux Trademarks Law 1971 (covering Belgium, Holland and Luxembourg); the OAPI agreement (covering the former French colonies in west and central Africa); and the Community Trade Mark, explained in the previous chapter.

The Madrid Agreement

In addition, there has been in existence since 1891 the Madrid Agreement Concerning the International Registration of Marks (hereafter 'the Madrid Agreement'). The effect of the Madrid Agreement must be distinguished from the three 'supranational' regional systems just mentioned, in that it provides a procedural short-cut for the trade mark applicant. One trade mark application results in a series of national applications, which will mature (hopefully) into national registrations. It does *not* create a single registration covering several countries. To that extent, it is erroneous to refer to the system created by it as 'international registration'. Rather, it is a single application resulting in a batch of national registrations.

The Madrid Agreement is administered by the World Intellectual Property Organisation (WIPO) in Geneva at the International Bureau set up by the Madrid Agreement. So far, its membership has been relatively low (about 30 countries) for reasons which will be explained below. Membership has tended to be largely (but not exclusively) confined to countries of Europe and North Africa which operate the 'deposit' system of trade mark registration. Not all Member States of the EC belong to the Madrid Agreement, and no country which operates the common law system of trade mark examination has ever joined. In particular, the United Kingdom, the United States of America and Japan never felt able to join the Madrid Agreement in its original form, which prevented trade mark owners from these countries from taking advantage of its system.

The Madrid Protocol

After many years of negotiations, and no doubt prompted by the imminence of the rival Community Trade Mark, the Madrid Agreement has been revised by the addition in 1989 of a Protocol (hereafter 'the Madrid Protocol'). The Madrid Protocol contains several significant differences from the original Madrid Agreement. As a result of these changes, there is every indication that the remaining EC States which never joined the original Madrid Agreement (the United Kingdom, the Republic of Ireland, Denmark and Greece) will join the Madrid Protocol. All four countries have signed the Protocol, although each will only become a full member once domestic legislation has been passed incorporating the provisions of the Protocol into their respective national laws. There is some doubt surrounding whether the United States of America will ratify the Protocol.

United Kingdom ratification of the Protocol

The Trade Marks Act 1994 in sections 53 and 54 will enable the United Kingdom to ratify the Madrid Protocol, primarily by conferring on the Secretary of State the power to make statutory instruments containing the necessary detailed rules. It is expected that the Madrid Protocol will be operative on 1 April 1995 (it needs a minimum of four ratifications to activate it, of which one must be a signatory to the original Madrid Agreement), and that the relevant United Kingdom delegated legislation will probably be passed shortly after the coming into force of the domestic part of the 1994 Act.

It must be stressed that the United Kingdom will accede to the Madrid Protocol and not the original Madrid Agreement. The Protocol operates as an alternative version of the Madrid Agreement, so that initially there will be two parallel systems for the international registration of marks. The Madrid Agreement will continue to apply to those countries which acceded to the latest (Stockholm) version of the Agreement agreed in 1967; the Protocol will only apply to those countries which ratify it. Article 9*sexies* of the Protocol provides in effect that ultimately the provisions of the Protocol will replace the provisions of the Agreement, but only after the Madrid Protocol has been in operation for at least 10 years and a majority of the members of the Madrid Agreement have been members of the Protocol for at least five years. Until then, the parallel versions will remain.

Structure of this chapter
Because there will be the two parallel systems for the international registration of trade marks, the workings of the Madrid Agreement will first be explained in general terms. The account should make clear why countries such as the United Kingdom felt unable to join. The differences found in the Madrid Protocol will then be examined, followed by a brief explanation of how the Protocol will become part of United Kingdom domestic law. Finally, a comparison will be drawn between the Madrid system and the Community Trade Mark, as the two systems can be regarded as rivals, each having its advantages and disadvantages.

The Madrid Agreement

The applicant
The starting-point for an international registration under the Madrid Agreement is that the intending applicant, whether a natural person or company, must have a trade mark registration in its country of origin, which equally must be a contracting State of the Madrid Agreement (Article 1(2)).

The term 'country of origin' is strictly defined by Article 1(3) of the Madrid Agreement to mean the country where the applicant has a real and effective industrial or commercial establishment. If no such establishment exists in a member country of the Madrid Agreement then the country of origin is the member country in which the applicant is domiciled or has its headquarters. If neither of these criteria is satisfied, then the country of origin is deemed to be the country of which the applicant is a national, *provided in each case the country is a member of the Madrid Agreement.*

The term 'real and effective industrial or commercial establishment' refers to the place of business of the applicant, not that of a subsidiary company. Hence under the Madrid Agreement, a British company could not claim to be an applicant by virtue of carrying on business in France, because the legal person having an effective establishment in France would be its French subsidiary. The doctrine of legal personality thus prevents the British company getting the benefit of the status of its subsidiary.

Procedure on application
An application for an international registration has to be sent to the International Bureau in Geneva by the national office (that is, the trade marks registry) of the country of origin (Article 1(2)). The application must include (amongst other things):

(a)   the applicant's name and address;

(b)   details of the registration in the country of origin;
(c)   the details of any Convention priority being claimed;
(d)   a reproduction of the mark;
(e)   a statement of the goods and services to which the mark is to be applied; and

(f)   a list of those countries of the Madrid Agreement in respect of which protection is requested (Articles 3(1), 3(2), 3*bis* and 3*ter*).

The onus is on the national office of the country of origin to satisfy itself that the application for international registration is in order. In connection with this, the national office is allowed to charge the applicant its own fee in addition to the fees payable to the International Bureau (Article 8(1)).

With regard to the statement of the goods or services, the international registration cannot be in respect of goods or services not covered by the national registration in the country of origin, although it can be for part of the goods or services covered by the national registration. The Madrid Agreement does not stipulate that the goods or services for which the international registration is sought must be included in a single national registration in the country of origin. The international registration could therefore be based on two or more national registrations.

Although the Madrid Agreement originally provided for an international registration to extend automatically to all its member countries, it is now up to the applicant specifically to request those countries in which protection for the mark is desired (Article 3*bis* and 3*ter*).

Once the International Bureau is satisfied that the application is in order, it will register the mark on the International Register and will arrange for it to be published in *Les Marques Internationales*, the trade marks journal of the International Bureau (Article 3(4)). The International Bureau does not examine the application, other than for compliance with formalities.

The registration date will be the date on which the International Bureau was in receipt of an application complying with all the requirements of the Madrid Agreement and the rules made pursuant thereto. *Pro forma* applications are then transmitted by the International Bureau to the national offices of the countries for which the applicant has requested registration, as well as copies of *Les Marques Internationales* (Articles 3(4) and 3(5)). The international registration is not, however, advertised in national trade mark journals.

From the date of the international registration, the mark is to be treated in each of the countries where the applicant has sought protection as though it had been filed directly at that country's national office (Article 4). However, provided the relevant national legislation so allows, a national office has the right to refuse protection for its territory, but only on the grounds which could be raised against a direct national filing under the terms of the Paris Convention (Article 5(1)). Notice of such a refusal must be sent to the International Bureau within one year of the date of the international registration (Article 5(2)). The Bureau will pass on the refusal to the applicant, who is to have the same rights of redress as if a direct national filing had been rejected (Article 5(3)). If the national office fails to notify its refusal (whether this is provisional or final) within the time limit, it loses its right to object to the extension of the international registration to that country (Article 5(5)).

The proprietor of an international registration can always make a subsequent request for extension of protection to another country of the Madrid Agreement. This may be as a result of the unforeseen expansion of business activities into the territory of that country, or as a result of that country later joining the Madrid Agreement. Any territorial extension runs coterminously with the original international registration (Article 3*ter*).

An international registration takes effect in the countries for which protection has been requested by the applicant as though it was a direct national registration. International registration does not, however, extend to the country of origin, where protection arises only by virtue of the original registration. Any changes to the original registration must be notified by the country of origin to the International Bureau where such changes affect the international registration (Article 9). The Bureau will record such changes on the International Register and will notify them to the offices of the countries where the mark is protected.

Subsequent dealings

If the international registration is assigned during its first five years to a person based in a contracting country other than the country of the original applicant, the office of the country of origin of the new proprietor must give its consent to the assignment, otherwise the international registration must be cancelled (Article 9*bis*). An international registration cannot be assigned to a person who is not entitled to file an international application (Article 9*bis*(2)).

Where there is a partial assignment of an international registration, each of the contracting countries has the right to refuse to recognise the assignment if the goods or services included in the part which is assigned are similar to those for which the assignor remains registered (Article 9*ter*). There can also be the partial assignment of an international registration in respect of some of the contracting countries only (Article 9*ter*(2)).

Where the owner of the international registration previously owned a national registration for the same mark, the international registration is deemed to have replaced the earlier registration, without prejudice to any rights acquired by reason of the earlier registration (Article 4*bis*).

Duration, renewal and 'central attack'

An international registration is for a period of 20 years and is renewable indefinitely for further 20-year periods (Articles 6(1) and 7). Once the mark has been on the International Register for more than five years, it becomes independent of the registration in the country of origin (Article 6(2)). However, if during those first five years the national mark ceases to be protected in the country of origin, the international registration is also destroyed (Article 6(3)). This is the so-called system of 'central attack' which renders an international registration vulnerable. It does not matter whether the national registration in the country of origin is lost voluntarily, or as a result of action by the local trade marks registry, or as a result of a judicial decision. In any event, the international registration and all resultant national registrations based on it are lost, even if the grounds on which the national registration in the country of origin was lost are not recognised in the other contracting countries.

Fees
When filing an application for an international registration or renewing the same, only one set of fees (calculated in Swiss francs) is payable in advance to the International Bureau. The fee consists of the 'basic fee' (which is the same on registration and renewal and which can be paid in two 10-year instalments), a supplementary fee for each class of goods or services beyond the three classes automatically allowed to the applicant, and a complementary fee for each country for which protection is requested. The total fees are less than the total of national fees which would have to be paid were the applicant to make a direct national filing in each of the contracting countries.

Although the fees are distributed by the International Bureau between the contracting States after deduction of operating expenses, such fees are generally far less than would be charged by the trade mark registries of those countries if they carried out a full examination of the trade mark applications. Hence, countries such as the United States of America felt unable to join the Madrid Agreement because this would result in domestic applicants subsidising international applicants.

Working language
The only working language of the Madrid Agreement is French.

Infringement
Because the effect of the Madrid system is to create a series of national registrations, infringement remains a matter for the domestic law of the member country concerned.

The Madrid Protocol

Two parallel systems
As explained above, the Madrid Protocol provides a parallel system to the Madrid Agreement and will eventually supersede it. It should be assumed therefore that the points outlined above apply equally to the Madrid Protocol unless stated otherwise.

Major differences between the two systems
The major differences between the Madrid Agreement and the Madrid Protocol are as follows:

(a)   An international registration can be based either on an application or a registration in the applicant's own country, provided this country is a contracting State (Article 2(1)). The original Madrid Agreement allowed the international registration to be based only on a home registration.

(b)   An international registration can also be based either on an application or a registration obtained at an intergovernmental organisation (such as the Community Trade Mark Office) (Article 2(1)). This means that a Community Trade Mark can be the 'basic' application or registration for an international registration.

(c)   A contracting State has the right to declare that the time limit during which it can object to the extension of the international registration to its territory is to be 18 months, not 12 months as under the Agreement (Article 5(2)(b)).

(d)   A contracting State may also object to the extension to its territory of the international registration on the grounds of an opposition brought by a third party, and if so can reject the international registration more than 18 months after the filing date. This is subject to the proviso that the contracting State must have notified the International Bureau when it acceded to the Protocol of the possibility that oppositions could be filed after this time limit (Article 5(2)(c)(i) and (d)).

(e)   In the case of refusal based on opposition proceedings, the notification of rejection must be within seven months of the start of the opposition period or one month from the expiry of the opposition period, whichever is the shorter (Article 5(2)(c)(ii) and (d)).

(f)   Registration is for a period of 10 years, renewable for further periods of 10 years (Articles 6(1) and 7(1)), rather than the periods of 20 years specified in the Agreement.

(g)   The international registration becomes independent of the 'home' registration after five years (Article 6(2)). However, in the case of a successful 'central attack' during the first five years, the proprietor has the right to 'transform' the international registration into a series of national applications all enjoying the same filing date, and, if applicable, the same priority date as the international registration (Article 9*quinquies*). Such transformation must be effected within three months of the loss of the international registration, must be for the same goods or services and must comply with all other requirements of the national law concerned. Under the Madrid Agreement, 'central attack' was fatal to all dependent national registrations.

(h)   A contracting State can 'opt out' of the distribution of fees collected by the International Bureau and instead charge its own fees (Article 8(7)). Such fees may not exceed the amount which the contracting State's office would be entitled to receive from an applicant for a 10-year registration or from a proprietor in respect of a 10-year renewal at that office.

(i)   The working languages of the Protocol are to be French and English.

Implementation of the Madrid Protocol in United Kingdom Domestic Law

The formal ratification by the United Kingdom of the Madrid Protocol will entail the creation of two new procedures under United Kingdom domestic trade marks law. Both of these will be covered in detail by secondary legislation to be made under section 54 of the 1994 Act. This can be expected some time early in 1995.

The delegated legislation will have to provide in effect for two-way traffic. First, a procedure will have to be laid down under which the United Kingdom owner of a United Kingdom trade mark application or registration can ask the United Kingdom Registry to send a request to the International Bureau in Geneva for an international registration based on the United Kingdom mark.

Secondly, a procedure will have to be established under which the United Kingdom Registry will receive requests from the International Bureau for the extension of an international registration originating in another Member State of the Madrid system to the United Kingdom. Such a registration is called, by virtue of section 53 of the 1994 Act an 'international trade mark (UK)' and will attract all the benefits of a domestic registration. Thus an international trade mark (UK) will be treated as an earlier trade mark for the purposes of relative grounds of refusal under section 5 and can be protected through an infringement action under section 10 in the normal way. Likewise it will be subject to the rules on revocation and invalidity found in sections 46 and 47, and the provisions on assignment and licensing in sections 24 and 28.

Section 54 contains an indicative but not exhaustive list of the detailed rules which will have to be included in any statutory instrument giving effect to the Madrid Protocol in United Kingdom law. The matters to be covered include:

(a)   where a United Kingdom application or registration is to be the basis of an international registration, how the international application is to be sent by the United Kingdom Trade Marks Registry to the International Bureau and the procedure to be followed where the United Kingdom 'base' application or registration fails or ceases to be in force;

(b)   where an international registration is to be extended to the United Kingdom, the procedures to be adopted by the Trade Marks Registry for handling the request for extension, the effects of a successful request for extension, and, should the international application or registration fail, the method for transforming the United Kingdom extension into a domestic application or registration;

(c)   general rules concerning communications between the International Bureau and the United Kingdom Trade Marks Registry, the payment of fees and so on.

The statutory instrument will also have to provide for the application of specific sections of the 1994 Act to any international trade mark (UK), in particular, section 21 (threats), sections 89 to 91 (the ability to request Customs and Excise to prevent the importation of counterfeit goods) and sections 92 to 96 (criminal offences, including counterfeiting).

Comparison between the Madrid System and the Community Trade Mark

The unitary character of the Community trade mark
The principal weakness (and yet also the strength) of a Community Trade Mark registration will be its unitary character. As explained in chapter 14, this means that the registration will cover all the Member States of the EC and cannot be fragmented by partial assignment.

Although the unitary character is obviously a major benefit once registration has been obtained, the converse is that a proposed Community mark must be acceptable in all Member States, not just on absolute grounds, but also on relative grounds. It is easy to envisage a Community trade mark application being foiled because the name, although acceptable in (say) English, is unacceptable in (say) German. This might explain why Rolls Royce cars have not registered the name 'Silver Mist' in Germany ('mist' means 'dung' in German); and why General Motors changed the name of the Vauxhall 'Nova' to the Vauxhall 'Corsa' (in Spanish, a 'Nova' car literally 'does not go'). Equally, a potential Community registration might be foiled by a prior right existing in (say) Portugal or Denmark which does not exist elsewhere.

The problems posed by the unitary character of the Community trade mark will get worse as more Member States, all with their own languages and cultures, accede to the Community. It is not clear yet what will happen when a new country joins the EC after the Community Trade Mark Office becomes operational. Existing

Community registrations might automatically be extended to the new Member State, thereby overriding local marks. Or an existing Community mark might be invalidated by a local mark in the new Member State. Either solution seems unfair. The alternative would be to make the Community registration apply only to those countries which were Member States at the date of registration, a pragmatic solution which immediately undermines the unitary character of a Community registration.

The unitary nature of the Community trade mark raises other practical problems. For a variety of quite legitimate reasons, some trade mark owners prefer to have different names for the same product in different countries. Alternatively, a multinational group of companies may choose to have local subsidiaries owning local registrations, rather than all trade marks being owned by the parent company. A company may not want to do business in all Member States of the EC. In all of these cases, the unitary nature of the Community trade mark cuts across such practical considerations, in that the Trade Mark Regulation assumes that there will be one brand name, owned by one member of the corporate group and used throughout the EC.

Finally, the unitary character of the Community registration raises difficulties in connection with the loss of registration. If a Community trade mark is refused registration or is later revoked for non-use, genericness or deceptiveness, or is declared invalid because it conflicts with the absolute or relative grounds of refusal, then it is lost for the whole of the EC. With regard to revocation for non-use, it is not yet clear what level of use will suffice to maintain the validity of a Community mark. However, by inference from Article 108 of the Trade Mark Regulation (which permits a failed Community application or registration to be converted into a national application), it seems that use in more than one Member State is required, although this is contradicted by the minutes of the meeting of the Council of Ministers approving the Community Trade Mark Regulation.

Advantages of the Madrid system

By contrast the Madrid system is much more flexible, and has the advantage of having been in operation for over 100 years, so that it is tried and tested. The trade mark owner can select which countries are relevant to the business and will not have to pay a filing fee for unwanted countries. If the international application is rejected in one of the designated countries, that does not affect the outcome of the applications elsewhere. International registrations can be obtained for different marks, the applicant designating the countries in which protection is required. Equally, different members of the corporate group can apply for separate registrations to operate in different territories. As long as there is no overlap, this is permissible.

Because the Madrid system results in the international registration ultimately being treated as a series of national registrations, the fact that the mark is later challenged in one country is not fatal to the validity of the other registrations. If new countries accede to the Protocol, it is up to the trade mark owner to decide whether to ask for the international registration to be extended to them. A request for extension will therefore be dealt with on its merits and will not affect the validity of the previous registrations for that mark obtained through the Madrid system.

Further, the Madrid system is not confined to the EC, nor indeed to mainland Europe, and has the potential, since the conclusion of the Protocol, to become a worldwide system.

Drawbacks of the Madrid system

Lest it be thought that the Madrid system has no drawbacks when compared with the Community trade mark, it must be repeated that both the Agreement and the Protocol are open only to nationals of those countries which have joined either one or the other. By contrast, the Community trade mark is open to any person who is a national of or domiciled in any member of the Paris Convention.

The principal perceived weakness of the Madrid system is 'central attack' (explained above). This, however, is much modified by the Protocol, with the significant ability to seek 'transformation' of the international registration into national marks. In any case central attack only applies for the first five years of the international registration. By contrast, a Community trade mark registration is open to attack at any time, with the result, if the attack is successful, that the entire registration is lost.

Cost

The most telling difference between the two systems is likely to be cost. The exact fees to be charged by the Community Trade Mark Office are not known at the time of writing, but because of the requirement (under Article 116) that all documents and transactions have to be translated into all Community languages, the fees are likely to be high. The fees under the Madrid system are known and relatively low (despite the exchange rate against the Swiss franc). There is only one working language under the Agreement, two under the Protocol. Unless the Community Trade Marks Office can undercut the fees charged by WIPO in Geneva, many firms may well find the Madrid system more suitable for their commercial needs.

APPENDIX ONE
Trade Marks Act 1994

CHAPTER 26

ARRANGEMENT OF SECTIONS

PART I   REGISTERED TRADE MARKS

Introductory

Section

Grounds for refusal of registration

Effects of registered trade mark

Infringement proceedings

Other general provisions

SCHEDULES

Trade Marks Act 1994

An Act to make new provision for registered trade marks, implementing Council Directive No. 89/104/EEC of 21st December 1988 to approximate the laws of the Member States relating to trade marks; to make provision in connection with Council Regulation (EC) No. 40/94 of 20th December 1993 on the Community trade mark; to give effect to the Madrid Protocol Relating to the International Registration of Marks of 27th June 1989, and to certain provisions of the Paris Convention for the Protection of Industrial Property of 20th March 1883, as revised and amended; and for connected purposes.   [21st July 1994]

BE IT ENACTED by the Queen's most Excellent Majesty, by and with the advice and consent of the Lords Spiritual and Temporal, and Commons, in this present Parliament assembled, and by the authority of the same, as follows:—

PART I   REGISTERED TRADE MARKS

Introductory

1.   Trade marks

(1)   In this Act a 'trade mark' means any sign capable of being represented graphically which is capable of distinguishing goods or services of one undertaking from those of other undertakings.

A trade mark may, in particular, consist of words (including personal names), designs, letters, numerals or the shape of goods or their packaging.

(2)   References in this Act to a trade mark include, unless the context otherwise requires, references to a collective mark (see section 49) or certification mark (see section 50).

2.   Registered trade marks

(1)   A registered trade mark is a property right obtained by the registration of the trade mark under this Act and the proprietor of a registered trade mark has the rights and remedies provided by this Act.

(2)   No proceedings lie to prevent or recover damages for the infringement of an unregistered trade mark as such; but nothing in this Act affects the law relating to passing off.

Grounds for refusal of registration

3.   Absolute grounds for refusal of registration

(1)   The following shall not be registered—

(a)   signs which do not satisfy the requirements of section 1(1),

(b)   trade marks which are devoid of any distinctive character,

(c)   trade marks which consist exclusively of signs or indications which may serve, in trade, to designate the kind, quality, quantity, intended purpose, value, geographical origin, the time of production of goods or of rendering of services, or other characteristics of goods or services,

(d)   trade marks which consist exclusively of signs or indications which have become customary in the current language or in the *bona fide* and established practices of the trade:

Provided that, a trade mark shall not be refused registration by virtue of paragraph (b), (c) or (d) above if, before the date of application for registration, it has in fact acquired a distinctive character as a result of the use made of it.

(2)   A sign shall not be registered as a trade mark if it consists exclusively of—

(a)   the shape which results from the nature of the goods themselves,

(b)   the shape of goods which is necessary to obtain a technical result, or

(c)   the shape which gives substantial value to the goods.

(3)   A trade mark shall not be registered if it is—

(a)   contrary to public policy or to accepted principles of morality, or

(b)   of such a nature as to deceive the public (for instance as to the nature, quality or geographical origin of the goods or service).

(4)   A trade mark shall not be registered if or to the extent that its use is prohibited in the United Kingdom by any enactment or rule of law or by any provision of Community law.

(5)   A trade mark shall not be registered in the cases specified, or referred to, in section 4 (specially protected emblems).

(6)   A trade mark shall not be registered if or to the extent that the application is made in bad faith.

4.   Specially protected emblems

(1)   A trade mark which consists of or contains—

(a)   the Royal arms, or any of the principal armorial bearings of the Royal arms, or any insignia or device so nearly resembling the Royal arms or any such armorial bearing as to be likely to be mistaken for them or it,

(b)   a representation of the Royal crown or any of the Royal flags,

(c)   a representation of Her Majesty or any member of the Royal family, or any colourable imitation thereof, or

(d)   words, letters or devices likely to lead persons to think that the applicant either has or recently has had Royal patronage or authorisation,

shall not be registered unless it appears to the registrar that consent has been given by or on behalf of Her Majesty or, as the case may be, the relevant member of the Royal family.

(2)   A trade mark which consists of or contains a representation of—

(a)   the national flag of the United Kingdom (commonly known as the Union Jack), or

(b)   the flag of England, Wales, Scotland, Northern Ireland or the Isle of Man,

shall not be registered if it appears to the registrar that the use of the trade mark would be misleading or grossly offensive.

Provision may be made by rules identifying the flags to which paragraph (b) applies.

(3)   A trade mark shall not be registered in the cases specified in—

section 57 (national emblems, &c. of Convention countries), or

section 58 (emblems, &c. of certain international organisations).

(4)   Provision may be made by rules prohibiting in such cases as may be prescribed the registration of a trade mark which consists of or contains—

(a)   arms to which a person is entitled by virtue of a grant of arms by the Crown, or

(b)   insignia so nearly resembling such arms as to be likely to be mistaken for them,

unless it appears to the registrar that consent has been given by or on behalf of that person.

Where such a mark is registered, nothing in this Act shall be construed as authorising its use in any way contrary to the laws of arms.

5.   Relative grounds for refusal of registration

(1)   A trade mark shall not be registered if it is identical with an earlier trade mark and the goods or services for which the trade mark is applied for are identical with the goods or services for which the earlier trade mark is protected.

(2)   A trade mark shall not be registered if because—

(a)   it is identical with an earlier trade mark and is to be registered for goods or services similar to those for which the earlier trade mark is protected, or

(b)   it is similar to an earlier trade mark and is to be registered for goods or services identical with or similar to those for which the earlier trade mark is protected,

there exists a likelihood of confusion on the part of the public, which includes the likelihood of association with the earlier trade mark.

(3)   A trade mark which—

(a)   is identical with or similar to an earlier trade mark, and

(b)   is to be registered for goods or services which are not similar to those for which the earlier trade mark is protected,

shall not be registered if, or to the extent that, the earlier trade mark has a reputation in the United Kingdom (or, in the case of a Community trade mark, in the European Community) and the use of the later mark without due cause would take unfair advantage of, or be detrimental to, the distinctive character or the repute of the earlier trade mark.

(4)   A trade mark shall not be registered if, or to the extent that, its use in the United Kingdom is liable to be prevented—

(a)   by virtue of any rule of law (in particular, the law of passing off) protecting an unregistered trade mark or other sign used in the course of trade, or

(b)   by virtue of an earlier right other than those referred to in subsections (1) to (3) or paragraph (a) above, in particular by virtue of the law of copyright, design right or registered designs.

A person thus entitled to prevent the use of a trade mark is referred to in this Act as the proprietor of an 'earlier right' in relation to the trade mark.

(5)   Nothing in this section prevents the registration of a trade mark where the proprietor of the earlier trade mark or other earlier right consents to the registration.

6. Meaning of 'earlier trade mark'

(1)   In this Act an 'earlier trade mark' means—

(a)   a registered trade mark, international trade mark (UK) or Community trade mark which has a date of application for registration earlier than that of the trade mark in question, taking account (where appropriate) of the priorities claimed in respect of the trade marks,

(b)   a Community trade mark which has a valid claim to seniority from an earlier registered trade mark or international trade mark (UK), or

(c)   a trade mark which, at the date of application for registration of the trade mark in question or (where appropriate) of the priority claimed in respect of the application, was entitled to protection under the Paris Convention as a well known trade mark.

(2)   References in this Act to an earlier trade mark include a trade mark in respect of which an application for registration has been made and which, if registered, would be an earlier trade mark by virtue of subsection (1)(a) or (b), subject to its being so registered.

(3)   A trade mark within subsection (1)(a) or (b) whose registration expires shall continue to be taken into account in determining the registrability of a later mark for a period of one year after the expiry unless the registrar is satisfied that there was no *bona fide* use of the mark during the two years immediately preceding the expiry.

7. Raising of relative grounds in case of honest concurrent use

(1)   This section applies where on an application for the registration of a trade mark it appears to the registrar—

(a)   that there is an earlier trade mark in relation to which the conditions set out in section 5(1), (2) or (3) obtain, or

(b)   that there is an earlier right in relation to which the condition set out in section 5(4) is satisfied,

but the applicant shows to the satisfaction of the registrar that there has been honest concurrent use of the trade mark for which registration is sought.

(2)   In that case the registrar shall not refuse the application by reason of the earlier trade mark or other earlier right unless objection on that ground is raised in opposition proceedings by the proprietor of that earlier trade mark or other earlier right.

(3)   For the purposes of this section 'honest concurrent use' means such use in the United Kingdom, by the applicant or with his consent, as would formerly have amounted to honest concurrent use for the purposes of section 12(2) of the Trade Marks Act 1938.

(4)   Nothing in this section affects—

(a)   the refusal of registration on the grounds mentioned in section 3 (absolute grounds for refusal), or

(b)   the making of an application for a declaration of invalidity under section 47(2) (application on relative grounds, where no consent to registration).

(5)   This section does not apply when there is an order in force under section 8 below.

8. Power to require that relative grounds be raised in opposition proceedings

(1)   The Secretary of State may by order provide that in any case a trade mark shall not be refused registration on a ground mentioned in section 5 (relative

grounds for refusal) unless objection on that ground is raised in opposition proceedings by the proprietor of the earlier trade mark or other earlier right.

(2) The order may make such consequential provision as appears to the Secretary of State appropriate

(a) with respect to the carrying out by the registrar of searches of earlier trade marks, and

(b) as to the persons by whom an application for a declaration of invalidity may be made on the grounds specified in section 47(2) (relative grounds).

(3) An order making such provision as is mentioned in subsection (2)(a) may direct that so much of section 37 (examination of application) as requires a search to be carried out shall cease to have effect.

(4) An order making such provision as is mentioned in subsection (2)(b) may provide that so much of section 47(3) as provides that any person may make an application for a declaration of invalidity shall have effect subject to the provisions of the order.

(5) An order under this section shall be made by statutory instrument, and no order shall be made unless a draft of it has been laid before and approved by a resolution of each House of Parliament.

No such draft of an order making such provision as is mentioned in subsection (1) shall be laid before Parliament until after the end of the period of ten years beginning with the day on which applications for Community trade marks may first be filed in pursuance of the Community Trade Mark Regulation.

(6) An order under this section may contain such transitional provisions as appear to the Secretary of State to be appropriate.

Effects of registered trade mark

9. Rights conferred by registered trade mark

(1) The proprietor of a registered trade mark has exclusive rights in the trade mark which are infringed by use of the trade mark in the United Kingdom without his consent.

The acts amounting to infringement, if done without the consent of the proprietor, are specified in section 10.

(2) References in this Act to the infringement of a registered trade mark are to any such infringement of the rights of the proprietor.

(3) The rights of the proprietor have effect from the date of registration (which in accordance with section 40(3) is the date of filing of the application for registration):

Provided that—

(a) no infringement proceedings may be begun before the date on which the trade mark is in fact registered; and

(b) no offence under section 92 (unauthorised use of trade mark, &c. in relation to goods) is committed by anything done before the date of publication of the registration.

10. Infringement of registered trade mark

(1) A person infringes a registered trade mark if he uses in the course of trade a sign which is identical with the trade mark in relation to goods or services which are identical with those for which it is registered.

(2)   A person infringes a registered trade mark if he uses in the course of trade a sign where because—

(a)   the sign is identical with the trade mark and is used in relation to goods or services similar to those for which the trade mark is registered, or

(b)   the sign is similar to the trade mark and is used in relation to goods or services identical with or similar to those for which the trade mark is registered,

there exists a likelihood of confusion on the part of the public, which includes the likelihood of association with the trade mark.

(3)   A person infringes a registered trade mark if he uses in the course of trade a sign which—

(a)   is identical with or similar to the trade mark, and

(b)   is used in relation to goods or services which are not similar to those for which the trade mark is registered,

where the trade mark has a reputation in the United Kingdom and the use of the sign, being without due cause, takes unfair advantage of, or is detrimental to, the distinctive character or the repute of the trade mark.

(4)   For the purposes of this section a person uses a sign if, in particular, he—

(a)   affixes it to goods or the packaging thereof,

(b)   offers or exposes goods for sale, puts them on the market or stocks them for those purposes under the, sign, or offers or supplies services under the sign;

(c)   imports or exports goods under the sign; or

(d)   uses the sign on business papers or in advertising.

(5)   A person who applies a registered trade mark to material intended to be used for labelling or packaging goods, as a business paper, or for advertising goods or services, shall be treated as a party to any use of the material which infringes the registered trade mark if when he applied the mark he knew or had reason to believe that the application of the mark was not duly authorised by the proprietor or a licensee.

(6)   Nothing in the preceding provisions of this section shall be construed as preventing the use of a registered trade mark by any person for the purpose of identifying goods or services as those of the proprietor or a licensee.

But any such use otherwise than in accordance with honest practices in industrial or commercial matters shall be treated as infringing the registered trade mark if the use without due cause takes unfair advantage of, or is detrimental to, the distinctive character or repute of the trade mark.

11.   Limits on effect of registered trade mark

(1)   A registered trade mark is not infringed by the use of another registered trade mark in relation to goods or services for which the latter is registered (but see section 47(6) (effect of declaration of invalidity of registration)).

(2)   A registered trade mark is not infringed by—

(a)   the use by a person of his own name or address,

(b)   the use of indications concerning the kind, quality, quantity, intended purpose, value, geographical origin, the time of production of goods or of rendering of services, or other characteristics of goods or services, or

(c)   the use of the trade mark where it is necessary to indicate the intended purpose of a product or service (in particular, as accessories or spare parts),

provided the use is in accordance with honest practices in industrial or commercial matters.

(3)   A registered trade mark is not infringed by the use in the course of trade in a particular locality of an earlier right which applies only in that locality.

For this purpose an 'earlier right' means an unregistered trade mark or other sign continuously used in relation to goods or services by a person or a predecessor in title of his from a date prior to whichever is the earlier of—

(a)   the use of the first-mentioned trade mark in relation to those goods or services by the proprietor or a predecessor in title of his, or

(b)   the registration of the first-mentioned trade mark in respect of those goods or services in the name of the proprietor or a predecessor in title of his;

and an earlier right shall be regarded as applying in a locality if, or to the extent that, its use in that locality is protected by virtue of any rule of law (in particular, the law of passing off).

12.   Exhaustion of rights conferred by registered trade mark

(1)   A registered trade mark is not infringed by the use of the trade mark in relation to goods which have been put on the market in the European Economic Area under that trade mark by the proprietor or with his consent.

(2)   Subsection (1) does not apply where there exist legitimate reasons for the proprietor to oppose further dealings in the goods (in particular, where the condition of the goods has been changed or impaired after they have been put on the market).

13.   Registration subject to disclaimer or limitation

(1)   An applicant for registration of a trade mark, or the proprietor of a registered trade mark, may—

(a)   disclaim any right to the exclusive use of any specified element of the trade mark, or

(b)   agree that the rights conferred by the registration shall be subject to a specified territorial or other limitation;

and where the registration of a trade mark is subject to a disclaimer or limitation, the rights conferred by section 9 (rights conferred by registered trade mark) are restricted accordingly.

(2)   Provision shall be made by rules as to the publication and entry in the register of a disclaimer or limitation.

Infringement proceedings

14.   Action for infringement

(1)   An infringement of a registered trade mark is actionable by the proprietor of the trade mark.

(2)   In an action for infringement all such relief by way of damages, injunctions, accounts or otherwise is available to him as is available in respect of the infringement of any other property right.

15.   Order for erasure, &c. of offending sign

(1)   Where a person is found to have infringed a registered trade mark, the court may make an order requiring him—

(a)   to cause the offending sign to be erased, removed or obliterated from any infringing goods, material or articles in his possession, custody or control, or

(b)   if it is not reasonably practicable for the offending sign to be erased, removed or obliterated, to secure the destruction of the infringing goods, material or articles in question.

(2)   If an order under subsection (1) is not complied with, or it appears to the court likely that such an order would not be complied with, the court may order that the infringing goods, material or articles be delivered to such person as the court may direct for erasure, removal or obliteration of the sign, or for destruction, as the case may be.

16.   Order for delivery up of infringing goods, material or articles

(1)   The proprietor of a registered trade mark may apply to the court for an order for the delivery up to him, or such other person as the court may direct, of any infringing goods, material or articles which a person has in his possession, custody or control in the course of a business.

(2)   An application shall not be made after the end of the period specified in section 18 (period after which remedy of delivery up not available); and no order shall be made unless the court also makes, or it appears to the court that there are grounds for making, an order under section 19 (order as to disposal of infringing goods, &c.).

(3)   A person to whom any infringing goods, material or articles are delivered up in pursuance of an order under this section shall, if an order under section 19 is not made, retain them pending the making of an order, or the decision not to make an order, under that section.

(4)   Nothing in this section affects any other power of the court.

17.   Meaning of 'infringing goods, material or articles'

(1)   In this Act the expressions 'infringing goods', 'infringing material' and 'infringing articles' shall be construed as follows.

(2)   Goods are 'infringing goods', in relation to a registered trade mark, if they or their packaging bear a sign identical or similar to that mark and—

(a)   the application of the sign to the goods or their packaging was an infringement of the registered trade mark, or

(b)   the goods are proposed to be imported into the United Kingdom and the application of the sign in the United Kingdom to them or their packaging would be an infringement of the registered trade mark, or

(c)   the sign has otherwise been used in relation to the goods in such a way as to infringe the registered trade mark.

(3)   Nothing in subsection (2) shall be construed as affecting the importation of goods which may lawfully be imported into the United Kingdom by virtue of an enforceable Community right.

(4)   Material is 'infringing material', in relation to a registered trade mark if it bears a sign identical or similar to that mark and either—

(a)   it is used for labelling or packaging goods, as a business paper, or for advertising goods or services, in such a way as to infringe the registered trade mark, or

(b)   it is intended to be so used and such use would infringe the registered trade mark.

(5)   'Infringing articles', in relation to a registered trade mark, means articles—

(a)   which are specifically designed or adapted for making copies of a sign identical or similar to that mark, and

(b)   which a person has in his possession, custody or control, knowing or having reason to believe that they have been or are to be used to produce infringing goods or material.

18.   Period after which remedy of delivery up not available

(1)   An application for an order under section 16 (order for delivery up of infringing goods, material or articles) may not be made after the end of the period of six years from—

(a)   in the case of infringing goods, the date on which the trade mark was applied to the goods or their packaging,

(b)   in the case of infringing material, the date on which the trade mark was applied to the material, or

(c)   in the case of infringing articles, the date on which they were made, except as mentioned in the following provisions.

(2)   If during the whole or part of that period the proprietor of the registered trade mark—

(a)   is under a disability, or

(b)   is prevented by fraud or concealment from discovering the facts entitling him to apply for an order,

an application may be made at any time before the end of the period of six years from the date on which he ceased to be under a disability or, as the case may be, could with reasonable diligence have discovered those facts.

(3)   In subsection (2) 'disability'—

(a)   in England and Wales, has the same meaning as in the Limitation Act 1980;

(b)   in Scotland, means legal disability within the meaning of the Prescription and Limitation (Scotland) Act 1973;

(c)   in Northern Ireland, has the same meaning as in the Limitation (Northern Ireland) Order 1989.

19.   Order as to disposal of infringing goods, material or articles

(1)   Where infringing goods, material or articles have been delivered up in pursuance of an order under section 16, an application may be made to the court—

(a)   for an order that they be destroyed or forfeited to such person as the court may think fit, or

(b)   for a decision that no such order should be made.

(2)   In considering what order (if any) should be made, the court shall consider whether other remedies available in an action for infringement of the registered trade mark would be adequate to compensate the proprietor and any licensee and protect their interests.

(3)   Provision shall be made by rules of court as to the service of notice on persons having an interest in the goods, material or articles, and any such person is entitled—

(a)   to appear in proceedings for an order under this section, whether or not he was served with notice, and

(b)   to appeal against any order made, whether or not he appeared;

and an order shall not take effect until the end of the period within which notice of an appeal may be given or, if before the end of that period notice of appeal is duly given, until the final determination or abandonment of the proceedings on the appeal.

(4)   Where there is more than one person interested in the goods, material or articles, the court shall make such order as it thinks just.

(5)   If the court decides that no order should be made under this section, the person in whose possession, custody or control the goods, material or articles were before being delivered up is entitled to their return.

(6)   References in this section to a person having an interest in goods, material or articles include any person in whose favour an order could be made under this section or under section 114, 204 or 231 of the Copyright, Designs and Patents Act 1988 (which make similar provision in relation to infringement of copyright, rights in performances and design right).

20.   Jurisdiction of sheriff court or county court in Northern Ireland

Proceedings for an order under section 16 (order for delivery up of infringing goods, material or articles) or section 19 (order as to disposal of infringing goods, &c.) may be brought—

   (a)   in the sheriff court in Scotland, or

   (b)   in a county court in Northern Ireland.

This does not affect the jurisdiction of the Court of Session or the High Court in Northern Ireland.

21.   Remedy for groundless threats of infringement proceedings

(1)   Where a person threatens another with proceedings for infringement of a registered trade mark other than—

   (a)   the application of the mark to goods or their packaging,

   (b)   the importation of goods to which, or to the packaging of which, the mark has been applied, or

   (c)   the supply of services under the mark,

any person aggrieved may bring proceedings for relief under this section.

(2)   The relief which may be applied for is any of the following—

   (a)   a declaration that the threats are unjustifiable,

   (b)   an injunction against the continuance of the threats,

   (c)   damages in respect of any loss he has sustained by the threats;

and the plaintiff is entitled to such relief unless the defendant shows that the acts in respect of which proceedings were threatened constitute (or if done would constitute) an infringement of the registered trade mark concerned.

(3)   If that is shown by the defendant, the plaintiff is nevertheless entitled to relief if he shows that the registration of the trade mark is invalid or liable to be revoked in a relevant respect.

(4)   The mere notification that a trade mark is registered, or that an application for registration has been made, does not constitute a threat of proceedings for the purposes of this section.

Registered trade mark as object of property

22.   Nature of registered trade mark

A registered trade mark is personal property (in Scotland, incorporeal moveable property).

23.   Co-ownership of registered trade mark

(1)   Where a registered trade mark is granted to two or more persons jointly, each of them is entitled, subject to any agreement to the contrary, to an equal undivided share in the registered trade mark.

(2)   The following provisions apply where two or more persons are co-proprietors of a registered trade mark, by virtue of subsection (1) or otherwise.

(3)   Subject to any agreement to the contrary, each co-proprietor is entitled, by himself or his agents, to do for his own benefit and without the consent of or the need to account to the other or others, any act which would otherwise amount to an infringement of the registered trade mark.

(4)   One co-proprietor may not without the consent of the other or others—

(a)   grant a licence to use the registered trade mark, or

(b)   assign or charge his share in the registered trade mark (or, in Scotland, cause or permit security to be granted over it).

(5)   Infringement proceedings may be brought by any co-proprietor, but he may not, without the leave of the court, proceed with the action unless the other, or each of the others, is either joined as a plaintiff or added as a defendant.

A co-proprietor who is thus added as a defendant shall not be made liable for any costs in the action unless he takes part in the proceedings.

Nothing in this subsection affects the granting of interlocutory relief on the application of a single co-proprietor.

(6)   Nothing in this section affects the mutual rights and obligations of trustees or personal representatives, or their rights and obligations as such.

24.   Assignment, &c. of registered trade mark

(1)   A registered trade mark is transmissible by assignment, testamentary disposition or operation of law in the same way as other personal or moveable property.

It is so transmissible either in connection with the goodwill of a business or independently.

(2)   An assignment or other transmission of a registered trade mark may be partial, that is, limited so as to apply—

(a)   in relation to some but not all of the goods or services for which the trade mark is registered, or

(b)   in relation to use of the trade mark in a particular manner or a particular locality.

(3)   An assignment of a registered trade mark, or an assent relating to a registered trade mark, is not effective unless it is in writing signed by or on behalf of the assignor or, as the case may be, a personal representative.

Except in Scotland, this requirement may be satisfied in a case where the assignor or personal representative is a body corporate by the affixing of its seal.

(4)   The above provisions apply to assignment by way of security as in relation to any other assignment.

(5)   A registered trade mark may be the subject of a charge (in Scotland, security) in the same way as other personal or moveable property.

(6)   Nothing in this Act shall be construed as affecting the assignment or other transmission of an unregistered trade mark as part of the goodwill of a business.

25. Registration of transactions affecting registered trade mark

(1)   On application being made to the registrar by—

(a)   a person claiming to be entitled to an interest in or under a registered trade mark by virtue of a registrable transaction, or

(b)   any other person claiming to be affected by such a transaction,

the prescribed particulars of the transaction shall be entered in the register.

(2)   The following are registrable transactions—

(a)   an assignment of a registered trade mark or any right in it;

(b)   the grant of a licence under a registered trade mark;

(c)   the granting of any security interest (whether fixed or floating) over a registered trade mark or any right in or under it;

(d)   the making by personal representatives of an assent in relation to a registered trade mark or any right in or under it;

(e)   an order of a court or other competent authority transferring a registered trade mark or any right in or under it.

(3)   Until an application has been made for registration of the prescribed particulars of a registrable transaction—

(a)   the transaction is ineffective as against a person acquiring a conflicting interest in or under the registered trade mark in ignorance of it, and

(b)   a person claiming to be a licensee by virtue of the transaction does not have the protection of section 30 or 31 (rights and remedies of licensee in relation to infringement).

(4)   Where a person becomes the proprietor or a licensee of a registered trade mark by virtue of a registrable transaction, then unless—

(a)   an application for registration of the prescribed particulars of the transaction is made before the end of the period of six months beginning with its date, or

(b)   the court is satisfied that it was not practicable for such an application to be made before the end of that period and that an application was made as soon as practicable thereafter,

he is not entitled to damages or an account of profits in respect of any infringement of the registered trade mark occurring after the date of the transaction and before the prescribed particulars of the transaction are registered.

(5)   Provision may be made by rules as to—

(a)   the amendment of registered particulars relating to a licence so as to reflect any alteration of the terms of the licence, and

(b)   the removal of such particulars from the register—

(i)   where it appears from the registered particulars that the licence was granted for a fixed period and that period has expired, or

(ii)   where no such period is indicated and, after such period as may be prescribed, the registrar has notified the parties of his intention to remove the particulars from the register.

(6)   Provision may also be made by rules as to the amendment or removal from the register of particulars relating to a security interest on the application of, or with the consent of, the person entitled to the benefit of that interest.

26.   Trusts and equities

(1)   No notice of any trust (express, implied or constructive) shall be entered in the register; and the registrar shall not be affected by any such notice.

(2) Subject to the provisions of this Act, equities (in Scotland, rights) in respect of a registered trade mark may be enforced in like manner as in respect of other personal or moveable property.

27. Application for registration of trade mark as an object of property

(1) The provisions of sections 22 to 26 (which relate to a registered trade mark as an object of property) apply, with the necessary modifications, in relation to an application for the registration of a trade mark as in relation to a registered trade mark.

(2) In section 23 (co-ownership of registered trade mark) as it applies in relation to an application for registration the reference in subsection (1) to the granting of the registration shall be construed as a reference to the making of the application.

(3) In section 25 (registration of transactions affecting registered trade marks) as it applies in relation to a transaction affecting an application for the registration of a trade mark, the references to the entry of particulars in the register, and to the making of an application to register particulars, shall be construed as references to the giving of notice to the registrar of those particulars.

Licensing

28. Licensing of registered trade mark

(1) A licence to use a registered trade mark may be general or limited.

A limited licence may, in particular, apply—

(a) in relation to some but not all of the goods or services for which the trade mark is registered, or

(b) in relation to use of the trade mark in a particular manner or a particular locality.

(2) A licence is not effective unless it is in writing signed by or on behalf of the grantor.

Except in Scotland, this requirement may be satisfied in a case where the grantor is a body corporate by the affixing of its seal.

(3) Unless the licence provides otherwise, it is binding on a successor in title to the grantor's interest.

References in this Act to doing anything with, or without, the consent of the proprietor of a registered trade mark shall be construed accordingly.

(4) Where the licence so provides, a sub-licence may be granted by the licensee; and references in this Act to a licence or licensee include a sub-licence or sub-licensee.

29. Exclusive licences

(1) In this Act an 'exclusive licence' means a licence (whether general or limited) authorising the licensee to the exclusion of all other persons, including the person granting the licence, to use a registered trade mark in the manner authorised by the licence.

The expression 'exclusive licensee' shall be construed accordingly.

(2) An exclusive licensee has the same rights against a successor in title who is bound by the licence as he has against the person granting the licence.

30. General provisions as to rights of licensees in case of infringement

(1) This section has effect with respect to the rights of a licensee in relation to infringement of a registered trade mark.

The provisions of this section do not apply where or to the extent that, by virtue of section 31(1) below (exclusive licensee having rights and remedies of assignee), the licensee has a right to bring proceedings in his own name.

(2)   A licensee is entitled, unless his licence, or any licence through which his interest is derived, provides otherwise, to call on the proprietor of the registered trade mark to take infringement proceedings in respect of any matter which affects his interests.

(3)   If the proprietor—
    (a)   refuses to do so, or
    (b)   fails to do so within two months after being called upon,
the licensee may bring the proceedings in his own name as if he were the proprietor.

(4)   Where infringement proceedings are brought by a licensee by virtue of this section, the licensee may not, without the leave of the court, proceed with the action unless the proprietor is either joined as a plaintiff or added as a defendant.

This does not affect the granting of interlocutory relief on an application by a licensee alone.

(5)   A proprietor who is added as a defendant as mentioned in subsection (4) shall not be made liable for any costs in the action unless he takes part in the proceedings.

(6)   In infringement proceedings brought by the proprietor of a registered trade mark any loss suffered or likely to be suffered by licensees shall be taken into account; and the court may give such directions as it thinks fit as to the extent to which the plaintiff is to hold the proceeds of any pecuniary remedy on behalf of licensees.

(7)   The provisions of this section apply in relation to an exclusive licensee if or to the extent that he has, by virtue of section 31(1), the rights and remedies of an assignee as if he were the proprietor of the registered trade mark.

31.   Exclusive licensee having rights and remedies of assignee

(1)   An exclusive licence may provide that the licensee shall have, to such extent as may be provided by the licence, the same rights and remedies in respect of matters occurring after the grant of the licence as if the licence had been an assignment.

Where or to the extent that such provision is made, the licensee is entitled, subject to the provisions of the licence and to the following provisions of this section, to bring infringement proceedings, against any person other than the proprietor, in his own name.

(2)   Any such rights and remedies of an exclusive licensee are concurrent with those of the proprietor of the registered trade mark; and references to the proprietor of a registered trade mark in the provisions of this Act relating to infringement shall be construed accordingly.

(3)   In an action brought by an exclusive licensee by virtue of this section a defendant may avail himself of any defence which would have been available to him if the action had been brought by the proprietor of the registered trade mark.

(4)   Where proceedings for infringement of a registered trade mark brought by the proprietor or an exclusive licensee relate wholly or partly to an infringement in respect of which they have concurrent rights of action, the proprietor or, as the

case may be, the exclusive licensee may not, without the leave of the court, proceed with the action unless the other is either joined as a plaintiff or added as a defendant.

This does not affect the granting of interlocutory relief on an application by a proprietor or exclusive licensee alone.

(5)   A person who is added as a defendant as mentioned in subsection (4) shall not be made liable for any costs in the action unless he takes part in the proceedings.

(6)   Where an action for infringement of a registered trade mark is brought which relates wholly or partly to an infringement in respect of which the proprietor and an exclusive licensee have or had concurrent rights of action—

(a)   the court shall in assessing damages take into account—
        (i)   the terms of the licence, and
        (ii)   any pecuniary remedy already awarded or available to either of them in respect of the infringement;

(b)   no account of profits shall be directed if an award of damages has been made, or an account of profits has been directed, in favour of the other of them in respect of the infringement; and

(c)   the court shall if an account of profits is directed apportion the profits between them as the court considers just, subject to any agreement between them.

The provisions of this subsection apply whether or not the proprietor and the exclusive licensee are both parties to the action; and if they are not both parties the court may give such directions as it thinks fit as to the extent to which the party to the proceedings is to hold the proceeds of any pecuniary remedy on behalf of the other.

(7)   The proprietor of a registered trade mark shall notify any exclusive licensee who has a concurrent right of action before applying for an order under section 16 (order for delivery up); and the court may on the application of the licensee make such order under that section as it thinks fit having regard to the terms of the licence.

(8)   The provisions of subsections (4) to (7) above have effect subject to any agreement to the contrary between the exclusive licensee and the proprietor.

Application for registered trade mark

32.   Application for registration

(1)   An application for registration of a trade mark shall be made to the registrar.

(2)   The application shall contain—
(a)   a request for registration of a trade mark,
(b)   the name and address of the applicant,
(c)   a statement of the goods or services in relation to which it is sought to register the trade mark, and
(d)   a representation of the trade mark.

(3)   The application shall state that the trade mark is being used, by the applicant or with his consent, in relation to those goods or services, or that he has a *bona fide* intention that it should be so used.

(4)   The application shall be subject to the payment of the application fee and such class fees as may be appropriate.

33. Date of filing

(1) The date of filing of an application for registration of a trade mark is the date on which documents containing everything required by section 32(2) are furnished to the registrar by the applicant.

If the documents are furnished on different days, the date of filing is the last of those days.

(2) References in this Act to the date of application for registration are to the date of filing of the application.

34. Classification of trade marks

(1) Goods and services shall be classified for the purposes of the registration of trade marks according to a prescribed system of classification.

(2) Any question arising as to the class within which any goods or services fall shall be determined by the registrar, whose decision shall be final.

Priority

35. Claim to priority of Convention application

(1) A person who has duly filed an application for protection of a trade mark in a Convention country (a 'Convention application'), or his successor in title, has a right to priority, for the purposes of registering the same trade mark under this Act for some or all of the same goods or services, for a period of six months from the date of filing of the first such application.

(2) If the application for registration under this Act is made within that six-month period—

(a) the relevant date for the purposes of establishing which rights take precedence shall be the date of filing of the first Convention application, and

(b) the registrability of the trade mark shall not be affected by any use of the mark in the United Kingdom in the period between that date and the date of the application under this Act.

(3) Any filing which in a Convention country is equivalent to a regular national filing, under its domestic legislation or an international agreement, shall be treated as giving rise to the right of priority.

A 'regular national filing' means a filing which is adequate to establish the date on which the application was filed in that country, whatever may be the subsequent fate of the application.

(4) A subsequent application concerning the same subject as the first Convention application, filed in the same Convention country, shall be considered the first Convention application (of which the filing date is the starting date of the period of priority), if at the time of the subsequent application—

(a) the previous application has been withdrawn, abandoned or refused, without having been laid open to public inspection and without leaving any rights outstanding, and

(b) it has not yet served as a basis for claiming a right of priority.

The previous application may not thereafter serve as a basis for claiming a right of priority.

(5) Provision may be made by rules as to the manner of claiming a right to priority on the basis of a Convention application.

(6)   A right to priority arising as a result of a Convention application may be assigned or otherwise transmitted, either with the application or independently.

The reference in subsection (1) to the applicant's 'successor in title' shall be construed accordingly.

36.   Claim to priority from other relevant overseas application

(1)   Her Majesty may by Order in Council make provision for conferring on a person who has duly filed an application for protection of a trade mark in—
  (a)   any of the Channel Islands or a colony, or
  (b)   a country or territory in relation to which Her Majesty's Government in the United Kingdom have entered into a treaty, convention, arrangement or engagement for the reciprocal protection of trade marks,
a right to priority, for the purpose of registering the same trade mark under this Act for some or all of the same goods or services, for a specified period from the date of filing of that application.

(2)   An Order in Council under this section may make provision corresponding to that made by section 35 in relation to Convention countries or such other provision as appears to Her Majesty to be appropriate.

(3)   A statutory instrument containing an Order in Council under this section shall be subject to annulment in pursuance of a resolution of either House of Parliament.

Registration procedure

37.   Examination of application

(1)   The registrar shall examine whether an application for registration of a trade mark satisfies the requirements of this Act (including any requirements imposed by rules).

(2)   For that purpose he shall carry out a search, to such extent as he considers necessary, of earlier trade marks.

(3)   If it appears to the registrar that the requirements for registration are not met, he shall inform the applicant and give him an opportunity, within such period as the registrar may specify, to make representations or to amend the application.

(4)   If the applicant fails to satisfy the registrar that those requirements are met, or to amend the application so as to meet them, or fails to respond before the end of the specified period, the registrar shall refuse to accept the application.

(5)   If it appears to the registrar that the requirements for registration are met, he shall accept the application.

38.   Publication, opposition proceedings and observations

(1)   When an application for registration has been accepted, the registrar shall cause the application to be published in the prescribed manner.

(2)   Any person may, within the prescribed time from the date of the publication of the application, give notice to the registrar of opposition to the registration.

The notice shall be given in writing in the prescribed manner, and shall include a statement of the grounds of opposition.

(3)   Where an application has been published, any person may, at any time before the registration of the trade mark, make observations in writing to the registrar as to whether the trade mark should be registered; and the registrar shall inform the applicant of any such observations.

A person who makes observations does not thereby become a party to the proceedings on the application.

39. Withdrawal, restriction or amendment of application

(1) The applicant may at any time withdraw his application or restrict the goods or services covered by the application.

If the application has been published, the withdrawal or restriction shall also be published.

(2) In other respects, an application may be amended, at the request of the applicant, only by correcting—

(a) the name or address of the applicant,

(b) errors of wording or of copying, or

(c) obvious mistakes,

and then only where the correction does not substantially affect the identity of the trade mark or extend the goods or services covered by the application.

(3) Provision shall be made by rules for the publication of any amendment which affects the representation of the trade mark, or the goods or services covered by the application, and for the making of objections by any person claiming to be affected by it.

40. Registration

(1) Where an application has been accepted and—

(a) no notice of opposition is given within the period referred to in section 38(2), or

(b) all opposition proceedings are withdrawn or decided in favour of the applicant,

the registrar shall register the trade mark, unless it appears to him having regard to matters coming to his notice since he accepted the application that it was accepted in error.

(2) A trade mark shall not be registered unless any fee prescribed for the registration is paid within the prescribed period.

If the fee is not paid within that period, the application shall be deemed to be withdrawn.

(3) A trade mark when registered shall be registered as of the date of filing of the application for registration; and that date shall be deemed for the purposes of this Act to be the date of registration.

(4) On the registration of a trade mark the registrar shall publish the registration in the prescribed manner and issue to the applicant a certificate of registration.

41. Registration: supplementary provisions

(1) Provision may be made by rules as to—

(a) the division of an application for the registration of a trade mark into several applications;

(b) the merging of separate applications or registrations;

(c) the registration of a series of trade marks.

(2) A series of trade marks means a number of trade marks which resemble each other as to their material particulars and differ only as to matters of a non-distinctive character not substantially affecting the identity of the trade mark.

(3) Rules under this section may include provision as to—

(a) the circumstances in which, and conditions subject to which, division, merger or registration of a series is permitted, and

(b) the purposes for which an application to which the rules apply is to be treated as a single application and those for which it is to be treated as a number of separate applications.

Duration, renewal and alteration of registered trade mark

42. Duration of registration

(1) A trade mark shall be registered for a period of ten years from the date of registration.

(2) Registration may be renewed in accordance with section 43 for further periods of ten years.

43. Renewal of registration

(1) The registration of a trade mark may be renewed at the request of the proprietor, subject to payment of a renewal fee.

(2) Provision shall be made by rules for the registrar to inform the proprietor of a registered trade mark, before the expiry of the registration, of the date of expiry and the manner in which the registration may be renewed.

(3) A request for renewal must be made, and the renewal fee paid, before the expiry of the registration.

Failing this, the request may be made and the fee paid within such further period (of not less than six months) as may be prescribed, in which case an additional renewal fee must also be paid within that period.

(4) Renewal shall take effect from the expiry of the previous registration.

(5) If the registration is not renewed in accordance with the above provisions, the registrar shall remove the trade mark from the register.

Provision may be made by rules for the restoration of the registration of a trade mark which has been removed from the register, subject to such conditions (if any) as may be prescribed.

(6) The renewal or restoration of the registration of a trade mark shall be published in the prescribed manner.

44. Alteration of registered trade mark

(1) A registered trade mark shall not be altered in the register, during the period of registration or on renewal.

(2) Nevertheless, the registrar may, at the request of the proprietor, allow the alteration of a registered trade mark where the mark includes the proprietor's name or address and the alteration is limited to alteration of that name or address and does not substantially affect the identity of the mark.

(3) Provision shall be made by rules for the publication of any such alteration and the making of objections by any person claiming to be affected by it.

Surrender, revocation and invalidity

45. Surrender of registered trade mark

(1) A registered trade mark may be surrendered by the proprietor in respect of some or all of the goods or services for which it is registered.

(2) Provision may be made by rules—

(a)   as to the manner and effect of a surrender, and

(b)   for protecting the interests of other persons having a right in the registered trade mark.

46.   Revocation of registration

(1)   The registration of a trade mark may be revoked on any of the following grounds—

(a)   that within the period of five years following the date of completion of the registration procedure it has not been put to genuine use in the United Kingdom, by the proprietor or with his consent, in relation to the goods or services for which it is registered, and there are no proper reasons for non-use;

(b)   that such use has been suspended for an uninterrupted period of five years, and there are no proper reasons for non-use;

(c)   that, in consequence of acts or inactivity of the proprietor, it has become the common name in the trade for a product or service for which it is registered;

(d)   that in consequence of the use made of it by the proprietor or with his consent in relation to the goods or services for which it is registered, it is liable to mislead the public, particularly as to the nature, quality or geographical origin of those goods or services.

(2)   For the purposes of subsection (1) use of a trade mark includes use in a form differing in elements which do not alter the distinctive character of the mark in the form in which it was registered, and use in the United Kingdom includes affixing the trade mark to goods or to the packaging of goods in the United Kingdom solely for export purposes.

(3)   The registration of a trade mark shall not be revoked on the ground mentioned in subsection (1)(a) or (b) if such use as is referred to in that paragraph is commenced or resumed after the expiry of the five year period and before the application for revocation is made:

Provided that, any such commencement or resumption of use after the expiry of the five year period but within the period of three months before the making of the application shall be disregarded unless preparations for the commencement or resumption began before the proprietor became aware that the application might be made.

(4)   An application for revocation may be made by any person, and may be made either to the registrar or to the court, except that—

(a)   if proceedings concerning the trade mark in question are pending in the court, the application must be made to the court; and

(b)   if in any other case the application is made to the registrar, he may at any stage of the proceedings refer the application to the court.

(5)   Where grounds for revocation exist in respect of only some of the goods or services for which the trade mark is registered, revocation shall relate to those goods or services only.

(6)   Where the registration of a trade mark is revoked to any extent, the rights of the proprietor shall be deemed to have ceased to that extent as from—

(a)   the date of the application for revocation, or

(b)   if the registrar or court is satisfied that the grounds for revocation existed at an earlier date, that date.

47. Grounds for invalidity of registration

(1) The registration of a trade mark may be declared invalid on the ground that the trade mark was registered in breach of section 3 or any of the provisions referred to in that section (absolute grounds for refusal of registration).

Where the trade mark was registered in breach of subsection (1)(b), (c) or (d) of that section, it shall not be declared invalid if, in consequence of the use which has been made of it, it has after registration acquired a distinctive character in relation to the goods or services for which it is registered.

(2) The registration of a trade mark may be declared invalid on the ground—

(a) that there is an earlier trade mark in relation to which the conditions set out in section 5(1), (2) or (3) obtain, or

(b) that there is an earlier right in relation to which the condition set out in section 5(4) is satisfied,

unless the proprietor of that earlier trade mark or other earlier right has consented to the registration.

(3) An application for a declaration of invalidity may be made by any person, and may be made either to the registrar or to the court, except that—

(a) if proceedings concerning the trade mark in question are pending in the court, the application must be made to the court; and

(b) if in any other case the application is made to the registrar, he may at any stage of the proceedings refer the application to the court.

(4) In the case of bad faith in the registration of a trade mark, the registrar himself may apply to the court for a declaration of the invalidity of the registration.

(5) Where the grounds of invalidity exist in respect of only some of the goods or services for which the trade mark is registered, the trade mark shall be declared invalid as regards those goods or services only.

(6) Where the registration of a trade mark is declared invalid to any extent, the registration shall to that extent be deemed never to have been made:

Provided that this shall not affect transactions past and closed.

48. Effect of acquiescence

(1) Where the proprietor of an earlier trade mark or other earlier right has acquiesced for a continuous period of five years in the use of a registered trade mark in the United Kingdom, being aware of that use, there shall cease to be any entitlement on the basis of that earlier trade mark or other right—

(a) to apply for a declaration that the registration of the later trade mark is invalid, or

(b) to oppose the use of the later trade mark in relation to the goods or services in relation to which it has been so used,

unless the registration of the later trade mark was applied for in bad faith.

(2) Where subsection (1) applies, the proprietor of the later trade mark is not entitled to oppose the use of the earlier trade mark or, as the case may be, the exploitation of the earlier right, notwithstanding that the earlier trade mark or right may no longer be invoked against his later trade mark.

Collective marks

49. Collective marks

(1) A collective mark is a mark distinguishing the goods or services of members of the association which is the proprietor of the mark from those of other undertakings.

(2) The provisions of this Act apply to collective marks subject to the provisions of Schedule 1.

Certification marks

50. Certification marks

(1) A certification mark is a mark indicating that the goods or services in connection with which it is used are certified by the proprietor of the mark in respect of origin, material, mode of manufacture of goods or performance of services, quality, accuracy or other characteristics.

(2) The provisions of this Act apply to certification marks subject to the provisions of Schedule 2.

PART II COMMUNITY TRADE MARKS AND INTERNATIONAL MATTERS

Community trade marks

51. Meaning of 'Community trade mark'

In this Act—

'Community trade mark' has the meaning given by Article 1(1) of the Community Trade Mark Regulation; and

'the Community Trade Mark Regulation' means Council Regulation (EC) No. 40/94 of 20th December 1993 on the Community trade mark.

52. Power to make provision in connection with Community Trade Mark Regulation

(1) The Secretary of State may by regulations make such provision as he considers appropriate in connection with the operation of the Community Trade Mark Regulation.

(2) Provision may, in particular, be made with respect to—

(a) the making of applications for Community trade marks by way of the Patent Office;

(b) the procedures for determining *a posteriori* the invalidity, or liability to revocation, of the registration of a trade mark from which a Community trade mark claims seniority;

(c) the conversion of a Community trade mark, or an application for a Community trade mark, into an application for registration under this Act;

(d) the designation of courts in the United Kingdom having jurisdiction over proceedings arising out of the Community Trade Mark Regulation.

(3) Without prejudice to the generality of subsection (1), provision may be made by regulations under this section—

(a) applying in relation to a Community trade mark the provisions of—

(i) section 21 (remedy for groundless threats of infringement proceedings);

(ii) sections 89 to 91 (importation of infringing goods, material or articles); and

(iii) sections 92, 93, 95 and 96 (offences); and

(b) making in relation to the list of professional representatives maintained in pursuance of Article 89 of the Community Trade Mark Regulation, and persons on that list, provision corresponding to that made by, or capable of being made under, sections 84 to 88 in relation to the register of trade mark agents and registered trade mark agents.

(4) Regulations under this section shall be made by statutory instrument which shall be subject to annulment in pursuance of a resolution of either House of Parliament.

The Madrid Protocol: international registration

53. The Madrid Protocol
In this Act—

'the Madrid Protocol' means the Protocol relating to the Madrid Agreement concerning the International Registration of Marks, adopted at Madrid on 27th June 1989;

'the International Bureau' has the meaning given by Article 2(1) of that Protocol; and

'international trade mark (UK)' means a trade mark which is entitled to protection in the United Kingdom under that Protocol.

54. Power to make provision giving effect to Madrid Protocol
(1) The Secretary of State may by order make such provision as he thinks fit for giving effect in the United Kingdom to the provisions of the Madrid Protocol.

(2) Provision may, in particular, be made with respect to—

(a) the making of applications for international registrations by way of the Patent Office as office of origin;

(b) the procedures to be followed where the basic United Kingdom application or registration fails or ceases to be in force;

(c) the procedures to be followed where the Patent Office receives from the International Bureau a request for extension of protection to the United Kingdom;

(d) the effects of a successful request for extension of protection to the United Kingdom;

(e) the transformation of an application for an international registration, or an international registration, into a national application for registration;

(f) the communication of information to the International Bureau;

(g) the payment of fees and amounts prescribed in respect of applications for international registrations, extensions of protection and renewals.

(3) Without prejudice to the generality of subsection (1), provision may be made by regulations under this section applying in relation to an international trade mark (UK) the provisions of—

(a) section 21 (remedy for groundless threats of infringement proceedings);

(b) sections 89 to 91 (importation of infringing goods, material or articles); and

(c) sections 92, 93, 95 and 96 (offences).

(4) An order under this section shall be made by statutory instrument which shall be subject to annulment in pursuance of a resolution of either House of Parliament.

The Paris Convention: supplementary provisions

55. The Paris Convention

(1) In this Act—

(a) 'the Paris Convention' means the Paris Convention for the Protection of Industrial Property of March 20th 1883, as revised or amended from time to time, and

(b) a 'Convention country' means a country, other than the United Kingdom, which is a party to that Convention.

(2) The Secretary of State may by order make such amendments of this Act, and rules made under this Act, as appear to him appropriate in consequence of any revision or amendment of the Paris Convention after the passing of this Act.

(3) Any such order shall be made by statutory instrument which shall be subject to annulment in pursuance of a resolution of either House of Parliament.

56. Protection of well-known trade marks: Article 6*bis*

(1) References in this Act to a trade mark which is entitled to protection under the Paris Convention as a well known trade mark are to a mark which is well-known in the United Kingdom as being the mark of a person who—

(a) is a national of a Convention country, or

(b) is domiciled in, or has a real and effective industrial or commercial establishment in, a Convention country,

whether or not that person carries on business, or has any goodwill, in the United Kingdom.

References to the proprietor of such a mark shall be construed accordingly.

(2) The proprietor of a trade mark which is entitled to protection under the Paris Convention as a well known trade mark is entitled to restrain by injunction the use in the United Kingdom of a trade mark which, or the essential part of which, is identical or similar to his mark, in relation to identical or similar goods or services, where the use is likely to cause confusion.

This right is subject to section 48 (effect of acquiescence by proprietor of earlier trade mark).

(3) Nothing in subsection (2) affects the continuation of any *bona fide* use of a trade mark begun before the commencement of this section.

57. National emblems, &c. of Convention countries: Article 6*ter*

(1) A trade mark which consists of or contains the flag of a Convention country shall not be registered without the authorisation of the competent authorities of that country, unless it appears to the registrar that use of the flag in the manner proposed is permitted without such authorisation.

(2) A trade mark which consists of or contains the armorial bearings or any other state emblem of a Convention country which is protected under the Paris Convention shall not be registered without the authorisation of the competent authorities of that country.

(3) A trade mark which consists of or contains an official sign or hallmark adopted by a Convention country and indicating control and warranty shall not,

where the sign or hallmark is protected under the Paris Convention, be registered in relation to goods or services of the same, or a similar kind, as those in relation to which it indicates control and warranty, without the authorisation of the competent authorities of the country concerned.

(4)   The provisions of this section as to national flags and other state emblems, and official signs or hallmarks, apply equally to anything which from a heraldic point of view imitates any such flag or other emblem, or sign or hallmark.

(5)   Nothing in this section prevents the registration of a trade mark on the application of a national of a country who is authorised to make use of a state emblem, or official sign or hallmark, of that country, notwithstanding that it is similar to that of another country.

(6)   Where by virtue of this section the authorisation of the competent authorities of a Convention country is or would be required for the registration of a trade mark, those authorities are entitled to restrain by injunction any use of the mark in the United Kingdom without their authorisation.

58.   Emblems, &c. of certain international organisations: Article 6*ter*
(1)   This section applies to—
(a)   the armorial bearings, flags or other emblems, and
(b)   the abbreviations and names,
of international intergovernmental organisations of which one or more Convention countries are members.

(2)   A trade mark which consists of or contains any such emblem, abbreviation or name which is protected under the Paris Convention shall not be registered without the authorisation of the international organisation concerned, unless it appears to the registrar that the use of the emblem, abbreviation or name in the manner proposed—
(a)   is not such as to suggest to the public that a connection exists between the organisation and the trade mark, or
(b)   is not likely to mislead the public as to the existence of a connection between the user and the organisation.

(3)   The provisions of this section as to emblems of an international organisation apply equally to anything which from a heraldic point of view imitates any such emblem.

(4)   Where by virtue of this section the authorisation of an international organisation is or would be required for the registration of a trade mark, that organisation is entitled to restrain by injunction any use of the mark in the United Kingdom without its authorisation.

(5)   Nothing in this section affects the rights of a person whose *bona fide* use of the trade mark in question began before 4th January 1962 (when the relevant provisions of the Paris Convention entered into force in relation to the United Kingdom).

59.   Notification under Article 6*ter* of the Convention
(1)   For the purposes of section 57 state emblems of a Convention country (other than the national flag), and official signs or hallmarks, shall be regarded as protected under the Paris Convention only if, or to the extent that—
(a)   the country in question has notified the United Kingdom in accordance with Article 6*ter*(3) of the Convention that it desires to protect that emblem, sign or hallmark,

(b) the notification remains in force, and

(c) the United Kingdom has not objected to it in accordance with Article 6*ter*(4) or any such objection has been withdrawn.

(2) For the purposes of section 58 the emblems, abbreviations and names of an international organisation shall be regarded as protected under the Paris Convention only if, or to the extent that—

(a) the organisation in question has notified the United Kingdom in accordance with Article 6*ter*(3) of the Convention that it desires to protect that emblem, abbreviation or name,

(b) the notification remains in force, and

(c) the United Kingdom has not objected to it in accordance with Article 6*ter*(4) or any such objection has been withdrawn.

(3) Notification under Article 6*ter*(3) of the Paris Convention shall have effect only in relation to applications for registration made more than two months after the receipt of the notification.

(4) The registrar shall keep and make available for public inspection by any person, at all reasonable hours and free of charge, a list of—

(a) the state emblems and official signs or hallmarks, and

(b) the emblems, abbreviations and names of international organisations,

which are for the time being protected under the Paris Convention by virtue of notification under Article 6*ter(3)*.

60. Acts of agent or representative: Article 6*septies*

(1) The following provisions apply where an application for registration of a trade mark is made by a person who is an agent or representative of a person who is the proprietor of the mark in a Convention country.

(2) If the proprietor opposes the application, registration shall be refused.

(3) If the application (not being so opposed) is granted, the proprietor may—

(a) apply for a declaration of the invalidity of the registration, or

(b) apply for the rectification of the register so as to substitute his name as the proprietor of the registered trade mark.

(4) The proprietor may (notwithstanding the rights conferred by this Act in relation to a registered trade mark) by injunction restrain any use of the trade mark in the United Kingdom which is not authorised by him.

(5) Subsections (2), (3) and (4) do not apply if, or to the extent that, the agent or representative justifies his action.

(6) An application under subsection (3)(a) or (b) must be made within three years of the proprietor becoming aware of the registration; and no injunction shall be granted under subsection (4) in respect of a use in which the proprietor has acquiesced for a continuous period of three years or more.

Miscellaneous

61. Stamp duty

Stamp duty shall not be chargeable on an instrument relating to a Community trade mark or an international trade mark (UK), or an application for any such mark, by reason only of the fact that such a mark has legal effect in the United Kingdom.

PART III   ADMINISTRATIVE AND OTHER SUPPLEMENTARY PROVISIONS

The registrar

62.   The registrar

In this Act 'the registrar' means the Comptroller-General of Patents, Designs and Trade Marks.

The register

63.   The register

(1)   The registrar shall maintain a register of trade marks.

References in this Act to 'the register' are to that register; and references to registration (in particular, in the expression 'registered trade mark') are, unless the context otherwise requires, to registration in that register.

(2)   There shall be entered in the register in accordance with this Act—

(a)   registered trade marks,

(b)   such particulars as may be prescribed of registrable transactions affecting a registered trade mark, and

(c)   such other matters relating to registered trade marks as may be prescribed.

(3)   The register shall be kept in such manner as may be prescribed, and provision shall in particular be made for—

(a)   public inspection of the register, and

(b)   the supply of certified or uncertified copies, or extracts, of entries in the register.

64.   Rectification or correction of the register

(1)   Any person having a sufficient interest may apply for the rectification of an error or omission in the register:

Provided that an application for rectification may not be made in respect of a matter affecting the validity of the registration of a trade mark.

(2)   An application for rectification may be made either to the registrar or to the court, except that—

(a)   if proceedings concerning the trade mark in question are pending in the court, the application must be made to the court; and

(b)   if in any other case the application is made to the registrar, he may at any stage of the proceedings refer the application to the court.

(3)   Except where the registrar or the court directs otherwise, the effect of rectification of the register is that the error or omission in question shall be deemed never to have been made.

(4)   The registrar may, on request made in the prescribed manner by the proprietor of a registered trade mark, or a licensee, enter any change in his name or address as recorded in the register.

(5)   The registrar may remove from the register matter appearing to him to have ceased to have effect.

65.   Adaptation of entries to new classification

(1)   Provision may be made by rules empowering the registrar to do such things as he considers necessary to implement any amended or substituted classification of goods or services for the purposes of the registration of trade marks.

(2)   Provision may in particular be made for the amendment of existing entries on the register so as to accord with the new classification.

(3)   Any such power of amendment shall not be exercised so as to extend the rights conferred by the registration, except where it appears to the registrar that compliance with this requirement would involve undue complexity and that any extension would not be substantial and would not adversely affect the rights of any person.

(4)   The rules may empower the registrar—

(a)   to require the proprietor of a registered trade mark, within such time as may be prescribed, to file a proposal for amendment of the register, and

(b)   to cancel or refuse to renew the registration of the trade mark in the event of his failing to do so.

(5)   Any such proposal shall be advertised, and may be opposed, in such manner as may be prescribed.

Powers and duties of the registrar

66.   Power to require use of forms

(1)   The registrar may require the use of such forms as he may direct for any purpose relating to the registration of a trade mark or any other proceeding before him under this Act.

(2)   The forms, and any directions of the registrar with respect to their use, shall be published in the prescribed manner.

67.   Information about applications and registered trade marks

(1)   After publication of an application for registration of a trade mark, the registrar shall on request provide a person with such information and permit him to inspect such documents relating to the application, or to any registered trade mark resulting from it, as may be specified in the request, subject, however, to any prescribed restrictions.

Any request must be made in the prescribed manner and be accompanied by the appropriate fee (if any).

(2)   Before publication of an application for registration of a trade mark, documents or information constituting or relating to the application shall not be published by the registrar or communicated by him to any person except—

(a)   in such cases and to such extent as may be prescribed, or

(b)   with the consent of the applicant;

but subject as follows.

(3)   Where a person has been notified that an application for registration of a trade mark has been made, and that the applicant will if the application is granted bring proceedings against him in respect of acts done after publication of the application, he may make a request under subsection (1) notwithstanding that the application has not been published and that subsection shall apply accordingly.

68.   Costs and security for costs

(1)   Provision may be made by rules empowering the registrar, in any proceedings before him under this Act—

(a)   to award any party such costs as he may consider reasonable, and

(b)   to direct how and by what parties they are to be paid.

(2)   Any such order of the registrar may be enforced—

(a)   in England and Wales or Northern Ireland, in the same way as an order of the High Court;

(b)   in Scotland, in the same way as a decree for expenses granted by the Court of Session.

(3)   Provision may be made by rules empowering the registrar, in such cases as may be prescribed, to require a party to proceedings before him to give security for costs, in relation to those proceedings or to proceedings on appeal, and as to the consequences if security is not given.

69.   Evidence before registrar

Provision may be made by rules—

(a)   as to the giving of evidence in proceedings before the registrar under this Act by affidavit or statutory declaration;

(b)   conferring on the registrar the powers of an official referee of the Supreme Court as regards the examination of witnesses on oath and the discovery and production of documents; and

(c)   applying in relation to the attendance of witnesses in proceedings before the registrar the rules applicable to the attendance of witnesses before such a referee.

70.   Exclusion of liability in respect of official acts

(1)   The registrar shall not be taken to warrant the validity of the registration of a trade mark under this Act or under any treaty, convention, arrangement or engagement to which the United Kingdom is a party.

(2)   The registrar is not subject to any liability by reason of, or in connection with, any examination required or authorised by this Act, or any such treaty, convention, arrangement or engagement, or any report or other proceedings consequent on such examination.

(3)   No proceedings lie against an officer of the registrar in respect of any matter for which, by virtue of this section, the registrar is not liable.

71.   Registrar's annual report

(1)   The Comptroller-General of Patents, Designs and Trade Marks shall in his annual report under section 121 of the Patents Act 1977, include a report on the execution of this Act, including the discharge of his functions under the Madrid Protocol.

(2)   The report shall include an account of all money received and paid by him under or by virtue of this Act.

Legal proceedings and appeals

72.   Registration to be *prima facie* evidence of validity

In all legal proceedings relating to a registered trade mark (including proceedings for rectification of the register) the registration of a person as proprietor of a trade mark shall be prima facie evidence of the validity of the original registration and of any subsequent assignment or other transmission of it.

73.   Certificate of validity of contested registration

(1)   If in proceedings before the court the validity of the registration of a trade mark is contested and it is found by the court that the trade mark is validly registered, the court may give a certificate to that effect.

(2) If the court gives such a certificate and in subsequent proceedings—
    (a) the validity of the registration is again questioned, and
    (b) the proprietor obtains a final order or judgment in his favour,
he is entitled to his costs as between solicitor and client unless the court directs otherwise.

This subsection does not extend to the costs of an appeal in any such proceedings.

74. Registrar's appearance in proceedings involving the register

(1) In proceedings before the court involving an application for—
    (a) the revocation of the registration of a trade mark,
    (b) a declaration of the invalidity of the registration of a trade mark, or
    (c) the rectification of the register,
the registrar is entitled to appear and be heard, and shall appear if so directed by the court.

(2) Unless otherwise directed by the court, the registrar may instead of appearing submit to the court a statement in writing signed by him, giving particulars of—
    (a) any proceedings before him in relation to the matter in issue,
    (b) the grounds of any decision given by him affecting it,
    (c) the practice of the Patent Office in like cases, or
    (d) such matters relevant to the issues and within his knowledge as registrar
as he thinks fit;
and the statement shall be deemed to form part of the evidence in the proceedings.

(3) Anything which the registrar is or may be authorised or required to do under this section may be done on his behalf by a duly authorised officer.

75. The court

In this Act, unless the context otherwise requires, 'the court' means—
    (a) in England and Wales and Northern Ireland, the High Court, and
    (b) in Scotland, the Court of Session.

76. Appeals from the registrar

(1) An appeal lies from any decision of the registrar under this Act, except as otherwise expressly provided by rules.

For this purpose 'decision' includes any act of the registrar in exercise of a discretion vested in him by or under this Act.

(2) Any such appeal may be brought either to an appointed person or to the court.

(3) Where an appeal is made to an appointed person, he may refer the appeal to the court if—
    (a) it appears to him that a point of general legal importance is involved,
    (b) the registrar requests that it be so referred, or
    (c) such a request is made by any party to the proceedings before the registrar in which the decision appealed against was made.

Before doing so the appointed person shall give the appellant and any other party to the appeal an opportunity to make representations as to whether the appeal should be referred to the court.

(4) Where an appeal is made to an appointed person and he does not refer it to the court, he shall hear and determine the appeal and his decision shall be final.

(5) The provisions of sections 68 and 69 (costs and security for costs; evidence) apply in relation to proceedings before an appointed person as in relation to proceedings before the registrar.

77. Persons appointed to hear and determine appeals

(1) For the purposes of section 76 an 'appointed person' means a person appointed by the Lord Chancellor to hear and decide appeals under this Act.

(2) A person is not eligible for such appointment unless—

(a) he has a 7 year general qualification, within the meaning of section 71 of the Courts and Legal Services Act 1990;

(b) he is an advocate or solicitor in Scotland of at least 7 years' standing;

(c) he is a member of the Bar of Northern Ireland or solicitor of the Supreme Court of Northern Ireland of at least 7 years' standing; or

(d) he has held judicial office.

(3) An appointed person shall hold and vacate office in accordance with his terms of appointment, subject to the following provisions—

(a) there shall be paid to him such remuneration (whether by way of salary or fees), and such allowances, as the Secretary of State with the approval of the Treasury may determine;

(b) he may resign his office by notice in writing to the Lord Chancellor;

(c) the Lord Chancellor may by notice in writing remove him from office if—

(i) he has become bankrupt or made an arrangement with his creditors or, in Scotland, his estate has been sequestrated or he has executed a trust deed for his creditors or entered into a composition contract, or

(ii) he is incapacitated by physical or mental illness,

or if he is in the opinion of the Lord Chancellor otherwise unable or unfit to perform his duties as an appointed person.

(4) The Lord Chancellor shall consult the Lord Advocate before exercising his powers under this section.

Rules, fees, hours of business, &c.

78. Power of Secretary of State to make rules

(1) The Secretary of State may make rules—

(a) for the purposes of any provision of this Act authorising the making of rules with respect to any matter, and

(b) for prescribing anything authorised or required by any provision of this Act to be prescribed,

and generally for regulating practice and procedure under this Act.

(2) Provision may, in particular, be made—

(a) as to the manner of filing of applications and other documents;

(b) requiring and regulating the translation of documents and the filing and authentication of any translation;

(c) as to the service of documents;

(d) authorising the rectification of irregularities of procedure;

(e) prescribing time limits for anything required be done in connection with any proceeding under this Act;

(f) providing for the extension of any time limit so prescribed, or specified by the registrar, whether or not it has already expired.

(3)   Rules under this Act shall be made by statutory instrument which shall be subject to annulment in pursuance of a resolution of either House of Parliament.

79.   Fees

(1)   There shall be paid in respect of applications and registration and other matters under this Act such fees as may be prescribed.

(2)   Provision may be made by rules as to—

    (a)   the payment of a single fee in respect of two or more matters, and

    (b)   the circumstances (if any) in which a fee may be repaid or remitted.

80.   Hours of business and business days

(1)   The registrar may give directions specifying the hours of business of the Patent Office for the purpose of the transaction by the public of business under this Act, and the days which are business days for that purpose.

(2)   Business done on any day after the specified hours of business, or on a day which is not a business day, shall be deemed to have been done on the next business day; and where the time for doing anything under this Act expires on a day which is not a business day, that time shall be extended to the next business day.

(3)   Directions under this section may make different provision for different classes of business and shall be published in the prescribed manner.

81.   The trade marks journal

Provision shall be made by rules for the publication by the registrar of a journal containing particulars of any application for the registration of a trade mark (including a representation of the mark) and such other information relating to trade marks as the registrar thinks fit.

Trade mark agents

82.   Recognition of agents

Except as otherwise provided by rules, any act required or authorised by this Act to be done by or to a person in connection with the registration of a trade mark, or any procedure relating to a registered trade mark, may be done by or to an agent authorised by that person orally or in writing.

83.   The register of trade mark agents

(1)   The Secretary of State may make rules requiring the keeping of a register of persons who act as agent for others for the purpose of applying for or obtaining the registration of trade marks; and in this Act a 'registered trade mark agent' means a person whose name is entered in the register kept under this section.

(2)   The rules may contain such provision as the Secretary of State thinks fit regulating the registration of persons, and may in particular—

    (a)   require the payment of such fees as may be prescribed, and

    (b)   authorise in prescribed cases the erasure from the register of the name of any person registered in it, or the suspension of a person's registration.

(3)   The rules may delegate the keeping of the register to another person, and may confer on that person—

    (a)   power to make regulations—

        (i)   with respect to the payment of fees, in the cases and subject to the limits prescribed by the rules, and

(ii)   with respect to any other matter which could be regulated by the rules, and

(b)   such other functions, including disciplinary functions, as may be prescribed by the rules.

84.   Unregistered persons not to be described as registered trade mark agents

(1)   An individual who is not a registered trade mark agent shall not—

(a)   carry on a business (otherwise than in partnership) under any name or other description which contains the words 'registered trade mark agent' ; or

(b)   in the course of a business otherwise describe or hold himself out, or permit himself to be described or held out, as a registered trade mark agent.

(2)   A partnership shall not—

(a)   carry on a business under any name or other description which contains the words 'registered trade mark agent'; or

(b)   in the course of a business otherwise describe or hold itself out, or permit itself to be described or held out, as a firm of registered trade mark agents, unless all the partners are registered trade mark agents or the partnership satisfies such conditions as may be prescribed for the purposes of this section.

(3)   A body corporate shall not—

(a)   carry on a business (otherwise than in partnership) under any name or other description which contains the words 'registered trade mark agent'; or

(b)   in the course of a business otherwise describe or hold itself out, or permit itself to be described or held out, as a registered trade mark agent, unless all the directors of the body corporate are registered trade mark agents or the body satisfies such conditions as may be prescribed for the purposes of this section.

(4)   A person who contravenes this section commits an offence and is liable on summary conviction to a fine not exceeding level 5 on the standard scale; and proceedings for such an offence may be begun at any time within a year from the date of the offence.

85.   Power to prescribe conditions, &c. for mixed partnerships and bodies corporate

(1)   The Secretary of State may make rules prescribing the conditions to be satisfied for the purposes of section 84 (persons entitled to be described as registered trade mark agents)—

(a)   in relation to a partnership where not all the partners are qualified persons, or

(b)   in relation to a body corporate where not all the directors are qualified persons, and imposing requirements to be complied with by such partnerships or bodies corporate.

(2)   The rules may, in particular—

(a)   prescribe conditions as to the number or proportion of partners or directors who must be qualified persons;

(b)   impose requirements as to—

(i)   the identification of qualified and unqualified persons in professional advertisements, circulars or letters issued by or with the consent of the partnership or body corporate and which relate to its business, and

(ii)   the manner in which a partnership or body corporate is to organise its affairs so as to secure that qualified persons exercise a sufficient degree of control over the activities of unqualified persons.

(3)   Contravention of a requirement imposed by the rules is an offence for which a person is liable on summary conviction to a fine not exceeding level 5 on the standard scale.

(4)   In this section 'qualified person' means a registered trade mark agent.

86.   Use of the term 'trade mark attorney'

(1)   No offence is committed under the enactments restricting the use of certain expressions in reference to persons not qualified to act as solicitors by the use of the term 'trade mark attorney' in reference to a registered trade mark agent.

(2)   The enactments referred to in subsection (1) are section 21 of the Solicitors Act 1974, section 31 of the Solicitors (Scotland) Act 1980 and Article 22 of the Solicitors (Northern Ireland) Order 1976.

87.   Privilege for communications with registered trade mark agents

(1)   This section applies to communications as to any matter relating to the protection of any design or trade mark, or as to any matter involving passing off.

(2)   Any such communication—
(a)   between a person and his trade mark agent, or
(b)   for the purpose of obtaining, or in response to a request for, information which a person is seeking for the purpose of instructing his trade mark agent,
is privileged from, or in Scotland protected against, disclosure in legal proceedings in the same way as a communication between a person and his solicitor or, as the case may be, a communication for the purpose of obtaining, or in response to a request for, information which a person is seeking for the purpose of instructing his solicitor.

(3)   In subsection (2) 'trade mark agent' means—
(a)   a registered trade mark agent, or
(b)   a partnership entitled to describe itself as a firm of registered trade mark agents, or
(c)   a body corporate entitled to describe itself as a registered trade mark agent.

88.   Power of registrar to refuse to deal with certain agents

(1)   The Secretary of State may make rules authorising the registrar to refuse to recognise as agent in respect of any business under this Act—
(a)   a person who has been convicted of an offence under section 84 (unregistered persons describing themselves as registered trade mark agents);
(b)   an individual whose name has been erased from and not restored to, or who is suspended from, the register of trade mark agents on the ground of misconduct;
(c)   a person who is found by the Secretary of State to have been guilty of such conduct as would, in the case of an individual registered in the register of trade mark agents, render him liable to have his name erased from the register on the ground of misconduct;
(d)   a partnership or body corporate of which one of the partners or directors is a person whom the registrar could refuse to recognise under paragraph (a), (b) or (c) above.

(2)   The rules may contain such incidental and supplementary provisions as appear to the Secretary of State to be appropriate and may, in particular, prescribe circumstances in which a person is or is not to be taken to have been guilty of misconduct.

Importation of infringing goods, material or articles

89.   Infringing goods, material or articles may be treated as prohibited goods

(1)   The proprietor of a registered trade mark, or a licensee, may give notice in writing to the Commissioners of Customs and Excise—

(a)   that he is the proprietor or, as the case may be, a licensee of the trade mark

(b)   that, at a time and place specified in the notice, goods which are, in relation to that registered trade mark, infringing goods, material or articles are expected to arrive in the United Kingdom—

(i)   from outside the European Economic Area, or

(ii)   from within that Area but not having been entered for free circulation, and

(c)   that he requests the Commissioners to treat them as prohibited goods.

(2)   When a notice is in force under this section the importation of the goods to which the notice relates, otherwise than by a person for his private and domestic use, is prohibited; but a person is not by reason of the prohibition liable to any penalty other than forfeiture of the goods.

(3)   This section does not apply to goods entered, or expected to be entered, for free circulation in respect of which the proprietor of the registered trade mark, or a licensee, is entitled to lodge an application under Article 3(1) of Council Regulation (EEC) No. 3842/86 laying down measures to prohibit the release for free circulation of counterfeit goods.

90.   Power of Commissioners of Customs and Excise to make regulations

(1)   The Commissioners of Customs and Excise may make regulations prescribing the form in which notice is to be given under section 89 and requiring a person giving notice—

(a)   to furnish the Commissioners with such evidence as may be specified in the regulations, either on giving notice or when the goods are imported, or at both those times, and

(b)   to comply with such other conditions as may be specified in the regulations.

(2)   The regulations may, in particular, require a person giving such a notice—

(a)   to pay such fees in respect of the notice as may be specified by the regulations;

(b)   to give such security as may be so specified in respect of any liability or expense which the Commissioners may incur in consequence of the notice by reason of the detention of any goods or anything done to goods detained;

(c)   to indemnify the Commissioners against any such liability or expense, whether security has been given or not.

(3)   The regulations may make different provision as respects different classes of case to which they apply and may include such incidental and supplementary provisions as the Commissioners consider expedient.

(4)   Regulations under this section shall be made by statutory instrument which shall be subject to annulment in pursuance of a resolution of either House of Parliament.

(5)   Section 17 of the Customs and Excise Management Act 1979 (general provisions as to Commissioners' receipts) applies to fees paid in pursuance of regulations under this section as to receipts under the enactments relating to customs and excise.

91.   Power of Commissioners of Customs and Excise to disclose information
Where information relating to infringing goods, material or articles has been obtained by the Commissioners of Customs and Excise for the purposes of, or in connection with, the exercise of their functions in relation to imported goods, the Commissioners may authorise the disclosure of that information for the purpose of facilitating the exercise by any person of any function in connection with the investigation or prosecution of an offence under section 92 below (unauthorised use of trade mark, &c. in relation to goods) or under the Trade Descriptions Act 1968.

Offences

92.   Unauthorised use of trade mark, &c. in relation to goods
(1)   A person commits an offence who with a view to gain for himself or another, or with intent to cause loss to another, and without the consent of the proprietor—

(a)   applies to goods or their packaging a sign identical to, or likely to be mistaken for, a registered trade mark, or

(b)   sells or lets for hire, offers or exposes for sale or hire or distributes goods which bear, or the packaging of which bears, such a sign, or

(c)   has in his possession, custody or control in the course of a business any such goods with a view to the doing of anything, by himself or another, which would be an offence under paragraph (b).

(2)   A person commits an offence who with a view to gain for himself or another, or with intent to cause loss to another, and without the consent of the proprietor—

(a)   applies a sign identical to, or likely to be mistaken for, a registered trade mark to material intended to be used—

(i)   for labelling or packaging goods,

(ii)   as a business paper in relation to goods, or

(iii)   for advertising goods, or

(b)   uses in the course of a business material bearing such a sign for labelling or packaging goods, as a business paper in relation to goods, or for advertising goods, or

(c)   has in his possession, custody or control in the course of a business any such material with a view to the doing of anything, by himself or another, which would be an offence under paragraph (b).

(3)   A person commits an offence who with a view to gain for himself or another, or with intent to cause loss to another, and without the consent of the proprietor—

(a)   makes an article specifically designed or adapted for making copies of a sign identical to, or likely to be mistaken for, a registered trade mark, or

(b)   has such an article in his possession, custody or control in the course of a business,

knowing or having reason to believe that it has been, or is to be, used to produce goods, or material for labelling or packaging goods, as a business paper in relation to goods, or for advertising goods.

(4)   A person does not commit an offence under this section unless—

(a)   the goods are goods in respect of which the trade mark is registered, or

(b)   the trade mark has a reputation in the United Kingdom and the use of the sign takes or would take unfair advantage of, or is or would be detrimental to, the distinctive character or the repute of the trade mark.

(5)   It is a defence for a person charged with an offence under this section to show that he believed on reasonable grounds that the use of the sign in the manner in which it was used, or was to be used, was not an infringement of the registered trade mark.

(6)   A person guilty of an offence under this section is liable—

(a)   on summary conviction to imprisonment for a term not exceeding six months or a fine not exceeding the statutory maximum, or both;

(b)   on conviction on indictment to a fine or imprisonment for a term not exceeding ten years, or both.

93.   Enforcement function of local weights and measures authority

(1)   It is the duty of every local weights and measures authority to enforce within their area the provisions of section 92 (unauthorised use of trade mark, &c. in relation to goods).

(2)   The following provisions of the Trade Descriptions Act 1968 apply in relation to the enforcement of that section as in relation to the enforcement of that Act—

section 27 (power to make test purchases),

section 28 (power to enter premises and inspect and seize goods and documents),

section 29 (obstruction of authorised officers), and

section 33 (compensation for loss, &c. of goods seized).

(3)   Subsection (1) above does not apply in relation to the enforcement of section 92 in Northern Ireland, but it is the duty of the Department of Economic Development to enforce that section in Northern Ireland.

For that purpose the provisions of the Trade Descriptions Act 1968 specified in subsection (2) apply as if for the references to a local weights and measures authority and any officer of such an authority there were substituted references to that Department and any of its officers.

(4)   Any enactment which authorises the disclosure of information for the purpose of facilitating the enforcement of the Trade Descriptions Act 1968 shall apply as if section 92 above were contained in that Act and as if the functions of any person in relation to the enforcement of that section were functions under that Act.

(5)   Nothing in this section shall be construed as authorising a local weights and measures authority to bring proceedings in Scotland for an offence.

94.   Falsification of register, &c.

(1)   It is an offence for a person to make, or cause to be made, a false entry in the register of trade marks, knowing or having reason to believe that it is false.

(2)   It is an offence for a person—

(a)   to make or cause to be made anything falsely purporting to be a copy of an entry in the register, or

(b)   to produce or tender or cause to be produced or tendered in evidence any such thing,

knowing or having reason to believe that it is false.

(3)   A person guilty of an offence under this section is liable—

(a)   on conviction on indictment, to imprisonment for a term not exceeding two years or a fine, or both;

(b)   on summary conviction, to imprisonment for a term not exceeding six months or a fine not exceeding the statutory maximum, or both.

95.   Falsely representing trade mark as registered

(1)   It is an offence for a person—

(a)   falsely to represent that a mark is a registered trade mark, or

(b)   to make a false representation as to the goods or services for which a trade mark is registered

knowing or having reason to believe that the representation is false.

(2)   For the purposes of this section, the use in the United Kingdom in relation to a trade mark—

(a)   of the word 'registered', or

(b)   of any other word or symbol importing a reference (express or implied) to registration,

shall be deemed to be a representation as to registration under this Act unless it is shown that the reference is to registration elsewhere than in the United Kingdom and that the trade mark is in fact so registered for the goods or services in question.

(3)   A person guilty of an offence under this section is liable on summary conviction to a fine not exceeding level 3 on the standard scale.

96.   Supplementary provisions as to summary proceedings in Scotland

(1)   Notwithstanding anything in section 331 of the Criminal Procedure (Scotland) Act 1975, summary proceedings in Scotland for an offence under this Act may be begun at any time within six months after the date on which evidence sufficient in the Lord Advocate's opinion to justify the proceedings came to his knowledge.

For this purpose a certificate of the Lord Advocate as to the date on which such evidence came to his knowledge is conclusive evidence.

(2)   For the purposes of subsection (1) and of any other provision of this Act as to the time within which summary proceedings for an offence may be brought, proceedings in Scotland shall be deemed to be begun on the date on which a warrant to apprehend or to cite the accused is granted, if such warrant is executed without undue delay.

Forfeiture of counterfeit goods, &c.

97.   Forfeiture: England and Wales or Northern Ireland

(1)   In England and Wales or Northern Ireland where there has come into the possession of any person in connection with the investigation or prosecution of a relevant offence—

(a)   goods which, or the packaging of which, bears a sign identical to or likely to be mistaken for a registered trade mark,

(b)   material bearing such a sign and intended to be used for labelling or packaging goods, as a business paper in relation to goods, or for advertising goods, or

(c)   articles specifically designed or adapted for making copies of such a sign,
that person may apply under this section for an order for the forfeiture of the goods, material or articles.

(2)   An application under this section may be made—

(a)   where proceedings have been brought in any court for a relevant offence relating to some or all of the goods, material or articles, to that court;

(b)   where no application for the forfeiture of the goods, material or articles has been made under paragraph (a), by way of complaint to a magistrates' court.

(3)   On an application under this section the court shall make an order for the forfeiture of any goods, material or articles only if it is satisfied that a relevant offence has been committed in relation to the goods, material or articles.

(4)   A court may infer for the purposes of this section that such an offence has been committed in relation to any goods, material or articles if it is satisfied that such an offence has been committed in relation to goods, material or articles which are representative of them (whether by reason of being of the same design or part of the same consignment or batch or otherwise).

(5)   Any person aggrieved by an order made under this section by a magistrates' court, or by a decision of such a court not to make such an order, may appeal against that order or decision—

(a)   in England and Wales, to the Crown Court;

(b)   in Northern Ireland, to the county court;
and an order so made may contain such provision as appears to the court to be appropriate for delaying the coming into force of the order pending the making and determination of any appeal (including any application under section 111 of the Magistrates' Courts Act 1980 or Article 146 of the Magistrates' Courts (Northern Ireland) Order 1981 (statement of case)).

(6)   Subject to subsection (7), where any goods, material or articles are forfeited under this section they shall be destroyed in accordance with such directions as the court may give.

(7)   On making an order under this section the court may, if it considers it appropriate to do so, direct that the goods, material or articles to which the order relates shall (instead of being destroyed) be released, to such person as the court may specify, on condition that that person—

(a)   causes the offending sign to be erased, removed or obliterated, and

(b)   complies with any order to pay costs which has been made against him in the proceedings for the order for forfeiture.

(8)   For the purposes of this section a 'relevant offence' means an offence under section 92 above (unauthorised use of trade mark, &c. in relation to goods) or under the Trade Descriptions Act 1968 or any offence involving dishonesty or deception.

98.   Forfeiture: Scotland

(1)   In Scotland the court may make an order for the forfeiture of any—

(a)   goods which bear, or the packaging of which bears, a sign identical to or likely to be mistaken for a registered trade mark,

(b) material bearing such a sign and intended to be used for labelling or packaging goods, as a business paper in relation to goods, or for advertising goods, or

(c) articles specifically designed or adapted for making copies of such a sign.

(2) An order under this section may be made—

(a) on an application by the procurator-fiscal made in the manner specified in section 310 of the Criminal Procedure (Scotland) Act 1975, or

(b) where a person is convicted of a relevant offence, in addition to any other penalty which the court may impose.

(3) On an application under subsection (2)(a), the court shall make an order for the forfeiture of any goods, material or articles only if it is satisfied that a relevant offence has been committed in relation to the goods, material or articles.

(4) The court may infer for the purposes of this section that such an offence has been committed in relation to any goods, material or articles if it is satisfied that such an offence has been committed in relation to goods, material or articles which are representative of them (whether by reason of being of the same design or part of the same consignment or batch or otherwise).

(5) The procurator-fiscal making the application under subsection (2)(a) shall serve on any person appearing to him to be the owner of, or otherwise to have an interest in, the goods, material or articles to which the application relates a copy of the application, together with a notice giving him the opportunity to appear at the hearing of the application to show cause why the goods, material or articles should not be forfeited.

(6) Service under subsection (5) shall be carried out, and such service may be proved, in the manner specified for citation of an accused in summary proceedings under the Criminal Procedure (Scotland) Act 1975.

(7) Any person upon whom notice is served under subsection (5) and any other person claiming to be the owner of, or otherwise to have an interest in, goods, material or articles to which an application under this section relates shall be entitled to appear at the hearing of the application to show cause why the goods, material or articles should not be forfeited.

(8) The court shall not make an order following an application under subsection (2)(a)—

(a) if any person on whom notice is served under subsection (5) does not appear, unless service of the notice on that person is proved; or

(b) if no notice under subsection (5) has been served, unless the court is satisfied that in the circumstances it was reasonable not to serve such notice.

(9) Where an order for the forfeiture of any goods, material or articles is made following an application under subsection (2)(a), any person who appeared, or was entitled to appear, to show cause why goods, material or articles should not be forfeited may, within 21 days of the making of the order, appeal to the High Court by Bill of Suspension; and section 452(4)(a) to (e) of the Criminal Procedure (Scotland) Act 1975 shall apply to an appeal under this subsection as it applies to a stated case under Part II of that Act.

(10) An order following an application under subsection (2)(a) shall not take effect—

(a) until the end of the period of 21 days beginning with the day after the day on which the order is made; or

(b)   if an appeal is made under subsection (9) above within that period, until the appeal is determined or abandoned.

(11)   An order under subsection (2)(b) shall not take effect—

(a)   until the end of the period within which an appeal against the order could be brought under the Criminal Procedure (Scotland) Act 1975; or

(b)   if an appeal is made within that period, until the appeal is determined or abandoned.

(12)   Subject to subsection (13), goods, material or articles forfeited under this section shall be destroyed in accordance with such directions as the court may give.

(13)   On making an order under this section the court may if it considers it appropriate to do so, direct that the goods, material or articles to which the order relates shall (instead of being destroyed) be released, to such person as the court may specify, on condition that that person causes the offending sign to be erased, removed or obliterated.

(14)   For the purposes of this section—

'relevant offence' means an offence under section 92 (unauthorised use of trade mark, &c. in relation to goods) or under the Trade Descriptions Act 1968 or any offence involving dishonesty or deception,

'the court' means—

(a)   in relation to an order made on an application under subsection (2)(a), the sheriff, and

(b)   in relation to an order made under subsection (2)(b), the court which imposed the penalty.

PART IV   MISCELLANEOUS AND GENERAL PROVISIONS

Miscellaneous

99.   Unauthorised use of Royal arms &c.

(1) A person shall not without the authority of Her Majesty use in connection with any business the Royal arms (or arms so closely resembling the Royal arms as to be calculated to deceive) in such manner as to be calculated to lead to the belief that he is duly authorised to use the Royal arms.

(2)   A person shall not without the authority of Her Majesty or of a member of the Royal family use in connection with any business any device, emblem or title in such a manner as to be calculated to lead to the belief that he is employed by, or supplies goods or services to, Her Majesty or that member of the Royal family.

(3)   A person who contravenes subsection (1) commits an offence and is liable on summary conviction to a fine not exceeding level 2 on the standard scale.

(4)   Contravention of subsection (1) or (2) may be restrained by injunction in proceedings brought by—

(a)   any person who is authorised to use the arms, device, emblem or title in question, or

(b)   any person authorised by the Lord Chamberlain to take such proceedings.

(5)   Nothing in this section affects any right of the proprietor of a trade mark containing any such arms, device, emblem or title to use that trade mark.

100. Burden of proving use of trade mark

If in any civil proceedings under this Act a question arises as to the use to which a registered trade mark has been put, it is for the proprietor to show what use has been made of it.

101. Offences committed by partnerships and bodies corporate

(1) Proceedings for an offence under this Act alleged to have been committed by a partnership shall be brought against the partnership in the name of the firm and not in that of the partners; but without prejudice to any liability of the partners under subsection (4) below.

(2) The following provisions apply for the purposes of such proceedings as in relation to a body corporate—

(a) any rules of court relating to the service of documents;

(b) in England and Wales or Northern Ireland, Schedule 3 to the Magistrates' Courts Act 1980 or Schedule 4 to the Magistrates' Courts (Northern Ireland) Order 1981 (procedure on charge of offence).

(3) A fine imposed on a partnership on its conviction in such proceedings shall be paid out of the partnership assets.

(4) Where a partnership is guilty of an offence under this Act, every partner, other than a partner who is proved to have been ignorant of or to have attempted to prevent the commission of the offence, is also guilty of the offence and liable to be proceeded against and punished accordingly.

(5) Where an offence under this Act committed by a body corporate is proved to have been committed with the consent or connivance of a director, manager, secretary or other similar officer of the body, or a person purporting to act in any such capacity, he as well as the body corporate is guilty of the offence and liable to be proceeded against and punished accordingly.

Interpretation

102. Adaptation of expressions for Scotland

In the application of this Act to Scotland—

'account of profits' means accounting and payment of profits;

'accounts' means count, reckoning and payment;

'assignment' means assignation;

'costs' means expenses;

'declaration' means declarator;

'defendant' means defender;

'delivery up' means delivery;

'injunction' means interdict;

'interlocutory relief' means interim remedy; and

'plaintiff' means pursuer.

103. Minor definitions

(1) In this Act—

'business' includes a trade or profession;

'director', in relation to a body corporate whose affairs are managed by its members, means any member of the body;

'infringement proceedings', in relation to a registered trade mark, includes proceedings under section 16 (order for delivery up of infringing goods, &c.);

'publish' means make available to the public, and references to publication—

(a)   in relation to an application for registration, are to publication under section 38(1), and

(b)   in relation to registration, are to publication under section 40(4);

'statutory provisions' includes provisions of subordinate legislation within the meaning of the Interpretation Act 1978;

'trade' includes any business or profession.

(2)   References in this Act to use (or any particular description of use) of a trade mark, or of a sign identical with, similar to, or likely to be mistaken for a trade mark, include use (or that description of use) otherwise than by means of a graphic representation.

(3)   References in this Act to a Community instrument include references to any instrument amending or replacing that instrument.

104.   Index of defined expressions

In this Act the expressions listed below are defined by or otherwise fall to be construed in accordance with the provisions indicated—

account of profits and accounts (in Scotland)	section 102
appointed person (for purposes of section 76)	section 77
assignment (in Scotland)	section 102
business	section 103(1)
certification mark	section 50(1)
collective mark	section 49(1)
commencement (of this Act)	section 109(2)
Community trade mark	section 51
Community Trade Mark Regulation	section 51
Convention country	section 55(1)(b)
costs (in Scotland)	section 102
the court	section 75
date of application	section 33(2)
date of filing	section 33(1)
date of registration	section 40(3)
defendant (in Scotland)	section 102
delivery up (in Scotland)	section 102
director	section 103(1)
earlier right	section 5(4)
earlier trade mark	section 6
exclusive licence and licensee	section 29(1)
infringement (of registered trade mark)	sections 9(1) and (2) and 10
infringement proceedings	section 103(1)
infringing articles	section 17
infringing goods	section 17
infringing material	section 17
injunction (in Scotland)	section 102
interlocutory relief (in Scotland)	section 102
the International Bureau	section 53
international trade mark (UK)	section 53
Madrid Protocol	section 53

Paris Convention	section 55(1)(a)
plaintiff (in Scotland)	section 102
prescribed	section 78(1)(b)
protected under the Paris Convention	
— well-known trade marks	section 56(1)
— state emblems and official signs or hallmarks	section 57(1)
— emblems, &c. of international organisations	section 58(2)
publish and references to publication	section 103(1)
register, registered (and related expressions)	section 63(1)
registered trade mark agent	section 83(1)
registrable transaction	section 25(2)
the registrar	section 62
rules	section 78
statutory provisions	section 103(1)
trade	section 103(1)
trade mark	
— generally	section 1(1)
— includes collective mark or certification mark	section 1(2)
United Kingdom (references include Isle of Man)	section 108(2)
use (of trade mark or sign)	section 103(2)
well-known trade mark (under Paris Convention)	section 56(1)

Other general provisions

105. Transitional provisions

The provisions of Schedule 3 have effect with respect to transitional matters, including the treatment of marks registered under the Trade Marks Act 1938, and applications for registration and other proceedings pending under that Act, on the commencement of this Act.

106. Consequential amendments and repeals

(1)   The enactments specified in Schedule 4 are amended in accordance with that Schedule, the amendments being consequential on the provisions of this Act.

(2)   The enactments specified in Schedule 5 are repealed to the extent specified.

107. Territorial waters and the continental shelf

(1)   For the purposes of this Act the territorial waters of the United Kingdom shall be treated as part of the United Kingdom.

(2)   This Act applies to things done in the United Kingdom sector of the continental shelf on a structure or vessel which is present there for purposes directly connected with the exploration of the sea bed or subsoil or the exploitation of their natural resources as it applies to things done in the United Kingdom.

(3)   The United Kingdom sector of the continental shelf means the areas designated by order under section 1(7) of the Continental Shelf Act 1964.

108. Extent

(1)   This Act extends to England and Wales, Scotland and Northern Ireland.

(2)   This Act also extends to the Isle of Man, subject to such exceptions and modifications as Her Majesty may specify by Order in Council; and subject to any such Order references in this Act to the United Kingdom shall be construed as including the Isle of Man.

109. Commencement

(1)   The provisions of this Act come into force on such day as the Secretary of State may appoint by order made by statutory instrument.

Different days may be appointed for different provisions and different purposes.

(2)   The references to the commencement of this Act in Schedules 3 and 4 (transitional provisions and consequential amendments) are to the commencement of the main substantive provisions of Parts I and III of this Act and the consequential repeal of the Trade Marks Act 1938.

Provision may be made by order under this section identifying the date of that commencement.

110. Short title

This Act may be cited as the Trade Marks Act 1994.

SCHEDULES

Section 49   SCHEDULE 1   COLLECTIVE MARKS

General

1.   The provisions of this Act apply to collective marks subject to the following provisions.

Signs of which a collective mark may consist

2.   In relation to a collective mark the reference in section 1(1) (signs of which a trade mark may consist) to distinguishing goods or services of one undertaking from those of other undertakings shall be construed as a reference to distinguishing goods or services of members of the association which is the proprietor of the mark from those of other undertakings.

Indication of geographical origin

3.—(1)   Notwithstanding section 3(1)(c), a collective mark may be registered which consists of signs or indications which may serve, in trade, to designate the geographical origin of the goods or services.

(2)   However, the proprietor of such a mark is not entitled to prohibit the use of the signs or indications in accordance with honest practices in industrial or commercial matters (in particular, by a person who is entitled to use a geographical name).

Mark not to be misleading as to character or significance

4.—(1)   A collective mark shall not be registered if the public is liable to be misled as regards the character or significance of the mark, in particular if it is likely to be taken to be something other than a collective mark.

(2) The registrar may accordingly require that a mark in respect of which application is made for registration include some indication that it is a collective mark.

Notwithstanding section 39(2), an application may be amended so as to comply with any such requirement.

Regulations governing use of collective mark

5.—(1) An applicant for registration of a collective mark must file with the registrar regulations governing the use of the mark.

(2) The regulations must specify the persons authorised to use the mark, the conditions of membership of the association and, where they exist, the conditions of use of the mark, including any sanctions against misuse.

Further requirements with which the regulations have to comply may be imposed by rules.

Approval of regulations by registrar

6.—(1) A collective mark shall not be registered unless the regulations governing the use of the mark—

(a) comply with paragraph 5(2) and any further requirements imposed by rules, and

(b) are not contrary to public policy or to accepted principles of morality.

(2) Before the end of the prescribed period after the date of the application for registration of a collective mark, the applicant must file the regulations with the registrar and pay the prescribed fee.

If he does not do so, the application shall be deemed to be withdrawn.

7.—(1) The registrar shall consider whether the requirements mentioned in paragraph 6(1) are met.

(2) If it appears to the registrar that those requirements are not met, he shall inform the applicant and give him an opportunity, within such period as the registrar may specify, to make representations or to file amended regulations.

(3) If the applicant fails to satisfy the registrar that those requirements are met, or to file regulations amended so as to meet them, or fails to respond before the end of the specified period, the registrar shall refuse the application.

(4) If it appears to the registrar that those requirements, and the other requirements for registration, are met, he shall accept the application and shall proceed in accordance with section 38 (publication, opposition proceedings and observations).

8. The regulations shall be published and notice of opposition may be given, and observations may be made, relating to the matters mentioned in paragraph 6(1).

This is in addition to any other grounds on which the application may be opposed or observations made.

Regulations to be open to inspection

9. The regulations governing the use of a registered collective mark shall be open to public inspection in the same way as the register.

Amendment of regulations

10.—(1) An amendment of the regulations governing the use of a registered collective mark is not effective unless and until the amended regulations are filed with the registrar and accepted by him.

(2) Before accepting any amended regulations the registrar may in any case where it appears to him expedient to do so cause them to be published.

(3) If he does so, notice of opposition may be given, and observations may be made, relating to the matters mentioned in paragraph 6(1).

Infringement: rights of authorised users

11. The following provisions apply in relation to an authorised user of a registered collective mark as in relation to a licensee of a trade mark—

(a) section 10(5) (definition of infringement: unauthorised application of mark to certain material);

(b) section 19(2) (order as to disposal of infringing goods, material or articles: adequacy of other remedies);

(c) section 89 (prohibition of importation of infringing goods, material or articles: request to Commissioners of Customs and Excise).

12.—(1) The following provisions (which correspond to the provisions of section 30 (general provisions as to rights of licensees in case of infringement)) have effect as regards the rights of an authorised user in relation to infringement of a registered collective mark.

(2) An authorised user is entitled, subject to any agreement to the contrary between him and the proprietor, to call on the proprietor to take infringement proceedings in respect of any matter which affects his interests.

(3) If the proprietor—

(a) refuses to do so, or

(b) fails to do so within two months after being called upon,

the authorised user may bring the proceedings in his own name as if he were the proprietor.

(4) Where infringement proceedings are brought by virtue of this paragraph, the authorised user may not, without the leave of the court, proceed with the action unless the proprietor is either joined as a plaintiff or added as a defendant.

This does not affect the granting of interlocutory relief on an application by an authorised user alone.

(5) A proprietor who is added as a defendant as mentioned in sub-paragraph (4) shall not be made liable for any costs in the action unless he takes part in the proceedings.

(6) In infringement proceedings brought by the proprietor of a registered collective mark any loss suffered or likely to be suffered by authorised users shall be taken into account; and the court may give such directions as it thinks fit as to the extent to which the plaintiff is to hold the proceeds of any pecuniary remedy on behalf of such users.

Grounds for revocation of registration

13. Apart from the grounds of revocation provided for in section 46, the registration of a collective mark may be revoked on the ground—

(a) that the manner in which the mark has been used by the proprietor has caused it to become liable to mislead the public in the manner referred to in paragraph 4(1), or

(b) that the proprietor has failed to observe, or to secure the observance of, the regulations governing the use of the mark, or

(c) that an amendment of the regulations has been made so that the regulations—

(i) no longer comply with paragraph 5(2) and any further conditions imposed by rules, or

(ii) are contrary to public policy or to accepted principles of morality.

Grounds for invalidity of registration

14. Apart from the grounds of invalidity provided for in section 47, the registration of a collective mark may be declared invalid on the ground that the mark was registered in breach of the provisions of paragraph 4(1) or 6(1).

Section 50 SCHEDULE 2 CERTIFICATION MARKS

General

1. The provisions of this Act apply to certification marks subject to the following provisions.

Signs of which a certification mark may consist

2. In relation to a certification mark the reference in section 1(1) (signs of which a trade mark may consist) to distinguishing goods or services of one undertaking from those of other undertakings shall be construed as a reference to distinguishing goods or services which are certified from those which are not.

Indication of geographical origin

3.—(1) Notwithstanding section 3(1)(c), a certification mark may be registered which consists of signs or indications which may serve, in trade, to designate the geographical origin of the goods or services.

(2) However, the proprietor of such a mark is not entitled to prohibit the use of the signs or indications in accordance with honest practices in industrial or commercial matters (in particular, by a person who is entitled to use a geographical name).

Nature of proprietor's business

4. A certification mark shall not be registered if the proprietor carries on a business involving the supply of goods or services of the kind certified.

Mark not to be misleading as to character or significance

5.—(1) A certification mark shall not be registered if the public is liable to be misled as regards the character or significance of the mark, in particular if it is likely to be taken to be something other than a certification mark.

(2) The registrar may accordingly require that a mark in respect of which application is made for registration include some indication that it is a certification mark.

Notwithstanding section 39(2), an application may be amended so as to comply with any such requirement.

Regulations governing use of certification mark

6.—(1) An applicant for registration of a certification mark must file with the registrar regulations governing the use of the mark.

(2) The regulations must indicate who is authorised to use the mark, the characteristics to be certified by the mark, how the certifying body is to test those characteristics and to supervise the use of the mark, the fees (if any) to be paid in connection with the operation of the mark and the procedures for resolving disputes.

Further requirements with which the regulations have to comply may be imposed by rules.

Approval of regulations, &c.

7.—(1) A certification mark shall not be registered unless—
    (a) the regulations governing the use of the mark—
        (i) comply with paragraph 6(2) and any further requirements imposed by rules, and
        (ii) are not contrary to public policy or to accepted principles of morality, and
    (b) the applicant is competent to certify the goods or services for which the mark is to be registered.

(2) Before the end of the prescribed period after the date of the application for registration of a certification mark, the applicant must file the regulations with the registrar and pay the prescribed fee.

If he does not do so, the application shall be deemed to be withdrawn.

8.—(1) The registrar shall consider whether the requirements mentioned in paragraph 7(1) are met.

(2) If it appears to the registrar that those requirements are not met, he shall inform the applicant and give him an opportunity, within such period as the registrar may specify, to make representations or to file amended regulations.

(3) If the applicant fails to satisfy the registrar that those requirements are met, or to file regulations amended so as to meet them, or fails to respond before the end of the specified period, the registrar shall refuse the application.

(4) If it appears to the registrar that those requirements, and the other requirements for registration, are met, he shall accept the application and shall proceed in accordance with section 38 (publication, opposition proceedings and observations).

9. The regulations shall be published and notice of opposition may be given, and observations may be made, relating to the matters mentioned in paragraph 7(1).

This is in addition to any other grounds on which the application may be opposed or observations made.

Regulations to be open to inspection

10. The regulations governing the use of a registered certification mark shall be open to public inspection in the same way as the register.

Amendment of regulations

11.—(1) An amendment of the regulations governing the use of a registered certification mark is not effective unless and until the amended regulations are filed with the registrar and accepted by him.

(2) Before accepting any amended regulations the registrar may in any case where it appears to him expedient to do so cause them to be published.

(3) If he does so, notice of opposition may be given, and observations may be made, relating to the matters mentioned in paragraph 7(1).

Consent to assignment of registered certification mark

12. The assignment or other transmission of a registered certification mark is not effective without the consent of the registrar.

Infringement: rights of authorised users

13. The following provisions apply in relation to an authorised user of a registered certification mark as in relation to a licensee of a trade mark—

(a) section 10(5) (definition of infringement: unauthorised application of mark to certain material),

(b) section 19(2) (order as to disposal of infringing goods, material or articles: adequacy of other remedies),

(c) section 89 (prohibition of importation of infringing goods, material or articles: request to Commissioners of Customs and Excise).

14. In infringement proceedings brought by the proprietor of a registered certification mark any loss suffered or likely to be suffered by authorised users shall be taken into account; and the court may give such directions as it thinks fit as to the extent to which the plaintiff is to hold the proceeds of any pecuniary remedy on behalf of such users.

Grounds for revocation of registration

15. Apart from the grounds of revocation provided for in section 46, the registration of a certification mark may be revoked on the ground—

(a) that the proprietor has begun to carry on such a business as is mentioned in paragraph 4,

(b) that the manner in which the mark has been used by the proprietor has caused it to become liable to mislead the public in the manner referred to in paragraph 5(1),

(c) that the proprietor has failed to observe, or to secure the observance of, the regulations governing the use of the mark

(d) that an amendment of the regulations has been made so that the regulations—

(i) no longer comply with paragraph 6(2) and any further conditions imposed by rules, or

(ii) are contrary to public policy or to accepted principles of morality, or

(e) that the proprietor is no longer competent to certify the goods or services for which the mark is registered.

Grounds for invalidity of registration

16. Apart from the grounds of invalidity provided for in section 47, the registration of a certification mark may be declared invalid on the ground that the mark was registered in breach of the provisions of paragraph 4, 5(1) or 7(1).

Section 105   SCHEDULE 3   TRANSITIONAL PROVISIONS

Introductory

1.—(1) In this Schedule—
'existing registered mark' means a trade mark, certification trade mark or service mark registered under the 1938 Act immediately before the commencement of this Act;
'the 1938 Act' means the Trade Marks Act 1938; and
'the old law' means that Act and any other enactment or rule of law applying to existing registered marks immediately before the commencement of this Act.

(2) For the purposes of this Schedule—

(a) an application shall be treated as pending on the commencement of this Act if it was made but not finally determined before commencement, and

(b) the date on which it was made shall be taken to be the date of filing under the 1938 Act.

Existing registered marks

2.—(1) Existing registered marks (whether registered in Part A or B of the register kept under the 1938 Act) shall be transferred on the commencement of this Act to the register kept under this Act and have effect, subject to the provisions of this Schedule, as if registered under this Act.

(2) Existing registered marks registered as a series under section 21(2) of the 1938 Act shall be similarly registered in the new register.

Provision may be made by rules for putting such entries in the same form as is required for entries under this Act.

(3) In any other case notes indicating that existing registered marks are associated with other marks shall cease to have effect on the commencement of this Act.

3.—(1) A condition entered on the former register in relation to an existing registered mark immediately before the commencement of this Act shall cease to have effect on commencement.

Proceedings under section 33 of the 1938 Act (application to expunge or vary registration for breach of condition) which are pending on the commencement of this Act shall be dealt with under the old law and any necessary alteration made to the new register.

(2) A disclaimer or limitation entered on the former register in relation to an existing registered mark immediately before the commencement of this Act shall be transferred to the new register and have effect as if entered on the register in pursuance of section 13 of this Act.

Effects of registration: infringement

4.—(1) Sections 9 to 12 of this Act (effects of registration) apply in relation to an existing registered mark as from the commencement of this Act and section 14 of this Act (action for infringement) applies in relation to infringement of an existing registered mark committed after the commencement of this Act, subject to sub-paragraph (2) below.

The old law continues to apply in relation to infringements committed before commencement.

(2) It is not an infringement of—

    (a) an existing registered mark, or

    (b) a registered trade mark of which the distinctive elements are the same or substantially the same as those of an existing registered mark and which is registered for the same goods or services,

to continue after commencement any use which did not amount to infringement of the existing registered mark under the old law.

Infringing goods, material or articles

5. Section 16 of this Act (order for delivery up of infringing goods, material or articles) applies to infringing goods, material or articles whether made before or after the commencement of this Act.

Rights and remedies of licensee or authorised user

6.—(1) Section 30 (general provisions as to rights of licensees in case of infringement) of this Act applies to licences granted before the commencement of this Act, but only in relation to infringements committed after commencement.

(2) Paragraph 14 of Schedule 2 of this Act (court to take into account loss suffered by authorised users, &c.) applies only in relation to infringements committed after commencement.

Co-ownership of registered mark

7. The provisions of section 23 of this Act (co-ownership of registered mark) apply as from the commencement of this Act to an existing registered mark of which two or more persons were immediately before commencement registered as joint proprietors.

But so long as the relations between the joint proprietors remain such as are described in section 63 of the 1938 Act (joint ownership) there shall be taken to be an agreement to exclude the operation of subsections (1) and (3) of section 23 of this Act (ownership in undivided shares and right of co-proprietor to make separate use of the mark).

Assignment, &c. of registered mark

8.—(1) Section 24 of this Act (assignment or other transmission of registered mark) applies to transactions and events occurring after the commencement of this Act in relation to an existing registered mark; and the old law continues to apply in relation to transactions and events occurring before commencement.

(2) Existing entries under section 25 of the 1938 Act (registration of assignments and transmissions) shall be transferred on the commencement of this Act to the register kept under this Act and have effect as if made under section 25 of this Act.

Provision may be made by rules for putting such entries in the same form as is required for entries made under this Act.

(3)   An application for registration under section 25 of the 1938 Act which is pending before the registrar on the commencement of this Act shall be treated as an application for registration under section 25 of this Act and shall proceed accordingly.

The registrar may require the applicant to amend his application so as to conform with the requirements of this Act.

(4)   An application for registration under section 25 of the 1938 Act which has been determined by the registrar but not finally determined before the commencement of this Act shall be dealt with under the old law; and subparagraph (2) above shall apply in relation to any resulting entry in the register.

(5)   Where before the commencement of this Act a person has become entitled by assignment or transmission to an existing registered mark but has not registered his title, any application for registration after commencement shall be made under section 25 of this Act.

(6)   In cases to which sub-paragraph (3) or (5) applies section 25(3) of the 1938 Act continues to apply (and section 25(3) and (4) of this Act do not apply) as regards the consequences of failing to register.

Licensing of registered mark

9.—(1)   Sections 28 and 29(2) of this Act (licensing of registered trade mark; rights of exclusive licensee against grantor's successor in title) apply only in relation to licences granted after the commencement of this Act; and the old law continues to apply in relation to licences granted before commencement.

(2)   Existing entries under section 28 of the 1938 Act (registered users) shall be transferred on the commencement of this Act to the register kept under this Act and have effect as if made under section 25 of this Act.

Provision may be made by rules for putting such entries in the same form as is required for entries made under this Act.

(3)   An application for registration as a registered user which is pending before the registrar on the commencement of this Act shall be treated as an application for registration of a licence under section 25(1) of this Act and shall proceed accordingly.

The registrar may require the applicant to amend his application so as to conform with the requirements of this Act.

(4)   An application for registration as a registered user which has been determined by the registrar but not finally determined before the commencement of this Act shall be dealt with under the old law; and sub-paragraph (2) above shall apply in relation to any resulting entry in the register.

(5)   Any proceedings pending on the commencement of this Act under section 28(8) or (10) of the 1938 Act (variation or cancellation of registration of registered user) shall be dealt with under the old law and any necessary alteration made to the new register.

Pending applications for registration

10.—(1)   An application for registration of a mark under the 1938 Act which is pending on the commencement of this Act shall be dealt with under the old law, subject as mentioned below, and if registered the mark shall be treated for the purposes of this Schedule as an existing registered mark.

(2) The power of the Secretary of State under section 78 of this Act to make rules regulating practice and procedure, and as to the matters mentioned in subsection (2) of that section, is exercisable in relation to such an application; and different provision may be made for such applications from that made for other applications.

(3) Section 23 of the 1938 Act (provisions as to associated trade marks) shall be disregarded in dealing after the commencement of this Act with an application for registration.

Conversion of pending application

11.—(1) In the case of a pending application for registration which has not been advertised under section 18 of the 1938 Act before the commencement of this Act, the applicant may give notice to the registrar claiming to have the registrability of the mark determined in accordance with the provisions of this Act.

(2) The notice must be in the prescribed form, be accompanied by the appropriate fee and be given no later than six months after the commencement of this Act.

(3) Notice duly given is irrevocable and has the effect that the application shall be treated as if made immediately after the commencement of this Act.

Trade marks registered according to old classification

12. The registrar may exercise the powers conferred by rules under section 65 of this Act (adaptation of entries to new classification) to secure that any existing registered marks which do not conform to the system of classification prescribed under section 34 of this Act are brought into conformity with that system.

This applies, in particular, to existing registered marks classified according to the pre-1938 classification set out in Schedule 3 to the Trade Marks Rules 1986.

Claim to priority from overseas application

13. Section 35 of this Act (claim to priority of Convention application) applies to an application for registration under this Act made after the commencement of this Act notwithstanding that the Convention application was made before commencement.

14.—(1) Where before the commencement of this Act a person has duly filed an application for protection of a trade mark in a relevant country within the meaning of section 39A of the 1938 Act which is not a Convention country (a 'relevant overseas application'), he, or his successor in title, has a right to priority, for the purposes of registering the same trade mark under this Act for some or all of the same goods or services, for a period of six months from the date of filing of the relevant overseas application.

(2) If the application for registration under this Act is made within that six-month period—

(a) the relevant date for the purposes of establishing which rights take precedence shall be the date of filing of the relevant overseas application, and

(b) the registrability of the trade mark shall not be affected by any use of the mark in the United Kingdom in the period between that date and the date of the application under this Act.

(3)   Any filing which in a relevant country is equivalent to a regular national filing, under its domestic legislation or an international agreement, shall be treated as giving rise to the right of priority.

A 'regular national filing' means a filing which is adequate to establish the date on which the application was filed in that country, whatever may be the subsequent fate of the application.

(4)   A subsequent application concerning the same subject as the relevant overseas application, filed in the same country, shall be considered the relevant overseas application (of which the filing date is the starting date of the period of priority), if at the time of the subsequent application—

(a)   the previous application has been withdrawn, abandoned or refused, without having been laid open to public inspection and without leaving any rights outstanding, and

(b)   it has not yet served as a basis for claiming a right of priority.

The previous application may not thereafter serve as a basis for claiming a right of priority.

(5)   Provision may be made by rules as to the manner of claiming a right to priority on the basis of a relevant overseas application.

(6)   A right to priority arising as a result of a relevant overseas application may be assigned or otherwise transmitted, either with the application or independently.

The reference in sub-paragraph (1) to the applicant's 'successor in title' shall be construed accordingly.

(7)   Nothing in this paragraph affects proceedings on an application for registration under the 1938 Act made before the commencement of this Act (see paragraph 10 above).

Duration and renewal of registration

15.—(1)   Section 42(1) of this Act (duration of original period of registration) applies in relation to the registration of a mark in pursuance of an application made after the commencement of this Act; and the old law applies in any other case.

(2)   Sections 42(2) and 43 of this Act (renewal) apply where the renewal falls due on or after the commencement of this Act; and the old law continues to apply in any other case.

(3)   In either case it is immaterial when the fee is paid.

Pending application for alteration of registered mark

16.   An application under section 35 of the 1938 Act (alteration of registered trade mark) which is pending on the commencement of this Act shall be dealt with under the old law and any necessary alteration made to the new register.

Revocation for non-use

17.—(1)   An application under section 26 of the 1938 Act (removal from register or imposition of limitation on ground of non-use) which is pending on the commencement of this Act shall be dealt with under the old law and any necessary alteration made to the new register.

(2)   An application under section 46(1)(a) or (b) of this Act (revocation for non-use) may be made in relation to an existing registered mark at any time after the commencement of this Act.

Provided that no such application for the revocation of the registration of an existing registered mark registered by virtue of section 27 of the 1938 Act (defensive registration of well-known trade marks) may be made until more than five years after the commencement of this Act.

Application for rectification, &c.

18.—(1) An application under section 32 or 34 of the 1938 Act (rectification or correction of the register) which is pending on the commencement of this Act shall be dealt with under the old law and any necessary alteration made to the new register.

(2) For the purposes of proceedings under section 47 of this Act (grounds for invalidity of registration) as it applies in relation to an existing registered mark, the provisions of this Act shall be deemed to have been in force at all material times.

Provided that no objection to the validity of the registration of an existing registered mark may be taken on the ground specified in subsection (3) of section 5 of this Act (relative grounds for refusal of registration: conflict with earlier mark registered for different goods or services).

Regulations as to use of certification mark

19.—(1) Regulations governing the use of an existing registered certification mark deposited at the Patent Office in pursuance of section 37 of the 1938 Act shall be treated after the commencement of this Act as if filed under paragraph 6 of Schedule 2 to this Act.

(2) Any request for amendment of the regulations which was pending on the commencement of this Act shall be dealt with under the old law.

Sheffield marks

20.—(1) For the purposes of this Schedule the Sheffield register kept under Schedule 2 to the 1938 Act shall be treated as part of the register of trade marks kept under that Act.

(2) Applications made to the Cutlers' Company in accordance with that Schedule which are pending on the commencement of this Act shall proceed after commencement as if they had been made to the registrar.

Certificate of validity of contested registration

21. A certificate given before the commencement of this Act under section 47 of the 1938 Act (certificate of validity of contested registration) shall have effect as if given under section 73(1) of this Act.

Trade mark agents

22.—(1) Rules in force immediately before the commencement of this Act under section 282 or 283 of the Copyright, Designs and Patents Act 1988 (register of trade mark agents; persons entitled to described themselves as registered) shall continue in force and have effect as if made under section 83 or 85 of this Act.

(2) Rules in force immediately before the commencement of this Act under section 40 of the 1938 Act as to the persons whom the registrar may refuse to recognise as agents for the purposes of business under that Act shall continue in force and have effect as if made under section 88 of this Act.

(3)   Rules continued in force under this paragraph may be varied or revoked by further rules made under the relevant provisions of this Act.

Section 106(1)   SCHEDULE 4
                              CONSEQUENTIAL AMENDMENTS

General adaptation of existing references

1.—(1)   References in statutory provisions passed or made before the commencement of this Act to trade marks or registered trade marks within the meaning of the Trade Marks Act 1938 shall, unless the context otherwise requires, be construed after the commencement of this Act as references to trade marks or registered trade marks within the meaning of this Act.

(2)   Sub-paragraph (1) applies, in particular, to the references in the following provisions—

Industrial Organisation and Development Act 1947	Schedule 1, paragraph 7
Crown Proceedings Act 1947	section 3(1)(b)
Horticulture Act 1960	section 15(1)(b)
Printer's Imprint Act 1961	section 1(1)(b)
Plant Varieties and Seeds Act 1964	section 5A(4)
Northern Ireland Constitution Act 1973	Schedule 3, paragraph 17
Patents Act 1977	section 19(2)
	section 27(4)
	section 123(7)
Unfair Contract Terms Act 1977	Schedule 1, paragraph 1(c)
Judicature (Northern Ireland) Act 1978	section 94A(5)
State Immunity Act 1978	section 7(a) and (b)
Supreme Court Act 1981	section 72(5)
	Schedule 1, paragraph 1(i)
Civil Jurisdiction and Judgments Act 1982	Schedule 5, paragraph 2
	Schedule 8, paragraph 2(14) and 4(2)
Value Added Tax Act 1983	Schedule 3, paragraph 1
Companies Act 1985	section 396(3A)(a) or (as substituted by the Companies Act 1989) section 396(2)(d)(i)
	section 410(4)(c)(v)
	Schedule 4, Part I, Balance Sheet Formats 1 and 2 and Note (2)
	Schedule 9, Part I, paragraphs 5(2)(d) and 10(2)
Law Reform (Miscellaneous Provisions) (Scotland) Act 1985	section 15(5)
Atomic, Energy Authority Act 1986	section 8(2)

Companies (Northern Ireland) Order 1986	article 403(3A)(a) or (as substituted by the Companies (No.2) (Northern Ireland) Order 1990) article 403(2)(d)(i) Schedule 4, Part I, Balance Sheet Formats 1 and 2 and Note (2) Schedule 9, Part I, paragraphs 5(2)(d) and 10(2)
Consumer Protection Act 1987	section 2(2)(b)
Consumer Protection (Northern Ireland) Order 1987	article 5(2)(b)
Income and Corporation Taxes Act 1988	section 83(a)
Taxation of Chargeable Gains Act 1992	section 275(h)
Tribunals and Inquiries Act 1992	Schedule 1, paragraph 34.

Patents and Designs Act 1907 (c.29)

2.—(1)   The Patents and Designs Act 1907 is amended as follows.

(2)   In section 62 (the Patent Office)—

(a)   in subsection (1) for 'this Act and the Trade Marks Act 1905' substitute 'the Patents Act 1977, the Registered Designs Act 1949 and the Trade Marks Act 1994'; and

(b)   in subsections (2) and (3) for 'the Board of Trade' substitute 'the Secretary of State'.

(3)   In section 63 (officers and clerks of the Patent Office)—

(a)   for 'the Board of Trade' in each place where it occurs substitute 'the Secretary of State'; and

(b)   in subsection (2) omit the words from 'and those salaries' to the end.

(4)   The repeal by the Patents Act 1949 and the Registered Designs Act 1949 of the whole of the 1907 Act, except certain provisions, shall be deemed not to have extended to the long title, date of enactment or enacting words or to so much of section 99 as provides the Act with its short title.

Patents, Designs, Copyright and Trade Marks (Emergency) Act 1939 (c.107)

3.—(1)   The Patents, Designs, Copyright and Trade Marks (Emergency) Act 1939 is amended as follows.

(2)   For section 3 (power of comptroller to suspend rights of enemy or enemy subject) substitute—

3.   'Power of comptroller to suspend trade mark rights of enemy or enemy subject

(1)   Where on application made by a person proposing to supply goods or services of any description it is made to appear to the comptroller—

(a)   that it is difficult or impracticable to describe or refer to the goods or services without the use of a registered trade mark, and

(b)   that the proprietor of the registered trade mark (whether alone or jointly with another) is an enemy or an enemy subject,

the comptroller may make an order suspending the rights given by the registered trade mark.

(2)   An order under this section shall suspend those rights as regards the use of the trade mark—

(a)   by the applicant, and

(b)   by any person authorised by the applicant to do, for the purposes of or in connection with the supply by the applicant of the goods or services, things which would otherwise infringe the registered trade mark,

to such extent and for such period as the comptroller considers necessary to enable the applicant to render well-known and established some other means of describing or referring to the goods or services in question which does not involve the use of the trade mark.

(3)   Where an order has been made under this section, no action for passing off lies on the part of any person interested in the registered trade mark in respect of any use of it which by virtue of the order is not an infringement of the right conferred by it.

(4)   An order under this section may be varied or revoked by a subsequent order made by the comptroller.'.

(3)   In each of the following provisions—

(a)   section 4(1)(c) (effect of war on registration of trade marks),

(b)   section 6(1) (power of comptroller to extend time limits),

(c)   section 7(1)(a) (evidence as to nationality, &c.), and

(d)   the definition of 'the comptroller' in section 10(1) (interpretation), for 'the Trade Marks Act 1938' substitute 'the Trade Marks Act 1994'.

Trade Descriptions Act 1968 (c.29)

4.   In the Trade Descriptions Act 1968, in section 34 (exemption of trade description contained in pre-1968 trade mark)—

(a)   in the opening words, omit 'within the meaning of the Trade Marks Act 1938'; and

(b)   in paragraph (c), for 'a person registered under section 28 of the Trade Marks Act 1938 as a registered user of the trade mark' substitute ', in the case of a registered trade mark, a person licensed to use it'.

Solicitors Act 1974 (c.47)

5.—(1)   Section 22 of the Solicitors Act 1974 (preparation of instruments by unqualified persons) is amended as follows.

(2)   In subsection (2)(aa) and (ab) (instruments which may be prepared by registered trade mark agent or registered patent agent) for ', trade mark or service mark' substitute 'or trade mark'.

(3)   In subsection (3A) (interpretation)—

(a)   in the definition of 'registered trade mark agent' for 'section 282(1) of the Copyright, Designs and Patents Act 1988' substitute 'the Trade Marks Act 1994'; and

(b)   in the definition of 'registered patent agent' for 'of that Act' substitute 'of the Copyright, Designs and Patents Act 1988'.

House of Commons Disqualification Act 1975 (c.24)

6.   In Part III of Schedule 1 to the House of Commons Disqualification Act 1975 (other disqualifying offices), for the entry relating to persons appointed to hear and determine appeals under the Trade Marks Act 1938 substitute—

'Person appointed to hear and determine appeals under the Trade Marks Act 1994.'.

Restrictive Trade Practices Act 1976 (c.34)

7. In Schedule 3 to the Restrictive Trade Practices Act 1976 (excepted agreements), for paragraph 4 (agreements relating to trade marks) substitute—

'4.—(1) This Act does not apply to an agreement authorising the use of a registered trade mark (other than a collective mark or certification mark) if no such restrictions as are described in section 6(1) or 11(2) above are accepted, and no such information provisions as are described in section 7(1) or 12(2) above are made, except in respect of—

(a) the descriptions of goods bearing the mark which are to be produced or supplied, or the processes of manufacture to be applied to such goods or to goods to which the mark is to be applied, or

(b) the kinds of services in relation to which the mark is to be used which are to be made available or supplied, or the form or manner in which such services are to be made available or supplied, or

(c) the descriptions of goods which are to be produced or supplied in connection with the supply of services in relation to which the mark is to be used, or the process of manufacture to be applied to such goods.

(2) This Act does not apply to an agreement authorising the use of a registered collective mark or certification mark if—

(a) the agreement is made in accordance with regulations approved by the registrar under Schedule 1 or 2 to the Trade Marks Act 1994, and

(b) no such restrictions as are described in section 6(1) or 11(2) above are accepted, and no such information provisions as are described in section 7(1) or 12(2) above are made, except as permitted by those regulations.'.

Copyright, Designs and Patents Act 1988 (c.48)

8.—(1) The Copyright, Designs and Patents Act 1988 is amended as follows.

(2) In sections 114(6), 204(6) and 231(6) (persons regarded as having an interest in infringing copies, &c.), for 'section 58C of the Trade Marks Act 1938' substitute 'section 19 of the Trade Marks Act 1994'.

(3) In section 280(1) (privilege for communications with patent agents), for 'trade mark or service mark' substitute 'or trade mark'.

Tribunals and Inquiries Act 1992 (c.53)

9. In Part I of Schedule 1 to the Tribunals and Inquiries Act 1992 (tribunals under direct supervision of Council on Tribunals), for 'Patents, designs, trade marks and service marks' substitute 'Patents, designs and trade marks'.

Section 106(2)   SCHEDULE 5
                          REPEALS AND REVOCATIONS

Chapter or number	Short title	Extent of repeal or revocation
1891 c. 50.	Commissioners for Oaths Act 1891.	In section 1, the words 'or the Patents, Designs and Trade Marks Acts, 1883 to 1888,'.
1907 c. 29.	Patents and Designs Act 1907.	In section 63(2), the words from 'and those salaries' to the end.
1938 c. 22.	Trade Marks Act 1938.	The whole Act.
1947 c. 44.	Crown Proceedings Act 1947.	In section 3(1)(b), the words 'or registered service mark'.
1949 c. 87.	Patents Act 1949.	Section 92(2).
1964 c. 14.	Plant Varieties and Seeds Act 1964.	In section 5A(4), the words 'under the Trade Marks Act 1938'.
1967 c. 80.	Criminal Justice Act 1967.	In Schedule 3, in Parts I and IV, the entries relating to the Trade Marks Act 1938.
1978 c. 23.	Judicature (Northern Ireland) Act 1978.	In Schedule 5, in Part II, the paragraphs amending the Trade Marks Act 1938.
1984 c. 19.	Trade Marks (Amendment) Act 1984.	The whole Act.
1985 c. 6.	Companies Act 1985.	In section 396— (a) in subsection (3A)(a), and (b) in subsection (2)(d)(i) as inserted by the Companies Act 1989, the words 'service mark,'.
1986 c. 12.	Statute Law (Repeals) Act 1986.	In Schedule 2, paragraph 2.
1986 c. 39.	Patents, Designs and Marks Act 1986.	Section 2. Section 4(4). In Schedule 1, paragraphs 1 and 2. Schedule 2.

Chapter or number	Short title	Extent of repeal or revocation
S.I. 1986/1032 (N.I. 6).	Companies (Northern Ireland) Order 1986.	In article 403— (a) in paragraph (3A)(a), and (b) in paragraph (2)(d)(i) as inserted by the Companies (No.2) (Northern Ireland) Order 1990, the words 'service mark,'.
1987 c. 43.	Consumer Protection Act 1987.	In section 45— (a) in subsection (1), the definition of 'mark' and 'trade mark' ; (b) subsection (4).
S.I. 1987/2049.	Consumer Protection (Northern Ireland) Order 1987.	In article 2— (a) in paragraph (2), the definitions of 'mark' and 'trade mark'; (b) paragraph (3).
1988 c. 1.	Income and Corporation Taxes Act 1988.	In section 83, the words from 'References in this section' to the end.
1988 c. 48.	Copyright, Designs and Patents Act 1988.	Sections 282 to 284. In section 286, the definition of 'registered trade mark agent'. Section 300.
1992 c. 12.	Taxation of Chargeable Gains Act 1992.	In section 275(h), the words 'service marks' and 'service mark'.

APPENDIX TWO

Council Directive 89/104/EEC

**First Council Directive
of 21 December 1988
to approximate the laws of the Member States relating to trade marks
(89/104/EEC)**

THE COUNCIL OF THE EUROPEAN COMMUNITIES,

Having regard to the Treaty establishing the European Economic Community, and in particular Article 100a thereof,

Having regard to the proposal from the Commission,[1]

In cooperation with the European Parliament,[2]

Having regard to the opinion of the Economic and Social Committee,[3]

[Recital 1] Whereas the trade mark laws at present applicable in the Member States contain disparities which may impede the free movement of goods and freedom to provide services and may distort competition within the common market; whereas it is therefore necessary, in view of the establishment and functioning of the internal market, to approximate the laws of Member States;

[Recital 2] Whereas it is important not to disregard the solutions and advantages which the Community trade mark system may afford to undertakings wishing to acquire trade marks;

[Recital 3] Whereas it does not appear to be necessary at present to undertake full-scale approximation of the trade mark laws of the Member States and it will be sufficient if approximation is limited to those national provisions of law which most directly affect the functioning of the internal market;

[Recital 4] Whereas the Directive does not deprive the Member States of the right to continue to protect trade marks acquired through use but takes them into account only in regard to the relationship between them and trade marks acquired by registration;

[Recital 5] Whereas Member States also remain free to fix the provisions of procedure concerning the registration, the revocation and the invalidity of trade

---

[1] OJ No. C 351, 31.12.1980, p. 1 and OJ No. C 351, 31.12.1985, p. 4.

[2] OJ No. C 307, 14.11.1983, p. 66 and OJ No. C 309, 5.12.1988.

[3] OJ No. C 310, 30.11.1981, p. 22.

marks acquired by registration; whereas they can, for example, determine the form of trade mark registration and invalidity procedures, decide whether earlier rights should be invoked either in the registration procedure or in the invalidity procedure or in both and, if they allow earlier rights to be invoked in the registration procedure, have an opposition procedure or an *ex officio* examination procedure or both; whereas Member States remain free to determine the effects of revocation or invalidity of trade marks;

[Recital 6] Whereas this Directive does not exclude the application to trade marks of provisions of law of the Member States other than trade mark law, such as the provisions relating to unfair competition, civil liability or consumer protection;

[Recital 7] Whereas attainment of the objectives at which this approximation of laws is aiming requires that the conditions for obtaining and continuing to hold a registered trade mark are, in general, identical in all Member States; whereas, to this end, it is necessary to list examples of signs which may constitute a trade mark, provided that such signs are capable of distinguishing the goods or services of one undertaking from those of other undertakings; whereas the grounds for refusal or invalidity concerning the trade mark itself, for example, the absence of any distinctive character, or concerning conflicts between the trade mark and earlier rights, are to be listed in an exhaustive manner, even if some of these grounds are listed as an option for the Member States which will therefore be able to maintain or introduce those grounds in their legislation; whereas Member States will be able to maintain or introduce into their legislation grounds of refusal or invalidity linked to conditions for obtaining and continuing to hold a trade mark for which there is no provision of approximation, concerning, for example, the eligibility for the grant of a trade mark, the renewal of the trade mark or rules on fees, or related to the non-compliance with procedural rules;

[Recital 8] Whereas in order to reduce the total number of trade marks registered and protected in the Community and, consequently, the number of conflicts which arise between them, it is essential to require that registered trade marks must actually be used or, if not used, be subject to revocation; whereas it is necessary to provide that a trade mark cannot be invalidated on the basis of the existence of a non-used earlier trade mark, while the Member States remain free to apply the same principle in respect of the registration of a trade mark or to provide that a trade mark may not be successfully invoked in infringement proceedings if it is established as a result of a plea that the trade mark could be revoked; whereas in all these cases it is up to the Member States to establish the applicable rules of procedure;

[Recital 9] Whereas it is fundamental, in order to facilitate the free circulation of goods and services, to ensure that henceforth registered trade marks enjoy the same protection under the legal systems of all the Member States; whereas this should however not prevent the Member States from granting at their option extensive protection to those trade marks which have a reputation;

[Recital 10] Whereas the protection afforded by the registered trade mark, the function of which is in particular to guarantee the trade mark as an indication of origin, is absolute in the case of identity between the mark and the sign and goods or services; whereas the protection applies also in case of similarity between the mark and the sign and the goods or services; whereas it is indispensable to give an interpretation of the concept of similarity in relation to the likelihood of confusion; whereas the likelihood of confusion, the appreciation of which depends on numerous elements and, in particular, on the recognition of the trade mark on the market, of the association which can be made with the used or registered sign, of the degree of similarity between the trade mark and the sign and between the goods or services identified, constitutes the specific condition for such protection; whereas the ways in which likelihood of confusion may be established, and in particular the onus of proof, are a matter for national procedural rules which are not prejudiced by the Directive;

[Recital 11] Whereas it is important, for reasons of legal certainty and without inequitably prejudicing the interests of a proprietor of an earlier trade mark, to provide that the latter may no longer request a declaration of invalidity nor may he oppose the use of a trade mark subsequent to his own of which he has knowingly tolerated the use for a substantial length of time, unless the application for the subsequent trade mark was made in bad faith;

[Recital 12] Whereas all Member States of the Community are bound by the Paris Convention for the Protection of Industrial Property; whereas it is necessary that the provisions of this Directive are entirely consistent with those of the Paris Convention; whereas the obligations of the Member States resulting from this Convention are not affected by this Directive; whereas, where appropriate, the second subparagraph of Article 234 of the Treaty is applicable,

HAS ADOPTED THIS DIRECTIVE:

Article 1   Scope
This Directive shall apply to every trade mark in respect of goods or services which is the subject of registration or of an application in a Member State for registration as an individual trade mark, a collective mark or a guarantee or certification mark, or which is the subject of a registration or an application for registration in the Benelux Trade Mark Office or of an international registration having effect in a Member State.

Article 2   Signs of which a trade mark may consist
A trade mark may consist of any sign capable of being represented graphically, particularly words, including personal names, designs, letters, numerals, the shape of goods or of their packaging, provided that such signs are capable of distinguishing the goods or services of one undertaking from those of other undertakings.

Article 3   Grounds for refusal or invalidity
   1.   The following shall not be registered or if registered shall be liable to be declared invalid:
      (a)   signs which cannot constitute a trade mark;
      (b)   trade marks which are devoid of any distinctive character;
      (c)   trade marks which consist exclusively of signs or indications which may serve, in trade, to designate the kind, quality, quantity, intended purpose, value, geographical origin, or the time of production of the goods or of rendering of the service, or other characteristics of the goods or service;
      (d)   trade marks which consist exclusively of signs or indications which have become customary in the current language or in the *bona fide* and established practices of the trade;

(e)   signs which consist exclusively of:
- the shape which results from the nature of the goods themselves, or
- the shape of goods which is necessary to obtain a technical result, or
- the shape which gives substantial value to the goods;

(f)   trade marks which are contrary to public policy or to accepted principles of morality;

(g)   trade marks which are of such a nature as to deceive the public, for instance as to the nature, quality or geographical origin of the goods or service;

(h)   trade marks which have not been authorized by the competent authorities and are to be refused or invalidated pursuant to Article 6*ter* of the Paris Convention for the Protection of Industrial Property, hereinafter referred to as the 'Paris Convention'.

2.   Any Member State may provide that a trade mark shall not be registered or, if registered, shall be liable to be declared invalid where and to the extent that:

(a)   the use of that trade mark may be prohibited pursuant to provisions of law other than trade mark law of the Member State concerned or of the Community;

(b)   the trade mark covers a sign of high symbolic value, in particular a religious symbol;

(c)   the trade mark includes badges, emblems and escutcheons other than those covered by Article 6*ter* of the Paris Convention and which are of public interest, unless the consent of the appropriate authorities to its registration has been given in conformity with the legislation of the Member State;

(d)   the application for registration of the trade mark was made in bad faith by the applicant.

3.   A trade mark shall not be refused registration or be declared invalid in accordance with paragraph 1(b), (c) or (d) if, before the date of application for registration and following the use which has been made of it, it has acquired a distinctive character. Any Member State may in addition provide that this provision shall also apply where the distinctive character was acquired after the date of application for registration or after the date of registration.

4.   Any Member State may provide that, by derogation from the preceding paragraphs, the grounds of refusal of registration or invalidity in force in that State prior to the date on which the provisions necessary to comply with this Directive enter into force, shall apply to trade marks for which application has been made prior to that date.

Article 4   Further grounds for refusal or invalidity concerning conflicts with earlier rights

1.   A trade mark shall not be registered or, if registered, shall be liable to be declared invalid:

(a)   if it is identical with an earlier trade mark, and the goods or services for which the trade mark is applied for or is registered are identical with the goods or services for which the earlier trade mark is protected;

(b)   if because of its identity with, or similarity to, the earlier trade mark and the identity or similarity of the goods or services covered by the trade marks, there exists a likelihood of confusion on the part of the public, which includes the likelihood of association with the earlier trade mark.

2. 'Earlier trade marks' within the meaning of paragraph 1 means:

(a) trade marks of the following kinds with a date of application for registration which is earlier than the date of application for registration of the trade mark, taking account, where appropriate, of the priorities claimed in respect of those trade marks:

(i)   Community trade marks;

(ii)   trade marks registered in the Member State or, in the case of Belgium, Luxembourg or the Netherlands, at the Benelux Trade Mark Office;

(iii)   trade marks registered under international arrangements which have effect in the Member State;

(b) Community trade marks which validly claim seniority, in accordance with the Regulation on the Community trade mark, from a trade mark referred to in (a)(ii) and (iii), even when the latter trade mark has been surrendered or allowed to lapse;

(c) applications for the trade marks referred to in (a) and (b), subject to their registration;

(d) trade marks which, on the date of application for registration of the trade mark, or, where appropriate, of the priority claimed in respect of the application for registration of the trade mark, are well-known in a Member State, in the sense in which the words 'well-known' are used in Article 6*bis* of the Paris Convention;

3. A trade mark shall furthermore not be registered or, if registered, shall be liable to be declared invalid if it is identical with, or similar to, an earlier Community trade mark within the meaning of paragraph 2 and is to be, or has been, registered for goods or services which are not similar to those for which the earlier Community trade mark is registered, where the earlier Community trade mark has a reputation in the Community and where the use of the later trade mark without due cause would take unfair advantage of, or be detrimental to, the distinctive character or the repute of the earlier Community trade mark.

4. Any Member State may furthermore provide that a trade mark shall not be registered or, if registered, shall be liable to be declared invalid where, and to the extent that:

(a) the trade mark is identical with, or similar to, an earlier national trade mark within the meaning of paragraph 2 and is to be, or has been, registered for goods or services which are not similar to those for which the earlier trade mark is registered, where the earlier trade mark has a reputation in the Member State concerned and where the use of the later trade mark without due cause would take unfair advantage of, or be detrimental to, the distinctive character or the repute of the earlier trade mark;

(b) rights to a non-registered trade mark or to another sign used in the course of trade were acquired prior to the date of application for registration of the subsequent trade mark, or the date of the priority claimed for the application for registration of the subsequent trade mark and that non-registered trade mark or other sign confers on its proprietor the right to prohibit the use of a subsequent trade mark;

(c) the use of the trade mark may be prohibited by virtue of an earlier right other than the rights referred to in paragraphs 2 and 4 (b) and in particular:

(i)   a right to a name;

(ii)   a right of personal portrayal;

(iii)   a copyright;

(iv)   an industrial property right;

(d)   the trade mark is identical with, or similar to, an earlier collective trade mark conferring a right which expired within a period of a maximum of three years preceding application;

(e)   the trade mark is identical with, or similar to, an earlier guarantee or certification mark conferring a right which expired within a period preceding application the length of which is fixed by the Member State;

(f)   the trade mark is identical with, or similar to, an earlier trade mark which was registered for identical or similar goods or services and conferred on them a right which has expired for failure to renew within a period of a maximum of two years preceding application, unless the proprietor of the earlier trade mark gave his agreement for the registration of the later mark or did not use his trade mark;

(g)   the trade mark is liable to be confused with a mark which was in use abroad on the filing date of the application and which is still in use there, provided that at the date of the application the applicant was acting in bad faith.

5.   The Member States may permit that in appropriate circumstances registration need not be refused or the trade mark need not be declared invalid where the proprietor of the earlier trade mark or other earlier right consents to the registration of the later trade mark.

6.   Any Member State may provide that, by derogation from paragraphs 1 to 5, the grounds for refusal of registration or invalidity in force in that State prior to the date on which the provisions necessary to comply with this Directive enter into force, shall apply to trade marks for which application has been made prior to that date.

Article 5   *Rights conferred by a trade mark*

1.   The registered trade mark shall confer on the proprietor exclusive rights therein. The proprietor shall be entitled to prevent all third parties not having his consent from using in the course of trade:

(a)   any sign which is identical with the trade mark in relation to goods or services which are identical with those for which the trade mark is registered;

(b)   any sign where, because of its identity with, or similarity to, the trade mark and the identity or similarity of the goods or services covered by the trade mark and the sign, there exists a likelihood of confusion on the part of the public, which includes the likelihood of association between the sign and the trade mark.

2.   Any Member State may also provide that the proprietor shall be entitled to prevent all third parties not having his consent from using in the course of trade any sign which is identical with, or similar to, the trade mark in relation to goods or services which are not similar to those for which the trade mark is registered, where the latter has a reputation in the Member State and where use of that sign without due cause takes unfair advantage of, or is detrimental to, the distinctive character or the repute of the trade mark.

3.   The following, *inter alia,* may be prohibited under paragraphs 1 and 2:

(a)   affixing the sign to the goods or to the packaging thereof;

(b)   offering the goods, or putting them on the market or stocking them for these purposes under that sign, or offering or supplying services thereunder;

(c)   importing or exporting the goods under the sign;

(d)   using the sign on business papers and in advertising.

4.   Where, under the law of the Member State, the use of a sign under the conditions referred to in 1(b) or 2 could not be prohibited before the date on which the provisions necessary to comply with this Directive entered into force in the Member State concerned, the rights conferred by the trade mark may not be relied on to prevent the continued use of the sign.

5.   Paragraphs 1 to 4 shall not affect provisions in any Member State relating to the protection against the use of a sign other than for the purposes of distinguishing goods or services, where use of that sign without due cause takes unfair advantage of, or is detrimental to, the distinctive character or the repute of the trade mark.

Article 6   Limitation of the effects of a trade mark

1.   The trade mark shall not entitle the proprietor to prohibit a third party from using, in the course of trade,

(a)   his own name or address;

(b)   indications concerning the kind, quality, quantity, intended purpose, value, geographical origin, the time of production of goods or of rendering of the service, or other characteristics of goods or services;

(c)   the trade mark where it is necessary to indicate the intended purpose of a product or service, in particular as accessories or spare parts;

provided he uses them in accordance with honest practices in industrial or commercial matters.

2.   The trade mark shall not entitle the proprietor to prohibit a third party from using, in the course of trade, an earlier right which only applies in a particular locality if that right is recognised by the laws of the Member State in question and within the limits of the territory in which it is recognised.

Article 7   Exhaustion of the rights conferred by a trade mark

1.   The trade mark shall not entitle the proprietor to prohibit its use in relation to goods which have been put on the market in the Community under that trade mark by the proprietor or with his consent.

2.   Paragraph 1 shall not apply where there exist legitimate reasons for the proprietor to oppose further commercialisation of the goods, especially where the condition of the goods is changed or impaired after they have been put on the market.

Article 8   Licensing

1.   A trade mark may be licensed for some or all of the goods or services for which it is registered and for the whole or part of the Member State concerned. A licence may be exclusive or non-exclusive.

2.   The proprietor of a trade mark may invoke the rights conferred by that trade mark against a licensee who contravenes any provision in his licensing contract with regard to its duration, the form covered by the registration in which the trade mark may be used, the scope of the goods or services for which the licence is granted, the territory in which the trade mark may be affixed, or the quality of the goods manufactured or of the services provided by the licensee.

Article 9 Limitation in consequence of acquiescence

1. Where, in a Member State, the proprietor of an earlier trade mark as referred to in Article 4(2) has acquiesced, for a period of five successive years, in the use of a later trade mark registered in that Member State while being aware of such use, he shall no longer be entitled on the basis of the earlier trade mark either to apply for a declaration that the later trade mark is invalid or to oppose the use of the later trade mark in respect of the goods or services for which the later trade mark has been used, unless registration of the later trade mark was applied for in bad faith.

2. Any Member State may provide that paragraph 1 shall apply *mutatis mutandis* to the proprietor of an earlier trade mark referred to in Article 4(4)(a) or an other earlier right referred to in Article 4(4)(b) or (c).

3. In the cases referred to in paragraphs 1 and 2, the proprietor of a later registered trade mark shall not be entitled to oppose the use of the earlier right, even though that right may no longer be invoked against the later trade mark.

Article 10 Use of trade marks

1. If, within a period of five years following the date of the completion of the registration procedure, the proprietor has not put the trade mark to genuine use in the Member State in connection with the goods or services in respect of which it is registered, or if such use has been suspended during an uninterrupted period of five years, the trade mark shall be subject to the sanctions provided for in this Directive, unless there are proper reasons for non-use.

2. The following shall also constitute use within the meaning of paragraph 1:

(a) use of the trade mark in a form differing in elements which do not alter the distinctive character of the mark in the form in which it was registered;

(b) affixing of the trade mark to goods or to the packaging thereof in the Member State concerned solely for export purposes.

3. Use of the trade mark with the consent of the proprietor or by any person who has authority to use a collective mark or a guarantee or certification mark shall be deemed to constitute use by the proprietor.

4. In relation to trade marks registered before the date on which the provisions necessary to comply with this Directive enter into force in the Member State concerned:

(a) where a provision in force prior to that date attaches sanctions to non-use of a trade mark during an uninterrupted period, the relevant period of five years mentioned in paragraph 1 shall be deemed to have begun to run at the same time as any period of non-use which is already running at that date;

(b) where there is no use provision in force prior to that date, the periods of five years mentioned in paragraph 1 shall be deemed to run from that date at the earliest.

Article 11 Sanctions for non-use of a trade mark in legal or administrative proceedings

1. A trade mark may not be declared invalid on the ground that there is an earlier conflicting trade mark if the latter does not fulfil the requirements of use set out in Article 10(1), (2) and (3) or in Article 10(4), as the case may be.

2. Any Member State may provide that registration of a trade mark may not be refused on the ground that there is an earlier conflicting trade mark if the latter

does not fulfil the requirements of use set out in Article 10(1), (2) and (3) or in Article 10(4), as the case may be.

3. Without prejudice to the application of Article 12, where a counterclaim for revocation is made, any Member State may provide that a trade mark may not be successfully invoked in infringement proceedings if it is established as a result of a plea that the trade mark could be revoked pursuant to Article 12(1).

4. If the earlier trade mark has been used in relation to part only of the goods or services for which it is registered, it shall, for purposes of applying paragraphs 1, 2 and 3, be deemed to be registered in respect only of that part of the goods or services.

Article 12   Grounds for revocation

1. A trade mark shall be liable to revocation if, within a continuous period of five years, it has not been put to genuine use in the Member State in connection with the goods or services in respect of which it is registered, and there are no proper reasons for non-use; however, no person may claim that the proprietor's rights in a trade mark should be revoked where, during the interval between expiry of the five-year period and filing of the application for revocation, genuine use of the trade mark has been started or resumed; the commencement or resumption of use within a period of three months preceding the filing of the application for revocation which began at the earliest on expiry of the continuous period of five years of non-use, shall, however, be disregarded where preparations for the commencement or resumption occur only after the proprietor becomes aware that the application for revocation may be filed.

2. A trade mark shall also be liable to revocation if, after the date on which it was registered,

(a)   in consequence of acts or inactivity of the proprietor, it has become the common name in the trade for a product or service in respect of which it is registered;

(b)   in consequence of the use made of it by the proprietor of the trade mark or with his consent in respect of the goods or services for which it is registered, it is liable to mislead the public, particularly as to the nature, quality or geographical origin of those goods or services.

Article 13   Grounds for refusal or revocation or invalidity relating to only some of the goods or services

Where grounds for refusal of registration or for revocation or invalidity of a trade mark exist in respect of only some of the goods or services for which that trade mark has been applied for or registered, refusal of registration or revocation or invalidity shall cover those goods or services only.

Article 14   Establishment a posteriori of invalidity or revocation of a trade mark

Where the seniority of an earlier trade mark which has been surrendered or allowed to lapse, is claimed for a Community trade mark, the invalidity or revocation of the earlier trade mark may be established a posteriori.

Article 15   Special provisions in respect of collective marks, guarantee marks and certification marks
1.   Without prejudice to Article 4, Member States whose laws authorise the registration of collective marks or of guarantee or certification marks may provide that such marks shall not be registered, or shall be revoked or declared invalid, on grounds additional to those specified in Articles 3 and 12 where the function of those marks so requires.
2.   By way of derogation from Article 3(1)(c), Member States may provide that signs or indications which may serve, in trade, to designate the geographical origin of the goods or services may constitute collective, guarantee or certification marks. Such a mark does not entitle the proprietor to prohibit a third party from using in the course of trade such signs or indications, provided he uses them in accordance with honest practices in industrial or commercial matters; in particular, such a mark may not be invoked against a third party who is entitled to use a geographical name.

Article 16   National provisions to be adopted pursuant to this Directive
1.   The Member States shall bring into force the laws, regulations and administrative provisions necessary to comply with this Directive not later than 28 December 1991. They shall immediately inform the Commission thereof.
2.   Acting on a proposal from the Commission, the Council, acting by qualified majority, may defer the date referred to in paragraph 1 until 31 December 1992 at the latest.
3.   Member States shall communicate to the Commission the text of the main provisions of national law which they adopt in the field governed by this Directive.

Article 17   Addressees
This Directive is addressed to the Member States.

Done at Brussels, 21 December 1988.

For the Council
The President
V. PAPANDREOU

APPENDIX THREE
Council Regulation (EC) No. 40/94

Council Regulation (EC) No. 40/94
of 20 December 1993
on the Community trade mark

THE COUNCIL OF THE EUROPEAN UNION,

Having regard to the Treaty establishing the European Community, and in particular Article 235 thereof,

Having regard to the proposal from the Commission,[1]

Having regard to the opinion of the European Parliament,[2]

Having regard to the opinion of the Economic and Social Committee,[3]

[Recital 1] Whereas it is desirable to promote throughout the Community a harmonious development of economic activities and a continuous and balanced expansion by completing an internal market which functions properly and offers conditions which are similar to those obtaining in a national market; whereas in order to create a market of this kind and make it increasingly a single market, not only must barriers to free movement of goods and services be removed and arrangements be instituted which ensure that competition is not distorted, but, in addition, legal conditions must be created which enable undertakings to adapt their activities to the scale of the Community, whether in manufacturing and distributing goods or in providing services; whereas for those purposes, trade marks enabling the products and services of undertakings to be distinguished by identical means throughout the entire Community, regardless of frontiers, should feature amongst the legal instruments which undertakings have at their disposal;

[Recital 2] Whereas action by the Community would appear to be necessary for the purpose of attaining the Community's said objectives; whereas such action involves the creation of Community arrangements for trade marks whereby undertakings can by means of one procedural system obtain Community trade marks to which uniform protection is given and which produce their effects throughout the entire area of the Community; whereas the principle of the unitary

---

[1] OJ No. C 351, 31.12.1980, p. 1 and OJ No. C 230, 31.8.1984, p. 1.

[2] OJ No. C 307, 14.11.1983, p. 46 and OJ No. C 280, 28.10.1991, p. 153

[3] OJ No. C 310, 30.11.1981, p. 22.

character of the Community trade mark thus stated will apply unless otherwise provided for in this Regulation;

[Recital 3] Whereas the barrier of territoriality of the rights conferred on proprietors of trade marks by the laws of the Member States cannot be removed by approximation of laws; whereas in order to open up unrestricted economic activity in the whole of the common market for the benefit of undertakings, trade marks need to be created which are governed by a uniform Community law directly applicable in all Member States;

[Recital 4] Whereas since the Treaty has not provided the specific powers to establish such a legal instrument, Article 235 of the Treaty should be applied;

[Recital 5] Whereas the Community law relating to trade marks nevertheless does not replace the laws of the Member States on trade marks; whereas it would not in fact appear to be justified to require undertakings to apply for registration of their trade marks as Community trade marks; whereas national trade marks continue to be necessary for those undertakings which do not want protection of their trade marks at Community level;

[Recital 6] Whereas the rights in a Community trade mark may not be obtained otherwise than by registration, and registration is to be refused in particular if the trade mark is not distinctive, if it is unlawful or if it conflicts with earlier rights;

[Recital 7] Whereas the protection afforded by a Community trade mark, the function of which is in particular to guarantee the trade mark as an indication of origin, is absolute in the case of identity between the mark and the sign and the goods or services; whereas the protection applies also in cases of similarity between the mark and the sign and the goods or services; whereas an interpretation should be given of the concept of similarity in relation to the likelihood of confusion; whereas the likelihood of confusion, the appreciation of which depends on numerous elements and, in particular, on the recognition of the trade mark on the market, the association which can be made with the used or registered sign, the degree of similarity between the trade mark and the sign and between the goods or services identified, constitutes the specific condition for such protection;

[Recital 8] Whereas it follows from the principle of free flow of goods that the proprietor of a Community trade mark must not be entitled to prohibit its use by a third party in relation to goods which have been put into circulation in the Community, under the trade mark, by him or with his consent, save where there exist legitimate reasons for the proprietor to oppose further commercialisation of the goods;

[Recital 9] Whereas there is no justification for protecting Community trade marks or, as against them, any trade mark which has been registered before them, except where the trade marks are actually used;

[Recital 10] Whereas a Community trade mark is to be regarded as an object of property which exists separately from the undertakings whose goods or services are designated by it; whereas accordingly, it must be capable of being transferred, subject to the overriding need to prevent the public being misled as a result of the transfer. It must also be capable of being charged as security in favour of a third party and of being the subject-matter of licences;

[Recital 11] Whereas administrative measures are necessary at Community level for implementing in relation to every trade mark the trade mark law created by this Regulation; whereas it is therefore essential, while retaining the Community's existing institutional structure and balance of powers, to establish an Office for Harmonisation in the Internal Market (trade marks and designs) which is independent in relation to technical matters and has legal, administrative and financial autonomy; whereas to this end it is necessary and appropriate that it should be a body of the Community having legal personality and exercising the implementing powers which are conferred on it by this Regulation, and that it should operate within the framework of Community law without detracting from the competencies exercised by the Community institutions;

[Recital 12] Whereas it is necessary to ensure that parties who are affected by decisions made by the Office are protected by the law in a manner which is suited to the special character of trade mark law; whereas to that end provision is made for an appeal to lie from decisions of the examiners and of the various divisions of the Office; whereas if the department whose decision is contested does not rectify its decision it is to remit the appeal to a Board of Appeal of the Office, which is to decide on it; whereas decisions of the Boards of Appeal are, in turn, amenable to actions before the Court of Justice of the European Communities, which has jurisdiction to annul or to alter the contested decision;

[Recital 13] Whereas under Council Decision 88/591/ECSC, EEC, Euratom of 24 October 1988 establishing a Court of First Instance of the European Communities,[1] as amended by Decision 93/350/Euratom, ECSC, EEC of 8 June 1993,[2] that Court shall exercise at the first instance the jurisdiction conferred on the Court of Justice by the Treaties establishing the Communities — with particular regard to appeals lodged under the second subparagraph of Article 173 of the EC Treaty — and by the acts adopted in implementation thereof, save as otherwise provided in an act setting up a body governed by Community law; whereas the jurisdiction which this Regulation confers on the Court of Justice to cancel and reform decisions of the appeal courts shall accordingly be exercised at the first instance by the Court in accordance with the above Decision;

[Recital 14] Whereas in order to strengthen the protection of Community trade marks the Member States should designate, having regard to their own national system, as limited a number as possible of national courts of first and second instance having jurisdiction in matters of infringement and validity of Community trade marks;

[Recital 15] Whereas decisions regarding the validity and infringement of Community trade marks must have effect and cover the entire area of the Community, as this is the only way of preventing inconsistent decisions on the part of the courts and the Office and of ensuring that the unitary character of Community trade marks is not undermined; whereas the rules contained in the Brussels Convention of Jurisdiction and the Enforcement of Judgments in Civil and Commercial Matters will apply to all actions at law relating to Community trade marks, save where this Regulation derogates from those rules;

[Recital 16] Whereas contradictory judgments should be avoided in actions which involve the same acts and the same parties and which are brought on the basis of a Community trade mark and parallel national trade marks; whereas for this purpose, when the actions are brought in the same Member State, the way in

[1] OJ No. L 319, 25.11.1988, p. 1 and corrigendum in OJ No. L 241, 17.8.1989, p. 4.
[2] OJ No. L 144, 16.6.1993, p. 21.

which this is to be achieved is a matter for national procedural rules, which are not prejudiced by this Regulation, whilst when the actions are brought in different Member States, provisions modelled on the rules on *lis pendens* and related action of the abovementioned Brussels Convention appear appropriate;

[Recital 17] Whereas in order to guarantee the full autonomy and independence of the Office, it is considered necessary to grant it an autonomous budget whose revenue comes principally from fees paid by the users of the system; whereas however, the Community budgetary procedure remains applicable as far as any subsidies chargeable to general budget of the European Communities are concerned; whereas moreover, the auditing of accounts should be undertaken by the Court of Auditors;

[Recital 18] Whereas implementing measures are required for the Regulation's application, particularly as regards the adoption and amendment of fees regulations and an Implementing Regulation; whereas such measures should be adopted by the Commission, assisted by a Committee composed of representatives of the Member States, in accordance with the procedural rules laid down in Article 2, procedure III(b), of Council Decisions 87/373/EEC of 13 July 1987 laying down the procedures for the exercise of implementing powers conferred on the Commission,[1]

HAS ADOPTED THIS REGULATION:

Title I   General Provisions

Article 1   Community trade mark

1.   A trade mark for goods or services which is registered in accordance with the conditions contained in this Regulation and in the manner herein provided is hereinafter referred to as a 'Community trade mark'.

2.   A Community trade mark shall have a unitary character. It shall have equal effect throughout the Community: it shall not be registered, transferred or surrendered or be the subject of a decision revoking the rights of the proprietor or declaring it invalid, nor shall its use be prohibited, save in respect of the whole Community. This principle shall apply unless otherwise provided in this Regulation.

Article 2   Office

An Office for Harmonisation in the Internal Market (trade marks and designs), hereinafter referred to as 'the Office', is hereby established.

Article 3   Capacity to act

For the purpose of implementing this Regulation, companies or firms and other legal bodies shall be regarded as legal persons if, under the terms of the law governing them, they have the capacity in their own name to have rights and obligations of all kinds, to make contracts or accomplish other legal acts and to sue and be sued.

[1] OJ No. L 197, 18.7.1987, p. 33.

Title II   The Law Relating to Trade Marks

SECTION 1   DEFINITION OF A COMMUNITY TRADE MARK OBTAINING A COMMUNITY TRADE MARK

Article 4   Signs of which a Community trade mark may consist
A Community trade mark may consist of any signs capable of being represented graphically, particularly words, including personal names, designs, letters, numerals, the shape of goods or of their packaging, provided that such signs are capable of distinguishing the goods or services of one undertaking from those of other undertakings.

Article 5   Persons who can be proprietors of Community trade marks
   1.   The following natural or legal persons, including authorities established under public law, may be proprietors of Community trade marks:
      (a)   nationals of the Member States; or
      (b)   nationals of other States which are parties to the Paris Convention for the protection of industrial property, hereinafter referred to as 'the Paris Convention'; or
      (c)   nationals of States which are not parties to the Paris Convention who are domiciled or have their seat or who have real and effective industrial or commercial establishments within the territory of the Community or of a State which is party to the Paris Convention; or
      (d)   nationals, other than those referred to under subparagraph (c), of any State which is not party to the Paris Convention and which, according to published findings, accords to nationals of all the Member States the same protection for trade marks as it accords to its own nationals and, if nationals of the Member States are required to prove registration in the country of origin, recognises the registration of Community trade marks as such proof.
   2.   With respect to the application of paragraph 1, stateless persons as defined by Article 1 of the Convention relating to the Status of Stateless Persons signed at New York on 28 September 1954, and refugees as defined by Article 1 of the Convention relating to the Status of Refugees signed at Geneva on 28 July 1951 and modified by the Protocol relating to the Status of Refugees signed at New York on 31 January 1967, shall be regarded as nationals of the country in which they have their habitual residence.
   3.   Persons who are nationals of a State covered by paragraph 1(d) must prove that the trade mark for which an application for a Community trade mark has been submitted is registered in the State of origin, unless, according to published findings, the trade marks of nationals of the Member States are registered in the State of origin in question without proof of prior registration as a Community trade mark or as a national trade mark in a Member State.

Article 6   Means whereby a Community trade mark is obtained
A Community trade mark shall be obtained by registration.

Article 7   Absolute grounds for refusal
   1.   The following shall not be registered:

    (a)   signs which do not conform to the requirements of Article 4;

    (b)   trade marks which are devoid of any distinctive character;

    (c)   trade marks which consist exclusively of signs or indications which may serve, in trade, to designate the kind, quality, quantity, intended purpose, value, geographical origin or the time of production of the goods or of rendering of the service, or other characteristics of the goods or service;

    (d)   trade marks which consist exclusively of signs or indications which have become customary in the current language or in the *bona fide* and established practices of the trade;

    (e)   signs which consist exclusively of:

       (i)   the shape which results from the nature of the goods themselves; or

      (ii)   the shape of goods which is necessary to obtain a technical result; or

     (iii)   the shape which gives substantial value to the goods;

    (f)   trade marks which are contrary to public policy or to accepted principles of morality;

    (g)   trade marks which are of such a nature as to deceive the public, for instance as to the nature, quality or geographical origin of the goods or service;

    (h)   trade marks which have not been authorised by the competent authorities and are to be refused pursuant to Article *6ter* of the Paris Convention;

    (i)   trade marks which include badges, emblems or escutcheons other than those covered by Article *6ter* of the Paris Convention and which are of particular public interest, unless the consent of the appropriate authorities to their registration has been given.

    2.   Paragraph 1 shall apply notwithstanding that the grounds of non-registrability obtain in only part of the Community.

    3.   Paragraph 1(b), (c) and (d) shall not apply if the trade mark has become distinctive in relation to the goods or services for which registration is requested in consequence of the use which has been made of it.

Article 8   Relative grounds for refusal

    1.   Upon opposition by the proprietor of an earlier trade mark, the trade mark applied for shall not be registered:

    (a)   if it is identical with the earlier trade mark and the goods or services for which registration is applied for are identical with the goods or services for which the earlier trade mark is protected;

    (b)   if because of its identity with or similarity to the earlier trade mark and the identity or similarity of the goods or services covered by the trade marks there exists a likelihood of confusion on the part of the public in the territory in which the earlier trade mark is protected; the likelihood of confusion includes the likelihood of association with the earlier trade mark.

    2.   for the purposes of paragraph 1, 'Earlier trade marks' means:

    (a)   trade marks of the following kinds with a date of application for registration which is earlier than the date of application for registration of the Community trade mark, taking account, where appropriate, of the priorities claimed in respect of those trade marks:

       (i)   Community trade marks;

      (ii)   trade marks registered in a Member State, or, in the case of Belgium, the Netherlands or Luxembourg, at the Benelux Trade Mark Office;

(iii)   trade marks registered under international arrangements which have effect in a Member State;

(b)   applications for the trade marks referred to in subparagraph (a), subject to their registration;

(c)   trade marks which, on the date of application for registration of the Community trade mark, or, where appropriate, of the priority claimed in respect of the application for registration of the Community trade mark, are well known in a Member State, in the sense in which the words 'well known' are used in Article 6*bis* of the Paris Convention.

3.   Upon opposition by the proprietor of the trade mark, a trade mark shall not be registered where an agent or representative of the proprietor of the trade mark applies for registration thereof in his own name without the proprietor's consent, unless the agent or representative justifies his action.

4.   Upon opposition by the proprietor of a non-registered trade mark or of another sign used in the course of trade of more than mere local significance, the trade mark applied for shall not be registered where and to the extent that, pursuant to the law of the Member State governing that sign,

(a)   rights to that sign were acquired prior to the date of application for registration of the Community trade mark, or the date of the priority claimed for the application for registration of the Community trade mark;

(b)   that sign confers on its proprietor the right to prohibit the use of a subsequent trade mark.

5.   Furthermore, upon opposition by the proprietor of an earlier trade mark within the meaning of paragraph 2, the trade mark applied for shall not be registered where it is identical with or similar to the earlier trade mark and is to be registered for goods or services which are not similar to those for which the earlier trade mark is registered, where in the case of an earlier Community trade mark the trade mark has a reputation in the Community and, in the case of an earlier national trade mark, the trade mark has a reputation in the Member State concerned and where the use without due cause of the trade mark applied for would take unfair advantage of, or be detrimental to, the distinctive character or the repute of the earlier trade mark.

SECTION 2   EFFECTS OF COMMUNITY TRADE MARKS

Article 9   Rights conferred by a Community trade mark
1.   A Community trade mark shall confer on the proprietor exclusive rights therein. The proprietor shall be entitled to prevent all third parties not having his consent from using in the course of trade:

(a)   any sign which is identical with the Community trade mark in relation to goods or services which are identical with those for which the Community trade mark is registered;

(b)   any sign where, because of its identity with or similarity to the Community trade mark and the identity or similarity of the goods or services covered by the Community trade mark and the sign, there exists a likelihood of confusion on the part of the public; the likelihood of confusion includes the likelihood of association between the sign and the trade mark;

(c)   any sign which is identical with or similar to the Community trade mark in relation to goods or services which are nor similar to those for which the

Community trade mark is registered, where the latter has a reputation in the Community and where use of that sign without due cause takes unfair advantage of, or is detrimental to, the distinctive character or the repute of the Community trade mark.

2.   The following, *inter alia,* may be prohibited under paragraph 1:

(a)   affixing the sign to the goods or to the packaging thereof;

(b)   offering the goods, putting them on the market or stocking them for these purposes under that sign, or offering or supplying services thereunder;

(c)   importing or exporting the goods under that sign;

(d)   using the sign on business papers and in advertising.

3.   The rights conferred by a Community trade mark shall prevail against third parties from the date of publication of registration of the trade mark. Reasonable compensation may, however, be claimed in respect of matters arising after the date of publication of a Community trade mark application, which matters would, after publication of the registration of the trade mark, be prohibited by virtue of that publication. The court seised of the case may not decide upon the merits of the case until the registration has been published.

Article 10   Reproduction of Community trade marks in dictionaries
If the reproduction of a Community trade mark in a dictionary, encyclopaedia or similar reference work gives the impression that it constitutes the generic name of the goods or services for which the trade mark is registered, the publisher of the work shall, at the request of the proprietor of the Community trade mark, ensure that the reproduction of the trade mark at the latest in the next edition of the publication is accompanied by an indication that it is a registered trade mark.

Article 11   Prohibition on the use of a Community trade mark registered in the name of an agent or representative
Where a Community trade mark is registered in the name of the agent or representative of a person who is the proprietor of that trade mark, without the proprietor's authorisation, the latter shall be entitled to oppose the use of his mark by his agent or representative if he has not authorised such use, unless the agent or representative justifies his action.

Article 12   Limitation of the effects of a Community trade mark
A Community trade mark shall not entitle the proprietor to prohibit a third party from using in the course of trade:

(a)   his own name or address;

(b)   indications concerning the kind, quality, quantity, intended purpose, value, geographical origin, the time of production of the goods or of rendering of the service, or other characteristics of the goods or service;

(c)   the trade mark where it is necessary to indicate the intended purpose of a product or service, in particular as accessories or spare parts,
provided he uses them in accordance with honest practices in industrial or commercial matters.

Article 13   Exhaustion of the rights conferred by a Community trade mark
1.   A Community trade mark shall not entitle the proprietor to prohibit its use in relation to goods which have been put on the market in the Community under that trade mark by the proprietor or with his consent.

2.   Paragraph 1 shall not apply where there exist legitimate reasons for the proprietor to oppose further commercialisation of the goods, especially where the condition of the goods is changed or impaired after they have been put on the market.

Article 14   Complementary application of national law relating to infringement
1.   The effects of Community trade marks shall be governed solely by the provisions of this Regulation. In other respects, infringement of a Community trade mark shall be governed by the national law relating to infringement of a national trade mark in accordance with the provisions of Title X.
2.   This Regulation shall not prevent actions concerning a Community trade mark being brought under the law of Member States relating in particular to civil liability and unfair competition.
3.   The rules of procedure to be applied shall be determined in accordance with the provisions of Title X.

SECTION 3   USE OF COMMUNITY TRADE MARKS

Article 15   Use of Community trade marks
1.   If, within a period of five years following registration, the proprietor has not put the Community trade mark to genuine use in the Community in connection with the goods or services in respect of which it is registered, or if such use has been suspended during an uninterrupted period of five years, the Community trade mark shall be subject to the sanctions provided for in this Regulation, unless there are proper reasons for non-use.
2.   The following shall also constitute use within the meaning of paragraph 1:
    (a)   use of the Community trade mark in a form differing in elements which do not alter the distinctive character of the mark in the form in which it was registered;
    (b)   affixing of the Community trade mark to goods or to the packaging thereof in the Community solely for export purposes.
3.   Use of the Community trade mark with the consent of the proprietor shall be deemed to constitute use by the proprietor.

SECTION 4   COMMUNITY TRADE MARKS AS OBJECTS OF PROPERTY

Article 16   Dealing with Community trade marks as national trade marks
1.   Unless Articles 17 to 24 provide otherwise, a Community trade mark as an object of property shall be dealt with in its entirety, and for the whole area of the Community, as a national trade mark registered in the Member State in which, according to the Register of Community trade marks,
    (a)   the proprietor has his seat or his domicile on the relevant date; or
    (b)   where subparagraph (a) does not apply, the proprietor has an establishment on the relevant date.
2.   In cases which are not provided for by paragraph 1, the Member State referred to in that paragraph shall be the Member State in which the seat of the Office is situated.

3.   If two or more persons are mentioned in the Register of Community trade marks as joint proprietors, paragraph 1 shall apply to the joint proprietor first mentioned; failing this, it shall apply to the subsequent joint proprietors in the order in which they are mentioned. Where paragraph 1 does not apply to any of the joint proprietors, paragraph 2 shall apply.

Article 17   Transfer
1.   A Community trade mark may be transferred, separately from any transfer of the undertaking, in respect of some or all of the goods or services for which it is registered.
2.   A transfer of the whole of the undertaking shall include the transfer of the Community trade mark except where, in accordance with the law governing the transfer, there is agreement to the contrary or circumstances clearly dictate otherwise. This provision shall apply to the contractual obligation to transfer the undertaking.
3.   Without prejudice to paragraph 2, an assignment of the Community trade mark shall be made in writing and shall require the signature of the parties to the contract, except when it is a result of a judgment; otherwise it shall be void.
4.   Where it is clear from the transfer documents that because of the transfer the Community trade mark is likely to mislead the public concerning the nature, quality or geogaphical origin of the goods or services in respect of which it is registered, the Office shall not register the transfer unless the successor agrees to limit registration of the Community trade mark to goods or services in respect of which it is not likely to mislead.
5.   On request of one of the parties a transfer shall be entered in the Register and published.
6.   As long as the transfer has not been entered in the Register, the successor in title may not invoke the rights arising from the registration of the Community trade mark.
7.   Where there are time limits to be observed *vis-à-vis* the Office, the successor in title may make the corresponding statements to the Office once the request for registration of the transfer has been received by the Office.
8.   All documents which require notification to the proprietor of the Community trade mark in accordance with Article 77 shall be addressed to the person registered as proprietor.

Article 18   Transfer of a trade mark registered in the name of an agent
Where a Community trade mark is registered in the name of the agent or representative of a person who is the proprietor of that trade mark, without the proprietor's authorisation, the latter shall be entitled to demand the assignment in his favour of the said registration, unless such agent or representative justifies his action.

Article 19   Rights in rem
1.   A Community trade mark may, independently of the undertaking, be given as security or be the subject of rights *in rem*.
2.   On request of one of the parties, rights mentioned in paragraph 1 shall be entered in the Register and published.

Article 20   Levy of execution

1.   A Community trade mark may be levied in execution.

2.   As regards the procedure for levy of execution in respect of a Community trade mark, the courts and authorities of the Member States determined in accordance with Article 16 shall have exclusive jurisdiction.

3.   On request of one of the parties, levy of execution shall be entered in the Register and published.

Article 21   Bankruptcy or like proceedings

1.   Until such time as common rules for the Member States in this field enter into force, the only Member State in which a Community trade mark may be involved in bankruptcy or like proceedings shall be that in which such proceedings are first brought within the meaning of national law or of conventions applicable in this field.

2.   Where a Community trade mark is involved in bankruptcy or like proceedings, on request of the competent national authority an entry to this effect shall be made in the Register and published.

Article 22   Licensing

1.   A Community trade mark may be licensed for some or all of the goods or services for which it is registered and for the whole or part of the Community. A licence may be exclusive or non-exclusive.

2.   The proprietor of a Community trade mark may invoke the rights conferred by that trade mark against a licensee who contravenes any provision in his licensing contract with regard to its duration, the form covered by the registration in which the trade mark may be used, the scope of the goods or services for which the licence is granted, the territory in which the trade mark may be affixed, or the quality of the goods manufactured or of the services provided by the licensee.

3.   Without prejudice to the provisions of the licensing contract, the licensee may bring proceedings for infringement of a Community trade mark only if its proprietor consents thereto. However, the holder of an exclusive licence may bring such proceedings if the proprietor of the trade mark, after formal notice, does not himself bring infringement proceedings within an appropriate period.

4.   A licensee shall, for the purpose of obtaining compensation for damage suffered by him, be entitled to intervene in infringement proceedings brought by the proprietor of the Community trade mark.

5.   On request of one of the parties the grant or transfer of a licence in respect of a Community trade mark shall be entered in the Register and published.

Article 23   Effects vis-à-vis *third parties*

1.   Legal acts referred to in Articles 17, 19 and 22 concerning a Community trade mark shall only have effects *vis-à-vis* third parties in all the Member States after entry in the Register. Nevertheless, such an act, before it is so entered, shall have effect *vis-à-vis* third parties who have acquired rights in the trade mark after the date of that act but who knew of the act at the date on which the rights were acquired.

2.   Paragraph 1 shall not apply in the case of a person who acquires the Community trade mark or a right concerning the Community trade mark by way of transfer of the whole of the undertaking or by any other universal succession.

3.   The effects *vis-à-vis* third parties of the legal acts referred to in Article 20 shall be governed by the law of the Member State determined in accordance with Article 16.

4.   Until such time as common rules for the Member States in the field of bankruptcy enter into force, the effects *vis-à-vis* third parties of bankruptcy or like proceedings shall be governed by the law of the Member State in which such proceedings are first brought within the meaning of national law or of conventions applicable in this field.

Article 24   The application for a Community trade mark as an object of property
Articles 16 to 23 shall apply to applications for Community trade marks.

Title III   Application for Community Trade Marks

SECTION 1   FILING OF APPLICATIONS AND THE CONDITIONS WHICH GOVERN THEM

Article 25   Filing of applications
1.   An application for a Community trade mark shall be filed, at the choice of the applicant,
(a)   at the Office; or
(b)   at the central industrial property office of a Member Stare or at the Benelux Trade Mark Office. An application filed in this way shall have the same effect as if it had been filed on the same date at the Office.

2.   Where the application is filed at the central industrial property office of a Member State or at the Benelux Trade Mark Office, that office shall take all steps to forward the application to the Office within two weeks after filing. It may charge the applicant a fee which shall not exceed the administrative costs of receiving and forwarding the application.

3.   Applications referred to in paragraph 2 which reach the Office more than one month after filing shall be deemed withdrawn.

4.   Ten years after the entry into force of this Regulation, the Commission shall draw up a report on the operation of the system of filing applications for Community trade marks, together with any proposals for modifying this system.

Article 26   Conditions with which applications must comply
1.   An application for a Community trade mark shall contain:
(a)   a request for the registration of a Community trade mark;
(b)   information identifying the applicant;
(c)   a list of the goods or services in respect of which the registration is requested;
(d)   a representation of the trade mark.

2.   The application for a Community trade mark shall be subject to the payment of the application fee and, when appropriate, of one or more class fees.

3.   An application for a Community trade mark must comply with the conditions laid down in the implementing Regulation referred to in Article 140.

Article 27   Date of filing
The date of filing of a Community trade mark application shall be the date on which documents containing the information specified in Article 26(1) are filed

with the Office by the applicant or, if the application has been filed with the central office of a Member State or with the Benelux Trade Mark Office, with that office, subject to payment of the application fee wthin a period of one month of filing the abovementioned documents.

Article 28   Classification
Goods and services in respect of which Community trade marks are applied for shall be classified in conformity with the system of classification specified in the Implementing Regulation.

SECTION 2   PRIORITY

Article 29   Right of priority
1.   A person who has duly filed an application for a trade mark in or for any State party to the Paris Convention, or his successors in title, shall enjoy, for the purpose of filing a Community trade mark application for the same trade mark in respect of goods or services which are identical with or contained within those for which the application has been filed, a right of priority during a period of six months from the date of filing of the first application.

2.   Every filing that is equivalent to a regular national filing under the national law of the State where it was made or under bilateral or multilateral agreements shall be recognised as giving rise to a right of priority.

3.   By a regular national filing is meant any filing that is sufficient to establish the date on which the application was filed, whatever may be the outcome of the application.

4.   A subsequent application for a trade mark which was the subject of a previous first application in respect of the same goods or services, and which is filed in or in respect of the same State shall be considered as the first application for the purposes of determining priority, provided that, at the date of filing of the subsequent application, the previous application has been withdrawn, abandoned or refused, without being open to public inspection and without leaving any rights outstanding, and has not served as a basis for claiming a right of priority. The previous application may not thereafter serve as a basis for claiming a right of priority.

5.   If the first filing has been made in a State which is not a party to the Paris Convention, paragraphs 1 to 4 shall apply only in so far as that State, according to published findings, grants, on the basis of a first filing made at the Office and subject to conditions equivalent to those laid down in this Regulation, a right of priority having equivalent effect.

Article 30   Claiming priority
An applicant desiring to take advantage of the priority of a previous application shall file a declaration of priority and a copy of the previous application. If the language of the latter is not one of the languages of the Office, the applicant shall file a translation of the previous application in one of those languages.

Article 31   Effect of priority right
The right of priority shall have the effect that the date of priority shall count as the date of filing of the Community trade mark application for the purposes of establishing which rights take precedence.

Article 32   Equivalence of Community filing with national filing
A Community trade mark application which has been accorded a date of filing shall, in the Member States, be equivalent to a regular national filing, where appropriate with the priority claimed for the Community trade mark application.

SECTION 3   EXHIBITION PRIORITY

Article 33   Exhibition priority
1.   If an applicant for a Community trade mark has displayed goods or services under the mark applied for, at an official or officially recognised international exhibition falling within the terms of the Convention on International Exhibitions signed at Paris on 22 November 1928 and last revised on 30 November 1972, he may, if he files the application within a period of six months from the date of the first display of the goods or services under the mark applied for, claim a right of priority from that date within the meaning of Article 31.

2.   An applicant who wishes to claim priority pursuant to paragraph 1 must file evidence of the display of goods or services under the mark applied for under the conditions laid down in the Implementing Regulation.

3.   An exhibition priority granted in a Member State or in a third country does not extend the period of priority laid down in Article 29.

SECTION 4   CLAIMING THE SENIORITY OF A NATIONAL TRADE MARK

Article 34   Claiming the seniority of a national trade mark
1.   The proprietor of an earlier trade mark registered in a Member State, including a trade mark registered in the Benelux countries, or registered under international arrangements having effect in a Member State, who applies for an identical trade mark for registration as a Community trade mark for goods or services which are identical with or contained within those for which the earlier trade mark has been registered, may claim for the Community trade mark the seniority of the earlier trade mark in respect of the Member State in or for which it is registered.

2.   Seniority shall have the sole effect under this Regulation that, where the proprietor of the Community trade mark surrenders the earlier trade mark or allows it to lapse, he shall be deemed to continue to have the same rights as he would have had if the earlier trade mark had continued to be registered.

3.   The seniority claimed for the Community trade mark shall lapse if the earlier trade mark the seniority of which is claimed is declared to have been revoked or to be invalid or if it is surrendered prior to the registration of the Community trade mark.

Article 35   Claiming seniority after registration of the Community trade mark
1.   The proprietor of a Community trade mark who is the proprietor of an earlier identical trade mark registered in a Member State, including a trade mark registered in the Benelux countries, or of a trade mark registered under international arrangements having effect in a Member State, for identical goods or services, may claim the seniority of the earlier trade mark in respect of the Member State in or for which it is registered.

2.   Article 34(2) and (3) shall apply.

Title IV   Registration Procedure

SECTION 1   EXAMINATION OF APPLICATIONS

Article 36   Examination of the conditions of filing
1. The Office shall examine whether:
    (a)   the Community trade mark application satisfies the requirements for the accordance of a date of filing in accordance with Article 27;
    (b)   the Community trade mark application complies with the conditions laid down in the Implementing Regulation;
    (c)   where appropriate, the class fees have been paid within the prescribed period.
2. Where the Community trade mark application does not satisfy the requirements referred to in paragraph 1, the Office shall request the applicant to remedy the deficiencies or the default on payment within the prescribed period.
3. If the deficiencies or the default on payment established pursuant to paragraph 1(a) are not remedied within this period, the application shall not be dealt with as a Community trade mark application. If the applicant complies with the Office's request, the Office shall accord as the date of filing of the application the date on which the deficiencies or the default on payment established are remedied.
4. If the deficiencies established pursuant to paragraph 1(b) are not remedied within the prescribed period, the Office shall refuse the application.
5. If the default on payment established pursuant to paragraph 1(c) is not remedied within the prescribed period, the application shall be deemed to be withdrawn unless it is clear which categories of goods or services the amount paid is intended to cover.
6. Failure to satisfy the requirements concerning the claim to priority shall result in loss of the right of priority for the application.
7. Failure to satisfy the requirements concerning the claiming of seniority of a national trade mark shall result in loss of that right for the application.

Article 37   Examination of the conditions relating to the entitlement of the proprietor
1. Where, pursuant to Article 5, the applicant may not be the proprietor of a Community trade mark, the application shall be refused.
2. The application may not be refused before the applicant has been given the opportunity to withdraw his application or submit his observations.

Article 38   Examination as to absolute grounds for refusal
1. Where, under Article 7, a trade mark is ineligible for registration in respect of some or all of the goods or services covered by the Community trade mark application, the application shall be refused as regards those goods or services.
2. Where the trade mark contains an element which is not distinctive, and where the inclusion of said element in the trade mark could give rise to doubts as to the scope of protection of the trade mark, the Office may request, as a condition for registration of said trade mark, that the applicant state that he disclaims any exclusive right to such element. Any disclaimer shall be published together with the application or the registration of the Community trade mark, as the case may be.

3. The application shall not be refused before the applicant has been allowed the opportunity of withdrawing or amending the application or of submitting his observations.

SECTION 2 SEARCH

Article 39 Search
1. Once the Office has accorded a date of filing to a Community trade mark application and has established that the applicant satisfies the conditions referred to in Article 5, it shall draw up a Community search report citing those earlier Community trade marks or Community trade mark applications discovered which may be invoked under Article 8 against the registration of the Community trade mark applied for.

2. As soon as a Community trade mark application has been accorded a date of filing, the Office shall transmit a copy thereof to the central industrial property office of each Member State which has informed the Office of its decision to operate a search in its own register of trade marks in respect of Community trade mark applications.

3. Each of the central industrial property offices referred to in paragraph 2 shall communicate to the Office within three months as from the date on which it received the Community trade mark application a search report which shall either cite those earlier national trade marks or trade mark applications discovered which may be invoked under Article 8 against the registration of the Community trade mark applied for, or state that the search has revealed no such rights.

4. An amount shall be paid by the Office to each central industrial property office for each search report provided by that office in accordance with paragraph 3. The amount, which shall be the same for each office, shall be fixed by the Budget Committee by means of a decision adopted by a majority of three-quarters of the representatives of the Member States.

5. The Office shall transmit without delay to the applicant for the Community trade mark the Community search report and the national search reports received within the time limit laid down in paragraph 3.

6. Upon publication of the Community trade mark application, which may not take place before the expiry of a period of one month as from the date on which the Office transmits the search reports to the applicant, the Office shall inform the proprietors of any earlier Community trade marks or Community trade mark applications cited in the Community search report of the publication of the Community trade mark application.

7. The Commission shall, five years after the opening of the Office for the filing of applications, submit to the Council a report on the operation of the system of searching resulting from this Article, including the payments made to Member States under paragraph 4, and, if necessary, appropriate proposals for amending this Regulation with a view to adapting the system of searching on the basis of the experience gained and bearing in mind developments in searching techniques.

SECTION 3 PUBLICATION OF THE APPLICATION

Article 40 Publication of the application
1. If the conditions which the application for a Community trade mark must satisfy have been fulfilled and if the period referred to in Article 39(6) has expired,

the application shall be published to the extent that it has not been refused pursuant to Articles 37 and 38.

2.   Where, after publication, the application is refused under Articles 37 and 38, the decision that it has been refused shall be published upon becoming final.

SECTION 4   OBSERVATIONS BY THIRD PARTIES AND OPPOSITION

Article 41   Observations by third parties

1.   Following the publication of the Community trade mark application, any natural or legal person and any group or body representing manufacturers, producers, suppliers of services, traders or consumers may submit to the Office written observations, explaining on which grounds under Article 7, in particular, the trade mark shall not be registered *ex officio*. They shall not be parties to the proceedings before the Office.

2.   The observations referred to in paragraph 1 shall be communicated to the applicant who may comment on them.

Article 42   Opposition

1.   Within a period of three months following the publication of a Community trade mark application, notice of opposition to registration of the trade mark may be given on the grounds that it may not be registered under Article 8:

   (a)   by the proprietors of earlier trade marks referred to in Article 8(2) as well as licensees authorised by the proprietors of those trade marks, in respect of Article 8(1) and (5);

   (b)   by the proprietors of trade marks referred to in Article 8(3);

   (c)   by the proprietors of earlier marks or signs referred to in Article 8(4) and by persons authorised under the relevant national law to exercise these rights.

2.   Notice of opposition to registration of the trade mark may also be given, subject to the conditions laid down in paragraph 1, in the event of the publication of an amended application in accordance with the second sentence of Article 44(2).

3.   Opposition must be expressed in writing and must specify the grounds on which it is made. It shall not be treated as duly entered until the opposition fee has been paid. Within a period fixed by the Office, the opponent may submit in support of his case facts, evidence and arguments.

Article 43   Examination of opposition

1.   In the examination of the opposition the Office shall invite the parties, as often as necessary, to file observations, within a period set them by the Office, on communications from the other parties or issued by itself.

2.   If the applicant so requests, the proprietor of an earlier Community trade mark who has given notice of opposition shall furnish proof that, during the period of five years preceding the date of publication of the Community trade mark application, the earlier Community trade mark has been put to genuine use in the Community in connection with the goods or services in respect of which it is registered and which he cites as justification for his opposition, or that there are proper reasons for non-use, provided the earlier Community trade mark has at that date been registered for not less than five years. In the absence of proof to this

effect, the opposition shall be rejected. If the earlier Community trade mark has been used in relation to part only of the goods or services for which it is registered it shall, for the purposes of the examination of the opposition, be deemed to be registered in respect only of that part of the goods or services.

3. Paragraph 2 shall apply to earlier national trade marks referred to in Article 8(2)(a), by substituting use in the Member State in which the earlier national trade mark is protected for use in the Community.

4. The Office may, if it thinks fit, invite the parties to make a friendly settlement.

5. If examination of the opposition reveals that the trade mark may not be registered in respect of some or all of goods or services for which the Community trade mark application has been made, the application shall be refused in respect of those goods or services. Otherwise the opposition shall be rejected.

6. The decision refusing the application shall be published upon becoming final.

SECTION 5 WITHDRAWAL, RESTRICTION AND AMENDMENT OF THE APPLICATION

Article 44 Withdrawal, restriction and amendment of the application
1. The applicant may at any time withdraw his Community trade mark application or restrict the list of goods or services contained therein. Where the application has already been published, the withdrawal or restriction shall also be published.

2. In other respects, a Community trade mark application may be amended, upon request of the applicant, only by correcting the name and address of the applicant, errors of wording or of copying, or obvious mistakes, provided that such correction does not substantially change the trade mark or extend the list of goods or services. Where the amendments affect the representation of the trade mark or the list of goods or services and are made after publication of the application, the trade mark application shall be published as amended.

SECTION 6 REGISTRATION

Article 45 Registration
Where an application meets the requirements of this Regulation and where no notice of opposition has been given within the period referred to in Article 42(1) or where opposition has been rejected by a definitive decision, the trade mark shall be registered as a Community trade mark, provided that the registration fee has been paid within the period prescribed. If the fee is not paid within this period the application shall be deemed to be withdrawn.

Title V Duration, Renewal and Alteration of Community Trade Marks

Article 46 Duration of registration
Community trade marks shall be registered for a period of ten years from the date of filing of the application. Registration may be renewed in accordance with Article 47 for further periods of ten years.

Article 47   Renewal

1.   Registration of the Community trade mark shall be renewed at the request of the proprietor of the trade mark or any person expressly authorised by him provided that the fees have been paid.

2.   The Office shall inform the proprietor of the Community trade mark, and any person having a registered right in respect of the Community trade mark, of the expiry of the registration in good time before the said expiry. Failure to give such information shall not involve the responsibility of the Office.

3.   The request for renewal shall be submitted within a period of six months ending on the last day of the month in which protection ends. The fees shall also be paid within this period. Failing this, the request may be submitted and the fees paid within a further period of six months following the day referred to in the first sentence, provided that an additional fee is paid within this further period.

4.   Where the request is submitted or the fees paid in respect of only some of the goods or services for which the Community trade mark is registered, registration shall be renewed for those goods or services only.

5.   Renewal shall take effect from the day following the date on which the existing registration expires. The renewal shall be registered.

Article 48   Alteration

1.   The Community trade mark shall not be altered in the register during the period of registration or on renewal thereof.

2.   Nevertheless, where the Community trade mark includes the name and address of the proprietor, any alteration thereof not substantially affecting the identity of the trade mark as originally registered may be registered at the request of the proprietor.

3.   The publication of the registration of the alteration shall contain a representation of the Community trade mark as altered. Third parties whose rights may be affected by the alteration may challenge the registration thereof within a period of three months following publication.

Title VI   Surrender, Revocation and Invalidity

SECTION 1   SURRENDER

Article 49   Surrender

1.   A Community trade mark may be surrendered in respect of some or all of the goods or services for which it is registered.

2.   The surrender shall be declared to the Office in writing by the proprietor of the trade mark. It shall not have effect until it has been entered in the Register.

3.   Surrender shall be entered only with the agreement of the proprietor of a right entered in the Register. If a licence has been registered, surrender shall only be entered in the Register if the proprietor of the trade mark proves that he has informed the licensee of his intention to surrender; this entry shall be made on expiry of the period prescribed by the Implementing Regulation.

SECTION 2   GROUNDS FOR REVOCATION

Article 50   Grounds for revocation
1.   The rights of the proprietor of the Community trade mark shall be declared to be revoked on application to the Office or on the basis of a counterclaim in infringement proceedings:

(a)   if, within a continuous period of five years, the trade mark has not been put to genuine use in the Community in connection with the goods or services in respect of which it is registered, and there are no proper reasons for non-use; however, no person may claim that the proprietor's rights in a Community trade mark should be revoked where, during the interval between expiry of the five-year period and filing of the application or counterclaim, genuine use of the trade mark has been started or resumed; the commencement or resumption of use within a period of three months preceding the filing of the application or counterclaim which began at the earliest on expiry of the continuous period of five years of non-use shall, however, be disregarded where preparations for the commencement or resumption occur only after the proprietor becomes aware that the application or counterclaim may be filed;

(b)   if, in consequence of acts or inactivity of the proprietor, the trade mark has become the common name in the trade for a product or service in respect of which it is registered;

(c)   if, in consequence of the use made of it by the proprietor of the trade mark or with his consent in respect of the goods or services for which it is registered, the trade mark is liable to mislead the public, particularly as to the nature, quality or geographical origin of those goods or services;

(d)   if the proprietor of the trade mark no longer satisfies the conditions laid down by Article 5.

2.   Where the grounds for revocation of rights exist in respect of only some of the goods or services for which the Community trade mark is registered, the rights of the proprietor shall be declared to be revoked in respect of those goods or services only.

SECTION 3   GROUNDS FOR INVALIDITY

Article 51   Absolute grounds for invalidity
1.   A Community trade mark shall be declared invalid on application to the Office or on the basis of a counterclaim in infringement proceedings,

(a)   where the Community trade mark has been registered in breach of the provisions of Article 5 or of Article 7;

(b)   where the applicant was acting in bad faith when he filed the application for the trade mark.

2.   Where the Community trade mark has been registered in breach of the provisions of Article 7(1)(b), (c) or (d), it may nevertheless not be declared invalid if, in consequence of the use which has been made of it, it has after registration acquired a distinctive character in relation to the goods or services for which it is registered.

3.   Where the ground for invalidity exists in respect of only some of the goods or services for which the Community trade mark is registered, the trade mark shall be declared invalid as regards those goods or services only.

Article 52   Relative grounds for invalidity

1.   A Community trade mark shall be declared invalid on application to the Office or on the basis of a counterclaim in infringement proceedings:

(a)   where there is an earlier trade mark as referred to in Article 8(2) and the conditions set out in paragraph 1 or paragraph 5 of that Article are fulfilled,

(b)   where there is a trade mark as referred to in Article 8(3) and the conditions set out in that paragraph are fulfilled;

(c)   where there is an earlier right as referred to in Article 8(4) and the conditions set out in that paragraph are fulfilled.

2.   A Community trade mark shall also be declared invalid on application to the Office or on the basis of a counterclaim in infringement proceedings where the use of such trade mark may be prohibited pursuant to the national law governing the protection of any other earlier right and in particular:

(a)   a right to a name;

(b)   a right of personal portrayal;

(c)   a copyright;

(d)   an industrial property right.

3.   A Community trade mark may not be declared invalid where the proprietor of a right referred to in paragraphs 1 or 2 consents expressly to the registration of the Community trade mark before submission of the application for a declaration of invalidity or the counterclaim.

4.   Where the proprietor of one of the rights referred to in paragraphs 1 or 2 has previously applied for a declaration that a Community trade mark is invalid or made a counterclaim in infringement proceedings, he may not submit a new application for a declaration of invalidity or lodge a counterclaim on the basis of another of the said rights which he could have invoked in support of his first application or counterclaim.

5.   Article 51(3) shall apply.

Article 53   Limitation in consequence of acquiescence

1.   Where the proprietor of a Community trade mark has acquiesced, for a period of five successive years, in the use of a later Community trade mark in the Community while being aware of such use, he shall no longer be entitled on the basis of the earlier trade mark either to apply for a declaration that the later trade mark is invalid or to oppose the use of the later trade mark in respect of the goods or services for which the later trade mark has been used, unless registration of the later Community trade mark was applied for in bad faith.

2.   Where the proprietor of an earlier national trade mark as referred to in Article 8(2) or of another earlier sign referred to in Article 8(4) has acquiesced, for a period of five successive years, in the use of a later Community trade mark in the Member State in which the earlier trade mark or the other earlier sign is protected while being aware of such use, he shall no longer be entitled on the basis of the earlier trade mark or of the other earlier sign either to apply for a declaration that the later trade mark is invalid or to oppose the use of the later trade mark in respect of the goods or services for which the later trade mark has been used, unless registration of the later Community trade mark was applied for in bad faith.

3.   In the cases referred to in paragraphs 1 and 2, the proprietor of a later Community trade mark shall not be entitled to oppose the use of the earlier right, even though that right may no longer be invoked against the later Community trade mark.

SECTION 4 CONSEQUENCES OF REVOCATION AND INVALIDITY

Article 54 Consequences of revocation and invalidity

1. The Community trade mark shall be deemed not to have had, as from the date of the application for revocation or of the counterclaim, the effects specified in this Regulation, to the extent that the rights of the proprietor have been revoked. An earlier date, on which one of the grounds for revocation occurred, may be fixed in the decision at the request of one of the parties.

2. The Community trade mark shall be deemed not to have had, as from the outset, the effects specified in this Regulation, to the extent that the trade mark has been declared invalid.

3. Subject to the national provisions relating either to claims for compensation for damage caused by negligence or lack of good faith on the part of the proprietor of the trade mark, or to unjust enrichment, the retroactive effect of revocation or invalidity of the trade mark shall not affect:

(a) any decision on infringement which has acquired the authority of a final decision and been enforced prior to the revocation or invalidity decision;

(b) any contract concluded prior to the revocation or invalidity decision, insofar as it has been performed before that decision; however, repayment, to an extent justified by the circumstances, of sums paid under the relevant contract, may be claimed on grounds of equity.

SECTION 5 PROCEEDINGS IN THE OFFICE IN RELATION TO REVOCATION OR INVALIDITY

Article 55 Application for revocation or for a declaration of invalidity

1. An application for revocation of the rights of the proprietor of a Community trade mark or for a declaration that the trade mark is invalid may be submitted to the Office:

(a) where Articles 50 and 51 apply, by any natural or legal person and any group or body set up for the purpose of representing the interests of manufacturers, producers, suppliers of services, traders or consumers, which under the terms of the law governing it has the capacity in its own name to sue and be sued;

(b) where Article 52(1) applies, by the persons referred to in Article 42(1);

(c) where Article 52(2) applies, by the owners of the earlier rights referred to in that provision or by the persons who are entitled under the law of the Member State concerned to exercise the rights in question.

2. The application shall be filed in a written reasoned statement. It shall not be deemed to have been filed until the fee has been paid.

3. An application for revocation or for a declaration of invalidity shall be inadmissible if an application relating to the same subject matter and cause of action, and involving the same parties, has been adjudicated on by a court in a Member State and has acquired the authority of a final decision.

Article 56 Examination of the application

1. In the examination of the application for revocation of rights or for a declaration of invalidity, the Office shall invite the parties, as often as necessary, to file observations, within a period to be fixed by the Office, on communications from the other parties or issued by itself.

2.   If the proprietor of the Community trade mark so requests, the proprietor of an earlier Community trade mark, being a party to the invalidity proceedings, shall furnish proof that, during the period of five years preceding the date of the application for a declaration of invalidity, the earlier Community trade mark has been put to genuine use in the Community in connection with the goods or services in respect of which it is registered and which he cites as justification for his application, or that there are proper reasons for non-use, provided the earlier Community trade mark has at that date been registered for not less than five years. If, at the date on which the Community trade mark application was published, the earlier Community trade mark had been registered for not less than five years, the proprietor of the earlier Community trade mark shall furnish proof that, in addition, the conditions contained in Article 43(2) were satisfied at that date. In the absence of proof to this effect the application for a declaration of invalidity shall be rejected. If the earlier Community trade mark has been used in relation to part only of the goods or services for which it is registered it shall, for the purpose of the examination of the application for a declaration of invalidity, be deemed to be registered in respect only of that part of the goods or services.

3.   Paragraph 2 shall apply to earlier national trade marks referred to in Article 8(2)(a), by substituting use in the Member State in which the earlier national trade mark is protected for use in the Community.

4.   The Office may, if it thinks fit, invite the parties to make a friendly settlement.

5.   If the examination of the application for revocation of rights or for a declaration of invalidity reveals that the trade mark should not have been registered in respect of some or all of the goods or services for which it is registered, the rights of the proprietor of the Community trade mark shall be revoked or it shall be declared invalid in respect of those goods or services. Otherwise the application for revocation of rights or for a declaration of invalidity shall be rejected.

6.   The decision revoking the rights of the proprietor of the Community trade mark or declaring it invalid shall be entered in the Register upon becoming final.

Title VII   Appeals

Article 57   Decisions subject to appeal
1.   An appeal shall lie from decisions of the examiners, Opposition Divisions, Administration of Trade Marks and Legal Division and Cancellation Divisions. It shall have suspensive effect.

2.   A decision which does not terminate proceedings as regards one of the parties can only be appealed together with the final decision, unless the decision allows separate appeal.

Article 58   Persons entitled to appeal and to be parties to appeal proceedings
Any party to proceedings adversely affected by a decision may appeal. Any other parties to the proceedings shall be parties to the appeal proceedings as of right.

Article 59   Time limit and form of appeal
Notice of appeal must be filed in writing at the Office within two months after the date of notification of the decision appealed from. The notice shall be deemed to

have been filed only when the fee for appeal has been paid. Within four months after the date of notification of the decision, a written statement setting out the grounds of appeal must be filed.

Article 60   Interlocutory revision

1.   If the department whose decision is contested considers the appeal to be admissible and well founded, it shall rectify its decision. This shall not apply where the appellant is opposed by another party to the proceedings.

2.   If the decision is not rectified within one month after receipt of the statement of grounds, the appeal shall be remitted to the Board of Appeal without delay, and without comment as to its merit.

Article 61   Examination of appeals

1.   If the appeal is admissible, the Board of Appeal shall examine whether the appeal is allowable.

2.   In the examination of the appeal, the Board of Appeal shall invite the parties, as often as necessary, to file observations, within a period to be fixed by the Board of Appeal, on communications from the other parties or issued by itself.

Article 62   Decisions in respect of appeals

1.   Following the examination as to the allowability of the appeal, the Board of Appeal shall decide on the appeal. The Board of Appeal may either exercise any power within the competence of the department which was responsible for the decision appealed or remit the case to that department for further prosecution.

2.   If the Board of Appeal remits the case for further prosecution to the department whose decision was appealed, that department shall be bound by the *ratio decidendi* of the Board of Appeal, insofar as the facts are the same.

3.   The decisions of the Boards of Appeal shall take effect only as from the date of expiration of the period referred to in Article 63(5) or, if an action has been brought before the Court of Justice within that period, as from the date of rejection of such action.

Article 63   Actions before the Court of justice

1.   Actions may be brought before the Court of Justice against decisions of the Boards of Appeal on appeals.

2.   The action may be brought on grounds of lack of competence, infringement of an essential procedural requirement, infringement of the Treaty, of this Regulation or of any rule of law relating to their application or misuse of power.

3.   The Court of Justice has jurisdiction to annul or to alter the contested decision.

4.   The action shall be open to any party to proceedings before the Board of Appeal adversely affected by its decision.

5.   The action shall be brought before the Court of Justice within two months of the date of notification of the decision of the Board of Appeal.

6.   The Office shall be required to take the necessary measures to comply with the judgment of the Court of Justice.

Title VIII   Community Collective Marks

Article 64   Community collective marks

1.   A Community collective mark shall be a Community trade mark which is described as such when the mark is applied for and is capable of distinguishing the goods or services of the members of the association which is the proprietor of the mark from those of other undertakings. Associations of manufacturers, producers, suppliers of services, or traders which, under the terms of the law governing them, have the capacity in their own name to have rights and obligations of all kinds, to make contracts or accomplish other legal acts and to sue and be sued, as well as legal persons governed by public law, may apply for Community collective marks.

2.   In derogation from Article 7(1)(c), signs or indications which may serve, in trade, to designate the geographical origin of the goods or services may constitute Community collective marks within the meaning of paragraph 1. A collective mark shall not entitle the proprietor to prohibit a third party from using in the course of trade such signs or indications, provided he uses them in accordance with honest practices in industrial or commercial matters; in particular, such a mark may not be invoked against a third party who is entitled to use a geographical name.

3.   The provisions of this Regulation shall apply to Community collective marks, unless Articles 65 to 72 provide otherwise.

Article 65   Regulations governing use of the mark

1.   An applicant for a Community collective mark must submit regulations governing its use within the period prescribed.

2.   The regulations governing use shall specify persons authorised to use the mark, the conditions of membership of the association and, where they exist, the conditions of use of the mark including sanctions. The regulations governing use of a mark referred to in Article 64(2) must authorise any person whose goods or services originate in the geographical area concerned to become a member of the association which is the proprietor of the mark.

Article 66   Refusal of the application

1.   In addition to the grounds for refusal of a Community trade mark application provided for in Articles 36 and 38, an application for a Community collective mark shall be refused where the provisions of Article 64 or 65 are not satisfied, or where the regulations governing use are contrary to public policy or to accepted principles of morality.

2.   An application for a Community collective mark shall also be refused if the public is liable to be misled as regards the character or the significance of the mark, in particular if it is likely to be taken to be something other than a collective mark.

3.   An application shall not be refused if the applicant, as a result of amendment of the regulations governing use, meets the requirements of paragraphs 1 and 2.

Article 67   Observations by third parties

Apart from the cases mentioned in Article 41, any person, group or body referred to in that Article may submit to the Office written observations based on the particular grounds on which the application for a Community collective mark should be refused under the terms of Article 66.

Article 68   Use of marks

Use of a Community collective mark by any person who has authority to use it shall satisfy the requirements of this Regulation, provided that the other conditions which this Regulation imposes with regard to the use of Community trade marks are fulfilled.

Article 69   Amendment of the regulations governing use of the mark

1.   The proprietor of a Community collective mark must submit to the Office any amended regulations governing use.

2.   The amendment shall not be mentioned in the Register if the amended regulations do not satisfy the requirements of Article 65 or involve one of the grounds for refusal referred to in Article 66.

3.   Article 67 shall apply to amended regulations governing use.

4.   For the purposes of applying this Regulation, amendments to the regulations governing use shall take effect only from the date of entry of the mention of the amendment in the Register.

Article 70   Persons who are entitled to bring an action for infringement

1.   The provisions of Article 22(3) and (4) concerning the rights of licensees shall apply to every person who has authority to use a Community collective mark.

2.   The proprietor of a Community collective mark shall be entitled to claim compensation on behalf of persons who have authority to use the mark where they have sustained damage in consequence of unauthorised use of the mark.

Article 71   Grounds for revocation

Apart from the grounds for revocation provided for in Article 50, the rights of the proprietor of a Community collective mark shall be revoked on application to the Office or on the basis of a counterclaim in infringement proceedings, if:

(a)   the proprietor does not take reasonable steps to prevent the mark being used in a manner incompatible with the conditions of use, where these exist, laid down in the regulations governing use, amendments to which have, where appropriate, been mentioned in the Register;

(b)   the manner in which the mark has been used by the proprietor has caused it to become liable to mislead the public in the manner referred to in Article 66(2);

(c)   an amendment to the regulations governing use of the mark has been mentioned in the Register in breach of the provisions of Article 69(2), unless the proprietor of the mark, by further amending the regulations governing use, complies with the requirements of those provisions.

Article 72   Grounds for invalidity

Apart from the grounds for invalidity provided for in Articles 51 and 52, a Community collective mark which is registered in breach of the provisions of Article 66 shall be declared invalid on application to the Office or on the basis of a counterclaim in infringement proceedings, unless the proprietor of the mark, by amending the regulations governing use, complies with the requirements of those provisions.

Title IX   Procedure

SECTION 1   GENERAL PROVISIONS

Article 73   Statement of reasons on which decisions are based

Decisions of the Office shall state the reasons on which they are based. They shall be based only on reasons or evidence on which the parties concerned have had an opportunity to present their comments.

Article 74   Examination of the facts by the Office of its own motion

1.   In proceedings before it the Office shall examine the facts of its own motion; however, in proceedings relating to relative grounds for refusal of registration, the Office shall be restricted in this examination to the facts, evidence and arguments provided by the parties and the relief sought.

2.   The Office may disregard facts or evidence which are not submitted in due time by the parties concerned.

Article 75   Oral proceedings

1.   If the Office considers that oral proceedings would be expedient they shall be held either at the instance of the Office or at the request of any party to the proceedings.

2.   Oral proceedings before the examiners, the Opposition Division and the Administration of Trade Marks and Legal Division shall not be public.

3.   Oral proceedings, including delivery of the decision, shall be public before the Cancellation Division and the Boards of Appeal, insofar as the department before which the proceedings are taking place does not decide otherwise in cases where admission of the public could have serious and unjustified disadvantages, in particular for a party to the proceedings.

Article 76   Taking of evidence

1.   In any proceedings before the Office, the means of giving or obtaining evidence shall include the following:
   (a)   hearing the parties;
   (b)   requests for information;
   (c)   the production of documents and items of evidence;
   (d)   hearing witnesses;
   (e)   opinions by experts;
   (f)   statements in writing sworn or affirmed or having a similar effect under the law of the State in which the statement is drawn up.

2.   The relevant department may commission one of its members to examine the evidence adduced.

3.   If the Office considers it necessary for a party, witness or expert to give evidence orally, it shall issue a summons to the person concerned to appear before it.

4.   The parties shall be informed of the hearing of a witness or expert before the Office. They shall have the right to be present and to put questions to the witness or expert.

Article 77   Notification
The Office shall, as a matter of course, notify those concerned of decisions and summonses and of any notice or other communication from which a time limit is reckoned, or of which those concerned must be notified under other provisions of this Regulation or of the Implementing Regulation, or of which notification has been ordered by the President of the Office.

Article 78   Restitutio in integrum
1.   The applicant for or proprietor of a Community trade mark or any other party to proceedings before the Office who, in spite of all due care required by the circumstances having been taken, was unable to observe a time limit *vis-à-vis* the Office shall, upon application, have his rights re-established if the non-observance in question has the direct consequence, by virtue of the provisions of this Regulation, of causing the loss of any right or means of redress.
2.   The application must be filed in writing within two months from the removal of the cause of non-compliance with the time limit. The omitted act must be completed within this period. The application shall only be admissible within the year immediately following the expiry of the unobserved time limit. In the case of non-submission of the request for renewal of registration or of non-payment of a renewal fee, the further period of six months provided in Article 47(3), third sentence, shall be deducted from the period of one year.
3.   The application must state the grounds on which it is based and must set out the facts on which it relies. It shall not be deemed to be filed until the fee for re-establishment of rights has been paid.
4.   The department competent to decide on the omitted act shall decide upon the application.
5.   The provisions of this Article shall not be applicable to the time limits referred to in paragraph 2 of this Article, Articles 29(1) and 42(1).
6.   Where the applicant for or proprietor of a Community trade mark has his rights re-established, he may not invoke his rights *vis-à-vis* a third party who, in good faith, has put goods on the market or supplied services under a sign which is identical with or similar to the Community trade mark in the course of the period between the loss of rights in the application or in the Community trade mark and publication of the mention of re-establishment of those rights.
7.   A third party who may avail himself of the provisions of paragraph 6 may bring third party proceedings against the decision re-establishing the rights of the applicant for or proprietor of a Community trade mark within a period of two months as from the date of publication of the mention of re-establishment of those rights.
8.   Nothing in this Article shall limit the right of a Member State to grant *restitutio in integrum* in respect of time limits provided for in this Regulation and to be observed *vis-à-vis* the authorities of such State.

Article 79   Reference to general principles
In the absence of procedural provisions in this Regulation, the Implementing Regulation, the fees regulations or the rules of procedure of the Boards of Appeal, the Office shall take into account the principles of procedural law generally recognised in the Member Stares.

Article 80　Termination of financial obligations

1. Rights of the Office to the payment of a fee shall be extinguished after four years from the end of the calendar year in which the fee fell due.

2. Rights against the Office for the refunding of fees or sums of money paid in excess of a fee shall be extinguished after four years from the end of the calendar year in which the right arose.

3. The period laid down in paragraphs 1 and 2 shall be interrupted in the case covered by paragraph 1 by a request for payment of the fee and in the case covered by paragraph 2 by a reasoned claim in writing. On interruption it shall begin again immediately and shall end at the latest six years after the end of the year in which it originally began, unless, in the meantime, judicial proceedings to enforce the right have begun; in this case the period shall end at the earliest one year after the judgment has acquired the authority of a final decision.

SECTION 2　COSTS

Article 81　Costs

1. The losing party in opposition proceedings, proceedings for revocation, proceedings for a declaration of invalidity or appeal proceedings shall bear the fees incurred by the other party as well as all costs, without prejudice to Article 115(6), incurred by him essential to the proceedings, including travel and subsistence and the remuneration of an agent, adviser or advocate, within the limits of the scales set for each category of costs under the conditions laid down in the Implementing Regulation.

2. However, where each party succeeds on some and fails on other heads, or if reasons of equity so dictate, the Opposition Division, Cancellation Division or Board of Appeal shall decide a different apportionment of costs.

3. The party who terminates the proceedings by withdrawing the Community trade mark application, the opposition, the application for revocation of rights, the application for a declaration of invalidity or the appeal, or by not renewing registration of the Community trade mark or by surrendering the Community trade mark, shall bear the fees and the costs incurred by the other party as stipulated in paragraphs 1 and 2.

4. Where a case does not proceed to judgment the costs shall be at the discretion of the Opposition Division, Cancellation Division or Board of Appeal.

5. Where the parties conclude before the Opposition Division, Cancellation Division or Board of Appeal a settlement of costs differing from that provided for in the preceding paragraphs, the department concerned shall take note of that agreement.

6. On request the registry of the Opposition Division or Cancellation Division or Board of Appeal shall fix the amount of the costs to be paid pursuant to the preceding paragraphs. The amount so determined may be reviewed by a decision of the Opposition Division or Cancellation Division or Board of Appeal on a request filed within the prescribed period.

Article 82　Enforcement of decisions fixing the amount of costs

1. Any final decision of the Office fixing the amount of costs shall be enforceable.

2.   Enforcement shall be governed by the rules of civil procedure in force in the State in the territory of which it is carried out. The order for its enforcement shall be appended to the decision, without other formality than verification of the authenticity of the decision, by the national authority which the Government of each Member State shall designate for this purpose and shall make known to the Office and to the Court of Justice.

3.   When these formalities have been completed on application by the party concerned, the latter may proceed to enforcement in accordance with the national law, by bringing the matter directly before the competent authority.

4.   Enforcement may be suspended only by a decision of the Court of Justice. However, the courts of the country concerned shall have jurisdiction over complaints that enforcement is being carried out in an irregular manner.

SECTION 3   INFORMATION OF THE PUBLIC AND OF THE OFFICIAL AUTHORITIES OF THE MEMBER STATES

Article 83   Register of Community trade marks
The Office shall keep a register to be known as the Register of Community trade marks, which shall contain those particulars the registration or inclusion of which is provided for by this Regulation or by the Implementing Regulation. The Register shall be open to public inspection.

Article 84   Inspection of files
1.   The files relating to Community trade mark applications which have not yet been published shall not be made available for inspection without the consent of the applicant.

2.   Any person who can prove that the applicant for a Community trade mark has stated that after the trade mark has been registered he will invoke the rights under it against him may obtain inspection of the files prior to the publication of that application and without the consent of the applicant.

3.   Subsequent to the publication of the Community trade mark application, the files relating to such application and the resulting trade mark may be inspected on request.

4.   However, where the files are inspected pursuant to paragraphs 2 or 3, certain documents in the file may be withheld from inspection in accordance with the provisions of the Implementing Regulation.

Article 85   Periodical publications
The Office shall periodically publish:

(a)   a Community Trade Marks Bulletin containing entries made in the Register of Community trade marks as well as other particulars the publication of which is prescribed by this Regulation or by the Implementing Regulation;

(b)   an Official Journal containing notices and information of a general character issued by the President of the Office, as well as any other information relevant to this Regulation or its implementation.

Article 86   Administrative cooperation
Unless otherwise provided in this Regulation or in national laws, the Office and the courts or authorities of the Member States shall on request give assistance to

each other by communicating information or opening files for inspection. Where the Office lays files open to inspection by courts, Public Prosecutors' Offices or central industrial property offices, the inspection shall not be subject to the restrictions laid down in Article 84.

Article 87   Exchange of publications

1.   The Office and the central industrial property offices of the Member States shall despatch to each other on request and for their own use one or more copies of their respective publications free of charge.

2.   The Office may conclude agreements relating to the exchange or supply of publications.

SECTION 4   REPRESENTATION

Article 88   General principles of representation

1.   Subject to the provisions of paragraph 2, no person shall be compelled to be represented before the Office.

2.   Without prejudice to paragraph 3, second sentence, natural or legal persons not having either their domicile or their principal place of business or a real and effective industrial or commercial establishment in the Community must be represented before the Office in accordance with Article 89(1) in all proceedings established by this Regulation, other than in filing an application for a Community trade mark; the Implementing Regulation may permit other exceptions.

3.   Natural or legal persons having their domicile or principal place of business or a real and effective industrial or commercial establishment in the Community may be represented before the Office by an employee, who must file with it a signed authorisation for insertion on the files, the details of which are set out in the Implementing Regulation. An employee of a legal person to which this paragraph applies may also represent other legal persons which have economic connections with the first legal person, even if those other legal persons have neither their domicile nor their principal place of business nor a real and effective industrial or commercial establishment within the Community.

Article 89   Professional representatives

1.   Representation of natural or legal persons before the Office may only be undertaken by;

(a)   any legal practitioner qualified in one of the Member States and having his place of business within the Community, to the extent that he is entitled, within the said State, to act as a representative in trade mark matters; or

(b)   professional representatives whose names appear on the list maintained for this purpose by the Office.

Representatives acting before the Office must file with it a signed authorisation for insertion on the files, the details of which are set out in the Implementing Regulation.

2.   Any natural person who fulfils the following conditions may be entered on the list of professional representatives:

(a)   he must be a national of one of the Member States;

(b)   he must have his place of business or employment in the Community;

(c)   he must be entitled to represent natural or legal persons in trade mark matters before the central industrial property office of the Member State in which he has his place of business or employment. Where, in that State, the entitlement is not conditional upon the requirement of special professional qualifications, persons applying to be entered on the list who act in trade mark matters before the central industrial property office of the said State must have habitually so acted for at least five years. However, persons whose professional qualification to represent natural or legal persons in trade mark matters before the central industrial property office of one of the Member States is officially recognised in accordance with the regulations laid down by such State shall not be subject to the condition of having exercised the profession.

3.   Entry shall be effected upon request, accompanied by a certificate furnished by the central industrial property office of the Member State concerned, which must indicate that the conditions laid down in paragraph 2 are fulfilled.

4.   The President of the Office may grant exemption from:

(a)   the requirement of paragraph 2(c), second sentence, if the applicant furnishes proof that he has acquired the requisite qualification in another way;

(b)   the requirement of paragraph 2(a) in special circumstances.

5.   The conditions under which a person may be removed from the list of professional representatives shall be laid down in the Implementing Regulation.

Title X   Jurisdiction and Procedure in Legal Actions Relating to Community Trade Marks

SECTION 1   APPLICATION OF THE CONVENTION ON JURISDICTION AND ENFORCEMENT

Article 90   Application of the Convention on Jurisdiction and Enforcement

1.   Unless otherwise specified in this Regulation, the Convention on Jurisdiction and the Enforcement of Judgments in Civil and Commercial Matters, signed in Brussels on 27 September 1968, as amended by the Conventions on the Accession to that Convention of the States acceding to the European Communities, the whole of which Convention and of which Conventions of Accession are hereinafter referred to as the 'Convention on Jurisdiction and Enforcement', shall apply to proceedings relating to Community trade marks and applications for Community trade marks, as well as to proceedings relating to simultaneous and successive actions on the basis of Community trade marks and national trade marks.

2.   In the case of proceedings in respect of the actions and claims referred to in Article 92:

(a)   Articles 2, 4, 5(1), (3), (4) and (5) and Article 24 of the Convention on Jurisdiction and Enforcement shall not apply;

(b)   Articles 17 and 18 of that Convention shall apply subject to the limitations in Article 93(4) of this Regulation;

(c)   the provisions of Title II of that Convention which are applicable to persons domiciled in a Member State shall also be applicable to persons who do not have a domicile in any Member State but have an establishment therein.

SECTION 2   DISPUTES CONCERNING THE INFRINGEMENT AND VALIDITY OF COMMUNITY TRADE MARKS

Article 91   Community trade mark courts

1.   The Member States shall designate in their territories as limited a number as possible of national courts and tribunals of first and second instance, hereinafter referred to as 'Community trade mark courts', which shall perform the functions assigned to them by this Regulation.

2.   Each Member State shall communicate to the Commission within three years of the entry into force of this Regulation a list of Community trade mark courts indicating their names and their territorial jurisdiction.

3.   Any change made after communication of the list referred to in paragraph 2 in the number, names or territorial jurisdiction of the courts shall be notified without delay by the Member State concerned to the Commission.

4.   The information referred to in paragraphs 2 and 3 shall be notified by the Commission to the Member States and published in the *Official Journal of the European Communities.*

5.   As long as a Member State has not communicated the list as stipulated in paragraph 2, jurisdiction for any proceedings resulting from an action or application covered by Article 92, and for which the courts of that State have jurisdiction under Article 93, shall lie with that court of the State in question which would have jurisdiction *ratione loci* and *ratione materiae* in the case of proceedings relating to a national trade mark registered in that State.

Article 92   Jurisdiction over infringement and validity

The Community trade mark courts shall have exclusive jurisdiction:

(a)   for all infringement actions and — if they are permitted under national law — actions in respect of threatened infringement relating to Community trade marks;

(b)   for actions for declaration of non-infringement, if they are permitted under national law;

(c)   for all actions brought as a result of acts referred to in Article 9(3), second sentence;

(d)   for counterclaims for revocation or for a declaration of invalidity of the Community trade mark pursuant to Article 96.

Article 93   International jurisdiction

1.   Subject to the provisions of this Regulation as well as to any provisions of the Convention on Jurisdiction and Enforcement applicable by virtue of Article 90, proceedings in respect of the actions and claims referred to in Article 92 shall be brought in the courts of the Member State in which the defendant is domiciled or, if he is not domiciled in any of the Member States, in which he has an establishment.

2.   If the defendant is neither domiciled nor has an establishment in any of the Member States, such proceedings shall be brought in the courts of the Member State in which the plaintiff is domiciled or, if he is not domiciled in any of the Member States, in which he has an establishment.

3.   If neither the defendant nor the plaintiff is so domiciled or has such an establishment, such proceedings shall be brought in the courts of the Member State where the Office has its seat.

4. Notwithstanding the provisions of paragraphs 1, 2 and 3:

(a) Article 17 of the Convention on Jurisdiction and Enforcement shall apply if the parties agree that a different Community trade mark court shall have jurisdiction;

(b) Article 18 of that Convention shall apply if the defendant enters an appearance before a different Community trade mark court.

5. Proceedings in respect of the actions and claims referred to in Article 92, with the exception of actions for a declaration of non-infringement, of a Community trade mark, may also be brought in the courts of the Member State in which the act of infringement has been committed or threatened, or in which an act within the meaning of Article 9(3), second sentence, has been committed.

Article 94   Extent of jurisdiction

1. A Community trade mark court whose jurisdicrion is based on Article 93(1) to (4) shall have jurisdiction in respect of:

— acts of infringement committed or threatened within the territory of any of the Member States,

— acts within the meaning of Article 9(3), second sentence, committed within the territory of any of the Member States.

2. A Community trade mark court whose jurisdiction is based on Article 93(5) shall have jurisdiction only in respect of acts committed or threatened within the territory of the Member State in which that court is situated.

Article 95   Presumption of validity — Defence as to the merits

1. The Community trade mark courts shall treat the Community trade mark as valid unless its validity is put in issue by the defendant with a counterclaim for revocation or for a declaration of invalidity.

2. The validity of a Community trade mark may not be put in issue in an action for a declaration of non-infringement.

3. In the actions referred to in Article 92(a) and (c) a plea relating to revocation or invalidity of the Community trade mark submitted otherwise than by way of a counterclaim shall be admissible insofar as the defendant claims that the rights of the proprietor of the Community trade mark could be revoked for lack of use or that Community trade mark could be declared invalid on account of an earlier right of the defendant.

Article 96   Counterclaims

1. A counterclaim for revocation or for a declaration of invalidity may only be based on the grounds for revocation or invalidity mentioned in this Regulation.

2. A Community trade mark court shall reject a counterclaim for revocation or for a declaration of invalidity if a decision taken by the Office relating to the same subject-matter and cause of action and involving the same parties has already become final.

3. If the counterclaim is brought in a legal action to which the proprietor of the trade mark is not already a party, he shall be informed thereof and may be joined as a party to the action in accordance with the conditions set out in national law.

4. The Community trade mark court with which a counterclaim for revocation or for a declaration of invalidity of the Community trade mark has been filed shall

inform the Office of the date on which the counterclaim was filed. The latter shall record this fact in the Register of Community trade marks.

5.   Article 56(3), (4), (5) and (6) shall apply.

6.   Where a Community trade mark court has given a judgment which has become final on a counterclaim for revocation or for invalidity of a Community trade mark, a copy of the judgment shall be sent to the Office. Any party may request information about such transmission. The Office shall mention the judgment in the Register of Community trade marks in accordance with the provisions of the Implementing Regulation.

7.   The Community trade mark court hearing a counterclaim for revocation or for a declaration of invalidity may stay the proceedings on application by the proprietor of the Community trade mark and after hearing the other parties and may request the defendant to submit an application for revocation or for a declaration of invalidity to the Office within a time limit which it shall determine. If the application is not made within the time limit, the proceedings shall continue; the counterclaim shall be deemed withdrawn. Article 100(3) shall apply.

Article 97   Applicable law

1.   The Community trade mark courts shall apply the provisions of this Regulation.

2.   On all matters not covered by this Regulation a Community trade mark court shall apply its national law, including its private international law.

3.   Unless otherwise provided in this Regulation, a Community trade mark court shall apply the rules of procedure governing the same type of action relating to a national trade mark in the Member State where it has its seat.

Article 98   Sanctions

1.   Where a Community trade mark court finds that the defendant has infringed or threatened to infringe a Community trade mark, it shall, unless there are special reasons for not doing so, issue an order prohibiting the defendant from proceeding with the acts which infringed or would infringe the Community trade mark. It shall also take such measures in accordance with its national law as are aimed at ensuring that this prohibition is complied with.

2.   In all other respects the Community trade mark court shall apply the law of the Member State to which the acts of infringement or threatened infringement were committed, including the private international law.

Article 99   Provisional and protective measures

1.   Application may be made to the courts of a Member State, including Community trade mark courts, for such provisional, including protective, measures in respect of a Community trade mark or Community trade mark application as may be available under the law of that State in respect of a national trade mark, even if, under this Regulation, a Community trade mark court of another Member State has jurisdiction as to the substance of the matter.

2.   A Community trade mark court whose jurisdiction is based on Article 93(1), (2), (3) or (4) shall have jurisdiction to grant provisional and protective measures which, subject to any necessary procedure for recognition and enforcement pursuant to Title III of the Convention on Jurisdiction and Enforcement, are applicable in the territory of any Member State. No other court shall have such jurisdiction.

Article 100   Specific rules on related actions

1.   A Community trade mark court hearing an action referred to in Article 92, other than an action for a declaration of non-infringement shall, unless there are special grounds for continuing the hearing, of its own motion after hearing the parties or at the request of one of the parties and after hearing the other parties, stay the proceedings where the validity of the Community trade mark is already in issue before another Community trade mark court on account of a counterclaim or where an application for revocation or for a declaration of invalidity has already been filed at the Office.

2.   The Office, when hearing an application for revocation or for a declaration of invalidity shall, unless there are special grounds for continuing the hearing, of its own motion after hearing the parties or at the request of one of the parties and after hearing the other parties, stay the proceedings where the validity of the Community trade mark is already in issue on account of a counterclaim before a Community trade mark court. However, if one of the parties to the proceedings before the Community trade mark court so requests, the court may, after hearing the other parties to these proceedings, stay the proceedings. The Office shall in this instance continue the proceedings pending before it.

3.   Where the Community trade mark court stays the proceedings it may order provisional and protective measures for the duration of the stay.

Article 101   Jurisdiction of Community trade mark courts of second instance —
Further appeal

1.   An appeal to the Community trade mark courts of second instance shall lie from judgments of the Community trade mark courts of first instance in respect of proceedings arising from the actions and claims referred to in Article 92.

2.   The conditions under which an appeal may be lodged with a Community trade mark court of second instance shall be determined by the national law of the Member State in which that court is located.

3.   The national rules concerning further appeal shall be applicable in respect of judgments of Community trade mark courts of second instance.

SECTION 3   OTHER DISPUTES CONCERNING COMMUNITY TRADE MARKS

Article 102   Supplementary provisions on the jurisdiction of national courts other than Community trade mark courts

1.   Within the Member State whose courts have jurisdiction under Article 90(1) those courts shall have jurisdiction for actions other than those referred to in Article 92, which would have jurisdicrion *ratione loci* and *ratione materiae* in the case of actions relating to a national trade mark registered in that State.

2.   Actions relating to a Community trade mark, other than those referred to in Article 92, for which no court has jurisdiction under Article 90(1) and paragraph 1 of this Article may be heard before the courts of the Member State in which the Office has its seat.

Article 103   Obligation of the national court

A national court which is dealing with an action relating to a Community trade mark, other than the action referred to in Article 92, shall treat the trade mark as valid.

SECTION 4   TRANSITIONAL PROVISION

Article 104   Transitional provision relating to the application of the Convention on Jurisdiction and Enforcement
The provisions of the Convention on Jurisdiction and Enforcement which are rendered applicable by the preceding Articles shall have effect in respect of any Member State solely in the text of the Convention which is in force in respect of that State at any given time.

Title XI   Effects on the Laws of the Member States

SECTION 1   CIVIL ACTIONS ON THE BASIS OF MORE THAN ONE TRADE MARK

Article 105   Simultaneous and successive civil actions on the basis of Community trade marks and national trade marks
1.   Where actions for infringement involving the same cause of action and between the same parties are brought in the courts of different Member States, one seized on the basis of a Community trade mark and the other seized on the basis of a national trade mark:
    (a)   the court other than the court first seized shall of its own motion decline jurisdiction in favour of that court where the trade marks concerned are identical and valid for identical goods or services. The court which would be required to decline jurisdiction may stay its proceedings if the jurisdiction of the other court is contested;
    (b)   the court other than the court first seized may stay its proceedings where the trade marks concerned are identical and valid for similar goods or services and where the trade marks concerned are similar and valid for identical or similar goods or services.
2.   The court hearing an action for infringement on the basis of a Community trade mark shall reject the action if a final judgment on the merits has been given on the same cause of action and between the same parties on the basis of an identical national trade mark valid for identical goods or services.
3.   The court hearing an action for infringement on the basis of a national trade mark shall reject the action if a final judgment on the merits has been given on the same cause of action and between the same parties on the basis of an identical Community trade mark valid for identical goods or services.
4.   Paragraphs 1, 2 and 3 shall not apply in respect of provisonal, including protective, measures.

SECTION 2   APPLICATION OF NATIONAL LAWS FOR THE PURPOSE OF PROHIBITING THE USE OF COMMUNITY TRADE MARKS

Article 106   Prohibition of use of Community trade marks   .
1.   This Regulation shall, unless otherwise provided for, not affect the right existing under the laws of the Member States to invoke claims for infringement of earlier rights within the meaning of Article 8 or Article 52(2) in relation to the use of a later Community trade mark. Claims for infringement of earlier rights within

the meaning of Article 8(2) and (4) may, however, no longer be invoked if the proprietor of the earlier right may no longer apply for a declaration that the Community trade mark is invalid in accordance with Article 53(2).

2. This Regulation shall, unless otherwise provided for, not affect the right to bring proceedings under the civil, administrative or criminal law of a Member State or under provisions of Community law for the purpose of prohibiting the use of a Community trade mark to the extent that the use of a national trade mark may be prohibited under the law of that Member State or under Community law.

Article 107   Prior rights applicable to particular localities
1. The proprietor of an earlier right which only applies to a particular locality may oppose the use of the Community trade mark in the territory where his right is protected insofar as the law of the Member State concerned so permits.

2. Paragraph 1 shall cease to apply if the proprietor of the earlier right has acquiesced in the use of the Community trade mark in the territory where his right is protected for a period of five successive years, being aware of such use, unless the Community trade mark was applied for in bad faith.

3. The proprietor of the Community trade mark shall not be entitled to oppose use of the right referred to in paragraph 1 even though that right may no longer be invoked against the Community trade mark.

SECTION 3   CONVERSION INTO A NATIONAL TRADE MARK APPLICATION

Article 108   Request for the application of national procedure
1. The applicant for or proprietor of a Community trade mark may request the conversion of his Community trade mark application or Community trade mark into a national trade mark application

(a)   to the extent that the Community trade mark application is refused, withdrawn, or deemed to be withdrawn;

(b)   to the extent that the Community trade mark ceases to have effect.

2. Conversion shall not take place:

(a)   where the rights of the proprietor of the Community trade mark have been revoked on the grounds of non-use, unless in the Member State for which conversion is requested the Community trade mark has been put to use which would be considered to be genuine use under the laws of that Member State;

(b)   for the purpose of protection in a Member State in which, in accordance with the decision of the Office or of the national court, grounds for refusal of registration or grounds for revocation or invalidity apply to the Community trade mark application or Community trade mark.

3. The national trade mark application resulting from the conversion of a Community trade mark application or a Community trade mark shall enjoy in respect of the Member State concerned the date of filing or the date of priority of that application or trade mark and, where appropriate, the seniority of a trade mark of that State claimed under Article 34 or 35.

4. Where:

— the Community trade mark application is deemed to be withdrawn or is refused by a decision of the Office which has become final,

— the Community trade mark ceases to have effect as a result of a decision of the Office which has become final or as a result of registration of surrender of the Community trade mark,

the Office shall notify to the applicant or proprietor a communication fixing a period of three months from the date of that communication in which a request for conversion may be filed.

5. Where the Community trade mark application is withdrawn or the Community trade mark ceases to have effect as a result of failure to renew the registration, the request for conversion shall be filed within three months after the date on which the Community trade mark application is withdrawn or on which the registration of the Community trade mark expires.

6. Where the Community trade mark ceases to have effect as a result of a decision of a national court, the request for conversion shall be filed within three months after the date on which that decision acquired the authority of a final decision.

7. The effect referred to in Article 32 shall lapse if the request is not filed in due time.

Article 109 Submission, publication and transmission of the request for conversion

1. A request for conversion shall be filed with the Office and shall specify the Member States in which application of the procedure for registration of a national trade mark is desired. The request shall not be deemed to be filed until the conversion fee has been paid.

2. If the Community trade mark application has been published, receipt of any such request shall be recorded in the Register of Community trade marks and request for conversion shall be published.

3. The Office shall check whether conversion may be requested in accordance with Article 108(1), whether request has been filed within the period laid down in Article 108(4), (5) or (6), as the case may be, and whether the conversion fee has been paid. If these conditions are fulfilled, the Office shall transmit the request to the central industrial property offices of the States specified therein. At the request of the central industrial property office of a State concerned, the Office shall give it any information enabling that office to decide as to the admissibility of the request.

Article 110 Formal requirements for conversion

1. Any central industrial property office to which the request is transmitted shall decide as to its admissibility.

2. A Community trade mark application or a Community trade mark transmitted in accordance with Article 109 shall not be subjected to formal requirements of national law which are different from or additional to those provided for in this Regulation or in the Implementing Regulation.

3. Any central industrial property office to which the request is transmitted may require that the applicant shall, within not less than two months;

(a) pay the national application fee;

(b) file a translation in one of the official languages of the State in question of the request and of the documents accompanying it;

(c) indicate an address for service in the State in question;

(d) supply a representation of the trade mark in the number of copies specified by the State in question.

Title XII The Office

SECTION 1 GENERAL PROVISIONS

Article 111 Legal status

1. The Office shall be a body of the Community. It shall have legal personality.

2. In each of the Member States the Office shall enjoy the most extensive legal capacity accorded to legal persons under their laws; it may, in particular, acquire or dispose of movable and immovable property and may be a party to legal proceedings.

3. The Office shall be represented by its President.

Article 112 Staff

1. The Staff Regulations of officials of the European Communities, the Conditions of Employment of other servants of the European Communities, and the rules adopted by agreement between the Institutions of the European Communities for giving effect to those Staff Regulations and Conditions of Employment shall apply to the staff of the Office, without prejudice to the application of Article 131 to the members of the Boards of Appeal.

2. Without prejudice to Article 120, the powers conferred on each Institution by the Staff Regulations and by the Conditions of Employment of other servants shall be exercised by the Office in respect of its staff.

Article 113 Privileges and immunities

The Protocol on the Privileges and Immunities of the European Communities shall apply to the Office.

Article 114 Liability

1. The contractual liability of the Office shall be governed by the law applicable to the contract in question.

2. The Court of Justice shall be competent to give judgment pursuant to any arbitration clause contained in a contract concluded by the Office.

3. In the case of non-contractual liability, the Office shall, in accordance with the general principles common to the laws of the Member States, make good any damage caused by its departments or by its servants in the performance of their duties.

4. The Court of Justice shall have jurisdiction in disputes relating to compensation for the damage referred to in paragraph 3.

5. The personal liability of its servants towards the Office shall be governed by the provisions laid down in their Staff Regulations or in the Conditions of Employment applicable to them.

Article 115 Languages

1. The application for a Community trade mark shall be filed in one of the official languages of the European Community.

2.   The languages of the Office shall be English, French, German, Italian and Spanish.

3.   The applicant must indicate a second language which shall be a language of the Office the use of which he accepts as a possible language of proceedings for opposition, revocation or invalidity proceedings.

If the application was filed in a language which is not one of the languages of the Office, the Office shall arrange to have the application, as described in Article 26(1), translated into the language indicated by the applicant.

4.   Where the applicant for a Community trade mark is the sole party to proceedings before the Office, the language of proceedings shall be the language used for filing the application for a Community trade mark. If the application was made in a language other than the languages of the Office, the Office may send written communications to the applicant in the second language indicated by the applicant in his application.

5.   The notice of opposition and an application for revocation or invalidity shall be filed in one of the languages of the Office.

6.   If the language chosen, in accordance with paragraph 5, for the notice of opposition or the application for revocation or invalidity is the language of the application for a trade mark or the second language indicated when the application was filed, that language shall be the language of the proceedings.

If the language chosen, in accordance with paragraph 5, for the notice of opposition or the application for revocation or invalidity is neither the language of the application for a trade mark nor the second language indicated when the application was filed, the opposing party or the party seeking revocation or invalidity shall be required to produce, at his own expense, a translation of his application either into the language of the application for a trade mark, provided that it is a language of the Office, or into the second language indicated when the application was filed. The translation shall be produced within the period pre-scribed in the Implementing Regulation. The language into which the application has been translated shall then become the language of the proceedings.

7.   Parties to opposition, revocation, invalidity or appeal proceedings may agree that a different official language of the European Community is to be the language of the proceedings.

Article 116   Publication; entries in the Register

1.   An application for a Community trade mark, as described in Article 26(1), and all other information the publication of which is prescribed by this Regulation or the Implementing Regulation, shall be published in all the official languages of the European Community.

2.   All entries in the Register of Community trade marks shall be made in all the official languages of the European Community.

3.   In cases of doubt, the text in the language of the Office in which the application for the Community trade mark was is filed shall be authentic. If the application was filed in an official language of the European Community other than one of the languages of the Office, the text in the second language indicated by the applicant shall be authentic.

Article 117

The translation services required for the functioning of the Office shall be provided by the Translation Centre of the Bodies of the Union once this begins operation.

Article 118   Control of legality
1.   The Commission shall check the legality of those acts of the President of the Office in respect of which Community law does not provide for any check on legality by another body and of acts of the Budget Committee attached to the Office pursuant to Article 133.

2.   It shall require that any unlawful acts as referred to in paragraph 1 be altered or annulled.

3.   Member States and any person directly and personally involved may refer to the Commission any act as referred to in paragraph 1, whether express or implied, for the Commission to examine the legality of that act. Referral shall be made to the Commission within 15 days of the day on which the party concerned first became aware of the act in question. The Commission shall take a decision within one month. If no decision has been taken within this period, the case shall be deemed to have been dismissed.

SECTION 2   MANAGEMENT OF THE OFFICE

Article 119   Powers of the President
1.   The Office shall be managed by the President.

2.   To this end the President shall have in particular the following functions and powers:

(a)   he shall take all necessary steps, including the adoption of internal administrative instructions and the publication of notices, to ensure the functioning of the Office;

(b)   he may place before the Commission any proposal to amend this Regulation, the Implementing Regulation, the rules of procedure of the Boards of Appeal, the fees regulations and any other rules applying to Community trade marks after consulting the Administrative Board and, in the case of the fees regulations and the budgetary provisions of this Regulation, the Budget Committee;

(c)   he shall draw up the estimates of the revenue and expenditure of the Office and shall implement the budget;

(d)   he shall submit a management report to the Commission, the European Parliament and the Administrative Board each year;

(e)   he shall exercise in respect of the staff the powers laid down in Article 112(2);

(f)   he may delegate his powers.

3.   The President shall be assisted by one or more Vice-Presidents. If the President is absent or indisposed, the Vice-President or one of the Vice-Presidents shall take his place in accordance with the procedure laid down by the Administrative Board.

Article 120   Appointment of senior officials
1.   The President of the Office shall be appointed by the Council from a list of at most three candidates, which shall be prepared by the Administrative Board. Power to dismiss the President shall lie with the Council, acting on a proposal from the Administrative Board.

2.   The term of office of the President shall not exceed five years. This term of office shall be renewable.

3.   The Vice-President or Vice-Presidents of the Office shall be appointed or dismissed as in paragraph 1, after consultation of the President.

4.   The Council shall exercise disciplinary authority over the officials referred to in paragraphs 1 and 3 of this Article.

SECTION 3   ADMINISTRATIVE BOARD

Article 121   Creation and powers

1.   An Administrative Board is hereby set up, attached to the Office. Without prejudice to the powers attributed to the Budget Committee in Section 5 — budget and financial control — the Administrative Board shall have the powers defined below.

2.   The Administrative Board shall draw up the lists of candidates provided for in Article 120.

3.   It shall fix the date for the first filing of Community trade mark applications, pursuant to Article 143(3).

4.   It shall advise the President on matters for which the Office is responsible.

5.   It shall be consulted before adoption of the guidelines for examination in the Office and in the other cases provided for in this Regulation.

6.   It may deliver opinions and requests for information to the President and to the Commission where it considers that this is necessary.

Article 122   Composition

1.   The Administrative Board shall be composed of one representative of each Member State and one representative of the Commission and their alternates.

2.   The members of the Administrative Board may, subject to the provisions of its rules of procedure, be assisted by advisers or experts.

Article 123   Chairmanship

1.   The Administrative Board shall elect a chairman and a deputy chairman from among its members. The deputy chairman shall *ex officio* replace the chairman in the event of his being prevented from attending to his duties.

2.   The duration of the terms of office of the chairman and the deputy chairman shall be three years. The terms of office shall be renewable.

Article 124   Meetings

1.   Meetings of the Administrative Board shall be convened by its chairman.

2.   The President of the Office shall take part in the deliberations, unless the Administrative Board decides otherwise.

3.   The Administrative Board shall hold an ordinary meeting once a year; in addition, it shall meet on the initiative of its chairman or at the request of the Commission or of one-third of the Member States.

4.   The Administrative Board shall adopt rules of procedure.

5.   The Administrative Board shall take its decisions by a simple majority of the representatives of the Member States. However, a majority of three-quarters of the representatives of the Member States shall be required for the decisions which the Administrative Board is empowered to take under Article 120(1) and (3). In both cases each Member State shall have one vote.

6. The Administrative Board may invite observers to attend its meetings.

7. The Secretariat for the Administrative Board shall be provided by the Office.

SECTION 4 IMPLEMENTATION OF PROCEDURES

Article 125 Competence
For taking decisions in connection with the procedures laid down in this Regulation, the following shall be competent:
(a) Examiners;
(b) Opposition Divisions;
(c) an Administration of Trade Marks and Legal Division;
(d) Cancellation Divisions;
(e) Boards of Appeal.

Article 126 Examiners
An examiner shall be responsible for taking decisions on behalf of the Office in relation to an application for registration of a Community trade mark, including the matters referred to in Articles 36, 37, 38 and 66, except insofar as an Opposition Division is responsible.

Article 127 Opposition Divisions
1. An Opposition Division shall be responsible for taking decisions on an opposition to an application to register a Community trade mark.

2. An Opposition Division shall consist of three members. At least one of the members must be legally qualified.

Article 128 Administration of Trade Marks and Legal Division
1. The Administration of Trade Marks and Legal Division shall be responsible for those decisions required by this Regulation which do not fall within the competence of an examiner, an Opposition Division or a Cancellation Division. It shall in particular be responsible for decisions in respect of entries in the Register of Community trade marks.

2. It shall also be responsible for keeping the list of professional representatives which is referred to in Article 89.

3. A decision of the Division shall be taken by one member.

Article 129 Cancellation Divisions
1. A Cancellation Division shall be responsible for taking decisions in relation to an application for the revocation or declaration of invalidity of a Community trade mark.

2. A Cancellation Division shall consist of three members. At least one of the members must be legally qualified.

Article 130 Boards of Appeal
1. The Boards of Appeal shall be responsible for deciding on appeals from decisions of the examiners, Opposition Divisions, Administration of Trade Marks and Legal Division and Cancellation Divisions.

2. A Board of Appeal shall consist of three members. At least two of the members must be legally qualified.

Article 131   Independence of the members of the Boards of Appeal

1.   The members, including the chairmen, of the Boards of Appeal shall be appointed, in accordance with the procedure laid down in Article 120, for the appointment of the President of the Office, for a term of five years. They may not be removed from office during this term, unless there are serious grounds for such removal and the Court of Justice, on application by the body which appointed them, takes a decision to this effect. Their term of office shall be renewable.

2.   The members of the Boards of Appeal shall be independent. In their decisions they shall not be bound by any instructions.

3.   The members of the Boards of Appeal may not be examiners or members of the Opposition Divisions, Administration of Trade Marks and Legal Division or Cancellation Divisions.

Article 132   Exclusion and objection

1.   Examiners and members of the Divisions set up within the Office or of the Boards of Appeal may not take part in any proceedings if they have any personal interest therein, or if they have previously been involved as representatives of one of the parties. Two of the three members of an Opposition Division shall not have taken part in examining the application. Members of the Cancellation Divisions may not take part in any proceedings if they have participated in the final decision on the case in the proceedings for registration or opposition proceedings. Members of the Boards of Appeal may not take part in appeal proceedings if they participated in the decision under appeal.

2.   If, for one of the reasons mentioned in paragraph 1 or for any other reason, a member of a Division or of a Board of Appeal considers that he should not take part in any proceedings, he shall inform the Division or Board accordingly.

3.   Examiners and members of the Divisions or of a Board of Appeal may be objected to by any party for one of the reasons mentioned in paragraph 1, or if suspected of partiality. An objection shall not be admissible if, while being aware of a reason for objection, the party has taken a procedural step. No objection may be based upon the nationality of examiners or members.

4.   The Divisions and the Boards of Appeal shall decide as to the action to be taken in the cases specified in paragraphs 2 and 3 without the participation of the member concerned. For the purposes of taking this decision the member who withdraws or has been objected to shall be replaced in the Division or Board of Appeal by his alternate.

SECTION 5   BUDGET AND FINANCIAL CONTROL

Article 133   Budget Committee

1.   A Budget Committee is hereby set up, attached to the Office. The Budget Committee shall have the powers assigned to it in this Section and in Article 39(4).

2.   Articles 121(6), 122, 123 and 124(1) to (4), (6) and (7) shall apply to the Budget Committee *mutatis mutandis*.

3.   The Budget Committee shall take its decisions by a simple majority of the representatives of the Member States. However, a majority of three-quarters of the representatives of the Member States shall be required for the decisions which the Budget Committee is empowered to take under Articles 39(4), 135(3) and 138. In both cases each Member State shall have one vote.

Article 134   Budget

1.   Estimates of all the Office's revenue and expenditure shall be prepared for each financial year and shall be shown in the Office's budget, and each financial year shall correspond with the calendar year.

2.   The revenue and expenditure shown in the budget shall be in balance.

3.   Revenue shall comprise, without prejudice to other types of income, total fees payable under the fees regulations, and, to the extent necessary, a subsidy entered against a specific heading of the general budget of the European Communities, Commission Section.

Article 135   Preparation of the budget

1.   The President shall draw up each year an estimate of the Office's revenue and expenditure for the following year and shall send it to the Budget Committee not later than 31 March in each year, together with a list of posts.

2.   Should the budget estimates provide for a Community subsidy, the Budget Committee shall immediately forward the estimate to the Commission, which shall forward it to the budget authority of the Communities. The Commission may attach an opinion on the estimate along with an alternative estimate.

3.   The Budget Committee shall adopt the budget, which shall include the Office's list of posts. Should the budget estimates contain a subsidy from the general budget of the Communities, the Office's budget shall, if necessary, be adjusted.

Article 136   Financial control

Control of commitment and payment of all expenditure and control of the existence and recovery of all revenue of the Office shall be carried out by the Financial Controller appointed by the Budget Committee.

Article 137   Auditing of accounts

1.   Not later than 31 March in each year the President shall transmit to the Commission, the European Parliament, the Budget Committee and the Court of Auditors accounts of the Office's total revenue and expenditure for the preceding financial year. The Court of Auditors shall examine them in accordance with Article 188c of the Treaty.

2.   The Budget Committee shall give a discharge to the President of the Office in respect of the implementation of the budget.

Article 138   Financial provisions

The Budget Committee shall, after consulting the Court of Auditors of the European Communities and the Commission, adopt internal financial provisions specifying, in particular, the procedure for establishing and implementing the Office's budget. As far as is compatible with the particular nature of the Office, the financial provisions shall be based on the financial regulations adopted for other bodies set up by the Community.

Article 139   Fees regulations

1.   The fees regulations shall determine in particular the amounts of the fees and the ways in which they are to be paid.

2.   The amounts of the fees shall be fixed at such a level as to ensure that the revenue in respect thereof is in principle sufficient for the budget of the Office to be balanced.

3.   The fees regulations shall be adopted and amended in accordance with the procedure laid down in Article 141.

Title XIII   Final Provisions

Article 140   Community implementing provisions

1.   The rules implementing this Regulation shall be adopted in an Implementing Regulation.

2.   In addition to the fees provided for in the preceding Articles, fees shall be charged, in accordance with the detailed rules of application laid down in the Implementing Regulation, in the cases listed below:

1.   alteration of the representation of a Community trade mark;
2.   late payment of the registration fee;
3.   issue of a copy of the certificate of registration:
4.   registration of the transfer of a Community trade mark;
5.   registration of a licence or another right in respect of a Community trade mark;
6.   registration of a licence or another right in respect of an application for a Community trade mark;
7.   cancellation of the registration of a licence or another right;
8.   alteration of a registered Community trade mark;
9.   issue of an extract from the Register;
10.   inspection of the files;
11.   issue of copies of file documents;
12.   issue of certified copies of the application;
13.   communication of information in a file;
14.   review of the determination of the procedural costs to be refunded.

3.   The Implementing Regulation and the rules of procedure of the Boards of Appeal shall be adopted and amended in accordance with the procedure laid down in Article 141.

Article 141   Establishment of a committee and procedure for the adoption of Implementing Regulations

1.   The Commission shall be assisted by a Committee on Fees, Implementation Rules and the Procedure of the Boards of Appeal of the Office for Harmonisation in the Internal Market (trade marks and designs), which shall be composed of representatives of the Member Stares and chaired by a representative of the Commission.

2.   The representative of the Commission shall submit to the Committee a draft of the measures to be taken. The Committee shall deliver its opinion on the draft within a time limit which the chairman may lay down according to the urgency of the matter. The opinion shall be delivered by the majority laid down in Article 148(2) of the Treaty in the case of decisions which the Council is required to adopt on a proposal from the Commission. The votes of the representatives of the Member States within the Committee shall be weighted in the manner set out in that Article. The chairman shall not vote.

The Commission shall adopt the measures envisaged if they are in accordance with the opinion of the Committee.

If the measures envisaged are not in accordance with the opinion of the Committee, or if no opinion is delivered, the Commission shall, without delay, submit to the Council a proposal relating to the measures to be taken. The Council shall act by a qualified majority.

If, on the expiry of a period of three months from the date of referral to the Council, the Council has not acted, the proposed measures shall be adopted by the Commission, save where the Council has decided against the measures by a simple majority.

Article 142   Compatibility with other Community legal provisions
This Regulation shall not affect Council Regulation (EEC) No. 2081/92 on the protection of geographical indications and designations of origin for agricultural products and foodstuffs[1] of 14 July 1992, and in particular Article 14 thereof.

Article 143   Entry into force
1.   This Regulation shall enter into force on the 60th day following that of its publication in the *Official Journal of the European Communities.*
2.   The Member States shall within three years following entry into force of this Regulation take the necessary measures for the purpose of implementing Articles 91 and 101 hereof and shall forthwith inform the Commission of those measures.
3.   Applications for Community trade marks may be filed at the Office from the date fixed by the Administrative Board on the recommendation of the President of the Office.
4.   Applications for Community trade marks filed within three months before the date referred to in paragraph 3 shall be deemed to have been filed on that date.

This Regulation shall be binding in its entirety and directly applicable in all Member States.

Done at Brussels, 20 December 1993.
For the Council
The President
A. BOURGEOIS

---

[1] OJ No. L 208, 24.7.1992, p. 1.

APPENDIX FOUR
Nice Classification, 6th Edition

List of Classes of Goods and Services

Goods

Class 1. Chemicals used in industry, science and photography, as well as in agriculture, horticulture and forestry; unprocessed artificial resins, unprocessed plastics; manures; fire extinguishing compositions; tempering and soldering preparations; chemical substances for preserving foodstuffs; tanning substances; adhesives used in industry.

Class 2. Paints, varnishes, lacquers; preservatives against rust and against deterioration of wood; colourants; mordants; raw natural resins; metals in foil and powder form for painters, decorators, printers and artists.

Class 3. Bleaching preparations and other substances for laundry use; cleaning, polishing, scouring and abrasive preparations; soaps; perfumery, essential oils, cosmetics, hair lotions; dentifrices.

Class 4. Industrial oils and greases; lubricants; dust absorbing, wetting and binding compositions; fuels (including motor spirit) and illuminants; candles, wicks.

Class 5. Pharmaceutical, veterinary and sanitary preparations; dietetic substances adapted for medical use, food for babies; plasters, materials for dressings; material for stopping teeth, dental wax; disinfectants; preparations for destroying vermin; fungicides, herbicides.

Class 6. Common metals and their alloys; metal building materials; transportable buildings of metal; materials of metal for railway tracks; non-electric cables and wires of common metal; ironmongery, small items of metal hardware; pipes and tubes of metal; safes; goods of common metal not included in other classes; ores.

Class 7. Machines and machine tools; motors and engines (except for land vehicles); machine coupling and transmission components (except for land vehicles); agricultural implements; incubators for eggs.

Class 8. Hand tools and implements (hand operated); cutlery; side-arms; razors.

Class 9. Scientific, nautical, surveying, electric, photographic, cinematographic, optical, weighing, measuring, signalling, checking (supervision), life-saving and teaching apparatus and instruments; apparatus for recording, transmission or reproduction of sound or images; magnetic data carriers, recording discs; automatic vending machines and mechanisms for coin-operated apparatus; cash registers, calculating machines, data processing equipment and computers; fire-extinguishing apparatus.

Class 10.   Surgical, medical, dental and veterinary apparatus and instruments, artificial limbs, eyes and teeth; orthopaedic articles; suture materials.

Class 11.   Apparatus for lighting, heating, steam generating, cooking, refrigerating, drying, ventilating, water supply and sanitary purposes.

Class 12.   Vehicles; apparatus for locomotion by land, air or water.

Class 13.   Firearms; ammunition and projectiles; explosives; fireworks.

Class 14.   Precious metals and their alloys and goods in precious metals or coated therewith, not included in other classes; jewellery, precious stones; horological and chronometric instruments.

Class 15.   Musical instruments.

Class 16.   Paper, cardboard and goods made from these materials, not included in other classes; printed matter; bookbinding material; photographs; stationery; adhesives for stationery or household purposes; artists' materials; paintbrushes; typewriters and office requisites (except furniture); instructional and teaching material (except apparatus); plastic materials for packaging (not included in other classes); playing cards; printers' type; printing blocks.

Class 17.   Rubber, gutta-percha, gum, asbestos, mica and goods made from these materials and not included in other classes; plastics in extruded form for use in manufacture; packing, stopping and insulating materials; flexible pipes, not of metal.

Class 18.   Leather and imitations of leather, and goods made of these materials and not included in other classes; animal skins, hides; trunks and travelling bags; umbrellas, parasols and walking sticks; whips, harness and saddlery.

Class 19.   Building materials (non-metallic); non-metallic rigid pipes for building; asphalt, pitch and bitumen; non-metallic transportable buildings; monuments, not of metal.

Class 20.   Furniture, mirrors, picture frames; goods (not included in other classes) of wood, cork, reed, cane, wicker, horn, bone, ivory, whalebone, shell, amber, mother-of-pearl, meerschaum and substitutes for all these materials, or of plastics.

Class 21.   Household or kitchen utensils and containers (not of precious metal or coated therewith); combs and sponges; brushes (except paintbrushes); brushmaking materials; articles for cleaning purposes; steel wool; unworked or semiworked glass (except glass used in building); glassware, porcelain and earthenware not included in other classes.

Class 22.   Ropes, string, nets, tents, awnings, tarpaulins, sails, sacks and bags (not included in other classes); padding and stuffing materials (except of rubber or plastics); raw fibrous textile materials.

Class 23.   Yarns and threads, for textile use.

Class 24.   Textiles and textile goods, not included in other classes; bed and table covers.

Class 25.   Clothing, footwear, headgear.

Class 26.   Lace and embroidery, ribbons and braid; buttons, hooks and eyes, pins and needles; artificial flowers.

Class 27.   Carpets, rugs, mats and matting, linoleum and other materials for covering existing floors; wall hangings (non-textile).

Class 28.   Games and playthings; gymnastic and sporting articles not included in other classes; decorations for Christmas trees.

Class 29.   Meat, fish, poultry and game; meat extracts; preserved, dried and cooked fruits and vegetables; jellies, jams, fruit sauces; eggs, milk and milk products; edible oils and fats.

Class 30.   Coffee, tea, cocoa, sugar, rice, tapioca, sago, artificial coffee; flour and preparations made from cereals, bread, pastry and confectionery, ices; honey, treacle; yeast, baking-powder; salt, mustard; vinegar, sauces (condiments); spices; ice.

Class 31.   Agricultural, horticultural and forestry products and grains not included in other classes; live animals; fresh fruits and vegetables; seeds, natural plants and flowers; foodstuffs for animals, malt.

Class 32.   Beers; mineral and aerated waters and other non-alcoholic drinks; fruit drinks and fruit juices; syrups and other preparations for making beverages.

Class 33.   Alcoholic beverages (except beers).

Class 34.   Tobacco; smokers' articles; matches.

Services

Class 35.   Advertising; business management; business administration; office functions.

Class 36.   Insurance; financial affairs; monetary affairs; real estate affairs.

Class 37.   Building construction; repair; installation services.

Class 38.   Telecommunications.

Class 39.   Transport; packaging and storage of goods; travel arrangement.

Class 40.   Treatment of materials.

Class 41.   Education; providing of training; entertainment; sporting and cultural activities.

Class 42.   Providing of food and drink; temporary accommodation; medical, hygienic and beauty care; veterinary and agricultural services; legal services; scientific and industrial research; computer programming; services that cannot be placed in other classes.

APPENDIX FIVE
Relevant Provisions of the Rome Treaty

Article 2
The Community shall have as its task, by establishing a common market and monetary union and by implementing the common policies or activities referred to in Articles 3 and 3a, to promote throughout the Community a harmonious and balanced development of economic activities. sustainable and non-inflationary growth respecting the environment, a high degree of convergence of economic performance, a high level of employment and of social protection, the raising of the standard of living and quality of life, and economic and social cohesion and solidarity among Member States.

Article 3
For the purposes set out in Article 2, the activities of the Community shall include, as provided in this Treaty and in accordance with the timetable set out therein:

(a) the elimination, as between Member States, of customs duties and quantitative restrictions on the import and export of goods, and of all other measures having equivalent effect; . . .

(c) an internal market characterised by the abolition, as between Member States, of obstacles to the free movement of goods, persons, services and capital; . . .

(g) a system ensuring that competition in the internal market is not distorted.

Article 30
Quantitative restrictions on imports and all measures having equivalent effect shall, without prejudice to the following provisions, be prohibited between Member States.

Article 36
The provisions of Articles 30 to 34 shall not preclude prohibitions or restrictions on imports, exports or goods in transit justified on grounds of public morality, public policy or public security; the protection of health and life of humans, animals or plants; the protection of national treasures possessing artistic, historic or archaeological value; or the protection of industrial and commercial property. Such prohibitions or restrictions, shall not, however, constitute a means of arbitrary discrimination or a disguised restriction on trade between Member States.

Article 85

1. The following shall be prohibited as incompatible with the common market: all agreements between undertakings, decisions by associations of undertakings and concerted practices which may affect trade between Member States and which have as their object or effect the prevention, restriction or distortion of competition within the common market, and in particular those which:

(a)   directly or indirectly fix purchase or selling prices or any other trading conditions;

(b)   limit or control production, markets, technical development, or investment;

(c)   share markets or sources of supply;

(d)   apply dissimilar conditions to equivalent transactions with other trading parties, thereby placing them at a competitive disadvantage;

(e)   make the conclusion of contracts subject to acceptance by the other parties of supplementary obligations which, by their nature or according to commercial usage, have no connection with the subject of such contracts.

2.   Any agreements or decisions prohibited pursuant to this Article shall be automatically void.

3.   The provisions of paragraph 1 may, however, be declared inapplicable in the case of:

—   any agreement or category of agreements between undertakings;

—   any decision or category of decisions by associations of undertakings;

—   any concerted practice or category of concerted practices;

which contributes to improving the production or distribution of goods or to promoting technical or economic progress, while allowing consumers a fair share of the resulting benefit, and which does not:

(a)   impose on the undertakings concerned restrictions which are not indispensable to the attainment of these objectives;

(b)   afford such undertakings the possibility of eliminating competition in respect of a substantial part of the products in question.

Article 86

Any abuse by one or more undertakings of a dominant position within the common market or in a substantial part of it shall be prohibited as incompatible with the common market insofar as it may affect trade between Member States. Such abuse may, in particular, consist in:

(a)   directly or indirectly imposing unfair purchase or selling prices or other unfair trading conditions;

(b)   limiting production, markets or technical development to the prejudice of consumers;

(c)   applying dissimilar conditions to equivalent transactions with other trading parties, thereby placing them at a competitive disadvantage;

(d)   making the conclusion of contracts subject to acceptance by the other parties of supplementary obligations which, by their nature or according to commercial usage, have no connection with the subject of such contracts.

Article 177

The Court of Justice shall have jurisdiction to give preliminary rulings concerning:

(a)   the interpretation of this Treaty;

(b)   the validity and interpretation of acts of the institutions of the Community and of the ECB;

(c)   the interpretation of the statutes of bodies established by an act of the Council, where those statutes so provide.

Where such a question is raised before any court or tribunal of a Member State, that court or tribunal may, if it considers that a decision on the question is necessary to enable it to give judgment, request the Court of Justice to give a ruling thereon.

Where any such question is raised in a case pending before a court or tribunal of a Member State, against whose decisions there is no judicial remedy under national law, that court or tribunal shall bring the matter before the Court of Justice.

Index